TEACHING ENGLISH AS A SECOND LANGUAGE
A New Pedagogy for a New Century

Second Edition

Editors

MANISH A. VYAS
Department of English
VPMP Polytechnic
Gandhinagar, Gujarat

YOGESH L. PATEL
Controller of Examination
Shree Somnath Sanskrit University
Veraval–Somnath, Gujarat

PHI Learning Private Limited
Delhi-110092
2015

₹ 395.00

TEACHING ENGLISH AS A SECOND LANGUAGE
A New Pedagogy for a New Century, **Second Edition**
Edited by Manish A. Vyas and Yogesh L. Patel

© 2015 by PHI Learning Private Limited, Delhi. All rights reserved. No part of this book may be reproduced in any form, by mimeograph or any other means, without permission in writing from the publisher.

ISBN-978-81-203-5152-3

The export rights of this book are vested solely with the publisher.

Second Printing (Second Edition) . . . . . . **September, 2015**

Published by Asoke K. Ghosh, PHI Learning Private Limited, Rimjhim House, 111, Patparganj Industrial Estate, Delhi-110092 and Printed by Raj Press, New Delhi-110012.

*To
Drashti and Gungun*

CONTENTS

Foreword	*ix*
Preface	*xi*
Preface to the First Edition	*xiii*
List of Contributors	*xi*

1. **English: Aladdin's Magic Lamp**
   — *Venkataramanan Durairaj*   1–4

PART 1
COMMUNICATIVE LANGUAGE TEACHING IN ESL CONTEXT

2. **What Can We Learn from Classroom Observations?: A Study of CLT in a Chinese University Context**
   — *Lixin Xiao*   7–44

3. **Communicative Language Teaching and English Language Teaching in Nigeria**
   — *Emmanuel Taiwo Babalola*   45–56

4. **Communicative Language Teaching: An Indian Teacher Resolves a Methodology Dilemma**
   — *Deepti Gupta*   57–68

5. **Integrating ICT in the Language Classroom: An Intercultural Journey?**
   — *Anne Fox*   69–86

PART 2
MULTIMEDIA IN ELT

6. **Computer-Assisted Language Learning: Its Future**
   — *Richard Watson Todd*   89–99

7. **Podcasting: An Effective Tool for Language Learning**
   — *S. Vijayalakshmi*   100–104

8. Making Language Teaching Relevant for the Digital Age
   — *Miriam Schcolnik*   105–125

PART 3
CONTENT BASED INSTRUCTION (CBI)

9. Content-Based Instruction
   — *Makiko Ebata*   129–135

10. Familiarity and Planning in Task-based Learning
    — *Margaret Horrigan*   136–161

11. A Fine 'How Do You Do': Contextual Factors within English Greetings
    — *Alex Baratta*   162–179

PART 4
FACTORS AFFECTING ESL TEACHING

12. Motivation and Demotivation Factors in Language Learning
    — *Makiko Ebata*   183–193

13. Narrative Inquiry for Teacher Development
    — *Simon Coffey* and *Constant Leung*   194–211

14. Redefining Learner Autonomy in the Indian ESL Context
    — *P. Bhaskaran Nair*   212–217

15. Teaching English at Undergraduate Level: Groping in the Dark?
    — *Indira Nityanandam*   218–220

16. Applying Knowledge of Psycholinguistics in Language Teaching and Learning
    — *Maya Khemlani David* and *David Yoong*   221–235

PART 5
GAMES AND ACTIVITIES IN ESL CLASSROOM

17. Language-based Games and Motivation: Using Games in the ESL Classroom
    — *Johansen Quijano-Cruz*   239–248

18. Dynamic, Interactive Classroom Activities
    — *Shira Koren*   249–259

19. Games and Students' Motivation in Foreign Language Learning
— *Justyna Walczak*   260–272

PART 6
VOCABULARY DEVELOPMENT

20. Vocabulary Learning through Experience Tasks
— *Paul Nation*   275–284

21. Enhancing ESL Learners' Lexical Competence
— *Rotimi Taiwo*   285–294

22. Morphological Analysis and Vocabulary Development: Critical Criteria
— *Tom S. Bellomo*   295–308

23. Mass Media, Language Attitudes and Language Interaction Phenomena: A Study in Code Switching, Code Mixing and the Teaching Process
— *Aadil Amin Kak* and *Sajad Hussain Wani*   309–324

PART 7
PEDAGOGICAL REORIENTATION OF GRAMMAR

24. Revising Our Paradigm: Teaching Grammar as Text Inquiry
— *Cornelia Paraskevas*   327–339

25. A Reflection of Pedagogic Value on Swan's Design Criteria and Westney's Approach to Grammar Teaching
— *Roberto Rabbini*   340–351

PART 8
DEVELOPING COMMUNICATION SKILLS

26. Developing the Speaking and Writing Skills at Technical Institutes: A Classroom Investigation with Suggestions
— *S. Joseph Arul Jayraj*   355–368

27. Integrating Skills: Business Presentations for Business Students
— *Vanessa Street*   369–380

PART 9
MULTICULTURALISM IN ESL

28. Linguistic Migrations: Teaching English in Multicultural Contexts
    — *Esterino Adami* — 383–391

29. Identity Maintenance for Non-Native Speakers of English
    — *Rebecca Belchamber* — 392–400

30. Pursuing a Post-Method Pedagogy in English Language Instruction in India
    — *Miguel Mantero* and *Sikarini Majumdar* — 401–414

31. Understanding and Examining Linguistic Diversity in American Classrooms
    — *Charlotte Pass* and *Miguel Mantero* — 415–428

32. Crosstalk in Multilingual Interactions among Non-native Speakers of English
    — *Svetlana I. Harnisch* and *Maya Khemlani David* — 429–443

PART 10
CURRICULUM DEVELOPMENT

33. Universals in the Process of Curriculum Development in ELT
    — *E.A. Gamini Fonseka* — 447–457

34. Communicative Language Teaching: Problems of Designing Syllabuses and Producing Materials
    — *Madan M. Sarma* — 458–470

35. Constructing Curriculum for an Intensive English Program
    — *Natalie Hess* and *Elizabeth Templin* — 471–483

PART 11
LANGUAGE TESTING

36. Testing Communicative Competence
    — *Manish A. Vyas* and *Yogesh L. Patel* — 487–497

Author Index — *499–500*

Subject Index — *501–502*

FOREWORD

Teaching English as a Second Language: A New Pedagogy for a New Century is a wonderful collection of a variety of texts from prominent ESL/EFL educators from around the world. The book is like a buffet of great dishes from many cultures, many topics, tried and true classics as well as modern needs. It has rich contributions from authors from such diverse locations as Nigeria, Japan, China, India, and the US on a variety of topics ranging from the bread and butter principles of Communicative Language Teaching to the modern need for teachers to incorporate multimedia technologies such as podcasting and Computer-Assisted Language Learning into their English Language Teaching practice in order to make content memorable, meaningful, and accessible to today's hungry English language learners. Other sections focus on the meat and potatoes of content-based learning and task-based learning, which are so prominent in elementary and high schools nowadays, as well as innovative grammar teaching perspectives and the essentials of flavourful vocabulary instruction. The side dishes of motivation, personal inquiry, games and activities, and also business English add spice to this meal that make it unforgettable. Such rich variety of ethnic flavours would not be complete without an emphasis on multiculturalism in language teaching. The rich main course focuses on the sometimes hard to swallow curriculum development and testing, yet the authors are able to present this content in a palatable and easily digestible manner. Such a fabulous meal would not be complete without a satisfying desert emphasizing communication skills, which seems to be one of the most important areas of ELT nowadays since recent graduates are finding that this is the skill that is most used in the workplace.

It is my great pleasure to recommend this text for pre-service teachers who would like a broad panorama of the ELT world as well as for those seasoned professionals who would like to keep abreast of modern trends in the field.

Dr. Julie Ciancio
Associate Dean
College of Education, Westcliff University
Irvine, California, USA

PREFACE

It has been nearly six years since the first edition of this book was published in India and very well-received world-wide. The popular reception of the book and the growing number of ESL learners across the continents call for a new edition. In this edition, Chapters 13 and 23 have been rewritten, while Chapters 30 and 31 have been slightly modified. Nevertheless, when we contacted the contributors of the first edition for revising their essays, many of them were in favour of retaining the original ones. The reason, we believe, being that these essays provide plenty of practical experience to draw upon and also offer an important insight into different aspects of teaching English as a second language. It is important to note that the first edition was used as much in, let us say, a university department in Kerala as in a university in Israel or the US. While we do not claim that this anthology will provide immediate answers to the problems of teaching and learning ESL, it will undoubtedly point a way to begin with.

We thank Dr. Julie Ciancio for kindly agreeing to write a foreword to this edition. Thanks are also due to Prof. Deepti Gupta, Dr. Rajendrasinh Jadeja and Dr. Piyush Joshi for their inputs and words of encouragement. We also thank Ms. Babita Misra and Ms. Ruchira at PHI Learning, Delhi for their editorial assistance.

MANISH A. VYAS
YOGESH L. PATEL

PREFACE TO THE FIRST EDITION

Much has already been written and talked about teaching English as a Second Language. One would, therefore, be justified in asking: Why publish another volume on the subject? A survey of available works in India convinced us that there was a room for a book for teachers of English that can address the current issues in teaching English in the non-native context. At first, the editors had planned to include views of teachers in the Indian sub-continent only. However, the unprecedented spread and shifts, thanks to globalization, in teaching ESL in terms of teaching methods, curriculum, and application of learning theories made us feel the need to incorporate as many diverse voices as possible. Today, there are more non-native users of English than the native ones. This has resulted in the use of two varieties of language—what David Crystal calls "one spoken in one's home country and a new kind of English that can be internationally understood". Keeping this paradigm shift in view, teachers of English have to equip themselves with new methods and strategies. At the same time, this shift has generated a demand for teachers who can teach learners of varied cultures and socio-economic and psychological backgrounds. This volume is, therefore, an earnest effort to answer these existing challenges in teaching ESL from the application point of view.

It is important to define the focus of our attention and the context in which the term 'ESL' is used. As Muriel Saville-Troike in *Introducing SLA* aptly defines: "A Second Language is typically an official or societally (we can also add 'politically' and 'culturally') dominant language needed for education, employment and other basic purposes. It is often acquired by minority group members or immigrants who speak another language natively." Our primary aim is, thus, in ESL for teachers who teach English to the learners whose first language or mother tongue is a language other than English, who have to use English for social, professional and academic purposes.

Needless to say, this book does not aim at developing a single coherent theory or methodology or a communicative model for language teaching. Nor does it negate existing language theories. At best, it attempts to provide application-oriented solutions to the problems of teaching ESL. Language and language learning being a complex phenomenon, there can be no easy solutions. As Vaishna Narang comments: "A language teacher helping an adult learn a new language faces a number of problems in handling this complex socio-psychological phenomenon called language, and yet another complex of socio-psychological processes involved in language learning."

In this collection of 36 essays by contributors from around 18 countries across the globe, teachers of English will find a wide variety of themes—CALL, CLT, ICT, Content Based Instruction, Learners' Motivation, Cultural Diversity, Communicative Activities and Games, Developing Communication Skills, Curriculum Development, and Communicative Testing. Though the contributors have drawn heavily from their own academic backgrounds, it is hoped that the insights and suggestions they have provided will also illuminate the whole of the teacher fraternity, and may also become instrumental in establishing a Department of English as a Second Language in India.

In outlining and designing this book, we are, first and foremost, highly indebted to all the contributors, whose cooperation, hard work and trust in us made this book possible. We are personally thankful to Dr. Lixin Xiao who, despite the devastating earthquake that hit almost the whole of China and his native land, made it possible to contribute his essay. Our sincere thanks are also due to Dr. Paul Nation for readily sending his essay and, thus, encouraged novices like us. How can we forget Dr. Miguel Mantero, Dr. Ebata Makiko and Dr. Maya David who contributed two chapters and, thus, helped widen the scope of the book? However, the project had to face one of its saddest moments caused by the sad demise of one of the contributors, Late Professor Johanees Eckerth. We deeply regret his untimely death.

In the end, we would like to thank the Publishers, PHI Learning, for their careful processing of the manuscript.

MANISH A. VYAS
YOGESH L. PATEL

LIST OF CONTRIBUTORS

1. **Dr. ESTERINO ADAMI** is a researcher in English Language and Translation at the Faculty of Education, University of Turin, Italy. His areas of specialisation focus on English as a Global Language, Varieties of English (in particular, Indian English, African Englishes), English for Primary Teachers, Translation Studies and Anglophone Cultures. He has published various articles on Indian English, the role of games in ELT, Didactics of the New Englishes, Postcolonial and Diasporic Literatures in English. Author of *Rushdie, Kureishei, Syal: Essays in Diaspora* (2006), he is currently working on the semiotic analysis of the language of comics.

2. **Dr. EMMANUEL T. BABALOLA** teaches at the Department of English, Obafemi Awolowo University, Ile-Ife, Nigeria where he earned PhD in English Studies. His major areas of research are: contemporary use of the English language in major domains of language use, language in education and applied linguistics. He has published seminal papers in Nigeria, United States of America, Spain, Poland, Finland, and other countries. Dr. Babalola is also a regular speaker and resource person at workshops and seminars for English language teachers and a curriculum developer. He is a regular English language consultant for some leading publishers and print and electronic media houses in Nigeria, apart from being a regular newspaper columnist in the country. He is a member of English Studies Association of Nigeria, Linguistic Association of Nigeria, Reading Association of Nigeria and a former member of the International Reading Association.

3. **Dr. ALEXANDER BARATTA** teaches at Manchester Institute of Education, University of Manchester, UK. He received his PhD in English Language and Linguistics from the University of Manchester, having completed his MA in English Composition and Rhetoric in his native California. He has taught EFL in South Korea, the United States and the United Kingdom in the area of academic composition, specifically focusing on how writers reveal themselves within their academic essays (an area known as writer stance). He is also the author of a book entitled *Visual Writing*.

4. **REBECCA BELCHAMBER** teaches at the University of Adelaide, in the Academic Preparation Programme, the Pre-Enrolment English Program (PEP). She is pursuing her PhD on identity issues for Saudi Arabian students studying abroad in Australia.

5. **Dr. TOM BELLOMO** teaches within the Department of Student Life Skills for Daytona State College, Florida. Previously, he taught ESOL/EAP for the same institution, and graduate level applied linguistics at the University of Central Florida and Stetson University. Other experiences include having been an adult ESOL instructor and program manager in New York, and having taught multi-ethnic students in Spain.

6. **DAVID YOONG SOON CHYE** is a Senior Lecturer with the Faculty of Languages and Linguistics, University of Malaya. In addition to Discourse Analysis, his areas of research are Critical Discourse Analysis, Social Psychology, Sociology, Photography, Photojournalism and Musicology.

7. **Dr. MAYA KHEMLANI DAVID**, is Hon. Academic Consultant, London College of Clinical Hypnosis and Consultant, CLMV Program, AEI, University of Malaya. She has written *A Guide for the English Language Teacher: A Malaysian Perspective*, *The Sindhis of Malaysia: A Sociolinguistic Account* along with other co-authored and co-edited works such as *Language and the Power of Media, Teaching of English in Second and Foreign Language Settings: Focus on Malaysia* and *Developing Reading Skills*. As a sociolinguist, she has a special interest in cross-cultural communication and the role of language in establishing and maintaining peace and national unity. Dr. David is the Linguapax Prize Winner for 2007.

8. **Dr. VENKATARAMANAN DURAIRAJ** teaches at the Department of English, University of Madras, Chennai. He earned his PhD and M.Phil from University of Madras. He had been an Assistant Editor with Orient Longman, Chennai for four years as well as sub-editor with *The Indian Express* and wrote Book Reviews. In addition to these, he has presented and published papers on Curriculum, Canadian English, Postmodernism and Canadian Literature. His areas of expertise are Russian Studies, Postmodernism and ELT.

9. **Dr. MAKIKO EBATA** teaches English as a Second/Foreign Language at Digital Hollywood University, Tokyo. Her field of expertise is in Content Based Instruction, motivation and teacher-education.

10. **Dr. SIMON COFFEY** is an applied linguist and language teacher educator at King's College, London. Having taught English and other languages for many years, his research interests are language pedagogies, motivation and the use of discourse and narrative analytic approaches to understand individuals' investment in language learning. He has been the UK lead in several European Union-funded projects and has published widely on language autobiographies and teacher professional development.

11. **Dr. EDIRISNIGHA ARACHCHIGE GAMINI FONSEKA** is Head of the Department of English & Linguistics at the University of Ruhuna,

Sri Lanka. A specialist in Teaching Language through Literature, he has authored four series of a study guides for the Sri Lanka GEC ('O' Level) and ('A' Level) Examinations in English Literature and produced a number of academic papers and articles on language teaching and literary theory. His interests are oral literature, orality, learner autonomy, applied linguistics, stylistics, and cross culture. Besides, he is a scholar, writer, teacher educator, lecturer and an amateur dramatist, singer, cartoonist, painter, and storyteller.

12. **Ms. ANNE FOX** is a Briton living in Denmark since 1993. After gaining her TEFL MA she became an English teacher specializing in technical English for local, and international companies and runs her own business offering EFL training and teacher training consultancy mainly in the areas of digital learning especially in languages and intercultural communication. She has over 15 years experience as partner, external quality advisor, evaluator and manager (including VITAE) in various international educational projects. She is co-host of the Absolutely Intercultural podcast.

13. **Dr. DEEPTI GUPTA** is Professor, Department of English, Panjab University, Chandigarh, India. She has an M.Phil. in Stylistics and a PhD in ELT. She has been widely published in both national and international journals. She has presented papers in Singapore and South Korea, where she was a panelist in the panel discussion on ELT in India. Besides, she is also a member of English Language Teachers Association of India (ELTAI), International Association of Teachers of English as a Foreign Language (IATEFL), Associate Editor for *Asian EFL Journal* and *Profile Research Journal*, Columbia.

14. **Dr. SVETLANA I. HARNISCH** is the Head of All-Russian Scientific Permanent Working Seminar on Knowledge Society: Sociological Aspect. She is a doctorate in General Linguistics and Socio-linguistics, USSR Academy of Sciences, Institute of Linguistics, Moscow. She had been on the Chair of Soviet Research Committee on Socio-linguistics, Soviet Sociological Association, and Academy of Sciences, USSR. She has more than 100 publications including three monographs and two manuals to her credit. Her areas of expertise include Sociology of Communication, Philosophy of Language, Economy of Knowledge, Socio-linguistics, Language Policy, Language Planning. Code-switching and Cross Talk.

15. **Dr. NATALIE B. HESS** is an Associate Professor of Bilingual Multicultural Education and ESL at Northern Arizona University in Yuma. She has authored and co-authored several ESL textbooks and teacher resource books and has been a teacher-educator in six countries.

16. **Professor MARGARET HORRIGAN** has been an English language teacher since 1991. She teaches adults and children and is a Cambridge ESOL DELTA, CELTA and CELTYL trainer at International House and a teacher of EAP courses at the LUISS University in Rome. She is currently the head of teacher training at IH Rome.

xviii   List of Contributors

17. **Dr. S. JOSEPH ARUL JAYRAJ**, PhD in Applied Linguistics, is a Reader in the Department of English, St. Joseph's College, Tiruchirappalli, India. He has co-authored, edited and published articles on a number of themes of ELT as well as literature. In addition to this, he has also participated in national and international seminars and workshops. He is a member of English Language Teachers' Association of India (ELTAI).

18. **Dr. AADIL AMIN KAK** teaches at the Department of Linguistics, University of Kashmir, India. He earned his PhD from the University of Delhi. He has co-authored three books and has published and presented numerous articles in different national and international conferences and journals. Among several books, Dr. Kak has authored are: *Keshir Zabaan: Akh Grammari Vetsnai* (*Kashmiri Language: A Grammatical Description*), *The Attitude of Islam Towards Science and Philosophy* and *Introduction to English Phonetics and Phonology*. He specializes in Syntax, Computational Linguistics, Language Acquisition and Socio-linguistics.

19. **Dr. SHIRA KOREN** is on the editorial board of *Novitas-Royal: Research on Youth and Language* (a refereed electronic journal) as of 2007. She has an MA and a PhD in Applied Linguistics and a teaching certificate in English. She has been teaching reading comprehension and academic writing in English at Bar Ilan University, Israel since 1980. She has published articles both in linguistics and children's literature in several journals and has also published five children's books in Hebrew. She has developed computer programs for the purpose of sharing material with her colleagues, and a program for reading comprehension of academic material (TEXTFUN) on the Internet. Her research interests include musicality and acquisition of pronunciation, motivation and attitude to L2, vocabulary learning, dictionary use, note-taking, dynamic teaching of FL, modern fairy tales and parodies and gender studies.

20. **Dr. CONSTANT LEUNG** is a Professor of Educational Linguistics, King's College, London. His academic and research interests include classroom pedagogy, content and language-integrated curriculum development, language assessment, and language policy. He also serves on the Editorial Boards of four international journals: *Language Assessment Quarterly*, *Language and Education*, *Prospect*, and *TESOL Quarterly*

21. **Mrs. SIKARINI MAJUMDAR** is currently a PhD candidate in the College of Education at the University of Alabama. Her research interests lie in English language policy, multicultural education and international education.

22. **Dr. MIGUEL MANTERO** is an Associate Professor of Educational Linguistics and Chair of the Department of Curriculum and Instruction in the College of Education at the University of Alabama. His research and publications focus on the discourse practices of language classrooms, the role of cognition in second language acquisition, and identity and second language learning.

23. **Dr. P. BHASKARAN NAIR** is currently Professor of English at Hindustan University, Chennai, India. He had had his MLitt. and Ph.D. in ELT from the Central Institute of English & Foreign Languages (currently EFL University), Hyderabad. He has published many research articles and books (theory as well as coursebooks for schools and universities). Dr. Nair is currently engaged in teacher training and content development for various organizations. He also edits a quarterly *Journal of ELTIF*, and is the founder President of a professional organization—English Language Teachers' Interaction Forum (ELTIF).

24. **Dr. PAUL NATION** is Emeritus Professor of Applied Linguistics in the School of Linguistics and Applied Language Studies at Victoria University of Wellington, New Zealand. He has taught in Indonesia, Thailand, the United States, Finland, and Japan. He specializes in language teaching methodology and vocabulary learning. His latest books include *Learning Vocabulary in Another Language* (second edition 2013), *Focus on Vocabulary* (2007), and *Teaching Vocabulary: Strategies and Techniques* (2008). His forthcoming books are *Teaching ESL/EFL Listening and Speaking* (with Jonathan Newton) and *Teaching ESL/EFL Reading and Writing* (Routledge). Two books strongly directed towards teachers appeared in 2013 from Compass Media in Seoul—*What should every ESL Teacher Know?* (available free from HYPERLINK "http://www.compasspub.com/ESLTK" www.compasspub.com/ESLTK) and *What should every EFL Teacher Know?*

25. **Dr. INDIRA NITYANANDAM** retired as Principal, Smt. S.R. Mehta Arts College, Ahmedabad, Gujarat, India. She has been teaching ELT and English literature for last more than three decades. Being a versatile and prolific scholar, she has published six books and more than 25 research papers on ELT, translation studies and women's writings. She is also a recognized M.Phil. and PhD guide at the Gujarat University, Ahmedabad. She is now a visiting faculty at Indian Institute of Management, Ahmedabad and Entrepreneurship Development Institute of India (Gandhinagar).

26. **Dr. CORNELIA PARASKEVAS** is a Professor of Linguistics and Writing at Western Oregon University, where she teaches courses in Introductory Linguistics, Basic Grammar, Teaching Writing, History of English, Grammar and Writing. She completed her MA and PhD in Theoretical Linguistics at the University of Kansas. Her research interests include the contact zone between linguistics and writing, educational linguistics, teaching writing, language and immigration.

27. **Dr. CHARLOTTE PASS** is a PhD in Curriculum and Instruction from the College of Education in the University of Alabama. Her research interests are teacher education and English as a second language pedagogy. Currently, she works at the Department of English, Stillman College, Tuscaloosa, Alabama.

28. **Dr. JOHANSEN QUIJANO-CRUZ** is an Assistant Professor of English at Tulsa Community College. He holds a PhD in Rhetoric and Composition from the University of Texas at Arlington and graduate degrees in the Teaching of English as a Second Language and English Literature from the University of Puerto Rico. His research interests include rhetoric and composition, games and education, media rhetoric, procedural rhetoric, communication studies, and networked narratives.

29. **Professor ROBERTO RABBINI** teaches communication, writing and cross-cultural courses full time at Seigakuin University and part-time at Bunka Women's University and Tokyo University, Japan. He is an MA in Linguistics (TESOL) from the University of Surrey (UK). He has published and presented extensively in the field of applied linguistics and his research interests include cross-cultural psychology and bilinguistic development. Professor Rabbini is also a co-author of the communicative textbook *Out Front* and has co-written popular textbooks for Oxford University Press. He has been the President of the JALT Omiya Chapter and helped establish the first EFL podcast in Japan in 2003, which currently has a global audience of 17,000 listeners.

30. **Dr. MADAN M. SARMA** is Professor and Head of the Department of English and Foreign Languages at Tezpur University, Assam, India. He has been involved in ESL programme designing at various levels in Assam; helping in designing syllabuses and producing materials that are implemented and used in all government-aided schools in Assam. He has also designed CLT-oriented courses for undergraduate programmes. He has written a book on spoken English for Assamese-speaking students and has recently completed a major research project in ELT. His areas of interest are: ELT and applied linguistics, translation, critical theory and new literatures in English. He is an established creative writer and critic of Assamese and is also a translator.

31. **Dr. MIRIAM SCHCOLNIK** recently retired from the Division of Foreign Languages at Tel Aviv University, where she developed and directed the Multimedia Language Learning Center and coordinated and taught courses of English for Academic Purposes for three decades. She also designed and taught a graduate course on Computer Technology and Language Learning in the Tel Aviv University TESOL program for international students. Her areas of specialization are educational evaluation, instructional design and computer technology in education. Her research interests are e-reading and e-learning, computer mediated communication, and the use of technology in traditional and alternative language assessment. She has published numerous textbooks, teacher resource books and articles and has designed and developed many language learning software packages and online learning environments. She is webmaster of the IFAW (Israel Forum for Academic Writing) website (http://mschcolnik.wix.com/ifaw).

32. **Dr. VANESSA STREET** has a PhD in Education (Autonomous Language Learning and the Computer) from the University of Kent, UK, and has been working at the Université du Littoral Côte d'Opale, France. Her research interests include the interface between learning and technology, CLIL (Content and Language Integrated Learning), English language teaching methodology and EAP (English for Academic Purposes).

33. **Dr. ROTIMI TAIWO** teaches at the Department of English, Obafermi Awolowo University, Ile-Ife. His areas of interest are Text and Discourse Analysis and Applied English Syntax. He has published in *Nordic Journal of African Studies, Linguistik Online, California Linguistic Notes, Issues in Political Discourse Analysis. The Internet TESLJ International Journal of Language Culture and Society, Ife Studies in English Language*, and so forth. He has co-edited two books: *Towards the Understanding of Discourse Strategies* and *Perspectives on Media Discourse* and is currently editing a handbook titled: *Handbook of Research on Discourse Behavior and Digital Communication: Language Structures and Social Interaction*. Dr. Taiwo is also a consulting editor for *Linguistik Online* and a member of the editorial board of the *International Journal of Language, Society and Culture*.

34. **Professor ELIZABETH TEMPLIN** has recently retired as the Assistant Director of the Centre for English as a Second Language, the University of Arizona.

35. **Dr. RICHARD WATSON TODD** is an Associate Professor of Applied Linguistics at King Mongkut's University of Technology, Thonburi. He holds a PhD from the University of Liverpool and is the author of numerous articles and books, most recently, *Much Ado about English* (Nicholas Brealey Publishing).

36. **Professor S. VIJAYALAKSHMI** has fifteen years of teaching experience and has handled diverse subjects like technical English, general English, communication skills, soft skills, professional ethics and business communication. Her forte is vocabulary enhancement techniques and CASLA (Computer Assisted Second Language Acquisition). She has specialized in English Language Teaching and is pursuing her PhD in the field of technology for language learning. She is Associate Professor in English, School of Social Science and Humanities, VIT University, Tamil Nadu, India.

37. **JUSTYNA WALCZAK** is a teacher of English in Poland. She is widely published in reputed ELT journals.

38. **SAJAD H. WANI** teaches at the Department of Linguistics, University of Kashmir, and is also an academic counsellor with Indira Gandhi National Open University, New Delhi. He earned his MPhil in Linguistics from the University of Kashmir. He has contributed to some journals and has also presented papers in various national and international conferences.

39. **Dr. LIXIN XIAO** is a Professor of English Language Education and Intercultural Communication at School of Foreign Languages, Tianjin Polytechnic University, P.R. China. He holds a PhD in L2 & EFL Education from the School of Applied Language and Intercultural Studies, Dublin City University, Ireland. He has been teaching English as a Foreign Language at university level in China for over 27 years, and has research and teaching experience in Canada and Ireland. His main research interests include teaching methodology, CLT application in China, critical thinking development in EFL education and ESP. He has published widely internationally in reputed TEFL/TESL journals.

Chapter 1

ENGLISH
Aladdin's Magic Lamp

— Venkataramanan Durairaj

> Every language is a temple in which the soul of those who speak it is enshrined.
> — Oliver Wendell Holmes Sr.

This study contextualizes the metamorphosis of the English language from a colonial power to a global market player and questions its dual status today with an apprehensive query about its next move. English has subsumed several languages and emerged as a global power-broker, but it occupies a paradoxical position in the contemporary world language scene, which interestingly has turned the applecart of English as an erstwhile colonial legacy and has fixed it within a different paradigmatic structure. English dominates the global arena in more ways than one. It has seeped into every sector of human endeavour—personal and public. Today, proficiency with the nuances of the English language—both spoken and written—promotes the user in several ways.

The story of the language is the best story that has come to be written. From sounds and gestures to a common means of communication, the evolution of language is a bestseller par excellence. Every language across the globe has its own unique story to narrate. It goes without saying that no single language can be considered inferior or superior. But reality springs many a surprise. Languages undergo changes—they transform, they also die. Sometimes, a single language can play a crucial role in razing down the citadels of other languages. David Malouf (1934–), an Australian writer, in his story 'The Only Speaker of his Tongue' describes a lexicographer's meeting with the last speaker (as quoted by Crystal 2005):

> When I think of my mother tongue being no longer alive in the mouths of men, a chill goes over me that is deeper than my own death, since it is the gathered death of all my kind. (p. 114)

It is this extermination that David Crystal bemoans as "Language Death". In this, the role of English as a colonial power takes on a significance that has raised so much dust yet to settle down. It comes as no surprise that English has 'displaced' many aboriginal languages in North America and Australia. As Crystal rightly states, language is "community history" and "cultural identity" (*ibid.*, pp. 58–59). Language and its development is a significant move in the history of humankind. It would not be amiss to state that *language is power*. But what happens when one language absorbs and flaunts this power? What happens when one language comes to dominate as a global language? The English language has done just this!

English has travelled a long way. It is no more merely a language of the British Empire but has taken on the status of a global language. Crystal clarifies, "A language becomes a world language for one reason only—the power of the people who speak it" (*ibid.*, p. 10). He attributes this power to political, technological, cultural and economic reasons. He points out that English is spoken as a first language besides major countries like UK, USA, Ireland, Australia, Canada, New Zealand, South Africa, also by a majority of people in Antigua, Bahamas, Barbados, Belize, Bermuda, Dominica, Grenada, Guyana, Jamaica, St. Christopher and Nevi, St. Lucia, St. Vincent, and Trinidad and Tobago. In this context, the rise of English takes on interesting dimensions. It has subsumed many languages and has assumed a gargantuan status at the global level. Now, the seminal question is—can we call this 'empowerment'? The quality of empowerment is an innate component of any language, which is a special gift to human beings. The ability to communicate is in itself empowerment. But the notion of empowerment needs to be questioned when one language emerges as a dominant one razing down other languages. One language should not be responsible for the death of other languages.

Today, there is a presupposed notion that facility with the spoken and written forms of English is empowerment. It has come to be seen as an indicator of power and success. English has come to be equated with empowerment. The big question is—is it? The answer is—it is and it isn't. Steven R. Covey defines empowerment as "the power within people, enormous reservoir of creativity, activity, potential contribution that lies within a worker, largely untapped by organizational leadership and management" and that "it is not a program; it is a condition for quality." In the word 'empowerment', the root 'power' refers to the ability to do, accomplish, perform and enable. In Latin and Greek, the prefix 'em' means "within". We need to question what is within English that empowers. Is English empowerment? It is *Yes* and *No*.

In the contemporary world, 'knowledge' is a business package stylishly packed, marketed and sold, embalmed within the enduring charm generated by the 26 alphabets of the English language which finds itself in a strange position—a position that is both laudable and enviable. From a colonial construct, English has metamorphosed into 'Englishes' and now plays the role of a global 'Big Brother'. It has become a post-global marketable product and its next step is apprehensive. What is interesting but pitiable to note is that English has become Janus-faced, as a global facilitator on one side and as a global watchdog on the other. Is this empowerment?

English has created a special place, a common platform across the globe. It has become a unifying agent, a common channel of expression. This has strengthened the corporate and industrial sectors and to some extent the academia. But this platform itself has created a 'class' ignoring other groups. In this case, commonality only divides. Thus, empowerment becomes enslavement leading to an imbalance. There arises a gulf between those who comprehend the language and those who cannot, and those who do not get an opportunity. So, English unites as well as divides. If divisions are bridged, then that would be true empowerment.

As a global player, English has impregnated the academia, media and corporate sectors, which were earlier posing as 'ivory towers'. The so-called language of the British Empire has been processed by all the market players and the end products are the brands of English that permeate the present, from "English for Engineers" (many universities—especially technical—have such a course) to "Business English"? or Communication Skills (prescribed in MBA and commerce curricula). There has been a perceptible paradigm shift, not only in the nature but also in the uses of the English language. The language and its components are the same. But English comes packaged according to the market needs. Now, Soft Skills has become the 'in-thing' that the corporate players and subsequently the academics are harping on. Here again, though there are other components to Soft Skills, it is the language that operates at the core. There is much hue and cry over learning spoken as well as written English.

What is more interesting is that India has come to be one of the major players in this dalliance with English, which is playing a major role in the IT corridors, corporate conglomerates, the academia, media and industry. English is the new *mantra*—the elitist buzzword. One witnesses a sporadic growth of interest in the use of English, and this has led to the metamorphosis of English into Englishes that only seem to be proliferating. It is more interesting to note that several countries like France, Germany and Korea evince a keen interest in learning 'English and Englishes' and they come to the Indian shores for this purpose. They do not show any indication of approaching either the United Kingdom or the United States of America—the two so-called guardians and promoters of the English language. The obvious question to ask would be—Why this hesitance? Can we now see English in this context as empowering? If these countries approach either England or America for assistance in learning English, this would be a revival of a kind of neocolonialism. The United Kingdom (UK) and USA have not yet come out of their ideological framework as an enslaving apparatus in spite of English having slipped between their clutching fingers of a stranglehold. So, resorting to help from these two countries would only be a revisiting and a renewal of 'subservience' to a new form of colonialism. This leads to a Hobson's choice of ignoring UK and USA vis-à-vis learning English. And India comes to play a crucial role here. It functions as both a hospitable and a versatile source-provider, well-equipped with all the requirements of offshore clients. Here we need to reiterate that India in serving these needs plays to its legacy of a humanist tradition. This is the 'empowerment' that we render the English language as against the so-called empowerment instituted by UK and USA.

The English language 'entices' and it 'sells'. As already stated, a tremendous boom is seen at the global level for the acquisition of skills in English. India, equipped with all the prerequisites, is now serving the needs of countries such as Germany, France, South Korea and China. In this sense, India has been truly empowered. But we need to see beyond this and reflect on what would happen once the needs of these countries have been fulfilled. Then where will we stand? In being merely a service provider sans any political agenda, we would soon turn deadwood once we deliver the goods. Then we will be functioning not as providers but merely as another competitor in the 'global rush' ruminating on ways of marketing English. This is an open question that needs to be addressed.

English—the genie in Aladdin's magic lamp—has worked wonders. The genie, tired, seems to have taken a break. Its silence is apprehensive. Is it hibernating? Will it answer another call? The questions are many! The answers are unpredictable. The users of the English language need to keep trying their luck. Who knows, several other genies may be within! By the way, Aladdin also needed English to reach across the world from Arabia!

REFERENCES

Covey, Steven R., "What is Experiment?" Retrieved from
    www.qualitydigest.com/jan/covey.html
Crystal, David, *The Language Revolution*, New Delhi: Foundation Books, 2005.

Part 1

COMMUNICATIVE LANGUAGE TEACHING IN ESL CONTEXT

Chapter 2

WHAT CAN WE LEARN FROM CLASSROOM OBSERVATIONS? A Study of CLT in a Chinese University Context

— LIXIN XIAO

2.1 INTRODUCTION

In this chapter, we describe the procedures used for classroom observation and the teachers' attitudes towards them. Then we give the details concerning classroom observations of five English language teacher participants in the English Department, of one of the major universities in North China to see whether the generally favourable attitudes held by teachers towards the communicative language teaching (CLT) approach are reflected in teachers' classroom practices. Two of the five participants, Ms. Lan and Ms. Shan who teach the same English Reading Course with the same textbook, are selected in particular for detailed comparison and analysis in order to find out the similarities and differences between them in line with the principles of CLT approach. Following this, there is a discussion of the interrelated contributory factors which have led to the discrepancy between what the teachers claimed to be [do] and what they actually did in their English class. Finally, some pedagogical suggestions are given about adopting CLT in the Chinese EFL (English as a foreign language) context at the college level.

2.1.1 Background

The Chinese Ministry of Education issued a revised version of Chinese National English Language Curriculum for English Majors at the college level, which requires that a communicative or innovative language teaching approach, i.e., a student-centred approach, should be employed in English classrooms (English Division 2000). The revised curriculum requires teachers to place emphasis on the cultivation of students' cross-cultural communicative competence. The curriculum represents a great challenge to the traditionally dominant role that Chinese teachers of English have been playing in a teacher-centred classroom because a communicative or student-centred approach to lesson, material and syllabus design advocates the involvement of learners in contributing to the classroom learning process. Learners can be invited to express their views on their needs for learning the language, their preferred learning styles, their beliefs about language learning or their preferred activity types (Barkhuisen 1998). However, so far, 200 empirical study in China has examined in an overt systematic way the relationship between Chinese EFL teachers' perceived attitudes to it and the concepts of CLT or student-centred approach and the daily instructional practices they really adopt in their English classes.

2.1.2 Related Study to Date

Judging from this line, this study is a follow-up project of a series of separate investigations in which both quantitative and qualitative research methods were used to elicit both students' and teachers' attitudes to and opinions on CLT, the traditional teacher-centred approach, the teaching of culture, and their own perceived respective roles in English class (Xiao 2005; Xiao 2006a; Xiao 2006b). The investigation showed that the current teaching approach widely used by the teachers failed to capture most of English-majored students' preferences; nor was it found effective to develop learners' ability to use English appropriately for communication purposes (*ibid.*). Although many teachers claimed, in their interview accounts, to have adopted communicative language teaching methods in class, the findings revealed that there was an obvious mismatch between teachers' attitudes to CLT and their real teaching practices. This result was supported by the related survey findings: although majority of the students and the teachers under study showed their respective favourable attitudes towards CLT, it was found that, in terms of instructional practices, many students who voiced their support of CLT disliked the so-called CLT methods employed by their teachers in English class (*ibid.*). It is obvious that CLT practices that teachers claimed to adopt in English class do not match their students' preferences or expectations. The results also supported the findings of some previous studies which explored the gap between teachers' instructional practices and students' pedagogical preferences (Spratt 1999; Rao 2002). On the teachers' part, the implications of related studies to this current research seem to be clear: What teachers claimed to be (i.e., their favourable attitudes to CLT) and what they claimed to do may not match with what they really have done in their English class in spite of the fact that most of teachers claimed to be CLT supporters or followers.

2.1.3 Statement of Purpose

Based on the above mentioned scenario, the author has tried to investigate

Chinese EFL teachers' instructional practices through personal classroom observations in order to find out the following

1. Whether the above-mentioned favourable attitudes held by teachers towards CLT are reflected in their instructional practices.
2. If any mismatch exists, what are the possible reasons for this mismatch?
3. On the basis of this investigation, I will suggest a pedagogical guideline to apply the communicative features of CLT to the teachers' instructional practices at the college level.

2.2 LITERATURE REVIEW OF CLT

Communicative language teaching (CLT) starts from a theory of language as communication. CLT is not really a coherent and cohesive theory aimed at supporting a set of techniques for foreign or second language (L2) teaching in a clear-cut way. Rather, it is more an eclectic collection of emphases in the teaching of language, which are drawn from many sources, and promote or lead to the teaching and learning of foreign language or L2 as a tool for communication (Widdowson 1978; Littlewood 1981). It stresses the importance of using the language in interaction rather than mastering the rules of usage. The goal of the approach is to increase learners' communicative competence. Littlewood points out that one of the most characteristic features of CLT is that:

> It pays systematic attention to functional as well as structural aspects of language, combining these into a more fully communicative view. (p. 1)

CLT advocates go beyond teaching grammatical rules of the target language and propose that, by using the target language in a meaningful way, learners will develop communicative competence. Richards and Rodgers (1986/2001) also claim that:

> The emphasis in CLT on the processes of communication rather than mastery of language forms leads to different roles for [teacher and] learners from those found in more traditional second language classrooms. (p. 166)

In China, English language is taught and learned in a non-native English environment in which the classroom where the language is taught seems to be the only formal place where learners are exposed to the target language and able to practise it, especially oral English. Outside the classroom, the learners have little access to an English-speaking environment in which they can reinforce their classroom learning as can their English as a second language (ESL) counterparts. Given such a situation, CLT, as an innovative teaching approach which needs to be specifically modified to suit the Chinese EFL education context, has been advocated in order to enhance the learners' communicative competence (English Division, 2000, *op. cit.*).

2.3 RATIONALE FOR CLASSROOM OBSERVATION IN THIS STUDY

Classroom observation is, no doubt, the most direct means of gaining insight into teachers' English language instruction as well as learners' classroom behaviour. To serve this purpose, it also enables one to find a match or mismatch between what teachers claimed to do and what they actually did in their English classes. Lincoln and Guba (1985) point out the importance of detailed observation: "Prolonged engagement provides scope, and persistent observation provides depth" (p. 302). Kleinsasser and Savignon (1991) also note that there is a difference between information about teaching practice and the reality of the practice. They claim that "Observation can mirror what they [teachers] do rather than what they profess to be [do]". (p. 293)

2.3.1 Teacher Participants

In this study, consequently, observations were carried out on five teacher participants in their English classes. Each participant was observed for four class hours to gain understanding of the way he/she handled his/her classroom instruction of an English lesson from the textbook (see Table 2.1 for details). During the classroom observations, I focused on the whole proceedings of the class events which were observable: setting, participants, events, acts and gestures (Glesne and Peshkin 1992). This enabled me to capture an overall view of class events than determining in advance what to look for in the observed context.

TABLE 2.1   Classroom Observation Details

Teachers	English course	Years of teaching	Class hours Observed	Students in English Class (U)
Ms. Lan	Comprehensive reading	8	4	2nd year
Ms. Shan	Comprehensive reading	14	4	2nd year
Ms. Ming	Introduction to Western cultures	21	4	2nd year
Ms. Chang	Linguistics	5	4	4th year
Mr. Cai	Selected readings from Western business journals and magazines	20	4	3rd year

Note: U = undergraduate students.

Of the five teachers, I chose two of them, namely, Ms. Lan and Ms. Shan[1], for detailed comparison and analysis since these two teachers,

---
1. All teacher participants in this research are given pseudonames to protect their privacy.

during the interviews, expressed their strong support of CLT approach which both also claimed to have used in their own instructional practice (Xiao 2006b, *op. cit.*). In addition, Lan had received the Dean's Award for her impressive efforts in initiating communicative teaching methods in her class. The teaching methods she used were reported to be the most liked by the students. This further aroused my interest in observing her class to see if there were any discrepancies or similarities between the two teachers who taught the same course with the same textbook.

2.3.2 Research Methodology: The Design for Classroom Observation

The procedure used for classroom observation was 'semistructured' in the sense that I focused on the proceedings of the class events as a whole instead of specific activities in the classroom. This enabled me to "capture more meaningful class events than determining in advance what to look for in the observed context" (Seliger and Shohamy 1989). In other words, I paid great attention to three dimensions at the procedural level—*classroom instruction, practice,* and *interaction*—as emphasized by Richards and Rodgers (1986). "**Instruction**" here means the way the teacher delivers the course in the class. "**Practice**" is defined as the language or language-related activities assigned by teachers for the students to do during the class. "**Interaction**" refers to the exchange of information between the teacher and the students or between the students, according to unequal information distribution or the *information gap* (*ibid.*). In this study, these three dimensions provide guidelines for the following discussion of the participants' teaching behaviours during the class.

The classroom observation took place in the English Department in one of the comprehensive universities in North China. When observing the class, I sat at the back of the classroom because all the classes observed were teacher-fronted. In order not to make the teacher feel uncomfortable and at the same time to make the class observation as authentic and natural as possible, I did not tape-record the classroom process. I took notes on the events that were going on in the class (types of practice, types of interactions, class events and so on). In addition, immediately following the observations, I reviewed and expanded all notes to include further information and detail. Altogether 20 teaching hours of English classes were observed as detailed in Table 2.1, which cover different courses designed for the students with different English proficiency levels.

2.4 TEACHERS' ATTITUDES TOWARDS CLASSROOM OBSERVATION

Prior to discussion of participants' teaching behaviours, it is worthwhile giving brief background information on teachers' general attitudes towards classroom observation so that readers may have a clear idea as to why the classroom observation proved to be a most sensitive aspect of this study.

Classroom observation proved to be quite unpopular as far as the teachers were concerned. Some teachers, especially seniors in their early or mid-fifties, whom I contacted in person or by telephone, tactfully declined the request declaring that they would feel quite 'uncomfortable' having their lessons observed. One teacher in his late 50s, who taught the course Introduction to Cultural Backgrounds of Major English-speaking Countries declined bluntly when I approached him with the request to observe his class. The teacher just said very modestly: "This lesson is not very interesting and not worth observing. Please do not waste your time." I was very surprised to hear that the teacher thought his own lecturing was "not interesting". If this was the case, I wondered, what would his students think of his lecture! This seemed to justify Liu's (1997) remarks about the role of observing classes and its implications in the Chinese EFL context. According to Liu, classroom observation was viewed negatively by teachers as it was always regarded as a means of assessing teaching. No matter what other purposes observation might have, the professional reputation of the observed teacher's 'face' was at stake (Scollon and Scollon 1995). Their reluctance to accept classroom observation was due to their deep-rooted misunderstanding of the purpose of the research project as well as previous negative experiences. Some teachers thought classroom observation was fruitless, amounted to faultfinding and even counter-productive since it made the teacher feel nervous and threatened and was, therefore, not representative of a normal lesson. Managing to convince them that I was coming to the class as an individual researcher, not in any official capacity, I finally contacted five teachers and got their prior permission to observe their English classes.

2.5 PRESENTATION OF THE CLASSROOM OBSERVATIONS

It is interesting to note that the close examination of the data collected through the class observations of the participants showed remarkable similarities in the types of instructional activities, class practices, and teacher-student or student-student 'interactions'. Some striking differences are also revealed between Ms. Lan and the other teachers in the way communicative activities were carried out in the classes.

The class practices can be further divided into two categories: (i) **text-based** and (ii) **non-text based**. The former is invariably non-communicative in the sense that there is no information gap between the speaker and the listeners. For instance, in Ms. Shan's class, she asked one student to read a paragraph of the textbook aloud before she went through the text in meticulous detail and in the traditional sentence-by-sentence manner. She sometimes asked the whole class a few questions which were listed on the right-hand side of the textbook or some grammatical questions, including paraphrasing some new words or verbal phrases. For example, when she came across the following sentence in the text:

> ... I did a 30-feet-long *mural* for which I laboriously copied hieroglyphics onto the sheet of brown paper. But no one ever told me what they *stood for*.

She asked the whole class, "what does the verbal phrase 'stand for' mean?". Then she asked a male student to give a synonym of the word 'mural'. The student answered *fresco*, but no difference or similarities were explained between the two words.

The **non-text-based** activities were somewhat communicative although at times they could be non-communicative as well. For instance, in Ms. Lan's class, students were divided into groups of 3–4 to discuss the topic "Ethnic minority discrimination" in relation to the text materials. This reflected the communicative nature of the class observed. However, when students were required to take turns doing an oral presentation in front of the class, almost all of them just *read* their pre-prepared notes rather than *talked* about the topic freely. There were no questions and answers after each presentation. Their activity was useful only insofar as the speakers had to make themselves understood by the whole class. No communication or exchange of ideas with each other took place. The teachers' patterns of classroom instruction and class activities are summarized in Tables 2.2 and 2.3, respectively. Table 2.4 lists the similarities and differences between teachers' instructional practices and their explanations.

TABLE 2.2 Teachers' Teaching Patterns in the Class[2]

Name	Course	Steps followed by the teachers
Ms. Lan	Comprehensive reading	1. Asking students to give oral presentation
		2. Briefly recapping the main points
		3. *Going over the text sentence by sentence*
	2nd year U	4. *Doing text-related exercises*
		5. Putting students in groups for discussion
Ms. Shan	Comprehensive reading	1. Asking students to give oral 'news report'
		2. English dictation
		3. *Going over the text sentence by sentence*
		(Continued)

---

2. Italics in Tables 2.2 and 2.3 indicate the similarities of teaching patterns observed in the classes of teacher participants.

TABLE 2.2 Teachers' Teaching Patterns in the Class (*Continued*)

Name	Course	Steps followed by the teachers
	2nd year U	4. *Asking students to paraphrase new words* 5. *Doing text-related exercises*
Ms. Ming	Introduction to Western cultures	1. *Asking a student to read a paragraph aloud* 2. *Going over the text sentence by sentence* 3. *Explaining new words, cultural information*
	2nd year U	4. *Doing text-related exercises by asking or answering questions*
Mr. Cai	International business reading	1. *Asking students to read a paragraph aloud* 2. *Going over the text sentence by sentence* 3. *Explaining some business terms*
	3rd year U	4. *Offering some background information*
Ms. Chang	Linguistics	1. *Going over the text materials by listing key points and terms*
	4th year U	2. *Going over the text materials closely* 3. *Explaining terms and key words*

Note: U stands for undergraduate students majored in English language.

TABLE 2.3 Types of Class Events[2]

Name	Classroom Instruction	Class Events — Text based	Class Events — Non-text based
Ms. Lan	[2]*Explaining new words of the text; demonstrating usage.* *Providing cultural information.* *Going over a text in a sentence by sentence way.*	Asking students questions listed in the textbook and asking them to paraphrase new words.	Asking students to discuss a topic in small groups;[3] Asking students to do a presentation (pre-prepared written speech).

(*Continued*)

---

3. Underlined part represents the difference between Lan's class and the other four teachers' classes.

TABLE 2.3 Types of Class Events (*Continued*)

Name	Classroom Instruction	Class Events Text based	Class Events Non-text based
Ms. Shan	*Explaining new words in the text. Demonstrating usage. Going over the text in a sentence by sentence way.*	Asking students to paraphrase new words in the text.	Asking students to come to the front and give news report (pre-prepared written speech).
Ms. Ming	*Explaining new words, places of historical interest in the text. Going over the texts in a sentence by sentence way.*	Asking students to answer the text-based questions listed in the textbook.	None
Mr. Cai	*Explaining the new words and business terms in the text. Going over the text sentence by sentence.*	Asking students to paraphrase new words/terms.	None
Ms. Chang	*Explaining definitions of linguistics and then referring back to the text materials.*	Occasionally asking some text-based questions.	None

TABLE 2.4 Similarities/Differences between Teachers' Instruction Practices and their Explanations[4]

	Similarities and Differences in Teaching Practice	*Teachers' Explanations*
Lan	Focus of instruction mainly on language forms and content of texts.	Students expected to learn more from a teacher.
	Students under tight control in doing text-based activities.	Pre-prepared written speech would lead to accuracy and high-quality homework. Students' proficiency in English was not good enough.
	The read their oral presentation rather than talking about it.	They didn't want to make errors.
	Communicative activities in groups or in pairs on a designated topic.	They liked working in a small group in my class.
Shan	Focus of instruction mainly on language forms and content of texts.	The aims and objectives of the course was prescribed and had to be followed via the textbook.

(*Continued*)

---

4. Bold type refers to the different in teaching methods used between Lan and the other four teacher participants in this study.

TABLE 2.4 Similarities/Differences between Teachers' Instruction Practices and their Explanations (*Continued*)

Similarities and Differences in Teaching Practice	Teachers' Explanations
Students under tight control doing non-communicative text-based activities. *They read their news report rather than talking about it.* No interaction between teacher and students took place.	Students were now given more time than before in class to practise oral English. "Teaching sparsely but well" (*shao er jing*): Oral English class teacher should be responsible for students' oral English ability, not I. Students' proficiency in English was too weak for successful communicative activities in class.
Ming — *Focus of instruction mainly on language forms and the content of texts.* Students under tight control. No interaction between teacher and students took place.	Class time was limited, students could do cultural comparisons after class. The aim of this course was to provide students with cultural information. Textbook was the main source teachers could rely on to finish the prescribed job in class. Students' knowledge about Western culture was inadequate for cultural comparison and contrast in class.
Cai — *Focus of instruction mainly on language forms and the content of texts.* Students under tight control. No interaction between teacher and students took place.	Students kept quiet in class, making it hard to engage them in communicative activities. They did not seem to like SCA[5]. My teaching would be evaluated on how much students had learned about the content of the texts and their knowledge of business terms. Students' knowledge of the content was too limited for meaningful group discussions in class.
Chang — *Focus of instruction mainly on the content of texts.* No interaction between teacher and students took place.	The nature of this course was to provide knowledge of the content rather than acquisitions of language skills. The objective of the course was designed to impart specific knowledge to students.

Red fonts show the difference among the teachers.

5. SCA stands for student-centred approach, a teaching approach required by the Chinese Ministry of Education for English language instruction to language-majored students at college level.

Although different subtypes of practice could be distinguished under both text based and non-text based activities, the teachers' classroom practice was characterized by two features when they engaged students in the former. First, the students had to be familiar with the text before they were able to complete the exercises in the class. Second, the classroom activities provided very few opportunities for the students to engage in genuine communication because these activities did not generally require information gaps and nor efforts to work towards the same of convergent goals with the exception of group discussions on a designated topic in Lan's class. Students merely answered the questions about new words, paraphrase or based on the text content which had just been closely analysed in the class.

As can be seen from Tables 2.2 and 2.3, despite the differences in the types of courses and teaching materials taught, the five teacher participants were extremely similar in two key aspects of teaching: (i) *instruction* and (ii) *practice*. During instruction, they mainly focused on language structure and grammatical points and followed the textbook very closely. Students were under tight control when they did text based exercises which covered sentence structure, text-related questions and answers. Another common characteristic was that the content of instruction was determined by text materials used in the class, reflecting heavy dependence on the teaching materials.

However, it was worth noting that there existed striking differences between the communicative group discussion in Lan's class and the non-communicative activities in the classes of the other four participants. Lan was the only teacher to engage students in a communicative group discussion on a designated topic relating to the text. Regarding oral practice activities, only Lan and Shan required students, to go to the front of the class in turns and give an oral presentation. Only their classrooms shared common approaches to the way the oral practice was carried out. As was evident in the observation, the real problem was not of the oral practice *per se* but the way students did their oral practice. During the presentation, each speaker actually *read* his or her pre-prepared written notes rather than *talked about* the topic freely. Consequently, there was no interaction between the speaker and the listeners. No questions and answers were elicited based on the content presented. Everyone took turns, one after another. It was more like students doing individual homework than engaging in communication with peers.

2.6 COMPARISON OF CLASS INTERACTION BETWEEN LAN's AND SHAN's

As is evident from the foregoing discussion, three dimensions at the procedural level were the focus of classroom observations. The results of observation showed that the *instruction style* of five teacher participants was remarkably similar: a traditional approach in which text content was dealt with very closely in a sentence by sentence manner with emphasis placed on structure and grammatical points. The following discussion focuses on the other two dimensions: class practice and interaction, which should indicate how well communicative or non-communicative activities were taking place. As shown in Table 2.5, the main similarities and discrepancies lay in the ways in which communicative activities were organized and conducted in the class. The Table 2.5 highlights the similarities and differences between the teaching styles of Lan and Shan.

TABLE 2.5   Similarities and Discrepancies

Teacher	Similarities		Discrepancies	
	Oral practice of students	*Interaction between T and S*	*Communicative activities*	*Interaction between S and S*
Lan	*Reading* oral presentation	Very limited	Group discussion on a given topic	Yes
Shan	*Reading* news report	Very limited	None	None

Note: S stands for students; T stands for teachers.

2.6.1   Discrepancies

As shown above, the discrepancy between Lan and Shan was that the former's class was comparatively more communicative in nature than the latter class because Lan engaged her students in the communicative activities via group discussions which seemed to be favoured by students who could practise their spoken English by communicating with one another in a group. It was Lan's class which the students liked most as they told the researcher later on. Lan's class was divided into 5 groups with 3 or 4 students in one group. The students started discussing the topic and some of them looked up for new words in the dictionary. Other students took notes while listening to their peers. It seemed that the discussion went well and students were active in the group work. After the group discussion, one student from each group gave a short summary to the whole class. It was interesting to point out that the report-back speakers from each group *talked about* the summary with only an occasional reference to a written note. This was because they did not have enough time to complete their summary in written form and had to list some key points which they needed to present.

Judging from the spontaneity and fluency of the students' *free talk*, it seemed that their oral presentation could be more communicative if they had done it in this free-style manner rather than *reading* written notes. After the group summary, the teacher finally gave a brief comment by supplementing the topic with some further information. It is worth mentioning that students' summary reports reflected their limited knowledge about the topic under discussion as they had little experience or knowledge of ethnic minority discrimination in China. They mainly talked about the cultural differences among different ethnic minorities or nationalities in China rather than ethnic minority discrimination. This inevitably points to the necessity of selecting a discussion topic that can match the students' current understanding and experience of the outside world to ensure a more fruitful group discussion. But in Shan's class, there was no such communicative group work. Students were given opportunities to practise their oral English without genuine interaction either between teacher and the students or between the students themselves.

2.6.2 Similarities

As shown in Tables 2.2, 2.3, and 2.4, the similarities between the two teachers—Lan and Shan—were mainly in the two aspects: (i) going over the text content in a sentence-by-sentence way, and (ii) oral practice. Apart from the similar ways, they dealt with the text materials, both the teachers also showed one common feature in the way they engaged their students in oral English practice in their classes: teachers had *inadequate* expectation of their students in terms of their [the students'] classroom behaviours. The students in both the classes, when giving oral presentation or news report, *read* the pre-prepared written notes instead of *talking* about the topic spontaneously in front of the class. Consequently, no real interaction took place between the teacher and the students or among the students themselves as detailed below.

Shan's class

In Shan's class, the students were required to take turns to come to the front of the class to tell the whole class four pieces of brief news in English. As revealed in the observation, a female student came to the front and began *reading* her pre-prepared note.

The classroom observation reveals that the teacher concerned had some misconception of communicative language teaching and did not see her role as one of guiding her students to *talk about* rather than to *read* their presentation. There was no interaction involved between speaker and listeners. The classroom atmosphere was not active and some students paid divided attention to the speaker. While the 'news reporter' was reading, I noticed, a girl sitting in front of me was reading the novel *Gone with the Wind,* and two male students on the right side were either looking up for new words in an electronic dictionary or doing something else. The teacher, Ms. Shan, made corrections every now and then and offered extra information while a student was *reading* her news report.

Lan's class

In Lan's class, the students were asked to give an oral presentation individually on the topic *What makes a good teacher or a good student in the 21st century?* Students had almost a week to prepare a presentation on this topic. In the class, they took turns to give a 4-minute oral presentation. Unlike in Shan's class, the striking feature of this oral practice was that the speakers again *read* their pre-prepared written speech rather than *talked* about it. The teacher noted the key points out of each speech and then wrote them down on the blackboard after each speaker finished his or her speech.

I observed that almost all student speakers had no direct eye contact with the audience and seldom used gestures to enhance their speech. A male student speaker, with his hands behind his back, just stared at his notes while *reading* his presentation. It was amazing to find in Lan's class that neither atmosphere nor effort was made to get the students to *talk about* rather than *read* their presentation. After the class, I had a brief discussion with Lan and asked her for her comment on the students' '*reading* presentation'. It was clear that she did not consider *reading out* the presentation to be a problem at all. She emphasized that each student's presentation performance was given a mark which would count towards his or her total end of semester mark. Students took it very seriously and spent a lot of time on preparing the topic. Lan explained that her students wanted to do a good presentation in front of the class. Therefore, they tended to believe 'reading out' obviously was a safe way to reflect the time and effort they devoted to their preparation. Explicitly asking them not to refer to their notes when they did their oral presentation might have been counter-productive, she claimed. They may feel very nervous and would not have been able to express themselves fluently. Many students would try to memorize their pre-prepared notes and it would be very likely that some of them might forget their 'lines' during the presentation. Students were worried that such a poor performance would not do justice to the work that they had done as part of their presentation. They felt safer referring to their notes. Lan concluded that her students' proficiency in English was not yet good enough and teachers could not expect too much at this stage. 'More haste, less speed'.

Her remarks showed clearly why she did not even expect her students to *talk about* rather than *reading* the topic in her class. She thought *reading out* would reflect how much effort each of her students put into preparing the topic and, consequently, lead to a good performance. It seemed that Ms. Lan was not clear of what difference it would make by explaining to students explicitly the beneficial functions of *talking* freely during the oral practice. Referring back to the *summary talk* by report-back speakers at the end of group discussion in Lan's class, it can be seen that although the students did not speak English very fluently or, in other words, they *talked* less fluently than they *read*, their efforts would pay off in the end. Through doing this, students would gradually overcome their nervousness and shyness.

2.7 CRITICAL COMMENTS ON LAN's AND SHAN's INSTRUCTIONAL PRACTICES

As is evident, a complex mix of affective, sociocultural, and educational factors were at work in determining the way students behaved in class such as fear of negative evaluation (Horwitz et al.: 1986) by teacher and peers, anxiety, fear of losing face, their lack of self-confidence in their proficiency in English and the habits they had acquired unconsciously over their school experience. Apart from the Chinese cultural influence on language learning and teaching, the following three points relating to the students' classroom behaviour and teachers' instruction practice are worth making clear:

1. Students' oral presentation assessment
2. Students' anxiety about speaking English
3. Teacher's inadequate feedback.

Assessment

The students were told that the presentation they were required to do would count towards the end of the semester course grade. Students cared much about scores. They viewed them as a vital part of their credibility vis-à-vis their classmates. Moreover, to receive an annual academic merit-based award, the average score of their total course grade is taken into account. It is not surprising that their 'free-talk' style would be negatively affected by their concern about the score they obtained in their oral presentation. They believed that a high score was a reflection of knowledge and ability. Prompted by this belief, students would tend to evaluate the outcome of the presentation solely in terms of the score they got rather than how much communicative work they did in class.

So the students cared more about scores than the communicative nature of the oral practice. They rated the score as a strong indicator of competence and credibility (face) in the eyes of their classmates. This is in contrast to the educational philosophy in the Western countries underlying CLT principles in which interactive activities were emphasised, fluency was viewed more important than accuracy and "students are encouraged not only to develop academic competence but also to demonstrate communicative competence in a social setting in order to do well in school" (Gilmore 1985: 139 cited in Liu, 2002: 51).

Anxiety in relation to speaking English in class

During a free talk after the class, many students mentioned that they would feel very anxious and nervous without referring to note when they spoke English in front of the whole class. This issue is not new. Early studies suggest that anxiety matters to students of all abilities and high language anxiety is related to students' negative concepts of themselves as language learners, and negative expectations for their language learning talents (Bailey 1983; *op. cit.*, Horwitz et al.; Price 1991). This is especially the case when there is heavy ego involvement. MacIntyre and Gardner (1994) stress that learner perceptions are important in the matter of reducing language anxiety, and studies of students' negative correlations between anxiety and output quality indicate that anxious students have more difficulty expressing themselves and tend to underestimate their level of ability (self-derogation) compared with more relaxed students (self-enhancement). Anxious students are capable of showing high levels of achievement, given sufficient time to study and practice (*ibid.*: 298). It is important for teachers to identify anxious students and any elements of the classroom environment which produce this reaction (*op. cit.*, Horwitz et al.). In addition, teachers should study (i) how learners' anxiety interacts with different teaching methods and personality variables such as learning styles, motivation, and personality types, and (ii) what techniques are effective in coping with it. In addition, making explicit to learners the beneficial functions of practice for real communicative purposes could help them reduce the level of anxiety "along with their development of EFL language skills" (*ibid.*).

Teacher's inadequate feedback

Another common feature which was identified in the classes of both teachers was inadequate feedback by the teachers. Some typical linguistic and lexical errors made by the student speakers escaped their attention which could lead to their fossilization of the errors. For instance, in Lan's class, while reading her written presentation on the topic of 'the qualities of being a good teacher', a female student began her speech with

> *During the journey of my study,* there are some teachers who I respect very much ... I dreamed of being a teacher in my childhood because a teacher can *control* a large group of students .... But later on I know that to be a teacher is easy, but to be a good teacher is not easy (Emphasised by me).

Her speech exposed a typical problem that Chinese students had in learning English—Chinese English or Chinglish, as it is often called. Speakers express their ideas in English but with a typical Chinese lexical variation which sounds awkward to native English speakers. In her speech, *during the journey of my study* is a word for word translation from the Chinese which would be in English 'in the course of my learning English' or simply 'during the years of my learning English'. Yet this escaped the teacher's attention. Uncorrected Chinglish expressions would be fossilized in the classroom which is very often the only place the students can be exposed to the target language, especially spoken English. In this study, Chinese English is used to refer to "English sentences that are grammatically correct but they make either no sense or mean something very different from the speakers' intentions" (Shi 1994 cited in Kent 1999: 198). The main reason why students had this problem was that they used English words but still thought in Chinese—something very difficult to spot because Chinese speakers are influenced by their mother tongue (*ibid.*). Unfortunately, this typical error escaped Lan's attention and was totally ignored.

In addition, none of the speakers said *thank you* at the end of their speech. There was an obvious lack of eye contact, gestures, and facial expressions—the indicators of communication skills in their speech. They were concerned only about *reading* their speech and being understood by their peers. There was virtually no interaction. No elements of strategic competence were emphasized or even pointed out in class by either the teacher or the students. This reflected students' deficiency in communication skills. On the other hand, it also revealed that teachers needed to correct their own misconceptions of communicative language teaching. They should have a clear understanding of the nature and aim of providing students with oral English practice in the class. Karavas-doukas (1996) has stressed the significance of correct attitudes and perceptions teachers hold on classroom instruction. He notes that teachers' educational attitudes and theories, although in many cases held unconsciously, would have an effect on their classroom behaviour and could influence what students actually learn.

2.8 DISCUSSION AND ANALYSIS

As is evident above, the comparison shows that both the teachers adopted the traditional teaching method to deal with the text materials. At the same time, they stressed the importance of students' oral practice in class. However, the striking difference was that Lan's class consisted of two parts: (i) communicative and (ii) non-communicative activities. During the communicative activities, students were engaged in communicative group discussions. While in Shan's class, there was no such a communicative aspect of learning activities. As for non-communicative activities, the teacher dealt with the text content in the traditional way.

From my observation, it can be seen that in Lan's class the students were more actively engaged in communicative activities than those in the rest of the classes observed. Their students' feedback in Lan's class indicated that they enjoyed the combination of traditional ways of dealing with the text content and communicative group activities in the class because the crossover blend helped them both acquire new language items and be given an opportunity to improve their oral English. Students would feel much safer to speak English in a small group rather than do it in front of the whole class. The results supported the findings of a separate study by the author that many English-majored students favoured the traditional way of dealing with the text content and, at the same time, they liked group work, too. They would like to be active in group work but would be afraid of speaking English in front of the whole class (Xiao 2005). This can be supported by the fact that, when asked to comment on the class, some students in Lan's class said, "We like it" because "we feel that we have learned something from the teacher and in the meantime, we have practised our own spoken English in the class".

In Shan's class, on the other hand, the class atmosphere was not lively and students paid scant attention to the 'news-reporter' and to the teacher. The observation showed that Lan had made an effort to include some communicative activities in her instruction and the result was positive based on students' responses. But the other teachers seemed unprepared for change in this direction. It should be noted that even Lan, as a model teacher in the English Department for her effort in initiating CLT in her class, still had much to learn about English language teaching and learning. She needed to revise her views of the roles of being a teacher and a student in her efforts to integrate both traditional and communicative approaches. The way her students *read out* their oral presentation showed that she had not fully understood the implications of interactive communicative work.

Despite the merits and demerits, an obvious problem worth addressing relates to the oral practice activities identified in both classes. As mentioned above, the results of classroom observation revealed a deep-seated misconception about CLT on the part of the teachers. Their misplaced expectations of students' oral work led to students' dependence on *reading* pre-prepared notes as they did their oral presentation. They should have been talking about it or engaging in a spontaneous exchange of ideas among their peers. In fact, this misconception was not an isolated case. In the eyes of many teachers, CLT meant less 'teacher talk' and more 'student talk' regardless of the 'nature' and 'spontaneity' of the talk *per se*. When asked why she did not encourage her students to *talk about* rather than to *read* their presentation in class as mentioned above, Lan replied, "Students lacked confidence for free talk in class. The pre-prepared speech would give students more time to organize their ideas and, therefore, would make them think deeply". She claimed that it would lead to accuracy in terms of content and form. Last but not the least, she argued that reading would boost their confidence and minimize the number of errors and, thus, reflect the real effort they had put into the task. It was obvious that it was the teacher's attitudes that set the scene for the learners' heavy dependence on accuracy rather than fluency.

However, since there was neither information gap nor interaction between speaker and listeners, the audience would, in all likelihood, become bored or lose interest or even become distracted while their peers were reading as was shown in the observation. It was hard to deny that a well-prepared presentation would allow students to draw upon their L2 or even L1 lexical, phonological, and structural resources to polish their individual speech with clarity and precision. However, it must be pointed out that by 'reading their note', the underlying aim of the learning task would be side-stepped and the question of cultivation of their ability to use the language appropriately for real communicative purposes avoided.

It can be seen that both teachers and students were focused more on 'accuracy' than 'fluency'. (Here 'fluency' does not refer to 'reading fluently' but to overall proficient spoken and spontaneous language.) Such a 'reading' practice seemed to be more relevant to the evaluation of their production skills (pronunciation, intonation, and content) than producing comprehensible output through interaction and meaningful exchange of information in the class even if the topic *per se* was very interesting.

This highlights the need for teachers to change their deeply-ingrained attitudes and perceptions of the nature of communicative learning activities and their teaching practice. The findings reveal this is the point at which the mismatch between what the teachers claimed to be and what they really did lies—their misconception of CLT. Karavas-doukas (*op. cit.*) points out that teachers can play a crucial role in determining the implementation of an approach which, in turn, influences the student-learning behaviour in class.

The classroom observations suggest that both teachers and students should be aware that classroom activity of this kind alone was not sufficient for developing learners' communicative competence as there was little interaction or negotiation of meaningful content in its real sense. It would be a completely different scenario if the teachers had explained explicitly to the whole class the beneficial functions of *talking about* their ideas rather than *reading* their written notes during the presentation so that on-the-spot feedback (questions and answers from the teacher and the students) could be exchanged. In so doing, the students' potential would be aroused and brought into play. This phenomenon revealed the teachers' lack of proper understanding of CLT and, therefore, led them to have low expectation of their students.

Howe (1993) stresses the significance of the teacher's role in influencing the learners' classroom behaviours. He asserts that irrespective of cultural traits inherent in the learners' learning styles, the teachers' expectations of their students are a vital factor in determining the students' classroom behaviours. The observation in most of the classes for this study revealed, that the teachers had inadequate expectations of their students in terms of stimulating their interest in and enthusiasm for communicative activities.

It can be seen that teachers' perceptions and expectations influenced significantly their classroom teaching as well as the way the students behaved in the class. In this study, neither the teachers nor the students considered this fact as a problem. The common conception was that the painstaking accumulation of incremental language items alone would equip learners to use the language in the future. *Practice makes perfect* and *strenuous effort would lead automatically to success in the end*, as the Chinese proverbs have it.

On the learners' part, it was interesting to note that the above *reading-not-talking* presentation also revealed that the students were subjected to what

Hofstede (1991) terms "high degree of uncertainty avoidance" which is characterized by avoiding taking risks in the classroom for fear of "making errors or losing face". If, however, the teachers could think differently and make explicit to the students the value of 'free talking', the students would feel more confident and be equipped to engage in communicative interaction. Then the classroom could become the lively and cooperative environment in which the students were encouraged to participate. Such a strategy requires enormous effort from both teachers and students alike for the communicative approach to work. This assumption is supported by the students' responses to my questions when I had a free talk with them after the class.

2.9 WEAKNESSES IDENTIFIED BY CLASSROOM OBSERVATIONS

As shown above, Lan's class was relatively communicative in nature while the classes of the other 4 participants were not. My classroom observation brought to light the evident weaknesses of their teaching methods. This finding *contradicted* the teachers' positive responses to the communicative approach in the questionnaire survey (Xiao 2005). However, it is encouraging to note that there is light at the end of this communicative teaching tunnel.

Observation of Lan's class revealed that the combination of both traditional and communicative approaches could be far more effective in offering learners more opportunities to speak English and engaging them in communicative activities. The following sections focus on the teaching methods used by the teacher participants and emphasize the analysis of mismatch between what teachers claimed to be [done] and what they actually did in class.

Traditional methods in reading class: Not seeing the wood for the trees

The way in which the teachers dealt with the text materials was problematic. They used a traditional grammar-translation method in which the teachers explained in detail the word's meaning and usage, sentence formation, and English grammar. This method failed to promote extensive reading skills, thus hindering the students from ever reading fluently (Li 1984) because in Dzau's (1990) words, "Students were taught to focus on each word in a text and to examine the text carefully for any unknown grammatical phenomenon" (p. 83). Using this method, they would often "miss the thread of the argument, the relationship between parts of a text and the text's main idea" (*ibid.*). The exclusive use of such methods would result in English reading courses that are mere extension of supplementary exercises for vocabulary building and grammar learning. Consequently, the logical meaning and cultural content inherent in the text would be lost "in a jumble of words and structures" (Zhang, 2003).

It should be noted that the different components of communicative competence are interrelated and the development of one competence will affect that of another (Savignon 2002). In spite of the teachers' positive responses to communicative approach, the classroom observation showed that they mainly focused on the traditional teaching methods. This reflects the Chinese traditional notion of foreign language learning which involves a progression from a quantitative accumulation of knowledge to the final qualitative improvement. The Chinese traditional value of learning suggests that memorizing the target language's vocabulary and studying its grammar will automatically foster fluency, flexibility and appropriate use of language (*op. cit.*, Dzau). It is believed that creativity will flow naturally in time from discipline to proficiency in rote memorization, and there is no need for the teacher to encourage fluency *per se* (Fang and Warschauer 2004).

As is evident from the survey findings, this traditional teaching method is a root cause of the students' dependence on teachers and the holding up of their lack of communicative competence. It teaches the learners to see 'only the trees, not the wood' in reading an English text.

Bottom-up information processing in reading English

Rumelhart (1980) points out that a reading text only provides directions for readers as to how they should retrieve or construct meaning from their own previously acquired knowledge and this previously acquired knowledge structure is called **schema theory**. According to this theory, comprehending words, sentences and the entire text involves more than just relying on one's linguistic theory. Efficient comprehension requires the ability to relate the textual materials to one's own knowledge (*ibid.*). Clark and Silberstein (1977) point out that there exist two information processing approaches, namely, (i) bottom-up processing and (ii) top-down processing. **Bottom-up processing** is triggered by the incoming data and is also called **data-driven** because the data enters the system through the best-fitting, bottom level schemata. It focuses the learners on the individual components of the spoken and written message, that is, the phonetics, graphemes, individual words and grammatical elements which need to be comprehended in order to understand these messages (Nunan 1991).

Top-down processing takes place as the system makes general predictions based on higher level, i.e. general schema, which means background knowledge in reading comprehension (*op. cit.*, Clark and Silberstein, 136). And according to Nunan (*op. cit.*)

> It focuses learners on macro-features of text such as the writer's or speaker's purpose, the topic of the message, the overall structure of the text and so on (p. 4).

Wang (2001) points out that the traditional teaching method of covering the text in a sentence-by-sentence manner is a focus on bottom-up processing strategy at the expense of seeking the macrofeatures of the text covered. It tends to rely too much on bottom-up processing on individual words and analysing sentence structure. It ignores the importance of applying top-down processing for the overall view of the text. This omission can hinder the development of good reading skills by failing to furnish the necessary background information and by leaving dormant any critical or analytical thinking processes.

Needless to say, readers must understand the individual parts of the text as part of grasping the overall meaning of the text materials. But early studies report that top-down thinking is crucial in processing the information. For instance, Nuttal (1983, 1996) suggests that, in practice, "Effective readers continually adopt a top-down approach to predict the probable theme and then move to the bottom-up approach to check their assumption by reading details." They are "two simultaneous and complementary ways of processing a text" (Chia 2001). This implies that in teaching reading,

> Teachers should instruct students to start their reading by using a top-down approach and later switch between the two approaches, as each kind of interpretation supports the other. (*ibid.*)

In other words, teachers should help students see both 'the wood and the trees' in English reading class.

Following a bottom-up processing approach, teachers view reading as a mechanical process and tend to concentrate on the surface-level features of reading rather than the whole unit of discourse. It cannot be denied that surface and cohesive elements are important markers of meaning. However, if considered as ends in themselves and not in relation to more holistic or global markers of organization in the discourse, they will not lead to efficient production and interpretation of text.

On the other hand, most of the comprehension questions and practice exercises are designed at the lexical or grammatical level while skills for obtaining logical meaning are seldom taught in a systematic way. Consequently, students may be able to identify a large number of words in isolation and explain their grammatical functions, but they are unable to assign appropriate meaning to these words with regard to how they are used properly in context. This indicates that the students were not aware of the importance of memory strategy. The habit of vocabulary building was reinforced by the traditional teaching approach. It is not surprising that students frequently complained that their own sense of logical relationships was very weak and they often felt at a loss when asked to answer the 'why' or 'how' questions which obviously require logical reasoning or inference from the context in a holistic manner rather than just literal information from the text. Therefore, innovative teaching methodology which helps students comprehend overall textual meaning, over and above lexical and grammatical meaning, is what is required. 'Innovative' here means moving beyond the traditional way of teaching English reading towards some sort of communicative-oriented group discussions in class by picking up a text-related topic.

Following this line of reasoning, we can see that the words and sentences are reliable landmarks but they do not constitute the total picture. According to Halliday and Hasan (1976), a text is a communicative occurrence involving textuality, without which the text does not stand up from a communicative perspective:

> A text is best regarded as a semantic unit: a unit not of form but of meaning. Thus, it is related to a clause or sentence not by size but by realization, the coding of one symbolic system in another. A text does not consist of sentences; it is realized by, or encoded in, sentences. (p. 2)

They note that the basic glue of a text is cohesion which concerns the ways in which surface components of the text are constituted or the relationship of one linguistic item to another in a text. These components cohere with one another by various grammatical dependences. Obviously, these dependences operate at the surface level of the text and constitute major signals for sorting out meanings and uses. However, the surface text alone is not enough. There must be interaction between cohesion and other standards of texuality to make communication efficient (*op. cit.*, Savignon). Another standard is coherence which concerns ideas within a text and the relation of all sentences or utterances in the text to a single 'global proposition' (*ibid.*, 39). Global proposition here refers to the structure of concepts and relations underlying the surface text. Savignon stresses that the establishment of a global meaning for a whole passage is an integral part of both expression and interpretation and makes possible the understanding of the individual sentences or utterances included in a text (*ibid.*). A text does not make sense by itself, but rather by the interaction of the text-presented knowledge with the readers' stored knowledge of the world. Thus, awareness of the notions of both cohesion and coherence would help students realize the underlying meaning of a passage and improve their reading efficiency.

2.10 POSITIVE SCENARIO: LIGHT AT THE END OF THE TUNNEL

In spite of the shortcomings, the findings of classroom observation suggest a positive outcome. For instance, Lan's efforts to integrate CLT into her teaching, although underdeveloped, is a positive contribution to methodological innovation and contributes much towards a long-term process of educational reform. It was revealed that Lan had two distinct components in her instruction: the *first* was traditional teaching aspect, and the *second* was the communicative aspect. It was the communicative aspect that made her class different from the other 4 teacher participants.

However, the traditional methods she used left a weak residue which reinforced "a bad reading habit" (Li 1984) as mentioned above. This raises other questions: how do teachers evolve from a grammar-oriented classroom to a communicative one? Which CLT activities most support language learning from a teacher's perspective in the existing EFL situations in China? How would teachers clarify the role of grammar in CLT? All these questions deserve further research in the future.

It is hoped that favourable feedback in Lan's class together with the praises she had received for her innovative efforts would encourage other faculty to increase their commitment to methodological innovation. She shows how integrating communicative methods can be integrated into existing teaching practice. In addition, to diffuse such a reform more broadly, the college administrators need to introduce greater incentives by providing faculty with adequate in-service training programmes at home and abroad, and help teachers pursue a deeper understanding of CLT. The future development of CLT depends on "correcting teachers' misconceptions of the communicative approach" (Thompson 1996). This will significantly advance teachers' own professional competence. In order to help more teachers and students realize and accept the deserved values of methodological innovation, administrators also should encourage the teachers and learners to express and discuss their own beliefs about language teaching and learning so that they can extend and deepen their knowledge about CLT (Fox 1993).

2.11 ANALYSIS OF THE MISMATCH

The classroom observation also illustrates a mismatch between the teachers' positive responses to communicative approach in the questionnaire survey and their actual teaching practice in their classes. A careful examination of the teacher participants' teaching behaviours and their explanations sheds light on the factors causing this gap. There are four interrelated contributory factors that led to the discrepancy between what most teachers said and what they actually did in the class. They are discussed now.

2.11.1 Ignorance of Learners' Needs

Firstly, the findings of the classroom observation revealed that despite teachers' general positive attitudes towards a student-centred approach (SCA), most teachers do not have a clear idea of what their students want to do with English, either in class or in the future. This is backed up by the findings (in a separate study) that the teachers have merely gauged that 49 per cent of their students preferred classroom activities and use of language learning strategy (Xiao 2006b). Moreover, teachers are not certain about how to achieve the objectives of SCA in their classroom instruction. Their ignorance of students' needs leads to vagueness of teaching goals which, in turn, makes it inevitable that teachers rely heavily or solely on designated textbook materials to achieve the course objectives. This can result in teachers' slowness to innovate and a persistent failure to create a classroom environment conducive to learners' active participation in communicative activities. Ross (1993) argues:

> Hesitant teachers see the text as their most reliable model for correct language use. Such a position is defensible primarily because their role is to reproduce in their students the knowledge in which they themselves have been grounded. (p. 108)

The gap between what most teachers claimed to be doing and what they actually did in class supported the findings of an earlier study that many teachers trained in a traditional way find it a painful step to adjust themselves to different innovative teaching methods and are usually unprepared when difficulties crop up. They often give up and resort to using outdated methods in their teaching (Chen 1996: 1).

As we have seen, substantial amount of time is spent on going over the text sentence by sentence and doing text-based exercises and activities that are mostly teacher-controlled and non-communicative in nature. Although the teachers claimed to be in support of CLT and adopted some features of SCA or CLT, most of them actually still use the traditional approach.

2.11.2 Traditional Role of Teacher

Secondly, heavy dependence on the text materials inevitably places the teacher in the position of a 'knowledge provider'. The Chinese teacher's perceived obligation as a transmitter of received knowledge may help us understand why the act of learning English for millions of Chinese students and teachers is basically the detailed study of textbook materials. Such a role as a knowledge provider fits well with traditional Chinese views on teaching and the teacher-student relationship, which is lubricated by respect and hierarchy. "The teacher is viewed as a knowledge provider and the students as the receivers of knowledge, and the teaching as a process of transmitting knowledge from teacher to students" (Wu and Fang 2002: 156). One might also call this the 'empty vessel' view of learning. This reflects the tradition of language teaching in China which has been characterized by "teacher-centredness, structure-based instruction and drill repetition" (Sun and Cheng 2002: 15). With such a tradition, it is not surprising that teachers surveyed have their own version or interpretation of CLT. Li (1998) reports that many Chinese teachers understand CLT as merely a concentration on listening and speaking or language games to attract students' attention. Some think that CLT is merely a method for teaching spoken English, but not reading and writing. Others point out that it is more difficult to persuade teachers than students in China to accept CLT (Anderson 1993; Burnaby and Sun 1989).

Although the teachers formally agreed with the idea that teacher should play the role of a facilitator in a communicative class, judging from their instructional behaviours, it was clear that the teachers were much more comfortable with their role as the dominant figure in class. It seems that they do not have a clear idea of how to integrate CLT into traditional language teaching or vice versa. As Maley (1982) points out:

> It is a sad observation that many teachers who exercise rigid control do so [TCA] from a sense of insecurity. They are worried about their inability to operate in a situation where everything is not in their control. This is a natural enough fear but one experience which usually proves unjustified when they try a more relaxed approach. It is a fear of the unknown more than anything else. (p. 41)

Following this line of reasoning, teachers treat classroom as the venue for imparting to students linguistic items as specified in the designated teaching materials. The role of teachers as knowledge provider is further strengthened by the existing assessment system which emphasizes knowledge about the target language rather than ability to use it for a communicative purpose (*op. cit.*, Wu and Fang). As one teacher interviewee said, "The current teaching trends are essentially unchanged. Most teachers are teaching the old way even if they use a new textbook".

2.11.3 Misconception of CLT

Thirdly, although the CLT approach is widely recognized and promoted by the revised curriculum at tertiary level in China (*op. cit.*, English Division: 13), little is actually known about what teachers understand by CLT and how to implement it in the classroom. Regardless of the rich theoretical base for CLT, "different interpretations and variations exist at the level of design and procedure" (Richards and Rodgers 1986). As a result, many Chinese EFL teachers have become very confused. The survey revealed that some teachers equated CLT with the teaching of spoken English. Others regarded CLT simply as a teaching method that did not require grammar teaching. Many teachers simply view CLT as increasing 'student talk time' and decreasing 'teacher talk time' in class as shown in Shan's and Lan's classes. This reflected the fact that although teachers expressed their favourable attitudes towards the communicative approach, very few classes under observation are actually communicative in nature. Teachers have a partial knowledge of CLT and their beliefs about language teaching and learning are based on their own EFL learning and teaching experience. Johnson (1994) points out that the prior beliefs based on formal language learning experiences were so powerful that teachers could not alter their beliefs without explicit alternative instructional practices (p. 451). This reveals that teachers' misconceptions must be corrected before the communicative approach can be applied in its real sense.

On the other hand, many teachers do not know how to set about improving their teaching and, consequently, cannot modify their own teaching style, nor incorporate related communicative activities in their class. The inevitable result is that they omit the communicative activities suggested in the textbooks and use the time saved for text-based pattern drill exercises or teaching supplementary materials which are not communicative-oriented in nature. For instance, in Shan's class, students were given a dictation in which the teacher read a short passage four times at a tempo much slower than normal speed.

2.11.4 Teaching Culture in English Class

Last but not the least, a comparison between teachers' views on culture teaching and learning and the teaching behaviour during the *Culture Course* showed clear discrepancies between what was said and what was done. The traditional method of going over the text in a sentence-by-sentence way dominated the culture course as Ming's class revealed. The teaching–learning outcome was not satisfactory as the interview data revealed that many student informants complained about the way the course was delivered.

My classroom observation showed that the culture teaching in the EFL domain amounted to treating foreign cultures as a collection of knowledge items. The teacher merely provided learners with a great deal of cultural information. In response to the call for culture teaching and learning in EFL programmes, some target culture introduction courses are offered for English majors in many English departments as an optional course at university level. However, due to the deep-rooted traditional teaching methods prevalent in English language classrooms, these culture courses follow almost exactly the same teaching methods as used in the 'intensive reading' class. The usual process of the teaching was merely text-reading, explaining grammar, structure, language points, and translation of terms, names and places. More meaningful methods such as comparison and contrast from an intercultural perspective, class discussion, and interaction between teachers and students were seldom attempted. The traditional teaching methods employed by the teacher in the culture course also downplayed the effectiveness of the teaching of culture regardless of the hours instructed or new courses introduced into the EFL programmes.

As Cao (1998) recounts, one of the main conventions in foreign language teaching in Chinese tertiary institutions is that culture teaching is done solely as imparting knowledge or facts. As long as learners get to know the facts, they are assumed to be equipped with competence for intercultural communications. This is reflected in Ming's culture class. It seems, teachers tend to think that if culture courses are offered in the EFL programmes, the learners' cross-cultural ability will be increased along with their EFL linguistic development. Needless to say, such a point of view is very misleading in the process of EFL teaching and learning.

Some Chinese EFL researchers propose a different approach to culture teaching in English class. Zhang (2000) suggests a task-based approach to teaching culture. Unlike the knowledge-transmission methods, this approach encourages an interactional, experiential learning concerned with the learners' own interest, and considers cultural knowledge as "the ability to organise thought, to interpret facts and act on them appropriately". The learners will be provided with the opportunities, instead of mere facts, to explore new ideas and new knowledge for themselves and, consequently, they will learn more effectively and enthusiastically.

The task-based learning and teaching view cultures as something always in the making, and being dynamic. A teacher should give sufficient consideration to teaching learners how cultural assimilation and differences have been formed and how cultural conflicts have occurred and have been dealt with in real situation. Such a comparative method would encourage students to reflect upon their own culture, and at the same time to discover new knowledge about another. Therefore, it would be a useful and necessary means towards understanding a new culture, which will finally help learners enhance their communicative competence.

Some Western researchers note the importance of integrating culture and language learning and contend that language set in a meaningful communicative environment is discourse and not an artificial construct (Widdowson 1978; Snow and Genesee 1989). Learners who are taught to treat language learning and content learning as independent processes need to be constantly reminded that without real meaning language functions and structures are likely to be learned as abstractions with little conceptual or cognitive value. Content provides a motivational basis for language learning. If the learners find content interesting and informative, they will have a strong desire to learn. "Language then will be learned because it provides access to content" (Xiao et al. 1996). A closer examination of this issue reveals the following three main factors that have contributed to this situation in China.

1. Teachers' competence

As revealed in Ming's class, the teachers' own levels of intercultural sensitivity and competence cast doubt on the effectiveness and quality of the teaching of culture in EFL programmes. Given the lack of adequate intercultural competence and expertise required in the teaching of culture, the desired aim can hardly be achieved. This reveals the necessity that EFL teachers themselves should become interculturally sensitive and at the same improve their own understanding and practice of teaching methodology. This also shows the urgency and necessity to set up a systematic staff training program with a clear theoretical and pedagogical guideline for teaching culture in English classroom. As shown in interview accounts, given the situation, it is not surprising that students in culture class feel that the aim of developing learners' cultural awareness is subordinated to improving language knowledge and cultural information. Cultivation of sociocultural competence is ignored and just left open to individual interest rather than being incorporated as an integral part of the language teaching and learning.

2. Textbooks

The selection of sociocultural items for cultural learning in EFL is still problematic as revealed in the classroom observation. The culture textbooks were more concerned about presenting facts and history and gave insufficient consideration to help teachers teach learners such knowledge and skills as how cultural assimilation and differences had been formed and how cultural conflicts had occurred and had been dealt with in real situation. In China, there are a few cultural textbooks that introduce, in general, the cultures of major English speaking countries and these books are widely used by EFL teachers in English departments at university level in China for their teaching of culture courses. I have carefully read two widely used culture textbooks. The content of these textbooks revealed a sort of simplification and stereotypes. The compilers probably are not aware of this. Furthermore, rarely are the sources of information or the background of the authors given in the textbooks, hence, the reader does not know whether the cultural information is from a cultural insider or outsider. For most Chinese students who have no direct exposure to the target cultures or the outside world, they are very likely to conceptualise the information or knowledge contained in the textbooks as authoritative.

3. The testing system in China

In two nation-wide English proficiency tests for English-majors at university level, namely, English Major Test-4 (EMT-4) and EMT-8, culture does not have a very explicit place as the tests focus on the knowledge about the target language. This undoubtedly discourages the teaching and learning of culture studies. Wang (1999) points out that many teachers in China adopt a *teach-whatever-is-tested* attitude and learners also learn whatever is tested. Therefore, Wang calls for the inclusion of testing of cultural competence in these tests because "it would be the major means to attract the attention from teachers and students" (p. 15).

Moreover, the lack of proper and effective teaching of culture in class is reflected in the topics that students chose for their graduation dissertations. During the examination of undergraduates' graduation theses, I learnt that among the total of 298 students, only 12 students 8.1 per cent of the total chose to write about cultural topics. However, even a dozen students who chose cultural topics just gave overall descriptions or comments without a comprehensive comparison and contrast, and not any theoretical framework cited or reviewed. This phenomenon was not congruent with the findings of the questionnaire data that students expressed their strong desire to learn about Western cultures and peoples (Xiao 2005, 2006b).

From a pedagogical perspective, it can be seen that there is a long way to go before the teaching and learning of culture can be integrated, and not just *added,* into the EFL programme for English majors at university level since it requires radical innovation both in curriculum design and in teaching methodology. Further research is needed in this area to seek proper integration of culture teaching into English language education.

2.12   CONCLUSION AND PEDAGOGICAL GUIDELINE

The classroom observation shows that despite the shortcomings exposed in Lan's class, she tried strenuously to integrate the communicative components of CLT into her instruction. As for the rest of teachers, it is clear that they still mainly adhere to the traditional approach. The gap between what they claimed to be doing and what they actually did not only reflects their misconceptions about CLT, but also manifests the various challenges confronting them in adopting CLT in their English classes. To integrate CLT into the teaching practice the teachers require to adopt attitudes in their classes which may contradict their established beliefs, educational philosophies, and classroom instruction practice. As revealed in Lan's class, neither the traditional nor the communicative approach will, on its own, be the panacea for the problem of EFL education. An appropriate integration of the strengths from both CLT and teacher-centred approach (TCA) would, however, go a long way towards addressing the problems.

As far as the teaching methodology is concerned, the English Department under study contains both a traditional approach and a communicative component. The former far outweighs the latter because very few teachers have successfully adopted the communicative component into their teacher-centred classes—Lan being the exception. Lan's classes show that she is trying to adopt the communicative methodology to traditional teacher-centred classes, but she needs to take the process much further. As revealed in her class, she gave students more time to practise their spoken English but there was no real interaction between speaker and listeners. She undertook text analysis in a very traditional way with emphasis on structure and language points. The striking difference in her class was that, after text analysis, she attempted to reorganize the teaching procedure and obtained a shift of focus. That is, she converted the lesson used for text analysis into communicative group discussion in which the text material was used only as the background for this activity and the teacher receded somewhat. The teacher's role became one of helping the students complete the task and monitor the process of the activity by providing some necessary scaffolding.

For the rest of the teachers observed, the weight of traditional language teaching preconceptions is still heavy. In their classes, students were given more time than before for oral practice, but the teachers still concentrated on grammar and discrete language points although they used new textbooks. This clearly indicates that the adoption of a communicative view of language is more important than using a new textbook or introducing new teaching techniques. If teachers do not change their attitudes vis-à-vis EFL teaching, the CLT approach will pass them by. Introducing new methods for classroom activities is helpful, but not sufficient. Adopting approaches should start from the beginning of curriculum design and should address the accumulated, educational beliefs of the teachers and the actual needs and preferences of students. Moreover, adaptation of teaching methodology will be more effective and welcomed by students if the theory of teaching and learning from which the communicative language teaching methodology is derived is reviewed and shared among teachers and students.

2.12.1 A Pedagogical Guideline

Lan's experiment proves that proper integration of communicative and traditional methods can improve teaching and learning outcomes. In adopting an approach that can combine strengths from both CLT and teacher-centredness, teachers need to adopt appropriate pedagogical practices to ensure smooth progression of classroom activities in which both form and meaning are properly dealt with. The aim is to combine communicative components with the explicit instruction of form and structure. For such a smooth classroom progression to happen in the Chinese EFL context, there needs to be general pedagogical guidelines for the teachers to follow. A number of L2 and EFL researchers have proposed different types of integration concern-ing classroom progression for the purpose of combining communicative and traditional methods. Some suggest a progression from communicative to formal instruction (Brumfit 1978) while some others suggest a progression (i) from formal classroom instruction to communicative activities (Nunan, 1992), (ii) from the activities of skills-getting to skills-using (Rivers and Temperley 1987), and (iii) from text-based mechanical pattern drills to free communication (Rao 1996). Littlewood (1984) takes a more flexible stance and suggests that the sequence of progression of classroom-learning activities is interchangeable rather than a fixed pattern and it is up to the teacher to decide—based on such factors as the learners, the specific content of the text materials and the kinds of activities used.

The classroom progression needs to be based on a multifaceted view of communicative activities in class. It should also seek to incorporate student input into the learning process. In some cases, it is appropriate to focus on assigned tasks and small-group learning. In other cases, a whole class format is the best. In still others, a combination is appropriate. Therefore, it varies with different variables such as learners' English proficiency level and knowledge about the topic under discussion, the content of text materials, teachers' competence in target language, teaching styles and classroom management skills. In short, it depends on a particular context (Bax 2003).

The following stages present a pedagogical model of teaching comprehensive reading course by following such a pedagogical guideline.

Pre-reading stage

Pre-reading or previewing activities begin with questions to be initiated by a teacher. Rather than asking these questions at the end of each lesson to test learners' understanding of the text the teacher will start the lesson with the thought-provoking questions. These questions should be aimed at students' understanding of the meaning and structure of a text to relate their reading activity to their prior knowledge and experience, increase their interest in the subject to be read and enable them to read with a purpose.

While-reading stage

While-reading stage consists of reading a text twice, each for a specific purpose. The first reading concerns two important speeding techniques, namely, **skimming** and **scanning**. Training of these skills is of particular importance because they are not only indispensable for EFL learners but also students' schemata can be activated in the process (Xiang and Wang 1999). Skimming facilitates text process by initiating students into the gist and organization of the text while scanning is helpful for seeking specific information for the pre-reading questions mentioned above. The second reading is a problem-solving process. The problems to be solved may include such dimensions as (i) lexical and syntactic, (ii) discourse, (iii) sociocultural (Xiao 2006b).

While-reading stage also emphasizes the learners' need for explicit structural and grammatical presentation and reading comprehension. The meaning of a text is embodied in the language form. Given the fact that EMT-4 and EMT-8 are two major nation-wide English tests for English majors at tertiary level in China, both the teachers and students are aware of the importance of structural presentation in English class. Consequently, explicit grammar and structural instruction still remains an important part of EFL teaching in class. However, the crucial point is not to spoon-feed students as occurred in the classroom observations.

What is evident above is in a striking contrast to what happened in those classes observed: the teachers paraphrased almost every language point of the text which they thought might be difficult to the students. Hence they gave the students so much 'help' that it became a crutch that the students could not do without. That is, the students were led to formulating word-by-word reading habits while some aspects of learning leading to discourse competences were ignored.

Post-reading stage

Post-reading stage analyses and checks students' comprehension, consolidates their language skills and engages them in communicative group activities. This stage includes students' answers to the pre-reading questions, and further questions raised by teachers at the post-reading stage, for instance, text-based questions of inference, questions of evaluation, and questions of personal response and so on to check students' understanding of the text. In addition, students can also be assigned various tasks to complete. Each task to be completed is a step on the road to learner independence. Teachers can ask students to predict or attempt to reconstruct the content on the basis of the given clues from the part of the text without having read, heard, or seen the whole. For instance, teachers can ask students to predict problem solution and story endings by using a text with a situation-problem-solution-evaluating pattern, namely, let students read/hear/watch only parts of a text which give the situation and problem(s). Then ask students to work in pair or in a group to work out a couple of alternative solutions of their own, and then evaluate other pair's or group's solutions. When they have presented their best solutions to each other during a report phase, the class can be asked to predict which solutions are mentioned in the original text. They finally read/hear/watch the whole piece and compare and evaluate (Willis 1999).

By using a sequential text, teachers can give students most of the text information and ask them to write an ending, or give an ending, and ask them to write the beginning. They can scaffold students by giving them a few carefully chosen words from the text. In doing this, it should be made sure that students do not feel they will fail if they say something entirely different from the original text. No doubt, this would help students improve their ability to make judgements on what they read, to express their own opinions and to grasp the structure of a text. In a word, learners' analytical, creative and critical thinking ability together with their communicative competence will improve.

These activities and tasks may cover inference, practical reasoning, negotiation of meaning, problem solving and information transfer, and they may be carried out in a number of ways such as group-work, pair work, individual work and role play. They must become a regular part of a language programme. In many cases, a condition and an active atmosphere need to be created for the performance of these tasks and activities.

2.13 CONCLUSION

To sum up, if teachers know how to make proper use of pre-reading and while-reading stages to raise questions, offer background information, solve problems concerning lexical, syntactic, discourse and sociocultural aspects, this will help learners initiate post-reading discussions. Students may be interested in what they are doing and their attention would be attracted since these activities will create a vivid classroom atmosphere and enrich their prior knowledge.

What is more, it helps them link their existing knowledge to the text and directs them into a much deeper understanding. As mentioned above, the pre-reading questions help learners to make a prediction and enable them to decide what they look for (either the global meaning of the text or the necessary facts and details). The while-reading stage is problem-solving and it helps students overcome the difficulties in their correct comprehension of the text. Post-reading encourages them to use their own analytical and critical thinking skills. In addition, communicative group activities can be organized to achieve meaningful goals assigned to different groups based on the text content, thus enhancing interaction between teacher and students as well as between students themselves.

The striking difference between the above procedures and the traditional teaching or study scheme *of preview, practice and review* (*yuxi, lianxi* and *fuxi*) is that the former can remove some of the boredom involved in the teaching and learning process and integrate communicative components into EFL classrooms. At present, what happens in English class is that students are asked to prepare (*yuxi*) each lesson in advance, then to go over it in class (*lianxi*) and then to review it again later (*fuxi*). This naturally leads to certain lack of interest since by the time the students arrive in class, they may have covered the text anyway, so they simply have to undergo a repetition of what they already 'know'. Actually, as some student acknowledged, by and large, they came to know that teachers would go over texts in such meticulous detail in class that they just looked up some new words in a dictionary rather than reviewed the text carefully before class. They knew that the teacher would tell them everything in class. It is not surprising that the students in this study found their English classes dull because these classes had almost "no discourse, no language use, but only display of language usage as sentence or text" (Widdowson 1983 cited in Wei 1997: 86). In other words, the students were not really challenged, intellectually or pedagogically.

It is important to note, no matter how workable an innovative approach sounds, that there is no denying that further classroom-based empirical research should be done to test it. It is strongly advised that teachers should design and implement an innovative approach in actual classroom settings, and summarize its effect in terms of reading skills development, motivation, and attitude changes on the part of the students, as well as teachers' feedback in order to have it validated. For the future research, studies on more varied and creative ways of utilizing an innovative approach for EFL classrooms are needed. Further, we may capture and readily access first-hand data in classroom settings for both research and pedagogical purposes.

REFERENCES

Anderson, J., "Is a communicative approach practical for teaching English in China? Pros and cons," *System* **21**.4 (1993): 471–480.

Bailey, K.M., "Competitiveness and anxiety in adult second language learning: Looking at and through the diary studies," *Classroom Oriented Research in Second Languages*, H.W. Seliger and M.H. Long (Eds.), Rowley, MA: Newbury House (1983): 67–103.

Barkhuizen, G.P., "Discovering learners' perceptions of ESL classroom teaching and learning activities in a South African context," *TESOL Quarterly* **32**.1 (1998): 85–107.

Bax, S., "The end of CLT: A context approach to language teaching," *ELT Journal* **57**.3 (2003): 278–287.

Brumfit, C.J., "Communicative language teaching: An assessment," *In Honour of A.S. Hornby*, P. Strevens (Ed.), Oxford: Oxford University Press, 1978.

Burnaby, B. and Sun, Y., "Chinese teachers' views of Western language teaching: Context informs paradigms," *TESOL Quarterly* **23**.2 (1989): 219–238.

Cao, W., "Two layers of English culture teaching," *Waiyu jiaoxue yu yanjiu (Foreign Language Teaching and Research)* **115**.3 (1998): 10–14.

Chen, Y.D., "The psychology of the Chinese classroom," *Teaching English in China*, **28** (1996): 7–8.

Chia, H.L., "Reading activities for effective top-down processing," *Forum* **39**.1 (2001): 22, Retrieved on October 28, 2003. http://exchanges.state.gov/forum/vols/vol39/no1/

Clark, M.A. and Silberstein, S., "Toward a realization of psycholinguistics principles for the ESL reading class," *Language Learning* **27**.1 (1977): 136–137.

Dzau, Y.F., "Teachers, students and administrators," *English in China*, Y.F. Dzau (Ed.), Hong Kong: AIP Press, 1990.

English Division of the Advisory Committee for the Teaching of Foreign Languages for Foreign Language Majors. *English Curriculum for English Majors in Chinese Universities and Colleges,* Beijing: Foreign Language Teaching and Research Press, 2000.

Fang, X. and Warschauer, M., "Technology and curriculum reform in China: A case study," *TESOL Quarterly* **38**.2 (2004): 301–321.

Fox, C.A., "Communicative competence and beliefs about language among graduate teaching assistants in French," *Modern Language Journal* **77** (1993): 313–324.

Glesne, G. and Peshkin, A., *Becoming Qualitative Researchers*, New York: Longman, 1992.

Halliday, M. and Hason, R., *Cohesion in English*, Harlow and London: Longman, 1976.

Hofstede, G., *Cultures and Organizations: Intercultural Cooperation and its Importance for Survival—Software of the Mind*, New York: McGraw-Hill, 1991.

Horwitz, E.K., Horwitz, M.B., and Cope, J. "Foreign language classroom anxiety," *Modern Language Journal* **70**.2 (1986): 125–132.

Howe, S., "Teaching in Vietnam," *Interchange* **22** (1993): 29–32.

Johnson, K.E., "The emerging beliefs and instructional practices of pre-service English as a Second Language Teachers," *Teaching and Teachers Education* **10**.4 (1994): 439–452.

Karavas-Doukas, E., "Using attitude scales to investigate teachers' attitudes to the communicative approach," *ELT Journal* **50**.3 (1996): 187–198.

Kent, D.B., "Speaking in tongues: Chinglish, Japlish and Konglish," *KOTESOL Proceedings of the Second Pan Asian Conference*, Seoul, 1999, Retrieved on October 30, 2003. http://www.kotesol.org/pubs/proceedings/1999/pacpro197.pdf

Kleinsasser, R.C. and Savignon, S.J., "Linguistics, language pedagogy, and teachers' technical cultures," *Linguistics and Language Pedagogy: The State of the Art—Georgetown University Round Table on Languages and Linguistics 1991*, J.E. Alatis (Ed.), Washington, D.C.: Georgetown University Press (1991), 289–301.

Li, D.F., "It's always more difficult than you plan and imagine: Teachers' perceived difficulties in introducing the communicative approach in South Korea," *TESOL Quarterly* **32** (1998): 677–703.

Li, X.J., "In defense of the communicative approach, *ELT Journal* **38**.1 (1984): 2–13.

Lincoln, Y.S. and Guba, E.G., *Naturalistic Inquiry*, Calif.: Sage Publications, 1985.

Littlewood, W., "Integrating the New and the Old in a Communicative Approach," in *Communicative Language Teaching* (Anthology Series 14), B.K. Das (Gen. Ed.), Singapore: Singapore University Press, 1984, pp. 171–191.

Liu, D.L., "Ethnocentrism in TESOL: Teacher education and the neglected needs of international TESOL students," *ELT Journal* **52**.1 (1998): 3–10.

Liu, J., "The new role of observing classes and its implications," *Wai Yu Jie (Journal of the Foreign Language World)* **66**.2 (1997): 14–17.

_____, "Negotiating silence in American classrooms: Three Chinese cases," *Language and Intercultural Communication* **2**.1 (2002): 37–54.

MacIntyre, P.D. and Gardner, R.C., "The subtle effects of language anxiety on cognitive processing in the second language," *Language Learning* **44**.2 (1994): 283–305.

Maley, A., "Whatever next? Some recent currents in foreign language teaching," *Waiyu jiaoxue yu yanjiu (Foreign Language Teaching and Research)*, **2** (1982): 39–50.

Nunan, D., *Language Teaching Methodology: A Textbook for Teachers*, New York: Prentice Hall, 1991.

_____, *Research Methods in Language Learning*, Cambridge: Cambridge University Press, 1992.

Nuttall, C., *Teaching Reading Skills in a Foreign Language*, Oxford: Heinemann, 1983/1960.

Price, M.L., "The subjective experiences of foreign language anxiety: Interviews with anxious students," *Language Anxiety: From Theory and Research to Classroom Implications*, E.K. Horwitz and D.J. Young (Eds.), Englewood Cliffs, NJ: Prentice Hall (1991), 101–108.

Rao, Z.H., "Reconciling communicative approaches to the teaching of English with traditional Chinese methods," *Research in the Teaching of English* **30**.4 (1996): 458–471.

———, "Chinese students' perceptions of communicative and non-communicative activities in EFL classroom," *System* **30**.1 (2002): 85–105.

Richards, J.C. and Rodgers, T.S., *Approaches and Methods in Language Teaching—A Description and Analysis,* Cambridge: Cambridge University Press, 1986/2001.

Rivers, W.M. and Temperley, M.S., *A Practical Guide to the Teaching of English*, Oxford: Oxford University Press, 1987.

Ross, H.A., *China Learns English: Language Teaching and Social Change in the People's Republic,* New Haven, CT: Yale University Press, 1993.

Rumelhart, D.E., "Schemata: The building blocks of cognition," *Theoretical Issues in Reading and Comprehension*, R.J. Spiro, B. Bruce and W.F. Brewer (Eds.), Hillsdale, NJ: Erlbaum, 1980.

Sano, M., Takahashi, M., and Yoneyama, A., "Communicative language teaching and local needs," *ELT Journal* **38**.3 (1984): 170–177.

Savignon, S. (Ed.), *Interpreting Communicative Language Teaching: Contexts and Concerns in Teacher Education,* London: Yale University Press, 2002.

Scollon, R. and Sollon, S.W., *Intercultural Communication: A Discourse Approach,* Oxford: Blackwell, 1995.

Seliger, H.W. and Shohamy, E., *Second Language Research Methods*, Oxford: Oxford University Press, 1989.

Snow, M.M. and Genesee, F., "A conceptual framework for the integration of language and content in second/foreign language instruction," *TESOL Quarterly* **23**.2 (1989): 201–217.

Spratt, M., "How good are we at knowing what learners like?, *System* **27** (1999): 141–155.

Sun, G.Y. and Cheng, L.Y., "From context to curriculum: A case study of communicative language teaching in China," *TESL Canada Journal* **19**.2 (2002): 67–86.

Thomson, A., *Critical Reasoning in Ethics: A Practical Introduction*, London: Routledge, 1999.

Wang, F., "Teaching intensive reading within the framework of modern psycholinguistics," *Teaching English in China*, **24**(3) (2001): 55–59.

Wang, Y.P., "Towards developing the students' socio-cultural competence in college English teaching," *Wai Yu Jie (Journal of Foreign Language World)* **73**.1 (1999): 43–47.

Wei, L.B., "In defence of intensive reading," *Teaching English in China*, **29** (1997): 86–90.

Widdowson, H.G., *Teaching Language as Communication*, Oxford: Oxford University Press, 1978.

Willis, J., *A Framework for Task-based Learning*, Harlow, Essex: Longman, 1999: 77.

Wu, X.D. and Fang, L., "Teaching communicative English in China: A case study of the gap between teachers' views and practice," *Asian Journal of English Language Teaching* **12** (2002): 143–162.

Xiang, Q.J. and Wang, Y.M., "Towards a Realization of a Holistic Model of Teaching Reading in the EFL Class in China," *Teaching English in China,* **36** (1999): 46–50.

Xiao, H.Y., Medd, H., and Fearon-Jones, "British studies in China: An introduction to the new textbook on contemporary Britain developed at Guang Dong Foreign Studies University." *Teaching English in China* **27** (1996): 89–93.

Xiao, L.X., "Do we reliably know what EFL students like in English classrooms at university level?" *The Journal of Asia TEFL* **2**.3 (2005): 67–94.

_____, "What do we learn from an empirical study of learning needs of Chinese English majors in a university context?", *The Asian EFL Journal* **8**.4 (2006a): 74–99.

_____, *Communicative Competence and Critical Thinking: An Empirical Sudy of Chinese English Majors and Their Teachers in a University Context*, Tianjin: Tianjin People's Press, 2006b.

Zhang, B., "Culture Learning in Foreign Language Classroom," Teaching English in China, **23**.1 (2000): 50–53.

Zhang, Y., "A text-centred approach to English reading," *Teaching English in China* **26**.4 (2003): 51–55.

Zhao, Y.B., "Increasing learners' cultural awareness," *Teaching English in China* **27** (1996): 63–65.

Zhang, Z.Y., "Intensive reading: Getting your students to see the forest as well as the trees," *Forum* **35**.1 (1997). Retrieved on June 28, 2008. http://exchanges.state.gov/forum/vols/vol35/no1/p40.htm#page_top.

Chapter 3

COMMUNICATIVE LANGUAGE TEACHING AND ENGLISH LANGUAGE TEACHING IN NIGERIA

— EMMANUEL TAIWO BABALOLA

3.1 INTRODUCTION

Communicative language teaching (CLT) is an approach to the teaching of second and foreign languages, which emphasizes interaction of both the means and the ultimate goal of learning a language. It is also referred to as "communicative approach to the teaching of foreign languages" or simply "communicative approach" (Ref. Wikipaedia). As an extension of the notional-functional syllabus, CLT places great emphasis both on helping students use the target language in a variety of contexts and on learning language functions. Unlike the audiolingual method (ALM), its primary focus is on helping learners create meaning rather than develop perfectly grammatical structures or acquire native-like pronunciation. This means that successfully learning a foreign language is assessed in terms of how well learners have developed their communicative competence, which can loosely be defined as their ability to apply knowledge of both formal and socio-linguistic aspects of a language with adequate proficiency to communicate. Communicative language teaching is fundamentally concerned with *making meaning* in the language, whether by interpreting someone else's message, or by expressing one's own, or by negotiating when meaning is unclear. Thus, CLT has brought to the front burner the significance of semantics, the hitherto neglected branch of linguistics, in second language learning. It should be emphasized that the goal of language learning in a communicative classroom is to have a perfect understanding for the learners of the meaning expressed in the lesson and internalizing the rules of grammar, as well as be able to apply this new knowledge in their situations and, consequently, become proficient users of the language. But over-stressing the intricate web of grammar rules and emphasizing learning by rote of pronunciation guides of the language do not translate into such competence.

3.2 THE ORIGIN AND DEVELOPMENT OF CLT

The origins of CLT are many insofar as one teaching methodology tends to influence the next. The communicative approach could be said to be the product of educators and linguists who had grown dissatisfied with the audiolingual and grammar-translation methods of foreign language instruction. They felt that students were not learning enough realistic, whole language. They did not know how to communicate using appropriate social language, gestures, or expressions. In brief, they were at a loss to communicate in the culture of the language studied. As interest in and development of communicative-style teaching mushroomed in the 1970s, authentic language use and classroom exchanges where students engaged in real communication with one another became quite popular. In the intervening years, the communicative approach was adopted to the elementary, middle, secondary, and post-secondary levels, and the underlying philosophy spawned different teaching methods known under a variety of names such as *notional-functional, teaching for proficiency, proficiency-based instruction,* and *communicative language teaching.*

On the other hand, Beale (2002: 13) claimed that "the concept of communicative competence was originally developed thirty years ago by the sociolinguist Del Hymes (1972), as a response to perceived limitations in Chomsky's competence/performance model of language", while its further development could be credited to Canale and Swain in the early 1980s. Beale then gave a summary of the four components of communicative competence as follows:

Grammatical competence
producing a structured comprehensible utterance (including grammar, vocabulary, pronunciation and spelling);

Sociocultural competence
using socially-determined cultural codes in meaningful ways, often termed 'appropriacy' (e.g. formal or informal ways of greeting);

Discourse competence
shaping language and communicating purposefully in different genres (text types), using cohesion (structural linking) and coherence (meaningful relationships in language);

Strategic competence
enhancing the effectiveness of communication (e.g. deliberate speech), and compensating for breakdowns in communication (e.g. comprehension checks, paraphrase, and conversation fillers). (p. 14)

From the above paradigmatic analysis of the kernel of communicative competence, we observe that it is a well-developed approach that could be channeled towards ensuring that nonnative learners of English acquire the language in a way that will fully integrate them into the culture of the language.

Furthermore, communicative language teaching makes use of real-life situations that necessitate communication. The teacher sets up a situation that students are likely to encounter in real life. Unlike the audiolingual method of language teaching, which relies on repetition and drills, the communicative approach can leave students in suspense as to the outcome of a class exercise, which will vary according to their reactions and responses. The real-life simulations change from day to day. Students' motivation to learn comes from their desire to communicate in meaningful ways about meaningful topics.

In a communicative classroom for beginners, for example, the teacher might begin by passing out cards, each with a different name printed on it. He then proceeds to model an exchange of introductions in the target language. Using a combination of the target language and gestures, the teacher conveys the task in hand and gets the students to introduce themselves and ask their classmates for information. They do not know the answers beforehand as they are each holding cards with their new identities written on them. Hence there is an authentic exchange of information. Later during the class, as a reinforcement listening exercise, the students might hear a recorded exchange between two Yoruba or Igbo (Nigerian indigenous languages) freshmen meeting each other for the first time at the bus terminus. Then the teacher might explain in English the differences among Yoruba and Igbo greetings in various social situations and, finally, some of the grammar points and structures used.

3.3 WRONG PROPOSITIONS INHERENT IN CLT

Like many language-teaching theories, CLT has had its fair share of criticism and reviews. Most importantly, its application to different linguistic environments has been questioned. However, most of these criticisms have been geared towards making CLT more useful and adaptable to many situations. Notable among these reviews are the views of Robert O'Neill (2000). According to him there are six fundamentally *trivial* propositions inherent in CLT. These are:

- Language is primarily a tool of communication. Learning a language means learning to perform communicative speech acts with it.
- There is something called a 'communicative syllabus' which replaces, and is superior to, a 'structural syllabus'.
- Communicative goals can be specified. We can accurately describe what learners should have learned and be able to do with language at the end of the lesson.

- Good communicative teaching is learner-centred, and not teacher-centred.
- What matters most is not whether learners learn to *use* the language *accurately* but whether they learn to *get* their message *across*.
- The classroom and the behaviour of teachers and learners in the classroom should be as similar as possible to the behaviour of people in the *real world* outside the classroom.

O'Neill discusses the propositions one after the other and shows why they have been counter-productive to the tenets of CLT. He argues:

> If these propositions are true at all, they are only superficially and trivially true—and true only in essentially uninteresting ways. In other words, they are just as true as statements like "When people speak, they use words". Such a statement tells us nothing about what kinds of relationships there may be between words, how people learn to assemble them into larger units, or what else they do to construct or interpret meaning. (p. 2)

He, therefore, justifies his condemnation of the above propositions which, according to him, have been widely held by many practitioners of CLT by presenting the following six diametrically opposing propositions to the ones given above:

- Generative competence—the ability to use underlying syntax and structure—is one of the foundations of communicative competence. Without it, there is no pragmatic competence worth talking about.
- A language syllabus is more than a list. That is why examples of speech acts cannot be the basis of a syllabus.
- Communicative goals are exercises in illusion rather than reality. It is not possible to specify communicative goals with any precision.
- Good teaching requires an understanding of both "whole-class" and "pair/group" methods. Very often, CLT supporters are prepared to admit that competent whole-class teaching is more efficient than pair and group work.
- A reasonable degree of accuracy is an essential part of fluency.
- There are essential differences between using your own language and trying to use a language you do not know well. These differences help explain the differences in the behaviour of people in the foreign language classroom and in the streets outside the classroom.

What O'Neill emphasises is that there could be a better alternative approach to language teaching (especially foreign language), than what CLT has got to offer language teachers. He, thus, advocates a "pluralistic teaching strategies and techniques which allow for greater diversity and choice not just for individual learners but also for individual teachers". This, according to him, was because no single method or strategy has been found useful in all situations. It was yet to be empirically proved that the techniques of CLT were foolproof or worked in all conditions of learning. O'Neill believes that as there are different learners with different interests, so also are there different learning styles. He then concludes by presenting his idea of adopting a *narrative approach* to any of his teaching:

> My own solution is to adopt a "narrative" approach to the lessons I teach. As it happens, a fairly short text is usually the beginning, but never the end of the lesson. But the lesson would not have a narrative structure at all if that was all I did. And it is quite possible to teach within a narrative structure and not use a "text" in the conventional sense.... Narratives relate different aspects of language to each other in ways, which single speech acts or a set of collocations without context cannot do. (p. 1)

3.4 ENGLISH AS A SECOND OR FOREIGN LANGUAGE

Quirk et al. (1985: 27) subsume the concept of English as a second language (ESL) within Interference English (IE). This classification has, however, been rejected by Afolayan (1979) who has argued against the "glossing of IE as English acquired by speakers of other languages (ENSOL) whether as a foreign or as a second language" (p. 11). According to him the ESL situation is more than a mere 'interference' situation and the variety of English used in an ESL situation should be regarded as distinct from an interference variety which, according to Quirk et al.'s classification, is full of imperfections.

Afolayan argues that ESL, in its standard form, can indeed be seen as a recognized variety of English, distinct from IE but with some elements of IE, which has the potential of becoming a respectable standard dialect of English, and can stand side by side other standard varieties including English as a mother tongue (EMT) standards such as British English (BrE) and American English (AmE). But he points out that ESL has the peculiarity of being a bilingual rather than a monolingual variety, and that the EMT varieties will continue to have as its touchstone.

On the other hand, Quirk et al. define a foreign language as "a language used by persons for communication across frontiers or with others who are not from their country: listening to broadcasts, reading books or newspapers, engaging in commerce or travel, for example" (p. 5). In countries where English is neither used as a native language nor as a second language, it may be in use as a foreign language (FL). Its functions in such countries may, however, be restricted to, say, maintaining bilateral relations with English-speaking or other non-English speaking countries, and gaining access to classified information in English-medium journals. This, as Quirk et al. explains, is because "it [English] is needed for access to at least half of the world's scientific literature, and that the most important scientific journals are in English" (p. 5).

Thus, English is in use as a foreign language in France and the Francophone African countries, in the Far East countries such as Japan and

China, in the Arab countries such as Saudi Arabia, Jordan and Yemen, in such European countries as Portugal, Italy, Belgium, Poland and Spain, and in some parts of Latin America.

The desire to learn English for one purpose or the other has, therefore, been on the increase. The British Council, which has offices in virtually every part of the world, has worked closely with American organizations such as the United States Information Agency (USIA) and the Voice of America (VOA) to promote the teaching of English to speakers of other languages. Even the BBC (British Broadcasting Corporation), the CNN (Cable News Network) and other English-speaking countries like Australia also assume a heavy responsibility for the teaching of English as a second or foreign language. Even now, teaching and learning of English for specific purposes (ESP) have assumed an international dimension; the heavy volume of scholarly literature on ESP can attest to this fact (see, for example, Munby 1978; Strevens 1980; Hutchinson and Waters 1987; Robinson 1991). In the view of Quirk et al., "no language is more widely studied or used as a foreign language than English" (p. 5).

However, as important as the language is the world over, its teaching and learning in ESL situations such as Nigeria, Ghana, India, and Pakistan have a lot of challenges, especially to the classroom teachers at the various levels of education, who have the dilemma of choosing from the myriads of approaches and methods and adapt them to their own peculiar situations. And it is indeed our purpose in this study to examine the applicability and suitability of one of the time-tested language teaching approaches—communicative language teaching—to the Nigerian ESL situation.

3.4.1 Nigeria's Language Provision

In Nigeria, the entire language policy governing the multilingual/multiethnic giant African nation is encapsulated in the language provisions of the *National Policy on Education* (2004), a publication of the Nigerian Educational Research and Development Council (NERDC). In this document, the goals of Nigeria's education are clearly articulated and these include the government's position and policy statements on the management and utilization of hundreds of languages in the country. Many scholars (Obanya 1980; Chumbow 1990; Babalola 2002a, 2002b; Akindele and Adegbite 2004; Oladipo 2007) have at various times given a critique of the so-called language provision as it relates to proper assignment of roles to the existing languages in the country and have advocated a comprehensive language policy document for the country instead of the harried language provisions subsumed in the *National Policy on Education* (NPE). In the words of Oladipo:

> One way out of this quagmire is for the government and policy makers to have clearly-stated language policies that would take into cognizance the socio-cultural realities of its people. (p. 57)

However, of more significant to us in this study is the provision that stipulates that the language of instruction at the lower levels of education (nursery and primary) shall be any Nigerian indigenous language within the vicinity of the learners, that is, language of immediate environment (LIE) (NPE, Section 4(19e)), while English shall be taught as a school subject. It should be said categorically that this provision is at variance with the principles of communicative language teaching in foreign language teaching; even the characteristics of pedagogy that have been known to promote functional language competence attest to this fact. It should be recalled that Nigeria is a second language user of English, having acquired the language as a legacy of colonialism. But with time, the language has grown in status and function in the country and has ceased being considered as a vestige of colonialism to a language of unification and integration. The Nigerian state is made up of over 300 ethnic groups each with at least two distinct languages and several language-like dialects giving a replica of the Biblical Tower of Babel! But thanks to English that readily filled the vacuum of a neutral language with which the country was brought together and has remained together.

Now, how can a country desiring to inculcate high level of proficiency in English in its learners at the same time be discouraging early exposure of the same learners to the language that is very important to their full integration in all facets of life: academic, social, political, and inter-personal relationships? It is at this early level of education that the learners can best be immersed in the language. According to Guarino da Verona (1374–1460), an early humanist of the Italian Renaissance, an educator celebrated throughout Europe for his scholarship, as quoted by Musumeci (1997):

> Interpretive skills come first, acquired through immersion in the language, exposure to excellent models, and interaction with interesting subject matter. Fluency in oral and written expression develops gradually, as a consequence of exposure to good models and pleasant interaction in the second language.

In his own vision for educational reform, Comenius (1592–1670), as quoted by Musumeci (1997), acknowledged that if one wished to learn a modern language, the best way is to send him to a place where the language is spoken, and make him read, write, and learn the class books in the new language of the vernacular school. So using vernaculars as languages of instruction for all other subjects while English is treated as one of those subjects makes a mockery of any effort at achieving communicative competence in the English language. Comenius also advocates learning the second language through contact with excellent linguistic models and meaningful interaction with interesting, relevant subject matter.

However, where to procure these kinds of 'excellent linguistic models' in a second language environment remains a thing of conjecture. Furthermore, language input that may serve to assist the learners in refocusing what they have learnt in the formal classroom may not be available. In a nutshell, good models of language are not there and the learner may have to rely solely on the teachers who are themselves products of the same experience. In fact, the experience in Nigeria as in most second language situations is that language learners may even be afraid to practise the good spoken English they have been taught in school for fear of being ridiculed and labeled as 'African English men' or 'been-to' by ignorant members of the society. Even if you know the correct pronunciation of some words, you may keep that to yourself and go along with the common incorrect pronunciation that you know the people will easily understand. Thus, there is bound to be a discrepancy on the way language is taught in the classroom and how it is used outside.

3.4.2 Communicative Language Teaching in an ESL Environment

As a broad approach to teaching language, David Nunan (1991: 279) identifies five features of CLT:

1. An emphasis on learning to communicate through interaction in the target language.
2. Introduction of authentic texts into the learning situation.
3. Provision of opportunities for learners to focus not only on the language but also on the learning-management process.
4. An enhancement of the learner's own personal experiences as important contributing elements to classroom learning.
5. An attempt to link classroom language learning with language activities outside.

One thing that is significant in the adoption of CLT in any second or foreign language-learning situation is that the practitioner must ensure that there is a link between what is taught in the classroom with what obtains outside the class. In other words, the experiences of the learners in the world of reality must resemble the drills and activities they have undergone in the classroom. However, this requirement is very difficult to come by in most second language situations like Nigeria. For example, in a typical Nigerian language teaching classroom, the learners are arranged to sit in roles facing the teacher who himself stands backing the chalkboard and, in turn, facing the students. This arrangement means that:

- The teacher dominates.
- All information will come from the teacher.
- Interaction between or among students is less valued.
- Group work requiring negotiation and cooperation is deemphasized.
- Role-plays that allow for language use and practice are almost non-existent.

Thus, the experience in the English language class is not significantly different from the teaching of any other subject such as History, Government and Economics. The learners look up at the teacher as some sort of encyclopaedia who is always right, and what they do mostly as participants in the learning situation is to write down whatever the teacher dictates or anything that is meaningful to them. In this scenario, we can conclude that the principles of CLT have been compromised. The interaction which is the ultimate goal in CLT is not in any special way encouraged since the teachers see themselves as the only purveyors of knowledge and the learners are reduced to mere listeners. But the reality is that many of the teachers (who are second language users of English) themselves may not be significantly better than the learners in terms of the competence in the target language.

The CLT approach cannot be successfully utilized in a second language environment where useful books and materials needed by the learners are not readily available. It should be noted that teachers themselves, who are not native speakers of the language, need books and materials to aid their teaching. Mostly, the language input from the natural setting where the language is to be used needs to be sorted and put together by competent writers and made availabe to both the teachers and learners. To do this will require a great deal of will because Nigeria is a very vast country and teachers can come from any part of the country to teach students with whom they do not share first language. And CLT often assumes that when the teacher and students understand each other, communication in a target language will be enhanced. But where this basic understanding is lacking, errors resulting from the influence of the first language may be very difficult to address and such learners may find it difficult making themselves intelligible to speakers beyond their immediate locality, especially foreigners.

In Nigeria, as is a common practice in many second language situations, classroom instruction in the English language consists of memorization of rules, repetition, drills, an early emphasis on linguistic accuracy coupled with a strong measure of error correction, and postponement of subject matter teaching until the grammar had been 'mastered'. Such practice has persisted over the years even though it has not produced functional competence in the learners. That is why majority of the learners still find it difficult to be successful in major English-based examinations. And this is part of the reasons that informed many second language countries including Nigeria electing to embrace language policies that favour the use of indigenous languages in education. But the success recorded from this practice, as far as Nigeria is concerned, has been insignificant compared to what is needed to sustain the practice. Again, Oladipo (2007: 54) comments on such failed efforts by citing the cases of Primary Education Improvement Project (PEIP) in the northern part of Nigeria, and Ife Six-Year Primary Project of the then University of Ife, both, though recorded remarkable gains, could not be sustained by the government.

Equally important is the input from native speakers environment which the learners have to be exposed to if their competence in the language must transcend their local environment. Both grammatical and communicative competence must be emphasised. Bax (2003) thumbs down CLT for not taking particular cognizance of the context in which teaching and learning take place. Another CLT scholar Belchamber (2007) underscores the need for resourceful teachers if the goals of CLT must be achieved:

> With the emphasis on communication, there is also the implication that spoken exchanges should be authentic and meaningful; detractors claim that the artificial nature of classroom-based (i.e. teacher-created) interactions makes CLT an oxymoron. Nevertheless, a proficient teacher will provide a context so that class interactions are realistic and meaningful but with the support needed to assist students to generate the target language.

Futhermore, the benefits of CLT cannot be maximally appropriated in Nigeria because the teaching settings in most of our schools (from primary to the university) are essentially exam-focused. As an illustration, there are at least three distinct levels of education in Nigeria that are compulsory for most students to pass through: primary, secondary, and the university. Though, there are some forms of kindergarten (pre-primary) schools that a child may attend before the primary level and there are some intervening schooling that could take the place of a university education as well. According to the National Policy on Education (NPE 2004), Nigerian indigenous languages are to be used as the languages of instruction while English is taught as a school subject at the primary level; at the other levels of education, English is the language of instruction. However, before a primary school pupil could gain entrance to the secondary school, they must pass English, and to gain admission to the university, English must be passed at credit level at the West African Examination Council (WAEC)-organised examinations. In addition, English is a compulsory subject that must be passed in the university matriculation examinations for all students seeking admission into the university in Nigeria.

    Thus, learners are usually preoccupied with passing their English language examinations than making conscious efforts at using the language to perform functions. This is most pervasive at the higher levels of education. Once a student passes exams, they do not feel inclined to remember the contents of the lesson or course. The country's belief in and emphasis on paper qualifications to the detriment of individuals' functionality is partly responsible for this trend. At the lower levels of education (primary to secondary schools), they queried the relevance of high competence in the English language to their situation where many of the students never used English outside the classroom; and even when they do, the correctness and standardness of their input did not bother them once they could barely make themselves intelligible. But using the language learnt in the class outside the learning environment is very vital to gaining mastery and confidence in the use of the target language. For example, a dancer needs to have practised the steps and finetune the techniques in the confines of her room before showcasing the same to a larger audience. Therefore, teachers have to ensure that their students learn as well as acquire the language in a way to cater for their need to pass their exams and at the same time enable them to use the language socially to perform different functions.

3.5 CONCLUSION

In this chapter, I have discussed the nature, usefulness and the applicabiiity of communicative language teaching approach to the teaching of English to speakers of other languages (TESOL), especially in a second language environment. The peculiar case of Nigeria has been discussed and steps in making the approach more relevant to the language situation of the country have been suggested. More importantly, adapting language teaching techniques to second or foreign language situations must take cognizance of the peculiar nature of these linguistic environments vis-à-vis their linguistic developmental goals.

Finally, language teachers in second language environments should also be conscious of the place of motivation in their classroom. In my years of teaching English at different levels of education in Nigeria, I have found that one of the fundamental problems confronting English language teachers is how to motivate their students to learn English, not to even talk of encouraging them to acquire it. Teachers need to provide opportunity for students to discuss a topic in small groups before there is any expectation that they speak in front of the whole class. Language teachers should be aware that the need for ongoing negotiation during interaction increases the learners' overt participation. It is this involvement we need to harness and build on. Emphasis over the years has shifted among Nigerian students to how quickly to make money and become somebody. Even the society does not count competence in the use of the language any rare feat. How many people actually can appreciate good use of the language? Apart from the tiny cycle of elites and well-educated, you are just as ordinary as any cobbler!

REFERENCES

Afolayan, A., *Problems, Principles and Prospects of English Studies in an African University, Inaugural Lecture Series 38*, Nigeria: University of Ife Press, 1979a.

Akindele, F. and Adegbite, Wale, *The Sociology and Politics of English in Nigeria*, Ile-Ife, Nigeria: Obafemi Awolowo University Press, 2004.

Babalola, E.T., "The politics of language of instruction in Nigerian schools," *Literacy and Reading in Nigeria*, C.E. Onukaogu (Ed.), **9**.1 (2002a): 161–171.

Babalola, E.T., "The development and preservation of Nigerian languages and cultures: The role of the local government," *Studia Anglica Osnaniensia: An International Review of English Studies* **37** (2002b).

Bax, S., "The end of CLT: A context approach to language teaching," *ELT* **57** (2003): 278–287.

Beale, Jason, "Is communicative language teaching a thing of the past?," *Babel*, **37**.1 (2002): 12–16.

Belchamber, R., "The advantages of communicative language teaching," *The Internet TESL Journal*, **XIII**.2 (2007), http://iteslj.org/

Chumbow, Beban, "The place of mother tongue in the National Policy on Education," *Multilingualism, Minority Languages and Language Policy in Nigeria*, Nolue Emenanjo (Ed.), Agbor: Central Books, 1990, 61–72.

Federal Republic of Nigeria, *National Policy on Education*, 4th ed., Lagos: NERDC Press, 2004.

Hutchinson, T. and Waters, A., *English for Specific Purposes: A Learning-centred Approach*, Cambridge: Cambridge University Press, 1987.

Hymes, D., "On communicative competence," J.B. Pride and J. Holmes (Eds.), *Sociolinguistics*, Harmondsworth, England: Penguin Books.

Munby, J., *Communicative Syllabus Design*, Cambridge: Cambridge University Press, 1978.

Musumeci, D., *The Role of Grammar in Communicative Language Teaching: A Historical Perspective*, 1997, mhhe_webmaster@mcgraw-hill.com

Nunan, D., "Communicative tasks and the language curriculum," *TESOL Quarterly* **25**.2 (Summer 1991): 279–295.

Obanya, Pai, "Nigeria in search of a suitable educational system," *Journal of African Studies* **7**.1 (1980): 48–53.

Oladipo, R., "Language use in the Nigerian educational system: Problems and prospects," *Nigerian Languages, Literatures, Culture and Reforms: A Festschrift for Ayo Bamgbose*, N. Ozo-mekuri (Ed.), Port Harcourt: M&J Grand Orbit Communications Ltd. & Emhai Press, 2007, 49–59.

O'Neill, R., "Communicative language teaching," *Ted Power English Language Learning and Teaching*, Online, 2000, pp. 1–6.

Quirk, R., Greenbaum, S., Leech, G., and Svartvik, J., *A Comprehensive Grammar of the English Language*, London: Longman, 1985.

Robinson, P.C., *ESP Today: A Practitioner's Guide*, New York: Prentice Hall, 1991.

Stevens, P., "Functional Englishes (ESP)," *Teaching English as an International Language: From Practice to Principle*, Oxford: Pergamon Press, 1980, 105–121.

Chapter 4

COMMUNICATIVE LANGUAGE TEACHING: An Indian Teacher Resolves a Methodology Dilemma

— Deepti Gupta

4.1 INTRODUCTION

In 1989, Panjab University, Chandigarh (India) introduced a new module, Communicative English, based on the Communicative Approach. I soon realised that this course was not successful. As a practising teacher since 1985, I believed in the Communicative Approach in my classroom. But now I feel frustrated and faced with a methodological dilemma. In 1994, I undertook a research study to further explore the issues involved and arrive at some resolution. By 2004, it appeared that the whole teaching paradigm had changed. So, I repeated the research exercise of 1994 and the results revealed a complete paradigm shift in the ELT situation of India. Thus, my work as researcher empowered me as teacher.

4.1.1 Statement of the Issue

Based on the Communicative Approach (henceforth CA) to language teaching[1], Panjab University in 1998 introduced a new module of Communicative English in its undergraduate curriculum. I had been teaching since 1985 in an undergraduate college affiliated to this university and, like other ELT-proficient teachers, welcomed the move as a step in the right direction. But, within a year or two, in spite of the best efforts of all concerned, it became clear that this course was not as successful as expected. The Curriculum Development Centre had envisioned lively, activity-oriented classrooms with communication as the goal. Instead, my classroom became a place of stilted and forced task-based routines. I was constantly striving to motivate learners who found it impossible to respond to interactive methods after years of lecture-based teaching.

In spite of introducing learner-friendly communicative tasks over a period of time, there was no response from the majority of learners in my class. Matters had reached the point where I would dread the very idea of using tasks in my classroom; a big crisis for an impassioned advocate of task-based and interactive teaching. Why did the methodology that worked perfectly in the rest of the world fail in my classroom?

Facing unresponsive learners was causing professional frustration for me. To put this frustration to constructive use, delve deeper into the issues involved that had made my classroom a combat zone, understand the reasons for my being stonewalled by my students for the first time and find some way out of the methodology deadlock that I found myself in, I took up a research study in 1994. It was becoming increasingly difficult for me to sustain my optimism about Communicative Language Teaching (CLT) and present a brave face to all my colleagues who had written off CLT but continued to teach the CLT-based curriculum in a resigned manner. Conscious of the emotional nature of my dilemma and in order to create some distance between the problem and myself, I decided to involve other teachers and their learners as well to lend objectivity to my study. I used questionnaires and carried out classroom observation coupled with video recordings.

By 2004, both academic and nonacademic institutes began to implement the CA. I noticed that learners were now more receptive to tasks and interacted actively. Within the last decade, imperceptible changes in the Indian situation had given my students an understanding of their language needs which, in turn, had led to greater appreciation of the CLT methodology. The whole teaching paradigm had changed. To know the causes behind this dramatic change, I repeated the research exercise of 1994, using the classes of my colleagues and my own. The results revealed a complete paradigm shift in the ELT situation of India and encouraged me to continue innovating in the classroom.

4.1.2 Research Procedure and Results

Two kinds of questionnaire were drafted for the first study of 1994 and the same were used again in 2004. Through questions, I tried to address the problems I faced while teaching English through CLT. The first questionnaire was for students and the second was for teachers. These questionnaires were designed to elicit responses that would help clarify four issues:

1. Can I be confident of success on replacing one variety of ELT pedagogy with another in my classroom?
2. What do my students want?
3. What are the unique parameters of my Indian classroom?
4. How significant is the role of context in my classroom?

The questionnaire for students

The questionnaire (see Appendix) was a short one designed to catch the students' perceptions about their English classes. I wanted them to speak out and give candid, off-the-cuff opinions because their cultivated silence was the problem in the CLT classroom.

1994. The data collected from 300 students in colleges through the student questionnaire clarified the whole situation and gave me sufficient facts to base my conclusions on. The learner profile that emerged was in accordance with the circumstances I faced in my classroom. Having taken inputs from both my college and three other colleges, I was confident that my conclusions would not be biased or lopsided in any way. The majority of learners emerged as language users who (even after 13–16 years of language study) could not use English comfortably in the class, were not interested in reading books in English and did not use English frequently outside the classroom. This implied that the social set-up did not throw up enough opportunities to use English.

The professional environment could not offer adequate avenues for the above age group and even when it did, English was not perceived as a tool for empowerment. Therefore, they saw no reason to stretch their performance and participation in task-based classrooms, a fact reflected in the statistics: 90 per cent looked upon task-based teaching a waste of time and the majority expected the teacher to lecture most of the time. Sixty per cent disagreed that English could empower them within a profession, a statistic that explained my helplessness with regard to learner motivation in class. The complete lack of interest in any classroom activity that was not lecture-oriented was explained by the absence of exposure to any professional context. At the time of the study, I could not quite understand its significance, but after the second study, the picture became clearer as this lack of interest emerged as one of several related factors. Only 25 per cent students agreed that English was required outside the classroom as well, a typical response from an EFL society.

2004. The data collected after a decade through the same student questionnaire and logistics revealed a sea change in the whole teaching paradigm. Once again, I had taken input from both my own classes and those of my colleagues. The majority of learners had gone through the same 13–16 years of language study, could use English comfortably in the class, most of them were now bilingual, were interested in reading books in English and used English frequently outside the classroom. This meant that the social setup now encouraged them to use English and the professional environment yielded adequate avenues for this age group. Thus English became a tool for empowerment.

Now, they stood convinced of the requirement for fluency in professional contexts and were motivated enough to stretch their performance and participation in task-based classrooms. Only 20 per cent looked upon task-based teaching a waste of time and the majority did not expect the teacher to lecture most of the time. Seventy per cent agreed that English could empower them within a profession and 30 per cent were now working while studying. These statistics explained the drastic changes I perceived in learner motivation in the 2004 class. Most of them were now receptive to the idea of communicative and task-based teaching and looked forward to simulations of real-world situations, activities that had been dismissed indifferently a decade ago. At the time of the earlier study, I could not quite grasp the significance of this lack of interest, but after this second study, the dramatic transformation in the whole paradigm needed some explanation involving extra-pedagogic factors. More so, in the light of the fact that as compared to 1994 when only 25 per cent students agreed that English was required outside the classroom as well, in 2004, 60 per cent felt that they required it outside the classroom, indicating the changing status of English in my students' milieu.

The transformed trend of the data collected through the same questionnaire meant that the extra-linguistic factors also had to be taken into consideration. While designing the tools for research, I was not too keen on including a questionnaire for teachers because I felt that the students' responses and classroom observation would be enough. Most of my colleagues were unhappy about the failure of CLT in their classes and those who were not well-versed in ELT felt that I was wasting my time. But, in order to get objective results, I accepted the fact that I needed feedback from teachers. This acceptance and the consequent exchange of ideas gave me a better understanding of what the profession as a whole was going through because of the unhappy experience with CLT.

So, besides filling up one such questionnaire, I distributed copies to 50 colleagues. I went to two other undergraduate colleges for inputs from teachers to give a broad sociological base to the data.

The questionnaire for teachers

In 1994, four per cent teachers had attended workshops/training programmes/ refresher courses and 96 per cent continued in the profession on the strength of academic qualifications acquired before being employed. In 2004, 50 per cent teachers had attended workshops/training programmes/refresher courses, 30 per cent had acquired further academic degrees like PhDs and 20 per cent had achieved neither. This was a clear indication that the context had changed for the teacher as well; there was better awareness of teacher education, orientation and training. The whole process of curriculum change in India is cumbersome and time-consuming, so in spite of the limited success of CLT, it had not been removed from courses. This, in the long run, was for the better because, while on the one hand, the teachers had been able to familiarize themselves with its approach and methodology and, on the other, the changed and changing contexts had ensured its success at a later stage. In 1994, 80 per cent teachers wanted the removal of CLT from the curriculum but in 2004, 70 per cent felt that it should be retained. Ninety per cent in 1994 labelled the CLT methodology 'unrealistic'. Eighty-five per cent in 2004 called it 'the need of the hour' (see Appendix for the data collected from the exercise).

In 1994, 80 per cent teachers agreed that they lectured more than 70 per cent of the time in the classroom, but in 2004, 70 per cent teachers agreed that they spent between 40–50 per cent of the time on lecturing. This trend matched the changes in student expectations as well. The teacher was no longer just a facilitator of examinations.

Parents of learners form an important component of the teaching paradigm in India. In 1994, I faced many angry parents who were bewildered by the fact that I wanted their wards to participate in task-based activities. Their ire was justified because at that time teaching English in India meant lecturing by the teacher most of the time. So, any kind of change in course content or teaching methodology would result in stiff opposition from them, forcing the administrative body to recommend the continuation of traditional methodology. Observing the winds of change resulting from the acceptance of the global status of English, parents, in 2004, began to encourage innovation and experimentation in the classroom as they had in mind the high proficiency level demanded by educational institutes as well as employers.

While teaching a literary text in 1994, 80 per cent teachers began with an introductory lecture, 10 per cent with a discussion and 10 per cent with an activity or task. In 2004, 50 per cent teachers began with an activity or task, 30 per cent with a discussion and 20 per cent with an introductory lecture. The video recording of classroom teaching confirmed these facts while presenting a learner profile that was more proactive and cooperative than that of the 1994 study. In 1994, teachers rarely ventured beyond the lecture, but the 2004 class gave them both encouragement and motivation to introduce alternatives to the monotonous lecture.

The two biggest fears of the students in 1994 were using English inside the classroom and outside. In 2004, I found that their two biggest worries were employment and choice of the right profession. The opportunities thrown up by the economic scenario because of the liberalisation of the Indian economy demanded a candidate to be both linguistically and communicatively proficient. While earlier in the century, students who had specialised in English sought either teaching or civil services jobs, now a whole new spectrum of job opportunities opened up: call centres needed trainers to equip their employees with communication skills, marketing staff recruited by multinationals needed to be taught spoken English, medical transcription agencies needed efficient translators and reporters and those desirous of immigration to the West needed professional help for clearing tests like IELTS and TOEFL.

While 85 per cent teachers expressed their helplessness at the indifference of their students towards task-based activities in 1994, in 2004, 70 per cent agreed that their students enjoyed these activities. In 1994, the reason for this indifference was that they did not require English outside the classroom, so it was an exercise in futility. In 2004, the students enjoyed these activities because sufficient practice would assist them in their personal and professional lives.

In 1994, 80 per cent teachers agreed that English was a foreign language for their students and in 2004, 73 per cent held that English was a second language for their students. Whereas in 1994, 20 per cent felt that it was a second language, in 2004, 17 per cent labelled it the first language for their students and 10 per cent called it a foreign language. In 2004, in India, a whole new generation was coming up, a generation that today travels a lot in countries where English is the first language, works in places where English is the lingua franca and, as a result, carries home to other generations the same English as a medium of communication. Hence, the empowerment that Bax[2] looks forward to for teachers in times to come has come sooner due to changes in the teaching paradigm. I concluded that unless the context works for the teacher, no teacher training or upgradation of methodology can be productive or fruitful.

Seventy-five per cent teachers in 1994 felt that in spite of their best efforts, CLT as a methodology was not successful in the classroom, but in 2004, for 90 per cent, CLT and related methodology was the best for students. In 1994, lack of student response was the main reason cited for the failure of CLT and in 2004, students' enthusiasm was the reason for its success. Of course, all the factors cited above are behind this change, but the changed face of Indian ELT today is also due to a nonacademic factor.

In India, purely private sector academies sprung up to make learners proficient English users within a stipulated period. An increasing number of qualified teachers found their way to these places. Young teachers working in undergraduate colleges started working part-time at these academies. At the academy, they used the latest teaching aids and materials to achieve fluency at the earliest. I saw in my college that their teaching methodology underwent a transformation because they used the interactive, task-based and communicative methods more than the usual lecture methods.

Considering the brisk business the academies were doing, the administrative bodies of undergraduate colleges came to realise that a whole untapped market needed to be explored. Along with their regular degree classes, they began to introduce revenue-earning courses in the field of English proficiency that were open to the public. This led to a spill over effect in the undergraduate classes, too, as some teachers were common to both courses and the same campus saw a lot of innovative teaching. The parents of my students also were more open to change because of the observed success rate of these academies.

In 1994, 90 per cent teachers believed that the classroom situation had not changed much during the last 10 years. In 2004, 87 per cent teachers felt that the classroom situation had changed 'beyond recognition' and 'for the better' and was more 'innovation-friendly'. This was not surprising, considering the verification of data that emerged from the classroom video recordings. I had selected six classrooms at random in order to record teaching-in-process. During both the surveys, video recordings were made of the proceedings in order to verify data collected through the questionnaire. These recordings were particularly helpful in tabulating the radical change in learner profile. I recorded my own classroom as well in order to analyse my teaching practice.

By the end of the second study, I was better equipped to understand my classroom and improve upon my methodology accordingly. The impatience and frustration that had led to the study had been productively channelised and I felt more empowered as teacher because of my work as researcher. I did not feel inadequate as a teacher for being less than successful in the implementation of CLT the first time. I realised that I had been caught up with the journey of English in India, from the despised instrument of oppression to the reluctantly adopted lingua franca and later to the status symbol of the upper classes and its position today as a second language.

Just as the language was constantly reinvented, the whole ELT paradigm also travelled the complete gamut of modification and so did I as teacher and researcher. Just as the whole scenario had come to appreciate English better, I had to re-learn teaching methodology to keep in touch with my learners' needs. These changes were represented by the radical transformation in the data collected through the same questions within a decade.

As a linguist, pedagogic, researcher and teacher, I felt an explanation had to be sought for the diverse results of both studies and also for the fact that CLT, so successful in the 1970s in the whole world, took two decades to take root in India. Based upon the results of my study, I compared the growth of ELT in a first language context with its growth in India to explain the gap between the two situations. It is now clear that not only CLT, but also all developments in ELT need time to take root in India, a fact that resolved my dilemma finally.

When CLT was introduced in India in the 1980s, it was a dismal failure for some years because of the lack of the right context, which led to my frustration around the year 1994. The valuable lesson that I learnt through my research continues to inform and enrich my teaching, saving further angst as I now know that unless the context works for the teacher, no teacher training or upgradation of methodology can be productive and fruitful: a significant conclusion drawn from the initial failure of CLT in my classroom. All data pointed towards a complete paradigm shift from EFL to ESL, while demonstrating that the poor response to my teaching practice was due to the absence of a particular context and not due to any weakness in CLT.

The issue that I studied was specifically related to my context because English has gone through a whole range of change in my classroom within a decade. English defines the progress of India as a society. In 1994, society was in transition from isolated English users to widespread English usage.

I had succeeded in answering the four questions posed while beginning the study and now I knew that teachers like me were the victims of the transitional phase. The 2004 study clarified and supported the coming of age of English in India, proving that the transition was complete and in terms of ELT methodology, India was finally at par with the rest of the world.

The results of the earlier study showcased a classroom of participants happy to maintain the *status quo*. There were very few gusts of fresh air in the form of innovative teachers and enthusiastic learners. And, as in my classroom, if the teacher was willing to try a new methodology, failure often came with the absence of learner cooperation. While this perception may sound discouraging, it warned me of the uphill task ahead.

For me, as a teacher, both these studies gave vent first to frustration and anxiety, also provided answers to my dilemma and demonstrated that the context of an ELT situation is overwhelming in its significance. The vital importance of action research as a tool and trouble-shooter was reinforced over and again.

ENDNOTES

1. Richards, J.C. and Rodgers, T.S. (2002, p. 244): "Mainstream teaching on both sides of the Atlantic ... opted for Communicative Language Teaching (CLT) as the recommended basis for language teaching methodology in the 1980s and it continues to be the most plausible basis for language teaching today, although ... CLT is today understood to mean little more than a set of very general principles that can be applied and interpreted in a variety of ways.'

2. Bax, S. (2003, pp. 295-296): "In my view methodology can, if treated with excessive reverence, act as a brake on teachers. If we are not careful, we hinder teachers from developing their abilities to analyse and respond to the context productively. ... some teachers do break out of the straitjacket, but why can't the profession empower them to do so? ... The teacher is not to be merely 'reactive' to the context ... teachers should not only be sensitive to the context, but also provide the key ingredients for language learning such as opportunities for input, output, attention to accuracy, and so on ...."

SUGGESTED READINGS

Allwright, D., *Observation in the Language Classroom,* USA: Longman, 1988.

Bax, S., "Bringing context and methodology together," *ELT Journal* **57**.3 (2003), London: OUP.

Cook, V., *Second Language Learning and Language Teaching,* New York: OUP, 2001.

Dunkin, M.J. and Bruce, J.B., *The Study of Teaching,* New York: Holt, Rinehart and Winston, 1974.

Johnson, K., *An Introduction to Foreign Language Learning and Teaching,* Malaysia: Pearson Education, 2001.

McDonough, J. and McDonough, S., *Research Methods for English Language Teachers,* UK: Arnold, 1997.

McKay, S.L., *Teaching English as an International Language: Rethinking Goals and Approaches,* China: OUP, 2002.

Mitchell, R. and Myles, F., *Second Language Learning Theories,* UK: Arnold, 1998.

Rahman, T., *Language, Ideology and Power,* Pakistan: OUP, 2002.

Rao, P.J., Subrahmanyan, A., and Sunitha, K., "Feasibility of adopting the CLT approach to the Class XII English course," *The Language Curriculum: Dynamics of Change, Volume 2: Teacher as Researcher,* Rama Mathew and R. Lalitha Eapen (Eds.), India: Orient Longman, 2002: 44–47.

Richards, J.C., *The Context of Language Teaching,* New York: Cambridge University Press, 1985.

Richards, J.C. and Lockhart, C., *Reflective Teaching in Second Language Classrooms,* New York: Cambridge University Press, 1994.

Richards, J.C. and Rodgers, T.S., *Approaches and Methods in Language Teaching,* 2nd ed., Delhi: Cambridge University Press, 2002.

Skehan, P., *Individual Differences in Second-Language Learning,* New York: OUP, 1989.

Sobhana, N., *Communicative Competence in English,* New Delhi: Discovery Publishing House, 2003.

Wajnryb, R., *Classroom Observation Tasks,* London: Cambridge University Press, 1992.

Wallace, M.J., *Action Research for Language Teachers,* London: Cambridge University Press, 1998.

APPENDIX

Questionnaires for the Students

Dear students,

Here are a few questions that require honest answers. Please answer by encircling the option of your choice, filling in the blanks or by using a few words. Thank you for your cooperation.

1. For how many years have you been learning English in class?

    ………….. years.

2. Do you read books written in English that are not a part of your curriculum?

    (a) Never
    (b) Rarely

(c) Sometimes
(d) Frequently.

3. You ………….. speak English in the class.
    (a) never
    (b) rarely
    (c) sometimes
    (d) frequently.

4. Given the choice you would use …………...
    (a) your mother tongue
    (b) English
    (c) both.

5. You use English ………….. outside the classroom.
    (a) frequently
    (b) sometimes
    (c) rarely
    (d) never.

6. What percentage of the total time should a teacher of English lecture in the classroom?
    (a) Less than 60
    (b) 60
    (c) 70
    (d) 80
    (e) 90
    (f) 100.

7. Are you working while studying for your Bachelor's degree?
    (a) Yes
    (b) No.

8. Are fluency and proficiency in English essential for future professional success?
    (a) No
    (b) Yes.

9. Do you require English in your daily life out of College?
    (a) Yes
    (b) No
    (c) Not sure.

10. Communicative tasks in the English classroom are a waste of time. Do you agree?
    (a) Yes
    (b) No.

Questionnaires for the Teachers

Dear colleague,

Some of the questions here require a tick against the appropriate choice. Some may require a few words from you. Thank you for your cooperation.

1. Have you attended any training course in the field of ELT? Yes/no. If yes, name them.
2. Should CLT be removed from the syllabus?
   (a) Yes
   (b) No.
3. CLT in India is …………..
   (a) a waste of time.
   (b) unrealistic
   (c) slightly useful
   (d) the need of the hour.
4. For what percentage of the total time do you lecture in class?
   (a) 100
   (b) 90
   (c) 80
   (d) 70
   (e) 60
   (f) 40–50.
5. While teaching literature in the classroom, you begin with …………..
   (a) an introductory lecture
   (b) a discussion with students
   (c) task-based activities
   (d) any other (please specify).
6. The biggest fear of your students is/are …………..:
   (a) using English in the classroom
   (b) employment opportunities
   (c) using English outside the classroom
   (d) choice of profession.
7. Your students' attitude to task-based activity is one of
   (a) enjoyment
   (b) disinterest
   (c) indifference.
8. What could be the reason for the above attitude? (One line, please)
9. What is the status of English in India with regard to your students?
   (a) Foreign language
   (b) Second language
   (c) First language
   (d) Any other.

10. In your classroom, CLT as a methodology is successful.
    (a) Yes
    (b) No.

    What is your prime reason for the response to the last question in one sentence?

11. In the last ten years, the classroom situation in India has changed.
    (a) Not at all
    (b) Slightly
    (c) Completely.

12. Please describe the change in one word or phrase.

Chapter 5

INTEGRATING ICT IN THE LANGUAGE CLASSROOM
An Intercultural Journey?

— ANNE FOX

Integrating information and communication technologies (ICT) in education has been an issue for almost 40 years and it is still the case today that the potential for integration is far greater than the implementation, as attested by many reports (e.g. Attwell et al.). Certainly, the nature of the beast has changed from the 'repeat after me' tape-based language laboratories of the 60s and 70s to the interactive exercises of the 80s and the mixed media CD-ROMs and nascent Internet of the 90s when, armed with some knowledge of HTML coding, one could set up a website for one's classes. Now, in the 21st century, the technologies are truly communicative and interactive but still take-up and implementation is low, including in the language classroom. This is in spite of the fact that one of the defining elements of 21st century technologies, known as Web 2.0 technologies, is their ease of use and low cost.

The abundance of cheap information contributes to the enrichment of authentic texts in the language classroom, but its impact on the role of the teacher may not be so welcome. The easier it becomes to access information outside the classroom, the more the role of teacher as expert is diminished and the role of teacher as learning facilitator is needed. As for the potential of using ICT for communication in language teaching, this is hardly used. This is both due to the cautious approach of IT personnel in opening the required communication ports in the school network and the perceived complexity of the task of setting up audio and, maybe, even video on computers.

It is easy to find impressive ICT examples like the *Flat classroom project* in which a class in Bangladesh collaborated with a classroom in the US to discuss the Thomas Friedman book *The World is Flat* and its implications for the students involved. The project became so well-known that it attracted the attention of the author of the book who joined in the discussion. This is a deservedly famous project, but one can achieve a great deal without the level of organisation which accompanies this particular project. Some teachers are worried about some of the behaviours which go with the new technologies such as the use of informal language or the fact that the online encyclopaedia, Wikipedia, can be edited by anyone, often is, and sometimes in a malicious and misleading way. Teachers are uncomfortable with these behaviours because they don't accord with the behaviour expected in the classroom. Imagine if a student edited the handout circulated by the teacher!

But now imagine an office worker attending an interview for a new job and telling a potential employer that the job sounded very interesting but that he had never been interested in learning how to use IT. Would the employer accept an employee who insisted on sending paper letters and doing the accounts in a traditional ledger? And what about the responsibility of teachers in sending out their students prepared for current employment conditions? These are extrinsic reasons for including ICT, but there are also many positive intrinsic reasons for adopting ICT in the classroom, especially in the case of learning English.

For language teachers, this could include the many online dictionaries or comprehensive grammar explanations as well as easily accessible source material for working with texts and authentic artefacts such as catalogues and brochures. The second major benefit of ICT for language is in the area of communication. It has never been easier for teachers to present their students with opportunities to interact in the target language either in written format or through sound and even video.

However, ICT is a tool to be used only when there is a pedagogic advantage to doing so. The skill is in knowing when and how to use ICT in the most appropriate way. Prensky (2001) identified a further potential obstacle when he wrote a seminal article proposing the digital native and digital immigrant dichotomy. In the article, he made a distinction between those who were born into the digital world and find it completely natural and those who have had the digital world thrust upon them and find it strange and alien. As Wikipedia puts it:

> A digital native might refer to their new "camera"; a digital immigrant might refer to their new "digital camera".

The dichotomy is most often interpreted by reference to age, with older people being the digital immigrants. There have been many objections to the use of the dichotomy mainly because it is too simple. However, it does suggest that integrating ICT into everyday practice may be more difficult for those who are alien to the digital world. Once the problem is viewed as one of cultural differences, the inevitable question is whether ICT integration could be encouraged through an intercultural training approach. This approach has been piloted by the European VITAE project and this chapter sets out the VITAE approach in a way which can be tried out by readers.

Since the development effort was international, one of the considerations for the course developers was which standards or curriculum to base the course on. In the end, the newly developed 'ICT competency standards for teachers' framework by UNESCO was adopted mainly because the list of

ICT competences is holistic and includes consideration of pedagogy, administrative context and ongoing professional development. The framework also recognises different levels of ICT competence from technology literacy to knowledge creation. A summary of the UNESCO ICT framework is shown in Figure 5.1.

Table 5.1 shows the competency standard statements for the pedagogy area of the grid shown in Figure 5.1. The pedagogy element is only one of the five elements, but some challenges to traditional teaching approaches may already be apparent in, for example, 'help students reflect on their own learning'.

Policy and vision	▶	Technology literacy	▶	Knowledge deepening	▶	Knowledge creation
Curriculum and assessment	▶	Basic knowledge	▶	Knowledge application	▶	21st Century skills
Pedagogy	▶	Integrate technology	▶	Complex probem solving	▶	Self management
ICT	▶	Basic tools	▶	Complex tools	▶	Pervasive tools
Organization and administration	▶	Standard classroom	▶	Collaborative groups	▶	Learning organizations
Teacher professional development	▶	Digital literacy	▶	Manage and guide	▶	Teacher as model learner

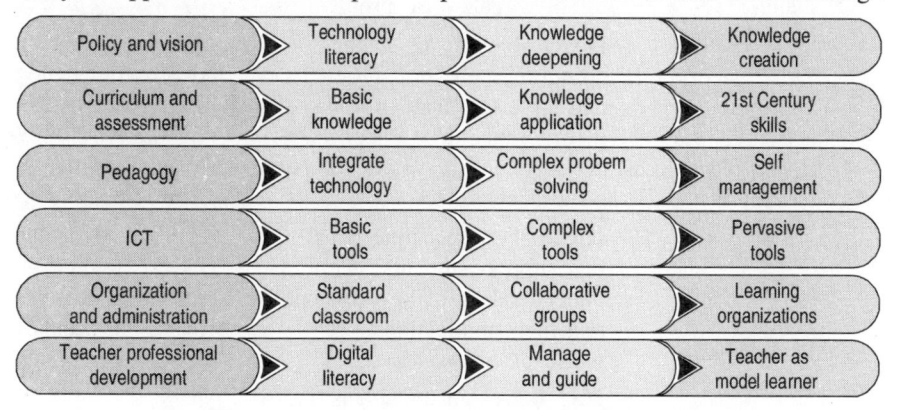

FIGURE 5.1 The UNESCO ICT competency standards for teachers—Implementation guidelines.

TABLE 5.1 UNESCO ICT competency standards for teachers: The pedagogy strand

Area	Technology Literacy	Knowledge Deepening	Knowledge Creation
Pedagogy	Teachers must know where, when (as well as when not), and how to use technology for classroom activities and presentations.	Teaching is student-centred and the teacher's role is to structure problem tasks, guide student understanding, and support student collaborative projects. In this role, teachers must have the skills to help students create, implement, and monitor project plans and solutions.	The role of teachers is to overtly model learning processes, structure situations in which students apply their cognitive skills, and assist them in their acquisition.
	Teachers should be able to: **I.C.1.** Describe how didactic	Teachers should be able to: **II.C.1.** Describe how collaborative, project-based learning and ICT	Teachers should be able to: **III.C.1.** Explicitly model their own

(*Continued*)

TABLE 5.1 (*Continued*)

Area	Technology Literacy	Knowledge Deepening	Knowledge Creation
	teaching and ICT can be used to support students' acquisition of school subject matter knowledge. **I.C.2.** Incorporate appropriate ICT activities into lesson plans so as to support students' acquisition of school subject matter knowledge. **I.C.3.** Use presentation software and digital resources to support instruction.	can support student thinking and social interaction as students come to understand key concepts, processes, and skills in the subject matter and use them to solve real-world problems. **II.C.2.** Identify or design complex, real-world problems and structure them in a way that incorporates key subject matter concepts and serves as the basis of student projects. **II.C.3.** Design online materials that support students' deep understanding of key concepts and their application to real world problems. **II.C.4.** Design unit plans and classroom activities so that students engage in reasoning with, talking about, and using key subject matter concepts while they collaborate to understand, represent, and solve complex real-world problems, as well as reflect on and communicate solutions. **II.C.5.** Structure unit plans and classroom activities so that open-ended tools and subject-specific applications will support students in their reasoning with, talking about, and use of key subject matter concepts and processes while they collaborate to solve complex problems. **II.C.6.** Implement collaborative, project-based unit plans and classroom activities while providing guidance to students in support of the successful completion of their projects and their deep understanding and key concepts.	reasoning, problem solving, and knowledge creation while teaching students. **III.C.2.** Design online materials and activities that engage students in collaborative problem solving, research, or artistic creation. **III.C.3.** Help students design project plans and activities that engage them in collaborative problem solving, research, or artistic creation. **III.C.4.** Help students incorporate multimedia production, web production, and publishing technologies into their projects in ways that support their ongoing knowledge production and communication with other audiences. **III.C.5.** Help students reflect on their own learning.

So, is there any advantage to viewing the barriers to ICT adoption as one of acculturation and what does intercultural training consist of? Culture is about a set of norms and behaviours which are automated to the extent that people of a similar culture do not have to think about many aspects of their behaviour such as gift rituals, greeting behaviour and eating habits. It is only when meeting people from a different culture, when these behaviours are manifestly different that confusion sets in. When two cultures mix and do not understand each other, the result is often irritation and other negative emotions. An important aspect of culture is that the automated behaviour is often based on a commonly agreed set of values which are rarely articulated because they are so obvious. In a culture where family counts above other human groupings, for example, offering a job to a close relative is seen as a joyous duty rather than a manifestation of corrupt nepotism. Intercultural training, therefore, consists just as much of uncovering the unspoken assumptions and values of the home culture as those of the new culture. Could a process of uncovering assumptions and values in the classroom help with integration of ICT in education?

The process of acculturation usually consists of the following steps:

1. Recognising your own culture in terms of its visible manifestations.
2. Identifying your own values which are your culture's invisible attributes.
3. Making preparations for your inter-cultural journey.
4. Recognising the other culture in terms of its artefacts and events.
5. Attempting to behave like a native in certain key situations such as greetings and meal times.
6. Understanding intercultural clashes which often denote differing values.
7. Obtaining information about the new culture from cultural informants.
8. Taking home some of the most useful aspects of the new culture.

One of the key aspects to successful integration of ICT in teaching is the level of support available and this also applies to intercultural training where the use of cultural informants is crucial to help a newcomer interpret what is going on. There have been many instances of lone enthusiasts who embrace ICT but who then feel more and more isolated as the IT department puts technical obstacles in their way, management refuses to fund the necessary equipment and colleagues look on in amusement or bemusement. The key to success is a supportive environment where everyone takes turns to be the teacher and the learner. The lone enthusiast often finds that type of support in the network of virtual communities which has grown up out of shared interests such as the Webheads in Action group which is dedicated to helping teachers of English incorporate digital technologies into their everyday practice. So, for example, you may be able to help a colleague start using blogs to increase motivation in the language classroom while they may be able to help you use the Audacity audio editing program so that you can move from a pure text environment into one which includes sound files. A key aspect of the VITAE approach is to bundle mentor training into the course so that it becomes a natural part of sharing knowledge and skills since external support is often the key to success.

Thus, the VITAE approach consists of an eight-module course which tackles the eight steps of intercultural training identified above in the form of an intercultural story. For each step, there is an instalment of the intercultural story, a pedagogical goal, a digital learning aspect in which technical guidance is given and a mentoring aspect. The mentor training part of the course is modelled by the course trainers in the way that support is provided by the course. It is the aim of the course that in answering the mentoring questions for each module, course participants will be given the tools to begin using similar questions with their colleagues.

Now it describe the eight-step approach to understanding and implementing digital culture adapted to the needs of TOEFL teachers in a way they can implement it to a certain extent. There is naturally a whole infrastructure which supports the course. This includes (i) presenting the content in a learning management system regardless of whether the training is held face to face, blended or fully distance and (ii) a virtual community of practice so that course participants can continue to share ideas and experiences once the course is over. A link to this virtual community is given in the References section at the end of this chapter.

1. Where are you now? The first important step in intercultural training is making the home culture explicit. One way of doing this in regard to teaching English is to describe where your current expertise comes from. So, the first task is to produce a diagram to illustrate this.

Pedagogical aspect: Many teachers would name their teacher-training and higher-education-level subject studies as their prime source of knowledge and expertise. But how do you keep uptodate in your subject especially if you have been teaching for a long time? Some people have started representing this in a graphic way rather than a written description and what comes out of these diagrams is the importance of informal sources of learning (see Figure 5.2). So, right from the first step of examining one's own personal learning environment (PLE) one can usually see the importance of mentor-like relationships on one's own learning. Many countries now recommend or even make it compulsory for students to compile learning portfolios to demonstrate their expertise. This is an exercise which most teachers have never been through themselves, so it is instructive to think about your own learning environment since this will probably help you facilitate the process in a more informed way when you have to implement it with your students.

Figure 5.2 shows the PLE of a language learner and a very wide range of sources from the very formal to the very informal. It shows also a wide range of sources of information and insperation from real world and local to virtual world and digital sources.

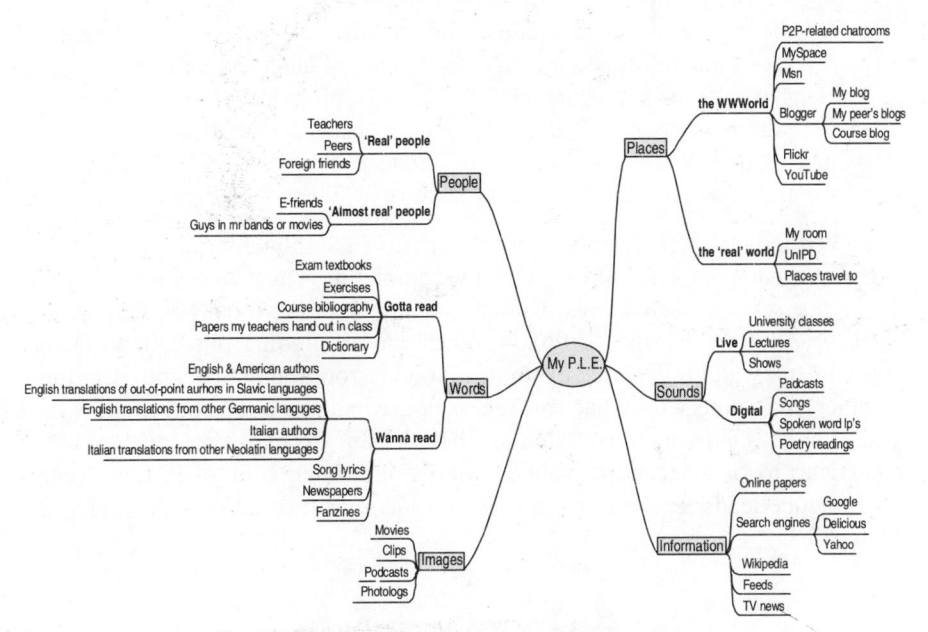

Chapter 5 Integrating ICT in the Language Classroom

FIGURE 5.2 PLE of a language learner.

Source: http://freemind.sourceforge.net/wiki/images/e/e7/My_P.L.E..jpeg from the blog post http://guesswhosblogging.blogspot.com/2007/12/on-personal-learning-environment.html

Technical aspect: You can see that Figure 5.2 has been made in some mind-mapping software. There are many such services. Some of the free ones include Freemind, Smartdraw and Mindomo. In fact, such a diagram could be generated in many different ways and each way will teach you something different about how to produce diagrams digitally. For example, you could handdraw the diagram, take a photograph and then upload the photograph to a photo-sharing service like Flickr or onto your blog if you have one. An alternative is to produce the diagram as a Powerpoint slide and upload that to a web page, blog or wiki. So, in doing this exercise, you are not only thinking in detail about where your skills come from but also trying out various digital tools.

Mentoring aspect: It is the first part of your intercultural journey. Here, valuable insights can come from being able to see and comment on the PLE diagrams of colleagues. Specific attention should be paid to the people in the diagrams who could be considered your mentors—How did they help you? Was it by example or by the giving of good advice or in some other way?, etc.

2. **Values and beliefs:** What do you expect when you walk into your classroom? What makes for an effective lesson? Just as there are different learning styles, so there are different teaching styles. Your teaching style will determine how easily you can adapt to using ICT tools because in many cases ICT undermines the model of teacher as

the sole source of credible information. With so much cheaply accessible information (which in the case of language learning includes a wealth of authentic materials), it is probably wiser to settle an argument about usage by using a concordance tool than by referring to a rule learned 20 years ago. The teacher as a learning facilitator is the model which the current state of ICT encourages and supports.

Pedagogy: The main task for this part of the intercultural journey is to find out what your teaching style is by completing a teaching styles survey. There are several such things available on the Internet mostly based on the work of Anthony Grasha (1996). Another way of finding out your teaching style is by watching some examples of classroom practice and deciding whether you agree with what you see or not, what you like about it and what you dislike. This exercise should include an exchange of views with colleagues to find out where your views overlap. Integration of ICT in every-day practice leads teachers into a role as a learning facilitator as illustrated in Figure 5.3.

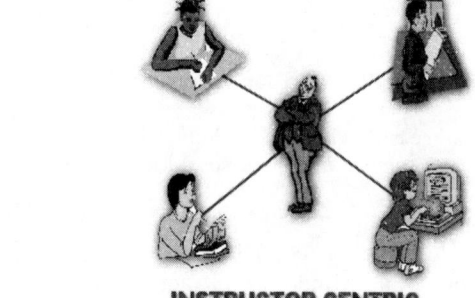

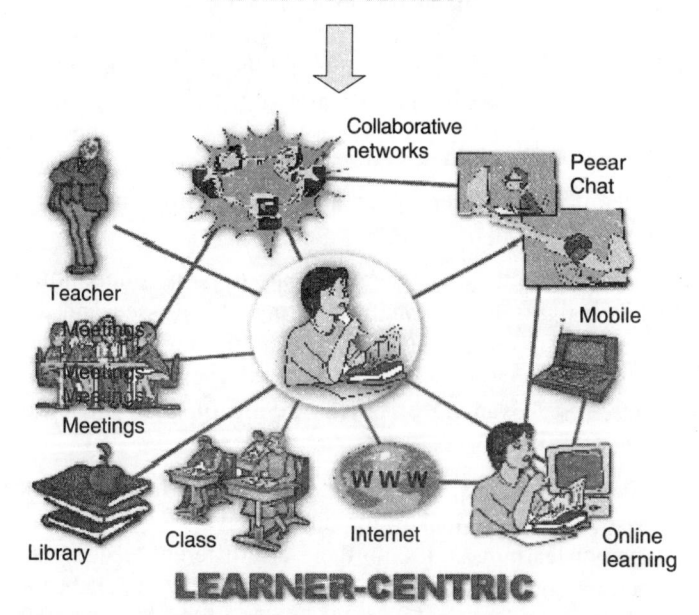

FIGURE 5.3 The emerging role of teacher as facilitator
(courtesy of Michael Coghlan, 2006).

This happens because ICT opens up many new avenues of learning so that the teacher becomes only one resource among many.

Technical: This intercultural journey is all about trying out various digital tools and an exercise of this sort is ideal as part of a learning diary presented in a blog. Some well-known blog services include Blogger and Wordpress. There are also several services offering so-called educational blog services which usually are free of advertising and may have inbuilt features to enable the teacher to keep track of their student blogs. Edublogs is one such a service. In carrying out this exercise with colleagues you can see what your colleagues have written and use the comment function to add your thoughts.

Mentoring: How has the availability of large amounts of cheap information affected your teaching style? Are there any ways in which you could involve your students in finding, monitoring and reporting back on areas of interest?

3. *Preparing for the journey:* When you make an intercultural journey, you need to think carefully about what to take with you and may need a visa and some inoculations. In this ICT intercultural journey, your preparations will include a comprehensive learning diary and an ICT competence test.

Pedagogy: In order to focus your thoughts on which areas to target, it would be a good idea to complete a competence assessment survey such as that offered by AdultEdOnline since this will help you identify which ICT skills you need to work on and how. The importance of reflective learning on the part of the teacher has been the focus of the first two stages of the intercultural journey. At this stage, the task is to set up a digital learning portfolio into which the results of the first two tasks can be incorporated. A digital or e-portfolio means an online location in which you gather evidence of your professional development in a systematic way. The digital portfolio will act as your intercultural diary as you travel more extensively in the world of using ICT in the classroom.

Technical: The e-portfolio could be the blog which you started for the second stage of the journey. The blog offered by Elgg at eduspaces is specially designed to be used as an e-portfolio, for example. It could be a wiki such as pbwiki which allows you to print out the wiki pages in PDF format, thus, allowing you to present the portfolio as a solid artefact. There are also various proprietary e-portfolio programs that provide a readymade format for your e-portfolio if you do not like the idea of being faced by a completely blank canvas.

Mentoring: A very important part of mentoring is the ability to identify and formulate goals. After taking the competence assessment, you should now be able to identify what is known as a SMART goal in the area of incorporating ICT in your teaching. This means a goal which is specific, measurable, achievable, realistic and timely. This goal can then be recorded in your e-portfolio and progress towards it noted on a regular basis.

4. ***Trying out some dishes and traditions:*** One of the most interesting parts of the intercultural journey is the opportunity to try out new foods, witness celebrations and generally participate in the daily life of the new culture. In our case, this will be the time when we get to try out some of the new digital tools in a safe and low-risk environment.

Pedagogy: This is the point in the training when the participants begin to work intensively with some of the major digital tools which have proved useful in teaching environments. In fact, the participants will already have used several important tools to get to this stage in the training. You will have noted that blogs have already been introduced for example. The course takes place in a learning management system (whether it is offered online, blended or face-to-face) to which the participants will already have gained access and they will have accessed digital material in picture, video or text format several times. However, this is now time to think in depth about how specific digital tools can be used in teaching situations. A key principle is to be guided by the pedagogical needs of the students. Therefore, the question should not be 'How can I use blogs with my students?' but rather 'Can I motivate my students to write more carefully when they know that their words may be read and reacted to by many people outside the educational institution?' The answer to that last question may be a blog but it may also be a wiki.

The key pedagogical areas to be targeted may include the following:

(i) ***Access to information:*** Typically this includes targets such as wanting your students to be more efficient at finding required information quickly, being aware of good sources of information in their subject area and being able to do more than use Google when searching for information on the Internet.

(ii) ***Managing information:*** Excess rather than paucity of information is the typical problem here. You may want to improve your students' ability to evaluate the trustworthiness of information and you may want to introduce them to tools which save time in collating reliable sources of information.

(iii) ***Improving the learning process:*** Language learning is not so much information-based, so improving the learning process probably has greater priority for the TEFL teacher than the first two items. Motivation is a key target and this can be greatly enhanced when students know that what they are doing has an audience outside the lecture theatre. This can include working with groups in other parts of the world in the target language or simply making postings on a blog or podcast publicly available and open to comments. Another important aspect of the learning process is goal setting. Goals are more likely to be met if they are public in some degree, for example, by being posted in an open blog or at the site 43things. For language learners, digital tools such as podcasts and videos offer unrivalled opportunities for improving pronunciation and intonation by opportunities to both listen and speak.

(iv) **Documenting learning:** There is an increased emphasis on being able to show what competences you have through a portfolio of evidence. Digital artefacts are very transportable. A well-organised blog or wiki which includes audio, video and pictorial evidence of facility in English may be very impressive to a prospective employer in addition to an imposing certificate.

Therefore, it is advisable to be clear about your students' precise needs before launching into using one specific type of tool over another.

Technical: There is no substitute for trying out the tools yourself sooner rather than later. Many of the tools are free of charge although often this is at the cost of accepting the presence of advertising on the interface. However, in many cases, the advertisements can be removed by using educational editions of the tools. The process of getting started usually involves choosing a username and password and giving a valid email address to which a confirmation message will be sent and to which you will have to respond. The whole process takes less than 5 minutes. You are then ready to make your first post in a blog, record your first audio message for a podcast or design your first page for a wiki. There are, of course, many finesses which can be added later such as a blogroll (list of favourite blogs) to a blog or embedding a video into a wiki but these can be learned later. The key action at this stage is to get started, try it out for yourself, try and visualise how you would use it with your students, and if in the end you decide that the wiki is better than the blog, then simply delete the blog.

I have worked with many teachers and businesses in this area and I have found that there is a great reluctance to sign up and try it out, but trying it for yourself is the only way to learn. I have also been part of long meetings discussing various problems which turned out not to be problems at all once the talk was transformed into action. A prime example of this was when we were planning to have students make short videos on a field trip and to edit and upload them once they were back in the classroom. We spent hours discussing whether the field trip destination organisation should buy some camcorders to lend out and how the film would be transferred back to the students once they were back in their institution, how difficult it would be to edit the videos and whether it would be too costly to upload the videos to the website. In the end, what happened was very simple. The students used their mobile phones to film and had very few problems transferring the video to the computer for editing that in most cases the teacher in charge did not even notice it being done. The students also managed the upload without the help of their teacher. This is a striking illustration of the digital immigrant and digital native syndrome in action. We, digital immigrants, wasted so much time devising strategies for a problem which, in the end, was no problem at all.

Mentoring: Can you identify the pedagogical priorities for your students and match these priorities to the functions offered by one or more of the common digital tools such as blogs, social bookmarking tools and podcasts?

    5. *Behaving like a native:* This part of the process involves taking a part of the curriculum you teach and transforming it with the use of ICT. For a language teacher, the main change of behaviour will probably lie in a willingness to allow students to initiate and produce materials for blogs, sound recordings or videos.

Pedagogy: The way in which we recommend participants to approach this is through the completion of a fairly comprehensive checklist inspired by the LOTI (Levels of Teaching Innovation) approach. Although the checklist is rather long, this is not meant to be a checklist exercise but rather a trigger for reflection and discussion. ICT expands your opportunities to give your students authentic problems to solve. If these problems are linked into your students' lives, you are assured of an even greater degree of engagement. ICT also extends your possibilities for differentiating your teaching and making sure that every student is operating at the peak level of their capabilities. For example, in a sound-recording exercise, those needing to improve their pronunciation could be assigned voice-over tasks while those needing to hone their writing skills could be assigned script-writing duties.

Technical: The technical challenges in this task are much the same as those for the previous task. The main difference is, probably, that once one begins to make concrete plans for a specific class, he has to make some specific decisions such as whether every student requires own blog (more motivating for the student but more work for the teacher), whether to start with a group blog, whether to require that all posts are approved first by the teacher, and whether to allow anyone to access a podcast or only registered users.

Mentoring: In what ways will your new teaching session be better with the integration of ICT than it was before? If it is difficult to respond to this question, maybe you should consider whether this is an appropriate session to transform.

    6. *Cultural clashes:* An inevitable aspect of intercultural encounters is the cultural clashes which occur especially when there are differences in values. There have been many examples of such clashes in integrating ICT in education. It is helpful to analyse the

viewpoints of both protagonists in such clashes in order to clarify one's core values in the classroom.

Pedagogy: Introducing ICT into the classroom is not a neutral act especially when one begins to experiment with user-generated content and interaction outside the classroom. This can challenge the values of all involved—, not just the teacher but also the students themselves, IT support and institutional management. One famous example was that of Chris Avenir, a student at Ryerson University in Canada who started a study group on the social networking site Facebook. His teachers saw that as cheating because the study group was discussing a set of questions which had only one set of correct answers and for which students would be awarded a grade. He was expelled from the university. The expulsion was only overturned after appeal, and even then, this was not unconditional. The case raises many questions about what constitutes cheating and what is the best way to learn. Even though the case concerned chemistry, it also raises questions about the wisdom of giving such closed questions outside a test or examination, which are equally applicable to a language class.

If you use a blog, you will have to make decisions about who can read it, who can edit it and who can contribute to it. If the blog is only accessible to the members of the institution, there will not be much interaction on it. Are you, as the teacher, going to insist on approving every post before it is made if the blog is open to the world? What about comments? Will they be allowed or moderated? There are many teachers who cannot accept the loss of control that opening up a blog or podcast can represent. If one switches attention to promoting live online meetings with selected groups, one might run into problems with the IT department for whom live audio represents a threat, technically speaking, since the software requires access to certain ports that are often blocked because they are targeted by malicious hackers.

Technical: Experience shows that it is a good idea to anticipate possible technical problems and objections and discuss them with the relevant technical personnel before going ahead. In this way, your ICT activities will be viewed as a partnership rather than a challenge to the IT department. It is much more difficult to act against restrictions which have already been put into place as a result of a few unfortunate incidents.

Mentoring: How will you cope if the sites you want to use are blocked or colleagues challenge why you are making material publicly available?

7. *Talking to the natives:* In this part of our intercultural journey, the idea is to get into contact with teachers who have implemented some of these ideas to question them about how they did it, what went well and what advice they would give to ensure success.

Pedagogy: This part of the training allows the participants to meet a very wide range of practitioners from all over the world since the meetings are live online. One would expect that meeting with the natives would come sooner in our intercultural journey, but experience has shown that course participants would prefer to have something concrete to discuss before they meet with teachers who have already implemented some of these approaches. Therefore, to meet experienced teachers just after one has begun to plan his own experiments in ICT is ideal. Another talking point could be the cultural clashes discussed in the previous course module to find out real-life responses to the dilemmas outlined and maybe to find out about additional dimensions to the issue of values in ICT integration. Outside a formal course, there are many opportunities to attend free online courses and conferences in which one meets with teachers who have implemented various ICT tools in their teaching. An example of a course would be the series offered by TESOL (Teachers of English to Speakers of Other Languages). Every January as a precursor to the face-to-face conference for teachers of English in the US. An example of a conference would be the one organised by the Webheads in Action group every two years or so. These are free and, in the online setting, there is usually ample opportunity to enter into dialogue with both the speakers and the other participants.

This module also allows participants to get an impression of the emotional power of such events. Meeting people with a shared interest live online is an impressive experience and is likely to remain so for a few years yet before it becomes the norm. As such it is a very motivating exercise for language students, especially if there has been some thorough preparation and asynchronous exchange of views beforehand so that the students have plenty to talk about. The technology also allows for recording these meetings so that they can be reviewed later for content, pronunciation or any other relevant aspect.

An example was the Streetlife project in which the author arranged a live conference with guests from Spain, Taiwan, Kuwait, Portugal and Australia to speak with her final year high school students. Two of the students said the following after their conversation:

> And this time I really did talk over the voice board, I never thought I was going to do that. And it turned out to be fun. It was, as you said, much easier to talk instead of writing. And it was much faster also. (extracted from Louise's learner diary).
>
> One wakes up to the fact that it is not only necessary for your counterpart to make compromises and adapt to your culture. Moreover, one must find a joint solution which both partners can feel satisfied with (Christina).

Not only had the students had a worthwhile experience as the following quotes from some of the international guests show:

> I just had a wonderful chat with Louise and Saranda. Louise started voice

chatting almost at once and Saranda followed. We had an extremely interesting talk. It was a fabulous experience. T. Almeida d'Eca, Portugal.

I just had a wonderful experience with two of Anne Fox's students. I had intended to limit the chat to one hour but I was so engaged in the conversation that I let it run for quite a bit longer. There's no doubt that the use of voice chat made the experience a far richer one for all parties. I could hear the hesitations as they strived for the right word, the right form of the word, giggles of occasional embarrassment at mistakes, laughter at comments I'd made. It was as if I could 'hear their intelligence'. Michael Coghlan, Australia (2006).

The guests on this occasion were experienced teachers for whom the use of digital tools was routine, so this event demonstrates the powerful emotional appeal of live synchronous communication.

Technical: The way in which this part of the course is implemented is that course participants meet other teachers through live communication tools such as Skype and Dimdim which offer free audio and video meetings. The intention is to introduce participants to several live communication tools so that they can begin to have an idea of how these tools can differ.

Mentoring: Do you have any contacts (for example, from your personal learning network) with whom you could arrange some live English speaking meetings in your chosen teaching module?

8. *What shall I bring home?* This is a pivotal section of the journey. When the course participant returns home they have several important tasks to perform—implementing the planned teaching module, sharing what they have learned with colleagues and continuing to develop themselves professionally in an active way.

Pedagogy: The rough outline of the planned teaching module should be in place once the participant returns to their home institution. On their return, the hard work of preparing, for example, a professional-looking wiki ready to be used with their students will need to be undertaken. An important aspect of ICT integration is to have a back-up plan in place in case there is a technical failure of some sort. For example, in the case of a planned live audio meeting, if Skype does not work, agree beforehand that perhaps Googletalk can be used instead. If a blog is temporarily unavailable, adopt a process-writing approach by requiring students to prepare a post offline first.

But this should not overshadow the equally important work of sharing their new found skills with their colleagues. This can be done in a number of different ways. If regular staff meetings are held then quick five-minute presentations can be offered. If there is a school Intranet, an internal wiki or blog could be set up to share experiences. An important part of the training is that it should end with an engaging event—with a live online conference in which the participants share their experiences back in their home institutions.

Technical: It is important that the virtual community of practice which has built up over the lifetime of the training remains intact when the participants return to their home institutions so that they feel able to call for help and support at this most concrete stage of the training.

Mentoring: The mentoring task for this last stage of the journey is the human aspect of maintaining the community of practice. Where relevant, this is supplemented by some individual coaching delivered by cell phone through short text messages so that the habit of continuous professional development becomes embedded behaviour. Since this is a course, it must have a distinct finishing point. However, the intention is, as stated above, that certain behaviours become embedded. These behaviours include continuous reflection on the part of the teacher in the form of professional development and experimentation, a tendency to make learning sessions more student-centred and continued contacts with professionals outside the institution to ensure that teaching is refreshed by external ideas.

A final observation is that it could be argued that a course to introduce teachers to digital tools should concentrate exclusively on these tools. However, many experts in the field, for example, McIntosh, maintain that the technology is changing the nature of learning itself so that it becomes more critical to learn how to manage information than to retain specific items of information in one's memory. If that is the case, simply presenting the tools is insufficient.

In summary, this chapter aims to help language teachers understand why they may feel uncomfortable with adopting the use of ICT in their everyday practice and to provide some approaches to overcome these negative feelings. The methodology has been presented in the form of the story of an intercultural journey. This should help make each stage follow naturally on from the previous one. The pedagogy is always the first consideration and they should be if the pedagogical goals can be achieved without the use of ICT. ICT should be a complement to, rather than a total replacement of, current activities. The technical aspects of implementing ICT are secondary to the overall pedagogical goals, especially if low threshold applications are used. These are usually free, quick to set up at a basic level and easy to abandon if they do not fit the goals of the teacher. There are mentoring considerations at every stage of the journey and graduates of the course should be able to begin using these key mentor questions back in the home institution in order to foster a collegial sharing of knowledge, resources and experiences. The intercultural approach should be of particular interest to language teachers since considerations of cultural differences are relevant even in the most technical settings. Two actions which would be of immediate assistance would be to join a supportive virtual network like the Webheads in Action and to sign up for one or two most interesting digital tools immediately and start exploring their potential.

REFERENCES

Attwell, G., Lone Dirckinck-Holmfeld, Peter Fabian, Andrea Kárpáti and Peter Littig, "E-Learning in Europe: Results and recommendations." *Impuls* 10, Thematic Monitoring under the Leonardo da Vinci programme, 2005.

Coghlan, Michael, http://www.slideshare.net/michaele/interactivity-in-virtual-classrooms, 2006.

Flat Classroom project http://flatclassroomproject2006.wikispaces.com/

Grasha, Anthony F., *Teaching with Style: A practical guide to enhancing learning by understanding teaching and learning styles,* CA: Alliance Publishers, 1996.

LOTI approach lesson plan template http://www.floresville.isd.tenet.edu/LoTi/FISDLessontemplate.doc

McIntosh, E., http://edu.blogs.com

Prensky, M., 'Digital natives, digital immigrants, 2001. http://www.marcprensky.com/writing/Prensky%20-%20Digital%20Natives,%20Digital%20Immigrants%20-%20Part1.pdf

T. Almeida d' Eca is a recently retired high school teacher. Her publications and presentations can be accessed at http://64.71.48.37/teresadeca/.

Teaching styles http://www1.indstate.edu/cirt1/facdev/pedagogies/styles/tstyle.html

UNESCO ICT Competency Standards for Teachers http://cst.unesco-ci.org/sites/projects/cst/The%20Standards/ICT-CST-Implementation%20Guidelines.pdf

VITAE project community of practice http://vitaeproject.ning.com

Webheads in Action http://webheadsinaction.org

Wikipedia Digital native http://en.wikipedia.org/wiki/Digital_native (retrieved June 30, 2008).

Tools Mentioned

43things http://www.43things.com/ Goal setting site

AdultEdOnline http://www.adultedonline.org/ Free competence assessment tool

Audacity http://audacity.sourceforge.net/ Free audio editing software

Blogger http://www.blogger.com Free blogging tool

Dimdim http://www.dimdim.com Free video conferencing tool

Edublogs http://www.edublogs.org Free educational blogging tool

Eduspaces e-portfolio blog http://www.eduspaces.net Free blogging and eportfolio tool

EVOnline courses http://evo08sessionscfp.pbwiki.com/ Free online annual courses offered by TESOL

Flickr http://flickr.com Free photo and video sharing service

Freemind http://freemind.sourceforge.net/wiki/index.php/Main_Page Free mindmapping tool

Googletalk http://www.google.com/talk/ Free text and audio chat tool

Pbwiki http://pbwiki.com/ Free wiki (editable group web pages)

Skype http://www.skype.com Free text and audio tool

Teaching styles inventory http://members.shaw.ca/mdde615/tchstylsquiz7.htm Free survey to diagnose your teaching style

Wordpress http://wordpress.com/ Free hosted blog with the option of adding static pages.

Part 2
MULTIMEDIA IN ELT

Chapter 6

COMPUTER-ASSISTED LANGUAGE LEARNING
Its Future

— RICHARD WATSON TODD

6.1 INTRODUCTION

The term *Computer-Assisted Language Learning* (CALL) covers a vast range of approaches to learning language—(i) at one extreme of control over learning material (Beatty 2003, Keobke 1998) are the behaviourist drill-like exercises prevalent in much multimedia CALL software and web-based language learning exercises and (ii) at the other end are word processing and web design where users have almost complete control over material. In between these two extremes are vast arrays of applications including concordancing, computer-mediated communication or CMC (bulletin boards, e-mail and chat), games, and web-based resources (Bax 2003; Jarvis 2002, 2004; Warschauer and Healey 1998; Watson Todd 2007). This range of CALL resources is mirrored by the variety of disparate ways in which CALL is used. CALL can be used (i) to produce discrete-point language-focused concordance handouts for the classroom (Hadley 2002), (ii) to provide supplementary remedial work for classroom learning (Hyland 2004), (iii) to act as input for autonomous noticing of language features (Adams 2001), and (iv) to provide the framework for very large-scale real-world projects (Luzon Marco 2002; Nutta and Spector-Cohen 2002). Such a complex range of applications makes it difficult to gain a full understanding of current CALL. Despite this complexity, in this paper, I intend to identify trends that are likely to be key directions that CALL will take in the future. If we wish to identify likely future trends for CALL, it is useful to take a step back and look at the past rather than starting from the present.

6.2 CALL—A BRIEF HISTORY

Several current CALL applications have a venerable history extending back decades. For instance, language learning software was first created in 1960 (when computers still took up whole rooms), concordancing started in 1969, and the first artificial intelligence program specifically designed for language learning appeared in 1976. Computer games for language learning emerged in 1983, e-mail projects were used by 1988, and tasks using the Internet as a knowledge resource were first reported in 1994 (very soon after the Internet became publicly available in 1992). More surprising perhaps is how little has changed since these first uses.

The first language learning software consisted of closed-ended questions in multiple-choice format—a pattern still prevalent in much commercial multimedia software. Early concordancing focused on word frequency counts and identifying common collocations, again the main focus of much corpus work. In the 1970s, promises were made that artificial intelligence programs would come of age in 20 years' time—a promise still made today. Language learning computer games are still predominantly behaviourist drills disguised in a game package, and most e-mail projects and Internet resourcing tasks used today differ little from the ones first reported. Overall, it appears that, while technology has come on in leaps and bounds in the last 10–15 years allowing more media use in CALL, the basic activities and tasks used in CALL have barely changed.

This pattern of stasis is confirmed by examining broader CALL issues in the literature. In 1982, Suppes argued that the main need in CALL was for clear applicable theories of computer-based learning—a need that is still echoed in the literature today. In 1988, Otto set three key questions concerning CALL that needed answering–how effective is CALL? What are the most appropriate roles for teachers and students in CALL? Can CALL reduce teaching costs?—and we appear to be no closer to providing answers now. Schreck and Schreck (1991) identified two key problems with CALL software—the facts (i) that learning opportunities are rarely maximised and (ii) that CALL focuses on what is easiest to design, not what is needed to be learnt—and current CALL software is often open to the same criticisms. We have to conclude that very little has changed in mainstream CALL in the last 15 years.

While computers have grown more powerful and multimedia has become more integrated, CALL paradigms (with the exception of CMC) have remained focused largely on receptive skills. The Internet is mainly a reading and listening resource, and multimedia CALL software has focused on reading and listening to audio and video files. Furthermore, in most English-learning environments, the majority being in the under-resourced developing world, access to computers has not been readily and easily available to most learners. This limited access has meant that CALL has not reached its full potential.

Very recent developments in the ways computers are used and in the miniaturisation of technology have led to two new directions which are just starting to be explored and which promise to challenge the status quo of predominantly receptive, limited-access CALL. It is these two directions that, I believe, will have a major impact on CALL in the long run and, thus, that hold the key to its future.

6.3 THE FIRST KEY DIRECTION: WEB 2.0 APPLICATIONS

On the traditional web, content is under the control of the webmasters and, thus, most CALL-using traditional web resources are receptive (although the web design projects like Kayser (2002), are productive). After 2005, however, a second generation of the web, dubbed Web 2.0, emerged. Web 2.0 encourages creativity, collaboration and sharing between users and so, rather than being recipients of content, its users generate content. A variety of applications fall under the Web 2.0 umbrella, and some of these are looked at in detail below. Since they all stress user-generated content, Web 2.0 CALL focuses far more on productive skills, especially writing, than traditional web-based CALL.

6.3.1 Blogs

Blogs, derived from web-logs, are diaries or regular opinion columns posted on the Internet. At present, according to the Technorati website, there are more than 100 million blogs in existence. In a typical blog, the writer posts a diary entry which others can read and comment on. This allows blogs to be used in two main ways within language teaching. First, learners can be encouraged to write and post their own blogs. If learners are writing learning journals or engaged in other forms of extensive writing in the classroom, it often makes sense to ask them to post their writing as blogs to create a wider and more meaningful audience for their writing. The experience of creating publicly available blogs may be motivating for learners and encourage the development of a new set of writing strategies (see Bloch (2007) for a case study of how this may happen). In addition, a blog can act as a personal portfolio for learners (Godwin–Jones 2006).

A second way of using blogs, and one which is more common in the language-learning community, is for the teacher to write the main blog entries which learners can then comment on (see Zorko (2007)). This allows a teacher-controlled, but still public, environment for learning to be extended outside the classroom. It also allows more specifically language learning-oriented support such as glosses and links to audio files to be integrated into the blog.

6.3.2 Sharing and Social Networking

Started in 2003, social networking websites are now some of the most popular ones. In July 2006, for instance, the social networking site MySpace received more hits than Google (Gefter 2006). Other well-known social networking sites include Facebook, Friendster and Bebo. On such sites, users create a personal profile detailing their interests and often including photos. Profiles can be linked to those of friends. For many teenagers it has become the most popular way of communicating online. In addition to general social networking sites, there are more specific sites. For instance, Muxlim is a Muslim networking site, Ravelry is a networking site for people interested in knitting, and myETP allows English language teachers to network. Most social networking sites have group creation facilities which teachers can use to set up outside-class discussion environments (Thelwall 2008).

There are many sharing sites similar in many ways to networking sites like Flickr, where users can post and view photos, and YouTube for videos. Although these sites do not provide the full communication facilities of networking sites, they can be useful for language learning. Instead of just giving a presentation in front of their classmates, learners can be encouraged to make a video of their presentation and post it in the public domain on YouTube; and learners can use sharing sites to find and exchange resources with other learners (Godwin–Jones 2005).

6.3.3 Wikis

The sharing of resources through sharing sites can be extended to full collaboration. Several Web 2.0 applications enable effective and efficient collaborative writing. Within a private domain, this can be achieved through a collaborative web-based word-processing tool like Google Docs (Chinnery 2008) or through new facilities on e-learning platforms like Blackboard (Laohajaratsang 2004). In the public domain, the most common resource for collaborative writing is wikis.

A wiki is a web-based environment for collaborative writing. Wikis can be used either within a private domain for collaborative writing within one group of students or within the public domain, most famously in the collaboratively created encyclopedia, Wikipedia. A feature of wikis that is particularly useful for language learning is the record of all drafts. This allows a focus on, and assessment of, the writing process as well as the written product.

An example of a private wiki used for language learning can be found in Mak et al. (forthcoming), who describe a wiki-based project to produce a school brochure for parents at a Hong Kong secondary school. Within the public domain, learners can be asked to collaborate as a class to produce a Wikipedia entry (McDonald 2007). Such projects promote peer-to-peer collaboration, increase motivation, empower learners to construct knowledge, and enable progress assessment (Zorko 2007).

6.3.4 MMOGs

Game-based learning has been a growing area of interest over the last 20 years and is now starting to reach fruition. Claimed benefits for game-based learning include increased motivation (Jong et al. 2006), enhancement of critical thinking (Pivec 2007), and increased engagement with learning (Prensky 2002). Games can be either designed specifically for language learning (Watson Todd 2005) or adapted to meet language learning objectives from existing well-known games like *The Sims* (Purushotma 2005). Within the latter paradigm, one of the most promising approaches involves Web 2.0 games, called Massively Multi-player Online Games or MMOGs.

The best-known MMOGs are *World of Warcraft* and *Second Life*. The first of these provides a platform for an online action game with millions of users, and the second is a partially user-created virtual world where users can live and interact in much the same way as in the real world. For monolingual environments where engaging in extensive communication in English outside the classroom is difficult, *Second Life* and similar virtual worlds provide opportunities for very large-scale interaction.

In an MMOG (like *Second Life*), users register and choose an avatar. They can then enter the virtual world, walk (and fly) around and meet people or go to specific destinations serving special interests. For most learners, simply communicating (through either chat or voice) with many other people can be a beneficial experience involving extensive use of communication and interaction strategies and negotiation of meaning (Peterson 2006). Alternatively, specific communities for educational purposes can be set up in *Second Life* for more focused learning (Stevens 2006).

6.3.5 Reasons for Using Web 2.0 Applications

While the applications described above may sound appealing to many teachers, there is a question of whether Web 2.0 is just a fashion adding little to existing CALL or whether it can be more than that. To answer this, it should first be noted that there are parallels between Web 2.0 applications and current CMC applications in CALL. Both allow discussions to extend beyond the classroom and involve extensive writing. However, there are three ways in which Web 2.0 applications manifest key theories of learning.

First, in recent years, language learning has been heavily influenced by social constructionism, especially by the work of Vygotsky (1978). In this perspective, learners learn best through active learning, or actively using the language they are learning (Nunan 2004), in social situations where they can interact with others. Web 2.0 applications are particularly suited to the learning of writing as social practice where writing is "purpose-driven communication in a social context" (Ivanič 2004: 225). These applications also promote collaborative learning through online interaction.

Second, Web 2.0 applications go beyond current CMC in extending learning outside the classroom. Research has shown that most autonomous learning activities outside the classroom focus on the receptive skills of listening and reading (Hyland 2004; Orlando 2006). By promoting written interaction with other language users, Web 2.0 applications extend the paradigm of out-of-class learning by providing new means of working with both other learners from the same class and outsiders. In the long run, such applications promote autonomous learning through empowering learners to develop outside of class (Field 2007).

Third, Web 2.0 provides a greater focus on process (as opposed to product) than other CALL applications. While traditional CMC may allow written social interaction outside the classroom, Web 2.0 builds on this by emphasising the process by which the written interactions are created. This can be seen most clearly in wiki applications where the different drafts leading to the finished product are easily accessible and analysable.

To summarise, although there are parallels between Web 2.0 applications and current CMC, the format goes beyond traditional CALL applications in promoting social interaction, learning outside class and process writing, encouraging learners to view the Internet as a place for productive creativity in addition to a receptive knowledge source.

6.4 THE SECOND KEY DIRECTION: MOBILE PHONE-ASSISTED LANGUAGE LEARNING (MPALL)

A key challenge for CALL is access. Even though the number of computers has grown exponentially over the last 20 years, CALL use is still restricted to educational environments, e.g. computer laboratories at universities. This is especially the case in the developing world where access to computers outside educational institutions is often limited, the so-called digital divide. While access to PCs can cause problems, there is a different type of computer that is readily available and convenient. Mobile phones have been called the PCs of the developing world (Marshall 2007). Originally, mobile phones offered a convenient alternative to traditional phones, but the addition of texting, gaming, e-mail and recording functions among others has meant that they now function in many ways as computers. In November 2007, the number of mobile phones in use reached 3.3 billion, equivalent to one mobile phone for every two people (Reuters 2007), suggesting that mobile phones have the potential to be a solution to the access problems of CALL.

In addition to their ubiquity, there are several other reasons for using mobile phones for language learning. They are accessible, convenient and portable, enabling any time any place learning (Chinnery 2006; Prensky 2004). They have become a central part of students' lives to the extent that many students see their mobile phones as part of their identity (Pettit and Kukulska-Hulme 2007), and the few investigations of mobile phone-based language learning have shown some surprisingly large beneficial learning effects (McConatha and Praul 2007; Thornton and Houser 2004, 2005). With such potential benefits, Mobile Phone Assisted Language Learning or MPALL (distinguished from Mobile Assisted Language Learning (MALL), which also covers PDAs, iPods, and wireless computing) holds great promise.

MPALL is still very much in its infancy, with much MPALL being dictated by what is easiest to do rather than what is most beneficial to students (as is still the case with a large proportion of CALL) see (Watts 1997). Thus, the most extant MPALL applications consist of explanations and drilling of discrete language points. The most common application is SMS messages sent to students, either of the word-a-day variety (Chinnery 2006; Lu 2006; McNicol 2004; Prensky 2004; Song and Fox 2005) or mini-lessons of grammar points (Chinnery 2006; Prensky 2004; Thornton and Houser 2004, 2005). There are also short, closed-ended quizzes or games testing discrete language points available through SMS, the web or downloads (Attewell 2005; Chinnery 2006; Kam et al. 2007, 2008; McNicol 2004; Uther et al. 2005). In addition to focusing on discrete-point language knowledge, these applications are also founded on behaviourist theories of learning. For instance, the listening application developed by Uther et al. appears to consist of minimal pair discrimination drills, the vocabulary learning of Song and Fox relies on SMS messages of English words with their Chinese translations, and the vocabulary lessons of Thornton and Houser are short definitions of words with examples of use. If implemented on computer, these applications would fall into the behaviouristic phase of Warschauer's (1996) categorisation of CALL.

Although most current MPALL involves behaviourist learning of discrete language points (a limited but still beneficial approach), there are signs that MPALL applications are expanding in range. Mobile phones have been used in classrooms for both communicative pairwork and as self-recording devices (Watson Todd 2006), an extensive learning management system for mobile phones has been set up in Europe (Attewell 2005), and a communicative language learning game using action reading mazes with specific language support has been designed (Watson Todd and Tepsuriwong, forthcoming). Such applications bode well for the future of MPALL. More critically, many mobile phones now allow access to standard webpages rather than the limited mobile-specific wap-pages, meaning that a vast range of existing CALL resources become available for MPALL. In these ways, the critical features of MPALL—portability, social interactivity, context sensitivity, connectivity, individuality and immediacy (Lan et al. 2007)—can become accessible to millions.

6.5 CONCLUSION

The long history of CALL has been dominated by behaviourist learning of discrete language points. Around 15–20 years ago, however, CALL started to change in two main directions—(i) through the massive exposure to authentic language on the Internet and (ii) through a growing use of CALL for social communication through e-mail projects and the like. These latter social purposes of CALL are likely to expand vastly with Web 2.0 applications in ways that are far more central to students' lives and more process-oriented. Thus, the types of learning achievable through CALL will become broader.

In addition to a wider range of types of learning being available, accessibility to technology-enhanced language learning may soon become massively easier with the addition of mobile phones as a learning tool. Combined with greater opportunities for CALL, more and more learning is likely to take place outside traditional classroom settings.

Present MPALL is at a similar stage to 1980s CALL (Watson Todd and Tepsuriwong, forthcoming) with the repertoire of applications just starting to go beyond behaviourist discrete-point learning. As more and more mobile phones allow Internet access, the number of applications available will skyrocket, and it will become far easier to produce language learning applications for mobile phones. Within a couple of years, it is likely that Web 2.0 language learning applications will be designed with mobile phone users in mind. Already, there is the phenomenon of moblogging, or mobile-blogging, which allows bloggers to write posts from anywhere (Godwin-Jones 2005; Chinnery 2006) although I am not aware of any attempts to use moblogging for language learning. Further, Web 2.0 applications on mobile phones will allow the benefits of Web 2.0—process-oriented social learning outside the classroom—to become available for learners at any time and in any place.

REFERENCES

Adams, K., "Mind the gap! Noticing in real time," *Action Research*, J. Edge (Ed.), Alexandria, VA: TESOL, 2001: 105–116.

Attewell, J., "Mobile technologies and learning: A technology update and M-learning project summary," London: Learning and Skills Development Agency, 2005. Retrieved on 6 March 2008.
http://www.lsda.org.uk/files/pdf/041923RS.pdf.

Bax, S., "CALL—Past, present and future," *System* **31**.1 (2003): 13–28.

Beatty, K., *Teaching and Researching Computer-assisted Language Learning*, London: Longman, 2003.

Bloch, J., "Abdullah's blogging: A generation 1.5 student enters the blogosphere," *Language Learning and Technology* **11**.2 (2007): 128–141.

Chinnery, G.M., "Going to the MALL: Mobile-assisted language learning," *Language Learning and Technology* **10**.1 (2006): 9–16.

_____, "On the Net: You've got some GALL: Google-assisted language learning," *Language Learning and Technology* **12**.1 (2008): 3–11.

Field, J., "Looking outwards, not inwards," *ELT Journal* **61**.1 (2007): 30–38.

Gefter, A., "Living online: This is your space," *New Scientist* **2569** (2006): 46–48.

Godwin-Jones, R., "Messaging, gaming, peer-to-peer sharing: Language learning strategies and tools for the millennial generation," *Language Learning and Technology* **9**.1 (2005): 17–22.

_____, "Tag clouds in the blogosphere: Electronic literacy and social networking," *Language Learning and Technology* **10**.2 (2006): 8–15.

Hadley, G.S., "An introduction to data-driven learning," *RELC Journal* **33**.2 (2002): 99–124.

Hyland, F., "Learning autonomously: Contextualising out-of-class English language learning," *Language Awareness* **13**.3 (2004): 180–202.

Ivanič, R., "Discourses of writing and learning to write," *Language and Education* **18**.3 (2004): 220–246.

Jarvis, H., "Towards a classification making sense of the Internet in language teaching and teacher development," *The Teacher Trainer* **16**.2 (2002): 15–19.

_____, "Investigating the classroom applications of computers on EFL courses," *Journal of English for Academic Purposes* **3**.2 (2004): 111–137.

Jong, M.S.Y., Shang, J.J., Lee, F.L., Lee, J.H.M., and Law, H.Y. "Learning online: A comparative study of a situated game-based approach and a traditional web-based approach," *Lecture Notes in Computer Science* **3942** (2006): 541–551.

Kam, M., Agarwal, A., Kumar, A., Lal, S., Mathur, A., Tewari, A., and Canny, J., "Designing e-learning games for rural children in India: A format for balancing learning with Fun," Paper presented at *Designing Interactive Systems Conference 2008*, Cape Town. Retrieved on March 3, 2008. http://www.cs.berkeley.edu/~mattkam/publications/DIS2008.pdf

_____, Rudraraju, V., Tewari, A., and Canny, J., "Mobile gaming with children in rural India: Contextual factors in the use of game design patterns," *Proceedings of DiGRA 2007 Conference*.

Kayser, A., "Creating meaningful webpages," *English Teaching Forum* **40**.3 (2002): 12–18.

Keobke, K., "Computers and collaboration: Adapting CALL materials to different learning styles," *Understanding Learning Styles in the Second Language Classroom*, J.M. Reid (Ed.), Upper Saddle River, NJ: Prentice Hall, 1998, 46–52.

Lan, Y.-J., Sung, Y.-T., and Chang, K.E., "A mobile-device-supported peer-assisted learning system for collaborative early EFL reading," *Language Learning and Technology* **11**.3 (2007): 130–151.

Laohajaratsang, T., "Next-generation e-learning: Sharing and re-use digital learning resources with pedagogically sound e-learning tools," *International Journal of the Computer, the Internet and Management* **12**.2 (2004): 72–80.

Lu, M., "Effectiveness of vocabulary learning via mobile phone," *3rd PacCALL Conference*, Nanjing, China, 2006.

Luzon Marco, M.J., "Internet content-based activities for English for specific purposes," *English Teaching Forum* **40**.3 (2002): 20–25.

Mak, B., Coniam, D., and Chan, J., "Using wikis to enhance and develop writing skills among secondary school students in Hong Kong, *System* (Forthcoming).

Marshall, J., "Smartphones are the PCs of the developing world," *New Scientist* **2615** (2007): 24–25.

McConatha, D. and Praul, M., "Mobile learning in the classroom: An empirical assessment of a new tool for students and teachers," Paper presented at *Washington Interactive Technologies Conference 2007*, Arlington, VA. Retrieved on March 6, 2008.

http://www.hotlavasoftware.com/article_info.php?articles_id=14

McDonald, K., "Wikipedia projects for language learning," *CALL-EJ Online* **9**.1 (2007).

McNicol, T., "Language e-learning on the move," *Japan Media Review*, 2004 Retrieved on March 3, 2008. http://ojr.org/japan/wireless/1080854640.php

Nunan, D., *Task-based Language Teaching*, Cambridge: Cambridge University Press, 2004.

Nutta, J.W. and Spector-Cohen, E., "Exploring culture from a distance: A U.S./Israeli e-mail exchange project," *TESOL Journal* **11**.4 (2002): 21–26.

Orlando, S.M., "The importance of informal learning in EFL," *Modern English Teacher* **15**.1 (2006): 45–48.

Otto, F., "Using the computer," *You Can Take It with You: Helping Students Maintain Foreign Language Skills Beyond the Classroom*, J. Berko Gleason (Ed.), Englewood Cliffs, NJ: Prentice Hall, 71–91.

Peterson, M., "Learner interaction management in an avatar and chat-based virtual world," *Computer Assisted Language Learning* **19**.1 (2006): 79–103.

Pettit, J. and Kukulska-Hulme, A., "Going with the grain: Mobile devices in practice," *Australasian Journal of Educational Technology* **23**.1 (2007): 17–33.

Pivec, M., "Play and learn: Potentials of game-based learning," *British Journal of Educational Technology* **38**.3 (2007): 387–393.

Prensky, M., "The motivation of gameplay: The real twenty-first century learning revolution," *On the Horizon* **10**.1 (2004): 5–11.

———, "What can you learn from a cell phone? – Almost Anything," Retrieved on March 3, 2008. http://www.marcprensky.com/writing/Prensky-What_Can_You_Learn_From_a_Cell_Phone-FINAL.pdf

Purushotma, R., "You're not studying, you're just ....," *Language Learning and Technology* **9**.1 (2005): 80–96.

Reuters, 2007, "Global Cellphone Penetration Reaches 50 pct," Retrieved on March 3, 2008.
http://investing.reuters.co.uk/news/articleinvesting.aspx?type+media&story ID= nL29172095

Schreck, R. and Schreck, J., "Computer-assisted language learning," *Teaching English as a Second or Foreign Language*, 2nd ed., M. Celce-Murcia (Ed.), Boston: Heinle and Heinle, 1991: 472–485.

Song, Y. and Fox, R., "Integrating m-technology into web-based ESL vocabulary learning for working adult learners," *Proceedings of the 2nd IEEE International Workshop on Wireless and Mobile Technologies in Education*, Jhongli, Taiwan, IEEE Computer Society, 2005.

Stevens, V., "Second life in education and language learning," *TESL-EJ* **10**.3 (2006).

Suppes, P., "Historical perspective on educational technology," *The Effective Teacher*, L.W. Anderson (Ed.), New York: McGraw-Hill, 259–268.

Thelwall, M., "MySpace, Facebook, Bebo: Social networking students," *Association of Learning Technology Online Newsletter* **11** (2008).

Thornton, P. and Houser, C., "Using mobile phones in education," *Proceedings of the 2nd IEEE International Workshop on Wireless and Mobile Technologies in Education*, Jhongli, Taiwan: IEEE Computer Society, 2004.

Thornton, P. and Houser, C., "Using mobile phones in English education in Japan," *Journal of Computer Assisted Learning* **21**.3 (2005): 217–228.

Uther, M., Zipitria, I., Uther, J., and Sigh, P., "Mobile adaptive CALL (MAC): A case study in developing a mobile learning application for speech/audio language training," *Proceedings of the 2nd IEEE International Workshop on Wireless and Mobile Technologies in Education*, Jhongli, Taiwan: IEEE Computer Society, 2005.

Vygotsky, L.S., "Interaction between learning and development," *Making It Happen: Interaction in the Second Language Classroom*, P.A. Richard-Amato (Ed.), New York: Longman, 1978: 342–353.

Warschauer, M., "Computer-assisted language learning: An introduction," *Multimedia Language Teaching*, S. Fotos (Ed.), Tokyo: Logos International, 1996: 3–20.

———, and Healey, D., "Computers and language learning: An overview," *Language Teaching* **31**.1 (1998): 57–71.

Watson Todd, R., "Three modes of CALL communication," *Reflections* **7** (2005): 1–12.

———, "Getting the most out of mobile phones for language learning," *Guidelines* **28**.2 (2006): 40–43.

———, "Computer-assisted language Use: An Internet survey," *CALL-EJ Online* **9**.1 (2007).

———, and Tepsuriwong, S., "Mobile mazes: Investigating a mobile phone game for language learning," *CALL-EJ Online*, Forthcoming.

Watts, N., "A learner-based design model for interactive multimedia language learning," *System* **25**.1 (1997): 1–8.

Zorko, V., "A rationale for introducing a wiki and a blog in a blended-learning context," *CALL-EJ Online* **8**.2 (2007).

Chapter 7

PODCASTING: An Effective Tool for Language Learning

— S. Vijayalakshmi

7.1 INTRODUCTION

This study proposes to offer 'podcasting' as an ideal and very effective tool for language learning. First there was the blackboard used by generations of teachers for classroom instruction. Then came the white board which said good bye to the 'chalk and talk' method. With the changing times, it is currently the phase of the use of iPods for teaching. Podcasting offers an ideal alternative to the traditional approach with considerable advantages even to those users with little technical skills. This research argues for the usefulness of podcasting as a knowledge-sharing medium and a cognitive learning tool. Podcasting is a buzz word which is fast becoming ubiquitous among the tech-savvy people in general and the younger generation in particular. The student population which is often referred to as 'generation next' can be said to be addicted to gadgets and gizmos and it is quite rare to find students who do not possess an iPod these days. The ease with which they use the tools of technology like computers, cell phones, iPods and other gadgets is really astounding and this fascination which they have for machines should be put to good use by the teaching fraternity.

7.1.1 Podcasting—Meaning

The term 'podcast' is a portmanteau of the words "Pod" and "broadcast" according to Wiki, and it refers to the use of an ipod for purposes of recording and broadcasting any material. In other words, a podcast is an audio file that you download from the Internet. After you download it, you can listen to it on your computer or on an MP3 player or portable music player (e.g. iPod). Like *broadcast, podcast,* can refer either to the series of content itself or to the method by which it is syndicated. A podcast is a series of digital-media files distributed over the Internet using syndication feeds for playback on portable media players and computers. According to Phillip Torrone, *podcasting* derives its name from Apple's iPod, but to create a podcast or even to listen to one, you don't need to necessarily own an iPod or any portable music player. The host or author of a podcast is often called a podcaster.

The timeline

It has been said that 'podcasting' was one of several terms for portable listening to audio blogs suggested by Ben Hammersley in *The Guardian*. It is also said that the term was popularized by the media entrepreneur and former MTV VJ Adam Curry. Podcasting is spreading quickly because of the rapid adoption of MP3 players, and the desire of owners to have fresh content.

7.1.2 Scope

Podcasting has ample scope for use in myriad ways. It is an online audio content delivered via an RSS feed. Many people find it similar to radio on demand, but podcasting gives far more options in terms of content and programming than radio does. Further, with podcasting, listeners can determine the time and the place, the meaning they decide, what programming they want to receive and when they want to listen to it according to Sharon Housley (2007). In a nutshell, podcasting is a new type of online media delivery. You publish selected audio files via the Internet and allow your users to subscribe via an RSS feed to automatically receive new files. Podcasting also lets you create your own syndicated online talk show or radio program, with the content of your choosing.

7.1.3 Uses

Podcasting is delivering audio content to iPods and other portable media players on demand so that it can be listened to at the user's convenience. The main benefit of podcasting is that listeners can sync content to their media player and take it with them to listen whenever they want to. Podcasts are typically saved in MP3 format, hence they can also be listened to on nearly any computer. The initial appeal of podcasting was to allow individuals to distribute their own radio-style shows, but the system quickly became used in a wide variety of other ways, including distribution of school lessons, (Wikipedia) official and unofficial audio tours of museums, conference meeting alerts and updates, and by police departments to distribute public safety messages. It is also possible to subscribe to a podcast so that it is delivered to you automatically each day, just like a newspaper.

Advantages for language learning

Podcasting is becoming increasingly popular in education and has the potential to evolve rapidly. Podcasting allows students to use their tech-based entertainment systems for educational purposes. With it we are able to move away from the traditional face-to-face training without losing the student-to-trainer relationship that is so effective in any learning process. Podcasts enable students and teachers to share information with anyone at any time. An absent student can download the podcast of the recorded lesson and is thus able to access missed lectures. They could also access lectures of experts which may not otherwise be available because of geographical distance or other reasons. It can be a tool for teachers or administrators to communicate curriculum, assignments and other information with parents and others. Teachers can record discussions, vocabulary and other language lessons, interviews, and debates. Things that are repetitive in nature, like the instructions especially for the lab, can be podcast. Students could create their own podcasts, say, for instance, a record of activities, their thoughts and point of view on certain topics of interest. Podcasting can be a publishing tool for student oral presentations. This need not be limited to audio alone as video podcasts also can be used in all these ways. The use of videos is referred to as **vodcasting** which is fast becoming widespread. Podcasting can be used for publishing any type of audio, and some developers are exploring the idea of using the same techniques to publish video and other types of content. Some students rely on instructors to introduce the relevant learning materials. Such a passive learning focus seems to negatively affect the teaching-learning process and reduces the lasting effect of learning, especially in the language classroom. One approach to mitigate this situation could be to use technological tools like iPod.

Other uses

The podcasting genre is particularly useful and effective for interviews. According to Torrone (2007), "I've interviewed makers from around the world via SKYPE or iChat (plus in person) and made them available as podcasts." Podcasting can be used for:

1. *Self-guided walking tours:* Information content.
2. *Music:* Band promotional clips and interviews.
3. *Talk Shows:* Industry or organizational news, investor news, sportscasts, news coverage and commentaries.
4. *Training:* Instructional informational materials.
5. *Story:* Storytelling for children or for the visually-impaired.

7.2 PODCAST PRODUCTION STEP-BY-STEP

Here is a four-step guide to create audio podcasts:

STEP 1: The podcaster can use an MP3 player with voice recording facility for recording, say, an interview.

STEP 2: The audio files from the MP3 player are then transferred to the computer. Almost all MP3 players come with USB plug-in option for transferring the files.

STEP 3: The audio files can then be edited using audio-editing suites. There are a few open source softwares, like Audacity, which can be used for this purpose.

STEP 4: This step hosts the podcast. There are sites that host podcasts. It is also possible to embed the podcasts on an individual's personal blog.

7.2.1 Recording in Person on a Laptop

It is possible to make a podcast with your laptop by yourself. If you're just recording yourself or conducting an in-person interview, you can use a laptop and a microphone. You could use an audio application or Audacity which is a free, open source, cross-platform audio recording and editing tool. Download Audacity and take some time to familiarize yourself with it.

7.3 PODCASTING IN INDIA

Podcasting can be utilized in India in large ways especially to counteract the problem of different accents which crop up due to the influence of the regional medium of instruction and the influence of mother tongue. Following the trend set by the Stanford and Berkeley universities, Welingkar Institute of Management, a Mumbai-based business school, is planning to record lectures and make them available to its students over iTunes. According to Preethi (2007) there are three popular Indian podcasters: (i) Indicast, (ii) Kamla Bhatt and (iii) Podmasti.

7.4 DOWNSIDES

The application of any technology will obviously have its pros and cons. On the technical side, the users must have sufficient bandwidth to download the podcast. Beyond access, there are potential issues with the format. Further, podcasting is not designed for two-way interaction, thus there could arise the problem of the lack of immediacy or the absence of rapport between the teacher and the taught. The quality of sound may not be as effective as that of actual or that of a professional broadcast.

7.5 CONCLUSION

There can be no denying the fact that the use of technology, especially podcasting, can greatly enhance the teaching-learning process. Improving learning effectiveness has long been a research goal and a pedagogical aspiration of the academic community. Universities and other organizations of higher education are facing increased pressure to demonstrate the effectiveness of their educational efforts. These pedagogical approaches of incorporating technology are certainly not new, but nevertheless not easily adopted by the older generation. But today's learners are so addicted to gadgets and gizmos and it would be better to incorporate this attitude into our learning system. Thus, the technophobic people should necessarily change their mindset and move with the changing times. So, the use of podcasting for language learning has the potential to enhance the effectiveness of traditional learning techniques.

REFERENCES

Housley, Sharon, "What is podcasting?", Retrieved on December 12, 2007.
http://www.podcastingnews.com/articles/What_is_Podcasting.html.

Preethi, J., "B-schools set to use podcasting," *The Hindu Business Line*, Chennai, April 24, 2007.

Subramaniam, Karthik, "Day 1 session on podcasting proves to be enlightening," *The Hindu*, Chennai edition: June 11, 2007.

Torrone, Philip, "What is podcasting?", Retrieved on December 12, 2007.
http://digitalmedia.oreilly.com/2005/07/20/WhatIsPodcasting.html (21.12.07)

"Seven things you should know about Podcasting," Retrieved on December 20, 2007. www.educause.edu/eli

Chapter 8

MAKING LANGUAGE TEACHING RELEVANT FOR THE DIGITAL AGE

— Miriam Schcolnik

8.1 INTRODUCTION

Language teaching cannot be the same as it was 30, 20 or even 10 years ago. The powerful information and communication technologies available have opened up new social and educational opportunities, creating new needs and requiring the development of new skills. "The development of literacy and communication skills in new online media is critical to success in almost all walks of life" (Shetzer and Warschauer 1999: 171). In order to prepare students to function in the digital age, we must ensure that language instruction takes advantage of the online environment with its rich resources and varied media and that the language curriculum incorporates the necessary digital literacy skills.

This study deals with a variety of issues relevant to language instruction in the digital age. The acronyms CALI (Computer Assisted Language Instruction) and CALL (Computer Assisted Language Learning) are not used because, just as we do not refer to 'pen-assisted language learning', or 'book-assisted language learning' (Warschauer 2007), the term computer-assisted learning does not seem suitable. The technology, as Warschauer claims, is no longer an outside instrument but rather a part of the "ecology of language use". It profoundly changes the way we read, write and communicate. Warschauer sums up the difference between the CALL approach and his proposed alternative, an electronic literacy perspective, which this study adopts, as follows:

> A CALL perspective asks how we can use the Internet to promote language learning. An electronic literacy perspective—while not ignoring that question—also asks how we can teach language to promote online reading, writing, and communication skills.

For the purpose of this study, I have coined an acronym DALI or Digital Age Language Instruction. This new concept focuses on the need of adopting foreign language teaching to the digital age by incorporating digital literacy skills to the language curricula.

For years, teachers feared that technology would replace them. In the past, many teachers felt that they were not capable of using computers for teaching since their students being younger and more computer literate, 'digital natives' rather than 'digital immigrants' (Prensky 2001) could actually teach them instead. I would like to claim that this is a misconception. As Uschi Felix (2008) said in her EUROCALL 07 plenary talk, we cannot assume that digital natives, who know how to use the technology, also know how to learn with the technology.

Digital age language teachers have at least four important responsibilities. First, they need to be aware of the online resources available to make language learning more authentic and relevant. Second, they need to critically select those resources that are suitable in content and level for the specific student population and develop suitable activities that will create opportunities for enhancing both language and digital skills. In the third place, they need to teach the skills necessary to function in the digital age, including reading and writing digital texts and communicating and publishing on line. Finally, they have to ensure that the introduction of the digital literacy skills is done seamlessly and in an integrated manner so that the language course is a coherent whole rather than a collection of loose components.

8.2 THE ABC OF DALI

Here we will deal with a variety of matters related to DALI. The alphabetical organization was chosen both because of the large number of issues to be covered and the lack of hierarchy. Here, the characteristics of the digital age that language educators should be aware of such as the unique digital tools and the possibilities now available and the skills required of students are discussed. It also provides examples of tasks developed which can be adapted to other language levels and content fields. Explanatory notes are in italics within each sample task.

8.2.1 A—Authentic Resources and Activities

Using the Internet in the language classroom allows for easier and faster access to authentic resources than in the past. These resources may include people (e.g. peers, tutors, e-pals, subject matter experts) to communicate and collaborate with texts, graphics, animation, voice, video, or a combination of media (multimedia). The resources may be anywhere in the world and access is usually instantaneous.

EXAMPLE 8.1 Using the Internet to access authentic resources

Language focus: Grammar—Awareness of wh- questions.
Digital skill focus: Finding specific information on the page.

In preparation for the task, find a variety of online interviews with people in fields your students may be interested in. For example, for young students, sports stars or movie stars; for adults, business people, scientists, or politicians. Provide students with several optional links to choose from. Each link should be annotated so that the students know what the choices are.

The task:

1. Choose one link and click to go to the interview.
2. Find (by pressing Ctrl-F or choosing the **Find on this page** option in your browser) 5 wh- questions. Make sure you look for **wh** with capital letters and that the sentences end in question marks.
3. Copy the questions: (*Depending on facilities available or on other factors, decide whether the task of copying should be onto a word processor or in a notebook.*)
4. Next to each question, write what information the question is asking for: place, reason, time, frequency, person, object, amount, or something else.
5. Underline the verb in each question. Is the question about the past, the present or the future?
6. Make sure you understand the questions. Use an online dictionary to help you.
7. Go back and read the answers to the questions you chose.
8. Tell the class about your interview.

In a more advanced class, a more authentic activity could consist of preparation of questions for an interview. Students could then interview someone virtually. The language focus in that case would be production/speaking rather than awareness or recognition of the grammatical structure, and the digital skill focus would be virtual oral communication in the target language.

The types of activities to be developed for the language class require careful consideration. There is justification for structured activities that focus on discrete grammatical or vocabulary points, as the task shown in Example 8.1. The Grammar and vocabulary are enabling skills and they need to be learned to comprehend and communicate. The task shown is not authentic but the resources are, and the students are given a choice of resources because the task is generic. However, the language course should also include activities that simulate real-life activities. The teacher needs to keep the following questions in mind:

- What does the 21st century ESL student need to do in real life with the language?
- How can the English teacher facilitate that task?

The authenticity of the task will probably motivate the student. Examples of authentic tasks could be: email tasks (see Example 8.7), listening to weekly podcasts in English on topics of the students' choice, the preparation of a hyperlinked manual to accompany a product. The main point is that the simple use of technology does not necessarily benefit the students. For that to happen, the tasks require a sound pedagogical rationale, clear objectives, easy-to-understand instructions, suitability to the specific student population and their needs, and a usable format.

8.2.2 B—Books Online

Among other available resources, students can now access books online on a variety of subjects. These come in various formats, for example, PDF files, which are replicas of printed materials and include page numbers, illustrations, tables and other graphics. These files allow the user options such as scanning the text for locating specific words, highlighting the text and, in some cases, adding notes and comments. Other formats may be simple HTML files, plain word-processor documents or files formatted for many available e-book readers such as Microsoft Reader (http://www.microsoft.com/Reader/default.mspx) that allow users to display the texts on the computer screen or on handheld devices. The books available include textbooks, reference books, fiction, books of short stories, and others. The Internet TESOL Journal keeps an updated list of links to online textbooks for teachers and students of ESL (http://iteslj.org/links/ESL/Online_Textbooks/).

Some of the available books were designed and developed professionally taking into account presentation factors and text layout factors, whereas others were simply typed in and uploaded to the web. Not all the texts available online can be read comfortably and effectively (Schcolnik and Kol 2006). In order to take advantage of the reading resources available online, students need to know how to deal with digital text. DALI should teach the necessary skills and strategies (see sub-section 8.2.20).

8.2.3 C—Collaboration and Communication

The Internet allows for the teacher-learner and learner-learner collaboration and communication in ways that were unimaginable only a few years ago—synchronous and asynchronous, written and oral through email, discussion forums, chat rooms, or computer-mediated voice conversations. Communication between students and the teacher is no longer limited to face-to-face encounters during class time or office hours. It is now possible to ask and answer questions, submit work, and provide feedback virtually. This one-on-one instruction allows for individual attention even in large classes.

Learners can now communicate online in the target language and learn the rules of online communication (see sub-section 8.2.16), certainly a relevant skill in the real world. They can collaborate with virtual teams as they do their assignments and tasks, a good preparation for a 21st century activity, where teams made up of people in different geographical locations often work together.

8.2.4 D—Do and Learn

In DALI, students do not merely listen to the teacher, take notes and absorb what she teaches; but they also do activities, interact with materials, with their peers and teacher both physically and virtually. The experience is totally hands on and students learn by actively using the target language as they perform the tasks that are mediated, enabled and enhanced by the technology.

8.2.5 E—Evaluating Online Information

Due to the abundance of resources and the ease of access to these resources, students must be taught to evaluate the accuracy, reliability, objectivity, and value of online information. DALI must include training on the critical evaluation and selection of resources. One way might be to provide students with a list of minimal criteria. A resource not fulfilling these criteria would prove to be unsuitable for their purposes. Examples of constructs to be considered are the source of the information (recognized publication, institution, university, or known organization), the date of publication or webpage update date, the information available about the author, the topics dealt with, and the length of the text.

EXAMPLE 8.2   Evaluating Online Information

Language focus: Reading, writing.

Digital skill focus: Critical assessment of online resources.

The task:

1. Explore the websites listed below and select one for evaluation. (*These could be specialized sites, all dealing with the same subject, or mixed, depending on your population. You need to compile the list of links with your target population in mind.*)
2. Evaluate the selected site. Fill out the following questionnaire and submit your answers.
3. Name of website: _____
4. URL: _____
5. Author: _____
6. Publisher/Organization/Institution: _____
7. Last update date: _____
8. What does the website include? [] an electronic textbook [] articles [] a timeline [] video/animation [] games [] tests/quizzes [] news [] problems [] a forum [] links to other resources [] puzzles [] book reviews [] interviews [] other (please specify)

9. Who is the website aimed at? [] a general audience [] students [] professionals [] other _____

10. Rate the site:

Accuracy/Credibility/Authority	[] excellent [] very good [] good [] fair [] poor
Interest of Content	[] excellent [] very good [] good [] fair [] poor
Objectivity of Content	[] excellent [] very good [] good [] fair [] poor
Presentation of Content	[] excellent [] very good [] good [] fair [] poor

Justify your ratings:

8.2.6 F—Find

One of the main advantages of reading and writing digital text is that it is easy to locate specific information by using the Find feature available in all word processors, browsers, and e-book readers. Specific information can be easily located by entering the term in the Find box. The time saved by using this feature can then be spent reflecting on the significance of the information! A lower-order task that consists in finding factual information in a text can be easily transformed (provided the right questions are asked) into a higher-order task requiring students to read between the lines or infer what that information implies.

DALI must make students aware of the Find feature of computer programs so that they can take full advantage of digital texts. Moreover, it must provide opportunities for students to practise the skill of scanning digital texts for specific information.

EXAMPLE 8.3 Learning to Use the Find Feature

Language focus: Scanning for specific information; specialized vocabulary.

Digital skill focus: Learning to find specific information on a page by using Find; becoming familiar with specialized resources on the Internet.

The task:

1. Go to the Introduction to Anatomy site and follow the Anatomy 1 link.
2. To find answers to the questions, use the **Find on this page** feature.
   - What is sagittal plane?
   - What are the principal axes?
   - What is the meaning of 'peripheral'?
   - What is dorsum?

8.2.7 G—Giving Credit

It is now easier than ever to copy and paste materials from various sources, and students are often tempted to do it so as to do assignments quickly and effortlessly. The temptation may be even greater when the assignment is in English. Plagiarism is a very serious problem and teachers need to be aware of it and know how to combat it. One way of attacking the problem is by discussing it in class, and showing students how to acknowledge their sources and give credit for what they use in their work to avoid plagiarism. There are many excellent resources that explain all about plagiarism and how to avoid it. See, for example, the Scholastic site (http://content.scholastic.com/browse/article.jsp?id=1604) aimed mainly at high school students, and the many university sites (e.g. Indiana University http://www.indiana.edu/~tedfrick/plagiarism/; Purdue http://owl.english.purdue.edu/owl/resource/589/01/) aimed at university students.

8.2.8 H—Hypermedia

The World Wide Web (WWW) is a hypermedia system allowing users to navigate in all directions and through all kinds of information by following links. On the one hand, the system allows for a lot of flexibility as users do not need to follow a linear and prescribed path. On the other hand, it could result in lack of focus, disorientation, and confusion. DALI can teach certain strategies for staying on track. One way is to provide guidelines for keeping the main purpose in mind while reading and following only the links that can help the student achieve that purpose. In other words, students need to be able to deal with the abundance of links available by selecting what to follow mindfully. In addition, dealing with nonlinearity implies the ability to go back to the original point of origin. Older students, who are probably 'digital immigrants', may have to learn hypermedia navigation as a completely new skill; younger students or 'digital natives' may already be proficient in the skill in L1 (first language), but may tend to lose their thread of thought when following links in English.

According to Nielsen (2008), people arriving at a website know what they want and pursue their interest in a nonlinear fashion as they "construct their own experience". DALI needs to ensure that students of English as a Foreign/Second Language are capable of doing that as well. Learning not to drift too far away from their reading objective is a "crucial literacy goal" (Murphy-Judy 1997: 137) that should be included in the curriculum.

8.2.9 I—Integration of Skills

DALI can take advantage of the technologies available to integrate the language skills. Students can read on paper or on the screen, discuss what they have read face-to-face or online, in writing or orally, or they can listen to a podcast or view a video and write about it and share their views with their peers, thus, activating all four language skills.

EXAMPLE 8.4   Skill Integration*

Language focus: Reading and speaking—learning how to report the news in English.

Digital skill focus: Reading online news reports.

The task:

1. Select a news category and a headline that interests you.
2. Read the article and note the basic facts.
3. Organize them and add your interpretation.
4. Explain why this is of interest.
5. Add a question that would be interesting for future research.
6. Give your report in class. *An alternative could be to prepare a podcast with the report, thus implementing yet another digital skill.*

* Adapted from Schcolnik and Kol 2003.

8.2.10   J—JPEG Files

JPEG files are compressed image files commonly used over the Internet. They are examples of the many types of files the 21st century students have at their disposal and use. DALI can take advantage of the abundance of media available online to encourage students to use language creatively and incorporate suitable media to make small productions of their own. For example, a reading comprehension task may consist of reading or listening to a description of a place or a situation, then placing an image in a Word or PowerPoint file and adding captions, thus, demonstrating comprehension of the passage. This could also be accompanied by a recording of a full description of the illustration in the student's own words.

8.2.11   J—Just-in-time Learning

Just-in-time learning is defined as "the acquisition of knowledge or skills as they are needed" (http://www.wordspy.com). The Internet allows instruction to be delivered exactly when and where you need it, and learning to take place anywhere and anytime.

8.2.12   K—Knowledge

Probably, one of the main aims of education in the digital age is to help students learn how to process information so as to transform it into knowledge. Knowledge acquisition is one of the important 21st century skills (Egbert 2007). By making information available anytime and anywhere and facilitating collaboration, the Internet allows students to build a "pool of shared knowledge" (Schcolnik, Kol and Abarbanel 2006). DALI should encourage the construction of knowledge by allowing for flexibility and choice, "cooperation in performing the task, exchange of ideas or findings, feedback, clarification, and evaluation" (*ibid.:* 16).

8.2.13 L—Language, Style and Register

Online communication offers opportunities for learning about suitable ways of communicating with different people and for different purposes, using various styles and registers. DALI must make students aware of the differences and variability of conventions and the suitability or lack of suitability of different communicative contexts. For example, while Netspeak (Crystal 2008) is appropriate and convenient to write an SMS (short text message sent and received on mobile phones) to a friend, it is not appropriate when writing on a professional forum, or when writing email to a professor or a client.

SMS abbreviations have become a special language and have been included in dictionaries (e.g. Crystal 2004; *Concise Oxford Dictionary*). David Crystal coined the term 'Textspeak' for this special type of language or genre, whose existence was mainly motivated by the small screen size of the mobile phone. According to Crystal (2008), this language is characterized by ingenious and often idiosyncratic abbreviations, no sentence punctuation, no apostrophes, and the use of capital letters for effect rather than for marking beginning of sentences, among other things. He claims that when the space constraint is not there, for example, when using a larger screen, people will probably drop most of their Textspeak trends. At school, the trend is continuing to use Textspeak in unsuitable contexts, for example, essays can be controlled by the teacher by helping students develop a "sense of linguistic appropriateness" (Crystal 2008: 82).

EXAMPLE 8.5 Learning about Suitable Digital Communication Styles

Language focus: Textspeak versus Standard English.

Digital skill focus: Awareness of style appropriateness.

The task:

John wrote the following email note to his teacher. Correct his message to make it more suitable. Correct spelling, change SMS abbreviations to full words, and add apostrophes and punctuation.

dear ms jones
i cant come 2u b4 class 2mrw sry…
can u tell me y u gave me an f
cu
john

Corrected message:
Dear Mrs. Jones,

I can't come to you before class tomorrow. Sorry.
Can you tell me why you gave me an F?
See you,
John

After going over the corrections, you may want to discuss the tone and whether, in addition to the corrections made to change Textspeak into Standard English, there are other improvements that could be made to the message.

8.2.14 L—Learning Styles

Learning styles are the ways in which we prefer to learn. People differ not only in their preferences, but also in the ways they organize their learning, in their beliefs about what is good for them, in their motivation for different types of activities and in their efficiency while performing different tasks. Using Reid's (1998) list of learning styles, I shall use the webquest to exemplify how DALI can cater to a variety of students. Teachers may not know what each of their students' learning styles are, but they can offer options for students to choose from.

A webquest is an activity that sends students out on a quest for new information with which they will be able to perform some task. As students navigate through the sources of information, they absorb, reflect, synthesize and finally use the information collected in order to produce something new, a creation of their own. If the resources embedded into the webquest are multimedia resources, learners of different styles will be able to comfortably work through the quest. Visual learners, who understand information better from reading, will be able to deal with the task as long as texts are available. Auditory learners, who are more at ease with oral information, will grasp the ideas more readily by utilizing the audio available. Kinesthetic and tactile learners, who learn best by experience, will be able to understand the information better whenever the textual material is accompanied by simulations, in which they can participate in some kind of virtual experiment. It is not always possible to have all modes available for every single task, but the more possibilities available, the better students will be able to learn.

8.2.15 M—Multimedia

Multimedia integrates text, graphics, animation, audio, still images and video. Multimedia brings the language classroom closer to the real world, and to the sights and sounds students are accustomed to in their daily lives. The learning environment, physical or virtual, becomes more natural and contextualized, and language can be learned in more integrated and authentic ways. The multimedia materials can be used for teacher presentation, for student practice, or can be created by students. Murphy-Judy (1997) claims that multimedia literacy is "the literacy most germane to our new world" (p. 136).

EXAMPLE 8.6   Multimedia Literacy

Language focus: Integrated language skills (writing, speaking).
Digital skill focus: Multimedia presentation or digital story.
The task:

- Choose a story you would like to share with your classmates. It can be a story that you read or heard, something that happened to you, or a story that you made up.
- Write the script of the story. Remember you can look up the words you don't know in the dictionary.
- Find suitable photographs, pictures and backgrounds to illustrate your story.
- Find suitable background music for the parts of the story that you think need it.
- Practise narrating the story as many times as necessary. Remember you can look up the words you are not sure about in an online dictionary to hear how they are pronounced.
- Prepare your presentation or digital story. Don't put too much text on the screen. Your slides should be mainly visual, and your narration should accompany each slide.
- Present your story in class.

8.2.16   N—Netiquette

Netiquette is a term that refers to the rules of etiquette or courtesy in electronic communications. DALI should include netiquette as part of the curriculum. For example, the English teacher can still teach the traditional rules of capitalization, but she also needs to explain the connotations that uppercase has in digital messages. Students need to know that capital letters are necessary at the beginning of sentences and for proper nouns, but they also need to learn that they cannot type a whole message in capital letters because it is considered shouting.

There are many websites that deal with netiquette. See, for example, the guidelines for email etiquette provided by the Purdue Online Writing Lab (http://owl.english.purdue.edu/owl/resource/636/01/).

EXAMPLE 8.7   Netiquette

Language focus: Writing email to make a polite request.
Digital skill focus: Netiquette rules.
The task:
You are not happy with the grade you got on your oral presentation. Write an email to your teacher expressing how you feel and asking her/him to change your grade or give you another opportunity. Make sure you observe netiquette rules.

8.2.17 O—Online Tools

One of the components of information literacy is tool literacy or "the ability to understand and use the practical and conceptual tools of current information technology" (Shapiro and Hughes 1996). In the case of language learners, we could interpret this to mean that students should know how to take advantage of online language tools such as dictionaries, spellcheckers, and concordances to help them with their reading, writing and speaking. DALI should introduce useful tools to the students and offer opportunities for practising their use. Just as in the past many English language courses included dictionary skills, they should now include online tool skills.

EXAMPLE 8.8   Using Online Language Tool

Language focus: Pronunciation.

Digital skill focus: Using an online dictionary to improve pronunciation.

The task:
- You have each received from me a list of words that you mispronounced when giving your oral presentations.
- Go to *Webster's Online* to hear how they are pronounced and then say them out a loud a few times. You should listen to each word several times and pronounce it as closely as possible to the voice you hear.
- Record yourself as you pronounce the list of words and email the recording.

8.2.18 P—Production

Traditionally, the four language skills were divided into two groups: (i) receptive or passive skills—listening and reading, and (ii) productive or active skills—speaking and writing. However, both listening and reading involve activity on the part of the participant. The listener or reader has to be active in order to comprehend, and has to interact with the text so as to construct its meaning. In any case, in the digital age, with the availability of multimedia, it is both feasible and important to think in terms of all four skills, and the technology enables tasks in which multiple skills are activated and integrated (see sub-section 8.2.9).

In the digital age, students do not simply produce language, but they perform a task in which language is only one of the means of expression used (others being graphics, music, sound effects, animation, or video) in order to put together a final product. Examples of such student creations can be blogs, webpages, podcasts, digital photo stories (see Example 8.6), PowerPoint presentations, hypertexts, and others. Using the technology, students can become producers and not only consumers of media. This not only adds to their motivation, but it allows them to implement the language learnt purposefully. Language may be the object of instruction in the course, but it becomes a means of communication and expression in the project, where the other means combine with it to create a successful communicative product.

8.2.19 Q—Queries

Another component of information literacy is "research literacy" (Shapiro and Hughes 1996) or "inquiry" (Egbert 2007), the ability to access information resources and do research. Students need to learn how to properly use online research tools like search engines. DALI should provide guidelines as to how to search for information and how to narrow down a search while keeping the purpose of the search in mind. By choosing which key words to enter into the search box of a search engine, a user defines the query or request for information. If the words entered are 'good', the results are usually satisfactory. Knowing how to use search engines in L1 does not ensure a successful transfer of the skill to L2. Problems may range from inaccurate spelling of the search terms to the inclusion of unnecessary function words (e.g. prepositions). A 'bad' search will yield insufficient or no results and will frustrate the learner.

Besides their usual uses for producing lists of resources, search engines like Google can be used to learn about language use. For example, if students search for an expression in English within quotation marks and the search yields 0 results, they can assume that the expression does not exist in English or that there is something wrong either in the syntax, or in their choice of lexical items or in their spelling.

8.2.20 R—Reading

More and more reading is now online, and the new medium changes the way in which people read (Burbules 1998). The purposes of reading digital text are varied and may range from quick information searches to learning for an exam. In order to read digital text effectively, students need to be aware of the platforms and formats used for displaying electronic texts (e.g. ebook readers, plain text, PDF files reproducing the printed page; one or two pages; portrait or landscape), of the options and tools available to the user (e.g. bookmarking, annotating, changing the background color, changing the font size), of text navigation methods (scrolling and paging), and, above all, of the unique reading strategies they can employ to understand the content, strategies due to the uniqueness of the medium are different from those used when reading from paper (Kol and Schcolnik 1997; Kol and Schcolnik 2000). Some EFL curricula already include digital reading skills. For example, in 2002, Kol and Schcolnik included a series of digital skills such as using an online dictionary, skimming a digital article, and using Find in their English for Academic Purposes curriculum, and have added many others since. Another example is the program of web literacy instruction developed by

Reinhardt and Isbell (2002) as part of an EFL academic skills curriculum. They included several skills such as searching for and evaluating online information, and processing digital texts.

8.2.21 S—Spellcheckers

Spellcheckers are tools that help improve writing and make messages and papers more 'presentable,' if not perfect. DALI should capitalize on their potential. Bad spelling makes a bad impression, so spellcheckers (the powerful electronic tools) should not be ignored. Students should understand that using a spellchecker before sending a message or submitting an assignment is like combing their hair before leaving their house in the morning—an attempt to make a better impression. This is not to say that students should not learn the spelling rules and understand the principles behind rules such as the doubling of the consonant in the word sitting and the addition of 'e' before 's' in potatoes.

8.2.22 T—Text Manipulation

When reading digital text, whether on a computer screen or on a small handheld computer (Schcolnik et al. 2007), we have tools for manipulating it (Cobb and Stevens 1996). Text manipulation is particularly important when learning from digital text. The available tools make it possible to interact with the text by using a variety of reading and study strategies. In addition to the strategies we use when learning from printed text, such as underlining or highlighting portions of the text in different colors and writing marginal notes, most e-reading programs offer useful options and tools such as bookmarking, drawing, copying onto a word processing file, and linking to other resources, namely, data bases, dictionaries and grammar reference books.

> **EXAMPLE 8.9 Text Manipulation***
>
> **Language focus:** Close reading to encourage attention to details and comprehension of the ideas in the text in preparation for a quiz.
>
> **Digital skill focus:** Use of digital tools (highlights and notes) for study purposes.
>
> **The task:** Use the digital dictionary to help you understand the new words.
>
> **A—Close reading with annotation**
>
> *Paragraph 1*
> 1. Highlight the words and expressions that show that mathematical knowledge has been relevant to engineering throughout time.
> 2. Highlight the verbs that show that mathematics was relevant in the past and still is.

Paragraph 2

3. Highlight two sentences that state the main difference between engineering and science.

Paragraph 3

4. Highlight the sentence that explains why engineers need to make mathematical calculations.

Paragraph 4

5. Highlight the three forms of communication that the engineers must master.

Paragraph 5

6. Highlight the four branches of mathematics that were taught before World War II.

Paragraphs 6–7

7. Highlight the causes of change after 1950.
8. Highlight the three branches of mathematics that are relevant for all engineering disciplines.

Paragraph 8

9. Number the factors that have resulted in changes for engineering practice lately.
10. Number the knowledge requirements emphasized by employers.
11. Highlight the author's suggestions for changes in engineering education.

B—Learning for the quiz: Reread the text and learn the main points using your highlights and notes to help you.

* Excerpted from Schcolnik et al. 2007.

8.2.23 U—Usability

The usability of instructional materials depends on factors such as the quality and legibility of the print, the clarity of the instructions, and the transparency of the organization. In the digital age, the development of online language learning materials requires special attention to usability issues. If the teacher develops the materials herself but is constrained by the structure of an existing platform, there may not be much that can be done about navigation or operation of the system, but attention can and should be paid to the design of the individual webpages and activities (Nielsen 1999; Dix et al. 1998; Shneiderman 1998).

8.2.24 V—Vocabulary Reinforcement

The digital medium offers many new ways of reinforcing vocabulary acquisition, such as the possibilities of glossing text through annotation; seamlessly accessing monolingual or bilingual online dictionaries; having student-created glossaries with lists of words or example sentences to be kept, periodically updated and printed; doing interactive exercises with immediate feedback and repeating the exercises or vocabulary games as many times as the student deems it necessary. According to Wood (2001), some of the advantages of technology for vocabulary acquisition are that

- Animations and video clips can add visual information to word meanings and help learners understand the concepts;
- Sound can reinforce the learning of new words; the computer environment allows students to repeat the activities as many times as needed, thus, facilitating practice;
- The presentation of words in multiple modes helps learners of various learning styles acquire new words;
- Word games stimulate and motivate learners and activate prior knowledge; and
- Learners can record themselves as they pronounce the new vocabulary and, thus, have further reinforcement.

8.2.25 W—Webpage Publishing

"Publishing literacy" is another dimension of information literacy (Shapiro and Hughes 1996) and an authentic communicative activity—now that the Internet has become a primary medium of communication. By creating content in English for a broader audience than their teacher or classmates, students learn responsible writing. Moreover, while they research a topic, synthesize the information, organize it, find visuals to accompany the text, decide on the layout, and publish their pages, they learn "the rules of the game (*ibid*)". They learn valuable web literacy skills as well as language skills.

EXAMPLE 8.10 Webpage Publishing

Language focus: Reading, writing, speaking.

Digital skill focus: Integrating different media for web publication.

The task:

Learn about a topic that interests you by reading several resources in English (at least two) and prepare and publish a webpage to share what you learned. Synthesize the information: It's quality and not quantity that counts! Use your own words to avoid plagiarism. Make your webpage esthetic and check your spelling, capitalization and punctuation! *This task is accompanied by additional guidelines with a list of required and optional components and an assessment rubric.*

8.2.26 X—Stands for Unknown

Another important skill is "emerging technology literacy" or the ability to "adapt to, understand, evaluate and make use of the continually emerging innovations in information technology" (Shapiro and Hughes 1996). Technologies change all the time, and some of the programs and storage media in use now will most certainly become obsolete in a few years. The content that we develop now may be pedagogically sound and suitable for current media, but will need to be changed and adapted to new media and ways of doing things. The same is true of the skills and strategies used. In a few years, new skills may become necessary, useful and important, and they will need to be added to the curriculum. Digital age instructors need to be flexible, open-minded and willing to change periodically. Change is very fast, and we cannot teach obsolete skills with obsolete technologies. The language teacher, just as any other teacher in the digital age, must make room for the X in her curriculum.

8.2.27 Y—Yelling on the Internet

Students may not be aware of the fact that typing messages in uppercase is equivalent to yelling and a violation of netiquette. Sometimes students type their messages in uppercase because they don't want to bother with capitalization rules, or with the Shift key. For them, pressing Caps lock once simplifies matters. Making them aware of the problem of netiquette as well as the fact that uppercase text slows down reading (Muter 1996) is extremely important.

EXAMPLE 8.11   Yelling on the Internet

Language focus: Reading.

Digital skill focus: Netiquette awareness.

Group task:

1. Read this message that was sent to the president by a junior high school student.
2. What three problems do you see with the message? (*All uppercase; subject that is not specific enough; no polite closing although there is a signature.*)
3. Revise the message so as to solve the problems.

From: Susan Cook
Date: Thursday May 21, 2008
To: thepresident@gmail.com
Subject: A problem

DEAR MR. PRESIDENT,

I LIVE IN _____. I AM WRITING BECAUSE WE DON'T HAVE A PUBLIC LIBRARY IN MY TOWN. WE HAVE A LIBRARY IN MY SCHOOL, BUT THAT IS NOT ENOUGH. MOST OF THE INTERESTING BOOKS IN THE SCHOOL LIBRARY ARE OUT WHEN I WANT TO BORROW THEM!

CAN YOU HELP US?

SUSAN COOK

8.2.28 Z – Zooming into Relevant Language Skills

There are questions that the language teacher needs to ask in order to analyze the needs of the digital age students. Many of the questions are important regardless of the century and technology, but others are more obviously pertinent to the 21st century. The answers may vary across different populations and in different contexts, but a valid curriculum cannot be developed until some answers have been obtained. The following are just some of the many questions that could be asked:

- What kind of communication skills will my students need to activate? (e.g. mainly speaking, mainly writing, online publishing)
- What kinds of communication media are they likely to use? (e.g. phones, face-to-face, print, the Internet)
- Who will they communicate with and in what kinds of situations?
- What types of discourse will they need to comprehend (e.g. speech produced by native speakers when conversing among themselves, by non-native speakers speaking slowly and with special accents, political addresses, jokes and theater plays, lectures, written articles in magazines and newspapers, academic articles and books)?
- What types of discourse will they need to produce?
- What level of performance/competence will be expected of my students when they are out of the classroom (e.g. in academic life, the workplace)?

8.3 CONCLUSION

In an article entitled "How to Bring Our Schools out of the 20th Century?" Wallis and Steptoe (2006) summarize the 21st century skills proposed in the report of the Commission on the Skills of the American Workforce. The context and target of the report is the US educational system, but I suggest that the skills could be applicable to other contexts as well.

The first skill mentioned is "knowing more about the world" requiring, among other things, understanding foreign cultures and the knowledge of foreign languages. Language learning and culture have been linked for over a century, yet now in the digital age, the Internet offers new opportunities for learning about other cultures as well as for cultural exchange and the formation of virtual cultural communities. DALI should not ignore these opportunities.

The second skill listed is "thinking outside the box", probably what Egbert (2007) refers to as "creative thinking", DALI can start by opening up the box of the language classroom to the world and by allowing for student creativity for choice of activities and for flexibility in modes of presentation.

The third skill is 'becoming smarter about new sources of information'. This refers to the evaluation of resources, a skill that has no doubt, a place in the EFL/ESL curriculum, as discussed above (see sub-section 8.2.5).

The fourth skill is 'good people skills'. This refers to the ability to communicate with others and to work in teams. DALI should encourage pair and group work in which students can cooperate, learn and produce together.

Language skills need to be combined with digital skills in order to be useful in the 21st century. Taking into account both present and future needs of students will result in curricula and teaching that are uptodate, interesting, motivating and relevant for the digital age.

REFERENCES

Boling, E. and Frick, T., *Understanding Plagiarism*, Indiana University Bloomington, School of Education, 2005, available: http://www.indiana.edu/~tedfrick/plagiarism/ [2008, August]

Burbules, N.C., "Rhetorics of the Web: Hyperreading and critical literacy," *Page to Screen: Taking Literacy into the Electronic Era*, I. Snyder (Ed.), London and New York: Routledge, 1998, 102–122.

Cobb, T. and Stevens, V., "A principled consideration of computers and reading in a second language," *The Power of CALL*, M.C. Pennington (Ed.), La Jolla, CA: Athelston, 1996.

Crystal, D., "Texting," *ELT Journal* **62**.1 (2008): 77–83.

_____, *A Glossary of Textspeak and Netspeak,* Edinburgh: Edinburgh University Press, 2004.

Dix, A., Finlay, J., Abowd, G., and Beale, R., *Human-Computer Interaction*, 2nd ed., Hemel Hempstead Hertfordshire: Prentice Hall, 1998.

Egbert, J., "Asking useful questions: Goals, engagement, and differentiation in technology-enhanced language learning," *Teaching English with Technology* **7**.1 (February 2007), IATEFL Poland.

Felix, U., "The unreasonable effectiveness of CALL: What have we learnt in two decades of research?," *EUROCALL 2007*, University of Ulster, Video available at http://www.eurocall2007.com/ [2008, August].

Kol, S. and Schcolnik, M., "Enhancing screen reading strategies," *Calico Journal* **18**.1 (2000): 67–80.

Kol, S. and Schcolnik, M., "Reading from screen vs. Reading from paper: A pilot study," *CAELL Journal* **8**.1 (1997): 10–14.

Murphy-Judy, K.A., "Literacies for foreign language learners in the information age," *Nexus: The Convergence of Language Teaching and Research Using Technology*, K.A. Murphy-Judy (Ed.), CALICO *Monograph Series* **4** (1997): 133–144.

Muter, P., "Interface design and optimization of reading of continuous text," *Cognitive Aspects of Electronic Text Processing*, H. Van Oostendorp, and de Mul, S. Norwood (Eds.), NJ: Albex, 1996, 161–180.

Nielsen, J., *Alertbox for June 9: Writing Style for Print* vs. *Web*, 2008. Available: http://www.useit.com/alertbox/print-vs-online-content.html [2008, August].

_____, *Designing Web Usability: The Practice of Simplicity*, Indianapolis: New Riders Publishing, 1999.

Pitterman, C., *When Your Writing Isn't Your Own*, 2008. Available: http://content.scholastic.com/browse/article.jsp?id=1604 [2008, August].

Prensky, M., "Digital natives, digital immigrants," *On the Horizon* **9**.5 (2001). Available: http://digbig.com/4wxqw [2008, July].

Purdue, OWL, *Avoiding Plagiarism*, Purdue University, 2007, Available: http://owl.english.purdue.edu/owl/resource/589/01/ [2008, August].

Reid, J.M., *Understanding Learning Styles in the Second Language Classroom*, New Jersey: Prentice Hall, 1998.

Reinhardt, J. and Isbell, K., "Building web literacy skills," *The Reading Matrix*, **2**.2 (2002), Available: http://www.readingmatrix.com/articles/isbell_reinhardt/index.html

Schcolnik, M., Kol, S., and Abarbanel, J., "A flexible approach to English for academic purposes: Web-enabled constructivism," *Proceedings of EdMedia 2003—World Conference on Educational Multimedia, Hypermedia and Telecommunications*, Honolulu, Hawaii.

_____, "Constructivism in Theory and in Practice," *English Teaching Forum* **44**.4 (2006): 12–21.

Schcolnik, M. and Kol, S., "Reading and learning from screen," *User-Centered Computer Aided Language Learning*, P. Zaphiris and G. Zacharia (Eds.), Hershey, Pennsylvania: Idea Group Publishing, 2006, 257–277.

Schcolnik, M., Kol, S., and Oren, A., "Are handhelds suitable for reading academic texts?," *Proceedings of EdMedia*, 2007: 888–895.

Shapiro, J.J. and Hughes, S.K., "Information literacy as a liberal art," *Educom Review* **31**.2 (1996).

Shetzer, H. and Warschauer, M., "An electronic literacy approach to network-based language teaching," *Network-based Language Teaching: Concepts and Practice*, M. Warschauer and R. Kern (Eds.), New York: Cambridge University Press, 171–185.

Shneiderman, B., *Designing the User Interface: Strategies for Effective Human-Computer Interaction*, 3rd ed., Reading, Massachusetts: Addison-Wesley, 1998.

Wallis, C. and Steptoe, S., "How to bring our schools out of the 20th century," *TIME in partnership with CNN*. Available: http://www.time.com/time/nation/article/0,8599,1568429,00.html [2008, August].

Warschauer, M., *CALL* vs. *Electronic Literacy: Reconceiving Technology in the Language Classroom*, CILT Research Forum. Available: http://www.cilt.org.uk/research/papers/resfor2/warsum1.htm [2008, August].

Wood, J., "Can software support children's vocabulary development?," *Language Learning and Technology* **5**.1 (Jan. 2001): 166–201.

Available: http://llt.msu.edu/vol5num1/wood/default.html [2008, August]

Part 3

CONTENT BASED INSTRUCTION (CBI)

Chapter 9

CONTENT-BASED INSTRUCTION

— Makiko Ebata

9.1 INTRODUCTION

Language is a superb invention for the simple reason that it allows us to communicate with each other and thereby broaden our world. But language teaching and acquisition is by no means simple. Being in a position which enables me to teach students about the preciousness of learning a new language, I have come to question how to go about this effectively in teaching English. Using a number of methods has allowed me to understand that content-based instruction (CBI) is the most efficient not only for language development but also for content mastery. In this study, I explain the theory of content-based instruction, assess its merits and drawbacks, and offer suggestions for content-based materials development.

9.2 THEORY OF CONTENT-BASED INSTRUCTION

According to Brinton et al. (2003):

> Content-based instruction aims at eliminating the artificial separation between language instruction and subject matter classes which exists in most educational settings.

Again, "Communication-based instruction can be an effective tool for providing English language learners access to content-area learning" (Hernandez 2003). Met (2008) suggests:

> Content in content-based programs represents material that is cognitively engaging and demanding for the learner, and is material that extends beyond the target language or target culture.

Since it is important to produce students who comprehend English without translating into their native languages, choosing meaningful content is essential. In ESL/EFL settings in Japan, however, translation of English into Japanese is still used, which provides students with comfort but never enables them to be real English users. Through communication-based instruction focused on content, students are able to pick up not only the communication skills that are necessary for effective language, but also learning new subject matter.

In addition, content-based material is believed to motivate students to acquire not only a target language but also content. Brinton, et al. (*op. cit.*) mention:

> The use of informational content which is perceived as relevant by the learner is assumed by many to increase motivation in the language course and, thus, to promote more effective learning.

According to Stoller (1997):

> There is a relationship between student motivation and student interest—common outcomes of content-based classes—and a student's ability to process challenging materials, recall information, and elaborate.

Content-based instruction has a strong correlation with student motivation which is a vital element in English education. Motivation allows students to pursue learning English, not to be afraid of making errors, and to use it as a means of communication with a number of people. Motivation makes students understand the actual purpose of studying English. In other words, motivated students realize that English is not just a subject or a way to pass an entrance examination.

According to Sticht (1997):

> All human intellectual activities such as thinking, communicating, problem solving, and learning, require both processes and content (knowledge). This implies that attempting to raise people's cognitive abilities to high levels simply by improving processes such as "reading," "writing," and "critical thinking" is futile. To perform these processes well requires high levels of content knowledge on which the processes can operate.

Brinton et al. (*op. cit.*) assert, "Language should be taught through a focus on contextualized use rather than on fragmented examples of correct sentence-level usage, the former a critical feature of a content-based approach." Met (*op. cit.*) suggests, "Content facilitates language growth." Content is strongly believed to have an effective impact on the brain. While students learn about a certain topic, they are required not only to use their background knowledge, but also to think, doubt, and solve tasks. In other words, they need to reflect critically on the content, encouraging them to utilize a range of intellectual skills. This makes it possible for them to store new information in their knowledge bank. According to Kennedy (2006):

> Enriched experiences enhance neural growth and, thus, enhance learning, indicating that brains construct themselves through life experiences. The more stimulation received, the greater the learning. Emotion, experiences, and learning of meaningful information strengthens useful connections and results in cortical pyramidal cell branching.

9.3 SUGGESTIONS FOR CONTENT-BASED MATERIALS DEVELOPMENT

Materials development is one of the key challenges instructors encounter during their career. Composing materials for content-based English class in particular is a tremendous trial for instructors unfamiliar with the content or those without support from the subject instructors. Materials used in class, however, have tremendous impact on the learning experience and, thus, must be thoroughly prepared prior to class. In order for materials to be effective for both English and content learning, instructors should be familiar with the expected outcome of English ability as well as understanding of the content.

Met (*op. cit.*) asserts, "Careful planning for language development can be useful in ensuring that students gain language competence that will be useful in settings beyond the school itself". It is necessary that students can employ what they learn in real life. Snow (2001) suggests:

> In order to develop communicative competence, learners must have extended opportunities to use the second/foreign language productively. Thus, in addition to receiving comprehensible input, they must produce comprehensible output; in other words, explicit attention must be paid to the productive language skills of speaking and writing.

According to Heo (2006), "The students must go through a real-world process instead of using independent, creative, or unrealistic thoughts". Brinton, et al. (*op. cit.*) assert:

> First and most important, the materials chosen should be exploitable. In other words, there should be a range of language functions and structures available, and these should map neatly onto the language syllabus.

Valuable and realistic lessons foster students' language development. For students to effectively communicate with others, materials used in class need to train them to become successful communicators.

Furthermore, materials need to motivate students to pursue the target language. According to Brinton et al. (*op. cit.*):

> Every attempt should be made to select materials which reflect the needs and interests of the students and to choose content areas in which the language teacher has some interest or expertise.

According to Met (*op. cit.*), materials should be:

> Enhancing language learning by providing motivating topics to communicate about, and enhancing language learning by providing meaningful, purposeful language practice opportunities drawn from a variety of topics.

Varying the choice of topics and themes is essential in order to engage students in learning the content through English; appealing topics and themes encourage them to actively participate in class. Active participation in class, moreover, enhances students' relationships with one another, creating a positive influence on classroom atmosphere.

There are several key points required in material-making. To Short (1991):

> In order to make English language input as comprehensible as possible, the teacher should present information through diverse media: realia, graphs, demonstrations, pre-reading, and pre-writing strategies. The focus of the instruction should be motivated by the content to be learned which will help identify the language skills required to learn that content and the reasoning abilities needed to manipulate it.

Hernandez (*op. cit.*) mentions, "It is essential to familiarize English language learners with clear content vocabulary related to the unit of study". He also suggests:

> Lessons may need to be sequenced with careful planning so that students can be exposed to information needed as a prerequisite for another subject matter, particularly in the areas of maths and science. Students should be guided to see that these thinking processes are common in everyday life situation; lessons can then be adapted to demonstrate how the critical thinking used in their personal lives can be transferred to academic thought.

The instructors need to carefully choose the way they present the planned content in their materials. It is particularly important to structure activities in an appropriate order. In addition, visual aids are instrumental in supplementing students' understanding. Vocabulary-building is strongly believed to be one of the key elements in English education. Thus, materials must include relevant vocabulary exercises at the right time. Most importantly, materials need to be built with the goal of fostering critical thinking, forcing students to utilize a combination of prior knowledge and skills.

9.4 ASSESSMENT OF CONTENT-BASED INSTRUCTION: STUDENTS PROJECT WORK IN CLASS

Most problematic for the instructors of content-based classes is evaluation, necessitating the right of language assessment and content assessment. According to Heo (*op. cit.*):

> Students in CBI classes cannot be evaluated in the traditional way because they were exposed to more input and content information through the class.

Brinton et al. mention:

> Instructors need to be continually aware of the interface between language and content in evaluation, the content factor in language tests and the language factors in content tests. In particular, they need to consider possible causes of misevaluation when designing tests or other assessment tasks.

The instructors need to be deeply familiar with the assessment method.

Designing methods of assessment requires much time and consideration. The format and content of evaluation necessitates well-organization and consideration (Heo, *op. cit.*):

> Assessment of CBI should not be simple and isolated; students must be required to integrate information, to form, and to articulate their own opinions about the subject matter, not to analyze the linguistic structure of the target language. Designing authentic and interactive content-based assessment was required because learners in CBI had to complete discourse level tasks and the skills evaluated in the assessment were in an academic setting.

According to Brinton et al. (*op. cit.*)

> The language learning objectives of content-based courses are performance-based. Students aim not only to improve their knowledge of the language but to learn how to use this knowledge to perform tasks in an academic setting. Evaluating their ability to do so will necessarily involve tasks requiring comprehension or expression of relatively complex content.

Authentic and performance-based task evaluation is essential in assessing acquired knowledge and linguistic skills in content-based classes.

Evaluation should include the following abilities: feasibility, validity, appropriateness, reliability, variety, and frequency (*ibid*). They also stress that the evaluation process should involve not only assessment by the instructor, but also self-assessment and peer-assessment. In addition, there are five categories of evaluation: (i) knowledge of elements of the linguistic code, (ii) knowledge of discourse, (iii) interactive communication skills, (iv) academic language use skills, and (v) other relevant study skills. Content-based language instructors efficiently need to take all the five factors into consideration in order to efficiently assess their students language both in terms of language output and content understanding. Furthermore, ability and content mastery need to be evaluated at appropriate intervals. Hernandez (*op. cit.*) asserts:

> It is important for the teacher to frequently check learners' comprehension by collecting and evaluating student work samples in the subject area. Monitoring a student's degree of complexity in the use of English language is another way of measuring progress in English language acquisition through communication-based instruction.

9.5 TEACHING ENGLISH USING CONTENT-BASED INSTRUCTION

An actual lesson is introduced in this class. The class consists of 17 freshmen from various countries including the Philippines, Cambodia, France, Taiwan, China, and a few Japanese returnees from the English-speaking countries.

This is an advanced university English class which aims to produce fluent and eloquent output from students to equip them for regular classes conducted in English during their study abroad in the third year. The class meets four times a week from Tuesday to Friday for 90 minutes. On Tuesday and Wednesday, the class focuses on input skills with the content before they make output in English. The material for these two days consists of (i) timed reading, (ii) listening, (iii) pre-reading, (iv) mid-reading while reading, and (v) post-reading. Key vocabulary words are highlighted after timed reading and during reading so that the learners can pick up the new vocabulary necessary to understand the content. Thursday and Friday are dedicated to output skills: speaking and writing. Key words are practised through speaking activities.

The English course continues for two years with four semesters. Each semester focuses on certain areas including speaking skills, debate skills, essay-writing skills, and presentation skills. On Thursday and Friday, skills are carefully instructed to prepare the students for academic success.

Project work is the main method of evaluation. For instance, during the first semester of the first year, the focus is on speaking skills requiring the students to make three speeches based on the content tackled in class.

9.6 POSITIVE ASPECTS OF CONTENT-BASED INSTRUCTION

New content in English allowed the students to be familiar with academic and specialized terms that they would never have encountered in ESL/EFL class. Their knowledge of the particular content also expanded increasing their overall confidence. Their attitudes towards learning content in English gradually changed: at the beginning, they were hesitant to read complicated passages and articles. However, by the end of the semester, they were able to read any material using background knowledge, experiences, critical thinking, and their expanded vocabulary set. Moreover, speeches and presentation enabled the students to master the essential skills that are significant in mainstream classes overseas. Such projects made the students learn about the content and English from each other.

9.7 CONCLUSION

Content-based instruction allows English learners to acquire not only English but also certain themes or topics. It is surely valuable since there is no isolation of language and content. Students also need to employ all required skills to comprehend the content and store the newly acquired knowledge. In addition, content-based instruction has a strong connection with student motivation. Although materials development is one of the challenges that many instructors encounter during their career, content-based English instructors also need to set a target for both English ability and understanding of the content. Materials should have motivating, comprehensible, and real-world relevance. The problematic part in content-based instruction is evaluation. Instructors should familiarize themselves with methods of assessment in order to evaluate students as accurately as possible.

REFERENCES

Brinton, D.M., Snow, M.A., and Wesche, M., *Content-based Second Language Instruction,* Michigan: University of Michigan Press, 2003.

Heo, Y., "Content-based instruction," *TESL Working Paper Series* **4**.2 (2006).

Hernandez, A., "Making content instruction accessible for English language learners," *English Learners: Reaching the Highest Level of English Literacy,* Gilbert G. Gracia (Ed.), Newark: International Reading Association, 2003, 125–149.

Kennedy, T.J., "Language learning and its impact on the brain: Connecting language learning with the mind through content-based instruction," *Foreign Language Annals* **39**.3 (2006).

Met, M., "Content-based instruction: Defining terms, making decisions," *NFLC Reports.* Retrieved on 01/24/2008 from http://www.carla.umn.edu/cobaltt/modules/principles/decisions.html

Short, D.J., "Integrating language and content instruction: Strategies and techniques," *NCBE Program Information Guide Series* **7** (Fall, 1991).

Snow, M.A., *Teaching English as a Second or Foreign Language,* Boston: Heinle and Heinle, 2001, 303–318.

Sticht, T.G., "The theory behind content-based instruction," *NCSALL,* **1**.D (1997).

Stoller, F.L., "A means to promote language content," *Forum* **35**.4 (1997).

Chapter 10

FAMILIARITY AND PLANNING IN TASK-BASED LEARNING

— MARGARET HORRIGAN

10.1 INTRODUCTION

One of the first entirely task-based courses was Prabhu's (1987) Communicational Teaching Project in Bangalore, India (Ellis 2003: 340) and since then a growing body of research on Task-based Learning (TBL) has emerged. The primary role of output is a major theoretical tenet of TBL, as the meaningful interaction that takes place during interaction may push learners to shift their attention from semantic processing to syntactic processing (Swain 1985: 249). However, interaction is not the only source of output. Learners can be encouraged to think about how they want to tell a story, record themselves and focus on their own language in a bid to encourage syntactic processing. Let us first turn our attention to encouraging learners to think about how they tell their stories. This harnessed thinking within TBL is labelled **planning**.

10.2 TYPES OF PLANNING

10.2.1 Task Repetition

Previous studies regarding task repetition took a broad definition of what familiarity with task entails (Guerrero 2006). Foster and Skehan (1996) viewed familiarity of task type, i.e. one-way narratives or information exchanges, and cognitive and interactive conditions, as defining familiarity. Bygate (1999b) viewed familiarity as the repetition of the exact same task and conditions. Gass et al. (1999) took content familiarity as their definition. Robinson (2003) saw familiarity in light of task content, i.e. a familiar area in a map task. Guerrero (2004) took familiarity to involve task type, discourse genre (Swales 1990) and the most "complex of task conditions" (Guerrero 2006)—the *there and then* condition of his 2004 study.

For the purposes of the current study, task repetition is defined as being familiar with task content, i.e. repetition of the same task, and is labelled *familiar* (F). Thus, the participants in this study will be familiar with the task type and discourse genre of all the tasks. The cognitive conditions will, however, be unfamiliar as the recording of the narratives should render the performance more permanent and may give a higher status to the language (Willis 1996: 34) than previous classroom tasks.

Bygate (1996: 138) suggests that all things being equal, there is no reason to doubt that task repetition can enhance output as the processing which is effectuated during speech production is less taxing on a second encounter with a task. This phenomenon in real life, for example, phone conversations, show the effectiveness of repetition in general (Bygate 1999b: 41). Bygate (1996: 136–137) argues that this is due to the shifting of attention from initial declarative or linguistic knowledge to proceduralised knowledge or language skill. This recalls the automaticity process that is intrinsic to fluency development (Izumi 2003: 170).

Bygate and Samuda (2005: 44) explicitly draw on Levelt's speech production model to account for effects of task repetition on learners' output. These authors suggest that a considerable amount of conceptualisation occurs during a first encounter with a task and that a re-run of the task enables learners to access working memory more easily. Thus prior experience acts as a primer of conceptual content and lexico-grammatical forms resulting in faster recovery of these items from the conceptualiser and increased capacity during formulation (*ibid.*: 45). In short, repeated tasks may prompt more fluent and accurate production (*ibid.*). This is true also for strategic planning.

10.2.2 Strategic Planning

Strategic planning has become an umbrella term for a variety of pre-task planning (Ellis 2005: 75). Wendel (1997), basing his research on Levelt's (1989) model of speech production, is credited with distinguishing between online planning and strategic planning (Ellis 2003: 25). Strategic planning directly involves conceptualisation which concerns what is to be said and may effect how this is to be said (formulation), resulting in production which is laden with errors (*ibid.* 109). Thus, remembering of the 'how' is generally not verbatim as planned and it often results in online planning, increased complexity and fluency but diminished accuracy during production.

Mehnert relates this significant improvement of complexity to the amounts of time allocated to planning as opposed to its being a general consequence of planning (1998: 83). Ellis (2005: 75) distinguishes between the process and product of strategic planning. Thus, studies on strategic planning need to account for what learners do while planning, strategies operated, as well as focusing on the effects evident on learner output (Ortega 2005: 78). Post-task interviews and participants' notes taken during planning, for the moment, remain the sole sources of interpreting learner strategies (Ellis 2005; Guerrero 2004).

Studies on the guidance given during strategic planning and the source of such guidance are less frequent in the literature. Foster and Skehan (1999: 221–222) suggest that planning instructions need to be devised so that attention is directed to both content and language. In their study they conclude that teacher-based planning is as effective as solitary unguided planning while the group-based planning resulted inferior (*ibid.* 241). Foster and Skehan (1996: 135) caution, however, that guided planning tended to increase the complexity of language but reduce its accuracy.

In summary, the literature on strategic planning suggests that provision of these components enhance learner output regardless of peer or teacher participation. Thus, unguided planning was deemed appropriate for the current study.

10.3 FINDINGS OF PREVIOUS RESEARCH

10.3.1 Fluency

Helgesen's (2003: 18) simplistic view of fluency as "smoother" language does not include the learner's "capacity to use language in real time" (Skehan and Foster 1999: 96). Thus, the fewer dysfluencies (*ibid.* 230) that occur during real-time speech production render the output *smooth*. Such phenomena have become the basis for oral fluency analysis. The occurrence of drawling, however, has not been systematically accounted for in the literature and may yield supplementary insight into planning processes (Bärenfanger et al. 2002).

In the literature consulted, fluency increases with strategic planning time. Mehnert (*op. cit.* 99), Ortega (1999: 139) and Ellis (2000: 203) concur that fluency is significantly better when ten minutes of solitary planning time is provided. Solitary and teacher-fronted planning resulted in better fluency than 'group' and no planning in Foster and Skehan's (1999: 235) study. Guerrero's (*op. cit.*) study on task complexity reported mixed findings regarding fluency. His 'planned here-and-now' condition produced more fluency than the other three conditions—a result that he attributes to the complexity of the 'there-and-then' and unplanned conditions involved in his study.

Fluency was also improved in task repetition studies although this effect was not extended to new tasks (Bygate 1999b: 43; Gass et al. 1999: 572). Bygate (1996: 141) reports an improvement of over 50 per cent regarding verbatim repetitions in the repeated task with substitutive repetitions also increasing. He associates this phenomenon (1999a: 144) to the familiarity with content in providing speakers with extra time and attention to monitor their output more effectively. Similar findings regarding fluency and conclusions were drawn that repetition of tasks release speakers' spare capacity to attend to fluency with positive results (Bygate 2001: 42).

10.3.2 Complexity

Complexity is the capacity to use more advanced language or language with depth (Helgesen, *op. cit.*, 18). The risk that learners run by attempting to use more complex language is that their output may be less accurate. This may also involve being more open to taking risks as fewer controlled language subsystems may be used (Skehan and Foster 1999: 96–97).

Previous research reports predominantly positive effects of strategic planning on complexity in general (Ellis 2005: 23). Mehnert (*op. cit.*), however, found that increasing the quantity of planning time produced significantly more complex language. Guerrero (2004) reports no changes in syntactic complexity across conditions even with ten minutes of strategic planning time.

Studies on the effects of task familiarity and repetition also report predominantly positive effects on complexity. Wording in this small body of research is, however, less consistent. Although Bygate (2001: 42) occasionally refers to complexity as being increased by familiarity, in his previous study (1996: 143) he refers to 'quality of talk' as being better. More recently, Bygate and Samuda (*op. cit.*: 67) report more 'formulation' of information with task repetition. Lynch and Maclean (2000: 225) report that more complex language was a consequence of planning, but do not overtly report on the effects of task rehearsal on learner output. Gass et al. (1999: 572) also report positive effects on lexical sophistication in their study.

10.3.3 Accuracy

Accuracy in performance is a general ability to avoid error. Learners may effectuate such avoidance through more conservative use or higher levels of control (Skehan and Foster 1999: 96) in order to produce more precise language. Such control may, however, not be particularly beneficial to IL development (Skehan 2003: 293).

Mixed results are reported regarding the effects of strategic planning on learners' accuracy (Ellis 2005: 22). In Foster and Skehan's (1996) study, accuracy was higher for the unguided than the guided planning. Their later study (1997) showed increased accuracy in the personal narrative task while the decision-making task showed insignificant changes. Mehnert's (*op. cit.*) one-minute planners were more accurate than the ten and five minute planners. Ortega (1999) noted increased accuracy of target-like use of noun modifiers while that of articles remained insignificant. Ellis' (1987) study showed increased accuracy of regular past simple verbs while accuracy of irregular verbs decreased with planning time. Wendel's (*op. cit.*: 142) prediction of increased accuracy was incorrect as accuracy rates for both conditions in his study produced almost identical results. Similar findings are reported by Guerrero (2004: 319) for target-like use of articles and percentage of error-free units although more complex tasks regarding the 'here-and-now' variable revealed significantly higher percentages of self-repairs and ratio of repaired-to-un-repaired errors.

Studies that focus on task repetition show positive effects on accuracy. Foster (1996: 133) reports that her narrative tellers were significantly more accurate. Bygate (1999b: 43) reports increase of self-correction and greater capacity for form during the repeated task. Later, Bygate (2001: 43) reports only marginal increases of accuracy which may be related to the measurement operated in his study. Gass et al. (1999: 572) also indicate that greater accuracy in morphosyntax was caused by task repetition. Lynch and Maclean (*op. cit.*: 245) suggest that the positive effects on accuracy recorded from their study were due to repetition alone. These effects were not sustained in later tasks (Gass et al. 1999: 572; Bygate 1999b: 43), hence claims that the learning that has taken place is questionable.

The cognitive process in speech production involves message conceptualisation, formulation and articulation (Levelt 1989). This process slows down when the L2 speakers' proficiency level is low (De Bot 1992). The level of interaction between declarative and procedural knowledge systems further complicates the process. Thus, automaticity, the rate of information retrieval, may increase over time with planning (Batstone 2005). Therefore, the learners' oral output is the only real-time indicator of both the speech production process and automaticity. Whether their output is modified externally, or internally, is still open to debate (Ellis 2003). TBL research has gradually revealed more complex issues regarding task manipulation (Ellis 2003, 2005). Although mixed findings tend to be reported for strategic planning (Elllis 2005), positive effects of the same are made. Familiarity studies provide more consistent positive effects although ambiguity of terminology prevails here (Ellis 2005, Bygate et al. 2001).

In general then, both types of planning have had positive effects on both fluency and complexity, although strategic planning has produced mixed results on accuracy (Ellis 2005: 22). Studies involving task repetition suggest that although performance is enhanced between similar or identical tasks (Lynch and Maclean 2000: 245, Gass et al. 1999: 572; Bygate 1999b: 43; Bygate 1996: 142) no carryover or performance effects occur. Thus, although repetition of the same task shows positive results on learner performance, these effects are not evident in new tasks. Thus, both strategic planning and familiarity combined should facilitate the cognitive process, which underlies oral language production by freeing capacity (Kormos 1999). The effects of this spare capacity on learners' fluency, complexity and accuracy are of interest to the current study.

10.4 RESEARCH DESIGN AND METHODOLOGY

As the purpose of this study is to examine the *effects* of pre-task planning time and task repetition on learners' oral narratives, a quantitative quasi-experimental design was operated as this allowed comparisons to be drawn with previous research of a similar nature. The main objective of this study is to gain an understanding of the effects that planning time and task familiarity have on the accuracy, fluency and complexity of learners' language. The objective, therefore, is to provide an analysis of learners' oral narratives produced under these specific conditions and relate the findings to pedagogical implications.

The research question was composed of: strategic planning time (five minutes), familiarity, no strategic planning, and no familiarity. Thus, four tasks were presented to learners over the two-week time span. The tasks were divided into two separate sessions. Unfamiliar unplanned narratives and familiar planned narratives were recorded in the first session. Familiar unplanned and unfamiliar planned narratives were recorded in the second session. This ensured that samples collected were uncontaminated by previous planning in both sessions.

10.4.1 Research Method

A repeated-measures design was used in which the within-subjects factors were familiarity with task (F) and strategic planning (P). Four levels of these independent variables were analysed in the following order:

Condition 1: Unplanned unfamiliar
Condition 2: Planned familiar
Condition 3: Unplanned familiar
Condition 4: Planned unfamiliar.

Given that in this experiment, participants were asked to narrate four stories, two of which they were already familiar with. An attempt to avoid practice or carryover effects from one story to another (Hagen 1994: 84) was made by dividing the experiment into two sessions. These sessions were separated by a period of two weeks. In addition to this, the unplanned stories were narrated first, in both sessions, so that the previous sitting did not enhance the participants' performance obliquely. Therefore, the condition of planning rendered the distribution of tasks less flexible and the more reliable Latin square design (*ibid.*) was not possible for this reason.

10.4.2 Participants

The participants of this study were 12 Italian students of law, between 19 and 22 at the LUISS University, a private university in Rome where the researcher works. The students were provided with Legal English lessons, three 45-minute lessons weekly, as part of their course. Their number of years of EL instruction range between 7 and 13. Six females and six males participated in the study. The participants were selected based on their current level of English language which is at the European Union's level of B1 (ALTE 2005). This was established by means of an initial placement test— the **Michigan Test of English Language Proficiency** (MTELP) which has stood the test of time within the LUISS university, and is implemented as a placement test to establish English language proficiency by numerous Universities (MTELP 2006). A further bid to set up the sample group with similar subjects was made by selecting participants who had obtained marks in a mid-term test that ranged between 26 and 29 out of a maximum of thirty.[1] The potential candidates that achieved these results were, thus, identified from the first, second and third year courses. Therefore, the final 12 subjects were Italian students at a law faculty who also studied English language and resulted within a similar range of the B1 level of the European Unions Scale of six levels.

10.4.3 Data Collection

Data collection occurred over two sessions in a lecture hall with pairs of participants and was conducted by the researcher alone. In contrast to previous studies (Foster and Skehan 1996; Skehan and Foster 1997; Mehnert 1998; Ortega 1999), operationalization of planning time was 5 minutes for planned narratives and 50 seconds for unplanned ones as this was deemed sufficient time to familiarise participants with the plots depicted in the comic strips (Guerrero 2004: 208). Five minutes were chosen above ten minutes of planning time as Mehnert's (1998: 104) 5-minute planners resulted as equally accurate as his 10-minute planners although complexity increased with 10 minutes. The current researcher also deemed 5 minutes as less conducive to participants dropping out of the study due to their personal time pressures and study obligations. Students were encouraged to take notes during strategic planning time regarding what they wanted to say and how to say it. These notes were removed, however, during performance and the participants were told this at the onset of the experiment. They were also informed that they could ask any questions they wanted during the planning period.

The steps taken during the two sessions were:

Session 1: Greetings and small talk for rapport.
Story 1: Unfamiliar unplanned—Mrs. Edwards.
Story 2: Familiar planned—Mrs. Brown.

Affective variables questionnaire for stories 1 and 2.

Session 2: Greetings and small talk for rapport.
Story 3: Familiar unplanned—Agent Smith.
Story 4: Unfamiliar planned—Halley met Barry.

Affective variables questionnaire for stories 3 and 4.

Protocol analysis

An affective variables questionnaire was conducted at the end of each session of data collection. A retrospective protocol report was conducted immediately after the experiment. Both questionnaire and protocol analysis were adopted from (Guerrero 2004: 391, 377) and were administered *in situ*. The protocol analysis was coded using Giorgi's (1985) four-stage method of comprehending, synthesising, theorising and recontextualising.

---

1. It is the norm to grade students out of 30 in tertiary education in Italy, 30 being the maximum.

10.4.4 Data Analysis

Word Counts and Time on Tasks

A preliminary analysis was carried out on total words and minutes per task. Table 10.1 illustrates means and standard deviations, and shows that both the unplanned unfamiliar (UU) and the familiar and planned (FP) conditions prompted more production of overall words than the familiar unplanned (FU) and unfamiliar planned (UP) conditions. The amount of time spent on the tasks is, however, considerably greater under the UU condition, the first in the design to be implemented. The opposite is true for the FP condition which prompted shorter narratives but in a much shorter time span than that of the UU condition.

TABLE 10.1 Means and Standard Deviations of Seconds and Total Words

Conditions and order of tasks	Session 1 UU Mean	SD	Session 1 FP Mean	SD	Session 2 FU Mean	SD	Session 2 UP Mean	SD
Total words	162.08	45.93	161.08	45.58	153.92	56.41	153.33	63.42
Seconds	119.25	32.12	102.83	28.22	103.17	38.27	100.92	34.32
Ratio of words to secs.	1.36		1.57		1.49		1.52	

The ratio of words-to-seconds measurement reveals that under the UU condition, the participants produced fewer words than they did under any other condition. This may indicate that more online planning occurred under this condition. The FP condition produces a noticeably higher ratio, at 0.05, from the UP condition under this measurement. It would appear, then, that under the FP condition, participants tended to produce more language and engage less in online planning. This, however, is an initial assumption based solely on words produced per second.

An account of the effects of the independent variables, strategic planning (P) and task familiarity (F) on the levels of the dependent variables, fluency, complexity and accuracy now follows.

Fluency

Fluency was measured at four levels: (i) total syllables, (ii) pruned syllables, (iii) fluency rate A and (iv) fluency rate B. Figure's 10.1 and 10.2 illustrate the distribution of data regarding the levels of total syllables and the distribution of data for pruned syllables, respectively.

The one-way ANOVA carried out on the first level of fluency, i.e. total syllables, revealed no significant differences between treatments. Thus, all treatments effected the participants' quantity of overall output in similar ways. The FP condition, although revealing a single outlier, produces data which

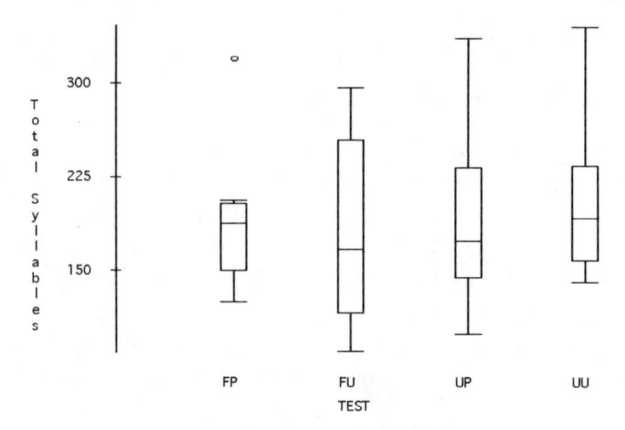

FIGURE 10.1 Distribution of Total Syllables across conditions with a single outlier.

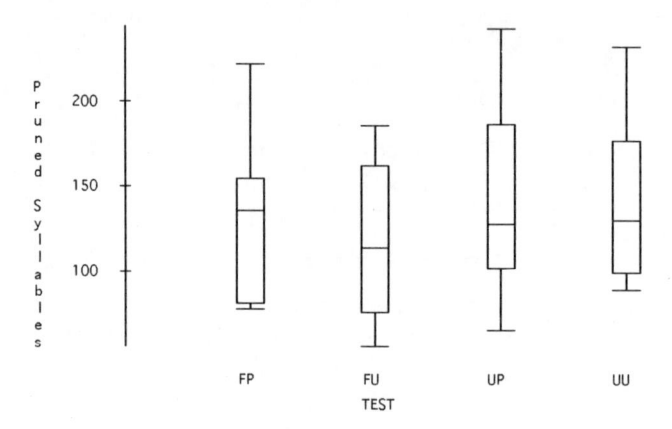

FIGURE 10.2 Distribution of pruned syllables across conditions.

displays less dispersion between scores (Figure 10.1). This is also evident from the mean and median scores which are closest under this condition at 187.42 ± 14.33 for the mean and 188 for the median. Therefore, this may be indicative of the FP treatment causing a larger majority of the participants to produce markedly similar quantities of text. However, the participants did not produce the largest quantity of overall syllables under the FP condition as the mean is the second lowest across the conditions.

The most positive findings for total syllables are to be found under the UU condition where the mean is 204.33 ± 16.27. The minimum and maximum scores are also the highest under this condition at 140 and 346, respectively. Thus, although no significant difference exists between the conditions, the UU condition reveals noticeably higher scores than any other condition. Therefore, the participants produced more overall text under this condition.

The pruned syllable measure is more indicative of articulate speech performance as it has been 'pruned' of syllables containing false starts, repetitions and reformulations. The one-way ANOVA conducted on pruned syllables returned no significant differences again. Although under the UP condition the highest mean 140.08 ± 15.69 was achieved, the data is skewed to the right (Figure 10.2). This implies that a small number of participants performed better than the majority under this condition. The UU condition, however, contains the second highest mean 137.25 ± 12.57, the highest minimum and maximum scores with a median which is also the second closest to the mean, indicative of less dispersion. Therefore, these findings seem to suggest that under the UU condition, the majority of participants spoke more articulately by using fewer repetitions, false starts and reformulations.

Fluency rates A and B measure syllables produced per minute and are, therefore, indicative of speech production in real time. Figures 10.3a and 10.3b represent box plots of the normal distribution of data measuring A and B, respectively.

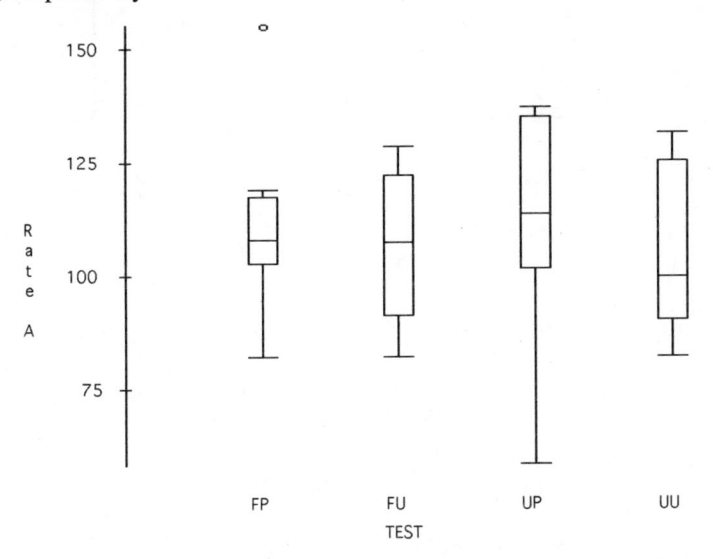

FIGURE 3a. Distribution of fluency rate A across conditions with a single outlier.

Fluency rate A is indicative of total syllables produced per minute and is represented in Figure 10.3a. Once again, the one-way ANOVA returned no significant differences between conditions for this measurement. The FP condition reveals data which is the least dispersed of all the conditions although one participant did perform noticeably better than the majority. The mean here, 110.59 ± 5.11, is 0.1 less than its nearest contender under the UU condition. It is also the second closest mean to its median 108.16, while its maximum and minimum scores are the highest and the second highest, respectively, across conditions. Therefore, it would seem that familiarity and strategic planning conditions combined enabled a more homogeneous majority of participants to speak more quickly overall.

An interesting finding here is under the FU condition where the least dispersion of data is evident. The median 107.48 is separated from the mean 107.43 ± 4.32 by 0.05. Thus, the participants performed in a very similar manner under this condition. This, however, may be attributable more so to the task operated than the FU condition *per se* and it will be discussed in detail under Triangulated Findings.

Fluency rate B measures pruned syllables produced per minute, the data from which is represented by Figure 10.3b. The one-way ANOVA again

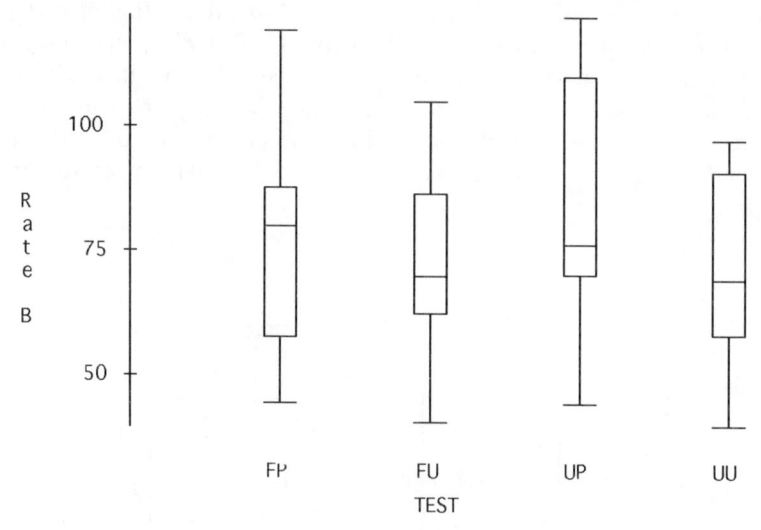

FIGURE 10.3b Distribution of fluency rate B across conditions.

revealed no significant differences between conditions. The descriptive statistics do, however, reveal similar findings to those discussed for fluency rate A. Although the UP condition reveals a markedly higher mean, 84.84 ± 6.8, the data here is more widely dispersed than the other conditions. Thus, the participants performed less uniformly under the UP condition. The FP condition, although positively skewed, reveals the second highest mean, 77.2 ± 5.8, which is also the second closest to its median. The FP median 80.24 is also the highest of all conditions. Thus, less dispersion is evident under the FP condition where a majority of participants appear to have produced more articulate speech in less time than any other conditions.

Complexity

Complexity was measured at three separate levels:

(i) Lexical density MSTTR (Mean Segment Type Token Ratio) a ratio of the total number of different words to the total number of words per narrative,
(ii) Syntactical complexity which is another ratio measurement to quantify the verb forms per narrative, and
(iii) Syntactical variety, the sum of different grammatical verb forms such as tense, modality and voice per narrative.

Chapter 10 Familiarity and Planning in Task-based Learning 147

The one-way ANOVAs carried out on the MSTTR and syntactical complexity measurements are summarised in. Given that the syntactical variety scores result from categorical data, a chi-squared test, and not an ANOVA, was used to measure significance.

A preliminary analysis of data measured for MSTTR revealed a single outlier in the UP condition that rendered the distribution of data not normal. Elimination of this outlier revealed normally distributed data. This data is illustrated by Figure 10.4a. The one-way ANOVA revealed no significant

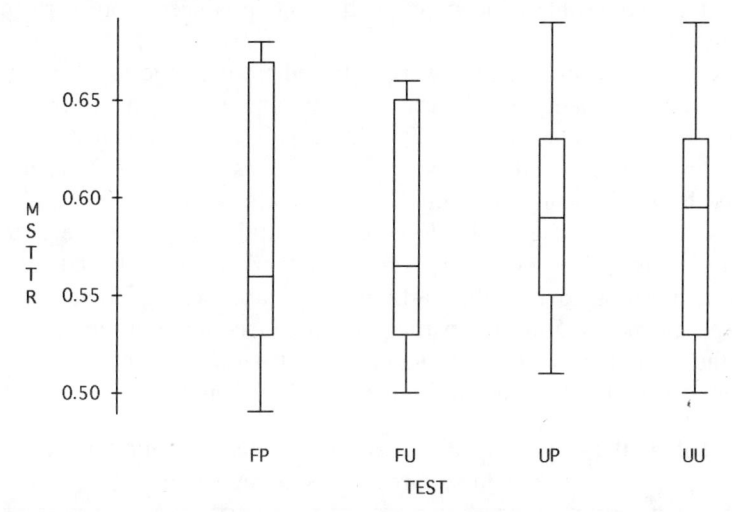

FIGURE 10.4a Distribution of lexical density (MSTTR) across conditions.

differences between conditions. In effect, the means and medians obtained across conditions under this measurement are quite close. Thus, no single condition had perceptible effects on the lexical density of participants' output.

Syntactical complexity measurements have been represented by Figure 10.4b. Although a single outlier is evident in the FU condition, it does

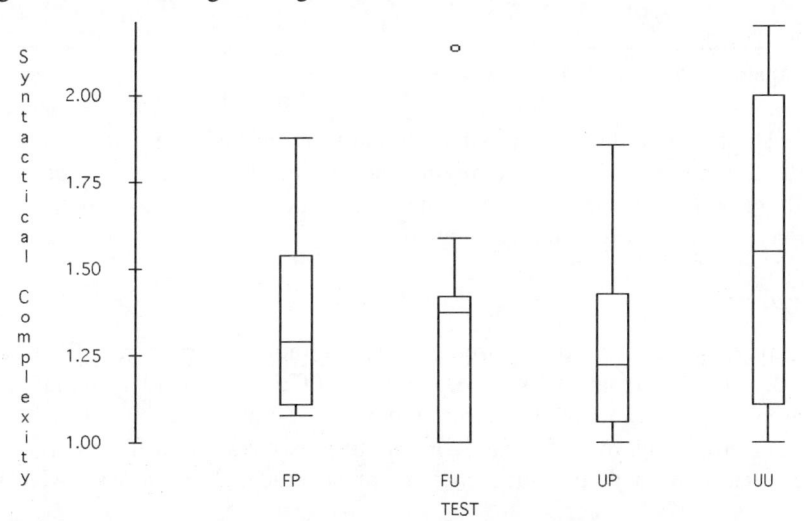

FIGURE 10.4b Distribution of syntactical complexity across conditions with a single outlier.

not interfere with the normal distribution of data and was, therefore, retained. The UU condition produced an identical mean and median at 1.55. A noticeably larger number of participants scored in or around the mean, which is also the highest of all the conditions. The one-way ANOVA carried out on syntactical complexity scores revealed that probability of difference between the conditions was 0.1525. Thus, although a significant difference is not evident a slight difference does exist. Therefore, under the UU condition, the first condition to be administered devoid of strategic planning and task familiarity, a noticeable majority of participants produced more verb forms in general.

Syntactical variety scores were obtained from categories of verb forms, namely, voice, modality and aspect. Such nominal data lends itself to the chi-squared statistic (Cohen et al. 2000: 251). This data returned no significant differences between conditions post chi-square test. Table 10.2 carries scores obtained by participants under this measure and a summary of the chi-square findings. Disappointingly, the FP condition did not encourage a majority of participants to produce more variety of verb forms. The UP condition, however, encouraged half the participants to use two different verb forms. Although an encouraging five participants produced three different verb forms under the FU condition, exact same number of participants produced the same number of verb forms again under the UU condition.

Table 10.2 Syntactical Variety Scores across Conditions and Chi-square Test Summary

Number of Different Verb Forms	FP	FU	UP	UU
1	2	5	2	0
2	4	2	6	4
3	4	5	2	5
4	1	0	2	1
5	0	0	0	2
6	1	0	0	0

Chi-square = 20.17 with 15 df, $p = 0.1656$.

Therefore, although no single condition pushed the participants to produce a noticeable increase in the variety of verb forms, the planning condition alone appears to have influenced 50 per cent of the participants to produce slightly more complex language.

Accuracy

Accuracy was measured at three levels: (i) ratio of error-free T-units to overall T-units, (ii) target-like use of articles (TLUA) and (iii) percentage of self-repairs. The ratio of error-free T-units to T-units distribution has been represented by Figure 10.5a. The UP condition is markedly different from the other conditions with this measurement of accuracy. The one-way ANOVA

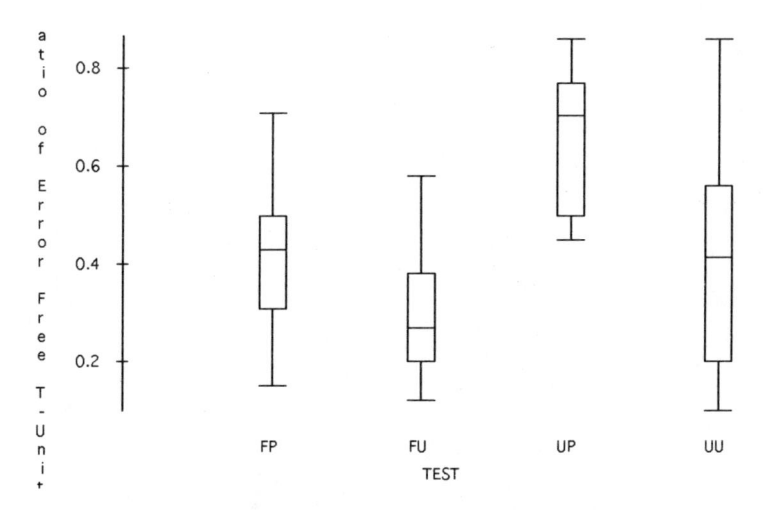

FIGURE 10.5a Distribution of ratio of error-free T-units to T-units across conditions.

also revealed significant difference (F_3, 44 $P \leq 0.0001$). The post-hoc test highlighted the UP condition as being significantly different in all three cases, the findings of which are set out in Table 10.3. Thus, the participants' output was significantly more accurate under the UP condition.

TABLE 10.3 Post-Hoc test Summary for Ratio of Error-free T-units to T-units

	Difference	Standard Error	Probability
FU – FP	–0.115000	0.0678	0.097003
UP – FP	0.255833	0.0678	*0.000479*
UP – FU	0.370833	0.0678	*0.000002*
UU – FP	0.005000	0.0678	0.941562
UU – FU	0.120000	0.0678	0.083748
UU – UP	–0.250833	0.0678	*0.000599*

The one-way ANOVA carried out on TLUA scores revealed no significant differences between conditions. Distribution under this measurement is represented by Figure 10.5b. The mean scores for TLUA, although not significantly different, appear to be slightly higher under conditions administered in the second session—FU and UP. These returned identical means, 84% ± 3.22 (FU), ± 3.53 (UP), which are the highest across conditions. The FU condition reveals more homogeneous data as its median is closer to its mean, indicative of a larger number of participants having produced similar quantities of TLUA under this condition. Thus, although significant differences do not exist, it would seem that the FU and UP conditions enabled learners to be slightly more accurate with their use of articles than the conditions administered during the first data collection session.

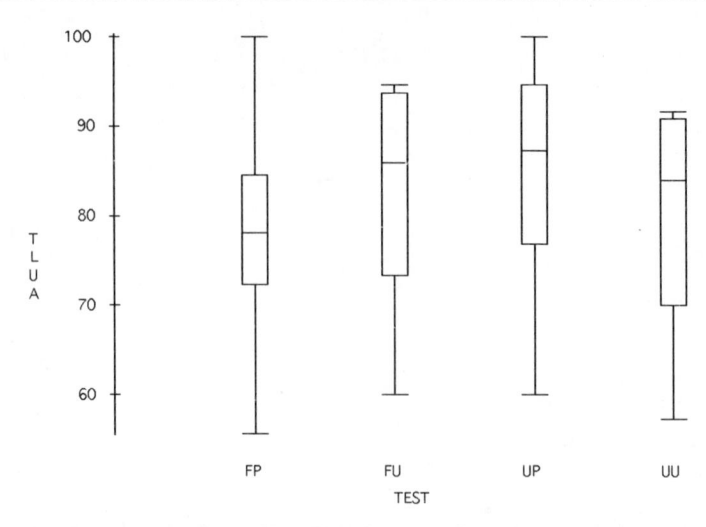

FIGURE 10.5b Distribution of target-like use of articles across conditions.

The previous measurements are indicative of accuracy of the finished product while the following measurement regards accuracy during the process of production (Guerrero 2004: 215). Thus, the percentage of self-repairs is indicative of participants attempting to correct and improve upon their own speech in real time. The data collected for the measurement of percentages of self-repairs was extremely skewed and, therefore, not normal. In order to effectuate the one-way ANOVA, this data was log transformed so that it was distributed normally. This ANOVA, however, returned no significant differences between groups. Figure 10.5c illustrates the means and standard errors achieved across conditions. It would appear that the participants tended to self-correct more during the first session of data gathering under the UU and FP conditions than during the second session. As mentioned previously, this data is highly skewed and, thus, findings here may be more indicative of individual participants' priorities to produce more accurate language than any influence of the conditions implemented in this study.

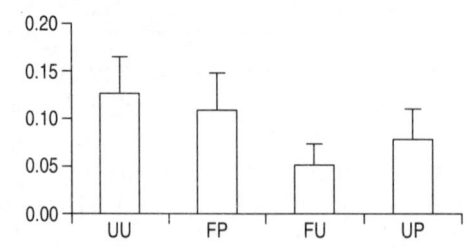

FIGURE 10.5c Percentage of self-repair means and standard errors across conditions.

Affective Variables

A Likert scale was used to elicit responses as this device would accommodate participant sensitivity via numbers (Cohen et al. 2000: 253). The mean scores from the affective variables questionnaire are depicted in Figure 10.6. The higher the value, the more negative the participants' perceptions are.

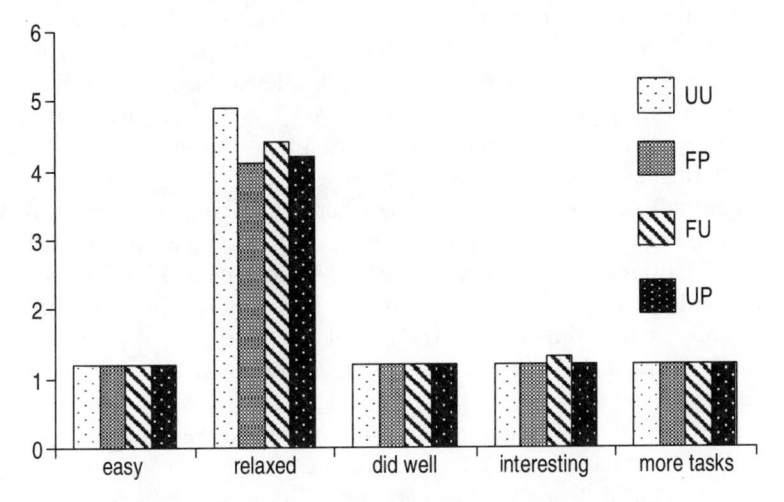

FIGURE 10.6 Affective variables mean scores.

An identical mean value, 1.2, resulted across conditions for participants' perceptions of levels of difficulty, performance and pedagogical usefulness. This result is also true for the level of interest although the FU condition scored slightly higher at 1.33. Thus, under all conditions, the tasks were perceived to be easy, well performed and interesting. The only difference to be found across these measures is the FU condition, the Agent Smith task which participants perceived to be less interesting to execute than the other tasks.

The participants' perceptions of stress induced by the different conditions provide the widest range across conditions. Under the UU condition the task was perceived to be the most stressful and clearly more difficult, 0.5, than the FU condition. The tasks used under the FP and UP conditions were perceived to be more or less equal by participants separated by 0.1. Thus, the task operated under the FP condition was perceived to be the least stressful to perform during the experiment.

Protocol analysis

The purpose of the protocol analysis was to examine participants' perceptions of the questions involved in the affective variables questionnaire in more detail, thus, shedding more light on their perceptions of the tasks administered under each condition.

Eleven participants fully expressed their preferences with regard to each task. The participants were divided on which of the four tasks was preferred. Five and six participants considered best both the *Mrs. Brown task* told under the FP condition and the *Halley met Barry* task told under the UP condition, respectively. Three participants considered the *Mrs. Brown* task the least attractive, while the *Halley met Barry* task was considered the worst by two. Six participants mentioned that the *Agent Smith* task used in the FU condition was the least interesting story and contained pictures that did not clearly reveal the storyline. One participant directly mentioned that more effort was required during this retelling as her "mind is in difficulty". Thus, the participants may have had more processing problems during this task, which concurs with the quantitative findings above. The FU condition in effect results the lowest and the second lowest throughout the mean scores of each measure of fluency, complexity and accuracy.

A contradiction of sorts is revealed here as the *Agent Smith* task was awarded the highest score by the majority of participants in the affective variables questionnaire. As reported earlier, 50 per cent of the participants ($n = 6$) mentioned that this story was the least interesting and contained complex images that did not clearly reveal the storyline. A total of eight participants awarded the score of one to the *Agent Smith* task used under the FU condition.

The level of difficulty that participants perceived was dictated primarily by the clarity of the pictures in the wordless comic strips. A recurring comment was that of "knowing the vocabulary" to describe the pictures. Two participants felt that the planning time and repetition of task rendered the storytelling easier as these conditions required "less effort".

The level of stress was increased for three participants by the presence of the digital recorders. This stress was less during the second session of data gathering as participants were becoming more accustomed to the recorder. Two participants commented on their awareness that the experiment was not "a test". The vocabulary theme arose again as participants felt that knowing the vocabulary made them relax. Another two participants commented that the stories told under the familiar condition, thus, repeated tasks, reduced their stress levels.

The participants' perception of what enabled them to perform well was, again, "knowing the vocabulary". Eight participants drew attention to this theme in their answers to question five protocol analyses. Clarity of the pictures and being familiar with the task were also mentioned by two participants.

The participants commented that the predominant pedagogical utility of the tasks was speaking practice. Seven participants felt that the tasks provided them with opportunities to speak freely. Two raised the theme of acquisition as they felt that the tasks provided them with occasions to learn. One of them commented that teacher correction needed to be present in order for any learning to occur, however. A single participant commented that being forced to think in English was a positive feature of the tasks.

10.4.5 Discussion of Findings

Fluency

The most noticeable effects are found under the UU condition. The means in general and interpretation of descriptive statistics tend to favour this condition. No familiarity and no strategic planning of task, therefore, appears to have caused changes on three levels of the dependent variables in this study. The participants produced more text in general as the total syllables and pruned syllables results were highest here.

The participants' perceptions, from the affective variables questionnaire, reveal that the UU condition appeared to raise their stress levels significantly more than the other conditions. However, this finding is not repeated in the protocol analysis interviews. This incongruence may be more a consequence of habituation over the conditions than the presence of the digital recorders. The UU condition was, in effect, the first treatment to be implemented, thus, the participants' perceptions of higher stress levels may have been caused by recording themselves for the first time rather than the lack of strategic planning or familiarity with task content. Thus, the argument that more processing occurred in the conceptualizer during the UU condition is weakened by its position in the overall design.

The total syllables and pruned syllables measures are indicative of the participants producing longer texts without the consideration of how long they took to do so. The fluency rates A and B, however, represent the speed at which these texts were produced. Therefore, these measures illustrate how quickly participants spoke and are more indicative of fluency as they account, albeit indirectly, for any pausing, thus online planning, which may have occurred during production. The FP condition was perceived to be slightly less stressful to perform than the UP condition and significantly less stressful than the UU and FU conditions. Therefore, the presence of the planning variable may have rendered the FP and UP conditions less stressful as less processing was required during the narration.

A closer look at differences between the FP and UP conditions shed further light on the findings. The highest means for total syllables and fluency rates A and B are to be found under the UP condition, the last to be implemented of the experiment. Interpretation of descriptive statistics, however, favours the FP condition as scores are not as widespread. Thus, some participants raised the means considerably during UP by speaking more quickly.

My opinion here, formed by personal observation during the last few candidates' performances, is that the participants were aware that the UP condition was the last to be implemented of the experiment. Although under this condition the ratio of error-free T-units is significantly different, this may be more indicative of the participants' playing safe through avoidance. In effect, the syntactical variety and complexity means are noticeably low while means for fluency levels are markedly high under the UP condition. Thus, it is suggested here that some participants tended to speak more quickly in order to get the task "over and done with", but in doing so they did not stretch their IL.

This partially corroborates the findings in the previous studies (Guerrero

2004; Yuan and Ellis 2003; Ellis 2000; Mehnert 1999; Ortega 1999; Wendel 1997; Foster and Skehan 1996) where consensus is in favour of strategic planning. Bygate's (2001: 42; 1996: 144) studies on task familiarity also report increased fluency. Gass et al. (1999: 572) found that "proficiency" increased with familiarity and Bygate and Samuda (2005: 69) argue that, in general, repetition enabled their participants to perform at a more sophisticated level. Wording, however, in the previous studies regarding the effects of familiarity on production is ambiguous. We must assume that when Bygate and Samuda, and Gass et al. refer to 'proficiency' and 'sophistication', they are referring to some aspect of fluency.

Disappointingly, the familiarity condition, UF, revealed some of the lowest scores across the conditions for fluency. A basic assumption proposed for the moment is that the low scores of FU are related more to the specific task than to the condition. Although results for UP are less clear-cut, it would appear that the participants' perceived the presence of planning time as a positive feature of task design. The argument, however, in favour of the planning condition alone producing enhanced fluency is weakened by the position of the treatment in the experiment as mentioned earlier. Thus, the findings from this study imply that the combination of familiarity and strategic planning enhanced the participants' ability to produce more language in less time and corroborate findings of previous research.

Complexity

Syntactical complexity was noticeably higher under the UU condition. Thus, the participants attempted to use more verb forms during this treatment. Syntactical variety was slightly better, however, under the UP condition. Lexical density measurements, MSTTR, were close across conditions, which concurs with Wendel's (1997: 118) findings regarding word families. However, previous research reports predominantly positive effects of strategic planning on complexity in general (Ellis 2005: 23). Mehnert's (1998) 10-minute planners resulted in more complex output. It must be remembered that in the current study, five minutes strategic planning time was allowed. Guerrero (2004) reports no changes in syntactic complexity across conditions regardless of planning time and, hence, the findings from the current study tend to support his findings.

Studies on the effects of task familiarity and repetition also report predominantly positive effects on complexity. Bygate (2001: 42) explicitly refers to complexity as being increased by familiarity, but previously he (1996: 143) refers to "quality of talk" as being superior. Bygate and Samuda (2005: 67) refer to more 'formulation' of information while Lynch and Maclean (2000: 225) report more complex language, but do not overtly report on the effects of task rehearsal on learner output. Gass et al. (1999: 572) continue this trend of ambiguous language by reporting positive effects on lexical sophistication in their study.

Although the findings of this study regarding complexity do not coincide with the majority of research on planning and familiarity they concur, nonetheless, with the research of Wendel (1997), Mehnert (1998) and Guerrero (2004) regarding strategic planning. Thus, the syntactical complexity is higher under the UU condition, under the UP condition there is slightly more syntactical variety for 50 per cent of participants ($n = 12$), while the lexical density remains unchanged across conditions. The UU condition was the first to be implemented in the experiment and, as discussed above, was perceived by the participants to be the most stressful during the affective variables questionnaire. This stress appears to have been caused by the presence of the recorder which Willis (1996: 34) suggests gives a higher status to the language produced as performance is rendered more permanent. Thus, the participants may have produced more complex language under the UU condition due to the first encounter with being recorded. This tendency was not carried over to the following tasks, however, suggesting that habituation (familiarity with being recorded) was taking place.

Accuracy

The mixed results regarding accuracy of this study reproduce the mixed findings of previous research (Ellis 2005: 22). Both the mean and analysis of descriptive statistics favour the UU and UP conditions. Significant difference was found for the ratio of error-free units under the UP condition although the percentage of self-repairs under the UU treatment revealed extremely skewed data.

The findings under the UU condition for percentage of self-repairs tend to concur with Mehnert's (1998) findings. In his study, the one-minute planners were more accurate than those who had five and ten minutes to plan, while the UP condition confirms Guerrero's (2004) findings for error-free T-units. It is suggested here that this particular measure cannot be taken at face value in the current study as syntactical complexity and variety scores were not significantly different under this treatment. The findings for error-free T-units under the UP condition may be more indicative of the participants' unwillingness to shift attention to formulation (Ellis 2005: 22) than any effect of the condition.

Target-like uses of articles were similar across the conditions in this study. Although the FU condition reveals more positive findings, these were not significantly different from the other treatments. This finding concurs with those of Ortega (1999) and Crookes (1989) who also report that articles remained unchanged in their studies. Ortega (1999), however, found that noun modifiers were improved in her study.

The findings within the research on task familiarity and repetition report predominantly positive findings on accuracy. Bygate (1996: 142) reports marginally fewer errors, significantly increased use of past simple regular forms but a drop in the use of past 'be' which coincided with an increase of lexical verbs. Bygate's later study (1998: 43) also reports positive findings as self-correction increased and a greater capacity for form was evident in the repeated task. It, however, revealed that accuracy was only marginally influenced (Bygate 2001: 43). This contrasting result, Bygate suggests, is due to the operation of the T-unit as a means to measure accuracy (*ibid.*). Lynch and Maclean (2000: 245) also report increases in accuracy and suggest that these were caused by practice alone. Gass et al. (1999: 572) report greater accuracy caused by repetition with task content, but when the content was changed accuracy dropped.

Although the findings of this study are mixed, they concur with previous studies regarding strategic planning (Wendel 1997; Mehnert 1998; Ortega 1999; Foster and Skehan 1999; Yuan and Ellis 2003; Guerrero 2004) but not with those concerning familiarity (Bygate 1996, 1999a, 1999b, 2001; Gass et al. 1999; Lynch and Maclean 2000). It is, perhaps, early in the day for such comparisons to be drawn as the body of research regarding familiarity and repetition of tasks is limited and varies in definitions of familiarity. These have predominantly used a variety of measurements and focused initially on small numbers of students (Lynch and Maclean 2000; Bygate 1996).

10.5 IMPLICATIONS FOR TASK-BASED LEARNING

Although this study does not reveal overtly negative findings regarding TBL, it has revealed to be an immensely complicated pedagogical methodology that cannot be taken on faith. Although earlier studies had predominantly validated this methodology (Ellis 2005: 27), it must be remembered that some of the strategic planning research was conducted on homogeneous groups (Yuan and Ellis 2003; Guerrero 2004). Real classrooms rarely present such homogeneity and this must be recognised in TBL research. It would appear from this study that outliers at the top end of the range performed particularly well across conditions and, apparently, would benefit from TBL in general. The majority of participants, however, benefited only in terms of increased fluency. In short, TBL research is a long way from justifying its unanimous acceptance as the methodology for language learning. In fact, to do so would be like accepting one of the language teaching methods that have long since been discredited (Stern 1983; Howatt 1984). Indeed, the overall tendency to embrace innovative approaches or methodologies in ELT, regardless of their theoretical underpinnings or merits, is perhaps indicative of the growing pains of a developing professional community.

Thus, although the combination of strategic planning and familiarity may have enhanced fluency in this study, no discernable effects were found for complexity and accuracy. This, however, does not limit the pedagogical implications of TBL to fluency development alone. Participants' intuition that post-task corrective feedback may have enhanced their learning may be indicative of a strong interface position between declarative and procedural knowledge and warrants further research of a longitudinal nature. The current research is limited in that it is cross-sectional and reports findings of the effects on, not long-term changes in, the participants' output. It is to such limitations of the current research that we now turn our attention.

10.6 RECOMMENDATIONS FOR FUTURE RESEARCH

There are some considerations deriving from this study which could enhance future research, particularly in the realm of familiarity of task content. Familiarity of task and strategic planning do appear to have positive effects on learners' fluency although the findings for these conditions, when separated, require further research. How this research is conducted needs to be thought out clearly as the familiarity variable does not limit itself to content alone.

The repeated measures within group design hamper the chronological implementation of conditions, thus, adding undesirable carryover effects which have been already highlighted. The operation of a between groups design may solve a number of issues while the participants would still act as their own controls. The first of these issues regards familiarity with being recorded. Operating a between groups design would ensure that each group could be exposed to the recording under the unfamiliar condition for their first experience with the experiment. Separating tasks across individual sessions, although more time consuming, would also provide more flexibility of condition implementation. Thus, the planning conditions could not overtly influence other conditions excessively.

The broader question of task, in both planning and familiarity studies, is complex. As was pointed out earlier, an element of familiarity with task is constantly prevalent when the same task type or genre is operated across conditions. This may be desirable in some studies regarding augmenting familiarity but may act as a confounding variable when it regards repetition. Operating different types of tasks across conditions adds further dimensions to studies as cognitive demands are altered by different tasks. There is no easy answer here as familiarity is intrinsically connected to proceduralised knowledge. Thus, one participant may be a particularly avid cinema fan and regularly relate film segments to peers while another may not. Establishing which types of tasks have not been proceduralised by a group of participants' stops short of looking for the proverbial 'needle in the haystack'. How participants would react to this hypothetical unfamiliar task is also questionable as lack of prior knowledge would, most likely, result in silence.

A final recommendation regards the measurement of complexity. In order to maintain consistency and facilitate comparisons to previous research measurements of syntactical complexity and variety were operated in this study. While analysing individual narratives, it became clear that some individuals were operating more complex language by attempting to use perfect and continuous aspects. It is suggested here that more detailed accounts of verb form components such as auxiliaries and grammatical morpheme additions to verbs need to be provided in future research. Two examples from LuDF's narrative under the UU condition follow in order to illustrate this issue:

1. last week mrs edwards have look an crash cars between two cars
2. and she was called for to for witness

Under syntactical complexity measures, individual verb forms are awarded a score of one. The final result is a ratio of overall to incorrect verb forms. The above examples would, thus, result as a ratio of 1:2 and reveal a final score of 0.5. Had LuDF used the present simple 'look' and 'the police *call* her', far less complex forms, she would nonetheless have scored identically under the syntactical complexity measurement. Thus, credit is not given with this measurement to the actual complexity of the individual verb forms. LuDF has attempted to use the perfect aspect in the first case and passive voice in the second. Although syntactical variety measures attempt to account for such complexity it too falls short as it does not account for error. Thus, a ratio of correct implementation of verb components to overall verb components may reveal both attempts to stretch interlanguage and how successfully this is done. For example, LuDF would score 3 for the overall components *have* and *was*, and the grammatical morpheme *ed*; two of these components are accurately implemented, thus, a ratio of 2:3 is obtained with a final score of 0.66. It is, therefore, suggested that this type of complexity measure, ratio of correct verb components to overall verb components, reveals more accurately individuals' attempts to be more complex and how successful their attempts are.

10.7 CONCLUSION

The results reported here have suggested evidence in favour of the combination of task repetition and strategic planning enhancing fluency. This finding is accounted for by the participants' being able to turn their spare capacity during a second encounter with a task and where provision for planning time is made toward fluency. This pointed to increased automaticity as the participants were able to access knowledge more efficiently. The effects on fluency, complexity and accuracy were deemed null in this study, however, due to insignificant findings. Although the ratio of error-free T-units to T-units was significantly different under the UP condition, it is suggested here that performance, and not condition, effects caused the difference. Thus, the participants tended to produce more accurate language through avoidance in order to draw an end to the experiment.

In conclusion, it would appear that combining strategic planning time and task familiarity may enhance learners' fluency. Effects on complexity and accuracy remain mixed, however. The repeated measures within group design may not be the ideal as this may confuse effects caused by conditions and the design. Thus, the combination of both familiarity and strategic planning warrants considerable future study.

REFERENCES

ALTE (The Association of Language Testers in Europe). *Framework and Can-Do.* 2005. http: // www.alte.org/can_do/framework/index.cfm.

Bärenfanger, O., Beyer, S., Aguado, K., and Stevener, J., *On the Functions of L2 Speech Production and Related Cognitive Processes for the Acquisition of L2 Speech Competence,* Research Project of the German Science Foundation (DFG), 2002. http://www.linguistik_online.de/1_01/DFG_English.html.

Batstone, R., "Planning as discourse activity," in R. Ellis, 2005, 277–295.

Bruton, A., "From tasking purposes to purposing tasks," *ELT Journal* **56**:3 (2002): 280–288.

Bygate, M., "Effects of task repetition: Appraising the developing language of learners" in D. Willis and J. Willis, 1996, 136–146.

_____, "Quality of language and purpose of task: Patterns of learners' language on two oral communication tasks," *Language Teaching Research* **3**.3 (1999a): 185–214.

_____, "Task as context for the framing, reframing and unframing of language," *System* **27**:1 (1999b): 33–48.

_____, "Effects of task repetition on the structure and control of oral language" in M. Bygate, P. Skehan, and M. Swain, 2001, 23–48.

Bygate, M. and Samuda, V., "Integrative planning through the use of task-repetition" in R. Ellis, 2005, 37–74.

Cohen, L., Manion, L. and Morrison, K. (Eds.), *Research Methods in Education,* 5th ed., London: Routledge Falmer, 2000.

Crookes, G., "Planning and interlanguage variation," *Studies in Second Language Acquisition* **11** (1989): 367–383.

De Bot, K., "A bilingual production model: Levelt's 'speaking' model adapted," *Applied Linguistics* **13**.1 (1992): 1–24.

_____, "Interlanguage variability in narrative discourse: Style in the use of the past tense," *Studies in Second Language Acquisition* **9** (1987): 12–20.

_____, *The Study of Second Language Acquisition,* Oxford: OUP, 1994.

_____, *Task Based Language Learning and Teaching,* Oxford: OUP, 2003.

_____, (Ed.), *Planning and Task Performance in a Second Language,* Amsterdam: John Benjamins Publishing Company, 2005.

_____, "Interlanguage Variability in Narrative Discourse: Style in the Use of Past Tense," *Studies in Second Language Acquisition,* **9** (1987): 12–20.

De Bot, K., "Task Based Research and Language Pedagogy," *Language Teaching Research*, **4**.3 (2000): 193–220.

Ellis, R., *Task Based Language Learning and Teaching*, Oxford: Oxford University Press, 2003.

_____, *Planning and Task Performance in a Second Language*, Amsterdam: John Benjamins Publishing Company, 2005.

Faulkner, F., Swann, J., Baker, S., Bird, M., and Carty, J., *Professional Development in Action: Methodology Handbook*, Milton Keynes: Open University, 1991.

Foster, P. and Skehan, P., "The influence of planning and task type on second language performance," *Studies in Second Language Acquisition* **18** (1996): 299–323.

_____, "The influence of source of planning and focus of planning on task-based performance," *Language Teaching Research* **3**.3 (1999): 215–247.

Foster, P., Tonkyn, A., and Wigglesworth, G., "Measuring spoken discourse: A unit for all reasons," *Applied Linguistics* **21**.3 (2000), 333–353.

Gass, S., Mackey, A., Alvarez-Torres, M.J., and Fernández-García, "The effects of task repetition on linguistic output, *Language Learning* **49**.4 (1999): 549–581.

Giorgi, A., *Phenomenology and Psychological Research*, Pittsburgh: Duquesne University Press, 1985.

Guerrero, R.G., *Task Complexity and L2 Narrative Oral production*, Ph.D. Thesis, University of Barcelona, 2004.

_____, Personal e-mail communication received May 11, 2006.

Hagen, L.K., "Constructs and measurement in parameter models of second-language acquisition," in D. Cohen and S. Gass, 1994, 62–87.

Helgesen, M., "One more time, with feeling—Bringing task recycling to the classroom," *The English Connection* **7**.3 (2003): 5–7, 18.

Howatt, A.P.R., *A History of Language Teaching*, Oxford: OUP, 1984.

Izumi, S., "Comprehension and production processes in second language learning: In search of the psycholinguistic rationale of the output hypothesis," *Applied Linguistics* **24**.2 (2003): 168–196.

Levelt, W.J.M., *Speaking: From Intention to Articulation*, Cambridge, MA: Massachusetts Institute of Technology Press, 1989.

Long, M.H., "A role for instruction in second language acquisition: Task-based language teaching," in K. Hyltenstam and M. Pienemann, 1985, 77–79.

Lynch, T. and Maclean, J., "Exploring the benefits of task repetition and recycling for classroom language learning," *Language Teaching Research* **4**.3 (2000): 221–250.

Mehnert, U., "The effects of different lengths of time for planning on second language performance," *Studies in Second Language Acquisition* **20** (1998): 52–83.

MTELP, *Michigan Test Website,* 2006. http://www.michigan-proficiency-exams.com/mtelp.html.

Ortega, L., "Planning and focus on form in L2 oral performance," *Studies in Second Language Acquisition* **21** (1999): 108–148.

_____, "What do learners plan? Learner-driven attention to form during pre-task planning," in R. Ellis, 2005, 77–109.

Prabhu, N.S., *Second Language Pedagogy,* Oxford: Oxford University Press, 1987.

Robinson, P., "The cognition hypothesis, task design, and adult task-based language learning," *Second Language Studies* **21**.2 (2003): 45–105.

Skehan, P., "Second language acquisition research and task-based instruction," in J. Willis, and D. Willis, 1996, 17–30.

_____, "A non-marginal role for tasks," *ELT Journal* **56**.3 (2003): 289–295.

Skehan, P. and Foster, P., "Task type and task processing conditions as influences on foreign language performance," *Language Teaching Research* **1**.3 (1997): 185–211.

_____, "The influence of task structure and processing conditions on narrative retellings," *Language Learning* **49**.1(1999): 93–120.

Stern, H.H., *Fundamental Concepts of Language Teaching,* Oxford: OUP, 1983.

Swain, M., "Communicative competence: Some roles of comprehensible input and comprehensible output in its development,' in S. Gass and Madden, 1985: 235–253.

Swales, J., *Genre Analysis: English in Academic and Research Settings,* Cambridge: Cambridge University Press, 1990.

Wendel, J.N., *Planning and Second-language Narrative Production,* Ph.D. Thesis, Temple University, 1997.

Willis, J., *A Framework for Task-based Learning,* London: Longman, 1996.

Yuan F. and Ellis, R., "The effects of pre-task planning and on-line planning on fluency, complexity, and accuracy in L2 monologic oral production," *Applied Linguistics* **24**.1 (2003): 1–27.

Chapter 11

A FINE 'HOW DO YOU DO'
Contextual Factors within English Greetings

— ALEX BARATTA

11.1 INTRODUCTION

This chapter analyzes the speech act of English greetings based on a variety of contextual factors as a suggested means to develop the communicative competence of L2 speakers within this pragmatic field. While several studies have already addressed the importance of context within real-life language use (Omaggio Hadley 1993; Jung 2002; Kasper and Rose 2002; Yu 2006; Grieve and Seebus 2008), there appears to be a lack of available literature which focuses specifically on the contextual factors involved when native English speakers greet each other. This study, therefore, seeks to fill a suggested gap within the current literature, by discussing the many contextual issues involved in English greetings. It also offers pedagogical suggestions for EFL teachers as to how this speech act might be approached within the classroom.

11.2 THE IMPORTANCE OF CONTEXT

Most, if not all, EFL students undoubtedly wish to communicate like native English speakers in a manner that sounds natural in terms of pronunciation and correct in terms of syntax. Both these elements can be considered part of communicative competence (Hymes and Gumperz 1972) though they alone would not include an arguably more important aspect which Hymes does— the role of context. As this study focuses on competence based on an understanding of the role that context plays within speech acts, the logical theoretical starting point is that of *pragmatic competence*. In other words, communicating in a competent manner means that EFL students must know more than just correct grammar. They must first consider the context in which the communicative act takes place. As Jung (2002, 1) states:

... communicating effectively and efficiently in any given language requires more than just linguistic knowledge. The ability to use this linguistic knowledge appropriately in the given sociocultural context is also essential. Hence, pragmatics is an indispensable aspect of language ability in order for second language (L2) learners to understand and be understood in their interactions with native speakers (NSs)".

Furthermore, Yu (2006) states that students "have to internalize sociolinguistic rules that can guide them in the choice of appropriate forms," (p. 1), leading to sociolinguistic competence. If we, therefore, apply the statements of Jung and Yu to the English greeting *How do you do?*, we might analyze it based on two perspectives: (i) syntactic and (ii) pragmatic. From a syntactic perspective, the greeting obeys the rules of Standard English grammar. This particular greeting is also considered polite within formal contexts (as is its arguably expected response, *I'm fine thank you, and you?*). Pragmatically speaking, however, it might come across as *unnecessarily* formal, even unnatural, within a great many informal contexts, and even within first time greetings such as greeting people at a party. While Jung (2002) states that "in developing pragmatic competence, learners have to become familiar with the cultural ethos associated with politeness as shared by members of the L2 community" (p. 6), this is sometimes not the case. Therefore, the view put forward is that it is possible to be *too* polite, as the greeting above arguably demonstrates, if used within informal contexts with the native speakers of English.

Kasper and Rose (2002) further state, "L2-specific sociopragmatic knowledge is required in order to choose the correct grammatical forms" (p. 28). This suggests that context is the deciding factor in choosing language that is appropriate, which may or may not conform to the rules of Standard English syntax, suggesting that there are situations in which communicative competence can be achieved, in fact, by *flouting* grammatical rules, a point mentioned by Beebe (1995). This can be seen in the following example:

Speaker A: *How you doing?*
Speaker B: *Pretty good.*

If the verbal exchange above is first considered from a syntactic point of view and, then from a pragmatic point of view, the analyses are quite different. The first sentence is grammatically incorrect (i.e. in terms of Standard English) because the copula verb is missing (i.e. are); the second sentence is grammatically incorrect as it is a fragment and, therefore, not a complete sentence. However, in the context of a greeting between two close friends, perhaps more so in the United States (than, say, the United Kingdom), it is perfectly an acceptable form of communication. It is not claimed that it would be a pragmatic error to ask an American 'how *are* you doing' rather, that the copula is, in informal contexts, pragmatically unnecessary. The implication that these two greetings have for L2 English speakers is that they reveal the importance of considering a speech act from a contextualized perspective in order to help the L2 English speakers develop more authentic English skills.

The claims that have been made thus far regarding the importance of context within communicative competence are hardly controversial. Communicative competence and the contextual factors within have long been recognized, dating back to the research of Hymes (1972). As Omaggio Hadley (1993) points out, "The idea that language learning should be contextualized is certainly not new in language teaching" (p. 125), adding that

> Most educators agree today that students must eventually know how to use the language forms they have learned in authentic communication situations (*ibid.*).

Nonetheless, it has been necessary to discuss communicative competence in order to provide the theoretical framework from which this study derives. However, while such an approach has been applied to a variety of speech acts in the English language, such as expressing gratitude (Eisenstein and Bodman 1993), apologizing (Bergman and Kasper 1993) and complaining (Olshtain and Weinbach 1993), it has yet to find its way to the study of how greetings are expressed in the English language.

11.3 WHY FOCUS ON GREETINGS?

Greetings are suggested to be a worthy focus of study for three reasons. First, it has already been stated that English greetings are a speech act that have not received a great deal of attention when compared with other speech acts within the English language. Omaggio Hadley (1993) considers greetings to be part of a context that involves "highly predictable everyday situation(s)." (p. 234) This predictability, thus implying a degree of simplicity, is perhaps one reason why English greetings have not been focused onto any great extent in research studies, in that they are assumed to be relatively straightforward. It is true that English greetings are generally short, consisting of, at the very most, just three separate verbal exchanges:

> Speaker A: *How are you?*
> Speaker B: *I'm fine thanks, and you?*
> Speaker A: *Fine.*

Therefore, it is perhaps also true that greetings do not require a great deal of time to learn and because they are generally short, the language used is perhaps easier to anticipate, suggesting that greetings are somewhat generalisable in terms of how to be initiated and how an addressee should respond. While this ties in with the predictability mentioned by Omaggio Hadley (1993), as does the comment of Kasper and Rose (2002) that American greetings in particular are "rather formulaic" (p. 151), it does not suggest that greetings are indeed as simple as they may be seen by some EFL teachers and students. Greetings can go beyond more 'traditional' adjacency pairs like *how are you? fine thanks*, and involve many other forms, which will be discussed in Section 11.5.

Second, greetings of some kind form the basis of great many human interactions. Many introductions begin with an initial greeting from which the conversation progresses and potential friendships can develop. Making new friends can be an important step in helping EFL students adjust to life in a new culture and, therefore, greetings are important to study. In fact, for nonnative English speakers who are living in an English-speaking country, any culture shock they may experience might be eased by making new friends who are part of the new culture.

Finally, by revealing the complexities of English greetings, this study seeks to subsequently avoid the implications of pedagogy which instructs EFL students in a rigid manner regarding real-world English. The following dialogue is taken from the online article, 'Survival English for Travelers' (Schmidt 2006). Here, an EFL teacher discusses the crux of the matter when he walked into his classroom on the first day:

> When I walked into the class, I said a very casual, "How's it going?"
>
> Nothing.
>
> "HOW ARE YOU?"
>
> A look of relief on their faces as they replied, "Fine. And you?" in the robotic fashion that they learned in middle school.
>
> (Introduction, para. 2)

There is nothing 'wrong' with *how are you* as a greeting, but the situations in which it might be more natural to use a greeting such as *how's it going?* or many other forms should also be considered. Greetings arguably form an integral part of an EFL class curriculum in the first instance, often being used on the first day of many EFL classes to allow students in part to practise their English by greeting their fellow classmates. This implies that the importance of greetings has not been ignored in the classroom and is, therefore, another reason to explore this speech act further in order to discover a multitude of ways in which native English speakers greet each other.

11.4 PREVIOUS RESEARCH

Research into the speech act of greetings in English is sparse, with Kasper and Rose (2002) stating that the bulk of research regarding speech acts in the English language is focused on requests. Relatively few studies which do focus on the speech act of greetings investigate greetings in an L2 language *other* than English, such as Kiswahili (Omar 1991), Indonesian (DuFon 1999), French (Hoffman-Hicks 1999) and Japanese (Ohta 2001b).

The research of DuFon (1999) might, however, suggest the ways in which L2 English speakers may encounter difficulties with English greetings. Her research involved six L2 Indonesian speakers who were focused on the acquisition of politeness as used within the language, to include greetings. The L2 Indonesian students, whose native language was English, "displayed a clear preference for greetings that were semantically closest to English" (p. 150), while "only slowly making use of what (to them) were more exotic greeting routines" (p. 152). This also has implications for nonnative English speakers, in that while Indonesian greetings such as *have you eaten yet?* may seem exotic to an English speaker, it might be the case that certain English greetings can be just as 'exotic' to a nonnative speaker of English. For example, the greeting *hey* (used by many young Americans, to which a response of *hey* is expected), may sound unusual to a nonnative English speaker and it is these more 'unusual' greetings that this chapter seeks to discuss. Such greetings as these should also be considered as a means to help L2 English speakers develop more authentic English skills. DuFon's study further addressed not just the ways in which L2 speakers of Indonesian initiated greetings, but also how they *responded* to greetings. This illustrates that developing the communicative competence of EFL students in English greetings is a twofold process: more than just teaching students how to initiate conversation we also need to stress the importance of knowing how to *respond* to conversation, and this can only be accomplished if EFL students first understand what is meant by the utterance directed at them. Fraser (1983) states that how an addressee determines the content of a speaker's utterance is itself a part of pragmatic competence as opposed to simply focusing on how to initiate a contextually logical utterance. The EFL students, then, must know how to communicate as both addressors and addressees.

The research of Grieve and Seebus (2008) considers the pragmatic implications for English greetings that take place when a telephone conversation is initiated. Their data involved analysis of telephone greetings used by 12 native speakers of English in Melbourne and Australia, over the course of one week, for a total of 116 calls. While the greetings in this chapter apply specifically to face-to-face interaction, the study of Grieve and Seebus (2008) is nonetheless relevant for two reasons. First, it reveals that a speech act as relatively straightforward as a telephone greeting can be more complex than perhaps otherwise thought; likewise, the same can be said of general greetings. Therefore, the country in which the telephone call is made (e.g. Australia versus the United States) influences what is deemed to be appropriate communication. This suggests that even a speech act assumed to be largely homogeneous throughout the English-speaking world might not be so among native English speakers. For example, a native of Australia might be momentarily confused to hear an American utter the expression *uh-huh* (arguably, a filler), in response to *thank you*. In addition, an American visiting Australia or the United Kingdom might not expect to have *thank you* answered by *no worries*. Both *uh-huh* and *no worries*, however, used within the context of expressing gratitude, equate to *you're welcome*. If native English speakers can have problems understanding each other, it stands to reason that the problem can be compounded for *non*-native speakers. Second, the study of Grieve and Seebus also reveals how many contextual factors play a part in telephone greetings, to include gender, the purpose of the telephone call and age of the speaker(s), and the importance of context with regard to how people initiate and respond to greetings. They specifically focus on the adjacency pair of summons-answer, such as *Hello?* or *This is John speaking*, as the response to the 'summons' of a telephone ringing.

The research conducted by Grieve and Seebus on telephone greetings confirmed that, in addition to the response of *hello*, Australians also tend to answer the telephone with *G'day* (which is also a commonly used Australian greeting in general). This in itself is not problematic from the point of view of an EFL student making the phone call, unless he/she is unfamiliar with the Australian greeting (regardless of when and where it is used). Further, it is perhaps less problematic if the nonnative speaker is the participant who responds to the summons of the telephone ringing, as he/she would then be able to greet in a way that he/she is familiar with. Nonetheless, making a telephone call, or responding to one, can be quite a complex matter, and this is especially true considering that the researches of Chaika (1982), Hymes (1986) and Grieve and Seebus (2008) focus on just the *initiation* of conversation, before the purpose of the call has even been identified.

The studies by Chaika (1982) and Hymes (1986) discuss the cultural specificity of pragmatic rules regarding how a telephone conversation must be initiated, in concurrence with the general socio-cultural rules for communication, as discussed by Yu (2006). The research of O'Loughlin (1989) further suggests that the Americans tend to answer the telephone with *hello*, while the British people tend to answer with their last name and/or the last four digits of their telephone number. If a nonnative English speaker calls a friend in the United Kingdom, only to be greeted by *Smith?* or *1384?*, it is not implausible to suggest a degree of confusion on his/her part.

A further study by Clyne et al. (2006) discusses the importance of regional variation in greetings. While their research focuses on forms of address used in Germany and Sweden, it could be applied to greetings in the English language also. In this way, it suggests that how people greet in New York might be different from Los Angeles, further revealing contextual complexity within this subject. As EFL students travel to, and/or study in, a variety of English-speaking countries, this is another reason as to why English greetings from many contextual perspectives need to be considered.

Regarding the need for such a contextualized focus on English greetings, the work of Grieve and Seebus (2008) is comparable with a study by Kiefer (1980) who focuses on the contextual factors involved with greetings (i.e. greetings in the traditional sense), albeit in the Hungarian language. Though his focus is not on English greetings, the contextual factors he discusses have relevance for this study, based on an analysis of the location of the greeting, the rank of the two participants and their respective ages.

11.5 A CONTEXTUALIZED APPROACH TO ENGLISH GREETINGS

This section details how a contextualized approach to English greetings can be realized, based on the work of Kiefer (1980) and Grieve and Seebus (2008). To envision the contextual complexities of English greetings (or any other for that matter), an inverted triangle is an apt metaphor (Figure 11.1).

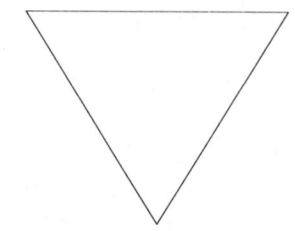

FIGURE 11.1 Inverted triangle to show contextual complexities of English language.

The implication is that the broader contextual factors reside at the top, with contextual factors becoming narrower as progression is made within the triangle. By simply drawing an inverted triangle on the board, it can become an effective method to help students visualize the contextual issues involved within English greetings due to its metaphorical nature (i.e. describing the levels of context in terms of a triangle). As Elbow states (1998), "metaphors make a big difference ..." (p. 18), as the use of figures of speech can help people form mental concepts of any subject. Wyrick (2002) concurs that such language helps produce images or pictures in people's minds, "helping them to understand unfamiliar or abstract subjects" (p. 325), such as 'context'. Therefore, the inverted triangle can become an effective starting point for the teaching of English greetings:

11.6 CONTEXTUAL FACTORS IN GREETINGS

11.6.1 Cultural Context

The broadest level is concerned with the country in which English is spoken as a native language and/or the region within a given English-speaking country. If the United States is the focus, then the common greetings within the country are obviously pertinent. The point to make is that greetings used in the United States differ from those used in other English-speaking countries, as English has several varieties spoken throughout the world with different implications regarding appropriate ways in which to initiate and respond to greetings.

11.6.2 Situational Context

The next proposed level refers to the location where the communication takes place, which can include a nightclub, a job interview, and a street corner. Kiefer (1980) regards this as the "social environment" (p. 147), which includes locations such as "workplace" and "dwelling place" in his analysis. The possibilities are infinite, as all communication has some kind of geographical location which, in turn, influences how communication (in this case greetings), is determined to be appropriate or not. Where we greet affects *how* we greet.

11.6.3 Relational Context

The bottom level of the triangle (Figure 11.1) refers to what is suggested to be the narrowest, though no less important, context: the rank, if any, that exists between the two individuals involved in greeting each other. If greetings involve a teacher–student, the teacher clearly 'outranks' the student. At a job interview, the interviewer outranks the interviewee. The implication is that the junior ranking person is usually required to adjust to a more formal use of language, and it is the senior ranking person who has the authority to permit informal address. This context can also refer to 'relations' from a broader perspective, such as age. For example, a younger individual may have to adjust his/her speech to greet an older person.

To see how all the three contextual factors can combine, let us consider a student meeting with his/her academic supervisor for the first time. In this case, the situational context (i.e. a university) and the relational context are arguably most relevant; it seems less likely that the location of the university, in terms of cultural context (e.g. USA versus UK, London versus Sydney, and so on) would have any significant impact on what kind of communication is considered appropriate. In this context, we have a university setting, and a junior (student) and a senior (professor/supervisor). A plausible, and natural, greeting might be as follows:

Student: *Hello Professor Higgins, my name is John, I'm your supervisee.*
Supervisor: *Hello John, nice to meet you.*
Student: *Nice to meet you, too.*

If, however, we look to alternate contextual factors, we can see how greetings change.

TABLE 11.1 Greetings among Friends: USA

Cultural Context	Situational Context	Relational Context
USA	On a city street	Two close friends, chance meeting

Within the above contexts, the following exchange is not unlikely:

Speaker A: *What's up?*
Speaker B: *Not much.*

What's up equates to *how are you,* and *not much* equates to *fine.* However, if a nonnative English speaker is unaware of such a greeting, the following hypothetical exchange is possible:

Native speaker: *What's up?* (intended as a greeting)
Nonnative speaker: *Nothing is wrong, I'm fine.*

In the above dialogue, the nonnative speaker has interpreted *what's up* to mean something along the lines of *what's the matter,* believing that the first speaker presumes something is troubling the nonnative speaker. In fact, the opposite is probably true. However, it is not enough for a student to be aware of what the intended meaning of the utterance is—here, *what's up* meaning *how are you*—but also the student must know how to respond based on the specific utterance, a point mentioned earlier. In other words, though *what's up* is synonymous with *how are you,* the following exchange would be pragmatically incorrect and sound somewhat unusual:

Speaker A: *What's up?*
Speaker B: *Fine thanks.*

Another common greeting used in the United States, certainly among the young people in California, if not throughout the country, is *what's happening?.* The expected response is again usually *not much.* However, this expression also has the potential to cause confusion if the EFL student is unfamiliar with what it actually means; in fact, a possible response to *what's happening* might be *where?* If the addressee interprets the question as the speaker's desire to seek information about the events or goings on at some undisclosed location.

House (1993, 177) offers an example of another misunderstanding, consisting of the addressee (a nonnative speaker) misinterpreting the native English speaker's question to be the initiation of a greeting. The example is taken from role-play elicited discourse data; this is the only example of a speech act which involves greetings within House's data:

NS: *Oh, hello Mike.*
NNS: *Oh, fine. You?*
NS: *I'm fine.* (puzzled pause).

The exchange above illustrates how a nonnative speaker can interpret a basic greeting of *hello* as synonymous with *how are you* and, subsequently, respond inappropriately (i.e. from a pragmatic point of view).

Furthermore, in the following context, though only the location has changed, so has the commonly used greeting:

TABLE 11.2 Greetings among Friends: England

Cultural Context	Situational Context	Relational Context
England	On a city street	Two close friends, chance meeting

Speaker A: *All right?*
Speaker B: *Not too bad.*

In England, if not most of the United Kingdom, *all right* is commonly used as an informal greeting, a reduction of *are you all right?* The expected response of *not too bad* is quite different from a more common response heard in the United States, which is often *pretty good*, and within the US, *how's it going* often replaces *all right?* The expected answer in the United Kingdom of *not too bad* reveals a little of cultural attitudes, as the BBC (2007) website declares the expression *not too bad* to be a reflection of "typical British understatement" (para. 2).

However, there are also greetings more specific to certain regions within the United Kingdom, such as *am you all right?*, which is often heard in the city of Birmingham; *right boy?* is used sometimes among men in Wales; in London, the expression *wotcha?* is sometimes used; and in Northern Ireland, the greeting *what about ya?* is common. *Am you all right*, with its use of nonstandard grammar, has additional implications for a nonnative English speaker's processing of the information, as he/she might easily believe that a native speaker is using incorrect English grammar, when the expression is simply a dialectal use.

From this analysis, and the examples shown, it is hoped that the importance of a multi-layered approach to context can be realized within greetings, as a means to develop students' communicative competence within this pragmatic field.

11.7 SUGGESTIONS FOR PEDAGOGIC PRACTICE

Using the inverted triangle as a starting point for an initiation into the world of English greetings, students are now ready to practise greetings for themselves, within a variety of contexts.

11.7.1 The Support for Role Plays

Regarding the focus on contextualized dialogues for use within the EFL classroom, there is a great deal of support for such. Sasaki (1998) declares that "role plays are regarded as simulating more authentic situations" (p. 459), with Graustein (1979) succinctly stating that "language should be seen as a tool ... in teaching as it is in the real world" (p. 377). Schmidt (1993) also supports the use of authentic contextualized examples of the subject under discussion as a means to raise EFL students' awareness of the importance of context. Finally, Jordan (1997) concurs that "the language items chosen for practice in ESP/EAP should reflect those used in the real world" (p. 24). I do not think that anyone would disagree with such statements, and role plays have arguably been a major feature of the EFL classroom for many years now.

Role plays can help prepare students for the kind of English that is used within their daily communicative needs while living (as well as being used to prepare them for future life) in an English-speaking country. It would seem that role plays allow students the opportunity to practise dialogues in the classroom before doing it 'for real,' which, I believe, is very important. While listening to role plays acted out on cassette tapes is useful, the speaking style heard on such recorded dialogues can sometimes sound rehearsed and a bit too 'clean'; it sounds less like an authentic conversation and more like two people reading their parts. Therefore, beyond advocating a contextually sensitive approach to the teaching of English greetings, I have always strived to encourage the use of dialogues that sound like they come from the real world, and not necessarily a textbook, and the importance of context as a means to help EFL students develop communicative competence can be seen within various EFL classroom approaches.

Troncale (2002), for example, discusses the area of Content-based Instruction (CBI) as a means to help students learn communication skills, in part because CBI argues for the need to teach language skills within a meaningful context. In this way, "integrating content and language provides students with repeated, natural exposure to the language" and furthermore, students "are engaged in meaningful, related theme-based tasks" (*ibid.*). Any number of social situations can, therefore, be used within a classroom which incorporates CBI as this approach recognizes the importance of helping students acquire the communication skills needed outside the classroom. In addition, Savignon (2006) discusses the importance of Communicative Language Teaching (CLT), saying that "the essence of CLT is the engagement of learners in communication in order to allow them to develop their communicative competence" (p. 209). Role plays, therefore, are an integral part of both CBI and CLT.

Role plays: A practical exercise

Here I describe a role-playing exercise which can help develop students' knowledge of English greetings. First, the class should be divided into pairs. They each student within each pair should be given a slip of paper. The paper tells each student his/her role within a given role play by simultaneously notifying the student of the context involved. A sample of an activity is given below:

SITUATION 1

1: *By chance, you see a close friend in the park.*

2: *By chance, a close friend of yours sees you in the park and greets you.*

The contextual factors involved with the role play above are as follows:

Cultural Context	Situational Context	Relational Context
For students to decide for themselves, should they feel it is relevant	In a park	Two close friends, chance meeting

One student will, of course, be the addressor, who, having recognized his/her friend, initiates a greeting. The other student will be the addressee and responds appropriately to the greeting offered.

SITUATION 2

1: *You are meeting a potential employer for a job interview you're about to have.*

2: *You are meeting a potential employee for a job interview you're about to give. Initiate an appropriate greeting.*

The following contextual factors can be seen:

Cultural Context	Situational Context	Relational Context
For students to once again decode for themselves	In an office, for the purpose of a job interview	Superior/manager and an interviewee

The purpose of first having students ponder their situation, decide on who will be in which role and then jotting down their dialogue offers several benefits. First, it tests the students' communicative competence directly by asking them to write down the dialogue that each of them deems to be suitable for the context they have been given. However, I would not allow each pair a great deal of time to prepare their dialogue because, in the real world, nonnative English speakers will not generally have the benefit of a great deal of preparation time before a response is produced to a question. For example, if approached by a stranger and asked, *Can you tell me where the nearest bank is?*, there is little time to pull out a pocket dictionary to answer the question; they must think on their feet! However, this is arguably good practice for developing speaking skills in English.

Furthermore, by not necessarily specifying on the slip of paper a cultural context (at least in the two situations above), this also allows for a degree of creativity on the students' part. For example, perhaps the students might wish for the park in Situation 1 to be the Central Park in New York and the speakers to be from that part of the world. How this might affect communication is left up to the students, thus giving them a bit of freedom in their role play and, arguably, providing a degree of autonomy. In addition, the act of having to create dialogue within the subject of greetings links with discourse completion tasks (DCT) in which students are usually required to provide missing words within a set dialogue. Though somewhat dated perhaps, DCTs can nonetheless test students' knowledge—syntactic, semantic and pragmatic—and for this classroom exercise, it is left to the students to determine *all* aspects of the conversation (albeit from a short speech act), and not just one or two lines.

After giving each pair sufficient time to formulate a dialogue, the slips of paper on which they wrote their role play should be collected so that the teacher can confirm what the students wrote on the paper corresponds to their actual dialogue. Then, it is up to each pair to come to the front of the class and simply act their parts, ideally striving to sound as natural as possible.

When all role plays have been performed, the teacher can open up the class for a group discussion. Here is where all the students can decide for themselves which dialogues sounded, to their knowledge at least, the most authentic. The teachers might also want to write down the more realistic sounding dialogues on the board as an example of what students might wish to emulate in the real world. This group discussion also helps in facilitating learning as students can see for themselves how they might wish to greet native English speakers based on a variety of contextual factors. This particular lesson on English greetings comprises the following four steps:

1. Discuss contextual factors in English greetings as part of an inverted triangle.
2. Have students prepare their role plays based on being given a situation to first consider.
3. Students to act out their role play in front of the class.
4. Class discussion to determine which role plays sounded authentic and which less so (and why).

After these four steps have been completed, the teacher is now in a better position to administer the final part of the lesson: to actually discuss a variety of English greetings based on many factors, to include country (e.g. Australia, Canada), situation (e.g. on the telephone, first-time meeting) and rank (e.g. two best friends). Following this, it is now up to the students to put what they have learned into practice in future instances of conversation with the native English speakers.

The suggested practical teaching approach also has a theoretical counterpart known as an *analytic approach*. Stern (1990) describes an analytic approach as one which involves a language being the subject of study (e.g. discussing grammatical rules). The analytic approach here refers to the discussion of the contextual factors involved with English greetings. He also discusses how an *experiential approach* within language teaching involves language being learned through communication–in this case, role plays. By combining the two approaches within pedagogy, Allen et al. (1990) believe that they "... provide essential support for one another in the L2 classroom (p. 77)."

11.7.2 Film in the Classroom

Avgerinou and Ericson (1997) summarise the use of visuals thus:

> The way we learn and, subsequently, remember bears a strong relationship to the way our senses operate. This means that we, as educators, cannot afford to ignore the fact that a very high proportion of all sensory learning is visual. (p. 287)

This introductory quotation helps provide support for the use of visuals within one's teaching (here, film), which is arguably a more innovative and modern approach. If we consider that most students nowadays are more 'visualized' than ever before, and then incorporating film clips, for example, as part of one's lesson, can be a way to grab their attention. Furthermore, according to Baratta (2004):

> ... in today's world, more than ever, we (especially children) are bombarded with visuals on a daily basis, such as advertisements on billboards and in magazines, Play stations, the Internet, pop-up ads, text message emoticons and much more. In fact, it can be said that today's children are growing up in a world much more visual than their parents. Therefore, if we are truly preparing students for the real world in which they will find their eventual careers, then it makes sense for us as educators to incorporate elements of that real world inside the classroom; the real world that students are exposed to in their lives *outside* the classroom. In doing so, we help to create a classroom environment that is just as real. (p. 5)

Therefore, by using film clips, which involve greetings, the EFL students can learn by seeing just as role plays involve learning by *doing*. It is up to the teacher, of course, to choose his/her favourite films to show in class, but here are a few suggestions:

Diamonds are Forever (1971)

In the film *Diamonds are Forever* (1971), Bond is introduced to a senior government official Sir Donald just after the film's opening credits have played. Sir Donald initiates the greetings with *how do you do*? to which Bond replies "sir". Clearly, the formal nature of this meeting determines that *how do you do* is indeed appropriate and clearly not overly formal at all in this specific context—a context that involves upper-class British speakers and a senior-ranking government official and his junior.

Pleasantville (1998)

In the first 15 minutes of the film *Pleasantville* (1998), there is a scene in which two American high school students greet each other with *hey* (a greeting I had referenced earlier). A key factor here is that beyond the cultural setting of USA, the two speakers are teenagers and so their youth is also a contributing factor to the greeting of *hey* which is often associated with young Americans, also a point I had already mentioned. Going further in the contextual analysis, the fact that the boy and girl like each other but are afraid to reveal their true feelings means that the greeting of *hey* communicates little in way of personal feelings (less so than say, *how are you doing nowadays?*). Therefore, for these two young American teens, *hey* allows them to say little and look 'cool', while at the same time acting as a legitimate greeting.

Little Voice (1998)

Throughout the film *Little Voice* (1998), a greeting commonly heard in the north of England where the film is set can be heard *areet?* (a variation of the British greeting 'allright?'). As I mentioned earlier, to be truly competent in communication of any kind, the students must know how to respond to conversation, not just initiate it. Therefore, even if they do not wish to emulate greetings such as *areet*, it stands to reason that if they live in that part of the world where such a greeting is used, they must know how to *respond* to such a greeting in a competent manner. In this case, *not too bad* would be an authentic British response.

It is also worth pointing out that the 'traditional' English accent (i.e. that spoken by the Queen) is used by only 3 per cent of the overall British population, thereby leaving 97 per cent of the population speaking with a regional accent (e.g. Manchester). The implication is that the students must learn more than just authentic greetings; understanding the accents that often accompany them is also important, and this is why films can be useful.

Rocky Balboa (2006)

Several times throughout the film *Rocky Balboa* (2006), we can hear Sylvester Stallone's *Rocky* character greet the customers in his restaurant with the common American expression *how you doin?* Moreover, this film allows students to hear an authentic Philadelphia accent (similar to a New York accent, but rhotic, as opposed to nonrhotic), which is considerably different from that of northern England!

It is acknowledged that sifting through several films just to find a greeting can be a hard work. However, it is worth the effort as it can provide real-life English in a real-life context, and all for students to see. The level of the EFL class should, of course, determine what level of listening material is appropriate, yet film can be a more accessible way for students to become accustomed to understanding how English sounds—in this case within the speech act of greetings—and film dialogue sounds less contrived than many cassette recordings of English dialogue.

The use of film/TV in the EFL classroom is especially useful as "no teacher alone can reproduce the variety of situations, voices, accents, themes and presentation techniques that are a feature of this medium" (Hill 1999, 2). Indeed, Bachman (1990, 87) discusses sociolinguistic competence in language as including sensitivity to dialect and register, which, like native accents, can be seen and heard on film. Hill (*op. cit.*) also states that the use of video in the classroom can involve real-life exemplars, which is very relevant to a teaching approach which seeks to prepare students for real life. Finally, he mentions that "television can provide a range of paralinguistic clues, often essential for successful comprehension and accurate understanding" (*ibid.*). This can include the body language which may accompany greetings (e.g. an informal back slap), as seen amongst close friends when they meet. Film, then, can be both entertaining and educational.

11.8 CONCLUSION

This chapter has sought to address the importance of contextual factors within English greetings, an area of focus which previous research appears not to have focused on in necessary depth. While research argues for a more contextually sensitive approach to EFL learning, greetings are an important speech act suggested to be worthy of greater inclusion within a class curriculum. This, in turn, can help develop students' communicative competence within this subject, important in that greetings are arguably an integral part of one's daily life, and language in general.

REFERENCES

Allen, P., Swain, M., Harley, B., and Cummins, J. (Eds.), "Aspects of classroom treatment: Toward a more comprehensive view of second language education," *The Development of Second Language Proficiency*, Cambridge: Cambridge University Press, 1990, 57–81.

A.S., *Second Language Acquisition Processes in the Classroom: Learning Japanese*, Mahway, NJ: Lawrence Erlbaum, 2001b.

Avgerinou, M. and Ericson, J., "A review of the concept of visual literacy," *British Journal of Educational Technology* **28**.4 (1997): 280–291.

Bachman, L., *Fundamental Considerations in Language Testing*, Oxford: OUP, 1990.

Baratta, A., *Visual Writing*, Unpublished book, 2004.

BBC World Service, "Learning English," 2007. Retrieved August 19, 2007 from www.bbc.co.uk/worldservice/learningenglish/grammar/learnit/learnitv52.shtml.

Beebe, L., "The social rules of speaking: Basics-not frosting on the cake," *The Language Teacher*, Japan Association for Language Teaching, 1995, **9**, 4–11.

Bergman, M. and Kasper, G., "Perception and performance in native and non-native apology," *Interlanguage Pragmatics*, G. Kasper and S. Blum-Kulka (Eds.), Oxford: OUP, 1993, 82–107.

Chaika, E., *Language: The Social Mirror*, Rowley, MA: Newbury House, 1982.

Clyne, M., Kretzenbacher, H., Norrby, K., and Schübpack, D., "Perceptions of variation and change in German and Swedish address," *Journal of Sociolinguistics* **10**.3 (2006): 287–319.

DuFon, M.A., "The acquisition of linguistic politeness in Indonesia as a second language by sojourners in a naturalistic context," (Doctoral dissertation, University of Hawaii'), *Dissertation Abstracts International* **60**.3985 (1999).

Eisenstein, M. and Bodman, J.W., "Expressing gratitude in American English by native and non-native speakers of American English," *Applied Linguistics* **7** (1993): 167–185.

Elbow, P., *Writing Without Teachers*, New York: OUP, 1998.

Fraser, B., "The domain of pragmatics," *Language and Communication*, J.C. Richards and R.W. Schmidt (Eds.), New York: Longman, 1983, 29–59.

Graustein, G., "The communicative approach to language teaching," *Journal of Pragmatics*, Oxford: OUP, 1979, **5**, 376–379.

Grieve, A., and Seebus, I., "G'day or Guten Tag: A cross-cultural study of Australian and German telephone openings," *Journal of Pragmatics*, Article in Press, 2008.

Hill, B., "Video in language learning," *Video Tech* **4**.1 (1999), 1–58.

Hoffman-Hicks, S., "The longitudinal development of French foreign language pragmatic competence: Evidence from study abroad participants," (Doctoral dissertation, Indiana University), *Dissertation Abstracts International* **61**.591 (1999).

House, J., "Toward a model for the analysis of inappropriate responses in native/non-native interactions," *interlanguage Pragmatics*, G. Kasper and S. Blum-Kulka (Eds.), Oxford: OUP, 1993, 161–183.

Hymes, D. and Gumperz, J.J., *Directions in Sociolinguistics: The Ethnography of Communication*, New York: Holt, Rinehart and Winston, 1972.

_____, "Discourse: Scope without depth," *International Journal of the Sociology of Language* **57** (1986): 49–89.

Jordan, R., *English for Academic Purposes,* Cambridge: Cambridge University Press, 1997.

Jung, J.Y., "Issues in acquisitional pragmatics," *Working Papers in TESOL and Applied Linguistics* **2**.2 (2002), Teachers College, Columbia University Retrieved August 9, 2007 from http://www.tc.columbia.edu/academic/a&hdept/tesol/Webjournal/JungFinal.doc.pdf

Kasper, G. and Rose, K., *Pragmatic Development in a Second Language*, University of Michigan, Blackwell Publishing, 2002.

Kiefer, F., "Greetings as language games," *Journal of Pragmatics* **4** (1980): 147–155.

Ohta, A.S., *Second Language Acquisition Processes in the Classroom: Learning Japanese*, Mahway, NJ: Lawrence Erlbaum, 2001b.

O'Loughlin, K., "Routine beginnings: Telephone openings in Australia," *Melbourne Papers in Applied Linguistics* **1**.2 (1989): 27–42.

Olshtain, E. and Weinbach, L., "Interlanguage features of the speech act of complaining," *Interlanguage Pragmatics*, G. Kasper and S. Blum-Kulka (Eds.), Oxford: OUP, 1993: 108–122.

Omaggio Hadley, A., *Teaching Language in Context*, Boston, MA: Heinle and Heinle, 1993.

Omar, A., "How learners greet in Kiswahili: A cross-sectional survey," *Pragmatics and Language Learning*, L.F. Bouton and Y. Kachru (Eds.), Monograph Series **2**, Urbana-Champaign, IL: Division of English as an International Language, University of Illinois, Urbana-Champaign, 1991, pp. 59–73.

Sasaki, M., "Investigating EFL students' production of speech acts: A comparison of production questionnaires and role plays," *Journal of Pragmatics* **30** (1998): 457–484.

Savignon, S., "Beyond communicative language teaching: What's ahead?," *Journal of Pragmatics* **39** (2006): 207–220.

Schmidt, R.W., "Interaction, acculturation, and the acquisition of communicative competence: A case study of an adult," *Sociolinguistics and Language Acquisition*, N. Wolfson and E. Judd Rowley (Eds.), MA: Newbury House, 1993, 137–174.

Schmidt, T., "Survival English for travelers: A basic EFL course with lesson plans and activities," 2006. Retrieved August 14, 2007 from http://bogglesworldesl.com/survivalESL.htm.

Stern, H.H., "Analysis and experience as variables in second language pedagogy," The development of second language proficiency, B. Harley, P. Allen, J. Cummins and M. Swain (Eds.), Cambridge: Cambridge University Press, 1990, pp. 93–109.

Troncale, N., "Content-based instruction, cooperative learning, and CALP instruction: Addressing the whole education of 7–12 ESL," Teachers College, Columbia University, Working Papers in TESOL and Applied Linguistics **2**.2 (2002). Retrieved August 9, 2007 from http://www.tc.columbia.edu/academic/a&hdept/tesol/Webjournal/archives5_1.htm.

Yu, M., "On the teaching and learning of L2 sociolinguistic competence in classroom settings," *Asian EFL Journal*, **8**.2 (2006). Retrieved December 19, 2007 from http://www.asian-efl-journal.com/June_06_mcy.php.

Wyrick, J., *Steps to Writing Well*, London: Harcourt Brace, 2002.

Part 4

FACTORS AFFECTING ESL TEACHING

Chapter 12

MOTIVATION AND DEMOTIVATION FACTORS IN LANGUAGE LEARNING

— Makiko Ebata

12.1 INTRODUCTION

Motivation in language learning plays a vital role. It produces effective second-language communicators by planting in the learners the seeds of self-confidence. It successfully makes them continuously engage themselves in learning even after they achieve the goal. In order for English instructors to motivate them, a number of methods are needed both within and outside class. According to Hussin, et al. (2001):

> Positive self-concept, high self-esteem, positive attitude, clear understanding of the goals for language learning, continuous active participation in the language-learning process, the relevance of conducive environment that could contribute to the success of language learning.

They state that six factors influence motivation in language learning: (i) attitudes, (ii) beliefs about self, (iii) goals, (iv) involvement, (v) environmental support, and (vi) personal attributes. Above all, three specific elements are strongly believed to build motivation towards language learning: (i) self-confidence, (ii) experiencing success and satisfaction, and (iii) good teacher–learner relationships as well as relationships between learners. All these three factors are believed to be correlated to each other in the process of motivation development. This study demonstrates analysis of the three factors that have a solid connection with motivation.

Profound analysis of demotivation in ESL/EFL settings is as essential as familiarity with the motivation factors since it is highly possible even for motivated ESL/EFL students to face demotivation due to several factors. In order to sustain students' enthusiasm for acquiring English, instructors must learn how to motivate and also how not to demotivate students. In addition, it is significant for instructors to be familiar with students' intrinsic demotives so that they can prevent students from being affected by possible demotives.

Literature review on demotivation factors, and a research into them are discussed in this study.

12.2 INVESTIGATION OF THE THREE FACTORS

12.2.1 Self-confidence

Self-confidence is the most significant factor in language-learning. It provides learners with the motivation and energy to become positive about their own learning. It also creates the drive in them to acquire the targeted language, enjoy the learning process, and experience real communication. "At the heart of all learning is a person's belief in his or her ability to accomplish the task" (Atsuta 2003). "In general, successful language learners appear to have higher self-esteem than those who are unsuccessful" (Richard-Amato 2003). Lack of belief in one's ability hinders a learner from achieving that task—pursuing a targeted language accomplishment. Moreover, it is widely believed that once students gain self-confidence, it progressively expands in conjunction with experiencing success and satisfaction as well as good relationships. Classroom community also plays an important role in building students' self-confidence. Jones (2006) suggests that it is essential for instructors to "encourage participants to take risks with the target language and push the limits of their proficiencies" (p. 6). Making students understand the necessity of errors during acquiring an L2 is significant in order to provide self-confidence for L2 students.

12.2.2 Experiencing Success and Satisfaction

Experience of success provides students with more power to pursue a new goal. It allows language learners to understand the purpose of trying and have pleasure in communicating with others. Some people might feel successful when they can communicate their thoughts to people; others might feel the sense of success when they complete a challenging task in a targeted language. The feeling of success time and again emerges specifically when the learners realize the degree of their improvement and achievement. Some people, on the other hand, appreciate compliments from others. Subrahmanian (2001) suggests that external praise for one's improvement is strongly related to fomenting the sense of success (p. 12). There is a similarity between the ex-perience of success and satisfaction; the experience of success at all times satisfies people in anything besides language-learning. To make it precise, it is strongly believed that the experience of success comes hand-in-hand with the sense of satisfaction.

According to Lile (2002), "A student will find it difficult to perform in a stressful environment" (p. 34) and "the lessons must be very simple, yet interesting, with a lot of changes from a writing exercise, to a speaking, listening, back to writing, and so on." Nunan (1999) states: "Students need to be able to use the skills taught in the classroom to do things other than those that they had been specifically taught".

This implies that in order for the learners to experience success and become satisfied, it is essential for instructors to create a relaxing learning environment so that the students can perform successfully. Moreover, a language class needs to contain a variety of materials and activities focusing on all necessary skills. By encouraging students to practise all skills, the class can be made more challenging and effective.

12.2.3 Good Relationships among Learners and between Teacher and Students

According to Hussin et al. (2001): "Teachers need to find creative ways to teach the language and increase the student's motivation to learn the language and to eventually appreciate the language."

There are a number of methods that English instructors can use to motivate students in class and instructors should flexibly employ the most suitable method for the class. Furthermore, Kabilan (2000) indicated, "Teachers should develop a mutual relationship with their learners". For this, the teachers need to understand the students who are from different backgrounds, have different interests, future goals, aims for English learning and, most importantly, different personalities. Once they understand them better, teachers are able to apply specific teaching and communicating strategies tailored to each student, thereby creating a trusting relationship between a teacher and student. Once the relationship develops, the classroom will become comfortable and enjoyable enough for students to learn positively from the teacher without any hesitation.

Hussin et al. (2001) mention:

> What occurs in the language classrooms must be extended beyond the walls of the classroom so that a link is created between what is learned in the classrooms with what occurs outside of the classrooms (p. 88).

Languages cannot be learned merely in classrooms. Learning a language requires communication in real-life situations. Thus, students need to acquire an array of communication skills that they can use with various kinds of people. It is essential that they learn not only how to communicate in the target language but also the background, history, and culture that defines it. According to Nunan (1999):

> Students who remain silent in group of ten or more will contribute actively to discussions when the size of the group is reduced to five or three. Type of communicative task can also influence students' willingness to speak.

Richard-Amato (2003):

> In classrooms in which mutual respect is lacking, differing values can lead to conflicts between student and teacher, and between student and peer (p. 66).

The classroom size and the size of group are to be carefully considered. Language learners tend to feel frightened to make a speech in front of a big group. Thus, teachers need to aid students who need support and encourage them to understand that no one can be as perfect as native speakers. In addition, teachers are required to teach all students the importance of having respect for one another in a classroom so that each of them can actively participate in lesson.

12.3 STUDENTS' VOICES FOR MOTIVATION

I did a survey on motivation using the students in my class. Sixteen college freshmen were interviewed regarding the class contents, materials, and the ideal teacher. Half of them had already experienced studying abroad; the other half had not, but their English abilities were as functional as those of returnees.

More students prefer visual aids for new information and their memorization. This means that when teachers introduce new information, visual aids are necessary for students to grasp the main points and details. In addition, the students enjoy thinking rather than talking and individual studying more than group studying; this proves that even returnees who had more opportunities to participate in group studying abroad feel comfortable with passive studying style. Furthermore, thinking comes before trial according to the survey. This means that students need to obtain time to use their critical thinking strategy before they actually start trying in language learning.

The students answered the question, "What kind of teacher do you prefer?" in the following ways:

- *A teacher who knows how to deal with students, especially teenagers.*
- *Teachers who do not push their thoughts to the students.*
- *Tolerant but responsible teachers. They also should never get mad and keep a smile on the face. Sense of humor is another element.*
- *Funny but serious.*
- *Kind and caring.*
- *A teacher who never ignores students' problems.*
- *Friendly and active.*
- *A teacher who can read students' minds and understand their needs.*
- *Fair and trustworthy*

Teachers need to acquire what students look for in teachers in order for students to be motivated in language learning. They certainly have a strong relation with students' motivation status. It is understood that teacher's personality and behavior towards students have a strong influence and in order to produce successful language speakers, they should passionately devote themselves in teaching.

12.4 DEMOTIVATION FACTORS IN ESL/EFL

In the education field, demotivation hinders people from pursuing their goals. It plays the bad-guy role in English education, leading great deal of students to give up. Furthermore, it is easy for highly motivated ESL/EFL students to become demotivated, puzzling instructors who have been teaching passionately with proven methods. According to Trang and Baldauf Jr. (2007):

> Research has shown that motivation is crucial for L2 learning because it directly influences how much effort students make, how often students use L2 learning strategies, how much students interact with native speakers, how much input they receive in the language being learned, how well they do on curriculum-related achievement tests, how high their general proficiency level becomes, and how long they reserve and maintain L2 skills after language study is over (p. 102).

Believing it that motivation plays vital role in L2 education, the analysis of demotivation process is considered as important as motivation in order to keep motivating L2 students.

Various factors cause demotivation amongst new language learners. According to Trang and Baldauf Jr., there are two groups of demotives: (i) internal attributions and (ii) external attributions. The internal attributions include students' attitudes towards English, their experiences of failure or lack of success, and the incidents related to their self-esteem; the external attributions contain teacher-related factors, the learning environment, and other external factors (*ibid.*). Since we, language instructors, have a direct influence on the students' external demotive attribution, it is incredibly significant for us to be aware of the external attributions.

Furthermore, according to Gorham and Millette (1997):

> The behavior of the teacher influences the behavior of the student, subsequently affecting learning outcomes. Student motivation is affected by a variety of factors, some of which are directly influenced by what a teacher does (how the teacher structures the course and how he or she behaves in class) and some of which are largely beyond the teacher's control (expectancies and attitudes students bring with them to the class) (p. 101).

In order to effectively maintain student motivation, special care should be applied to the course structure. Motivating student behavior as well is essential for L2 instructors although there is limit of our capability to sustain student's motivation. An interesting research was conducted by Trang and Baldauf Jr. (*op. cit.*), which concludes:

Among teacher-related factors, teaching method had the highest frequency in demotivating students (26%), followed by teacher behavior (7%), teacher competence (4%), and grading and assessment (1%). Out of 88 demotivated students, 59 had, to a greater or lesser extent, been affected by demotivation through teaching method (p. 87).

Gorham and Millette (*op. cit.*) also hypothesize:

> Motivation is related to the perceived challenge of a task. When individuals perceive themselves as capable of accomplishing a task, they are more likely to perceive the task as rewarding and remain motivated to accomplish it. If the task is perceived beyond the individual's capabilities (suboptimal challenge), dissatisfaction increases, there is a greater sense that goals or expectations were not fulfilled, and motivation decreases (p. 139).

In this regard, Jones (*op. cit.*) asserts:

> By far the greatest source of demotivation is teachers, including personality (e.g. lack of commitment to the students or teaching, excessive criticism, and belligerent or condescending attitude), and teaching style (e.g. repetitive, monotonous, insufficient or unclear instructions or explanations, lack of enthusiasm, and inferior use of materials or equipment). Other souces of demotivation were inadequate school facilities, reduced self-confidence, negative attitude towards L2, the compulsory nature of L2, interference of another FL being studied, negative attitude towards L2 community, attitudes of group members, and course book (p. 221).

Another appealing viewpoint is created by Peacock (2001):

> Matching teaching and learning style improves learning, attitudes, behavior, and motivation. Matching teaching style with learning style gives all learners an equal chance in the classroom and builds student self-awareness.
>
> The consensus is that when student and teacher styles are better matched, students are likely to work harder both in and outside the classroom and also to benefit much more from their EFL classes (p. 222).

It is strongly believed that students need to feel both relaxed and sure about what occurs in the classroom to be motivated to study second language in and outside the classroom. Even though it is challenging for the instructors to cater their teaching styles, it is necessary. It is also essential to carefully plan the tasks in the materials, paying special attention to their interests, backgrounds, and language levels to stir up their motivation. Borrowing Jones's (*op. cit.*) words:

> Extrinsic motivation had limitations, especially with more mature learners, and that one of our biggest challenges and responsibilities as language teachers was to find or design material that is intrinsically motivating.

12.5 CONQUERING DEMOTIVATION

Can demotivated students be remotivated to learn L2? According to Trang and Baldauf Jr. (*op. cit.*), the answer is YES. They report:

Most of the factors that helped the students overcome their demotivation concerned internal factors (71%) rather than external factors (29%). Five internal factors that significantly contributed to students' overcoming demotivation were: an awareness of the importance of English (27%), personal reasons (16%), self-improvement (12%), self-determination (12%), and positive attitude towards English (4%).

It is understood that the L2 learners need to come up with their own ways to motivate themselves again after demotivation to learn L2, which the instructors cannot completely control. Nevertheless, we can get involved with the other 29%, which are external motivating factors. According to Trang and Baldauf Jr. (*ibid.*): "External factors included positive changes in teacher behavior (6%), teaching method (7%), learning conditions (9%), and external encouragement (7%)" (p. 187).

This brightens our teaching world since the above four factors are within our control. Specifically, it is unproblematic to change the behaviors and students' learning conditions and encourage them to keep studying a target language. Furthermore, it is not as difficult as we expect to change teaching methods.

12.6 MOTIVATED STUDENTS' VOICES

After reading a number of research findings, I wondered how the students in my classes feel about studying English. In order to find their opinions, I prepared nine questions and asked the students to anonymously answer them. I asked 17 advanced-level freshmen from the Philippines, Cambodia, Nepal, Taiwan, France, China, and Japan. I also asked 20 advanced-level sophomores who were from Korea, China, Nepal, and Japan. The class utilized content-based instruction with new topics tackled every week for a total of 12 topics per semester. For evaluation, I had the students done the following projects: speech, essay, debate, and presentation.

1. *Are you motivated to study English?*

    Yes 37/37

    Since they are in advanced classes, they were more motivated to study English than those in other classes.

2. *Do you like your classmates?*

    Yes 34/37

    No 0/37

    Most of them 3/37

    At the beginning of the semester, they reportedly felt uncomfortable with their classmates because of unfamiliarity with them; however, they got used to each other after a number of group projects, discussions and parties outside class.

3. Do you like the instructor?

   Yes 37/0

   No 0/37

   It is quite difficult to analyze myself; however, they seem to like me because of my friendly and caring personality. They also feel comfortable with me since I removed the barriers between them and me.

4. Do you feel relaxed in your class? Why or why not?

   Yes 37/37

   No 0/37

   Comments:
   - Yes, everyone is friendly, so it is easy to stay in the class.
   - Yes, it is not so strict but it has deep contents.
   - Very relaxed because I know everyone in the class and they are all my friends.
   - Yes, because I have freedom.
   - Yes, I feel like I am at home.
   - Of course! They are so friendly and nice.

   It is strongly believed that communication and out-of-class activities foster a healthy, friendly teacher-student relationship. Grouping students with different classmates for each activity was also found to help them to understand each other's opinions and personalities.

5. Do you like the class contents? Why or why not?

   Yes 30/37

   No 4

   Some of them 3

   Comments:
   - I like some of them.
   - I like the class contents because they are not only for writing and speaking in English, but also for thinking and feeling.
   - Yes, because all the materials are student-centric.
   - I am not interested in some of them like psychology and anthropology.
   - Some of them. I like psychology very much. But ecology was not so interesting. It all depends.
   - Some of them are too difficult to understand.
   - Yes. My teacher only teaches me few grammatical errors and new colloquial words, however, I can acquire a bird's eye view

from her class. Unlike other teachers, she gives me lots of opportunities to get into academic disciplines; introductory studies, controversial issues and other methods that enable us to use English properly and enjoyably. "Not English but *in English*", this is the reason I prefer her class. In addition, my teacher understands what we want to do and what is effective for our future. Since we are learning methods to produce creative things in other classes, she gives us chances to make such products applying both creative studies and acquired awareness toward controversial things in her English class. The language to make and present works is eventually English, so this experience is quite beneficial for us, who really want to work in the English spoken country as a professional person in own aimed field or fields.

Choosing content is challenging for instructors since we need to learn about the students' interests, backgrounds, and future plans. Nevertheless, now and then it is possible for us to choose but need to exercise care in our choice of what we deal within class.

6. Which activity do you like the best?

Debate 10/37

Presentation 6/37

Speech 2/37

Essay 5/37

Group discussion 10/37

Listening to a lecture 2/37

No comment 2

7. Why do you think you need to study English?
   - For the future.
   - Lots of travelers come from other countries, so you need English to sell products.
   - It will be easier to travel around the world.
   - I will have more opportunities in life.
   - To communicate with the world.
   - To earn money.
   - For business.
   - I think that English is a necessary subject because it is an international language which will help an individual in his life. To progress in one's future, one must know how to speak English.

Each of them has his/her own purpose of learning English, which has positive effects on their motivation building.

8. *Do you like the method your teacher uses in class?*

   Yes 34/37

   No 0/37

   Sometimes 3/37

9. *Do you like to study alone or with your classmates?*

   Alone 1/37

   With classmates 34/37

   It depends on the tasks 2/37

12.7 CONCLUSION

Motivation is vital in language learning. It makes language learners positive about their own learning. It also creates the drive in them to acquire the targeted language, enjoy the learning process, and experience real communication. Moreover, the experience of success and satisfaction has a strong correlation with motivation. By experiencing their improvement and achievement, students always gain confidence. In order for language students to become satisfied with a lesson, it is necessary to produce a stress-free classroom and develop integrated-tasks lesson. Trust between teacher and students is important for communication in the targeted language. In short, three factors—self-confidence, experiencing success and satisfaction, and good teacher–learner relationships as well as relationships between learners—play essential roles in developing language learners' motivation. Moreover, in order to maintain motivation, the L2 instructors are to be familiar with demotivation factors—both internal and external attributions. They have a direct relation with students' external attributions. Fortunately, it is possible for once-demotivated students to overcome their obstacles in motivation.

REFERENCES

Atsuta, H., "Improving the motivation of unsuccessful learners in the Japanese high-school EFL context," ERIC Document Reproduction Service No. ED **476** 750, 2003.

Gorham, J. and Millette, D.M., "A comparative analysis of teacher and student perceptions of courses of motivation and demotivation in college classes," *Communication* **46**.4 (1997): 245–261.

Hussin, S., Maarof, N., and D'Cruz, J., "Sustaining an interest in learning English and increasing the motivation to learn English: An enrichment program," *The Internet TESL Journal* **7**.5 (2001).

Jones, B.A., "Practice to theory to practice: Sharing my story," K. Bradford-Watts, C. Ikeguchi and M. Swanson (Eds.), *JALT 2005 Conference Proceedings,* Tokyo: JALT, 2006.

Kabilan, M.K., "Creative and critical thinking in language classrooms," *The Internet TESL Journal* **6**.6 (2000).

Lile, W., "Motivation in the ESL classroom," *The Internet TESL Journal* **8**.1 (2002).

Nunan, David, *Second Language Teacher Education,* Cambridge: Cambridge University Press, 1999.

Peacock, M., "Match or mismatch? Learning styles and teaching styles in EFL," *International Journal of Applied Linguistics* **11**.1 (2001).

Richard-amato, Patricia A., *Making It Happen: From Interactive to Participatory Language Teaching: Theory and Practice,* New York: Pearson ESL, 2003.

Subrahmanian, U., "Helping ESL learners to see their own improvement," *The Internet TESL Journal* **7**.4 (2001).

Trang, T.T.T., and Baldauf Jr., R.B., "Demotivation: Understanding resistance to English language learning—The case of Vietnamese students," *The Journal of Asia TEFL* **4**.1 (Spring 2007): 79–105.

Chapter 13

NARRATIVE INQUIRY FOR TEACHER DEVELOPMENT

— SIMON COFFEY AND CONSTANT LEUNG[1]

13.1 INTRODUCTION

Within the field of second language teacher education there is an ongoing tension between research-driven theoretical developments and the application of these in pedagogical practice (Gass, 1995; Bardovig-Harlig and Hartford 1997; Fradd and Lee, 1998). This 'tension' lies at the heart of the deliberate shift from the term teacher 'training' to teacher 'education' (Richards, 1998). A key issue with the promotion of research-driven teacher development is the question of who produces the knowledge, i.e., are teachers to be recipients of applied linguistics research? Such a knowledge-transmission model of teacher education ideology risks producing a producer–consumer hierarchy that is not tenable in the long term as teachers need to be convinced by their own experience of the need for change and the effectiveness of solutions proposed. In this chapter, we will focus on second language teacher development, in particular, and how teacher-initiated inquiry can encourage this development. We use the term teacher development in the sense proposed by Tarone and Allwright (2005) to denote a deeper understanding, and to use this understanding to inform one's pedagogic practice.

13.2 TEACHER INQUIRY AS TEACHER PROFESSIONALISM

We suggest that teacher inquiry promotes what has been called *reflexive practice* (Bolton, 2002; Griffiths and Tann, 1992) and is a fundamental strategy for developing the individual and collaborative awareness-building that contributes to teacher professionalism. Second language teacher profession-alism, a 'selectively combined set of disciplinary-based knowledge, ethical principles, and time and place-specific work practices' (Leung, 2009,

---

1. This is a revised version of the first edition chapter entitled 'Talking to the other, and writing for oneself' by Johannes Eckerth and Constant Leung.

2013), has been suggested to include both *sponsored professionalism* as well as *independent professionalism*. Sponsored professionalism refers to institutionally endorsed and publicly heralded definitions of teachers' disciplinary knowledge and practical experience as expressed by regulatory bodies. Independent professionalism, in contrast, refers to more individually oriented notions of professionalism, in particular, individual teachers' committment to careful and critical examination of the assumptions and practices embedded in sponsored collective professionalism with reference to discipline-based knowledge, and a readiness to take action to effect change where appropriate. In particular, independent professionalism includes the willingness for individual practitioners to be engaged in reflexive examination of their own beliefs and action.

The purpose of the present paper is to explore the process of critical examination of one's own beliefs and actions as a part of independent professionalism. *Reflexivity*, as we understand it, refers to the willingness and the capacity of individuals to turn their thinking (and action) on itself (Johnson, 2000). One approach to reflexivity that has been subject to increased attention over the last years is *narrative inquiry*, i.e., the process of accounting for one's own professional experience through narration. As narrations can go beyond a simple re-telling of experiences, they are epistemically transformative in nature, thus representing forms of 'talking writing ourselves into understanding' (Mann, 2002). Exploiting this epistemic function of narration, it can be argued that narrative inquiry enables a subject to render his professional beliefs and assumptions an object available for self-examination. In the following, we investigate *narrative inquiry* as a potential tool in developing increased reflexivity. In particular, we present an account of one individual ESL teacher engaging in the process of narrative inquiry, both collaboratively and individually, and will consider in which ways these explorations may contribute to language teacher self-development. Our purpose in reporting one individual teacher's report experience as a case study is to explore the dynamics of teacher self-development.

13.3 NARRATIVE INQUIRY IN LANGUAGE TEACHER DEVELOPMENT

Language teachers' narrative inquiries, i.e., their reflexive accounts of professional experiences, vary along two dimensions: narrative mode and focus of inquiry. By *narrative mode* we refer to the channel that is used to conduct the narration: collaborative oral exchanges of experiences and practices (Mann, 2002) as compared to individually produced written accounts (Farrell, 1998). By *focus of inquiry*, we refer to the domain of relevant professional experience that is targeted by the inquiry. In this chapter, we will look at two broad, but clearly interrelated domains: accounts of *language teaching practices and beliefs* as compared to reflections on *language learning experiences*. We propose a research methodology which enables us to investigate both dimensions in combination.

Using a case study approach, this chapter scrutinizes one second language teacher's narrative reflection on teacher's second language learning experiences, and how these link to his beliefs about his own language teaching practices. Our own conceptual point of departure is that this teacher's personally held assumption that an inquiry into the one domain—L2 learning—would inform his awareness of and development in another—L2 teaching.

Narrative inquiries of language teachers' pedagogical practices have been suggested as a significant aspect of their professional development (Barkhuizen, 2011; Barkhuizen, Benson and Chik, 2014; Clandinin and Connelly, 2000; Johnson, 2002, 2009; Johnson and Golombek, 2011; Hazelrigg, 2005). Appel (1995), one of the rare autobiographical accounts in book length, provides an intense in-depth study of a secondary school EFL teacher's struggle with the complex and at the same time constraining conditions under which day-to-day teaching takes place. Motivated by the unsatisfactory experience of the 'transmission-model' in teacher education, Appel sets out to explore his teaching experience, and succeeds in effecting conceptual and pedagogical change. The structure of the book clearly evidences this teacher's developmental path:

Part One: *Survival* describes the difficulties I encountered when I started in my first teaching post, discipline being the most prominent one among them.

Part Two: *Change* is no longer exclusively about coping with the classroom situation, but about influencing it as well. It describes what were, for me, new perceptions as well as new methods.

Part Three: *Routine* looks at what role the changes described in part two can play in day-to-day teaching. It shows how humanistic principles can enhance routine work. (Appel, 1995: xv-xvi, original emphasis)

Being a potentially powerful tool for introspection, reflection, and self-evaluation, narrative 'knowledging' has been used both by novice teachers (Santana-Williamson, 2001) as well as by experienced teachers as a source of renewed inspiration and inquiry (Jarvis, 1992; Allwright, 2003). Such reported use of narratives has also been complemented by suggestions and guidelines as how to make full use of reflective writing in professional development

(Bailey, Curtis and Nunan, 2001; Richards and Farrell, 2005). Generally speaking, narrative accounts provide valuable insights into more implicit cognitive, affective, and attitudinal processes involved in language teaching, which are not necessarily amenable to direct observation.

A related goal is pursued by teachers' narrative inquiries of their own *language learning experiences*. Often being part of an accredited course in a teacher education program, these reflective writings either focus on subject matter learning within the program, or on language learning along the program (Bailey, 1983, 1990; Rivers, 1983; Waters, et al., 1990; Birch, 1992; Bailey and Nunan, 1996; Bailey, et al., 2001). Language learning diary studies affords the opportunity to see teaching "from the other side" (Richards, 1992: 146) and of giving more experienced L2 teachers the chance to "renew their connection with language learning, and thereby, to become more sensitive to the potential problems, their learners may experience" (Lowe, 1987: 89). This later goal may be especially valuable for native speaker teachers (teaching their own mother tongue) with no or only marginal prior foreign/second language learning experience.

So far, these two lines of inquiry, teaching-related and learning-related narratives have been pursued separately in teacher education. In our view they are complementary, as learning and teaching are closely interrelated, and personal experience of and reflection on the one can and will inevitable inform and impact on the other. Therefore, in the present paper, we will report on a language teacher who engaged in a narrative inquiry of his teaching practices and, later on, decided to keep a diary of his language learning experiences. We met Graham (pseudonym) as a student in the MA ELT and Applied Linguistics programme at our institution. He was first contacted by Andon,[2] 2009, one of our colleagues, a researcher and teacher educator himself, who was investigating second language teachers' pedagogical beliefs and practices in relation to task-based learning and teaching. At the time of the study, Graham had six years of experience in teaching ESL. After graduating, he took a CELTA course and taught ESL in the UK for several years before taking a DELTA course. After this, he has been teaching general and business English in private language schools, first in Spain, and later on in the UK. At his current work place, a well-established private language school in London, he was considered to be an experienced, proficient, popular and successful ESL teacher.

There are two stages of narrative inquiry reported here. Firstly, Graham and Andon met regularly to have collaborative discussions about their beliefs and attitudes to practice (i.e. teacher–teacher collaboration of the sort defined by Stewart, 2006, even though Graham was officially an MA student in

---

2. We would like to thank our colleague Nick Andon for sharing some of his data with us.

Andon's programme). Secondly, as it happened, Graham was also studying Spanish at this time, and kept a diary of his own experience of learning Spanish. He reported that his desire to conduct a diary study has been inspired by what had emerged from his participation in the narrative inquiry into his teaching (with Andon). Seeing an L2 classroom through the eyes of a learner, he not only aimed at an increased understanding of actions and perceptions of his own students, but also at an in-depth reflection of his own teaching practices. In doing so, he sought to distance himself from his usual professional role. By reflecting on his learning needs and on how they were addressed by the pedagogical practices of his teachers, Graham sought to gain a deeper understanding of his own pedagogical practices. Thus, in exploring his own *language teaching and learning*, this teacher adopted the role of a reflective and explorative agents in and of his own field, a role that clearly resonates with bottom-up and staff-driven approaches to teacher self-development (Cheng and Wang, 2004).

Our discussion will specifically focus on *practices of and beliefs about oral error correction* as one particular aspect of teacher development, a theme that emerged as an issue of concern to Graham. Thus, rather than imposing our own categories onto the data, we set out to better understand one aspect of the pedagogical practices that appear to be of significance to the teacher himself. In line with such an approach, we will adopt a two-fold perspective: While looking at the reflective narratives in view of what the may tell us *about* teacher development, we see them at the same time as *instances of* teacher development.

13.4 NARRATING ONE'S BELIEFS AND PRACTICES THROUGH COLLABORATIVE DIALOGUE

Language teachers' pedagogical beliefs, assumptions and knowledge have been the subject of intensified research since the mid-90s. To date, several studies have focused on different aspects of teacher cognition, an umbrella term for several interrelated psychological constructs referring to the "complexity of teachers' mental lives" (Borg, 2006: 50). More recently, some of this research has focused on teachers' knowledge about language ('KAL', Bartels, 2005) and teachers' beliefs about language learning (Kalaja and Fereirra Barcelos, 2003).

Through the regular meetings in which Andon and Graham discussed the latter's beliefs about his professional practices, Andon identified five main principles in Graham's teaching:

1. Build up the lesson spontaneously starting with ideas from the students.
2. Base lessons on the learners' and the teachers' personal experiences and stories.

3. Provide a balance of textbook-based language work and task-based language teaching.
4. Teach lexically.
5. Correct on the spot and include reformulations and elaborations.

These principles seem to be fairly consistent with central aspects of Task-based Language Teaching (the focus of Andon's study). For instance, Graham's teaching is characterized by using outcome oriented tasks (Skehan, 2002) that are embedded in a task-supported and partially task-based pedagogical framework (Ellis, 2003) and include incidental focus on form techniques (Long, 1991, Doughty and Williams, 1998) when working on emerging student language, and by integrating elements of a lexical approach (Lewis, 2002). Also with respect to issue 5 (above), providing corrective feedback, Graham's teaching appears to be principled in the sense that it followed a general pattern of corrective feedback:

> (One) example was when a student in a role play said 'first the coffee' the teacher, after seeming to puzzle over this for a minute, provided 'before we get down to business, let's have some coffee'. A lot of the language focus provided by the teacher consisted of this kind of lexical repair and extension, providing a number of alternative words and expressions in reaction to something a student said or was trying to say (Andon, 2009: 107).

Rather than working on lexical issues through pre-specified vocabulary-building activities, Graham picks up non target-like student language and provides corrective feedback in the form of alternative expressions. In this way, he draws on his intuition about English as a native speaker, and is thinking up alternatives and corrections on the spot. During the initial discussions it was not clear where this technique originated; in the collaborative narratives he did not mention his study of the language teaching literature. So it comes as a surprise that he clearly does consult the relevant professional literature and seeks to incorporate (see below) theories and findings to his teaching. For instance, when reflecting on aspects of his teaching, Graham explicitly refers to theoretical constructs, such as Krashen's 'i + 1' or authors of teaching methodology handbooks:

> ... then it was the Michael Lewis books the lexical approach which I thought oh yes I like this sort of thing so I was able to incorporate that ... and I started getting into language and looking at language and I really started enjoying it (Andon, 2009: 98).

However, though never mentioned in relation to the professional literature, Graham strongly holds on to the 'correct on the spot' technique, which he feels is popular among his students. This form of corrective feedback seems to be one of his core pedagogical principles to which he even refers to in terms of 'conviction':

> *I say that I'll correct on the spot when I can, and in fact I never have complaints about that (...) and I'm just so convinced that you should* (Andon, 2009: 112).

This conviction of the necessity and the beneficial effects of instant error correction are so strong that, when attending a conference, he even feels obliged to bring this issue up in a discussion with a key speaker:

> *Sharwood-Smith at IATEFL he gave this plenary speech and afterwards he had feedback from the plenary and I asked a question about on-the-spot correction, and he said no if the student isn't aware of the rule don't you shouldn't correct them on the spot (...) and I was arguing with him* (Andon, 2009: 243).

It seems as if Graham clings so strongly to the principle of instant correction that, as he cannot find much in support of it in published accounts of TBLT, he tries to find some back-up from acknowledged experts in the field. It is only in a later discussion and when talking about his language learning experience, when the origins of his convictions on error correction become more transparent. When speaking of his untutored learning of Spanish in Spain and later on in classes in the UK, he mentions the perceived lack of error correction:

> *Well there's one thing reformulation and another is correction but yeah correcting on the spot is ... erm ... maybe it is because I'd been in Spain and not had being corrected for such a long time, that I was very insistent with my teacher that they would correct me, and that if they didn't I would say correct me you know and them not being able to do it at the pace I wanted them* (Andon, 2009: 282).

In the light of this evidence it looks as if Graham's assumptions, and in fact, convictions on error correction have originated long time ago in his own language learning experience. Being a rather conscious and analytic language learner, he suffered from the lack of corrective feedback in conversations with native speaker. Moreover, he also complains that even in his language class he is not sufficiently corrected, and again he feels so strong about this issue that he explicitly asks his teachers to correct him more frequently. He even goes so far as to question their pedagogical skills and competence in this respect.

What emerges from these narratives is the picture of a skilled and experienced teacher with a highly reflective approach to his own teaching practices. Beyond the initial training that he has received he continually engages with the professional literature, attends professional conferences, and seeks to relate findings from research on L2 learning and teaching to his own classroom practices. With respect to TBLT, he has a good understanding of its key principles, and seeks to relate them in a fairly consistent manner to his teaching. In particular, he appreciates TBLT as a pedagogy that emphasizes authentic conversation, authentic meaning for Graham spontaneous and learner-initiated. He centers his teaching on tasks that are outcome related and which engage students in goal-oriented speaking activities. He also seeks to integrate a language focus that builds on students' language production rather than on pre-selected lexical and grammar issues, and tries to provide reformulations on production problems as they arise out of students' interactions. However, in stark contrast to this overall framework, he insists on immediate on-the-spot correction whenever he perceives a non target-like element in his students' output. As he refers to this error correction technique repeatedly and with strong affective emphasis, it seems to represent a core principle of Graham's teaching.

However, even through the repeated observations and narrative encounters it did not become entirely clear why he was so uncompromising about the very issue of error correction, and in which way it was possibly rooted in his language learning experience. As the interdependency between language learning experience, language teaching practice, and teacher self-education is at the core of continuing professionalism as a language teacher, we were eager to explore this issue further. We were therefore pleased to learn that Graham had decided to keep a diary of his experience of learning Spanish in the classroom, and to use some of the diary entries for his MA dissertation. As this diary study turned out to shed more light on his assumptions on error correction, both as a language learner and as language teacher, we will now turn to Graham's diary of a language learner.

13.5 GRAHAM'S DIARY NARRATION OF HIS OWN LANGUAGE LEARNING

Graham had picked up Spanish in South America, and in his diary, study, reports on his experience of studying Spanish in group and one-to-one classes in the UK. Rather than commenting on them, we will first listen to Graham's own voice. The following eight diary entries all focus on one specific issue, oral corrective feedback. As becomes clear from the first entry in which Graham reports on his own teaching practice, this issue is of central concern in his assumption of successful language learning and teaching.

In the following, and in accordance with Graham's original study, we distinguish between his recollection of classroom events (in italics and indented) and his framing of and reflecting on these events (regular font, no indentation). The subheadings (bold type) have been added by us for structuring purposes only.

13.5.1 Diary Extracts

Framing of diary entry 1 and 2

"This is an extract which describes how I teach. I think this is central to my diaries as these are the 'lenses' through which I see my experience in classes."

Diary entry 1, "And my method as a teacher was..."

By this time I was teaching a lot of one to one classes and my method was to use a piece of paper like a board and gloss the language I used as teacher and also write down my reformulations of their English. This was all done as the conversation progressed (...). I felt it was important to keep up the flow of the conversation but at the same time, drawing the student's attention to corrections and reformulations and sometimes explanations before returning to the theme/conversation of the class. It was all done at a pace.

Diary entry 2, "How would you say it?"

I found that this new language teacher was unable to do this. She wasn't correcting me as much as I wanted her to do and she didn't write (reformulate and correct) fast enough to keep up with my conversation. (...) I felt that correction was very important because I had learnt Spanish in informal language settings, and I hadn't ever been corrected. I wanted to be corrected a lot, as soon as I made the mistake, but she was unable to do this. I often knew that I wasn't saying something correctly or that I was avoiding the past tense form I was very aware of this avoidance strategy and I would even explain it to my teacher but it seemed she was unable to pick me up on it so I ended up having to ask her, "How would you say it ?" In fact that was one of the most common expressions I used "How would *you* say it?"

Framing of diary entry 3

"Another example of me speaking and not being corrected."

Diary entry 3, "Language almost stale in its automaticity"

I can't help but feel frustrated that in the more communicative parts of the class, I am not being corrected or reformulated. I am using expressions I have always used, language that seems almost stale in its automaticity. The linking together of fixed chunks and perhaps increasingly I'm realising without any ability to change them or to manipulate them. Or perhaps it's because I'm increasingly conscious of the language that I'm avoiding (verb tenses) and I'm frustrated that I'm not being picked up on this.

Framing of diary entry 4

"After a couple of group classes I get quite worried that she is not correcting any of us. I had paid a lot of money for the course and being corrected was central to my experience of being a student."

> **Diary entry 4, "In a class you 'suspend face'"**
>
> What should I do about her? She said she didn't want to correct us, that she didn't want to embarrass us. Why embarrass? It's embarrassing if you get corrected outside the class in natural environments. It's massively face threatening, but in a class you 'suspend face' if that makes sense. One of the rules I think to an effective classroom is that you do this to some extent.

Framing of diary entry 5

"So I have a private word with the teacher before my third class and ask her to correct me when I speak. She seemed a little taken aback, but she said that she would. This extract was written after the first class we'd been corrected in."

> **Diary entry 5, "Learning can go together with the discussion"**
>
> At the end I was happy with how the class had gone for the last 30 minutes. The way she corrected us while we talked. Pronouns and gender mostly it seemed. Is this just superficial correction though? I suppose reformulations are too much to ask for. I told her at the end that I was happy with the way learning can go together with the discussions.

Comment on diary entry 5

"This is the first time I become fully aware of my pronoun and gender problem. I knew that I had problems in this area, but was unaware of how frequently I was making mistakes in these areas. Through this on the spot correction I become much more aware of a lot of other problems I have."

Framing of diary entry 6

"I also make this comment about one of the 'prouder' but weaker members of the class. He sees himself as being quite good because he lived in Peru for a year. Just the same way that I felt after a year in Colombia"

> **Diary entry 6, "I wonder how he feels about being corrected"**
>
> I wonder how he feels about being corrected. He seems a bit embarrassed. It would be interesting to ask him.

Framing of diary entry 7

"Since I am being corrected in my group class, I am looking to her more and at times I become more hesitant. Especially at the beginning of a turn. I am perhaps a bit worried here that correction is having a negative effect on me. I also have my doubts about the manner in which we're being corrected."

Diary entry 7, "I do look to her after I say things"

Now that she's correcting us more, I do look to her after I say things as about 60% of what I say is corrected in some way. I don't remember all the corrections though, sometimes I'm in the middle of saying something a bit more expansive, a longer turn and she'll correct me, 'encontrar titulo' was corrected to 'tener titulo', that was clear, but there are other times when we don't quite catch the corrections.

Framing of diary entry 8

"This next extract is from a class where I destabilized completely. I was being very inaccurate and hesitant. I put it down to having bought my first grammar book a few days before and also to being quite tired. Getting corrected in this instance just seemed to be kicking me while I was down."

Diary entry 8, "When I make the mistake she'll jump"

It might be something to do with me having bought my first grammar book and getting my head around the pronouns and the reflexive verbs, and suddenly I'm off the rails. I think it's also because I'm conscious that she is correcting me and I'm aware that when I make the mistake she'll jump. With every utterance of a verb I almost closed my eyes as the word left my mouth and if no correction came I'd look to her and say, 'Ok?'

Comment on diary entry 8

"This last example worried me. It was the most negative experience I had about being corrected. What it had reduced me to. I was hardly able to speak. Perhaps for the first time, I question my belief that students should be corrected all the time."

13.5.2 End of Diary Extracts

Rather than paraphrasing the original wording, we would like to sum up the learner's initial and revised assumptions on error correction:

Initial assumptions on error correction before the diary study

1. Oral errors should be corrected all the time.
2. Overt and rather simple surface errors should be corrected on the spot.

3. Correction of more profound errors should be accompanied by explanations and black board glossing.
4. Covert errors in form of avoidance strategies, unvaried linguistic patterns and unanalyzed chunks should be identified and acted upon by offering alternative formulations.
5. Error correction should be embedded in conversational response moves.
6. The very nature of the language classroom constitutes an environment in which error correction is non-face threatening.

Emerging assumptions on error correction during the diary study

1. Error correction operates on a cognitive *and* affective level.
2. Though the classroom is an environment designed for the primary purpose of accelerated learning, the agents in this environment are at the same time constructing, maintaining, and protecting their social identities during and through classroom interactions.
3. Thus, under certain circumstances, error correction can be embarrassing for learners and can lead to language anxiety.
4. As a consequence of points 1–3, students should probably *not* be corrected all the time.

As the following and final reflection clearly demonstrates, for this teacher-researcher the diary study of his own classroom language learning has been a path, and as we suggest, an utterly successful path, to an increased awareness of his own teaching:

> This [error correction] is an area I've always been interested in. I do it a lot when I teach. I interrupt and correct. Sometimes I think that I do it too much. I wanted to know what it was like to be corrected. (...) Basically, I think this diary is a quest to find out what it's like to be taught by me.

This resonates closely with what has been reported in other teachers' language learning diary studies as we see in this extract from Lowe (1987):

> Perhaps the most interesting general point is that people suddenly realize they're learners again, and whether they are experienced or new teachers, the diary makes them realize how essential it is to remember what it was like to learn. At least once in every diary somebody said something like, 'I had quite forgotten it was so difficult to do so-and-so', or 'My poor students. I must try and remember that I hate this, and yet I force people to do it all the time.' (...) I think the diary acts as a self-awareness

instrument: if you know what's going on in your own learning, it makes you aware of what's possibly going on in the learners in your classroom. (p. 95)

In sum, then, we suggest that Graham's language learning diary study has been an example of language teaching awareness on a micro-genetic scale. By this, we do not suggest that the reported sequence was the first emergence of teaching awareness in this teacher's professional life. Rather we suggest that by and through the diary study, the writer undergoes a process of awareness of teaching *in the making*, a process to which readers of the diary are subsequently made privy. This shared experience, we believe, has a strong potential to propel individual and collaborative teacher development. As a part of the evolving paradigm of *exploratory practice* (Allwright and Lenzuen, 1997; Allwright, 2003) and *action research* in teacher development (Crookes and Chandler, 2001; Edge, 2001; Burns, 2005; Warneke, 2007), it is worth being pursued. However, having made this plea for increased teacher-led explorations of their own practices, we agree with Borg that language professionals will only become increasingly involved in different forms of exploratory practice when conditions such as material, structural and intellectual support and the potential for dissemination are in place (Borg, unpublished; as cited in Burns, 2005: 69).

13.6 IMPLICATIONS OF NARRATIVE INQUIRY FOR SELF-KNOWLEDGE AND PROFESSIONALISM

The previous sections have been concerned with second language teacher development. Perhaps at this point of the discussion it would be helpful to remind ourselves of Tarone and Allwright's (2005) definition of teacher development as concerned with *understanding* (which they distinguish from *training* and *education*);

> By understanding, we are referring to something beyond merely having a particular skill or having a certain piece of knowledge. **Understanding is whatever helps us to use our skill and knowledge appropriately.** Knowing how to get learners to work in groups (a pedagogic skill) and knowing that it could help their linguistic development (pedagogic knowledge) does not in itself mean we are not going perhaps to make unwise decisions about the use of group work in our lessons. (p. 7, emphasis added)

'Appropriately' is the operative word here. We can use our focal teacher Graham to illustrate the significance of this point. Our data suggest that Graham can deploy his teaching skills (e.g. using textbooks and other teaching material) to enact his lexical approach to language teaching, which incorporates a principle for 'on-the-spot' correction of student errors. His preferred teaching approach (e.g. his reference to Michael Lewis's, 2002 work) suggests that he has a knowledge of language teaching as a professional field. But does this particular combination of knowledge and skills benefit his students? In other words, is he using his knowledge and skills appropriately? One conventional way to answer this question is to look at the measurable learning outcomes of his students, e.g., assignment marks and test scores. Given that Graham is well-regarded as a teacher in a commercially run school where student 'results' matter, we can take it that his students have achieved expected level of marks and test scores. But for Graham to develop further as a professional teacher, he must understand his pedagogic beliefs and actions and the impact they may have on his students. This kind of understanding of one's own professional beliefs, values and actions is primarily reflexive—one has to detach oneself from one's own experience and examine it with the sensibilities 'from the other side'.

We believe that this case study shows the exploratory, formative and empowering potential of collaborative and individual narratives in the study of teacher development. Graham's narrative accounts pull aspects of his past and his present lives, his dispositions and his experience as a language teacher and as a language learner together in a personally coherent representation that has enabled Graham to achieve a deeper understanding of his own beliefs and actions. At the same time for us as teacher educators and researchers, these accounts provide us with an opportunity to explore the connections between theories and principles in second language teaching and their uptake and use by practitioners. Freeman (2002: 11) puts it succinctly, thus:

> If teachers' mental lives are stories or narrative webs of past and present experience, if their knowledge is reflective of their position in the activity of teaching, then it makes sense that reflective practice must become a central pillar in teacher education.

We know from current research that teacher development is a multi-faceted, dynamic and complex career-long process involving a whole host of individual, social and institutional factors (see earlier references). And it clearly involves on-going acquisition of new and different skills and knowledge, and these tend to be prioritised in teacher training and education schemes that would support some form of collective professionalism. However, for teachers to develop a sense of independent professionalism, they need to achieve some understanding of their pedagogic beliefs and actions, a key ingredient of which is reflexive self-knowledge. The narrative inquiries we have shown in this discussion can make a major contribution to that self-knowledge.

REFERENCES

Allwright, D., "A brief guide to exploratory practice", *Language Teaching Research*, **7**.2 (2003): 109–112.

Allwright, D. and R. Lenzuen, Exploratory practice: work at the Cultura Inglesa, Rio de Janeiro, Brazil. *Language Teaching Research*, **1**.1 (1997): 73–79

Andon, N., *What roles do theory and research play in language teaching? A case study on the task-based approach in language teaching (unpublished thesis)*. (PhD), King's College London, London, 2009.

Appel, J., *Diary of a Language Teacher*, Heineman: Oxford, 1995.

Bailey, K.M., "Competitiveness and anxiety in adult second language learning: Looking at and through the diary studies", in H.W. Seliger and M.H. Long (Eds.), *Classroom Oriented Research in Second Language Acquisition*, Rowley, MA: Newbury House, 67–103.

_____, "The Use of Diary Studies in Teacher Education Programmes," in: Richards, J. and D. Nunan (Eds.), *Second Language Teacher Education*, Cambridge: Cambridge University Press (1990): 215–226.

_____, A. Curtis and D. Nunan, *Pursuing Professional Development: The self as source*, Boston, MA: Heinle and Heinle, 2001.

Bailey, K.M. and Nunan, D. (Eds.), *Voices from the Language Classroom*, Cambridge: Cambridge University Press, 1996.

Bardovi-Harlig, K. and Hartford, B. (Eds.), *Beyond Methods: Components of second language teacher education*, New York: McGraw-Hill, 1997.

Barkhuizen, G., "Narrative Knowledging", *TESOL Quarterly*, **45**.3 (2011): 391–414.

Barkhuizen, G., Benson, P. and Chik, A., *Narrative Inquiry in Language Teaching and Learning Research*, New York, NY: Routledge, 2014.

Bartels, N. (Ed.), *Applied Linguistics and Language Teacher Education*, New York: Springer, 2005.

Birch, G., "Language learning case study approach to second language teacher education", in J. Flowerdew, M.N. Brock and S. Hsia (Eds.), *Perspectives on Second Language Teacher Education*, 283–294, (Hong Kong: City Polytechnic of Hong Kong: Bolton (2002): 1992.

Bolton, G., *Reflective Practice, Writing and Professional Development*, London: Paul Chapman, 2002.

Borg, S., *Teacher Cognition and Language Education: Research and Practice*, London: Continuum, 2006.

Burns, A., "Action Research: An evolving paradigm?" *Language Teaching*, **38**.2 (2005): 57–74.

Burton, J., A cross-case analysis of teacher involvement in TESOL research, *TESOL Quarterly*, **32**.3 (1998): 419–446.

Cheng, L. and H. Wang, Understanding professional challenges faced by Chinese teachers of English, *TESL-EJ* 7.4. < http://www-writing.berkeley.edu/TESl-EJ/ej28/a2.html>, retrieved on 23/10/2008, 2004.

Clandinin, D.J. and Connelly, F.M., *Narrative Inquiry: Experience and story in qualitative research,* San Francisco: Jossey-Bass, 2000.

Crookes, G. and Chandler, P., Introducing action research into post-secondary foreign language teacher education, *Foreign Language Annals*, **34**.2 (2001): 131–40.

Doughty, C. and J. Williams (Eds.), *Focus on Form in Classroom Second Language Acquisition*, Cambridge: Cambridge University Press, 1998.

Edge, J. (Ed.), *Action Research*, Alexandria, VA: Teachers of English to Speakers of Other Languages, Inc. (TESOL), 2001.

Ellis, R., *Task-based Language Learning and Teaching*, Oxford: Oxford University Press, 2003.

Farrell, T., 'ESL/EFL Teacher Development Through Journal Writing', *RELC Journal*, **29**.1 (1998): 92–109.

Fradd, S. and Lee, O., Development of a knowledge base for ESOL teacher education, *Teaching and Teacher Education*, **14** (1998): 761–773.

Freeman, D., The hidden side of the work: teacher knowledge and learning to teach, *Language Teaching,* **35** (2002): 1–13.

Gass, S.M., Learning and teaching: The necessary intersection, in F.R. Eckman, D. Highland, P.W. Lee, J. Mileham and R.R. Weber (Eds.), *Second Language Acquisition Theory and Pedagogy*, Mahwah, NJ: Erlbaum (1995): 3–20.

Griffiths, M. and Tann, S., Using reflective practice to link personal and public theories, *Journal of Education for Teaching*, **18** (1992): 69–84.

Jarvis, J., Using diaries for teacher reflection on in-service courses, *ELT Journal*, **46**.2 (1992): 133–143.

Johnson, K.E. and P.B. Golombek (Eds.), *Teachers' Narrative Inquiry as Professional Development*, Cambridge: Cambridge University Press, 2002.

_____, *Second Teacher Language Education: A sociocultural perspective*, New York, NY: Routledge, 2009.

_____, The transformative power of narrative in second language teacher education, *TESOL Quarterly*, **45**.3 (2011): 486–509.

Kalaja, P. and Fereirra Barcelos (Eds.), *Beliefs about SLA*, Springer, 2003.

Leung, C., Second language teacher professionalism, in A. Burns and J.C. Richards (Eds.), *Cambridge Guide to Second Language Teacher Education*, Cambridge: Cambridge University Press (2009): 49–58.

―――, Second/additional language teacher professionalism—What is it? In M. Olofsson (Ed.), *Symposium 2012: Lärarrollen I svenska som andraspråk*, Stockholm: Stockholms universitets förlag (2013): 11–27.

Lewis, M., *Implementing the Lexical Approach: Putting theory to practice*, Thompson, 2002.

Long, M., Focus on form: A design feature in language teaching methodology, in de Bot, K., Ginsberg, R. and Kramsch, C. (Eds.), *Foreign Language Research in Cross-Cultural Perspective*, Amsterdam: Benjamins (1991): 39–51.

Lowe, T., 'An experiment in role reversal: Teachers as language learners', *ELT Journal*, **41**.2 (1987): 89–96.

Mann, S., Talking ourselves into understanding, in Johnson and Golombek (Eds.) (2002): 159–209.

Prawat, R., Conversations with self and settings: A framework for thinking about teacher empowerment, *American Educational Research Journal*, **28**.4, 737–757.

Richards, K., Pepys into a TEFL course, *ELT Journal*, **46**.2 (1992): 144–152.

Richards, J., *Beyond training*. Cambridge: Cambridge University Press, 1998.

Richards, J. and T. Farrell, *Professional Development for Language Teachers: Strategies for teacher learning*. Cambridge: Cambridge University Press, 2005.

Roberts, J., *Language Teacher Education*, London: Arnold, 1998.

Santana-Williams, E., Early reflections: Journaling a way into teaching, in Edge (Ed.) (2002b) (2001): 74–83.

Skehan, P., A non-marginal role for tasks, *ELT Journal*, **56**.3 (2002): 289–295.

Steward, T., Teacher-Researcher Collaboration or Teachers' Research? *TESOL Quarterly*, **40**.2 (2006): 421–430.

Tarone, E. and Allwright, D., Second language teacher learning and student second language learning: shaping the knowledge base, in D.J. Tedick (Ed.), *Second language teacher education: international perspectives*, Mahwah, N.J.: Lawrence Erlbaum Associates, Publishers (2005): 5–23.

Tinker Sachs, G. (Ed.), *Action research: fostering and furthering effective practices in the teaching of English*, Hong Kong: City University of Hong Kong, 2002.

Towndrow, P., Reflections of an on-line tutor, *ELT Journal*, **58**.2 (2004): 174–181.

Warneke, D., Aktionsforschung und Praxisbezug in der DaF-Lehrerausbildung [Action research in German-as-a-foreign-language teacher training]. Kassel: Kassel University Press, 2007.

Waters, A., J. Sunderland, T. Bray, and J. Allwright, "Getting the Best out of the Language-Learning Experience," *ELT Journal*, **44**.4 (1990): 305–315.

Woods, D., *Teacher cognition in language teaching*. Cambridge: Cambridge University Press, 1996.

Chapter 14

REDEFINING LEARNER AUTONOMY IN THE INDIAN ESL CONTEXT

— P. Bhaskaran Nair

Since the relationship between language and culture is that of part–whole, cultural constructs facilitate as well as hinder the processes of language learning. Though these interactions among culture, cognition and language are difficult to be perceived or traced in the case of the development of the first language, they both form a decisive link and play a crucial role in the development of a second or foreign language. The teacher of a second language, therefore, is supposed to make the best use of the facilitating role of culture and, at the same time, try to minimize those elements of culture which adversely affect the learning of the target language. It is in this context that, the term 'learner-centredness' is to be redefined in the Indian context, taking into consideration the extent autonomy or independence a learner can have in learning a second language (as opposed to a content subject), especially in a formal setup of instruction. As freedom or autonomy is most welcome in one's personal life, where one deals with familiar things in familiar situations; so is the case with the positive change that autonomy may bring in promoting the use of one's first language, and thereby enabling the user to scale the heights of creative use of that language. But this need not be so in the case of learning a second language where the learner is willingly or by force engaged in cracking the code of a strange system. The question then is that how much autonomy does the learner need to feel comfortable and natural in the process of learning a new language and how much can be given in a formal setup like a classroom for attaining target of 'how to mean in a second language'.

In a broad sense, autonomy has always been the ultimate aim of any educational programme in the sense that the learner is expected to proceed from a highly rigid frame of subject matter and a strictly controlled process of learning towards self-chosen areas of studies and self-directed processes of learning. In an attempt to view curriculum from a descriptive point of view, rejecting the traditional prescriptive, Nunan (1988) sketches it as what teachers actually do rather than what should be done. He rightly claims that his is a bottom-up view of curriculum development since it has been based on studies what teachers do and think at various levels of planning, implementing and evaluating their language programmes, leaving little room in his discussion for what curriculum specialists dictate what teachers ought to do. Nunan's approach has been considered an important landmark in curri-culum development in ESL. Ever since this shift of focus in curriculum studies, greater emphasis has been given to the related concept of learner-centredness either as a subsequent or a consequent development.

Before examining the scope of learner autonomy in the context of learning a second language, let us begin the discussion from a very broad perspective wherein one can state that the ultimate aim of all education is the individual's autonomy: autonomy in life in its physical aspects such as social and economic fields as well as in its metaphysical aspects such as cognitive and psychological fields. In the case of adult learners, Brindley (1984) suggests:

> One of the fundamental principles underlying the notion of permanent education is that education should develop in individuals the capacity to control their own destiny and that, therefore, the learner should be seen as being at the centre of the educational process (p. 15).

Therefore, any effort in the direction of attaining autonomy through language education necessarily fulfils part of the overall goal. When it comes to the question of ESL, the notion of autonomy needs to be discussed in more accurate details in linguistic as well as cognitive terms and, above all, in socio-cultural terms as well. Learner autonomy in first language and personal autonomy through first language cannot be taken as a starting point in discussing autonomy in a second language.

One can notice that, as in any other fields of research, in the area of second language acquisition, there has been a great proliferation of literature and, as well as a result, notions which had been taken for granted in earlier discussions started getting special and specific treatment in detail, later on. In the recent past, the term 'learner-centredness' assumed the status of a serious research topic and, by the 1990s, two trends were clearly visible in its analysis. While some in the profession viewed 'learner-centredness' in positive terms, denoting the direction in which the whole process of second language learning has to move, quite a few professionals are rather skeptic about the focus of the term. They point out that the term could be interpreted in a too individualistic manner and, therefore, suggests a substitute term 'learning-centredness' in the sense that the whole process of learning will be the focus of study (Tudor 1996).

A growing interest among researchers resulted in the coinage of quite a few technical terms related to the degree of freedom the learner needs. Two key terms used to recur in the discussions on learner autonomy since the 1970s are (i) learner needs and (ii) learner training. Learner-centred curriculum removes the core grammatical features of the second language from the nuclear position and places the message that the learner wants to convey in the centre of the whole process. Learner training fixes its goal in such a position so as to enable the learner to learn more effectively and encourages him to take on more responsibilities on his own. Learner training, thus, can be viewed as a mid-point on the continuum, linking between learner-centredness and learner autonomy. It aims at the learners' independence (Ellis and Sinclair 1989):

> Learner training is, then, related to the concept of learner autonomy in that it aims to provide learners with the ability, which is strategies and confidence, to take on more responsibilities for their own learning although it does not thrust autonomy upon them. Instead, its aim is to prepare learners for independence (p. 3).

It means, in a learner-centred programme, the learner gets actively involved in both goal-setting and choice of methodology. This assumes a great dimension of challenge especially in a socio-cultural setup in which even adults are not capable of assuming self-responsibility when it comes to one's own learning, as it has been evident in the realm of higher education where the advanced-level learners are neither interested in becoming part of decision making nor do they feel proud of giving shape to their own future course. Getting rid of the clutches of current beliefs and concepts of education and thereby growing into a self-chosen direction may not be easy for young learners. As a prelude, therefore, a great deal of awareness raising has to be undertaken when we start thinking of providing the ESL learners with more and more autonomy. Learner training marks this stage of transition from the traditional teacher- or expert-dictated curriculum to learner-suggested programme of action (Tudor 1996):

> Learner training could, therefore, be defined as the process by which learners are helped to deepen their understanding of the nature of language learning, and to acquire the knowledge and skills they need in order to pursue their learning goals in an informed and self-directive manner. Learner training, therefore, constitutes the starting point and an enabling condition for the reflective involvement of language learners in their language study (p. 37).

Coming back to the point of learner needs in the context of learning a second language, the term has been interpreted in two ways: first the communicative needs which the learner is likely to encounter during and after education when he is in the target language community or during his association with a speaker of the target language in the host community. Secondly, and more importantly, the learner has to be aware of or to be made aware of the linguistic, cognitive and metacognitive prerequisites for mastering the code of the target language. It is this second interpretation of the term 'learner needs' that links it with study skills on the one side and learner training on the other. The learner's choice of strategies to reach the self-set goals links study skills from the linguistic perspective with learner training from the metacognitive perspective. Therefore, the discussion of the term 'learner-needs' should not be confined exclusively to the factors which are conventionally covered by the umbrella term 'communicative competence'. In this context, Brindley (1984) observes:

> ... Instructional programmes should be centred around learners' needs and that learners themselves should exercise their own responsibility in the choice of learning objectives, content and methods as well as in determining the means used to assess their performances (p. 15).

Learner autonomy has gained wide currency against the backdrop of humanistic thinking related to education. Writing in 2001, Lynch critically analyzed the important studies in the area of learner autonomy during the preceding decade. Quoting Pennycook (1997: 39), he states that the term learner autonomy "has rapidly achieved a moral status backed by dominant beliefs in liberal progressive education" (in Lynch 2001: 390). He uses the term to include learner independence as well, and identifies learning and communication strategies, self-directed learning, self-access centres, learner-centredness and collaborative learning as areas of study related to one another and which form the literature on the topic. He also narrows down the definition of learner autonomy as follows:

> Autonomy is often described in terms of learners' degree of freedom to select, practise and act within the confines of the language teaching institution, rather than their capacity to continue to learn English in their daily interaction with the academic discourse community (*ibid.*, 390–391).

A comprehensive study of the notions of learner-centredness, learner independence and learner autonomy has not been attempted in this chapter; all that has been aimed at here is to present the three concepts on a continuum and thereby trace the progression of research studies in this area during the last 10–15 years. An enquiry into the feasibility of applying these theoretical constructs in the ESL classroom, especially in the Indian contexts, may be relevant in this context.

Learner autonomy in first language acquisition has always been taken for granted; and autonomy in general terms through the use of first language is a social construct rather than a pedagogic issue. But attaining autonomy in second language learning cannot be analyzed within the frame of a classroom; it must be perceived against the background of socio-cultural realities which mould an individual *in toto*. Therefore, autonomy needs to be interpreted in terms of the learners' past experience related to second language classroom and, in general, to their overall experience. Adult learners come to the classroom with their own expectations about language learning, their roles in the classroom and the roles of their teacher. These expectations and experiences are culture-bound. Thus, adult learners may find it difficult to come to terms with the learner-centred curriculum in which they have to play multiple roles ranging from decision makers to self-assessors. Ellis and

Sinclair (1989) point out that the unfamiliarity with the new modes of learning may lead to frustration and they may revert to traditional modes.

Tarone and Yule (1989) also point out the dangers of transition from a classroom situation "in which teachers overtly control the activities of a group in a relatively formal manner" and in which the learners have "to maintain a subordinate and passive role" to a classroom in which "the teacher assumes a less authoritarian role, and expects interactive group work among students" (p. 9). In such classes, there is every chance of the teacher ignoring the noncooperative and noninteracting learner or the teacher may be forced to abandon the experiment of learner autonomy because of large group's hostility.

Commenting on the "perennial tension in language teaching", namely, making a choice between the traditional subject-centred curriculum and the proposed learner-centred curriculum, Nunan (1988) states as follows:

> Proponents of learner-centred curricula are less interested in learners acquiring the totality of the language than in assisting them gain the communicative and linguistic skills they need to carry out real-world tasks. Implicit in this learner-centred view is that no one person (even the native speaker) ever masters every aspect of the language (p. 22).

In the case of beginners and young learners, how can these statements be validated? Young learners of ESL in India (and even adult learners at the advanced level) are reluctant to interact with one another and with the teacher just because they are (rightly) conscious about their poor and inadequate linguistic as well as communicative competence. Though they are a little or vaguely aware of the needs of the real world, they cannot be made aware of how they have to have a grip on the more abstract prerequisites for learning a foreign code in a better and more independent way. A certain level of familiarity with the tool is imperative in starting to use the tool; and in such a context, the learner naturally prefers a subject-centred curriculum by surrendering his autonomy.

The question of culture-boundness in learning ESL has been well-addressed by researchers. Tudor (1996), for example, deals with culturally-based traditions of teaching and learning. Language learners are individuals who differ from one another on a number of parameters; at the same time, they are members of a socio-cultural community which enforces on them certain degree of homogeneity in terms of expectations. Tudor asserts the need of creating an interface in an instructional programme wherein the language learner's individual self and social self can be brought together:

> ... A learner centred approach to teaching must work with the socio-cultural aspects of their identity as much as with the more individual aspects of their identity (p. xi).

To conclude, any attempt of leading instructional programmes closer to learner autonomy, or any experiment of making the second language learner more and more independent, must take into consideration the socio-cultural traditions which have moulded the past educational experiences of the learner. Moreover, any such attempt should ensure a smooth and gradual transition causing minimal tension to the learners as well as the teachers.

REFERENCES

Brindley, G., *Needs Analysis and Objective Setting to Adult Migrant Education Programmes*, Sydney: NSW Adult Migrant Education Service, 1984.

Ellis, G. and Sinclair, B., *Learning to Learn English*, Cambridge: Cambridge University Press, 1989.

Lynch, T., "Promoting EAP learner autonomy in second language university context," *Research Perspectives on English for Academic Purposes*, J. Flowerdew and M. Peacock (Eds.), Cambridge: Cambridge University Press, 2001, 370–493.

Nunan, D., *The Learner-Centred Curriculum*, Cambridge: Cambridge University Press, 1988.

Pennycook, "Cultural alternatives and autonomy," *Autonomy and Independence in Language Learning*, P. Benson and P. Valler (Eds.), London: Longman, 1997, 35–63.

Tarone, B. and Yule G., *Focus on the Language Learner*, Oxford: OUP, 1989.

Tudor, S., *Learner-Centredness as Language Education*, Cambridge: Cambridge University Press, 1996.

Chapter 15

TEACHING ENGLISH AT UNDERGRADUATE LEVEL
Groping in the Dark?

— INDIRA NITYANANDAM

English in Gujarat is taught with varying levels of interest and proficiency, lack of interest and proficiency, as a painful necessity, as a necessary evil, as a ladder towards the job market, as a sure step towards assured success in today's globalized world, as a tool for computer use, as a magic key that may open many doors, etc. In all these, no one (not even the framers of policy, nor the teacher, nor the learner) is aware of the theories of language acquisition, the inter-related role of FL or second language (SL) or even third language (TL) in any language learning, the concepts of inter-language or of Universal Grammar (UG). It is these that have to be taken into account before any meaningful curriculum design, syllabi framing, classroom teaching or actual language acquisition can take place. This chapter raises questions that may need to be addressed before any meaningful language acquisition can happen through ELT. The questions gain further relevance when we remember that 6-month courses in a foreign language equip the student with the ability to communicate at an elementary level, but even after 8 or 10 or 12 years of ELT, 80% of our students are incapable of using English for communication. In India, where multi-lingualism—even more than bi-lingualism—is the rule rather than the exception, the teaching-learning of English needs to be reviewed if we wish to make it more effective and useful. Theories of Second Language Acquisition may prove useful for our understanding of the problem and our attempts to find lasting solutions.

The influences of L1 in the initial stages of L2 acquisition are understandable and acceptable, but the constant use of the translation method in L2 teaching has made interlanguage representation an intrinsic part of L2 acquisition in our classrooms. Whether it is the word order or the formation of questions, one notices with dismay that appropriate functional structures are not learnt or used. Does this arise from faulty linguistic inputs or is it a permanent feature of interlanguage representation? Is it possible that interlanguage representation can be defective in one domain and not in another? Hence, a student with Gujarati as L1 learns word order but fails to move out of the erroneous use of double past tense—'I didn't wrote my essay'. This may lead us to question and analyze the concept of UG or Universal Grammar—a natural language grammar which is internalized by every language learner—"a given in advance", a core property for language acquisition by humans.

In L2 or SL learning, as in the case of English in India, the learner builds upon pre-existing conceptual knowledge while in L1 or FL, knowledge of the world and knowledge of the language develop simultaneously. Do our students, at every level of English language learning, treat language as an object of explicit learning? Moreover, we have to constantly remind ourselves that L1 pattern of acquisition results from natural exposure whereas classroom exposure is necessarily artificially created. Again, in L1, a learner has lexically specific patterns from which abstract categories are later developed while in L2, learning knowledge of abstract categories have already been acquired. In this process, there is a constant conflict between the rules of L1 and L2. Moreover, in ELT, there is very little scope for actual use of the language outside the classroom situation. Thus, the learner is ill-equipped to use L2 in actual-life situations when the need arises.

In the context of ELT in India, the specific demands of constantly juggling two languages in a single mind as a psycho-linguistic study has probably not been really analysed or understood by teachers, nor have they looked at the resultant problems. Do our learners possess two lexicons or one? Should the lexicon be considered in terms of its representation or its semantics? Does a bilingual speaker\user in the learning of L2 (in our case English) selectively activate his lexicon in one language, or is it an integrated lexicon where it is possible to have a nonselective and parallel activation of word forms in both languages? Studies and research have attempted to answer these and more questions. (Doughty and Long, 2003: 106)

1. How are lexical forms in each language represented and activated during reading?
2. Are semantic representations shared across the bilinguals' two languages?
3. On what basis are lexical and semantic representations connected for words and concepts in each language?
4. How are words spoken in the second language when a more dominant alternative always exists in the first language?
5. How is the activation of lexical form and meaning controlled so that bilinguals recognize and speak words in the intended language?

However, one is not sure whether the answers to these questions have been analysed scientifically enough by us to make our classroom ELT more effective. The Berlitz method or the Direct method has to probably be more challengingly accepted by teachers in Indian college classrooms. Then a 'cultural island' where only L2 is used can develop by the use of Total Physical Response (TPR) or the view that language skills are acquired more rapidly if the kinesthetic sensory system is involved, and language comprehension should develop before oral participation (as it does in the case of children in L1 learning). This is based on the 'trace theory of memory' which claims activities such as motor activity and verbal rehearsal will strengthen memory connection and facilitate recall. This is probably more essential in ELT at the earlier stages or the first few years of our students' exposure to the English language as L2.

L2 pedagogy has to be rethought in India to a great extent. If comprehensible input of L2 causes acquisition as suggested by the natural Approach, and later by Krashen's theory of L2 acquisition, ELT in India needs to think about cross-linguistic interference as we often use the Translation Method in ELT classrooms. In L2 acquisition, the learner undergoes the same stages of temporary optionality that a child does in L1 acquisition. For adult learners, as Scorace (1996) has suggested, optionality is due to L1 as an additional source of optionality: L2 optionality persisting even at advanced competence levels. In India, in English as L2, this is particularly noticeable in verb positions, choice of tenses, the use of definite and indefinite articles, etc. In L1 learning, in a child, preference for one option becomes obvious in course of time. In adult learners, the dispreferred option never disappears and hence the Indian learner of English continues to make the same grammatical errors. The fact that optionality is selective may also explain why certain syntactical errors continue even at an advanced stage of L2 acquisition.

Each one of the above points prove that learning English as L2 for the Indian student is a far more complex process than merely imitating linguistic structures. It is in the context of the above problems that curriculum designing and syllabus framing has to be undertaken in the Indian context. If we agree with Prabhu's definition of syllabus as a plan with its function being to specify what is to be taught and in what order, this becomes even more imperative.

Mohammed (2008) lists the types of syllabuses, giving a detailed analysis of their characteristics, advantages and disadvantages. They are merly being listed here to indicate the possibilities: procedural, structural, cultural, situational, skill-based, multi-dimensional, formal, task-based, etc. To make ELT in India more effective and focused, curriculum designers and syllabus framers need to study and analyse these types. Only then will ELT achieve its purpose in India.

REFERENCE

Doughty, Catherine, J. and Long Michael, H., *Second Language Acquisition*, USA: Blackwell, 2003.

Mohammed, Mohsin Far, "An overview of syllabuses in ELT," *Karen's Linguistic Issues* (January 2008).

Sorace, A., "The use of acceptability judgements in L2 acquisition research," *Handbook of Second Language Acquisition*, W. Ritchie and T. Bhatia (Eds.), New York: Academic Press, 1996.

Chapter 16

APPLYING KNOWLEDGE OF PSYCHOLINGUISTICS IN LANGUAGE TEACHING AND LEARNING

— MAYA KHEMLANI DAVID AND DAVID YOONG

16.1 INTRODUCTION

Psycholinguistics is a cross-disciplinary field that amalgamates psychology, namely, cognitive psychology with linguistics. One of the jobs of psycholinguists is to study the cognitive processes of the brain in acquiring and generating grammatical and meaningful sentence out of vocabulary and grammatical structures, as well as the processes that make it possible to understand utterances, words, text, etc. (Steinberg and Sciarini 2006). Knowledge of psycholinguistics is, however, not strictly restricted to the domains of psycholinguistics as it can be applied in language pedagogy vis-à-vis receptive skills; reading and listening skills and vocabulary acquisition (David 2006). Hence, teachers must realise the importance of cognitive processes and their influence on language learning. The informed teachers must know of the numerous, minute, yet distinct processes that take place in the human brain which make possible both production and comprehension.

As language production (speaking and writing) and reception (reading and listening) are important elements in language pedagogy, this paper discusses these language processors from the top-down and bottom-up point of view, which includes schemas, miscues and ambiguity. These concepts are important in language learning and teaching vis-à-vis language production and reception.

16.2 LANGUAGE PRODUCTION AND COMPREHENSION

Basically, all communication models posit that communication occurs when information produced by one party which is received by another (Shannon and Weaver 1949). The information may be enacted through a number of means such as verbal (aural) and non-verbal language (vis-à-vis tactile, olfactory, gustatory, visual and other perceptual messages) (Ruthrof 2000).

Using magnetic resonance imaging (MRI), neurolinguistics have shown through aphasias that specific areas of the brain play important roles in both language production and comprehension. Broca's area, which lies in the frontal lobes, deals with language structures (i.e. sentences, words) while the Wernicke's area, which lies in the temporal region area, addresses semantic coherence, meaning and schema. Studies (Gardner et al.: 1975) have shown that damage to the Broca's area will affect the production of speech. The speech of Broca's aphasics consists mainly of content words, few grammatical morphemes and complex sentences, which resemble the telegraphic speech. In short, the Broca's area is in charge of top-down processes. Damage to the Wernicke's area, on the other hand, will render the speech of Wernicke's aphasics unintelligible as their utterances will be void of content and coherence despite the well-formed grammatical morphemes and complex sentences.

The relationship between top-down as well as bottom-up processes and the brain regions can be seen in Figure 16.1.

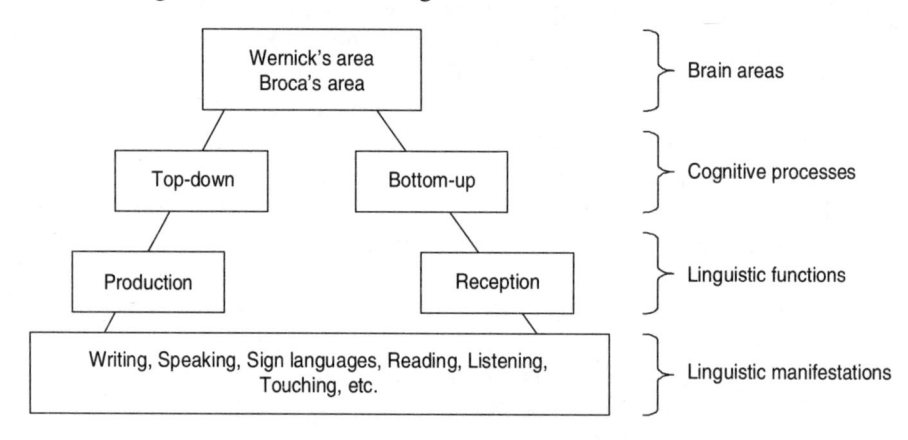

FIGURE 16.1 Model of language processes.

In short, the Broca and Wernicke's areas are used in both top-down and bottom-up processes.

16.2.1 Top-down Processes

Top-down processes are frequently known as processes that deal with information output. Language knowledge as well as schemas (triggered through bottom-up processes) are used in top-down processes to convey messages through words arranged in sentences/phrases as well as nonverbal cues.

At this juncture, it is perhaps imperative to note that top-down and bottom-up processes are not exclusively divided as they work hand-in-hand in both language reception and production. Westen (1996: 164–165) acknowledged that despite top-down processing starting 'at the top' from the observer's expectations and knowledge, top-down skills are used to also organise and interpret incoming sensations (bottom-up) based on prior knowledge and expectations rather than waiting for perceptions to form their own features.

From the psycholinguistic perspective, the Wernicke's and Broca's areas are involved in top-down processes. Firstly, before language is produced, the Wernicke's area passes its intended meanings to the Broca's area where abstract meanings are formulated in sentences. If the Wernicke's area is damaged, the message will be unintelligible.

Next, the Broca's area directs the necessary body parts to produce the meaning. If the individual is going to produce the meaning aurally, the Broca's area will direct the lungs to exhale air, the glottal to modify the air into sounds, and nasal and oral cavities to further modify the airflow. If the individual is going to produce the meaning in written form, the Broca's area will direct the muscles of the fingers (or other body parts if fingers are absent) to formulate shapes by manipulating the movements of the pen/pencil or coordinate the fingers to press certain buttons on the keyboard. Should the Broca's area be damaged, words will be slurred if spoken and letters will be laboured, uncoordinated, and take on a sloppy appearance (see Strub and Geschwind 1983).

Reverting to the functions of top-down processes, these processes in time are influenced by the attitude of the larger sociocultural practices in regards to language learning. Holmes (2001) wrote that people usually

> Do not hold opinions about languages in a vacuum ... they develop attitudes towards language which reflect their views about those who speak the languages, and the contexts and functions with which they are associated. (p. 343)

These attitudes are usually influenced by economic factors. Consider the Malaysian Sindhi community: The younger generations are shifting to English, an international language, and, thus, losing their mother tongue Sindhi because they do not view their mother tongue as having 'real importance' in terms of economic survival (see David 2001). Another group, the younger generations of Jawanese living in Perak, are shifting away from their Jawanese dialect to the 'standard' Malaysian Malay (see Mohd. Yasin: 1998) because they view the latter, and not their mother tongue, as a means of economic survival.

Politics and social factors also influence perception and attitudes towards languages. Of late, the previous Malaysian Minister of Culture, Arts and Heritage, Dr. Rais Yatim proposed that advertisers who display 'broken Malay' in their advertisements be punished. It is his perception that the Malay language should be safeguarded because it is a cultural value that defines the Malays. The enforcement of 'proper language,' in turn, causes individuals to comply to political powers. Also, because standard Malay is used extensively in various domains such as political administration, news media and in home domains, nonstandard Malay such as Bahasa Pasar (lit. Agoralingua) and Peranakan Malay are treated as inferior codes that are associated with being 'unrefined' and 'uneducated'. These practices and beliefs (bottom-up processes based on top-down processes) contribute to the development of schemas in top-down processes. In short, some individuals may view certain languages positively which, in turn, would make them acquire these codes. On the other hand, individuals with negative reaction to certain languages will diverge away from these codes.

16.2.2 Bottom-up Processes

Bottom-up processes on the other hand, are processes that deal with information input. According to Westen (1996), bottom-up processing refers to the process that begins 'at the bottom' with raw data 'feeding' up to the brain (p. 165). Information received through sensory motors (e.g. eyes, fingers, and ears) is encoded in the brain for comprehension. As mentioned earlier, both bottom-up and top-down processes in reality are not exclusively divided. The top-down processes also play a role during information input. Information received from sensory perceptions is filtered and categorised accordingly to the existing schemas and knowledge of the real world. Hence, individuals do not input every bit of information they receive, but they are selective. The top-down processing can, thus, be seen as a means of preventing information overload.

In terms of language processing, the Broca's area identifies and deciphers the input, both words and sentences. Then information is passed on to the Wernicke's area where the contents are analysed and organised.

The bottom-up processes are especially important in language acquisition. Ideally, young children who are free from the political and social contraints with regards to languages are able to acquire languages provided that they receive exposure to the language. Infants spoken to in baby-talk slowly recognise the codes their parents use and through repetitive stimulants of the language, they soon acquire competence in the codes. As for second language learners, they too have to be exposed to the language in order to build a sense of familiarity of the codes.

The Bottom-up processes are impeded, however, by attitudes as well as social and political factors. As mentioned earlier, an individual who views certain languages as 'valueless', for instance, may not acquire the language. Similarly, an individual who views pronunciation of certain words as 'wrong,' will react negatively towards the 'wrong' words when they are used (for instance, see Labov 1963 on the perception of New Yorkers on the 'r' sounds). Political and social factors too influence bottom-up processes. The enforcement of 'proper language' requires compliance of language use in advertisements or else advertisers will have to face punishment. Hence, the language use on advertisements will be received by the audience through bottom-up processes, who would, in turn, replicate these standards of codes.

16.3 APPLICATION OF LANGUAGE PROCESSING IN PEDAGOGY

There are various language teaching methods that can incorporate the use of language processes. They include the use of:

- Multi-modalities in language production.
- Existing schemas in language production and language comprehension.
- Miscues tests in language comprehension.
- Strategies to unveil ambiguity in language comprehension.

16.3.1 Multi-modalities in Language Production

It must be noted that language processes are dependent on contexts and situations as languages themselves are meaningless if they are not contextual or situtational. Ruthrof (2000: 151–152) provided some important maxims of languages, which include:

- Language does not mean by itself.
- Language is parasitic on nonlinguistic signs.
- Meaning is an event.
- Meaning events occur when language grids are activated by nonverbal signs.
- When meaning occurs, linguistic expressions act as directional schemata.
- Nonverbal signs are made up of tactile, olfactory, gustatory, aural, visual and other perceptual readings as well as their fantasy variants.
- Only the linguistic signifier is arbitrary.
- The signified are not arbitrary.
- All natural-language meanings display traces of concrete social situations.

These maxims demonstrate that language use itself is dependent on other contextual markers. The communicative teaching of Helen Keller is one prime example that supports these maxims. Helen Keller became both visually and hearing impaired when she was an infant, but through various linguistic bottom-up strategies, as taught to her by her teacher Anne Sullivan, which included tactile and olfactory communication (bottom-up processes), Helen developed her linguistic knowledge which eventually allowed her to communicate (top-down).

Also, the dual coding theory proposed by Paivio (1986) attempts to give equal weight to verbal and nonverbal processing:

> Human cognition is unique in that it has become specialized for dealing simultaneously with language and with nonverbal objects and events. Moreover, the language system is peculiar in that it deals directly with linguistic input and output (in the form of speech or writing) while at the

same time serving a symbolic function with respect to nonverbal objects, events, and behaviours. Any representational theory must accommodate this dual functionality. (p. 53)

The theory assumes that there are two cognitive subsystems: (i) representation and nonverbal objects/events processing (i.e., imagery) and (ii) the other specialized for dealing with language. Paivio also postulates two different types of representational units: (i) "imagens" for mental images and (ii) "logogens" for verbal entities, which he describes as being similar to "chunks". Logogens are organized in terms of associations and hierarchies while imagens are organized in terms of part-whole relationships.

Multimodality resembles the Dual Coding theory (Clark and Paivio 1991) where there are three types of processing:

1. **Representational**—The direct activation of verbal or nonverbal representations;
2. **Referential**—The activation of the verbal system by the nonverbal system or vice-versa; and
3. **Associative**—The activation of representations within the same verbal or nonverbal system.

A given task may require any of or all of the three kinds of processing.

The Dual Coding theory has been applied to many cognitive phenomena which includes mnemonics, problem-solving, concept learning and language. The theory accounts for the significance of spatial abilities in theories of intelligence. Clark and Paivio (*ibid.*) present dual coding theory as a framework for educational psychology. For example, many experiments reported by them support the importance of imagery in cognitive operations. In one experiment, the participants saw pairs of items that differed in roundness (e.g., tomato, and goblet) and were asked to indicate which member of the pair was rounder. The objects were presented as words, pictures, or word-picture pairs. The response times were slowest for word-word pairs, intermediate for picture-word pairs, and fastest for picture-picture pairs.

In language pedagogy, learners can use a variety of strategies to acquire languages. Ackerman (1991), for instance, wrote that children were able to memorise words much better if they were provided with olfactory stimulants and concludes that "smells stimulate learning and [memory] retention" (p. 11). Language education can also include nonverbal communication (e.g. visual) and tactile communication (e.g. asking students to watch films (see David 2007) where certain words/sentences/phrases are used in the context). Students can then practise what they have learnt in role playing sessions in language classrooms. What happens here is that students are given stimuli and told to be sensitive towards certain linguistic features prior to watching the films (bottom-up). Next, students practise what they have understood in the role-playing session (top-down).

Teachers may use film excerpts to teach students schemas. Using excerpts from the British comedy film the *Hitchhiker's Guide to the Galaxy*,

David (ibid.) for instance, showed how teachers may use films to teach the speech act of refusal and ways of mitigating such face-threatening acts (also see Brown and Levinson 1987). The curriculum vis-à-vis cultural norms of politeness are particularly important because learning how to refuse is a speech act that requires sensitivity of cultural norms as well as language proficiency (Tanck 2006). Example 16.1 illustrates this point.

EXAMPLE 16.1 Scene from *The Hitchhiker's Guide to the Galaxy*

Turn
1. Arthur (A): There we go. (Handing the administrative Vogon a form)
2. Vogon (V): Ooo. Kidnapping the president? She's not eligible for release at this time.
3. A: Ok. (Annoyed) Look. This, this is the president (showing Zephod to the Vogon). Okay? see? There? (pointing at Zephod's picture) He says that the whole kidnapping business was just a horrible misunderstanding.
4. V: Oh yeah.
5. A: He's ORDERING you to let her go.
6. V: But this isn't the presidential release of prisoner form. Those are blue.

Here, the protagonist (Arthur) was annoyed when the Vogon refused his application (Turn 2) and told him that he had to fill another form in order to get the application approved (Turn 6) after Arthur convinced the Vogon that Zephod (who happened to be the president of the galaxy) was ordering the Vogon to release Trisha. The Vogon used reasons in Turn 2 (ineligibility) and in Turn 6 (wrong application form) as ways of saying "No".

The example demonstrates that politeness is also an important stimulus that should be taught by educators, and this can be demonstrated through viewing films as they provide both visual and audio inputs and also the positive feelings elicited by the humour of a film. Students can use tactile communication as a support tool to acquire language skills. For instance, simple activities can include describing items while holding them. Students can also play with props and acquire languages this way. Children especially acquire linguistic competency at play and activities that promote positive reactions.

These multi-modalities allow bottom-up processes to be more effective in retaining information, which subsequently becomes schemas.

16.3.2   Existing Schemas in Language Production

Schemas are related to top-down processing that includes mental sets of representations of concepts, ideas and/or systems of beliefs. Schemas develop as a result of bottom-up exposures (e.g. opinions of others, books and media) and are used as heuristic (mental shortcuts) strategies to hasten tasks. Because of its nature, schemas also contribute to the development of stereotypes (Sternberg 1998). Such stereotypes should not be perceived negatively because they enable individuals to perform tasks more effectively. For instance, adult readers generally do not read every letter in a word, rather they identify the length of the word and patterns to identify words through previously known knowledge. Individuals can still read this line:

> ... becuase they use top-down processes to aid them in identifiyng familiar words, althuogh the lettres are srcambbeld.

This hastens reading tasks (top-down).

Stereotypes also enable students to make generalisation in language learning that contribute to future top-down processes. For instance, in acquiring (or modifying) sounds in words, learners who are told that the word prefixes starting with 'de-' are pronounced as "dee," will eventually make generalisations to other words that start with 'de-'.

In terms of syntax, students can also use stereotypes to learn phrase and sentence structures. For instance, if students are given the formula S = NP + VP, they will use this as a guideline to create other new sentences and they could use this formula whenever they are in doubt. Hence, they will say, "the cat sat on the mat" rather than "sat on the mat the cat".

However, there are caveats that language teachers must be aware of. Teachers must advise their students to be flexible in language learning and not be rigid with stereotypes because there are 'de-' words that are not pronounced as 'dee' such as 'devil' and there are sentences that do not follow the NP + VP formula strictly such as 'on the mat, sat the cat'. In short, students must be made aware that formulas are guidelines, but they must be flexible and be able to make amendments to their stereotypes and revise their previously held schemas.

Students must also be made aware of cultural values and update/revise their schemas with notion of cultural politeness so that conflicts in future interactions with strangers and individuals outside of the classroom can be avoided or mitigated. In other words, top-down processes should include methods of being polite. The educators must pay attention to the cultural references in the material the teachers present to students and avoid potential cultural bias. For instance, in the Malay language, there are various varieties of the second person referent "you" namely, "anda," "kamu," "engkau" and "kau". To the native Malay speaker, the leftmost continuum (anda) represents politeness while the rightmost continuum (kau) is considered rude in interactions between strangers or with superiors.

In terms of reading, the schema theory proposes that readers possess different conceptual frameworks, called schemata, which they bring to the reading of a text and which they use to make sense of what they read. Such schemata are used by readers in interactive bottom-up and top-down processing. Schemata provide a framework for readers to check their understanding of the text, fill in information gaps within the text, and clarify ambiguities (Steffenson and Joag-Dev 1984). Efficient readers use prior knowledge of content and textual features stored in schemata to make meaning out of the text (Rumelhart 1977; Goodman 1984).

A new famous study by Steffenson and Joag-Dev (*op. cit.*), based on the schema theory, demonstrates the effect of cultural background on reading comprehension. In the study, subjects from Indian and American backgrounds were asked to read and recall two texts describing an Indian and American wedding, respectively. The texts were presented in the form of letters, a common genre familiar to the students, and were similar in terms of structural complexity (i.e. length and syntax). It was predicted that the subjects would:

1. Recall more of the native than the foreign text.
2. Produce more expansions as a result of "remembering" items which were not mentioned in the text, but were culturally appropriate and consistent with it.
3. Make more distortions of the foreign text.

The types of errors made by the subjects with the foreign texts confirmed the researchers' three predictions and suggested that the subjects made these errors because they were unable to call on relevant cultural content schemata to check their understanding of the text. The writers concluded that an important part of reading comprehension is cultural knowledge—readers will understand a text better if they share the content schema assumed by the writer, but will distort the text if there is no shared schema.

16.3.3 Miscue Tests in Reading Comprehension

Goodman (1969) developed the Miscue Analysis method to study the types of reading strategies the readers use and the cognitive processes that are involved in reading. According to him, reading is a meaning-seeking process in which readers use graphic (letters/characters), phonemic (sounds), syntactic (language structures), and semantic (meaning) cues to make sense of texts.

This methodology scans for incorrect guesses because it gives the evaluator a clue of the reader's level of comprehension of certain texts. Goodman asserts that textual divergence is not necessarily a negative aspect of the reading process because it provides an understanding of reading processes (*ibid.,* 123). In the analysis, the readers are asked to read authentic texts orally. One of the maxims of miscue analyses is that the reader's understanding of a text is cued by language and personal experience (Goodman 1973: 93). Analyses often involve procedures that include the collection and examination of an oral reading experience followed by a retelling of the texts.

According to the PDF document prepared by the Department for Education and Skills,[1] analysts sometimes try to elicit miscues deliberately

---

1. Downloadable from http://www.dfes.gov.uk/readwriteplus/bank/Miscue%20Analysis.pdf

to "access learners' reading skills in relation to the demands of their jobs or courses and/or life in general" (p. 4). The educators can use the analyses to help students select texts and reading materials that are suitable for their level. However, the document also cautions that the analysis is inappropriate for beginners because they may not have phonic skills and may have to rely entirely on semantic cues. Example 16.2 provides a sample of miscue analysis.

EXAMPLE 16.2 Miscue analysis sample

Actual passage from book

Now John Cameron lived alone—apart from his household robot. And his life certainly did run smoothly. Some people changed their robot's programme every day, and left it in the 'Transit' position, that is, ready to receive orders. But not John. He was a rigid man who hated change. He wanted every day to be the same as the one before. So HIS robot was programmed once and for all. One weekend, he sat down after breakfast as usual, and watched his robot clear up the dishes. There were times when he felt almost fond of it. It was the silence he liked. Robots never argued—not like wives.

(From *'Knockouts' The Man Who Loved Robots'* by Jan Carew)

Passage as read by student

Now John Cameron lived alone—apart from his household robot. And his life certainly did run smoothly. Some people changed their robot's **performance** every day, and left it in the 'Transit' position, that is, **reading** to receive orders. But not John. He was a rigid man who **hadn't changed**. He wanted every day to be the same as the one before. So HIS robot was programmed once and for all. One weekend, he sat down after breakfast as usual, and watched his robot **clean clear** up the dishes. There were times when he felt almost **found fond** of it. It was the silence he liked. Robots never argued—not like wives.

(Taken from the Adult Literacy Unit's *Newsletter No. 5* 1979 in the Department for Education and Skills)

In this example, the reader substituted the following words, 'performance' for 'programme', 'reading' for 'ready', 'hadn't changed' for 'hated' among others. Also, there were self-corrections made. The example illustrates how the student read using the grapho/phonic, semantic and syntactic to decipher meaning.

In short, miscues are good indicators to test a student's top-down processes based on the bottom-up stimulus from reading. Successful reading (lack of miscues) indicates that the bottom-up processes are efficient. However, word errors which do not diverge from the coherence of the text indicate that the student is attempting to understand the passage (acceptable top-down processes). In contrast, word errors that diverge from the coherence of the text indicate that the learner has not understood the text and this could be due to poor top-down processes.

16.3.4 Strategies to Unveil Ambiguity in Language Comprehension

One of the ways to develop effective and efficient top-down processes is to decipher and identify ambiguity. Ambiguity arises when two or more different meanings can be interpreted from a certain word or phrase. Take lexical ambiguity for instance. When the context is lacking, lexical items can be ambiguous. In English, there are words that carry multiple meanings, e.g. 'foot' (below/bottom vs. human anatomy). The students can be taught to be aware of these occurrences and decipher ambiguous words/sentences through schemas and contextual sensitivity. In other words, they can use their top-down processes to aid them in deciphering the bottom-up processes. Example 16.3 illustrates this.

EXAMPLE 16.3 Unveiling ambiguity

"I saw her duck."

duck = animal (noun)   or   **duck = take cover (verb)**

"Students hate annoying professors."

annoying = the act of annoying (verb)   or   **annoying = modifier of professor (adjective)**

"Please wait for hostess to be seated."

waiting for the hostess to take her own seat or the guest wait for a hostess to usher them to a seat

---

(Retrieved from http://www.gray-area.org/Research/Ambig/)

Using top-down processes, students may find the first excerpt 'duck' as either the act of taking cover or of the animal depending on the context in which the sentence occurred. If it occurred in a farm, there is a high possibility that duck refers to an animal. Likewise, the second excerpt ('annoying') may refer to irritating professors (if they dislike their professors). The final excerpt may be interpreted accurately through power relations. Suppose the guest is a powerful figure, then the hostess will usher the guest to his/her seat, but if the hostess is a VIP, the guest has to pay tribute by waiting for the hostess to take his/her seat first.

16.4 MEMORY WORK AS LANGUAGE PROCESSING

Memory plays an important role in language processing because it allows schemas and concepts to be produced and, at the same time, allows information obtained from the bottom-up processes to be stored for either short-term or long-term recall. Memory is the ability of an organism to store, retain and, subsequently, recall information (Wikipedia: 2006). There are three critical distinctions about memory as listed by Atkinson et al. (1990):

1. Memory deals with encoding, storage and retrieval.

2. Memory is classified according to duration (i.e. short-term memory and long-term memory).
3. Memory is classified according to different memory storages that carry different information (e.g. one system for facts and another for skills).

Encoding is the process where information is received from stimulus (sight, sound, taste, touch and smell) while **storage** refers to the maintenance of information obtained from the encoding process and **retrieval** refers to the recall of the information stored. So, for instance, if a student were to learn a new word from a teacher, say, 'cat,' the student encodes the word according to its phonetic properties (ke-at) and its semantic meaning (furry four-legged creature with whiskers). Next, this information is stored in the student's memory according to the properties (semantic and pronunciation) of the word. When information has to be retrieved, the student using top-down processing and schemas accesses the storage to retrieve the word 'cat,' and may either say the word or describe it.

Generally, memory functions when our sensory motors pick up stimuli such as sound, sight, touch, taste and smell from the environment. The information is then encoded in the brain before it is stored. Should the information be produced later, the memory storage is accessed and information is retrieved. Here is where the distinction between long-term and short-term memories comes into play: If the information is retrieved after a certain period (say, an hour later) and can be reproduced later in the future (say, 10 years later), the information has become a long-term memory. However, should information dissipate or be forgotten after a delayed-response (15 seconds or more), it shows that the information has yet to become a long term memory (also see Atkinson et al. 1990).

Students may use their memories to organise information during encoding (bottom-up) for storage and recall (top-down) purposes (see Atkinson and Shiffrin, 1971: 271). This is particularly useful for word association exercises. Figure 16.2 illustrates this.

Home cat	Home dog	Jungle tiger	Jungle wolf
furry	furry	furry	furry
predator	predator	predator	predator
carnivorous	carnivorous	carnivorous	carnivorous
mammals	mammals	mammals	mammals
four legged	four legged	four legged	four legged
tame	tame	wild	wild

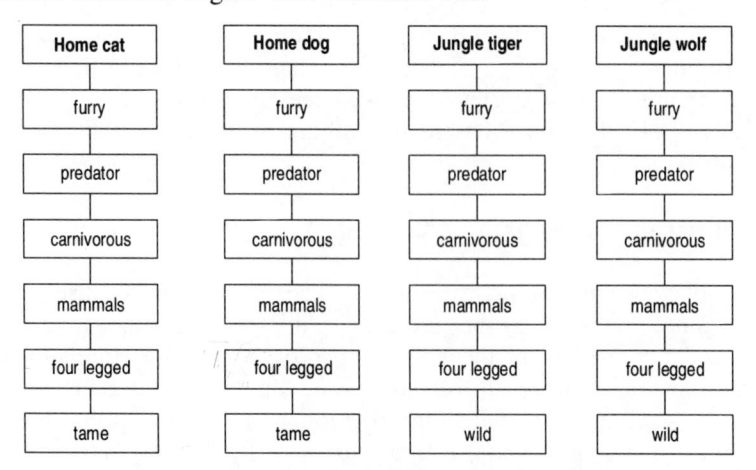

FIGURE 16.2 Organisation of information.

(Adapted from David 2006)

If the words, 'home cats,' 'home dogs,' 'jungle tiger' and 'jungle wolf' are categorised according to their generic properties such as 'furry,' 'predators,' 'carnivorous,' 'mammals' and 'four legged' as well as 'tame' and 'wild,' the individuals are able to retrieve animal groups pertaining to their category. Hence, 'furry,' 'carnivorous,' 'mammal,' 'four legged' and 'tame' entail either 'cats' or 'dogs,' but not 'tiger' or 'wolf'. This skill enables the teachers to assist their students to acquire semantic relations, which is helpful in developing long-term memory of a target word.

Another close concept in the organisation of words is **mind mapping**. It is a particularly useful way of encoding, storing and retrieving information, and if practised continuously, it can become long-term memory over a long period of time. Figure 16.3 shows this.

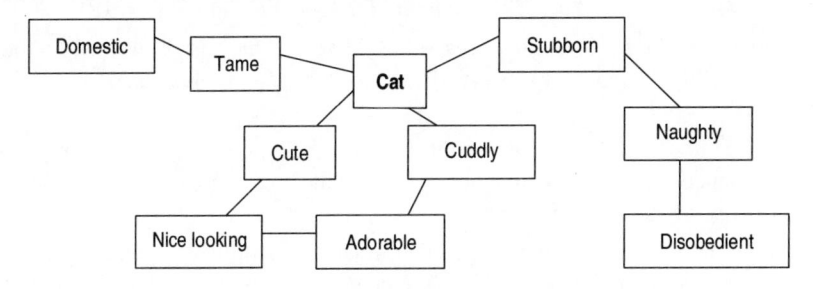

FIGURE 16.3 Mind mapping.

Here, the word 'cat' has many associative words, which allow students to acquire and expand their vocabulary. To generate new associative words, students can refer to thesaurus and dictionaries to build their corpus. For instance, 'stubborn' has an associative feature of 'naughty' and 'naughty' has an associative feature of 'disobedient'. The words can continue to expand.

16.5 CONCLUSION

As the study shows, language processes are dynamic and interdependent, that is, the top-down and bottom-up processes are always active (or passively active) in both language comprehension and production. If the students can be made to learn of top-down and bottom-up processes through activities and concepts, there is a chance that they will acquire linguistic capabilities and skills quickly and effectively. To do that, the teachers must first be made to realise the importance of cognitive processes as well as a number of variables such as attitude, the norms and values of society on language learning.

REFERENCES

Ackerman, D., *A Natural History of the Senses*, NY: Vintage, 1991.

Atkinson, R.C. and Shiffrin, R.M., "The control of short term memory," *Scientific American*, August 1971, **225**(2): 82–90.

Atkinson, R.L., Atkinson, R.C., Smith E.E., Bem, D.J., and Hilgard, E.R., *Introduction to Psychology*, 10th ed., San Diego: Harcourt Brace Jovanovich, 1990.

Brown, P. and Levinson, S., *Politeness: Some Universals in Language Usage*, Cambridge: Cambridge University Press, 1987.

Clark, J.M. and Paivio, A., "Dual coding theory and education," *Educational Psychology Review* **3**.3 (1991): 149–170.

David, M.K., *The Sindhis of Malaysia: A Sociolinguistic Account*, London: Asean, 2001.

_____, "Knowledge of psycholinguistics: Vital for language teaching", Paper presented at the SPELT International Conference, Islamabad, October 2006.

_____, *A Guide for the English Language Teacher*, Petaling Jaya: SIRD, 2007.

Department for Education and Skills (n.d.) Miscue Analysis, Retrieved October 18, 2006 from http://www.dfes.gov.uk/readwriteplus/bank/Miscue%20Analysis.pdf

Gardner, H., Albert, M., and Weintraub, S., "Comprehending a word: The influence of speed and redundancy on auditory comprehension in aphasia," *Cortex* **11** (1975): 158–162.

Goodman, K., "Analysis of oral reading miscues: Applied psycholinguistics," *Language and Literacy: The Selected Writings of Kenneth Goodman*, Vol. I., F. Gollasch (Ed.), Boston: Routledge and Kegan Paul, 1969, 123–134.

Goodman, K., "Miscues: Windows on the reading process," F. Gollasch (Ed.), 1973, 93–102.

_____, "Unity in reading," *Becoming Readers in a Complex Society*, 83rd Yearbook of the National Society for the Study of Education: Part I, A.C. Purves and O. Niles (Eds.), Chicago: University of Chicago Press, 1984, 79–114.

Holmes, J., *An Introduction to Sociolinguistics*, 2nd ed., London: Longman, 2001.

Labov, W., "The social motivation of a sound change," *Word* **19** (1963): 273–309.

Mohd. Yasin, M.S., *Language Allegiance and Language Shift: A Malaysian Case Study*, Bangi: Fakulti Pengajian Bahasa, Universiti Kebangsaan Malaysia, 1998.

Paivio, A., *Mental Representations*, New York: OUP, 1986.

Rumelhart, D.E., "Toward an interactive model of reading," *Attention and Performance VI*, S. Dornic (Ed.), Hillsdale, NJ: Erlbaum, 1977, 573–603.

Ruthrof, H., *The Body in Language*, London/New York: Cassell, 2000.

Shannon, C.E. and Weaver, W., *The Mathematical Theory of Communication*, Urbana: University of Illinois Press, 1949.

Steffenson, J. and Joag-Dev, C., "Cultural knowledge and reading," *Reading in a Foreign Language*, J.C. Alderson and A.H. Urquhart (Eds.), London: Longman, 1984, 48–61.

Sternberg, R.J., *In Search of the Human Mind*, Orlando: Harcourt Brace Jovanovich, 1998.

Steinberg, D.D. and Sciarini, N., *Introduction to Psycholinguistics*, 2nd ed., London: Longman, 2006.

Strub, R. and Geschwind, N., "Localization in Gerstmann syndrome," *Localization in Neuropsychology*, A. Kertesz (Ed.), New York: Academic Press, 1983, 295–322.

Tanck, S., *Speech Act Sets of Refusal and Complaint: A Comparison of Native and Non-Native English Speakers' Production*. Retrieved February 1, 2006 from http://www.american.edu/tesol/wptanck.pdf.

Westen, D., *Psychology, Mind, Brain and Culture*, NY: Wiley, 1996.

Wikipedia, Memory. Retrieved October 1, 2006 from http://en.wikipedia.org/wiki/Memory.

Part 5

GAMES AND ACTIVITIES IN ESL CLASSROOM

Chapter 17

LANGUAGE-BASED GAMES AND MOTIVATION: Using Games in the ESL Classroom

— Johansen Quijano-Cruz

17.1 INTRODUCTION

Motivation to learn plays an extremely important role in the learning process. This is especially true when one is engaged in the acquisition of a new language. In ESL and EFL classrooms the world over, it is often the case that students with a higher motivation to learn the language obtain higher grades and reach higher proficiency levels than those who are not motivated to learn. According to Normandia (1991):

> Poor motivation and the lack of information related to the importance of mastering language skills have prevented students from learning them effectively (p. 1).

Furthermore, Gee (2005) agrees that "learning is a deep human need, like eating or mating, and like all such needs, it is meant to be deeply pleasurable to human beings" (p. 13). Essentially, for people to learn, the learning process should be fun and meaningful, as Ausubel suggests—not only should the learning of something new be engaging and entertaining, but it should also have some sort of practical use.

In all his works about games and learning, Gee suggests that real learning happens as a cultural process. This means that in order to learn, people should perceive the process as an integral part of their culture. Games are one such a cultural process. When children grow up, they learn to play naturally because it is a part of their culture. Not only do they learn to share with other children, but they also learn the rules and content of the games they play. Researches on play with children and adults indicate that "play is an important mediator for learning and socialization throughout life" (Reiber 1996: 44). He argues:

> Play and imitation are natural learning strategies at which children are experts. Having children play games to learn is simply asking them to do what comes naturally. (*ibid.*, 50)

Of course, children are not the only ones who learn while playing; teenagers, and even adults, play games from time to time. Whenever they discover a new game with a new set of rules, they get involved in a learning process in order to master the rules and content of the game. While the games certainly differ from generation to generation (generally, children play with toys and cards, teens play sports and video games, and adults play mature games like Blackjack), the experience, and motivations, behind the learning of the game are the same.

According to Gee (*ibid.*), "good video games are hard work and deep fun. So is good learning" (p. 4). He suggests that games of all types are similar to learning in many aspects, including that they are fun. Many popular games, video or otherwise, "bank on children's love of mastery and expertise" (Gee 2007: 111). One example where games succeed, and education does not, is the Pokemon system. Even though this system is far more complex than many of the things taught in an elementary school, yet children seem to learn the names, physical characteristics, attributes, evolution stages, and history of the 493 Pokemon far better than whatever they learn at school. This implies that video games, most of the times, teach better than formal lectures as they give the players a motivation beyond "it is required" to learn. It may be possible, then, to use games in an educational setting in order to motivate students and improve their learning processes.

One of the most important learning aspects in games is the language as "the meaning of language is always associated with actions, experience, images, and dialogue" (*ibid.*, 116.) When this can be exploited, teachers can provide students with a wonderful learning experience by integrating games into their lessons. Using language-based games in ESL and EFL classrooms is quickly becoming a popular practice. The use of charades, 20 questions, and hangman is common throughout many ESL and EFL classrooms. Indeed, many online ESL communities now include a Language Games section, and books that give ideas on how to use games in the language classroom such as Imogene Forte's *ESL Content-Based Language Games* and Lucia Gorea's *ESL Games and Classroom Activities* are being released yearly. There are even books that deal with the theoretical and research aspects of games and learning such as Clark Quinn's *Engaging Learning*, Harry O Neil's *Computer Games and Team and Individual Learning*, and James Paul Gee's *What Video Games Have to Teach Us About Learning and Literacy*.

Using games in the language classroom opens doors for new possibilities in teaching and learning. Games, if done correctly, can become a powerful tool for groups to work together. Three popular games based on television shows that can be easily adapted for the use in ESL and EFL classrooms are (i) Jeopardy, (ii) Family Feud, and (iii) Wheel of Fortune. Using simplified rules, teachers can present students with a game show-like experience which they will enjoy and that will motivate them to learn the target language.

17.2 ESL JEOPARDY

Jeopardy is a television quiz game show based on trivia, which covers various subjects like history, literature, and science. Although the original game is composed of only three rounds, offers six categories to choose from, and the answers must be given in the form of questions, the classroom version can be modified to fit the context of the lesson. As such, played best with small groups, it can be successfully executed with up to 30 students.

This game is ideal when discussing literature or grammar rules. First, the teacher will introduce a story to the students and have a reading session. The teacher can ask the students to read the story independently in sustained silent reading (SSR) or read the story aloud with the students, asking the students to volunteer to read full paragraphs. If the activity is being used for grammar lessons, the teacher should first have given at least four topics. Instead of having a normal reading discussion or grammar review, the teacher will draw a Jeopardy grid on the board. The grid can have four–six categories, and each category should have questions with score values from 100–500 points. The categories shown in Table 17.1(a) and (b) are suggestions and could be changed by the teacher for other categories depending on the objective of the lesson.

Table 17.1(a)   For Use with a Short Story, Novel, or Other Reading

Setting	Plot	Characters	Relationships	Narrative Strategies
500	500	500	500	500
400	400	400	400	400
300	300	300	300	300
200	200	200	200	200
100	100	100	100	100

Table 17.1(b)   For Use with Grammar Lessons

Nouns	Pronouns	Adjectives	Verbs	Adverbs
500	500	500	500	500
400	400	400	400	400
300	300	300	300	300
200	200	200	200	200
100	100	100	100	100

In order to enhance students' experience with the game, the teacher can design a similar grid in PowerPoint and project it on the board. Using the program, the teacher can design the game so that whenever a student chooses a question (for example, pronouns for 100 points) (Figure 17.1) the teacher can click on the desired section and the question will pop up on the screen. Once the grid is drawn on the board, the teacher will explain the following rules to the group:

ESL Jeopardy

Nouns	Pronouns	Adjectives	Verbs	Adverbs
500	500	500	500	500
400	400	400	400	400
300	300	300	300	300
200	200	200	200	200
100	100	100	100	100

Pronouns – 100 Points

- Replace all the male nouns in the following sentences with pronouns.
  - Last night, John went with Mary to watch a movie.

FIGURE 17.1

- The class will be divided in 3–5 groups.
- The first group will choose a category and they will get an opportunity to answer the question with the lowest available score. For example, if group #1 chooses nouns, they will have to answer the question worth 100 points.
- Afterwards, group #2 may choose nouns for 200 points or any of the other categories for 100 points.
- If the members of any group give an incorrect answer or do not answer the questions, other groups will be given a chance to answer.
- If no one answers the question correctly after all the teams have had a chance, the teacher will give the answer.
- Groups will not be given the chance to choose two questions in a row. If group #1 chooses a category, the next turn will be given to group #2 regardless of whether group #1 answered correctly or not. This will avoid a single group of students answering all the questions and not allowing other students to participate.
- Students do not have to choose all the lower level questions before moving to a higher level, nor do they have to answer all the questions from a specific category before moving to the next.
- The activity will continue until all the grid is exhausted or until class time runs out.

While using a computer-generated version of the game, like the PowerPoint, the teacher does not need any sort of guide as the questions to be asked will already be in the program. However, when teachers have only a board and chalk at their disposal, they may want to have a guide sheet. In such cases, after the students choose their category, the teacher will read the questions aloud. As the students will not have any visual cues of the questions, they will also be practicing their listening skills. An example guide sheet is given in Table 17.2 based on the short story *The Woman with the Rose* by

TABLE 17.2   An Example Guide Sheet

Characters	Characters 2	Setting	Plot
What is the name of the old lady with the rose? (The story does not say.)	How did John feel when he saw the old lady with the rose? (Disappointed.)	What country did John fight against in WW2? (Germany) *BONUS* Who led Germany? (Hitler)	What is the name of the restaurant where John is supposed to meet Hollis at the end of the story? (It doesn't say.)
Describe Hollis Maynell. Mention 3 characteristics. (White skin, blonde, delicate, gentle lips, blue eyes, green suit.)	Describe the old lady. Mention at least 3 characteristics. (Well past 40, gray hair, worn hat, fat, thick ankle feet.)	To what war was John sent to fight? (WW2.)	How long did John fight in the war? (13 months / a year and a month.)
Describe Hollis' handwriting. (Soft, delicate, reflects thoughtful soul and insightful mind.)	Where does Hollis work? (The story does not say.)	What will Hollis be wearing when she meets John? (Rose.)	Where is John sitting at the beginning of the story?
Describe the book that was to identify John. (Small, worn, blue leather-bound book.)	What is John's rank in the army? (Lieutenant.) *BONUS* What rank comes after lieutenant? (Captain)	Where are John and Hollis supposed to meet? (Grand Central Station.)	The library where John found the book is in _____. (Florida)
John's last name is .... (Blanchard.)	Mrs. Maynell's first name is ... . (Hollis.)	Where does Hollis live? (New York.)	How did John learn about Hollis? (Book in library.)

S.I. Kishor. Several versions of the story can be found throughout the Internet.

Students enjoy this activity as it allows them to use the language and to engage with reading comprehension and literature analysis techniques, or practice grammar rules depending on the focus given by the teacher. Prizes such as candy or bonus points may be considered for the winning group at the discretion of the teacher in order to provide extrinsic motivation. Intrinsic motivation will come from the students' natural competitiveness and desire to engage in fun learning.

17.2 ESL FAMILY FEUD

Family Feud is a television show, which pits two families against each other in a contest to name the most popular responses to a survey-type question asked to 100 people. When used in the ESL classroom, the game is best played in groups of 10–14 students. Like Jeopardy, although the original television version has a certain amount of rounds, and some rounds offer additional bonuses, the modified classroom version should stick to the basic rules and can have as many or as few rounds as the teacher finds it necessary.

In order to play this game, the teacher will need a blackboard, chalk, and survey lists. Sample surveys can be found in many Family Feud-based tabletop games or top 10 lists, but teachers can also conduct their own surveys for use in the classroom. A sample survey could ask for the 5 most popular colors, the answers being red, blue, yellow, orange, and green.

As with every activity, the teacher should start by giving the students the rules of the game:

- The students will be split into two groups of 5–7 members.
- In each round, a student from each group will go to the front of the classroom.
- Students will then be asked a question related to a survey, for example, "Mention the most popular restaurant".
- In order to decide who goes first, the teacher could set a bell between the two students and the student who rings the bell first will have the chance to answer. If there is no bell, the teacher can set an object (e.g. an eraser), between the students, and the first one to grab it will get the chance to answer.
- If the answer given by the student appears in the survey list, the team will get a chance to answer the rest of the survey. If the answer does not appear in the survey, the rival group will get a chance to answer.
- If neither of the groups answers correctly, another survey will be used.
- Once a group answers the first guess correctly, that group gains control. The other members of the group will then try to guess the remaining answers.
- If they fail thrice, the rival group will have a chance to 'steal' the points.
- Each answer on the board is worth 1 point.
- The group with the most points at the end of the period or when the surveys run out wins.

Below is a sample round using the answers from the color survey mentioned above.

John and Mary walk up to the desk. The bell is on the center of the desk. The teacher asks "Mention the most popular colors". John rings the bell first and screams "PURPLE!" The teacher answers, "There is no purple on the board, Mary has a chance to answer". Mary answers "Orange" and the teacher replies that it is on the board in the fourth place. Mary's team now has a chance to guess the other answers. Pedro says "Green", and the teacher writes it in the fifth space. Janice answers "White," but it is not on the board. Mary's group has one miss. Alice answers "Blue" and the teacher writes it on the second space. The students from Mary's group will keep on guessing the colors in the survey until they guess all of them or until they have three misses. Mary's team accumulates three strikes and has not guessed "Yellow" yet, so John's team has a chance to steal the points. John's group decides to guess "Black", which is not on the survey. Four answers were given for a total of four points. This process is repeated with different surveys, but with students other than Mary and John walking up to the desk for control.

Some teachers might want to add a question about a previous lesson or a previously discussed story at the end of each round so that the team that won the round has a chance to earn a bonus point. Teachers who have access to a computer and a projector might want to prepare PowerPoint slides with the questions in order to enhance the experience for the students. However, the teacher will still have to write the score and the answers on the board by hand (Figure 17.2).

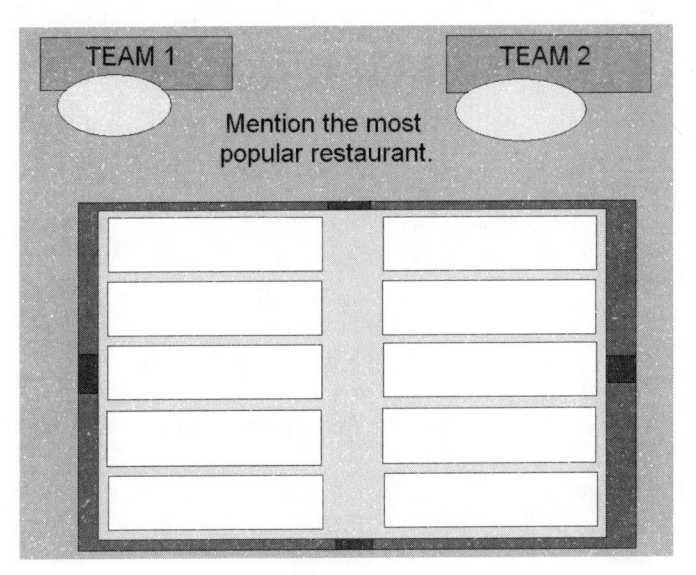

FIGURE 17.2.

Not only do students enjoy this activity, it also motivates them to think critically, engage with and discover the value of teamwork, and practices their listening skills. Just as with other games, the teacher can think of awaiting a prize to the winner team.

17.3 ESL WHEEL OF FORTUNE

Wheel of Fortune is a game show where contestants compete against each other to solve a word puzzle similar to those found in the game Hangman. Unlike the other two games mentioned in the previous sections, the original version of Wheel of Fortune has an element that would be impractical to include in a classroom version of the game: the giant wheel. For this reason, the rules have been modified more than Jeopardy, where they were hardly changed, and Family Feud, where the scoring system was altered.

This game requires only a blackboard and a chalk to play. Unlike ESL Jeopardy and ESL Family Feud, this game can be played with large groups with little effort, as the groups will work together as a team. The teacher will draw blank lines on the blackboard where each line will represent a letter in a word or phrase. For example, the phrase "Welcome to the English class" would be interpreted as "__ __." The rules of the game are as follow:

- The teacher will split the classroom into three or four groups.
- Each group will start with 1000 points.
- The teacher will write blank spaces of words, phrases, or sentences on the board.
- A student from the first group will say a consonant letter, and if that letter is in the phrase, the group gets 100 points for each time the letter appears.
- That student will have a chance to guess what the sentence or word is.
- If they pass the chance to guess, a student from the next group goes.
- If they try to guess incorrectly, the group loses 200 points.
- Students have the opportunity to 'buy' a vowel for 100 points.
- Students will get 100 points for each vowel in the word or sentence.
- The group that says the word or sentence correctly will get 500 points.
- If a player says a letter which it is not included the sentence, no points are deducted.
- At teacher's discretion, the first group to get 10,000, 15,000, 20,000, or 25,000 points wins.
- Alternately, the teacher could decide that the first group to win any number of times will win, with each word or sentence counting as 'one word'.

While using the game with students who are beginning to learn the language, it is best to use words or simple phrases. However, the game can also be played with advanced students by giving them longer and more difficult phrases. It may even be used while discussing literature or film. A teacher could make all the phrases revolve around a given work of literature (for example, *Gilgamesh*, or a movie like *Braveheart*), and classify the answers as

Events or Quotes. The teacher would then play the game using phrases from the chosen story or film, like "They may take our lives, but they'll never take our freedom!" (Braveheart 1995).

As with the other games, if the teacher has access to a computer and a projector, he or she may prepare PowerPoint slides before the class for enhanced visual effects (Figure 17.3).

FIGURE 17.3

Of the three activities described in this chapter, Wheel of Fortune is the one that lower-level students have commented on liking the most. Not only does it give them a chance to practice the alphabet, but it also allows them to think critically about their choices and about language patterns. As with all the other games, extrinsic motivation could be provided at the teacher's discretion.

17.4 CONCLUSION

In his *Reflections on Gaming with the Younger Generation*, Mike Perry (2002) writes about high school students he used to play games with during lunch:

> I doubt Tom, John, Chris and the others will remember much about the square roots and parabolas we studied in math class. I wouldn't be surprised, though, if they always remember the good times over games at lunch. I know I haven't forgotten all those laughs and the lessons.

He may be right. Games are an integral part of growing up as much as they are a part of learning development. They are fun, engaging activities that allow for better learning. Above all, they, like learning, are something that comes naturally to every human being. Hence, teachers should try to incorporate games into their lessons. After all, what better way to help students learn than by making learning fun?

REFERENCES

Gee, J.P., *Why Video Games are Good for Your Soul,* Australia: Common Ground, 2005.

Gee, J.P., *Good Video Games + Good Learning*, NY: Peter Lang, 2007.

Normandia de Jesus, P., *The Use of Language Laboratory as an Effective Resource in the Development of English Language Skills of College Students*, Unpublished Masters' thesis, University of Puerto Rico, Rio Piedras, Puerto Rico, 1991

Perry, M., "Reflections on gaming with the younger generation," *The Games Journal*, 2002. Retrieved on Sep 9, 2007 from http://www.thegamesjournal.com/articles/SeriousGaming.shtml

Reiber, L.P., "Seriously considering play: Designing interactive learning environments based on the blending of micro worlds, simulations, and games", *Educational Technology Research and Development* **44**.2 (1996): 43–58.

Chapter 18

DYNAMIC, INTERACTIVE CLASSROOM ACTIVITIES[1]

— Shira Koren

18.1 INTRODUCTION

Teachers often face the problem of students who are bored, uncooperative and fidgety, while the lesson that they have taken time and trouble to prepare is not yielding the expected results. Discipline problems arise, pupils talk to one another, and the goal of the lesson to impart knowledge and increase understanding is not achieved.

Research in education and in language learning has presented different approaches that could help frustrated teachers. David Perkins (1986) focuses on the meaning of knowledge and shows how teachers should aim at understanding as the goal of their lesson. Perkins (1997) further develops the meaning of understanding and shows how learning can lead to understanding. One important part of his argument is his call for challenging tasks in the classroom.

Another point of view is the product of language-learning strategy research. Researchers dealing with this area have identified many different styles and strategies that are used by different learners and have described them in books aiming at helping students learn new languages (Brown 2002; Paige et al. 2002) or helping teachers teach better (Oxford 1990; Cohen 1998).

But perhaps the most relevant research area related to the subject of classroom activities is that of motivational research, which has been developed by R.C. Gardner. Dornyei (2006) claims:

> The basic assumption underlying this chapter is that long-term, sustained learning—such as the acquisition of an L2—cannot take place unless the educational context provides ... sufficient inspiration and enjoyment to build up continuing motivation in the learners.

---

1. Most of the activities described in this article were learned by the author in a summer institute on strategies-based instruction at the University of Minnesota in 2000 and in two courses on dynamic teaching for the academic staff at Bar Ilan University in 2001and 2002.

The set of activities described below is based on these three approaches. The focus is on the learner, not the teacher. Following strategy research, the students are expected to understand not just *what* they study in the language classroom, but also *how* they can study more efficiently. Following Perkins, the tasks aim at presenting the students with challenging and interesting activities, and just as Dornyei recommends, the activities are hopefully inspiring and enjoyable enough to motivate the language learners. Many of the examples of the activities and games below make use of learning vocabulary items, since these are the simplest type of material for these activities. However, other aspects of language, such as idea-example pairs, cause-effect, fact-opinion and grammatical items can also be used for the same activities.

18.2 ACTIVITIES

18.2.1 First Day in Class

1. Introducing your neighbor

When the teacher meets the class for the first time, he or she can ask the students to sit in pairs, interview each other and write down the information. Each student will then rise and introduce his or her partner to the whole class. This way of "breaking the ice" on the first day of the course can achieve two goals: a speaking activity and a social activity as a way of getting to know one another. Another advantage is the replacement of the traditional self-introduction which embarrasses many pupils who are too shy to speak about themselves or who do not have a good command over the second language.

18.2.2 Introducing a New Text

2. Students' predictions and names on the board

Introducing a new text can be done by writing the topic (preferably an intriguing one) on the board. The teacher can then ask some students to write on the board their names and predictions of what the text will say about the topic. A text-skimming activity will follow, in which the students will see who guessed correctly, and their names will be circled on the board by the teacher.

3. Questions on board

Another way of introducing the new article is by writing some relevant questions on the board and letting the students discuss them in groups for several minutes. Each group should choose a spokesperson who will present the group's answers to the whole class. If the answers of some groups are very different from those of other groups, a debate can follow (in English, of course) between students from the different groups or between the groups' spokespersons. After skimming the text, the class can see which groups provided answers that are similar to those in the text. The teacher can write short answers of the various groups on the board so that a comparison between the groups' answers and the text can easily be made.

4. *Controversial subjects and reversing students' roles*

Introducing a new article with a controversial subject (such as the death penalty and drug legalization) can be done by dividing the class into two groups. One will raise arguments for the issue on the board and one against. The activity is limited in time and should not take more than a few minutes. When the time is up, the spokesperson of each group should tell the whole class the group's views. The teacher can write these points in short on the board. Then the groups will have to switch roles and raise arguments for the opposite point of view—but will make sure that the new points have not been mentioned yet by the other group. The teacher will write the new arguments on the board enabling everyone to see that they have not been raised in the first round. After skimming the text, a comparison can be drawn between the arguments in the text and those made by the students. The teacher can make a good use of colors by using one color of chalk or whiteboard marker for the students' arguments and one for those of the text, or two different colors for the two groups or one color for the students' pro arguments and one for their con arguments.

18.2.3 (Pre-) Skimming the Article

5. *Puzzle*

The teacher can take a text, divide it into several parts, cut and separate the parts, and give it to a group. The same task is given to all groups. The goal of the groups is to organize the parts according to the right order. The first group that completes the task successfully is the winner. This task could precede the skimming of an article. As it may demand comprehension of connecting words, it can serve as an activity that introduces this subject.

6. *Cocktail party*

I always encourage my students to use yellow markers to mark the telltale words that help predict the structure of the paragraph(s), such as additives (also, in addition, moreover), lists (there are several reasons, the first, another, one more, finally), and cause-effect (consequently, because, the reason for, as a result). This is a pre-skimming activity which is very helpful both for the skimming activity that follows it and for the understanding of the structure of the whole text. Once the students have done that, they walk around in the room with their marked texts and compare their markings. This activity is called **cocktail party**, since it requires mingling with others just for a short time and moving on to the next person, as is done in real cocktail parties. It combines learning from peers with fun, and does not need to be too long. The teacher can join the 'party' at a certain point and enable the students to compare their markings with his or hers, so eventually everybody will have the right markings on their texts.

18.2.4 Intensive Reading of Text

7. Paper ball

Once the students have read the text, they can be divided into two groups, each one sitting in a circle. Each student can be asked to write one difficult sentence on a clean sheet of paper (and state the paragraph number so that the sentence can be easily located). The teacher walks around, collects those sheets of paper, crumples and puts them one inside the other until a paper ball is created for each group. Now each group begins to "play" with their own ball. The first student who gets the ball from the teacher "peels" the most external sheet of paper, reads the sentence written there and tries to explain the difficulty. If he or she cannot, they can find the sentence in the text and see if the context helps. If it is too hard, they can ask their group to help. Once the sentence has been clarified, the student with the paper ball throws it to whoever he or she chooses and the game continues. This is not a game for a whole class. Therefore, the teacher should divide the class into two or three groups so that the pupils should not wait too long for their turn with the ball. Of course, there could be lots of variations for the contents of the game. For example, each student can write one word from the text that he or she does not understand, or a difficult idea, a word with an affix or whatever may be the challenge. One variation of the game is that each group will build his/her own ball again after having finished the game and will exchange the ball with that of another group so that everybody could now resume the game with a new ball. Another variation could be the use of paper balls created by the teacher with the difficulties that he or she wants the class to cope with.

8. Cards

Cards prepared by the teacher can be a useful, pleasant activity for the students and a time-saving preparation for the teacher because once prepared, they can be used many times. If the teacher wants to reinforce new vocabulary items from a text, he or she can print many new vocabulary items on one set of cards (one card for each word, printed with a very large font) and synonyms on another set of cards. The two sets of cards can be printed with two different colors to distinguish between them more easily. It would be helpful for the students to have the paragraph number where the new words can be found next to the words in the first set of cards, and try to figure out their meanings from context. The students can sit in small groups and receive some of the two sets of cards from the teacher. Their task is to match the new vocabulary items from the text with their synonyms. They will have to locate the words in the text to be able to find out the meaning. Once a group has completed the task, the teacher can switch their sets of cards with those of another group so that eventually all groups will do the work with all the cards. A variation could be a set of words and antonyms instead of synonyms.

9. Variation: Magnets on Whiteboard

Each group, after matching the cards, can put their pairs of cards on the magnetic whiteboard with the help of magnets. If the board is not magnetic, other means can be used to put the cards on the board, such as adhesive tapes and sticky gums. Since the words are written in big font on the cards, they can be seen by the class from a distance. At the end of the activity, all the pairs of cards will be on the board, so the students will be able both to see the fruit of their labor and to judge the correctness of the work of other groups. The two colors of the words—one for the new vocabulary items and the other for the synonyms (or antonyms)—will help the students distinguish between the new words they are supposed to learn and their synonyms.

10. Walking around with cards

Each student receives one card from the teacher containing a word or an idea from the text (written in short). All students have to get up, walk around, each holding his or her card in front, and have to find a partner who has the matching card with a synonym or antonym, or an example for the idea on their card. Once everybody has found his or her partner, they walk together in pairs in a circle until all students find their pairs and join the circle. When everybody has joined the circle, the game is over. For reinforcement, the pairs of cards can be put on the board with magnets so that everybody will be able to see, copy and learn.

11. Variation: Students prepare their own cards

Half the students in the class sit in one group and each has to write on a card in big letters, one new word from a text (a word that seems important to learn). They also have to state paragraph number next to the word so that it will be easily located later. Once they have prepared their cards, they get up and walk around holding their cards. The other half, who had to review the text while the first half were preparing their cards, now have to find the meanings of the words in the cards held by the first group (they can use the text or the dictionary). Each student has to find the meaning of the word of other student, write it in big letters on another card and then the pair of students put both cards on the board next to each other. At the end of the game, all the cards will be on the board with synonyms or explanations (or translations) of the meaning.

12. A "sitting" carousel

Students are seated in the center of the classroom in two circles facing each other. The internal circles have their back to the center; the external circle are facing the students in the internal circle. In this way, the students create pairs facing each other. Now they can exchange some kind of information. For example, all students in the internal circle ask their counterparts in the external circle some question about the text or the meaning of a word from the text. The students from the external circle must give the answer. Once the task was completed, the students from the external circle move one chair forward, so new pairs are created. Again, the students in the internal circle ask a question and receive an answer. There can be many variations to this game. Information can be exchanged in writing, cards can be passed from one circle to the other, etc. The game is completed once the students have moved a whole circle and are returning to their first partners. The teacher can prepare cards with questions or words for this game and give them to the students in one of the circles.

13. Variation: A "walking" carousel

Instead of sitting, the students can stand in two circles—one facing the other—and perform the same activities. This is good for variation and essential in classrooms where there are no single chairs that can be arranged in a circle.

14. Triplets: Trainer, trainee and observer

The class is divided into groups of three. In each triplet, one student is the trainer. He or she has to teach the second student a new structure (e.g. a grammatical structure). The trainee has to learn the form. The third student is the observer, who will comment on the teaching and explain to the trainer or trainee if it was adequate or not and why. Then the students exchange roles twice so that everyone has experienced the three roles. The teacher can prepare this activity by writing on the board three new structures that have to be learned in this game. The students can prepare for the activity by reading about the three structures in their books for some minutes before the game starts.

15. Competitions

The teacher divides the class into two groups and asks each group, at their turn, to answer a question or to give the meaning of a word, or to suggest a new word from the text that is important to learn. If the answer is correct, the teacher gives the group one point on the board. If the group has made a mistake, they lose a point. At the end of the activity, a total is made for both groups and the winners get a "hooray" from the teacher. Alternatively, instead of writing points on the board, the teacher can stick colored magnets.

16. "Microphone" rounds

The class discusses a certain topic. Each student who gets permission to tell the class his or her views about the topic, stands up in front of the class, holding a 'microphone' in the hands and talks, but is not allowed to relate to what the previous students said. If any body accidentally does relate to past ideas, he/she is silenced and has to sit down and their turn is given over to someone else.

Variation: Everybody who gets the microphone **must** relate to what his or her predecessor said. If they forget, they are silenced and have to sit down.

17. Variation: Practical and impractical

Students have to relate to a current problem. In one round they can give only practical suggestions; in another round they can give only impractical ones. A variation would be to alternate between the practical and impractical, which may create confusion and add to the fun. In this way, one student who gets the microphone gives a practical suggestion, while the one who comes right after him or her must give an impractical one. Those who get confused lose their turn and must sit down.

18. Info-café

Four tables are prepared in four corners of the classroom. On each table, there is a different type of information (e.g. four categories of words: nouns, verbs, adjectives and adverbs, or four groups of affixes, four tenses, three conditionals and "wish" structures). Around each "station," there are chairs, one of which is occupied by the "station master". Students walk around in the room and stop occasionally at different stations, where they sit and receive knowledge. Their specific task depends on the teacher: they may have to copy information into their notebooks or collect cards or fill in answers to questions on the tables in the station, etc. Once everyone has visited all stations, the game is over and the teacher can review the material on the board.

19. Memos

The teacher gives memo sheets to the students where they write their names. Then the class is divided into some groups and all the memo sheets of the groups are collected by the group leader. The aim of the students is to get back their memo sheets, but they can get them only if they answer the question of the group leader correctly. To increase the fun, the group leader, who asks questions that have been prepared by the teacher and given to him or her before the game, can write some humorous comments on the memo sheet that will reflect the quality of the answer before returning it to its owner, comment.

20. Drawings

Most texts include ideas or sentences that can be drawn visually. One of the easiest drawings of this kind is the cause-and-effect flow chart. But there are innumerable possibilities for simple drawings of ideas or structures that clarify a point in the text visually. The teacher can ask the students to draw such pictures in their notebooks and then call on some students to put their drawings on the board. A drawing can also be the product of a group, with pupils consulting on how to produce the best drawing. The results can be very interesting since there can be many different drawings representing the same idea. Once there are several drawings on the board representing one idea, the class can decide which one is the best.

21. Drama

Sometimes parts of a text can lend themselves to performing an act. For example, in a text that describes five experiments in social sciences, the class can be divided into five groups, each assigned the task of understanding one experiment and then performing it in front of the class so that everybody will understand the experiment, including its objectives and results. This vivid way of handling the comprehension of the experiments can lead to a much better understanding than mere reading.

22. Musical chairs

The class is seated in a circle with one student in the center, who has to perform some task like answering a question about a text or correcting a grammatical error in a sentence. Once the student has performed the task, he or she chooses the next person to sit on the "musical chair" and exchanges places with him or her.

18.2.5 Revision

23. Reports limited in time

In the beginning of a new lesson, the teacher can check what the students remember from the previous lesson by telling the students to form pairs, in which one student reports to his or her partner what he or she remembers in no more than one minute, and then the second student adds what she or he remembers also within half a minute. The first can add information in one quarter of a minute. The teacher can monitor the time for everybody, telling the students to start speaking and then to stop according to the watch.

18.2.6 Reading in Class

24. Read and report

If the students do not read articles assigned at home, the teacher can divide the class into groups of three and give each group a different article or a different part of an article that has to be studied in class. The groups have to read their part, answer the guiding questions that they get from the teacher and then the spokesperson of each group has to present the article to the whole class. In this way, some reading can be achieved instead of none or instead of the teacher's resorting to penalties, quizzes, poor grades, threats or anything else that may ruin the positive atmosphere in class.

Tips

1. Be consistent throughout the year. Whatever policy you determine in the first lesson (regarding homework, absences, late coming, exams, etc.), be sure to follow in the rest of the course.
2. Try to find material which is relevant to the students' lives and which will interest them.
3. Treat the students with respect, let them talk, express their wishes and expectations from the course. Ask them what they think about things and how they cope with difficulties.
4. Learn from everything that did not work out. You cannot always have a successful class. See what did not succeed and learn from it for the next time. Change your tactics when necessary.
5. You cannot do everything in class. There is a limited amount of material that can be covered. Do in class only what works nicely because this is what the students will remember anyway.
6. Try to break the traditional seating arrangement.
7. Be open to unexpected answers—if they are right.
8. Make sure that your lesson aims at understanding and confirm if it is a well-planned lesson; but if it is too difficult to understand, it means you have not reached your goal.
9. Encourage the students to reach their own solutions. Don't give them the solution.
10. Always check your goals of the lesson and see if you have achieved them.
11. Every teacher should use the methods that suit him or her. Not every method suits every teacher.

12. At the end of group work, always sum up the work with the class. Summarize what were the goals and what was achieved. Make sure the pupils understood the material and ask if they have questions.
13. Be sensitive to discipline problems. Group work is a good way to solve some of them because all the students have challenges at the same time unlike a frontal lesson, in which only one student talks at a time while the rest are inactive and may be bored.
14. When you see that students ask intelligent questions about what they have learned, reiterate what they have learned using their own words and in varying degrees of detail, and use new examples for what they have learned; it means they have understood.
15. Never show them how much they do not know. Always try to show them how much they have acquired and compliment the progress they have made. Be encouraging.
16. Always carry with you several colors of chalk or whiteboard marker and use the different colors meaningfully on the board, each color for a different purpose or structure. Never use several colors for the same purpose—it will only confuse the students. If you use a magnetic whiteboard, always have magnets with you (such as those with colored round plastic heads) so that you will be able to put students' work or cards that you have prepared on the board. For traditional blackboards or nonmagnetic whiteboards, there are other means of sticking material on them.

To sum up, in this chapter, I have tried to show alternative ways of teaching that can take the teacher away from the frontal lesson. These techniques may help the teacher create more effective and interesting lessons and will definitely make the students more active and involved. Teachers who want to adopt this dynamic approach can start using it gradually, introducing a few of the activities as part of their frontal lessons and increasing the number and types of these activities if they, and the students, feel comfortable using them. Even if the teachers realize that only a few of these activities work out for them they can still gain something, since class interest and participation will lead to a better understanding of the lesson and to higher achievements in the course.

REFERENCES

Brown, H.D., *Strategies for Success*, White Plains, NY: Longman/Pearson Education, 2002.

Cohen, Andrew, *Strategies in Learning and Using a Second Language*, London: Longman, 1998.

Dornyei, Zoltan, "Creating a motivating classroom environment," *The Handbook of English Language Teaching*, J. Cummins and C. Davison (Eds.), New York: Springer, 2006, 639–651.

Oxford, R.L., *Language Learning Strategies: What Every Teacher Should Know*, Boston: Heinle and Heinle, 1990.

Paige, Michael R., Cohen, Andrew D., Kappler, Barbara, Chi, Julie C., and Lassegard, James P., *Maximizing Study Abroad: A Student's Guide to Strategies for Language and Culture Learning and Use*, Center for Advanced Research on Language Acquisition: University of Minnesota, 2002.

Perkins, David, "Knowledge as design" in idem *Knowledge as Design,* Chapter 1, Hillsdale, New Jersey: Lawrence Erlbaum Associates, 1986, 1–34.

_____, "What is understanding?" *Teaching for Understanding: Linking Research with Practice,* Martha Stone Wiske (Ed.), San Francisco: Jossey-Bass Inc., 1997, 39–58.

Chapter 19

GAMES AND STUDENTS' MOTIVATION IN FOREIGN LANGUAGE LEARNING

— Justyna Walczak

19.1 INTRODUCTION

Teachers stretch their resources to the utmost to achieve the best possible teaching results, however, the process of school learning is undeniably very complex and depends not only on teacher's effort, but also on learner's needs, interest, background and many other factors. Pupil's attitude towards learning contingents mainly on the kind of motivation s/he has as well as on the fact whether s/he likes learning and is interested in acquiring knowledge. It becomes apparent that, as in all other fields, the key to success in foreign language learning (FLL) is motivation. Taking into consideration the importance of motivation in foreign language teaching, I came to the conclusion that games enhance language learning in a way that students do not really feel that they are *studying*, rather it can be regarded as learning through fun.

    Having started my first job as an English teacher in a primary school, the first thing I did was to give students a questionnaire to complete, that asked about their background, interests, their attitude towards learning English and also their reason for learning this language. I was not surprised to learn that almost half of the learners were not interested in learning English. However, the reasons for their presence at the classes were (i) the school curriculum (they had no other option), and (ii) their parents wanted them to learn English or they thought it a fashion. Being at elementary level, majority of my students had already previous failures in their studies, which left them completely demotivated. Indeed, my "inquiry" clarified everything making it obvious that I had to begin planning, for the future might bring unfavourable results. By working with students and observing them I concluded that what they need is the improvement of their motivation for learning.

    Taking into consideration the above facts, I will now focus on the nature and types of motivation, its role, and its impact on the process of foreign language learning. I will discuss the factors affecting motivation such as the teacher, students' interests and their background. I will also concentrate on the use of games to raise students' motivation with examples of activities involving games.

19.2 WHAT IS MOTIVATION?

Motivation is the driving force right from the beginning to the evaluation phase in the process of learning a foreign language. Vockell (2004) is of the opinion that the origin of the term motivation is connected with talking on action, with doing something. Harmer (1991: 3) defines motivation as a kind of "internal drive" that stimulates us to be active and achieve certain goal; while Ur (1996) states that the term motivation itself "is rather difficult to define" (p. 274). What is apparent is the fact that motivation makes both teaching and learning easier, much more effective and pleasurable.

19.3 THE IMPORTANCE OF MOTIVATION IN FOREIGN LANGUAGE TEACHING

I must admit that I totally concur with Corria (1999) who states that the learner's motivation is one of the most significant aspects of the process of learning and teaching a foreign language. Every teacher should be mindful of the fact that the motivation in learning a foreign language is quite different than in the conditions of the first language learning, when a child while learning its first language in order to fulfill its needs or wishes. Learners think in a different way, and so their motivation depends on and derives from their needs.

Following Vockell (2004), motivation is undeniably of a great significance and has indeed a great influence on learners in a variety of ways. Studies carried out by Gardner and Lambert (1972) are the best examples of how strongly motivation is related to the achievement of success in language learning. These studies proved that students with the most positive attitudes towards learning English were not only highly motivated but also learnt more successfully.

Ur (1996) states that contrary to general expectations, the most successful students are not definitely those who have a knack for languages. Gardner and Lambert (1972: 131) are of the same opinion that "having an ear" is just one of the myths often used to describe some students' failures and others' success.

Then, how it happens that everyone learns a first language? It might be suggested that everyone has some basic ear for learning languages. Successful students (Ur 1996) are those who are willing to participate, to do the task successfully; they have confidence in their ability to achieve success. They perceive the need for improvement. They are also ambitious and, therefore, direct their all endeavours towards achieving eminently. Such learners are undoubtedly highly motivated to achieve their goals; it is clear that without motivation they are not willing to do anything.

Most of the times, learners fail to achieve their goal of language learning owing to a lack of motivation. This eagerness and willingness to do something, this "internal drive" (Harmer 1991: 3) is considered to be the key to success although the teacher should remember that everything depends on the students' needs or goals (Niebrzydowski 1972). Well, as many students have as many preferences and different types of students' motivation having impact on their foreign language learning.

19.4 TYPES OF MOTIVATION AND THEIR IMPACT ON FOREIGN LANGUAGE LEARNING

It is widely agreed that motivation has a great effect on a student's capacity to learn. Methodologists mention different types of motivation while looking at this term from various perspectives. Brown (1994) presents three views of motivation: (i) behavioristic, (ii) cognitive and (iii) constructivist. Vockell (2004) mentions about interpersonal motivation where competition and co-operation play a very significant role. He further states that both these factors simulate intrinsic motivation.

Motivation is categorized into extrinsic and intrinsic forms by methodologists like Hamer (2000), Ur (1996), Komorowska (1993) and Brown (1994). Extrinsic motivation is to engage in an activity as a means to an end (Brzeziński 1987). Students work on a task because they believe that participation will result in some desirable outcomes like teacher appreciation.

While looking at all types of motivation, we should say that a global intrinsic motivation where a learner concentrates on the learning of the language itself. The learners engage themselves in the learning activities for its own sake. It is the most commonly recognized with the learners of a foreign language (Ur 1996). The division made by him is as follows: extrinsic motivation, which derives from the factors outside the classroom and intrinsic motivation, which concerns what takes place inside the classroom (p. 276). The same distinction is made by Harmer (1991).

One of the most significant factors having impact on extrinsic motivation is the attitude to the language. Gardner and Lambert's (1972) studies revealed that parental support and parents themselves, with positive attitudes towards the language learning, more effectively encouraged their children to learn the foreign language than did parents with less favourable attitudes.

After looking more deeply into extrinsic motivation, the following factors can be mentioned as having influence on students' attitudes towards FLL: stereotypes, value systems and previous failures.

Niebrzydowski (1972) lists teacher's personality, grades and marks, punishment and reward, student's background and his/her family situation as factors affecting extrinsic motivation; while Ur (1996) enumerates success and its rewards, failure and its penalties, teacher's demands, tests and competition (Chastain 1988) as having the power to motivate. Littlejohn (2001) also is of the opinion that rewards and punishment are the means of sustaining motivation. However, the teacher should be careful with these terms and try to find out his own rewarding system as it itself can be demotivating for the weaker students (*ibid.*).

Niebrzydowski (1972) studies the most significant features of intrinsic motivation like learners' ambitions, high aspirations, future plans and also student's interest in learning and their conviction about its utility. On the other side, Harmer (1991) mentions such factors as physical conditions of learning, the teacher and techniques used by him/her and also the success factors affecting intrinsic motivation.

19.5 FACTORS AFFECTING STUDENTS' MOTIVATION

It is rather difficult to point out only one single factor responsible for raising student's motives to learn (Littlejohn 2001). Students' interests, needs, their background, previous educational experience, and the teacher himself/herself are undoubtedly of great importance here. Furthermore, the factors of motivation such as challenge and curiosity that learners feel at different stages of their learning process cannot be omitted or underestimated.

19.5.1 Teacher

A teacher's role in the personal and social growth of the students has recently taken priority. Teachers are expected to meet students' affective, social and also cognitive needs (Chastain 1988). The teacher should take into consideration student's individual motivational differences and provoke their interest in the subject (*ibid.*).

According to Grygier (2001), the teacher takes the greatest part in the process of activating students. Niebrzydowski (1972) claims that teacher's impact can be so strong that it becomes a crucial factor in establishing student's relation to learning. The greatest influences on the students are the teachers who are generally liked by students and try to meet their needs (*ibid.*).

Both Niebrzydowski (1972) and Grygier (2001) highlight the importance of the teacher in the process of activating students. Ur (1996) briefly describes the models of teachers that can be defined as motivating. One model of the motivating teacher is the one who constantly encourages students to do their best, gives demanding and challenging tasks. The other model is the teacher who is able to provide students with personal support, makes them feel safe and important as individuals (Niebrzydowski 1972).

Another model of the motivating teacher mentioned by Ur (1996) is the teacher who directs his/her all endeavours to make the lesson and the subject as captivating and engaging as possible. Both Grygier (2001) and Ur (1996) state that the teacher has to be highly motivated himself/herself to be able to motivate students. Grygier (2001) claims that even the best planned lesson cannot substitute the motivating role of the teacher, considering the fact that the lack of positive role models for English learners is definitely a factor having a negative effect on student motivation.

The teacher must provide proper conditions for learning and must stimulate the students' interest in learning by giving interesting classes (Harmer 1991). It is important that the students know from the very beginning what the teacher wants them to achieve; teacher and students together must have the same goal and work towards its accomplishment. The teacher must give such goals as are not beyond the learners' abilities. Moreover, the teacher must be aware of the enormous impact of success on motivation (*ibid.*). Littlejohn (2001) emphasises that success in the task is an under-exploited source of motivation. Another thing worth mentioning is the fact that the teacher, bearing in mind students' motivational differences, should be flexible and, instead of acting as a controller or organizer, he should become facilitator, prompter or even participant.

A teacher's main concern should be motivating and facilitating his/her students' study of English. However, to be able to do this, s/he has to take into consideration a very significant factor affecting students' motivation, that is, students' interests.

19.5.2 Students' Interests

Grygier (2001) states that concentrating on students' interests, needs, abilities and disabilities is really worth doing as it enables the teacher to estimate the reasons of possible low motivation and react to it in order to improve it. She focuses teacher's attention on the fact that if students are disruptive during a lesson, it means that they are simply not interested in doing a task.

Corria (1999) claims that focusing on students' likes and dislikes concerning FLL is undoubtedly very useful. He states that students are bored spending too much time on unpleasant things. Hard though it may be, the teacher must try to find out what the students' interests are in order to plan his lessons/activities on the basis of this knowledge (Harmer 1991). Littlejohn (2001) directly encourages the teacher to "find out what students think". Niebrzydowski (1972) states that every student is interested in something, has individual preferences. Moreover, he adds that students usually learn more willingly those subjects at which they are successful. The learners' awareness of the possible success increases motivation and fosters studying and learning outside the classroom.

Chastain (1988) claims that the learner has a reason for learning and using that knowledge. Corria (1999) suggests that students should be given proper opportunities to use the language to communicate, and to talk about their experiences, failures and successes. It is obvious that the teacher may not be interested in the same topics as students; however, he cannot disregard them lest he should have demotivating impact on students and their academic results (Chastain 1988).

Knowing students' interests and needs will enable the teacher to arrange activities that will positively influence them and result in their active involvement, whole-hearted participation, self-esteem and greater confidence.

19.5.3 Students' Background

Besides students' interests, their background is another crucial factor that plays important role in affecting their motivation. Niebrzydowski (1972) is convinced that students' background and family situation are strictly connected with students' failures or success in learning. Harmer (1991) mentions students' social background as one of the vital components of knowledge about students. It is stressed that this fact must be taken into consideration before lessons are planned.

The study of Gardner and Lambert (1972: 140) portrays "language aptitude," intelligence, helpful "home background" and "parental support" as the major factors in foreign language acquisition. Niebrzydowski (1972) maintains that parental positive attitude towards learning, creating good learning environment at home, and the parents' belief in the value of their children's abilities greatly influence students learning.

It can be concluded that it all resolves into the matter of students' attitudes and motivation. What the teacher can do is to stretch his/her resources to the utmost in order to make the lessons as captivating as possible. The more interesting are the techniques and strategies, the better; they help improve students' motivation and involvement. Some activities are presented below.

ACTIVITY 1 Animals

Age: 12

Level: Elementary

No. of participants: 14

Time: 30 min.

Overall aim(s): To improve learners' motivation by the use of games; to practise vocabulary connected with animals in an interesting manner in order to encourage learners to participate in the lesson; to practise Present Simple (to express habitual action).

Subsidiary aims: To practise both productive and receptive skills (writing down words, reading them aloud, speaking and listening in order to find a suitable partner).

Assumed knowledge: Learners know the names of some animals, their body parts (hoof beak, wing, etc.); they know Present Simple.

Anticipated problems: During the game in which drawing is involved, some learners do not want to draw as they claim that they cannot draw. Learners have problems with the completion sheet (see Appendix 1B). They do not know what to write; some learners have problems with the use of Present Simple.

Solution: Teacher explains that it should be for fun, so the learners should not concentrate too much on the pictures. Teacher helps with the completion sheets and vocabulary.

Materials: A picture of animals (see Appendix 1A), completion sheets (see Appendix 1B).

Stages	Procedure	Aims	Time	Interaction Pattern
Pre-speaking	Teacher divides learners into 3 groups, then shows a picture (see Appendix 1A) and asks learners to look at the picture carefully for 1 min as they are going to play a memory game. After 1 min. learners are to write down as many animals as they can remember (from a picture). Next, all animals are written down on the blackboard and read out before the group. The group which has the most animals wins.	To practise vocabulary connected with animals (spelling and pronunciation of the words) in a form of a game, so in a motivating way.	1 min. 5 min. 3 min. 8 min. 4 min.	Teacher talks Group work Choral responses Pair work Individual work
Speaking	Next, teacher asks learners to work in pairs; each person chooses one animal from the blackboard and describes it to her/his partner, whose task is to draw the animal and say what animal it is. If he manages to draw and guess correctly, he describes the chosen animal to her partner. However, if he does not, the partner says (reveals) the animal and s/he has to walk around the classroom and make the sound this animal makes. Next, teacher gives learners the completion sheets (see Appendix 1B) and learners work on them invidually—they write as if they were animals they had chosen earlier. Then teacher asks learners to get up, mill around and find a suitable partner; they read their completions to each other and decide whether the person is a suitable partner. Teacher provides them with the example that it might be dangerous for a chicken to pair with a fox; new formed pairs sit together and report to the class why they have chosen each other.	To practise speaking and listening while describing animals. To practise expressing habitual actions; to motivate students by using a game; to practise writing simple words connected with animals' lives; to practise reading and listening to what the others read/say (to find a suitable partner).	5 min. 4 min.	Whole class interaction Pair work

Evaluation

After covering the material (connected with animals) in learners' course books, I decided to extend their vocabulary. Moreover, students still needed some practice as far as spelling of the words and pronunciation were concerned. Nevertheless, to avoid boring repetition and practice, I organized everything in a form of captivating games. Hard though I tried, there were still some students not willing to participate. However, students had enormous fun, while some were pretending animals and walking round the classroom.

Variation

To revise vocabulary connected with animals quickly and efficiently, we can play a game called "Last Letter". We may use a ball and the teacher throws the ball to one student and says a word, e.g. "frog". The student must reply with a word starting with 'G', such as "giraffe" and throw back the ball to the teacher who next throws it to the next student. We must remember that the last letter of the word must be the first letter of the next word.

I tried to make use of different types of games to base my activity on entertainment in order to create interest which in its turn adds motivation.

Appendix 1A

Look at the pictures carefully for a minute and try to remember as many animals as possible.

Appendix 1B

Completion Sheet

I usually eat ....

I never eat ....

I am afraid of ....

.... is/are afraid of me.

At night, I ....

During the day, I ....

ACTIVITY 2	That is My Job!
Age:	12–13 years
Level:	Elementary
No. of learners:	14
Time:	41 min.
Overall aim(s):	To practise vocabulary connected with people's jobs, professions in the form of a game in order to make the lesson interesting; to make use of learners' environment.
Subsidiary aim(s):	To cooperate in order to achieve the best results; to brainstorm the idea; to give reason, justifications; to practise both receptive and productive skills.
Assumed knowledge:	Present Simple, some verbs connected with people's jobs, will/going to.
Anticipated problems:	Some learners had problems how to make up a puzzle; learners may choose a job which has not been mentioned during the lesson and they

Solutions:	do not know how to say it in English; while a group work, only one occupation may be chosen by the group, e.g. a pilot. Teacher helps with puzzles, vocabulary, tries to elicit the needed word from the rest of the class. If learners fail to answer a word, the teacher provides the same. While a group works, different group members give reasons, justifications for the group's choice.
Materials:	A puzzle (see Appendix 2A) on slips of paper on which different professions are written (see Appendix 2B).

Stages	Procedure	Aims	Time	Interaction Pattern
Leading-in 1st speaking activity	Teacher shows learners a puzzle (see Appendix 2A) and asks them to solve it. The answer is: "Teacher"; then teacher says, "That's my job". Next, teacher explains that learners are going to play a game. Each person is to choose one slip of paper with names of professions written on it (see Appendix 2B) and the task is to make up a puzzle (just like the teacher had done). Each learner is to present his/her puzzle on the blackboard and the rest of the class is to solve it, that is to say, the correct profession (job). Teacher makes sure that everything is clear and gives learners some time to work on their puzzles. When all learners are ready, the game is played.	To provide learners with an example to explain the rules of the game; to practise vocabulary connected with peoples' jobs in the form of a game; to improve learners' motivation; to help learners if required.	2 min. 3 min. 7 min. 15 min. 4 min.	Close ended teacher's questioning, Teacher-talks Individual work Whole class interaction Pair work
2nd speaking activity	Teacher asks learners to work in pairs and find out who their partners would like to be in the future and why. Teacher gives learners some time, then they report to the class and all the jobs mentioned are written down on the blackboard; next learners are asked to form groups according to the profession (doctors one group, painters next group, etc.). Each group's task is to persuade the other that their job is the best choice; they are to give reasons and the discussion begins. Each group has maximum 2 min. to do it; if they manage to persuade somebody that they are right they win. Moreover, they are called 'experts' for the whole week at school.	To practise the ability of giving reasons, justifications. To brainstorm the idea. To give reasons, justifications, to speak and listen to the others; to improve learners' confidence by cooperating in groups.	10 min.	Group work

Evaluation

Considering the fact that the book provided neither enough presentation nor practice, as far as vocabulary connected with people's jobs is concerned, I decided to extend it. My priority was to present and practice vocabulary in an engaging and attractive way so that my learners get motivated and interested in the lesson. That was the reason why I used games to practise new words. Generally speaking, learners took part in the lesson, but after each game, I should have asked them if they liked it, how they could play it better, or how they would improve it. There was a moment when learners got too excited, they became extremely noisy. Then I had to stop the game and calm them down.

Variation

Teacher writes the names of the occupations and emotions on the slips of paper: one slip of paper per one student. Students' task is to draw papers from a bag and have them describe the emotion and the job on the blackboard without using those words. The rest of the class must guess the emotion and the occupation, e.g. "Smart firefighter," "Happy Postman". Each correct guess scores one point. Consequently, the student with the highest points wins. It can also be played as a mime game.

I made use of not only students' interests, but also their background in order to provide them with 'real' context and topic they are familiar with. The fact that students had the opportunity to work in pairs, next in groups aimed at creating positive attitudes towards learning and at improving their motivation.

Appendix 2A

I simply draw on the blackboard a rebus using the suitable drawings that give me the name TEACHER in the end (we can draw the tea + chimney—cross out the useless letters + r, it gives us teacher.)

Appendix 2B

Choose one slip of paper (with the name of profession written on it) and make up your own puzzle:

firefighter	photographer	typist
policeman	plumber	mechanic
secretary	doctor	judge
hairdresser	painter	nurse
teacher	pilot	farmer
dentist	cook	bus driver
actor	engineer	vet

Appendix 2C

Draw one slip of paper and **mime** the emotion and the job. Remember not to use words!

Happy Postman
Quiet Secretary
Good Doctor
Bad Judge
Funny Hairdresser
Friendly Nurse
Clever Vet
Kind Bus Driver
Shy Photographer
Tired Farmer
Hungry Cook
Helpful Teacher
Tall Actor
Short Plumber

REFERENCES

Brown, H.D., *Principles of Language Learning and Teaching*, Englewood Cliffs, NJ: Prentice Hall, 1994.

Brzeziński, J., *Nauczanie języków obcych dzieci*, Warszawa: Wydawnictwa Szkolne i Pedagogiczne, 1987.

Chastain, K., *Developing Second Language Skills*, San Diego: Harcourt, HBJ, 1988.

Corria, I.L., "Motivating EFL learners," *English Teaching Forum* **4** (1999): 17–18.

Gardner, R.C. and Lambert, W.E., *Attitudes and Motivation in Second Language Learning*, Rowley, Massachusetts: Newbury House Publishers, 1972.

Grygier, U., *Tajemnice skutecznej aktywizacji*, Nowa Szkoła, 10/2001.

Harmer, J., *The Practice of English Language Teaching*, Harlow: Longman, 1991.

Komorowska, H., *Podstawy metodyki nauczania języków obcych* Warszawa: Poland, 1993.

Littlejohn, A., "Motivation: Where does it come from? Where does it go?", *English Teaching Professional* 19 (March 2001).
http://www3.telus.net/linguisticsissues/motivation.html

Niebrzydowski, L., *Wpływ motywacji na uczenie się*, Warszawa: Nasza Księgarnia, 1972.

Ur, P., *A Course in Language Teaching, Practice and Theory*, Cambridge: Cambridge University Press, 1996.

Vockell, E., "Educational psychology: A practical approach," 2004. Available at http://education.calumet.edu/Vockell/EdPsyBook

Part 6

VOCABULARY DEVELOPMENT

Chapter 20

VOCABULARY LEARNING THROUGH EXPERIENCE TASKS

— PAUL NATION

20.1 INTRODUCTION

This chapter has a very practical goal. It looks at one major type of learning task—experience tasks—and shows how they are made and the role they play in learning, in particular vocabulary learning. It could be argued that experience tasks are the most important kinds of language learning tasks because they are essential for fluency development across the four skills of listening, speaking, reading and writing, and they are the most common means of learning from meaning-focused input and meaning-focused output.

20.2 The Classic Experience Task

Let us begin by looking at the classic example of an experience task that is involved in the experience approach to reading with young learners as described by Sylvia Ashton-Warner (1963) in relation to what was largely a first language learning environment.

The reading class begins with the young children each drawing a picture of something that happened to them during the weekend. As each learner completes their picture, they come to the teacher to describe what is happening in it. The teacher listens carefully to the learner's description and then, in clear teacherly handwriting, writes *exactly* what the learner said underneath the picture. This becomes the learner's reading text for the day. The learner then takes the picture away and works on reading the written text. She reads it to herself, then to other learners, and then to her parents and family. Day by day, these illustrated highly meaningful texts are gathered together to make the child's personalized reading book.

This reading activity is an experience task because most of the knowledge needed to do the task is already within the learner's experience. The language needed to do the task comes from the learner (it is their story), the ideas in the reading text come from the learner, and the organization of the text comes from the learner. The only new, partly unknown features in the task are the learning goals of the task. They are the recognition of the written form of the story and turning that written form into ideas by reading. This important goal of learning to read is brought within the learners' capability by the rest of the aspects of the task being well within their previous experience. Imagine the difficulties the beginning learner would face if the language, ideas, and text organization were all unfamiliar.

The essence of an experience task, then, is that most of the knowledge and skill needed to do the task is already within the learners' experience. When learners do experience tasks, to an outsider, they seem to perform quite fluently without any obvious support. What the outsider might not realize is that the support has occurred before the task is done.

20.3 MAKING EXPERIENCE TASKS

There are two major ways of making experience tasks: (i) by bringing the task to the learner and (ii) by bringing the learner to the task.

20.3.1 Bringing the Task to the Learner

As we have already seen, the task is largely brought within the learner's present knowledge. That is, the reading task uses the language, the ideas and a text structure the learner already knows. In second or foreign language learning, the most obvious experience task of this type is use of graded readers for extensive reading. The graded reader series such as Oxford Bookworms, Cambridge English Readers, Penguin Readers, Foundations Reading Library from Thomson ELT, and the Heinemann English Readers are made up of books especially written within a controlled vocabulary and a controlled set of grammatical structures. This means that learners can choose to read books that contain vocabulary and grammatical structures that are completely or largely within their previous experience. They can then focus on the learning goal of reading more fluently or of picking up the few vocabulary and grammatical items that are outside their experience. The availability of graded readers at a variety of proficiency levels means that learners can read largely within their previous language experience at most levels of proficiency. This is very important in a language course for several reasons. Firstly, it is through such experience tasks that most of the kind of learning needed for normal language use occurs. This learning adds to implicit knowledge which is the knowledge needed for unmonitored use of the language (Ellis 2005). Secondly, learners can engage in authentic receptive language use with such texts. They can experience the same kinds of understanding, feelings and reactions that a native speaker would have while reading. These include comprehension, enjoyment (or boredom if it is not a good story), and some kind of evaluative reaction to the story, that is, they can have an authentic reading experience. Thirdly, reading at the right level of difficulty can result in successful reading and in the strong motivation that can come from success. Finally, reading at the right levels and near a native speaker's reading speed can result in large quantities of language input. The greater the language input, the greater the possible language learning.

There are several ways of bringing the level of the task to the learners' present level of proficiency. One way is to use the learners' output as a source of input. This is the method used in Sylvia Ashton-Warner's experience approach to reading. It is also possible to use other learners' output as a source of input for others. This happens when learners read other learners' stories. Another way is for the teacher or course designer to deliberately control the level of the task as in graded readers. This can also be done through the careful selection and sequencing of material (Ghadirian 2002).

20.3.2 Bringing the Learner to the Task

The second major way of setting up an experience task is to bring the learner to the task. That is, to provide the learner with knowledge and experience *before* the task so that the task will then be within their experience. There are two ways of doing this:

1. Through pre-teaching or some form of pre-teaching
2. Through reminding the learners of the relevant ideas that they already know and helping them organise these in a useful way as in semantic mapping.

When using experience tasks for language teaching, it is useful to have a way of checking to see what parts of the task are within the learners' experience and what part of the task is being focussed on as the learning goal. There can be four sets of goals for a language course

1. Language item goals
2. Idea or content goals
3. Skill goals; and
4. Text or discourse goals.

The mnemonic LIST can be used to remember these goals. The skill goals can include the skills of listening, speaking, reading and writing, strategy development, and fluency and accuracy. A useful guideline to follow is that any experience task should have only one of these goals and the other three should already be within the learners' experience. So, if the teacher wants the learners to master the ideas or content of a text, the language items (vocabulary, grammar, language functions), the language skills and the text or discourse knowledge should all be within the learners' experience. Similarly, if the learners have the goal of increasing their reading speed (a part of the reading skill), then the reading speed passages should be written in simple language, deal with largely familiar ideas, and be written with a familiar type of organisation, that is, as a simple narrative or a regular step-by-step description.

So, when checking an experience task, it is useful to ask the two questions:

1. What is the learning goal of the task?
2. Are the three other aspects of the task within the learners' experience?

Table 20.1 shows how various aspects of a reading task can be brought within the learners' experience, either through control which brings the task to the learner or through recall and pre-teaching which brings the learner to the task. It summarises the ways of making experience tasks with a focus on reading. The same table can be made for the skills of listening, speaking and writing.

Table 20.1   Experience Tasks Involving Reading

Ways of Bringing the Task within the Learners' Experience		Typical Procedures for Reading Activities
Bringing the task to the learner: Control through selection or simplification	L	A reading text is written within a controlled vocabulary and a controlled list of structures.
	I	Learners describe their experience to the teacher who writes it to become the learners' reading texts.
	S	The learners read texts which are closely based on the texts they read in their first language.
	T	The teacher writes informative science texts as stories or personal accounts.
Bringing the learner to the task: Recall or sharing of personal experience	L	The learners work together to label diagrams and pictures based on the text they will read.
	I	The learners are asked to predict what will occur in a text after they know the topic of the text.
	S	The learners discuss how they take notes and summarise when they read in their first language.
	T	The learners share their predictions of which kinds of information will occur in what order in the text.
Bringing the learner to the task: Pre-teaching	L	The teacher explains vocabulary that will occur in the reading text.
	I	The learners collect and display pictures and articles relating to the topic of the text.
	S	The learners do guided exercises or first language reading activities to develop the needed reading skills.
	T	The learners are helped with the discourse analysis of a text of the same topic type as the text they will read.

In Table 20.1, the suggestions are organised under the aspects of Language, Ideas, Skills and Text. The suggestions in the section on control deal with ways in which the text can be written and adapted. The suggestions in the other two sections—recall and pre-teaching—describe how the learners can be prepared for the text. All the suggested activities occur *before* the learners read the text so that the actual reading of the text will become an experience task. Table 20.2 shows how a production task, speaking, can be brought within the experience of the learners.

TABLE 20.2 Experience Tasks Involving Speaking

Ways of Bringing the Task within the Learners' Experience		*Typical Procedures for Reading Activities*
Control through selection or simplification	L	A topic is chosen that allows the learners to use vocabulary and structures they already know.
	I	A topic is chosen that the learners know a lot about from first language experience.
	S	The learners are not put under time pressure during the talk.
	T	The task involves kinds of speaking, e.g. telling stories, that are already familiar from first language use.
Recall or sharing of personal experience	L	The teacher helps the learners build up a semantic map around the topic based on useful vocabulary and phrases.
	I	The learners work in groups to list all the things they know about the topic.
	S	The learners recall relevant sentences and collocations they have used before.
	T	The learners work in groups to order the points they will talk about.
Pre-teaching	L	The learners write about the topic before they talk about it. The teacher provides needed vocabulary for the writing.
	I	The learners go on a visit to some place related to the topic they will talk about
	S	The learners do a 4/3/2 activity on the topic with the 2-minute talk being the experience task, and the 4 and 3-minute talks are a kind of pre-teaching.
	T	The learners practise supporting main points with examples.

Although the suggestions in Table 20.2 are organised under control, recall and pre-teaching, it is possible to combine suggestions from different categories. For example, the teacher can choose a topic that the learners know a lot about from first language experience, such as how weddings are celebrated in their country. Then the class builds up a semantic map of the relevant second language vocabulary. Finally they perform a 4/3/2 activity in pairs on the topic. The two-minute talk is the experience task. All the rest, the semantic mapping (a shared task), and the four- and three-minute speaking (shared tasks) are preparation for the two-minute experience task.

20.4 EXPERIENCE TASKS AND COURSE DESIGN

There are three other kinds of tasks besides experience tasks. These are (i) shared, (ii) guided and (iii) independent tasks (Nation 1990). The shared tasks involve learners working together in pairs or groups to do a task. The guided tasks involve learners doing exercises that the teacher or course designer has prepared such as completion, transformation, ordering, copying and similar actions. These tasks support the learner during the task by limiting what he/she has to do. The independent tasks involve learners working through a task without any special preparation or support. Most tasks are a mixture of two or more of the above types of tasks, but to keep things simple, we will treat them as distinct kinds of tasks.

Let us now look at how experience tasks fit into the four strands of a course. I have argued (Nation 2007) that a well-balanced language course consists of four strands: (i) meaning-focused input, (ii) meaning-focused output, (iii) language-focused learning, and (iv) fluency development. In such a course, approximately equal amounts of time are given to each strand. The language-focused learning strand of a course involves deliberate attention to language features, for example, through the direct teaching of vocabulary, learners deliberately studying vocabulary, intensive reading involving dictionary use and teacher explanation, and the deliberate learning of strategies. There are elements of experience tasks in such activities (they should not be too far beyond the learners' previous experience), but they are mainly guided and occasionally shared tasks.

20.4.1 Experience Tasks and Meaning-focused Input and Output

Meaning-focused input, learning through meaning focused listening and reading, involves the following conditions:

1. The learners' attention is on the message. That is, they want to understand the meaning of what they are reading or listening to.
2. There is a small amount of the task which is outside the learners'

experience, but this can be handled by guessing from the context, ignoring it, or negotiation. From a vocabulary perspective, the learner should have at least 98% coverage of the running words in the text (Hu and Nation 2000). That is, the unknown words in the text should not occur at a density greater than one unknown word in every 50 running words. In a reading text, this is about one unknown word in every five lines. When listening this is about two or three unknown words per minute.
3. There is a large quantity of input. This is because the learning from meaning-focused input tends to be small, but with quantity of input these small bits of learning accumulate.

The conditions for meaning-focused output are similar to those of meaning-focused input.

Experience tasks are important in meaning-focused input and output because they set up the important conditions of having only a small amount of the task outside the learners' experience. In addition, because the support and preparation for experience tasks occur before the task is done, the task itself can be done in much the same way as a native-speaker would listen or read for comprehension, or speak or write to communicate a message and, thus, there can be a reasonable quantity of input.

20.4.2 Experience Tasks and Fluency

The fluency development tasks require the following conditions:

1. They must be performed with a focus on the message of the task rather than on the language features.
2. They should involve only familiar language features because the aim of such tasks is to make known features readily accessible.
3. They should require the learner to perform at a faster than usual speed.
4. They should involve large quantities of practice.

Because fluency tasks should involve only familiar language features, most fluency development tasks are experience tasks—where the language required to do the task is already within the experience of the learner.

20.5 VOCABULARY CONTROL

Here we shall look at research on experience tasks and vocabulary learning. The very small amount of research on vocabulary density for second language learners (*ibid.*) and first language learners (Carver 1994) suggests that in order for learners to gain adequate comprehension of a text, no more than 1–2% of the running words (tokens) in a text should be outside their present knowledge. This assumes that proper nouns are considered as known items or at least items that do not require much or any previous knowledge. This is an unknown word density of around one unknown word in every 50 running words and fits with West's (1955: 21) suggestion based on experience of writing and using graded readers for learners of English.

One unknown word in 50 still means that there is one unknown word in every five 10-word lines and six unknown words on every 300-word page. Thus, even with the vocabulary control typical of graded readers, there can be a substantial unknown vocabulary load (Nation and Wang 1999).

It has been suggested that using books written for young native speakers of English could reduce the unknown vocabulary load. Elley and Mangubhai (1981), for example, used children's books written for native speakers in their book. Cho and Krashen (1993) recommend the *Sweet Valley* series, written for young native speakers, as texts for extensive reading programmes for non-native speakers.

Vocabulary analysis of children's texts does not support this. The young native speakers beginning school have a vocabulary of several 1000 words and the books written for them make use of a correspondingly rich vocabulary (Nation 1997). The attractive presentation of such books and their interesting stories may help sustain interest and motivation and encourage the effort to read, but the amount nonnative learners could read must be greatly reduced by the vocabulary load of such difficult texts.

The ideal for nonnative learners of English is that there are attractive, engaging texts written in a controlled vocabulary that takes account of their initially low levels of vocabulary knowledge when they begin reading. There are many books like these, and with initiatives to encourage the production of high quality texts, e.g. the Extensive Reading Foundation awards, the number should grow. For learners of English with a vocabulary size over 2000 words, careful sequencing of texts written for native speakers may be a feasible way of making listening and reading become experience tasks.

The major resource, however, for learners of English at the elementary and intermediate levels has to be text written within a controlled vocabulary. Without this, there can be few of any experience tasks in a foreign language programme.

20.6 PRE-TEACHING VOCABULARY

The research on pre-teaching vocabulary shows that for pre-teaching to have an effect on comprehension, each pre-taught word has to get substantial attention (Graves 1986), what some call "rich instruction". Rich instruction involves spending several minutes teaching a word, drawing attention to several aspects of what is involved in knowing a word (its spoken and written forms, word parts, meaning, grammar and collocations). This is time-consuming and in effect only a few words can get this kind of attention before learners read a text. Nonetheless, for some important topic-related words, pre-teaching may be a useful option.

20.7 STIMULATING PREVIOUS KNOWLEDGE

There has been very interesting research on first language readers by Stahl and his colleagues (1991 and 1989) to see the relative effects on comprehension of vocabulary knowledge and learners' background knowledge of the topic of the text. Their findings have been that vocabulary knowledge and topic knowledge have different effects. Vocabulary knowledge increases the comprehension of sentence and proposition level detail (the microstructure), while topic knowledge affects global comprehension of the text (the macrostructure) including seeing an organization behind the facts in the text. Because these two have different effects, one is not a satisfactory compensation for lack of the other. This is supported by Laufer's (1992) findings with the foreign language learners.

For the learners of English as a second or foreign language, vocabulary knowledge is clearly a dominating factor in determining whether a task will be an experience task or not. Background knowledge cannot substitute for lack of vocabulary knowledge, and pre-teaching is limited in the number of words that can be satisfactorily covered in a reasonable amount of time. It is, thus, essential to make use of controlled material if a course is to have a suitable number of the experience tasks that are needed for developing proficiency through meaning-focused input, meaning-focused output and fluency development.

REFERENCES

Ashton-Warner, S., *Teacher*, New York: Simon and Schuster, 1963.

Carver, R.P., "Percentage of unknown vocabulary words in text as a function of the relative difficulty of the text: Implications for instruction," *Journal of Reading Behavior* **26**.4 (1994): 413–437.

Cho, K.S. and Krashen, S., "Acquisition of vocabulary from the Sweet Valley High Kids series: Adult ESL acquisition," *Journal of Reading* **32** (1993): 662–667.

Elley, W.B. and Mangubhai, F., *The Impact of a Book Flood in Fiji Primary Schools*, Wellington: New Zealand Council for Educational Research, 1981.

Ellis, R., "Principles of instructed language learning," *System* **33** (2005): 209–224.

Ghadirian, S., "Providing controlled exposure to target vocabulary through the screening and arranging of texts," *Language Learning and Technology* **6**.1 (2002): 147–164.

Graves, M.F., "Vocabulary learning and instruction," *Review of Research in Education,* **13** (1986): 49–89.

Hu, M. and Nation, I.S.P., "Vocabulary density and reading comprehension," *Reading in a Foreign Language* **13**.1 (2000): 403–430.

Laufer, B., "Reading in a foreign language: How does L2 lexical knowledge interact with the reader's general academic ability?," *Journal of Research in Reading* **15**.2 (1992): 95–103.

Nation, I.S.P., "The four strands," *Innovation in Language Learning and Teaching* **1**.1 (2007): 1–12.

Nation, I.S.P., "The language learning benefits of extensive reading," *The Language Teacher* **21**.5 (1997): 13–16.

_____, "A system of tasks for language learning," *Language Teaching Methodology for the Nineties*, Sarinee Anivan (Ed.), RELC Anthology Series No. 24 (1990): 51–63.

Nation, P. and Wang, K., "Graded readers and vocabulary," *Reading in a Foreign Language*, **12**.2 (1999): 355–380.

Stahl, S.A., Hare, V.C., Sinatra, R., and Gregory, J.F., "Defining the role of prior knowledge and vocabulary in reading comprehension: The retiring of number 41," *Journal of Reading Behavior* **23**.4 (1991): 487–508.

Stahl, S.A., Jacobson, M.G., Davis, C.E., and Davis, R.L., "Prior knowledge and difficult vocabulary in the comprehension of unfamiliar text," *Reading Research Quarterly*, **24**.1 (1989): 27–43.

West, M., *Learning to Read a Foreign Language*, 2nd ed., London: Longman, 1955.

Chapter 21

ENHANCING ESL LEARNERS' LEXICAL COMPETENCE

— Rotimi Taiwo

21.1 INTRODUCTION

The teaching of lexis to ESL learners must focus on specific goals. This chapter examines such goals and proposes a set of components that will help enhance the lexical competence of ESL learners. The major emphasis in the proposition is a global presentation of lexicon to learners with a view to making them competent users of the language in both L1 and L2 contexts. It took into consideration the challenge of ESL learners of being able to communicate and be understood in both the ESL and EMT contexts. In addition, the study suggested some methodologies that will aid teachers of L2 in helping their learners enhance their competence in English lexicon.

The teaching of English for many decades has been restricted to the teaching of grammatical, phonological and orthographic competence (Richards 1985; Sonaiya 1988). The active teaching of the lexical component of English in an ESL environment has often been restricted to the identification and memorization of forms and associated meanings. Typically, vocabulary learning is more of an incidental exercise than a deliberate one. There are hardly explicit instructions on vocabulary in many ESL classrooms (Naggy et al. 1985; Zimermann 1997). Teachers are quick to refer their students to learners' dictionaries and encourage them to read literary works as ways of acquiring English vocabulary.

This study looks at the goals of vocabulary learning in an ESL environment, recognizing that an ESL environment is remarkably different from the EMT environment in the sense that learning English in an EMT environment is reinforced by other outside influences as it is the language predominantly spoken. The situation in an L2 environment requires a lot of classroom activities. The lexical components for L2 learners must be the ones that will meet their communicative needs. The first crucial thing to consider while attempting to meet the lexical needs of learners is to determine their goals for learning English vocabulary. It is on the basis of these goals that the appropriate components for vocabulary learning can be proposed. Wilkin's (1972) comment that "appropriate vocabulary has to be selected on the basis of the learners' values in terms of their social needs" (p. 110) is a very essential for this kind of exercise.

21.2 THE GOALS OF ESL VOCABULARY LEARNING

The differences in the environment of ESL and EMT learners of English will necessitate the formulation of different goals for the learners in the two different environments. There may not be a compelling need for ESL learners to use words exactly the same way as native speakers since they are using the language to construct their unique experience, which is considerably different from that of the EMT learner. There is also a challenge for the ESL learner to be able to communicate and be understood both by the ESL and EMT speakers. Acquisition of vocabulary comes naturally in an EMT environment because the environment, as mentioned initially, reinforces acquisition—the language is predominantly used in every domain of language use. However, in an ESL situation, the local languages exist side by side with English and the learners have acquired them earlier as their mother tongues. Even in situations where we have children who acquire English as their first language in ESL contexts (which is fast becoming the case in most urbanized ESL contexts), their performance is still largely determined by several contextual factors, one of which is the models they are exposed to. Therefore, in an ESL setting, English is just an institutionalized variety, which operates side by side with several other languages in the society.

The goals of teaching vocabulary in an ESL environment should be to ensure that the learners retain and are able to retrieve the appropriate lexical items when they are needed for expressing themselves when using the language with both native and nonnative speakers. In other words, they should be able to express satisfactorily a wide range of ideas and experiences using the appropriate English lexical items in both native and nonnative contexts. Since linguistic environments differ, many a times the lexical resources learners' need to express ideas and experiences also differ. The goal of the teachers, therefore, will be first to motivate the learners to learn these appropriate items. Teachers' motivation is based on their awareness of these needs and preferences. Since the ESL learners are generally known to have limited vocabularies, teachers will need to systematically present to them the words they need, provide opportunities for elaborating their word knowledge and help them develop fluency with known words (Hunt and Beglar 1998).

21.3 L2 LEXICAL COMPONENT: A REAPPRAISAL

Scholars have identified various aspects of word knowledge learners must possess (Richards 1985; Nation 1990). L2 researchers have agreed that there is a difference between the vocabulary used for comprehension (receptive vocabulary) and that used for production (productive vocabulary). That an L2 learner comprehends a word does not necessarily predict its correct use

(Nation 1990). Scholars also agreed that the receptive-productive distinction is not necessarily a dichotomous one but a continuum, where words move from receptive into productive use (Read 2000; Zarewa et al. 2005). Lexical competence is a complex phenomenon and different propositions have been made on the different dimensions to it—receptive-productive control, quality-quantity and lexical organization (Qian and Schedl 2004). A summary of the various propositions of scholars of what constitutes vocabulary knowledge is: the spoken form, the written form, the grammatical behavior, the collocational behavior, the frequency of usage, the stylistic register constraints, the conceptual meaning, and the association of the word with other related words (Richards 1976; Gairns and Redman 1986; Nation 1990). This chapter draws upon some of the submissions and modifies them based on any research findings from a study of some senior secondary school pupils in south western Nigeria to propose a set of components. The findings revealed that the subjects had both remedial and developmental problems with the mastery of English lexical composition. The remedial problems manifested in their inability to use particular lexical items correctly, while their developmental problems manifested in their nonuse of the lexical items needed to convey their ideas in the compositions that they wrote. Some of the lexical errors identified are given now.

- **Errors traceable to Mother Tongue interference**
    - E.1: They told him to **carry** his mouth **come**.
    - E.2: In those days, **their eyes are black**.
- **Errors of redundant lexical items**
    - E.3: Our forefathers trek **using their legs**.
    - E.4: He was given life **jail** imprisonment.
- **Non-familiarity with English spelling and pronunciation**
    - E.5: My father has just bought a **brown** new car. [**brown** for **brand**]
    - E.6: The accident which occur along Ife and Modakeke road was very **fertile**. [**fertile** for **fatal**]
- **Omission of items that make collocation meaningful**
    - E.7: They have to receive high amount .... than teachers. [................. **of money**]
    - E.8: The food .... is very high and many people cannot afford it [**price**]
- **Errors of word arrangements**
    - E.9: **The most plight of people** in Nigeria is poverty. [**the plight of most people**]
    - E.10: They were given first aid by **a commercial literate bus driver**. [**a literate commercial bus driver**]
- **Errors of improper master of fixed collocation**
    - E.11: My brother decided to **sit on top of the fence** on the matter. [**sit on the fence**]

E.12: I found myself **between the dead and the blue sea**. [between the devil and the deep blue sea]

- **Superficial collocations**

    E.13: The **driver of the car** become **road worthy**. [car + road-worthy/driver + car]

    E.14: I learnt from the head girl in the school how to **type the keyboard** [type + typewriter, computer/strike + keyboard, type + on + keyboard]

The errors identified above can be broadly classified as:

- Interference,
- Redundancy,
- Spelling,
- Omission,
- Word order and
- Collocation.

The error of MT interference, arrangements and redundancy are traceable to the confusion between word association and order in the writers' mother tongue and English. Languages differ in how their words associate. In many African and Asian languages, serial verbs are used to convey information in the predicate. A serial verb is a string of verbs within a single clause that express simultaneous or immediately consecutive actions. They have a single grammatical subject and are understood as having the same grammatical categories such as aspect, modality and tense (see Aikhenvald and Dixon 2006: 1), so the use of two verbs as in *carry come*, in E1 is possible in many African and Asian languages, while in English this is not possible. Likewise, parts of the body are often associated with what they do without rendering any part of the structure redundant. The relationship between 'legs' and 'walk' is not just a matter of mental association in many L1 languages. The two nouns are also structurally-connected in speech as used in E2. Resolving the difference between mental and structural connection of items in L1 and L2 is very essential in L2 vocabulary learning and a way of doing this in vocabulary teaching is to stress to the learners the differences in word order and association in both L1 and L2.

Spelling and pronunciation are aspects of linguistic knowledge that are less emphasized in the teaching of ESL. English is one of the languages that lack the kind of correlation between pronunciation and spelling that makes learning easier. This problem of irregularity of spelling is further compounded by the large number of borrowed words in English whose pronunciation is retained. The spelling errors in E5 and E6 are phonological. It is clear from the error that the learner had an idea of the words they wanted to use as one can observe a kind of closeness in the sounds. The learners' attention must be drawn to the different possibilities for pronunciation in English. For instance, the letter combination *'ou'* can be pronounced in at least 11 different ways: *dough, bought, famous, you, cough, journey, should, tour, flour, loud,* and *though*. Such typical instances can be drawn on as examples to teach L2 learners about the variation in English spellings.

The importance of collocation has been emphasized by several scholars, like Sinclair (1991). Words are restricted in the ways they can be used. They do not just appear at random in texts. Words select other words they co-occur with and there are a larger number of semi-preconstructed phrases that constitute single choices in English (*ibid.*, 110). Teaching collocation is very essential as it helps learners to defining the semantic characteristics of a word and the kinds of words that can be found together (Nattinger 1988: 10). The errors in E7, E8, E11, E12, E13 and E14 are traceable to improper mastery of English collocations. It is not just enough for a learner to know that *money* and *amount* collocate or that *sit on the fence* is a fixed collocation in English. It is also important for them to understand the possible syntactic patterns of occurrences these expressions may fit into.

I present below the proposed components of lexical knowledge for L2 learners and then discuss some methods of presenting them in an L2 classroom:

A. *Morphological component*

Prefixing: *e.g.*: *re-*, *ab-*, *anti-*, as in re-educate, abnormal, and anti-rabbies.
Suffixing: *e.g.*: *-s*, *-er*, *-ing*, as in boys, faster, and carrying.
Compounding: *e.g.*: windscreen, handcuffs, and stiff-necked.
Blending: *e.g.*: motel = motor + hotel, brunch = breakfast + lunch.
Acronyming: *e.g.*: **word acronyms**, *e.g*, *NATO*;
alphabetism: *e.g.*: *EEC*.
Conversion: *e.g.*: **verb – noun**, *e.g*: *cheat*; **adjective – noun**: *e.g.*: *final*.
Borrowing: *e.g.*: **French** – *chauffeur*; **Arabic** – *giraffe*; **German** – *seminar*.

B. *Grapho-phonological component*

Spelling: *e.g.*: words commonly mis-spelt like *across, receive,* etc.
British American spelling: *e.g.*: **British** – *colour*, American – *color*.
                                        British – *centre*, American – *center*.
Pronunciation: *e.g.*: **homophones**: *there/their; principal/principle; sow/sew, price/prize, site/sight/cite*

C. *Lexical relations component*

1. *Paradigmatic relations*

    Synonyms: *e.g.*: *clear – transparent; investigate – examine*
    Antonyms: *e.g.*: *wide – narrow; long – short*
    Hyponyms: *e.g.*: *insect – ant, cockroach, bee, etc.*
    Whole-Part: *e.g.*: *car: dashboard, bonnet, boot, etc.*

2. *Syntagmatic relations*

Collocation-free combination: *e.g.: take – a loan, a risk, etc.*
Strong collocation: *e.g.:*

   adj + noun – *narrow   escape*
   v + noun – *foot + bill*
   adv + v – *adversely +affect*
   noun + v – *frog + croak*

Lexical Phrase: *e.g.:*
Binominals: *e.g.: part and parcel*
Idioms: *e.g.: take the bull by the horns*
Phrasal verbs: *e.g.: take off, carry out*
Similes: *e.g.: as blind as a bat*
Proverbs: *e.g.: there is no smoke without fire*
Fixed phrases: *e.g.: be that as it may*

D. Conceptual meaning component

Polysemy: *e.g.: bank* (of a river), *bank* (where money is kept)
Affective meaning: *e.g.:* **connotative** and **denotative** meaning – *child* – (a person who is not an adult), *child* (somebody who behaves like a *child*)

E. Register and style component

Formal and informal usage: *e.g.:* formal – *lavatory,* informal – *loo*
Geographical variations: *e.g.:*   British – *sweet,* American – *candy*
                                         British – *petrol*, American – *gas*

F. Culture-specific non-native English lexicon

21.4 METHODOLOGIES FOR THE PRESENTATION OF LEXICAL COMPONENTS

In the presentation of lexis to ESL learners, the first and most important thing to emphasize is the context in determining meaning of lexemes. Lexical items according to Ajulo (1995: 64) 'mean' nothing by themselves. It is only when they are used in specific contexts that they stand for anything. Vocabulary teaching should focus on deepening and internalising knowledge of words and this is only seen in the context in which such words are used. For instance, the word *hook* has different meanings in the following registers: fishing, boxing, telecommunications, cricket/golf, household and agriculture (see Taiwo 2003: 149). This is further illustrated in Table 21.1. Such tables will facilitate the presentation of polysemous English words to L2 learners. The learners may also be asked to construct their own tables of polysemous usages in English, identifying their meanings, usages and collocations.

TABLE 21.1 Some Meanings, Usages and Collocates of the
Word *Hook* in Different English Registers

Register	Meaning	Usage	Collocates
Fishing	A curved piece of metal for catching fish.	He caught the fish with a *hook*.	*fish, catch, line, bait*, etc.
Agriculture	A curved instrument for cutting grain from branches.	In order to prune the tree, the farmer used a *hook* to cut the branches.	*grain, cut, grass, branches*, etc.
Boxing	A short hand blow that is made with the elbow bent.	To send his opponent out of the ring, he gave him a left *hook* on the jaw.	*boxer, jay, ring, left, right*, etc.
Household	A bent piece of metal or plastic used for hanging things such as clothes, and pictures.	Can you please hang your coat on the *hook*. The picture fell off the *hook*.	*coat, picture, curtain, hang, towel*, etc.
Cricket/Golf	A way of hitting the ball so that it curves sideways instead of going straight ahead.	The champion in the golf tournament is a *hook* specialist.	*play, hit, bat, ball*, etc.
Telecommunication	The part of the telephone on which a telephone receiver rests or is hung.	The telephone receiver is not properly resting on the *hook*.	*telephone, hang, receiver, ring*, etc.

Dictionaries, sometimes, present a false idea that the English vocabulary is a list of words, each with one or more meanings attached to it. The true picture, however, is that lexical items are related to each other in many ways, and this is how they are remembered and stored. The lexical relations component is one essential aspect of vocabulary learning. Learners should be taught how to identify the boundaries of words related in meaning, e.g., *cup, mug,* and *bowl*; *book, monograph, journal,* etc. It is also important to stress how some general meanings relate to specific ones, *e.g.*: *machine* to *motorcycle, lawn mower,* etc. (see Taiwo 2001: 371). Learners often resort to the use of general expressions when they lack the knowledge of the specific ones.

Some ESL learners in generally have the tendency to expect the same degree of fit between sound and sight as it exists in most of their mother tongues. This expectation, according to Weinrich and Oladeji (1990: 61), sometimes leads to faulty transposition of certain items from speech to writing and the assignment of wrong meanings to certain lexemes misconstrued as similar in the spoken form. This is why we sometimes find students using the following homophones wrongly: *sew/sow, cheap/chip, flower/flour, sight/site/cite, lick/leak, their/there,* etc. Spelling should be actively taught with pronunciation simultaneously. The usual practice in pronunciation classes are drills, and spelling is hardly taught. These two aspects of lexical knowledge complement one another and learners will retain knowledge of a word better if they are taught the spelling and pronunciation together.

Teachers should create the awareness in the pupils that each lexical item has its own collocational behaviour. Teaching should not isolate words and separate them from other words they occur with. According to Carter (1987: 53), the description of restrictions on the range of collocability of particular items can provide a way of differentiating words from each other. Firth's (1957) popular statement on collocation that "you know a word by the company it keeps" further strengthens this position. For example (see Table 21.1), the collocates differ in different registers, since the meaning determines the collocates. For instance, in fishing, the possible collocates are *fish*, *catch*, *line*, *bait*, etc., while in household, the possible collocates are *coat*, *picture*, *curtain*, *towel*, *hang*, etc.

Words operate in fully or partially fixed combinations, which range from phrasal verbs to longer institutionalized expressions (see Nattinger and DeCarrico 1992; Lewis 1993, 1997; Howert 1998). Bygate (2001) calls such sequences "lexical phrase, lexical chunks or multi-word expressions". These include fixed phrases such as *be that as it may, all said and done*; phrasal verbs such as *carry out, put off*; and bi-nominals like *bits and pieces*. These lexical phrases behave like lexemes; therefore, learners should be encouraged to learn them as single units with their distinct meanings.

It is also important for the teacher to emphasize the socio-cultural use of lexical items. The same word may have a basic logical meaning in one context of use, for instance, when the surface side of the word is meant when used. On the other hand, the meaning may be largely figurative and, sometimes, require subjective judgment (see Odebunmi 2001: 50). While the surface meaning of a word is called the denotative meaning, its meta-conceptual use is regarded as the connotative meaning. For example, the words *thin, slim, slender, skinny* and *bony* can be graded on the basis of subjunctive judgement. While *thin* is neutral in meaning, *slim* and *slender* have positive connotations, and *skinny* and *bony* have negative connotations. However, all these words have the same basic meaning—describing "a person's skin that is not covered with much flesh". Knowing the appropriate one to use is very important for socio-cultural relations.

Since the goal of teaching is not just to make learners functional only in their environment, the dimension of some other related varieties, especially the American English, comes in. This may not be elaborate, but it is important for learners as they may have to interact with speakers of such variety or come in contact with literature written in, such variety. With globalization, the usages of American influence in the area of culture cannot be denied. Learners cannot differentiate between the usages of American English and the British English in the contemporary times. It is, however, important for them to distinguish between these two and this can only come when they are able to draw the comparison in the language classroom. A related strategy is the presentation of culture-specific nonnative English lexicon. This is particularly important for comparison. For instance, many nonnative English speakers assume that some of the lexicon they use are used in other English-speaking contexts. Their exposition to the native as well as the nonnative lexicon in the classroom will be with a view to help them know the ones appropriate for different contexts. This will encourage versatility of the learners. Learners will interact most times with English speakers who probably know only the nonnative lexicon. The goal of the component is to produce learners whose communicative competence is not limited in any English-speaking context they may find themselves. In addition to this, teachers should also concentrate on items that are closer to and similar to those in the mother tongue. It is believed that it will be easier to learn such items than the relatively dissimilar ones (see Waring 2002: 2). Such items can be introduced early to start up the ESL learners' vocabulary base before moving on to the complex ones.

21.5 CONCLUSION

The study did a total reappraisal of the presentation of vocabulary to L2 learners and on the basis of the author's research findings, proposed a set of components for the pedagogy of English language in L2 contexts. L2 learners should not be limited in their competence in terms of the appropriate lexicon needed to express themselves in L1 and L2 English speaking domains. Therefore, the component proposed addresses the needs of a total learner and takes care of the morphological, grapho-phonological, lexical relations, conceptual meaning, register and style and culture-specific nonnative lexicon.

REFERENCES

Aikhenvald, A. and Dixon, R.M.W., *Serial Verb Constructions—A Cross-Linguistic Typology,* Oxford: OUP, 2006.

Ajulo, E.B., *Investigating Lexis in English, Problems of Theory and Pedagogy*, Lagos: Stirling-Horder Publishers, 1995.

Bygate, P., *Researching Pedagogical Tasks in Second Language Learning, Teaching and Testing,* London: Longman, 2001.

Carter, R., *Vocabulary: Applied Linguistic Perspective,* London: Longman, 1987.

Firth, J.R., *Papers in Linguistics,* London: OUP, 1957.

Gairns, R. and Redman, S., *Working with Words, A Guide to Teaching and Learning Vocabulary,* Cambridge: Cambridge University Press, 1986.

Howert, P., "Phraseology and second language proficiency," *Applied Linguistics* **16**.2 (1998).

Hunt, A. and Beglar, D., "Current research and practice in teaching vocabulary," *Language Teacher Online* **22**.01 (1998): 1–9.

Lewis, M., *The Lexical Approach,* Hove, England: Language Teaching Publications, 1993.

_____, *Implementing the Lexical Approach: Putting Theory into Practice,* Hove, England: Language Teaching Publications, 1997.

Naggy, W.E., Herman, P., and Anderson, R.C., "Learning words from context," *Reading Research Quarterly* **20** (1985): 233–253.

Nation, I.S.P., *Teaching and Learning Vocabulary*, Rowley, MA: Newbury House, 1990.

_____, *New Ways in Teaching Vocabulary*, New York: Newbury House, 1994.

Nattinger, J., "Some current trends in vocabulary teaching," R. Carter, and M. McCarty (Eds.), 1988, 62–82.

Nattinger, J. and DeCarrico, J., *Lexical Phrases and Language Teaching*, Oxford: OUP, 1992.

Odebunmi, A., *The English Word and Meaning—-An Introductory Text*, Ogbomoso: Critical Sphere, 2001.

Qian, D. and Schedl, M., "Evaluation of an in-depth vocabulary knowledge measure for assessing reading performance," *Language Testing* **21** (2004): 28–52.

Read, J., *Assessing Vocabulary*, New York: Cambridge University Press, 2000.

Richards, J.C., "The Role of vocabulary teaching," *TESOL Quarterly* **1**.1 (1976): 77–89.

_____, *The Context of Language Teaching*, Cambridge: Cambridge University Press, 1985.

Sinclair, M., *Corpus, Concordance, Collocation*, Oxford: OUP, 1991.

Sonaiya, C.O., *The Lexicon in Second Language Acquisition: A Lexical Approach to Error Analysis*, Ph.D. Dissertation, Cornell University, 1988.

Taiwo, R., "Lexico-semantic relations errors in senior secondary school students' writing," *Nordic Journal of African Studies* **10**.3/76 (2001): 366–373.

Taiwo, O.O., *Collocational Errors in the Written English of Senior Secondary School Pupils in Six Yoruba-speaking States in Nigeria*, Ph.D. Dissertation, Obafemi Awolowo University, Ile-Ife, Nigeria, 2003.

Waring, P., "Basic principles and practice on vocabulary instructions," *The Language Teacher* (2002): 1–5.

http//:www1.harenet.ne.jp/waring/vocab/principles/commonsense.htm accessed April 2nd, 2004.

Weinrich, L.M. and Oladeji, N., "The complex nature of certain aspects of lexical deviation in ESL: The Nigerian example," *Journal of Nigerian English Studies Association* **1**.1 (1990): 61–70.

Wilkins, D.A., *Linguistics in Language Teaching*, London: Longman, 1972.

Zarewa, A., Schwanenflugel, P., Nikolova, Y., "Relationship between lexical competence and language proficiency," *Studies in Second Language Acquisition* **27** (2005): 567–595.

Zimermann, C.B., "Do reading and interactive vocabulary instruction make a difference?: An empirical study," *TESOL Quarterly* **31** (1997): 121–140.

Chapter 22

MORPHOLOGICAL ANALYSIS AND VOCABULARY DEVELOPMENT
Critical Criteria

— Tom S. Bellomo

22.1 INTRODUCTION

Morphological Analysis as a vocabulary acquisition strategy has both its advocates and antagonists. Criticism from opponents is often warranted when programs omit one or more of the three critical criteria—similarity of form, similarity of meaning and number of derivatives—that establish the framework behind a successful curriculum. The intent behind this study is to disseminate and explicate these three criteria, along with the methodology employed in a vocabulary acquisition program that was part of a college preparatory reading course.

The important link between the extent of one's vocabulary range and reading comprehension is well established (Davis 1944, 1968; Nagy and Herman 1987; Stahl 1982, 1990). Incorporating direct instruction of vocabulary into the curriculum, both to adults (Folse 2004) and children (Beck et al. 2002; Biemiller and Boote 2006; Nagy et al. 2003), is proliferating. With the adult in mind, logic dictates that instruction in strategies is perhaps the most prudent use of class time. According to Folse (2004):

> If it is accepted that acquisition of more vocabulary is our goal but that there are simply too many words in the language for all or most of them to be dealt with one at a time through vocabulary instruction, then what is the next logical step? Thus, one of the main classroom activities for teachers of vocabulary is the direct teaching of learning strategies related to vocabulary. (pp. 89–90)

This chapter addresses the successful use of morphological analysis as a vocabulary instruction strategy among foreign born and native English speaking college preparatory students (see Bellomo 2005). It discusses, in detail, the case for prudent selection of word parts and corresponding vocabulary and also covers the specifics of the program and results of an original study.

22.1.1 Background

Vocabulary strategies are techniques employed by the reader to unlock the meaning of an unknown word when encountering it in text, and/or a deliberate attempt to learn a word for the purpose of future recall. Schmitt (1997) compiled a list of 58 vocabulary acquisition strategies, and then in the form of a questionnaire, asked English language learners (ELLs) to identify from among those strategies the ones they themselves employed. Strategies that were selected were then to be rated based on their perceived helpfulness. The sample was comprised of 600 Japanese students. A total of 150 students were drawn from each of the following age groups: middle school, high school, university, and adult (professionals in language programs that were sponsored by corporations). The study was designed to "isolate changes in strategy use and perceptions as Japanese learners progress through the school system and into adult English classes" (*ibid.*, p. 223). Broadly, the list of strategies was dichotomized between discovery strategies ($n = 44$) used to unlock the meaning of unknown words, and consolidation strategies ($n = 14$) used to commit words to memory once they had been learned. Schmitt noted that the analysis of affixes and roots was one of only a few strategies that clearly functioned as both a discovery and consolidation strategy. Of the 58 total strategies, eight would most likely be used exclusively by nonnative speakers of English, e.g. "using a bilingual dictionary". The remaining strategies were representative of those used by both native English speakers and ELLs.

Resultant trends yielded through the survey indicated that certain strategies appeared more beneficial than others relative to student age. For example, word lists were used progressively less often and deemed less helpful at each subsequent stage of the four levels. Conversely, student perceptions of the helpfulness of root/affix knowledge—as both word attack and mnemonic strategies—increased noticeably up through the levels. Schmitt concluded, "Given the generally favorable response to strategies utilizing affixes and roots, both to help discover a new word's meaning and to consolidate it once it is introduced, it may be time to reemphasize this aspect of morphology" (*ibid.*, p. 226).

22.2 MORPHOLOGICAL ANALYSIS

Morphological, or structural, Analysis is the process of breaking down morphologically complex words into their constituent morphemes (word meaning parts). For instance, the word *worker* is comprised of two meaning units: the base *work*, and the inclusion of *-er*, which conveys the meaning of an agent (person or thing) that does whatever is implied in the base. Thus, the worker is one who works; a film projector is that which projects film onto a screen. As students proceed through the grades, course texts will take on increasingly sophisticated language. Often, these multi-syllabic words will be of the Graeco-Latin origin, which collectively comprise approximately two-thirds of the English lexicon (Carr et al. 1942). Studies have shown that moving along the word frequency continuum from more frequent to less frequent displays an increased percentage of Graeco-Latin words, while the percentage of Germanic mono-syllabic words decreases (*ibid.*, Oldfather 1940). It is in the academic arena that students will come across an influx of content-specific vocabulary throughout the curriculum. Recognizing frequent roots and affixes that transfer among the disciplines can support students as they make sense and attempt to retain the meanings of this deluge of new words. Corson (1997) noted:

> Pedagogical processes of analyzing words into their stems and affixes do seem important in academic word learning. These processes help embody certain conscious and habitual metacognitive and metalinguistic information that seems useful for word acquisition and use. Getting access to the more concrete roots of Graeco-Latin academic words in this way makes the words more semantically transparent for a language user, by definition. Without this, English academic words will often remain "hard" words whose form and meaning appear alien and bizarre. So, this kind of metacognitive development that improves practical knowledge about word etymology and relationships seems very relevant for both L1 [native English speaker] and L2 [non-native English speaker] development (pp. 707–708).

22.2.1 Prudent Word Part and Vocabulary Selection

In creating a workable vocabulary strategy curriculum that capitalizes on the strengths of morphological analysis, one must be cognizant of three underlying criteria requisite for a successful program. These components were touched upon by Orleans (1922), but appear to have not been implemented in many books and programs that have deservedly earned the rebuke of cynics discrediting word part analysis. He stated, "The possibility of transfer from the Latin to the English is determined by such elements as similarity of form, similarity of meaning, and perhaps number of derivatives" (p. 559). I will discuss each of these in turn, and then delineate a vocabulary acquisition program that was used among a heterogeneous class of college preparatory students.

Similarity of form

According to Webster's Third International Dictionary of the English Language (1993), the root *morph* in morphology is defined as *form*. In Venezky's (1967) article on the patterns of English orthography, he observes, "Orthography is not merely a letter-to-sound system riddled with imperfections, but, instead, a more complex and more regular relationship wherein phoneme and morpheme share leading roles" (p. 77). To illustrate a morpheme's leading role, were the English writing system to reflect a purely phonetic sound/symbol relationship, the words induce, reduction, and educate might be written, respectively, as [ĭn dōōs'], [rē dək' šən], and [ĕj' ōō kât].

However, the root [duc], which means "to lead," would not be apparent either aurally or orthographically since it is spoken and, consequently, would be written as dōōs, dək, and jōōk. Moreover, in the word educate, jōōk would be divided among three separate syllables! Yet a visual cue demonstrating a semantic connection among the words is evident due to the stable form of the morpheme [duc] regardless of its pronunciation.

As students learn the meaning of a particular word part and corresponding words, the visual cue of the morpheme serves as a mnemonic when encountering the same words later on in text; also, it can often assist as a word attack device when encountering new words derived from the same morpheme. For the latter, this association often will be viable only to the degree that the instructed word part is visually similar to the part found in the derivation or word family. For example, Brown (see Thompson, 1958) compiled a list of 14 master words that were taught to his adult education students. Based on 20 prefixes and 14 roots, it was claimed that these word parts pertained to "over 14,000 words in the Webster's Collegiate Dictionary and a projected 1,00,000 words in an unabridged dictionary" (p. 62). Such claims appear hyperbolic. Indeed, based on the divergent form of some of the master roots, the success of transferring knowledge of word parts from the known to the unknown is problematic. One of Brown's master words was *precept*. The prodigious vocabulary derived from /capere/, the root in this word, comes into question when one considers the variant spellings provided by Brown: *cept, cap, capt, ceiv, ceit,* and *cip*. This dissimilarity in form would most likely diminish the amount of words students can realistically expect to know based on the word *precept*. If students were introduced to a more formalized Latin-centered curriculum, changes in declensions and conjugations would reveal an order behind the spelling changes of /capere/ (Hayriye Karliova 2008), but the inclusion of such instruction would likely be deemed beyond the scope of a college preparatory program.

To take advantage of a similarity of form, a word part should be taught in the form it appears throughout the vocabulary curriculum and will most likely appear in the words students are apt to encounter in their own reading. For instance, the word part /malus/, which means *bad*, would be taught to students as /mal/, which is visually evident in such words as malign, malignant, malicious, malediction, and malefactor. Practical utility, not classical purity, should be the aim of such instruction.

Similarity of meaning (semantic transparency)

I will take the liberty to extend Orleans' (1922) prior observation to suggest that not only should the same meaning be conveyed within the family of words being introduced, but that this meaning should be transparent. In other words, there should be a clear (transparent) parts-to-whole relationship between the morphemes in a word and overall meaning in the word itself. For example, the five words above that are based on /mal/ all convey an aspect of 'bad'. Conversely, an empirical study by Swisher (1988) found the root /fer/ to be "the most difficult to master based on the number of words generated and retention of its meaning after instruction over time" (p. 204). That is not surprising when considering one of the study's instructional words, 'vociferous', where the root /fer/, which means *to bear* or *carry*, is not semantically transparent (see Levin et al. 1988, for an original study in semantic transparency).

Nagy and Anderson (1984) grouped words into six divisions based on semantic relatedness. A zero would indicate a perfectly clear parts-to-whole relationship, while six would suggest that no evident relationship exists between the word parts and the overall meaning of the word itself. Words from half of the six-point continuum were deemed semantically transparent (SEM 0-2) and the remaining divisions were deemed semantically opaque (SEM 3-5). Semantic relatedness was defined in terms of the following question: "Assuming that a child [grades 3-9] knew the meaning of the immediate ancestor, but not the meaning of the target word, to what extent would the child be able to determine the meaning of the target word when encountering it in context while reading?" (*ibid.*, p. 310). According to their scheme, it was determined that multiple words from the same family in the SEM 0-2 category would be inferable if the child already knew only one of the related words. For older students (late high school and beyond), it is quite possible for a number of words in the SEM 3 category to be grouped within the transparent word family due to the older students' advanced decoding capabilities and enriched schemata.

> ... which means that although the meaning of the derived form [from SEM 3] is not completely predictable from the meanings of its component parts, the meanings of the component parts do, in fact, contribute something to the derived meaning. Even in these cases, then, knowledge of word formation processes will be helpful to the reader trying to figure out the meaning of words in context (*ibid.*, p. 314).

Similarly, knowledge of only one morpheme within a multi-syllabic word can assist in differentiating between commonly confused words. The prefix [*im-*] means "in"; the prefix [*e-*] signifies "out". Knowing that distinction may suffice in obviating the confusion between immigrate and emigrate: one immigrates into a country while emigrating out of his/her original country.

Number of derivatives (ubiquity)

Building a vocabulary strategy program based on morphological analysis which includes word parts that are stable in form and transparent in meaning will not be of much use if these parts assist in recalling or learning only a few words. Ideally, selected morphemes should transfer to multiple words that will allow the student to obtain much mileage from this strategy. Holmes and Keffer (1995) sought to increase Scholastic Aptitude Test (SAT) scores through a computer program that enlarged students' vocabulary by using classical word parts. In determining which roots to incorporate into the program, the criterion for root selection was determined by whether or not a minimum of five English derivatives per root were found on a particular frequency list.

Ubiquitous word parts, like high frequency vocabulary, may assist in automaticity. Morphologically complex words appearing on the low-end of a frequency list are often more easily recognized when one considers its overall family—those derivations based on the same roots. Nagy et al. (1989) contended that the best measure of frequency is not the individual word itself, but the family or those words closely related in form and meaning:

> The word inactivity, for example, is a relatively low-frequency word, occurring less than once in a 100 million words of school text ... If word recognition were determined only by the frequency of the individual word, independent of morphological relationships, this word would be accessed slowly. However, when related words such as active, inactive, activity and activities are taken into account, the family frequency of inactivity is 10 thousand times as great as the frequency of this individual member. (p. 264)

Word families and their association with frequency, then, do not merely multiply a word's frequency but appear to operate exponentially. At present, this author is assembling word parts and vocabulary based on the three aforementioned criteria, and these will be utilized in a college preparatory reading program comprised of both native and nonnative speakers of English. Until its completion, good success has been achieved these past 12 years by modifying aspects of the book *Word Power Made Easy* by Lewis (1978). How I have tailored the contents of this text to meet the needs of my students, and the methodology I implemented for a vocabulary acquisition program based on morphological analysis are discussed next.

22.2.2 The Program

Text and supplemental

Word Power Made Easy is a compact trade book of over 500 pages. Major chapters introduce ten keywords based upon a common theme. For example, the topic of one particular chapter focuses on personality types. Readers are introduced to such types as egotists, extroverts, misanthropes, along with seven others. Several ensuing sessions, until the subsequent chapter, will pick apart these ten keywords to expand the reader's vocabulary based on the roots, affixes, and general word families derived from the keywords.

To facilitate my students' study of this book, I developed a handout composed of ten boxes. Each box corresponds to the vocabulary and word parts the students are required to know for a particular week, and these are indexed to the chapters and sessions from *the book*. Hence, the ten boxes are a streamlined coverage of ten weeks of instruction. Selected word parts were based on the aforementioned criteria of stable form, semantic transparency, and ubiquity; each box includes relevant transparent vocabulary (Table 22.1) as well. In all, 65 roots, 42 prefixes, and 24 suffixes were introduced, which accounted for 315 distinct words—or approximately five words per root. These words are distinct in that they comprise the same family

TABLE 22.1   Week Three of Weekly Word List

CHAPTER 4:

Session 4, p. 55 (Keywords)

Gynecologist psychiatrist dermatologist

Session 5, p. 60

Root	Prefix	Suffix	Vocabulary
Logo/logy	epi		psychology
Ped			pedestal, pedestrian, *pedometer*
Ocul			*binoculars, monocle*
Ops/optic (p. 62)		ician (p. 60, 63)	optician, optics, biopsy
	Mis* ("*wrongly*")		*misnomer, misuse, misunderstand*
Derm	(negative prefix)	itis	

Session 6, p. 68

			epidermis, hypodermic
			pachyderm, dermatitis, taxidermist
Psych (p. 87)		osis (p. 68)	psychosis, psychotic, psychiatrist
Genesis (p. 89)			psychogenesis

CHAPTER 5: Session 7, p. 81 (Keywords)

podiatrist psychologist optician optometrist

Session 9, p. 93

Meter/metr			thermometer, kilometer, *thermos*
Therm	peri		*periodic, perimeter, thermostat*
Pous/pod	tri		*tri-athlete* trilogy trio
Oct		ium	podium, *tripod, trinity tricycle*
			octopus, octagon, periodontal

(e.g. malicious, malefactor), but are not derivations based on suffixation (e.g. malicious, maliciously). Instead, students were required to utilize inflectional and derivational knowledge in order to correctly identify or produce different word forms based on parts of speech (e.g. noun abstraction, noun thing, noun agent, verb, adjective). Therefore, the amount of potentially different words the student could be expected to know (and be tested on) more than tripled the fixed number of words explicitly taught.

From Table 22.1, it can be seen that, at times, only a few keywords were taken from the initial chapter (in Chapter 4, three out of ten were selected; in Chapter 5, four were selected). Sometimes this was justified because the root of the keyword did not meet the selection criteria. For example, one particular keyword from a previous chapter was *ascetic*, which is based on the root *asketes*. No other word based on the root asketes is given throughout the book, so to include its word part in instruction would be moot due to its lack of productivity. In Chapter 4, the word pediatrician was omitted from among the keywords introduced. This word is based on the root, paidos, which means child. First, the root's form is not visually apparent in the vocabulary item (*paidos* versus *pedia*); additionally, *ped* in pediatrician could be confused with the root *ped* (*foot* as in pedal, moped) that is introduced in the same chapter. Morphological analysis is not as neat and clean as idealism would prefer; one purpose of the supplemental sheet is to keep these introductory lessons relatively straightforward. Once students have established a working foundation, then issues such as false transparency and the spelling of highly assimilatory affixes can be addressed.

Other keywords could have been included from among the set, but were not simply to keep the learning burden manageable. In this respect, some of the item selection was subjective and would undoubtedly differ from another instructor's selection. I have found that students seldom return this book as a campus buyback at the end of the semester as the author's lucid and casual style make for a pleasurable read. As well, some of the more ardent students choose to comb through its contents to learn on their own what was not covered in class.

Briefly, a few other things to note would be the inclusion of words and word parts in the box that are not covered in the text. Such productive morphemes are highlighted with an asterisk beside them, are typed in bold and italicized font, and have a brief definition or synonym beside them or underneath in parentheses (see *Mis* under the prefix section in Table 22.1). Similarly, words derived from the morphemes but not covered in the text are included in the vocabulary section of the box and are italicized. Sometimes these are deemed as novel words that students, especially ELLs, are not expected to know, like *misnomer*. Alternately, some easy high-frequency words are included which serve as mnemonics to facilitate recall of the word part, as in *misunderstand*. In an earlier lesson, *bicycle* was added to the vocabulary section to serve as a cue to recall the word part *bi* (two) due to the obvious visual—two wheels.

Ongoing assessment

Crucial to successfully building students' vocabulary and word part knowledge is making provision throughout the semester for multiple exposures to the target words and word parts. This is done in the form of weekly tests, an extensive mid-term exam (100 questions) and even larger final exam (200 questions). With tests typically given at the end of the week, I have at times given students crossword puzzles (see **www.puzzlemaker.com**) over the weekend to combat the natural tendency of some to procrastinate and, thus, cram for the weekly test. Since the vocabulary program is implemented in a reading class, I typically do not devote too much time to personal instruction as I prefer that students access content knowledge through reading the book. For a college preparatory class, this method serves to incidentally prepare students as independent learners who will derive much of their course content through texts. Much of what I do cover pertains to material not addressed in the text but included in the weekly box. Also, on the first class after each weekend, I entertain students' questions about anything not clearly explained in *Word Power*. The nature of their questions evidences how thoroughly students have read the assignment.

The first section of each test covers word parts. Synonyms or brief definitions are given, and students select from a comprehensive list of all the word parts covered that week and match them with their meaning. The second section is formatted similarly, but covers vocabulary. In keeping with informed test creation, several more word parts and vocabulary are given than definitions or synonyms so as to reduce reliance upon the process of elimination. Beginning with the second test and throughout, a third part entails review. Each week, the format of the third section differs. Sometimes the review may be presented as multiple choice items, or matching columns, and sometimes the format is more productive in nature. For example, to assess students' recollection of word parts, a word part is given followed by a line to the right of it that provides room for students to supply their own brief definition or synonym. To the right of the line is a set of brackets. Inside these brackets, students are to insert P (prefix), R (root), or S (suffix) to correctly identify the type of word part. Thus, a review question for word parts may look like this:

ego: _____ [ ].

(**Answer**   ego: *self* [R].)

For the vocabulary section, the first four of ten weekly tests will have students fill in the blank to the right of a definition/synonym by selecting from a list of all the vocabulary items introduced that week. For the following three tests, students' knowledge of derivations is incorporated as I, then, provide two, three, and sometimes four words that can technically be the correct answer, but only one will be deemed correct based on the parts of speech. For instance, an item might read:

"To go against something you've already said, such as telling others not to raise their voice yet you clearly do" (v).

Students knowing the answer will go through the alphabetical list and, in this case, find two related items: contradict and contradiction. Based on the cue at the end of the question (v), students must select the verb form. For the last three quizzes (eight through ten), this section is similar, but now the part of speech cue (e.g. "v" for verb) is omitted and students must supply the correct form based on the context.

Recall and depth of learning

Though much of the format of the weekly tests requires students to access recall, and the two major exams are exclusively multiple choice, I have not felt this to be a compromise of in-depth learning. Proponents of deep processing suggest that the more involved learners are in storing and productively using a lexical unit, the better their retention. Instruction, therefore, that involved more elaborate manipulation of the target words was believed to be more efficacious than simple recognition activities such as cloze passages or multiple choice. Folse (1999) challenged the belief that one particular activity was necessarily deeper than another. In his work among

ELLs, he investigated whether more elaborate activities explicitly resulted in greater depth of processing:

> Since original sentence writing may require more cognitive processing of a word than merely filling in a blank with that word, these results [greater retention] are to be expected. However, it remains to be seen whether the higher gains for original written output are the results of deeper processing or simply more time on task (p. 7).

Using a within-subjects design, Folse established three conditions with time on task being the critical variable. The elaborative condition required participants to compose an original sentence for each target word. In another condition, students practiced the vocabulary using a fill-in-the-blank procedure. For the final condition, students completed three fill-in-the-blank exercises using the target words. This last condition was chosen because a pilot study demonstrated that it took the ELL students approximately three times longer to create original sentences than to complete one cloze exercise. Thus, this final condition was an attempt to equalize time on task with the so-called deep-processing manipulation. His findings demonstrated that the (supposedly) more sophisticated productive task did not result in greater retention than the exercise providing multiple exposures. Both conditions, however, significantly differed from the remaining condition that afforded less exposure. The findings of Folse underscored the importance of repeated exposure to target words in order to strengthen memory links and facilitate retention.

For the two major exams (multiple choice), what instructors may lack in the ability to assess students' depth of vocabulary and word part knowledge can be compensated by breadth. A 200-question final exam in the multiple choice format covered about half of the course content. The multiple choice tests are completed relatively quickly by the students—are exceptionally quick in scoring and objective by design. The benefits of such tests are founded (Vacc et al., 2001). Of course, the ideal way to assess students' understanding of any subject matter would be a one-on-one, or a student-panel oral examination similar to what doctoral students encounter in their dissertation defense. Along the continuum from such a dynamic interaction to a static multiple choice format is the cost/benefit trade off among time, feasibility, reliability, and penetration of content. What does not differ along that continuum, however, is what the student actually knows. Although the instructor can gain greater insight from the one-on-one probing than from a multiple choice exam, that does not alter what the student brings to the test. With my international students, many often study equally as hard regardless of how they will be assessed. Ultimately, exams are not for the benefit of the instructor, but for the student. For many international students, their objective is to learn the language and to succeed in an institution of higher education where all course content will be delivered in English. They clearly see the correlation between an enhanced vocabulary and their academic success (Zimmerman 1997). To that end, I tend to view my major exams as further teaching aids. I see these as final opportunities to reinforce what has already been covered and to once again strengthen students' memory associations.

Associations based on mere recall do not necessarily minimize the degree to which students can know a word. Graves (1987) created a hierarchy founded on the difficulty involved in learning new words. Learning new words representing known concepts was classified as one of the easier tasks since schemata already exist for the concepts. This was true for both native English speakers and ELLs. Learning new words that represent new concepts was viewed as one of the more difficult tasks. This latter task is more indicative of the language needs of younger students whose concept development is far inferior to that of the college-age student. The chances are far greater that the adult student will already possess concept development for the item; for the ELL, often an English language equivalent is sufficient to know well the word or morpheme. The simple one-to-one relationship between a word part and its meaning, or the vocabulary item and its synonym, could be embellished by the adult student's rich schemata. Also, to facilitate this, both the morphemes and selected vocabulary items tend to be singular in meaning, thus eliminating the confounding effects of polysemy usually encountered with one syllable, high frequency vocabulary (Just and Carpenter 1987; Howards 1964).

22.2.3 Original Experiment

Positive student feedback over the years testified to the utility of the technique presented here. What had been lacking, however, was substantive empirical research. To assess the program's efficacy, a pretest/post-test design comprising word parts and vocabulary was administered, and replicated, over the course of several semesters (Bellomo 2005). Native English speaking students comprised one group and foreign students formed two additional groups—students whose language origin was Latin-based (i.e. Romance languages) and students whose language origin was not Latin-based (i.e. Asian languages). Results were compared and contrasted in view of group identity based on language origin. The pretest was used to quantify the extent that pre-existing knowledge of Latinate word parts and morphologically complex vocabulary differed among groups. The identical instrument served as a post-test to measure the extent that direct instruction in morphological analysis resulted in change among the same groups after one semester of instruction. Two sections on both the pretest and post-test yielded a total of four distinct mean scores that formed the primary basis for comparison.

Categorizing students within the college preparatory reading class based on language origin revealed distinctive strengths and weaknesses relative to group identity when learning Latin-based word parts and vocabulary. Though word parts and vocabulary introduced in the course were not exclusively Latinate in origin, the test instrument intentionally limited the items to those derived from Latin. This was an attempt to assess whether or not morphological analysis would offer an unfair advantage to, say, Spanish or French speaking students. In fact, results of a one-way fixed-factor analysis of variance, in conjunction with multiple comparison procedures, indicated that the Latin-based group did indeed perform the strongest. This group had the greatest mean score on all four measurements; however, only for the word part section of the pretest was the difference statistically significant. The non-Latin-based group performed the poorest as evidenced by scoring the lowest on three of the four measures, with a statistically significant difference for the vocabulary pretest.

No group began the semester demonstrating mastery of word parts or multi-syllabic Latin-based vocabulary; this was in keeping with observations by Levin et al. (1988). Thus, college preparatory students in general could stand to profit from such instruction, and indeed, all did. A pretest/post-test comparison for each respective group indicated that all three groups made significant gains on both sections of the test instrument. The results of the study suggest that college preparatory students, regardless of their language origin, enter higher education with limited knowledge of Latinate word parts and vocabulary. The results further suggest that students comprising the heterogeneously populated college preparatory reading class can profit from direct instruction in morphological analysis irrespective of language origin.

22.3 CONCLUSION

Prior research has demonstrated that college-level content words tend to be morphologically complex, singular in meaning, and likely to be Classical in origin. Reading is the salient skill utilized across the curriculum and often the primary means of content dissemination. Reading, in turn, is principally linked to the extent of one's vocabulary. Consequently, teaching morphologically complex vocabulary at the college preparatory level along with providing a working knowledge of morphemes can assist students toward college readiness.

For such a strategy to be successful, this author has heeded to, and expanded upon, a statement by Orleans in 1922 concerning critical criteria requisite to word part and vocabulary inclusion. To reiterate, word parts are to demonstrate stable form (visually similar in each of the target words), semantic transparency (clear parts-to-whole relationship with the primary meaning consistent in each of the target words), and ubiquity (morphemes are to be found in a minimum of five words from the same family, not mere inflections or from derivations that change only the part of speech).

Both the student feedback and the empirical research conveyed the viability of this strategy, which was robust enough to meet the needs of students from very diverse backgrounds—a diversity increasingly found within many of today's higher education institutions.

REFERENCES

Beck, I.L., McKeown, M.G., and Kucan, L., *Bringing Words to Life: Robust Vocabulary Instruction*, NY: Guilford Press, 2002.

Bellomo, T., "Latinate word parts and vocabulary: Contrasts among three groups comprising the community college preparatory reading class" (Doctoral dissertation, University of Central Florida, 2005), *Dissertation Abstracts International* **133** (2005).

Biemiller, A. and Boote, C., "An effective method for building meaning vocabulary in primary grades," *Journal of Educational Psychology*, **98**(1), (2006), 44–62.

Carr, W.L., Owen, E., and Schaeffer, R.F., "The sources of English words," *The Classical Outlook* **19**(5), (1942), 455–457.

Corson, D., "The learning and use of academic English words," *Language Learning* **47**(4), (1997), 671–718.

Davis, F.B., "Fundamental factors of comprehension in reading," *Psychometrika* **9**(3), (1944), 185–197.

_____, "Research in comprehension in reading," *Reading Research Quarterly* **3**(4), (1968), 499–545.

Folse, K.S., *The Effect of the Type of Written Practice Activity on Second Language Vocabulary Retention*. Unpublished doctoral dissertation, University of South Florida (1999).

_____, *Vocabulary Myths: Applying Second Language Research to Classroom Teaching*, Ann Arbor, MI: University of Michigan Press (2004).

Graves, M.F., "The roles of instruction in fostering vocabulary development," in M.G. McKeown and M.E. Curtis (Eds.), *The Nature of Vocabulary Acquisition*, Hillsdale, NJ: Lawrence Erlbaum Associates (1987), 165–184.

Karliova, Hayriye, Personal communication with the writer of this essay, July 25, 2008.

Holmes, T.C. and Keffer, R.L., A computerized method to teach Latin and Greek root words: Effect on verbal SAT scores," *Journal of Educational Research* **89**(1), (1995), 47–50.

Howards, M., "How easy are 'easy' words?," *Journal of Experimental Education* **32** (1964), 375–381.

Just, M.A. and Carpenter, P.A., *The Psychology of Reading Language Comprehension*, Newton, MA: Allyn and Bacon (1987).

Levin, J.R., Carney, R.N., and Pressley, M., "Facilitating vocabulary inferring through root-word instruction," *Contemporary Educational Psychology* **13**, (1988), 316–322.

Lewis, N., *Word Power Made Easy: The Complete Handbook for Building a Superior Vocabulary*, NY: Pocket Books (1978).

Nagy, W.E. and Anderson, R.C., "How many words are there in printed school English?," *Reading Research Quarterly* **19**(3), (1984), 304–330.

Nagy, W.E., Anderson, R.C., Schommer, M., Scott, J.A., and Stallman, A.C., "Morphological families in the internal lexicon," *Reading Research Quarterly* **24**(3), (1989), 262–282.

Nagy, W., Berninger, V., and Abbott, R., "Relationship of morphology and other language skills to literacy skills in at-risk second-grade readers and at-risk fourth-grade writers," *Journal of Educational Psychology* **95**(4), (2003), 730–742.

Nagy, W.E. and Herman, P.A., "Breadth and depth of vocabulary knowledge: Implications for acquisition and instruction," in M.G. McKeown and M.E. Curtis (Eds.), *The Nature of Vocabulary Acquisition*, Hillsdale, NJ: Lawrence Erlbaum Associates, 1987, 19–35.

Oldfather, W.A., "Increasing importance of a knowledge of Greek and Latin for the understanding of English," *Kentucky School Journal* (1940, December), 37–41.

Orleans, J.S., "Possible transfer value of the study of Latin to English vocabulary," *School and Society* **16**(411), (1922), 559–560.

Schmitt, N., "Vocabulary learning strategies," in N. Schmitt and M. McCarthy (Eds.), *Description, Acquisition and Pedagogy*, Cambridge: Cambridge University Press 1997, 199–227.

Stahl, S.A., *Differential Word Knowledge and Reading Comprehension*, Unpublished doctoral dissertation, Harvard University, 1982.

_____, *Beyond the Instrumentalist Hypothesis: Some Relationships between Word Meanings and Comprehension* (Tech. Report No. 505). University of Illinois at Urbana Champaign, Center of the Study of Reading, 1990.

Swisher, K.E., *Systematic Vocabulary Instruction through Morphological Analysis with Post-secondary Students*. Unpublished doctoral dissertation, The Ohio State University, 1988.

Thompson, E., "The 'Master Word' approach to vocabulary training," *Journal of Developmental Reading,* **2**(1) (1958), 62–66.

Vacc, N.A., Loesch, L.C., and Lubik, R.E., *Writing Multiple-choice Test Items* (ERIC Document Reproduction Service No. ED457440), 2001.

Venezky, R.L., "English orthography: Its graphical structure and its relation to sound," *Reading Research Quarterly,* **2**(3), (1967, Spring), 75–105.

Webster's Third New International Dictionary of the English Language, Unabridged, Springfield, MA: Merriam-Webster, 1993.

Zimmerman, C.B., "Do reading and interactive vocabulary instruction make a difference? An empirical study," *TESOL Quarterly* **31**(1), (1997), 121–141.

Chapter 23

MASS MEDIA, LANGUAGE ATTITUDES AND LANGUAGE INTERACTION PHENOMENA
A Study in Code Switching, Code Mixing and the Teaching Process

—Aadil Amin Kak and Sajad Hussain Wani

23.1 INTRODUCTION

This chapter discusses the interaction between mass media, linguistic attitudes and language interaction phenomena in the present day Kashmir. The chapter also tries to present the implications of this complex interaction of mass media, language attitudes and language interaction phenomena in the teaching process.

23.2 BACKGROUND

Mass media has broader implications for different socio-cultural phenomena, including patterns of language use in a society. Media has a role in inducing particular language behaviour in a given social set-up. Media is a direct reflection of the existing social set-up and associated cultural and political patterns. Media is also pivotal in terms of inducing particular language behaviour in a society. The media-lects or media induced varieties of language are gaining currency in the present day societies, and this is more true for youngsters who are psychologically more prone to media induction. Media does not only set the language patterns in a society, but the media represents a material and social interface for communication among people, and as a consequence, the same gets reflected in the linguistic preferences of the people. Language patterns are very important in determining the social patterning in a society, and are indicators of many other associated phenomena in a social set-up.

The linguistic effects of the media are not limited to spreading a language, but the media themselves also give rise to new uses of the language.

The media represents a material and social infrastructure for communication among people, and as a consequence, their characteristics quite naturally have an imprint on language. Therefore, that as human communication becomes mediatised (Hjarvard, 2003b), media bound varieties of language will arise. Whereas, linguists have focused on various dialects and socio-lects, the media induced language or what are now called as medialects need to be studied. These media related varieties or medialects are strongly influenced by English language. Language forms a field in which cultural and social conflicts are articulated and switching and mixing between languages serve as an important tool for shaping a particular discourse and serve as primary tools for maintenance of the equations of power and solidarity in a particular speech event. Switching between languages can serve as a marker of one's identity in a particular socio-cultural context. Thus, a particular linguistic choice or a particular pattern of switching and mixing can reveal a lot of information pertaining to a particular socio-cultural, economic, ethnic and psychological context. Thus, greater use of a language in the media not only represents the linguistic dominance, but acts to reinforce or strengthen a social and cultural hierarchy, which seems very natural with the passage of time.

Many studies (Fowler, 1991; Golding, 1992; Hall, 1982) reveal that language patterns in a society reflect an ideological background, and many social, political, economic and psychological variables in a society are mainly established or mediated by the mass media. These ideologies are expressed through public text and talk, and hence, patterns of language use in media have a direct role in establishing a particular ideological framework governing markets, politics, policies, economy and cultural phenomena in a society. These ideologies, in turn, shape the attitudes and stereotypes in a particular social set-up. In the present day world, media forms one of the most important determinants of setting particular attitudes, including linguistic attitudes in a society. The media plays a key role in setting not only the particular linguistic patterns but also setting linguistic preferences and linguistic attitudes in a society.

It has been found that bilinguals often mix and switch between languages. Code mixing is a process, whereby words of one language are inserted into another language or code mixing involves interaction between two languages below the clausal level. Code switching, on the other hand, is a process whereby full sentences of one language are used in alternation with the other language or code switching involves interaction between two languages above the clausal level. In other words, code mixing is intra-sentential and code switching is inter-sentential. Coming to psycholinguistic aspect of code mixing, it was earlier believed that bilingualism is disadvantageous for a child and language mixing was considered as a state of "semi-lingualism", indicating a lesser proficiency in both the languages. Labov (1971) has described code mixing as an 'irregular mixture', and has expressed his view that no one was ever able to show that such irregular mixture is governed by any systematic rules. Many pejorative names were given to mixing of Spanish and English such as 'Tex-Mex', 'Spanglish'. It was believed that mixing shows incomplete mastery of the two language systems. Bilingual children, who engage themselves in code switching, are questioned about their academic abilities and potentials, and they are more likely to be placed in remedial classes (Lara, 1989). Experts generally agree that teachers should restrict CS to the inter-sentential type. That is, teachers should switch languages only from sentence to sentence and not intra-sententially, or within a sentence (Ovando, 1985).

On the other hand, Gumperz (1982) and other scholars suggest that code switching has important discourse functions for bilinguals. Bilinguals strategically employ their language usage in order to be more appropriate and exact in particular social interactions. Many scholars are of the view that the development of languages is less researched in bilingual children when compared to their monolingual counterparts (Romaine, 1989; Tabors and Snow, 2001). The education community has not paid proper attention to explore the possibilities of bilingualism in children. The bilingual children's mixing of languages in the process of language acquisition has been viewed unfavourably by the mainstream society, and it has been "the least systematically studied" (Romaine, 1989). Code switching studies have "pedagogical implication for bilingual teaching, the development of bilingual instructional materials, and the evaluation of bilinguality" (Soh, 1987).

Looking at the cognitive dimensions of language interaction phenomena, research has shown that a bilingual brain is cognitively more advantaged than a monolingual. Vygotsky (1989) explains that avoidance of interference, differentiation, meta-linguistic awareness are some of the features, which make a bilingual cognitively more advantaged than a monolingual.

This claim of well-regulated nature of language interaction phenomena, and their implications for pedagogical purposes can also be linked to the work of those scholars who regard code switchers as having the same grammatical competence as monolinguals and to many proponents of code mixing grammars. Many proposals of code mixing grammars have been postulated so far, which will further support the use of these language interaction phenomena for the pedagogic purposes.

"The analysis of bilingual behaviour has shown that a group actually has not only two sets of rules from L1 and L2, but three L3.........." (Oksaar, 1972)

"Code mixing involves functioning in a diasystem, and as a consequence developing other linguistic code comprising formal features of two or more codes." (Kachru, 1975)

Poplack (1980) has also raised the possibility of existence of a code mixing grammar as a 'third grammar', which constrains the interaction of the two systems in mixture. Myers-Scotton (1993) concluded that just as other naturally occurring linguistic data, code switching is governed by structural principles of well-formedness, i.e., possible combinations can be predicted.

Code switching and code mixing can be useful for teaching purposes. Code switching has not to be viewed as an example for language interference, but must be regarded as an extension of a bilingual language faculty. Code switching and mixing serve as active cognitive strategies on the part of the bilingual speaker, and are used in a more expressive manner intended to convey meaning in a more unambiguous and effective manner. Different socio-linguistic functions have already been attributed to the phenomena of code switching and mixing and their implication for language teaching and learning has also been hinted at. Cook (1989, 1991) tries to assert the ways in which code switching can be integrated in second language teaching activities, and describes the Institute of Linguistics examinations in Languages for International Communication test as one which utilizes code switching. He also advocates using code switching as a second language teaching tool through reciprocal language teaching. Code switching can be used in a stage-wise manner for language teaching purposes, and can serve as a foundation for second language learning and teaching in an active strategic manner. (Cook, 1991). The use of Code switching as an active tool for language teaching has received support in many such studies, which explain the diverse and creative ways in which code switching is used to perform various communicative functions by bilinguals.

23.3 METHODOLOGY

There is an interrelation between Mass media, Language attitudes, Language interaction phenomena and Language teaching process. The relation is illustrated via language usage as observed in the present day Kashmiri speech community. It is through years of personal observation and research findings as the primary source of the data, and participant observations, and interviews conducted at university of Kashmir during the last decade the methodology has been developed. The database used in this study has been previously employed in a number of related studies on different aspects of language interaction phenomena. However, the central claim in this chapter is made upon the interviews which were carried at the University of Kashmir, in 2009 and 2013. Twenty departments of university were selected and interviews were conducted from both teachers and students. The twenty departments were selected from all the faculties, like Faculty of Arts, Faculty of Science, Faculty of Law and Faculty of Social Science. Two teachers and two students from each department were interviewed and about 48% of the interviewees were females. Further investigation in this regard has been performed by interviewing about 90 informants residing in Srinagar, Baramulla and Anantnag districts of the Kashmir province. The data pertaining to mass media was obtained from Srinagar Printing Press and Radio Kashmir Srinagar. The data from some previous studies has also been used in this study.

23.3.1 Language Patterns in the Present Day Kashmir

Kashmiri language forms the mother tongue of most of the population in Kashmir, whereas Urdu and English form the second languages of the Kashmiri speakers which have been introduced in Kashmir through the institutional intervention. Both Urdu and English have survived in Kashmir for more than a century, and have their due importance in the day-to-day lives of an average Kashmiri speaker. The nature of contact between Kashmiri, English and Urdu languages has been studied from many dimensions, and has resulted in many interesting studies on language contact and cultural contact phenomena. The said trio of languages in the present day Kashmir, presents a rich field for the studies of language contact. Kashmiri language nowadays is regularly used with English and Urdu in the speech of educated Kashmiries with Urdu forming the primary choice for code switching, and English forming the primary choice for code mixing for the majority of educated Kashmiri population (Kak and Wani, 2005). This can be understood by taking into consideration the higher number of Urdu proficient Kashmiri native speakers as compared with the English proficient ones. Thus code switching and code mixing are commonly observed phenomena in educated youngsters of Kashmir, and are somehow unmarked mode of speech.

23.3.2 Analysis

The following examples represent different language interaction phenomena which characterize the speech of Kashmiri educated multilingual speakers with Kashmiri, English and Urdu languages interacting with each other in the form of code switching and code mixing. The following examples show the language interaction phenomena operating in the present day Kashmiri speech community.

1.	ha:l-	as	gAy	*curtain*	**fit**	K-E CM
	Hall	dat	happened	curtain	fit	
The curtains were appropriate for the hall.							

2.	application	kar	**websayt-**	I	peThI	*download*	K-E CM
	application	do	website	abl	on	download	
Download the application from the website.								

3.	*comma*	kar	*enter.*	K-E CM
	comma	do	enter	
Enter the comma.				

4.	***exam***	chi	***tension***	tula:n	*K-E CM*
	exam	are	tension	Raise	
	Exams cause frustration.				

5.	Yi	***serial***	chu	***flop***	*K-E CM*
	This	serial	Is	flop	
	This serial is a flop one.				

6.	ath	***serial-***	as	che	sonam	***director***	*K-E CM*
	This	serial	dat	is	sonam	director	
	This serial is directed by sonam.						

7.	tAm-	is	korukh	***ultrasound.***	*K-E CM*
	He	dat	Did	ultrasound	
	He has undergone ultrasound.				

8.	m'An	***application***	tra:v	*K-E CM*
	my	application	drop	
	Submit my application.			

9.	kar	gatsch-	av	market	……….	***just***	***now.***	*K-E CS*
	when	go	fut-pl	market	……….	just	Now	
	When shall we go to the market?…………………. Just now.								

10.	yi	kus	aav	…….	***I***	***don't***	***know***	*K-E CS*
	this	Who	came	…….	I	dont	Know	
	Who has come …… …… ……………… I don't know.								

11.	tse	par	book	…….	***nahin***	***abi***	***nahin***	*K-U CS*
	you	read	book	…….	no	now	No	
	You read the book! …… …… ……………… No, not now.								

12.	zi	kariv	tschopI	…….	***Aur***	***Dou***	***ga:vou***	*K-U CS*
	two	do	silence	…….	And	Two	sing	
	Two of you remain silent and the other two will sing.								

Examples (1–12) clearly represent the ease with which elements of Urdu and English languages have incorporated in the day-to-day speech of Kashmiri speech community, in both informal and formal domains. Both students and teachers regarded code switching and code mixing as the facilitator in the classroom environment, and considered these phenomena as the norm rather than exception not only in classrooms but also in their day-to-day lives. The same response was collected from the informal settings outside the university departments. People from all the three selected districts in Kashmir regarded code switching and code mixing as inevitable, and were found to have positive attitudes towards the Urdu and English languages.

Sanskrit and Persian had been the languages of prestige in the ancient and the medieval times, and at present, Urdu and English enjoy the same position. On the one hand, Urdu is the official language of the state of Jammu and Kashmir with a receptive populace, an essential language up to 10th class, medium of instruction in Government schools till 2003, a court language in lower courts, for writing revenue records, avenues for exposure as in print media, books, etc. and other similar functions. On the other hand, the envisaged potential of English on its part appear to have influenced the socio-psychological attitudes of Kashmiries in a more effective manner. The higher prestige assigned to English language in Kashmir is manifested in a number of ways. Domains from where English and Urdu had been acquired in the past have mainly been educational institutions, but from last two decades, it is observed that English and Urdu have greatly infiltrated Kashmiri society, and their use in different domains has increased considerably.

Media is one of the most powerful sources of the present linguistic situation in Kashmir, and has largely determined the prevailing linguistic norms as well as linguistic attitudes of Kashmiri population, particularly in the youth. In case of electronic media, the introduction of cable network, DTH and other modern networks; people have more access to English and Urdu (Hindi) channels and local media has been relegated to the background. The youngsters and even elder generation is more acquainted with bollywood and Hollywood than the regional actors and singers. Moreover, regional channels broadcast more programmes in Urdu language than Kashmiri. Radio Kashmir Srinagar is designated as an Urdu station, and not as a Kashmiri station. The regional media is relegated to the background, with youth favouring more and more new national and international channels. BBC, CNN, Star Plus, Star Movies, HBO are household names in Kashmir and Times and Newsweek mean authenticity and status. The introduction of laptops, mobile phones, electronic gadgets, computer games, social networking sites has contributed immensely to the increasing amounts of switched and mixed speech. The influence of English has also caused a shift in the patterns of language use. For counting, naming colours, days of the week, etc. English is predominantly used and the youth is finding it difficult to use Kashmiri for these functions (Kak, 2002). In the office/administrative domain, Urdu though the official language, is rapidly being replaced by English. Urdu is used for court and revenue records, but this is changing with the advent of the younger generation who find themselves more comfortable in English than in Urdu. The dexterity with which youngsters switch and mix between Kashmiri, English and Urdu languages has become the normal mode of speech in accordance with the prevailing patterns in the Electronic media.

Print media presents an equally interesting picture of this increasing influence of English language in Kashmir with more and more youngsters preferring English newspapers, followed by Urdu. The print media in Kashmir operates mainly in the form of Urdu and English dailies and weeklies. A constant increase in the number of English newspapers certainly points to a particular linguistic set-up where a prestige language is increasing its impact at a steady speed. In 1994 only 1 English paper was published from Kashmir, but from 1995 onwards, a steady increase in the number of English newspapers was observed. At present, about 15 English dailies are published from Kashmir indicating a 15-fold increase in the recent years. Looking at the number of English weeklies during the same time, it is observed that the number of English weeklies was just 1 (as in the case of English dailies) in 1994. Presently, the number of English weeklies is 12. Urdu dailies and weeklies appear to have had a strong footing in 1994. The number of Urdu dailies in 1994 was 36 and the number of Urdu weeklies was 37. In 2005, the number was 48 Urdu dailies and 38 Urdu weeklies. Surprisingly, the increase in the number of Urdu dailies is 25% (as compared 1300% in the case of English dailies) and there is hardly any increase in the number of Urdu weeklies. Urdu dailies also lack a consistent increasing order with decrease in numbers as well (44 in 2001, 48 in 2003, 46 in 2004 and 48 in 2005) as compared to the English dailies, which show a consistent increase from 4 in 2001 to 8 in 2005 and 11 in 2008. Urdu weeklies, interestingly, show a somewhat constant number in the last decade.

A study (Dhar and Hassan, 2008) has shown that in case of Print media, the language preference of people in Srinagar city is shifting from Urdu to English. About 95% of the younger generation in the age group of 15–25 years read newspapers in English language, whereas for people in the age group of 30–55, only 40% read English dailies, whereas 60% read Urdu dailies. This change in the language preference to English from Urdu directly reflects the impact which new international media has on the younger generation of Kashmir. This is due to increased exposure available today in the form of national and international media and a trend observed in people where people prefer a global point of view rather than a local point of view.

Attitudes and views of Kashmiries have also been observed to show a change, with English speakers been stereotyped highest in the attributes 'intelligent, ambitious, practical and modern' (Kak, 2002), indicating what English, and its speakers symbolize for the Kashmiri native speaker. All the age and gender groups strongly feel that English should be the medium of instruction (Kak, 2002) and this is observed even more strongly in the case of the youth. Media has contributed immensely in giving this status to English language in valley. The prestige associated with Urdu is localized, which is fading nowadays due to accelerated impact of English speaking community in the form of British, American and other English television series, which have become the first choice of highly educated speakers in Kashmir valley. An easy access to English serials and movies via laptops and internet is contributing immensely to the increasing impact of English language in the valley. Kashmiri speakers consider English better in terms of its communicative potential and in terms of being modern, scientific and logical.

The above discussion about Media, language attitudes and language interaction phenomena illustrates how Kashmiri, Urdu and English languages are interacting in a complex manner resulting in an interesting picture of language contact phenomena. All the three languages, that is, Kashmiri, Urdu and English have their role and importance and switching and mixing among them serves the same. The interviewees attributed different functions to both code mixing as well as to the code switching. These functions range from linguistic to stylistic and from social to psychological. Many respondents, including teachers and students argue that comprehension becomes much easier when they switch and mix languages, e.g., a teacher explained while explaining the lecture on translation, he has to translate a sentence, like "Take my breath away", he has to shift from Kashmiri to English as he cannot explain the same in the Kashmiri language, and thus, it becomes a social necessity. Another reason which many teachers used for code mixing was that English was euphemistically milder, and less degrading than equivalent Kashmir vocabulary item or Kashmiri sentences.

13.	ye	chi	chyen	badi	*bari*	**blunder**	K-E CM
	it	Is	your	big	heavy	blunder	
	You committed a big blunder.							

Similarly, a mechanism which a teacher finds euphemistically milder and appropriate was to control the students by a switch to a prestige language. Consider the switch from Kasmiri to English or even from Urdu to English:

14.	ya	kariv	decide	......	*Or*	*bear*	*consequences*	K-E CS
	either	do	decide		Or	bear	Consequences	
	Either decide or bear the consequences.								

15.	ma	kariv	shour	....	*behave*	*like*	*students*	K-E CS
	dont	do	noise		behave	like	Students	
	Stop making noises! Behave like students.								

16.	meri	baat	Sunoo	………	*you*	*must*	*obey*	*U-E CS*
	my	talk	listen		you	must	obey	
	Listen to me….. you must obey!							

Thus, by switching to a prestigious language, teachers and even some parents think that they can control the students in a better way, and can ensure their more involvement and participation in the classroom discourse and other important tasks.

By switching frequently to English or a complete switch to English shows a change in relationship, i.e., from informal to formal or from solidarity to the power. Many teachers and students commented that switching to the prestigious language serves both the function of domain change as well as attitude change. Similarly, a heavy mixing from English language can indicate the change in attitude and switch from informal to formal, but in many cases the switch to prestigious language or mixing heavily can serve the opposite function, i.e., it can be a signal of solidarity between two persons belonging to same social and professional class. Thus, the switches and mixes between Kashmiri, English and Urdu language were found to be very useful in terms of linguistic, stylistic, social, psychological and other such contextual parameters. The following functions were attributed to the code switching and code mixing in terms of Kashmiri speech community:

1. It accounts for many linguistic deficits, i.e., objects or concepts for which there is no exact equivalent word in Kashmiri language. Common examples include vocabulary pertaining to academic, technical and scientific matters.
2. Switching and mixing accounts for the social appropriateness as certain concepts, which cannot be rendered in Kashmiri, definitely trigger switching to English language. English literature teachers explained that they cannot explain certain concepts in Kashmiri language, which are socially inappropriate in Kashmiri language, but quite normal when discussed in English. Common examples include certain Greek Myths, poetry of metaphysicals, pre-raphaelite poetry and many other themes, where a teacher needs a recourse to English language due to a certain socio-cultural code.
3. Switching and mixing accounts for certain psychological connotations in the classroom as switching to a prestige language or to a less prestige language can show a change in the relationship or a change in the context.
4. It sometimes act as an euphemistic device in classroom where a teacher switches to a prestigious language for linguistic euphemism.
5. Switching and mixing serve better comprehension. Switching and mixing between languages help in understanding a concept in a more detailed way than doing the same in one language.

6. A language switch is like opening a window to a new world. When a teacher makes a switch to other language, it is like opening a different perspective on the same problem.
7. Several teachers stated that code switching and mixing facilitates teaching-learning process by adding a certain degree of flexibility, creativity and dynamicity to the teaching process.
8. Code switching can sometimes serve as a stylistic device to exhibit linguistic skills in different languages and hence can act as a controlling tool over the diverse student population.
9. A switched and mixed language is the only language that we have, and we do not know of any language which claims to be a pure language.

Many more functions of switching and mixing were underlined during this research, and it was concluded that all the Kashmiri speakers are quite aware of the resourcefulness of these language interaction phenomena, and have attributed certain functions to these languages in their verbal repertoire as per the demands of different speech events.

The use of a switched and mixed language was appreciated by all the youngsters in the university campus, and in the main stream society, and the attitudes towards the mixing were very positive. This favourable attitude towards Kashmiri–English code mixing, Kashmiri–English code switching and Kashmiri–Urdu code switching can be accounted in terms of prestige and social usefulness.

Media is playing a very vital role in increasing the social significance of English and Urdu languages in Kashmir. English is creating its space not only in social set of Kashmir but in the psychological self of every Kashmiri speaker. This is encouraged by the parents and accepted eagerly by the children. This is because of the realization among all generations that learning English is a prerequisite to 'the good things in life', and English fluency is prestigious for children within and outside their peer group. Duration of use of English and Urdu has also been observed to be gradually increasing, not only in the formal contexts, but in the informal contexts as well along with claimed proficiency in English (Kak, 2002) which brings with it fruitful gains.

In the present context, code switching and code mixing is being reinforced by the media as a consequence of which it has become the unmarked code in Kashmiri society, where it is used more often by younger generation, and the same trend is followed in classroom where it is considered as the most natural form to be comprehended by the students. The media not only has introduced English and Urdu in Kashmir on a strong footing, but it is one of the main determinants of its usage patterns inside and outside the classroom. Thus, the pattern of language usage in media gets directly reflected in day-to-day life in general, and in classrooms, in particular. It is important to mention that the introduction of cable network and access to national and international media has considerably lead to the increase in speaking fluency. It is generally observed that younger generation is much better in pronunciation of English language because of the exposure of the international media.

Media has sensitized the youth about the right way of speaking, and it is one of the contributions of media that younger generation is quickly picking the pronunciation aspect of English language, which was one of the most difficult areas to be taught by a language teacher. Media has played a pivotal role in not setting only the fashion trends but also in setting certain patterns of language usage. The same pattern needed to be followed in classrooms (language as well as general classrooms) which will lead to better proficiency in speaking skills, and in communicating meaning in a better and more natural way. Today, when the academicians are talking about the Eclectic Approach in Language Teaching; one should not hesitate in taking the initial step where language usage patterns of media are followed in the classroom practices which in turn will lead to linguistic, cognitive and academic excellence.

23.4 CONCLUSION

This study has shown that both code switching and mixing as language interaction phenomena should be considered as highly valued resources in both formal and functional perspectives. This finding is an important finding in terms of its deviation from those studies which encourage code switching but not code mixing in the class room environment. This study has shown that code switching and mixing have same functionality and should not be considered different in their usefulness or functionality. The phenomenon of mixing illustrates the dynamicity of languages and should not be looked as disadvantageous to either a speaker or to the language. The code mixing shows flexibility and expansion potential of a language and also illustrates cognitive flexibility and expressive potential of a bilingual or multilingual speaker. This is in consonance with those studies, which propose the existence of a code mixing grammar and its utilization for pedagogic purposes.

The study revealed that Media has played an important role in determining the patterns of language use inside and outside the classroom. On a socio-psychological level, Media has played a major role in making English language the most valorized language of the educated class in Kashmir valley. The media induced variety of language, and language patterns are considered as the most natural way of speaking. The media has been successful in setting particular linguistic attitudes in Kashmiri society, particularly the young generation who are showing more and more shift towards English language in both spirit and form. Based on the information gathered from the interviewees and from a theoretical point-of-view, it can be easily discerned that language interaction phenomena can be used as a powerful tool for teaching purposes. An approach-based language interaction phenomena cannot help in second language teaching only, but can be utilized for developing a strong attitude towards one's own mother tongue and for meta-linguistic development of language learners. More work needs to be done in this direction and only further research in this area can reveal many other aspects of this complex and variable phenomenon.

Note:

List of Abbreviations:

1. K_E CM = Kashmiri English Code Mixing
2. K_E CS = Kashmiri English Code Switching
3. K_U CS = Kashmiri Urdu Code Switching
4. U_E CS = Urdu English Code Switching

REFERENCES

Bauer, E.B. and K. Montero, "Reading versus Translating: A Preschool Bilingual's Interpretation of Text," J.V. Hoffman, D.L. Schallert, C.M. Fairbanks, J. Worthy and B. Maloch (Eds.), Fiftieth Yearbook of the National Reading Conference, Vol. 50, Chicago: National Reading Conference, 2001.

Baker, Colin, *Foundations of Bilingual Education and Bilingualism*, Clevedon, UK: Multilingual Matters, 2001.

Bhatnagar, S.C., G.T. Mandybur, H.W. Buckingham, and O.J. Andy, "Language Representation in the Human Brain: Evidence from Cortical Mapping," Brain and Language, **74** (2000): 238–259.

Berthold, M., Mangubhai, F. and Batorowicz, K., Bilingualism and Multiculturalism: Study Book. Toowoomba, QLD: Distance Education Centre, University of Southern Queensland, 1997.

Bialystok, E., F.I.M. Craik, R. Klein and M. Viswanathan, "Bilingualism, Aging, and Cognitive Control: Evidence from the Simon Task," Psychology and Aging, **19** (2004): 290–303.

Bloomfield, L., *Language*, New York: Holt, Rinehart and Winston, 1933.

Burgess, C. and Lund, K., "Producing High-Dimensional Semantic Spaces from Lexical Co-Occurrence," *Behavior Research Methods, Instruments, and Computers*, **28** (1996): 203–208.

Cook, V., 'Reciprocal Language Teaching: Another Alternative', *Modern English Teacher*, **16**.3\4 (1989): 48–53.

_____, *Second Language Learning and Language Teaching*, Melbourne: Edward Arnold/Hodder Headline Group, 1991.

Crowl, T. and W. MacGinitie, "The Influence of Students' Speech Characteristics on Teachers' Evaluations of Oral Answers," *Journal of Educational Psychology*, **66**.3 (1974): 304–308.

Crystal, D., *The Cambridge Encyclopedia of Language*, Cambridge: Cambridge University Press, 1987.

Cummins, J., "The Influence of Bilingualism on Cognitive Growth: A Synthesis of Research Findings and Explanatory Hypotheses," *Working Papers on Bilingualism*, **9** (1976): 1–43.

Cummins, J., "Cognitive/Academic Language Proficiency, Linguistic Interdependence, The Optimal Age Question and Some Other Matters," *Working Papers on Bilingualism,* **9** (1979): 197–205.

Deucher, M., "Welsh-English Code Switching and the Matrix Language Frame Model," *Lingua,* 2007.

Fantini, A., *Language Acquisition of a Bilingual Child: A Sociolinguistic Perspective,* San Diego: College Hill Press, 1985.

Fowler, Roger, *Language in the News, Discourse and Ideology in the Press,* London: Routledge, 1991.

Golding, Peter, "Communicating Capitalism: Resisting and Restructuring State Ideology: The Case of Thatcherism Media", *Culture and Society,* **14**.4 (1992): 503–521.

Gumperz, J., *Discourse Strategies,* Cambridge: Cambridge University Press, 1982.

Hjarvard, S., "A Mediated World: The Globalization of Society and the Role of Media," S. Hjarvard (Ed.), *Media in a Globalized Society,* København: Museum Tusculanum Press, 2003a.

_____, *Det Selskabelige Samfund* [*The culture of sociability*], Frederiksberg: Samfundslitteratur, 2003b.

Hall, Stuart, "The Rediscovery of Ideology: Return of the Repressed in Media Studies", in M. Gurevitch, T. Bennett, J. Curran, and J. Woollacott (Eds.), *Culture, Society and the Media,* London: Methuen (1982): 56–90.

IRA and NAEYC, "Learning to Read and Write: Developmentally Appropriate Practices for Young Children," The Reading Teacher, **52**.2 (1998): 193–216.

Kachru, Braj B., "Lexical innovations in south Asian English," *International Journal of the Sociology of Language,* **1975**.4 (1975): 55–74.

Kak, A.A., *Acceptability of Kashmiri–English Mixed Sentences: A Sociolinguistic Study,* Diss. University of Delhi, 1995.

_____, *Language Maintenance and Language Shift in Srinagar,* Diss. University of Delhi, 2002.

Kak, A.A. and S.H. Wani, "Case for Base: A Study of Kashmiri–English Code Mixing," Paper presented at South Asian Linguistic Analysis 25 (SALA 25) at The Deptt. of Linguistics, Urbana-Champagne, USA: The University of Illinois, 2005.

_____, "Strategies of Neutrality and Code Mixing Grammar," K. Rai, et al. (Eds.) "Recent Studies in Nepalese Linguistics." *Proceedings of the 12th Himalyan Languages Symposium and 27th Annual Conference of Linguistic Society of Nepal,* November 26–28, 2006.

Kenner, Charmian, *Becoming Biliterate: Young Children Learning Different Writing Systems,* Sterling: Trentham Books, 2004.

Kishna, S., Lexicale Interferentie in Het Sarnami, MA dissertation, Amsterdam: University of Van Amsterdam, 1979.

Labov, W., "The Notion of 'System' in Creole Languages," in D. Hymes (Ed.), *Pidginization and Creolization of Languages,* Cambridge: Cambridge University Press (1971): 447–472.

Lara, S.G.M., "Reading Placement for Code Switchers," *Reading Teacher*, **42**.4 (1989): 278–282.

Levelt, Willem, J.M., *Speaking: From Intention to Articulation*, Cambridge: MIT Press, 1989.

MacNamara, J., *Bilingualism and Primary Education*, Edinburgh: Edinburgh University Press, 1966.

McClure, E., "Aspects of Code Switching in the Discourse of Bilingual Mexican-American Children," M. Saville-Troike (Ed.), *Linguistics and Anthropology*, Washington, DC: George Town University Press (1977): 93–115.

Mechelli, A., "Structural Plasticity in the Bilingual Brain: Proficiency in a Second Language and Age of Acquisition Affect Grey-Matter Density," *Nature*, **431** (2004): 757.

Milroy, L., *Observing and Analysing Natural Language: A Critical Account of Sociolinguistic Method*, Oxford: Blackwell Publishers, 1987.

Muysken, P., *Bilingual Speech: A Typology of Code Mixing*, Cambridge: Cambridge University Press, 2000.

Myers-Scotton, C., *Social Motivations for Code Switching*, Oxford: Oxford University Press, 1993.

Ojemann, G.A., "Brain Organization for Language from the Perspective of Electrical Stimulaton Mapping," *The Behavioral and Brain Sciences*, **2** (1983): 189–207.

Oksaar, E., "On Code Switching: An Analysis of Bilingual Norms", in Quistgaard, et al. (Eds.), *Proceedings of Association International De Linguistique Apliques Third Congress*, Julius Gross Verlag: Heidelberg, 1972.

Ovando, C.J. and V. Collier, *Bilingual and ESL Classrooms: Teaching in Multicultural Contexts*, New York: McGraw-Hill, 1985.

Poplack, S., "Sometimes I'll start a sentence in Spanish Y Termino Espanol: Towards a Typology of Code-Switching", *Linguistics*, **18** (1980): 581–618.

Ramirez, A.G. and R. Milk, Notions of Grammaticality among Teachers of Bilingual Pupils, *TESOL Quarterly*, **20**.3 (1986): 495–513.

Romaine, S., *Bilingualism*, Oxford: Blackwell, 1989.

_____, *Language in Society*, Oxford: Oxford University Press, 1994.

Seliger, H.W. and R.M. Vago, "The Study of First Language Attrition: An Overview," H.W. Seliger and R.M. Vago (Eds.), *First Language Attrition*, Cambridge: Cambridge University Press (1991): 3–15.

Soh, K.C., Asian Pacific Papers: Regional papers presented at the 8th World Congress of Applied Linguistics, University of Sydney, August (1987): 16–21.

Tabors, P. and C. Snow, 2001, "Young Bilingual Children and Early Literacy Development," S.B. Neuman and D.K. Dickinson (Eds.), *Handbook of Early Literacy Research*, New York: The Guilford Press (2001): 159–178,

Van Dijk, Teun A., "Discourse Semantics and Ideology", *Discourse and Society*, **6**.2 (1995): 243–289.

Wani, S.H., Formal and Functional Aspects of English–Kashmiri Code Mixing, MA, Dissertation, 2004.

_____, "CM Grammar and Relativized Constraints: A Study in Kashmiri–English Mixing," in N.A. Dhar (Ed.), *Interdisciplinary Journal of Linguistics IJL*, Vol. 1, Srinagar, India: University of Kashmir, 2008, 119–132.

_____, 2010. "Divergence in Kashmiri English Machine Translation: A Study in Passivisation Process", in N.A. Dhar (Ed.), *Interdisciplinary Journal of Linguistics IJL*, Vol. 3, Srinagar, India: University of Kashmir, 2010, 235–250.

_____, "Code Mixing Constraints, from Grammatical to the Minimalist Framework: A Study in Kashmiri-English Mixed Code," Diss. University of Kashmir, 2008. Published online in Asian EFL Journal available online at "http://www.asian-efl-journal.com/Thesis/Thesis-Wani.pdf.%20Retrieved%20 on%20 3-03-2012" http://www.asian-efl-journal.com/Thesis/Thesis-Wani.pdf. Retrieved on 3-03-2012.

Part 7
PEDAGOGICAL REORIENTATION IN GRAMMAR

Chapter 24

REVISING OUR PARADIGM
Teaching Grammar as Text Inquiry

— Cornelia Paraskevas

24.1 INTRODUCTION

This study explores the ways of rethinking grammar instruction and establishing a connection between grammars to writing. To accomplish this, we first need to revise the nature and scope of grammar instruction. The analysis includes not only words, phrases, clauses and sentences but also paragraphs, and considers linguistic features in specific text types. Grammar instruction within such a framework occurs in two stages—teacher-led and student-led. Specifically, during the teacher-led stage, teachers make use of close study and inquiry to analyze authentic texts in terms of the syntactic and textual choices writers have made. During the student-led stage, students use guides to analyze their own writing along various features. This model of grammar instruction revises the scope of grammar from that of parsing and error avoidance to one of choice appropriate for genre, audience and purpose.

> It is possible to invite students into the recuperation of grammar. We may invite them by demonstrating how knowledge of grammar grants access to power. We may tempt them by showing how grammar is an art or excite them by demonstrating how, to us, teaching is a love affair with words …. Learning grammar must be linked to the process of discovery, to intellectual thought.
>
> These are our goals for teaching grammar: to teach knowledge of conventional usage in order to increase power, opportunity and voice; to teach habits of fluency, inquiry, and experimentation; and to engage students in such a way that this knowledge and these habits are sustaining and flexible.
>
> —Ehrenworth and Vinton, 2005

Grammar recuperation? Showing students how grammar is art? Linking grammar instruction to intellectual thought and inquiry? To appreciate the power of the statements by Ehrenworth and Vinton, and to understand their call for a paradigm shift, we need to first visit the current state of grammar pedagogy in the United States and then propose a different paradigm, one where grammar is an inseparable part of writing and the other where the focus of instruction moves beyond the sentence level, considering sentences as they exist within paragraphs of a particular genre.

24.2 CURRENT PREDOMINANT PARADIGM

In the early 1960s, a small part of a sentence, taken out of context, changed the way students in the United States are taught about their language: "the teaching of formal grammar has a negligible ... or even harmful effect on the improvement of writing." And so began the 'grammarless period,' characterized by the absence of any large-scale, productive discussion about the role of grammar in writing and the absence of any significant paradigmatic shift in the way we teach grammar. Of course, some students were still taught grammar, in an approach that focuses in three areas:

(i) Structure identification (parts of speech and parsing of isolated sentences);
(ii) Error identification and elimination; and
(iii) "Fluency," which usually means variation in sentence openings and length. The first approach is typically grounded in a traditional, Latin-based paradigm that—in very general terms—recognizes only eight parts of speech (determiners, for example, are never mentioned) and focuses on parsing isolated sentences.

I see problems with such instruction: for example, all native speakers know how to use the various word classes—nouns, verbs, adverbs, determiners, pronouns, etc.—from the time they are 4 years old. They don't need to be reminded to use nouns or verbs for their sentences: after all, as Hudson (1994) has pointed out, 37% of all words in written texts are nouns. But they're not shown how each genre, i.e. each text type, distributes nouns and verbs differently. In addition, the curriculum doesn't spiral but repeats in circles, never moving from sentences to text; instead of developing, for instance, a deeper understanding of language and of the multiple ways grammar knowledge can help them control their choices as writers, instruction continues to focus on isolated sentences and parts of speech instruction year after year and grade after grade.

The second area of focus in current language pedagogy comprises error hunting/error avoidance. Students are shown simple/simplistic sentences with editing errors—always in isolation, always out of context—and are expected to correct them. In a fairly typical routine exemplified in the various state-adopted texts, students are presented with a sentence they're expected to correct—the remedial function of grammar instruction. In fact, I visited a school where the 2nd grade teacher proudly displayed the flipchart where there were sentences with capitalization and comma errors such as the following:

Betty lost her puppy.
They bought apples pears and oranges.

My daughter was asked to identify the problems with each sentence, and she was absolutely confused with the question itself. Her confusion stemmed from her relationship to language: it had never been one of prohibition but of possibility. So she looked at me clueless at what she was expected to see or do with the sentences she was seeing.

Such an error-hunting approach does not acknowledge that some errors are, in fact, myth rules, frequently genre dependent. For example, students are taught not to begin their sentences with a conjunction, yet professional writing often includes such constructions. Similarly, students are taught never to include fragments or comma splices in their texts; yet, narratives frequently include such constructions as a way to control the pacing of a story. In fact, this error-hunting approach establishes a particular attitude towards language: students engage with language analysis as a way to avoid making mistakes (they are error hunters) while teachers engage in language instruction as a way to keep it from changing—they are language keepers (MacDonald 2007). A corollary of that approach is that students whose writing doesn't have errors don't really need to understand anything about language—their writing is error free. But such an attitude strips students of their ability to choose their language, to craft their sentences; control, after all, brings choice.

Two more problems come to mind regarding error hunting and error avoidance: (i) they encourage minimalism, emphasizing teaching of grammar as needed—which does not help writers understand their language craft, but, most importantly, gives students a false understanding of grammar; (ii) instead of seeing grammar as a way to explore their options, they see it as a way of developing good proofreading skills and becoming careful editors (but not exciting language users). It is precisely in this area where writers and teachers of writing believe that understanding about language hampers their creativity—if understanding about language means simply knowing how not to make mistakes or how to correct them, then any concern about language will affect their ideas.

I believe the difficulty with some current grammar pedagogies clearly lies in the predominant understanding of the aim of language instruction as keeper of propriety and tradition. Such an approach has led a generation of students to believe that the purpose of grammar is correctness, propriety, and stability. A number of my students, for instance believe that grammar is

> a set of rules to abide so that our spoken language won't sound nonsense; grammar is a set of ideas and rules for putting sentences together correctly; grammar is the precise use of language; grammar is a way to keep language from changing improperly.

The third focus of grammar instruction, fluency, often defined in state guidelines as 'natural, fluent sound, variation in sentence structure, variation in length'. This focus developed late, usually under pressure from state writing tests where one of the traits scored is fluency. Unfortunately, the vague definition of the term renders it similar to tinsel on a Christmas tree (Corbett 1986)—variation in length and structure regardless of genre, audience and purpose considerations. For example, student writers are encouraged to vary their sentence openers to avoid repetition, without being taught that such variations have important effects on the cohesion between sentences or that repetition can be an effective rhetorical and stylistic tool used by a number of professional writers.

24.3 PARADIGM SHIFT—GRAMMAR AS CHOICE

If grammar is not error hunting and avoidance, what is it? And how can we connect it to writing? Echoing Ehrenworth and Vinton (2005), I claim that grammar is choice—syntactic and textual choice appropriate to genre, purpose and audience in writing.

It is important to remember that speech and writing are syntactically and textually different. In fact, Kress (1994) claims, "One feature of writing in its fully developed form is its unspeakableness" (p. 80). Writers who have full control of the written language, as they can "make appropriate linguistic choices in any circumstance and have the confidence to allow their own personal voice to influence their writing style" (Perera, 2008). Viewed from that angle, then, grammar and writing are "symbiotic" and inseparable, existing at two levels: (i) below the paragraph and (ii) above the paragraph. The general framework for this approach to grammar pedagogy aims at showing students the syntactic and stylistic choices they have at both the sentence level and the text level, always considering the constraints established by a particular genre. (For example, academic writing requires a greater number of nominalized constructions while narrative writing requires a greater number of verbs to move the action forward.)

The proposed model for grammar instruction at the first level—word level, clause level, and sentence level—does not require a radical shift from the current model. Students are taught about the syntactic 'inventory' of language using a linguistically accurate pedagogical grammar: word classes, syntactic structure of clauses, and clause combinations. The truly fundamental change involves the aims of grammar instruction: instead of focusing on parsing or error hunting, grammar instruction aims at demonstrating how the syntactic choices writers make are conditioned by the particular genre conventions/traditions. The general framework within which grammar instruction will operate involves inquiry and apprenticeship (Ray 1999, 2006).

What does that inquiry consist of? It consists of:

- Gathering texts that we believe have interesting use of language (mentor texts).

- Immersing students in studying the texts and engaging in close study—noticing interesting out-of-the-ordinary structures (and here's where we need to know what is ordinary) and explaining their effects.

Since each writer makes specific, context-dependent and text-dependent choices, mini-lessons and isolated sentences, out of context, do not work well in grammar instruction.

24.4 TEACHING GRAMMAR-FOR-WRITING

Let us now examine, in specific ways, how the above framework translates into pedagogical application. The first step is to gather various texts and model, for students, how to explore and understand the language choices a writer has made, and how to engage in close study of a text in order to uncover some syntactic and textual features.

As a starting point for the inquiry, I have chosen two types of texts—a nonfiction and a narrative, respectively, in order to examine the distribution of two important parts of speech—nouns (underlined) and verbs (highlighted):

Wildlife photography **represents** the nonconsumptive use of wildlife, which **is** the use, without removal or alteration, of natural resources. For much of this century, the management of wildlife for the hunter **has been emphasized** by wildlife managers. In recent years, however, management for nonconsumptive uses such as wildlife photography and bird-watching **has received** more attention. (Biber 2007: 48)

He **looked** out the window, down past the float on the right. They **had been flying** half an hour and they **were** already **getting** over forest. There **were** still some farms here and there, but less and less of them, even as he **watched**. When he **looked** ahead of the plane, through the whirling propeller, he **saw** the endless trees **stretching** away to the horizon. With the fear **gone**, or **controlled**, something about the forest **drew** him and that **was** a surprise as well (Paulsen 1991: 19).

Why does the first text have more nouns than the second one? Alternatively, why does Gary Paulsen include so many verbs in the story? The answer lies in the different nature of the texts: in story-telling, we need a lot of verbs since the action is moving forward and verbs are the ones to carry the energy. So here's the first important 'lesson' for writers: we need to apprentice under different texts, and pay attention to the kinds of word classes different texts demand. If we want to write an expository piece, for example, we need to let the nouns do more of the work; for a story, on the other hand, we need the verbs to do the work, to move the story forward.

The grammar-for-writing instruction, however, needs to move beyond the parts-of-speech analysis and towards longer structures. One of the difficulties the novice writers face is in the area of elaboration, where they display 'minimalism,' leaving the reader to supply all the missing information. To remedy this problem, we urge them to include more detail in their writing, but we don't always show them their options. In the following two passages repeated from above, we can do a close study of the different modifiers chosen that add detail to the piece.

> *Wildlife* photography represents the nonconsumptive use *of wildlife, which is the use, without removal or alteration, of natural resources.* For much of this century, the management of wildlife for the hunter has been emphasized by wildlife managers. In recent years, however, management for nonconsumptive uses such as wildlife photography and bird-watching has received more attention. (Biber, *op. cit.*)

We notice in the above text that modification of nouns is achieved through different constructions: a noun ('wildlife') to modify the noun 'photography'; a prepositional phrase 'of wildlife' to modify the noun 'use'; a relative clause 'which is the use, without removal or alteration, of natural resources,' to modify the noun phrase 'the nonconsumptive use of wildlife'. Noun modification, and the resulting noun phrase length, is an important measure of change in writing: as novice writers become more comfortable with the conventions of written texts—their noun phrases become longer because of increased use of modifiers.

In the following text, on the other hand, we will focus on modifiers that add adverbial information—where, when, why, how of an event—since the narrative text, as all texts of that genre, is characterized by increased use of verbs.

> He looked out the window, down past the float on the right. They had been flying half an hour and they were already getting over forest. There were still some farms *here and there*, but less and less of them, *even as he watched*. When he looked ahead of the plane, *through the whirling propeller*, he saw the endless trees stretching away to the horizon. With the fear gone, or controlled, something about the forest drew him and that was a surprise as well (Paulsen, *op. cit.*).

In this text, we notice that the writer has chosen different types of modifiers to add details to the events described through the verb: adverbs ('here and there'), a subordinate clause ('even as he watched'), or a prepositional phrase ('through the whirling propeller').

At this point, we have completed the first close study of our text, having gathered mentor texts, examined them closely, and analyzed them for a particular feature. So far, the paradigm does not differ drastically from the current one—after all, the focus is on the word, clause and sentence levels. However, if grammar study is to help students expand both their syntactic repertoire (in addition to avoiding errors) and their 'textual' repertoire—construct texts that reveal control of language—we need to move beyond the sentence level. It is here where the grammar/writing connection becomes clear because we can help writers see what language strategies they can use to create a well-crafted text.

Chapter 24 Revising Our Paradigm: Teaching Grammar as Text Inquiry 333

At this level of grammar analysis, we will use the paragraph as a unit and focus on two elements which appear to have the most significant impact on fluency and readability, namely, sentence openers and cohesive ties. Let us look at a short paragraph to identify the openers used (Markham 2006):

> Pig Latin is one of many secret languages used for fun among young people. In Pig Latin, the fist consonant of blend in a word is put at the end, and the sound 'ay' is added after that. Ancay ouyay eakspay igpay Atinlay? (p. 17).

The first sentence in the above paragraph begins with the subject—an expected choice. The second sentence, on the other hand, begins with a prepositional phrase which, in this case, serves as the background for the remaining of the sentence, explaining how Pig Latin works. By choosing a prepositional phrase that refers to 'Pig Latin,' the author maintains topic connectedness while, at the same time, providing variation in the structure of the sentence so that it doesn't begin in the same way as its preceding sentence.

We have seen in the paragraph above the two general options for opening a sentence: expected and unexpected; subjects are the expected choice (which is also typical of speech). Unexpected choices include an adverbial phrase, a dependent clause, a participle phrase, an infinitive phrase or even a conjunction. The choice of opener affects the way the paragraph develops since each opener sets the stage for what will unfold in the sentence. Even though 50% of all English sentences open with the subject, accomplished writers negotiate different openers to help sentences in a paragraph connect to each other.

The next element we want to consider is cohesive ties—the connections between sentences in a paragraph that effectively help hold the paragraph together. Experienced writers provide clear ties across sentences, anticipating where readers need explicit connections and where they don't. Inexperienced writers, on the other hand, often cannot put themselves in the reader's position and, as a result, they do not provide clear ties between sentences.

As a starting point for our inquiry into cohesive ties, we can look at the following example:

> Evan's climbing into Mommy's lap, looking for a hug. And how about a kiss?
>
> A SPIDER kiss! Tiptoe, tiptoe.
> A CROCODILE kiss! Nibble, nibble.
> A BUTTERFLY kiss. Flick flick.
> A LION kiss! Shake, shake.
> And a Mommy kiss.
> Evan's climbing down to the floor, ready to play!
>
> (Kolln and Hancock, p. 14–15)

What holds this text together? How can we conclude that it is a unified whole? Through the cohesive ties, in part, which include the repetition of the word 'kiss' on each line, and also through the structural repetition that includes a noun modifier to the word 'kiss'. Repetition between the first and the last sentences serves as an important signal for the beginning and end of the piece—and the story itself. The writer, then, has carefully chosen grammatical features to enhance the meaning of the text. Appreciating the effect of that choice critically depends on our understanding of grammar.

In general, cohesion—the connection between sentences—is critical for the organization of paragraphs. It can be lexical, established through repetition, synonymy, and close meaning connection between words; and grammatical, established through structural repetition and pronouns.

If the openers aren't carefully chosen and the cohesive ties between sentences not established, the resulting text will not hold together. In the text below, each sentence opens with the subject, an expected choice, typical of speech. This choice, however, doesn't allow the young writer to establish connections between sentences—a logical sequence of development. In fact, the paragraph reads like a list of items and, as a result, the sentences can be rearranged in any order—a mark of lack of development 'by design'.

> The word 'elephant' comes from the Middle East. African elephants have large ears and a low forehead that's sort of flat. The back arches down in the middle. Each ear may weigh up to 110 pounds. The average male is 10 feet tall at the shoulder and weighs 12,000 pounds. Elephants may live 50–60 years. Indian elephants have small ears, a high forehead with 2 bumps, weigh 10,000 pounds and may live 70–80 years. Elephants eat 330 lbs. of grass, fruit, bark, roots and flowers a day. They drink 25 gallons of water a day. Herds may have 5–15 elephants in them.
>
> Athena, Paraskevas-Nevins, "Elephants"

What kind of advice can we give this writer? How can we help her improve the cohesion of the paragraph without rewriting it for her? As a starting point, we need to remember that for young writers, a sentence is equivalent to a paragraph—hence the 'listy' feeling of the paragraph. With that in mind, there are two possible approaches we can take. First, ask her to look at the sentence openers chosen and see whether they refer to something in the preceding sentence. We are asking her, in effect, to treat each sentence as a link in a chain—and to make sure that the links are clearly connected. Additionally, we can point to the lack of pronouns, a definite 'clue' of lack of cohesion. After she has worked, with our guidance, on paragraph development through carefully choosing openers, we can ask her to rewrite sentences, using pronouns—she can replace the repetition of 'elephants' with the pronoun 'they,' something which will establish the clear connection between sentences.

24.5 TEXT GUIDES—A PEDAGOGICAL TOOL

We have so far modeled the ways grammar can connect to reading and understanding choices professional authors have made in their texts. Now, it is time to guide students towards their own inquiry, one that will undoubtedly help them become aware of the various choices they have in terms of sentence and paragraph organization. Such awareness can lead to improved writing since the students will be making conscious choices about their own texts. To develop student awareness and guide their inquiry, teachers can use the following guide as a pedagogical tool. The guide can also be used to conduct comparative studies between students' own writing and mentor texts or between different types of texts. Ideally, the text to be analyzed should be approximately at minimum 200 words, taken after the introductory paragraph of the piece. (For a similar exercise, Corbett (1988) asked his students to analyze a 1000-word piece of their own.) To demonstrate how the guide can be used, we will compare two different expository texts (one for children, and the other for the professionals in the field) along the various features listed in the guide and notice the specific ways in which they differ from each other. Obviously, teachers can choose which features of the guide they want to use in order to show students the particular properties of each text-type:

Text 1

> To produce sounds, there must be a source of energy. In speech, this energy comes from air in the lungs. Air from the lungs goes through the trachea into the larynx. There, two flaps of tissue (the vocal folds) make the air vibrate (a condition necessary for speech.) The vibrating air moves through the throat (pharynx), into the mouth region, and then through the opening between the lips. What happens in each of these chambers produces a different kind of sound. The soft palate can be raised (producing most of the sounds of English), lowered (producing nasal sounds as in the French *bon*), or lowered with the mouth closed (producing *m* and *n* sounds). The lips can be closed or held apart in various degrees to produce different kinds of rounding or spreading. The jaw controls the size of the space between the teeth and the position of the lips. The tongue can take more shapes and positions than any other speech organ. It affects all vowels and consonants.
>
> Some languages contain sounds that are not made by an air stream from the lungs. Various "click" languages of southern Africa use sounds produced only in the mouth. !Xu has as many as 48 click sounds. Singer Miriam Makeba, whose native language is Xhosa, recorded many click songs in the 1960s (Markham 2006: 17).

Text 2

> So what can instructors and writing program administrators do? Four things. First, we need to acknowledge the materiality of reading in college courses and in arenas beyond college. If one of the goals of

college composition is to teach students how to read constructively and actively in all corners of their lives, then a model for reading instruction in college writing courses needs to accommodate the fact that college students read lots of textbooks, and productive, working adults read lots of reports, manuals, memoranda and so on. Second, we need to develop a model of what reading ideally is and does in our programs and classrooms. We need to start with our outcomes and teach backward from them. Assuming we have a sequential curriculum that culminates with the most difficult and challenging piece of work students do in the course, we should take a close look at the final assignment and ask ourselves, "What exactly is the ideal relationship between reading and writing in this assignment?"

(Joliffe, 2007)

Study I—Sentence analysis (Items in parentheses indicate options)

(a) Sentence structure	Text 1	Text 2
Total number of sentences	14	8
Total number of simple sentences	12	3
(Percentage of simple sentences)		
Total number of compound sentences	0	0
List of coordinators used		
(Percentage of compound sentences (CD))		
Total number of complex sentences (CX)	2	4
(Percentage of complex sentences)		
Total number of mixed sentences (CDXC)	0	0
Longest sentence	33	59
Shortest sentence	6	2
Average length		
Number of passive sentences	1	0

Here, we see the syntactic complexity of the second text because of the range in sentence length that it exhibits—from 2 to 59 words—as well as the number of complex sentences that characterize it. We can help students develop such complexity by teaching them to deliberately vary the sentence length—short sentences call attention to themselves while variation in length helps with the rhythm of a piece.

(b) Clause structure	Text 1	Text 2
Number of finite verbs	20	16
Number of nonfinite phrases/clauses		
Infinitive	1	2
Participle	4	0
Number of subordinate clauses	0	1
Subordinators used	N/A	if-then
Number of relative clauses	2	1
Number of nominal clauses	0	2

Here, we see the effects of consolidation and combination; for example, the sentences in the second text average 2 tensed verbs each, while in the first text there is approximately one tensed verb per sentence. We can teach students to create texts that approximate those created by professional writers through sentence combining—taking two sentences and making one of them dependent (subordinate, relative or nominal).

(c) **Phrase structure**

Complex NP's (pre-noun and post-noun modifiers)

	Text 1	Text 2
Types of premodifiers used	adj, -ing form	noun, adj.
Post-modifiers		
Relative clauses	x	x
Participle clauses	x	no
Prepositional phrases	x	x
Appositives	0	0

Here the teachers are allowed to discuss the concept of elaboration, of detail added to nouns. The length of the noun phrase is a mark of syntactic development and, typically, students use adjectives to lengthen the noun phrase. As the Texts 1 and 2 show, however, English has multiple ways of elaborating nouns—both preceding and following the noun.

Study II—Textual structure

(a) **Paragraph length**

	Text 1	Text 2
Longest paragraph (in no. of sentences)	10	N/A
Shortest paragraph (in no. of sentences)	4	N/A
Average paragraph (in no. of sentences	N/A	N/A

(b) **Paragraph Development/Opener**

	Text 1	Text 2
Unmarked		
Subject (full NP or pronoun)	11	1
Marked		
Coordinating conjunction		
Dependent clause	nominal	subordinate
Conjunctive adverb (moreover, however)		2
Verbal group	infinitive	participle
Proposing/fronting (object, adjective, verb)		
Adverb	1	1
Prepositional phrase	1	
It/What Cleft		
Existential 'there'		

Here, teachers can focus on the choices students can make regarding the openers to their sentences. Openers, as mentioned earlier, are important for the textual organization of a piece since they contribute to the cohesion of paragraphs. In fact, carefully selected openers provide a method of development for the whole paragraph.

(c) **Cohesive devices**

Lexical	Text 1	Text 2
Repetition	x (i.e. energy/this energy)	
Synonym		instructors and program administrators/we
Meaning relation	chambers/throat, mouth, lips	outcomes/curriculum

Syntactic
  Structural repetition
  Pronominalization

Here, teachers ask students to figure out the ties that help connect sentences to each other; by doing this, students make sure that their connections are clear and will be evident to their readers. (Downing and Locke 2002 offer a model for this type of grammatical analysis)

24.6 CONCLUSION

The proposed paradigm for teaching grammar closely aligns with Ehrenworth and Vinton's (2005) plan for "grammar recuperation". Such recuperation requires a change in the core principles that govern grammar instruction:

- It uses examples from authentic texts, establishing a close connection with reading.
- It acknowledges that different genres require different linguistic structures.
- It trains students to read like writers, to engage in language inquiry.
- It shows students why choices are effective and appropriate within a specific genre.
- Examines units larger than a sentence.
- It analyzes the syntactic structure and information packaging (textual organization) of passages.

Looking at the texts at two different levels—sentence and paragraph levels—allows us to analyze not only the syntactic features of a piece but also its textual properties. But the new paradigm moves students beyond simple analysis and into apprenticeship and creation. Using the knowledge gained from such mentor texts in terms of syntactic and textual features, they can construct our own pieces, thus, expanding their syntactic choices and 'textual' repertoire as required for different types of text. A corollary of this approach is that the goal of grammar instruction changes: instead of focusing on parsing and error hunting, the focus now is on choice—a choice appropriate for genre, audience and purpose.

REFERENCES

Biber, Douglas, *University Language—A Corpus-based Study of Spoken and Written Registers,* New York: Oxford University Press, 2007.

Corbett, Edward P.J., "Teaching style," *The Territory of Language: Linguistics, Stylistics and the Teaching of Composition,* Donald A. McQuade (Ed.), Carbondale: Southern Illinois UP, 1986, 23–33.

Corbett, Edward P.J. and Robert Connors, J., *Classical Rhetoric for the Modern Student,* 4th ed., New York: Oxford University Press, 1988.

Downing, Angela and Locke Philip, *A University Course in English Grammar,* London: Routledge, 2002.

Ehrenworth, Mary and Vinton, Vicki, *The Power of Grammar: Unconventional Approaches to the Conventions of Language,* Portsmouth: Heinemann, 2005.

Hudson, Richard, "About 37% of word tokens are nouns," *Language* **70** (1994): 331–339.

Joliffe, *Review Essay,* CCC 58:3 (2007), 479.

Kolln, Martha and Hancock, Craig, "The story of English grammar in United States schools," *English Teaching: Practice and Critique* (2005), *Ladybug Magazine,* Chicago: Carus Publishing (www.education.waikato.ac.nz).

Kress, Guenther, *Learning to Write,* London: Routledge, 1994.

MacDonald, Susan Peck, "The erasure of language," *CCC* **58**.4 (2007): 585–625.

Markham, Lois, "Language," *Kids Discover,* New York, 2006.

Myhill, Debra, "From talking to writing: Linguistic development in writing," Unpublished manuscript, 2008.

Paulsen, Gary, *The River,* New York: Random House, 1991.

Perera, Katharine, *Children's Writing and Reading—Analysing Classroom Language,* Cornwall: Blackwell, 1984.

Ray, Katie Wood, "Study driven," *A Framework for Planning Units of Study in the Writing Workshop,* Portsmouth: Heinemann, 2006.

_____, *Wondrous Words,* Urbana: NCTE, 1999.

Chapter 25

A REFLECTION OF PEDAGOGIC VALUE ON SWAN'S DESIGN CRITERIA AND WESTNEY'S APPROACH TO GRAMMAR TEACHING

— ROBERTO RABBINI

25.1 INTRODUCTION

The question of the role of grammar in language teaching returned to the forefront in the late 1980s and early 1990s, most notably with the case for explicit instruction as presented by Ellis (1990) over implicit learning, inductive approach over deductive. The debate over the usefulness and value of pedagogic grammar is no more apparent than in the positions adopted by Swan (1994) and Westney (1994). Swan presents a traditional yet pragmatic argument, asserting the necessity for pedagogic rules to assist the learner in his or her ultimate goal of acquiring the target language. Conversely, Westney is mistrustful of such pedagogical tenets and generalisations as stipulated by Swan, and would rather avoid the use of such rules in the classroom due to their weak foundation in linguistic terms. This study examines these pedagogical perspectives as postulated by, firstly, Westney and, secondly, Swan highlighting the polarity of their views with specific reference to the teaching of the English modal system, which "remains highly resistant to tidy, systematic treatment" (Westney in Odlin 1994: 79). Evidence, in the form of rules (descriptive, pedagogical, referential and prescriptive) and various exercises specific to modals such as *must* and *have to* will be provided to support the stance of the pragmatist.

25.1.1 The Two Approaches

Swan's design criteria for a pedagogic grammar essentially attempts to find the most suitable way to present formal rules of language. In this sense, his approach is with the learner in mind which echoes the previous seminal work of pedagogic grammar of Corder (1973) and Allen (1974). For Swan (Bygate et al. 1994) then:

> Pedagogic grammar is not just about language; it is about the interaction between language and the language learners. (p. 51)

Westney, in contrast, adopts the perspective from the system's stand-point and is very suspicious of any adjustment made to grammatical formulas in order to accommodate the learner (*ibid.*: 73)

> There are sound reasons, both practical and theoretical, for learners and teachers to assume a cautious, if not skeptical, attitude towards any pedagogical treatment of language regularities.

Westney, in rejecting the criteria put forward by Swan, in one respect, parallels the no-interface position of Krashen (1982) in that grammatical definitions have so far been insufficiently described, suggesting that it would be wrong for the teacher to convey such flawed descriptions to the learner. Are the foundations of the rules of grammar precarious and inadequately related preventing the teacher from using them? Should the teacher dispose with providing rules in the classroom? Or do learners gain from the provision of such rules, even if they be generalized or oversimplified? These questions will be addressed in the following sections.

25.2 WESTNEY: PROBLEMS WITH PEDAGOGICAL GRAMMAR

Initially, Westney concentrates on the problems with rules of pedagogic grammar, which, he believes, instill the learner with a false sense of security. A prerequisite for his argument, therefore, is "avoiding 'basic' rules that inevitably prove inadequate" (Westney 1994: 77). He highlights three problems in the attempt to set true generalisations. The first obstacle to hurdle is "establishing the nature and extent of a generalisation" (Westney 1994: 77). He contrasts a nonpedagogic formulation from Quirk et al. (1985) with a pedagogically applicable formulation from Lewis (1986) and concludes that it is extremely difficult to find a solution in combining the two. Secondly, the problem of metalanguage is raised in "finding an appropriate formulation for a generalisation" (Westney 1994: 78). Finally, Westney claims that it is almost impossible to find a "safe generalisation" (Westney 1994: 79). He argues that when the evidence is weak (such as the distinction between *must* and *have to)*, the 'clear-cut rules ... are overvalued" (Westney 1994: 80). An example of such a pedagogic rule may help to clarify the issue (Swan 1980):

> I really **must stop** smoking.
>
> You **must be** here by 8 o'clock at the latest.
>
> Generally when **must** is used, the obligation comes from the speaker (as in the two examples above). If we talk about or report an obligation that comes from the 'outside' (a regulation, or an order from somebody else, for example) **must** is possible, but **have to** is more common (p. 394).

At first glance, this rule may appear to be well formed with a distinct lack of metalanguage, but Westney cites evidence from Palmer (1990) and Celce-Murcia (1990) that other factors such as variety and mode are influential here, suggesting that it is not a safe generalisation. Although this seems to be a genuine point, it is not clear what we are to replace these "ad hoc entities for which no strong claims can be made" (Westney 1994: 85) with.

Westney continues by rejecting the argument for equivalence, i.e. that rules are basically equivalent but formulated differently at each stage of the interaction between theory and application (*ibid.*: 83). He describes one aspect of the problematic relationship between theory and pedagogy as an "inevitable tension between the interests of generalisation and detail, or of simplicity and 'truth'" (*ibid.*: 92). Is there an alternative to this inevitable tension? Perhaps not. The very nature of inevitability implies a sense of preordained imminence, in the face of which the best that can be done should be done. If the rules are too heavy to carry, should we drop them and be done with them? Or should an attempt be made to lighten them in some way that enables the learner to continue his or her journey on the learning path. Swan offers a practical compromise as an option for the optimist, a closer inspection of which will be made next.

25.3 SWAN'S DESIGN CRITERIA FOR PEDAGOGIC LANGUAGE RULES

As mentioned earlier, the perspective here is very much with the learner taking a central role as "effective grammar teaching, then, focuses on the specific problems (real and potential) of specific learners" (Swan 1994: 53). Swan identifies six design criteria for pedagogic language rules which consists of (i) truth, (ii) demarcation, (iii) clarity, (iv) simplicity, (v) conceptual parsimony and (vi) relevance.

1. **Truth:** It is hoped that rules will always be as close to the truth as possible. This is not always the case, however, and the truth criterion is susceptible to distortion.

    Modal auxiliary verbs have several characteristics in common.

    - There is no *–s* in the third person.
    - There is no **do/does** in the question.
    - There is no **don't/doesn't** in the negative (Soars and Soars 1998: 155)

    Here, however, the truth appears to remain in tact, *ergo*, it is a truthful rule.

2. **Demarcation:** It is important to define the boundary within which a given form is acceptable. According to Swan, this feature is "particularly important, and notoriously difficult to satisfy, in pedagogic lexical definition" (Westney 1994: 47).

Modal verbs express five broad areas of meaning: probability, obligation, ability, permission and volition (Soars and Soars 1998: 75).

This rule specifies the boundary of use of modal verbs, albeit in a rather general manner; after all, the list seems incomplete by not including the concepts of refusal, promise, suggestion, willingness and prohibition. However, as an introduction to the vast field of modals, it seems to be satisfactory precisely because of its broad categorization.

3. **Clarity:** Rules should be clear and precise, therefore, inadequate terminology must be avoided.

There is a difference between the first and the second members of the following pairs:

'ability'	Can / Could	you recommend a good book?
'permission'	May / Might	I ask you to speak up?
'volition'	Will / Would	you be good enough to come and see me as soon as you can?
'possibility'	It may / might	start raining tomorrow

In these cases, the past forms do not express past time but greater consideration, politeness, or tentativeness than the corresponding present forms. This is an example of the HYPOTHETICAL use of auxiliaries (Quirk et al., 1972: 104). Although this seems true and demarcates to a degree, the abstract notion of *hypothetical* detracts from the precision of the rule and subsequently the clarity criterion is lost and it becomes obscure. The concept of a hypothetical usage may be unclear for learners and it may, therefore, be deemed to be an inadequate terminology.

4. **Simplicity:** It is essential that rules do not become too complex for several reasons; fear of demotivating the learner, obscuring the clarity criterion as well as adversely effecting the truth aspect.

Can, could, will and **would** are called modal auxiliary verbs. So are:

Shall, should, may, might, ought to and **must**. Modals are always followed by an infinitive without to.

I must go .... He will come .... (Powell and McHugh 1992: 61)

This example is clear and simple but very possibly to the detriment of the truth. It fails to single out the exception to the rule *ought to*, and does not address the syntactical behavior of *offers* and *requests* and distorts the truth to that end. Nevertheless, as a rudimentary initiation to the modal system, this example may be considered acceptable since it is "psychologically valuable" (Swan 1994: 49) in that it enables the learner to gain the feeling of control over the form.

5. **Conceptual parsimony:** The learner's awareness, or lack of it, must be taken into account prior to devising any explanation, the efficacy of which depends on the writer/teacher assuming "little conceptual sophistication on the part of his/her readers or listeners" (Swan 1994: 51).

Complex finite verb phrases

There are four basic types:

Type A (MODAL/PERIPHRASTIC) consists of a modal or periphrastic

Auxiliary + the base of the verb-phrase head. For example:

He must examine. (Quirk et al., 1972: 73).

Evidently, the language used in this rule is inadequate from the learners' point of view due to the unfamiliar nature of many of the terms. This reflects the idea presented by Corder (1973) that teacher–teacher grammatical discussions *vis-a-vis* teacher–student grammatical explanations should remain distinct entities.

6. **Relevance:** This final requirement again confronts the problems learners face when dealing with rules. If the teacher is in a position to contrast the L1 and L2 of his or her learners, then the former can better present rules with specific explanations to the latter. Swan (1980) provides examples of differences in article usage between Slav languages and French to highlight his argument. A similar example may be presented here with reference to the modal system:

Gianfranco must leave yesterday.
Kazuyoshi must leave yesterday.

Therefore, presumably, these mistakes can be remedied by the same pedagogical rule; ostensibly that "*must* can only be used to refer to present and future obligations. To talk about the past, *had to* is used" (*ibid.*: 394). However, it may also be desirable to be aware that the Italian and Japanese past modal equivalents of *must* are made by altering the stem of the present forms:

Gianfranco **deve** partire	— Gianfranco *must* leave.
Gianfranco ha **dovuto** partire ieri	— Gianfranco had to leave yesterday.
Kazuyoshi wa denakereba **nara<u>nai</u>**	— Kazuyoshi *must* leave.
Kino Kazuyoshi wa denakereba **nara<u>nakata</u>**	— Kazuyoshi had to leave yesterday.

Westney (1994) rejects this final criterion on the grounds that differences between L1/L2 should remain divorced from the other features. Evidently, this view stems from the grammatical system and, thus, ignores specific cases of student needs. Swan (1994: 45) however, is clearly the pragmatist presenting these points with the learner unequivocally at the centre of attention, which seems to be the most suitable way to progress.

Thus far, Swan (1994) design criteria has been shown to be a useful device in measuring the effectiveness of pedagogical rules which may be helpful to learners, and that although rules are often far from perfect, they can have a positive affect on learners' development and understanding of grammar. Westney's view, on the other hand, that "accurate and/or effective rules are neither realistic nor desirable in a learning/teaching situation" (Westney 1994: 92) has been seen as over cautious and negative. More examples of rules are given next in order to further justify the position of adopting Swan's approach to pedagogical grammar.

25.3.1 Further Reasons to Adopt the Design Criteria

Implicit in Swan's stance is the belief that grammatical guidelines are in some way beneficial to learners. Taking that the design criteria is an appropriate way to gauge rules it follows that by applying this criteria to a given rule will reveal the value and worth of the rule for the learner. The following rule is taken from a linguistic dictionary but may still be relevant for learners:

> Modal verbs share a set of morphological and syntactic properties which distinguish them from the other auxiliaries, e.g. no –s, -ing, or –en forms. (Crystal 1985: 244).

It is certainly true and demarcated (though it omits the rule that modals have no infinitives, i.e., *to must eat, or *to can drive). It seems simple enough but the terminology used will no doubt cause problems for most learners who may find it psychologically demotivating. Nevertheless, it is workable and must not be rejected outright as

> Learners certainly need to realize that most guideline rules are simplifications which will have to be revised as their knowledge and confidence grow". (Chalker, cited in Bygate et al. 1994: 32)

Westney's point that establishing the nature and extent of a generalisation causes problems is relevant here. The above rule seems to combine descriptive and pedagogical definitions and to a certain degree succeeds, but as a result, this rule may be restricted to advanced learners. Thus, Chalker's (1994) idea that generalised and simplistic rules act as important way-signs initially but that learners must be wary of them too, also seems credible.

Modal auxiliaries are also problematic for learners and teachers because concepts such as *possibility* and *obligation* are hard to process and convey, respectively. But, generalisations about such difficult concepts which come close to satisfying Swan's design criteria give the learner a better chance of grasping such ideas than without them. Other more extensive examples demonstrate this (Ellis and Gaies 1999: 133).

Modals of possibility

1. The modal verbs that express future possibility are **may, might, can, could**.
2. All these verbs are used with a main verb:
    People with Alzheimer's disease <u>may forget</u> very simple words.
3. The modal verbs may, might, can and could differ in meaning from 'will'. They say what may possibly happen. 'Will' says what will definitely happen:
    People with Alzheimer's disease <u>may get</u> lost. People with a high fever <u>will feel</u> sick.
4. These four modals are close in meaning. For most speakers, may and can refer to something that is possible and likely:
    A person with Alzheimer's disease <u>may forget</u> things.
    A person with Alzheimer's disease <u>can forget</u> things
    For most speakers, might and could refer to something that is possible but not so likely:
    A person with Alzheimer's disease <u>might wear</u> two shirts or dresses.
    A person with Alzheimer's disease <u>could wear</u> two shirts or dresses.
5. Use the simple present tense to say what generally happens:
    Everybody <u>forgets</u> things.
    Use a modal verb to express what we think will possibly happen.
    A person with Alzheimer's disease <u>may forget</u> where she lives.
6. The modal verbs might and could should be used when the sentence is referring to the past:
    We <u>thought</u> that she <u>might</u> be suffering from Alzheimer's disease.

Common errors

1. Using verb+ing, the infinitive with to or a past participle after a modal verb:
    - People with Alzheimer's disease may forgetting things.
    - People with Alzheimer's disease may to forget things.
    - People with Alzheimer's disease may forgotten things.
2. Using be able and can in the same sentence:
    - People with Alzheimer's disease can be able to forget things.
3. Using will instead of a modal verb of possibility:
    - People with Alzheimer's disease will forget things.
4. Using may when referring to past possibility:
    - We thought she may be suffering from Alzheimer's disease.

This grammatical reference to modals of *possibility* represents a comprehensive list of dos and don'ts for learners. It is true, well demarcated, clear and simple in that it tries to keep inadequate terminology to a minimum while being seemingly relevant. The manner in which this particular guideline is presented suggests that it largely complies with Swan's requirements for an appropriate pedagogical grammar and is a strong attempt to support the notion that such rules will be relevant for students. It is, however, by no means complete. Westney argues that there is no "final description of any area of language" (Westney 1994: 86) and that it is impossible to contain the elusive nature of grammar:

> Seemingly well-defined areas of grammar can be shown to contain great complexity, which is complicated by inherent variability and vagueness of use (*ibid.*: 86).

This is a valid contention which merits further inspection. There are indeed more complex issues concerning *possibility* which the above rule fails to incorporate; the passive can cause a shift in their range of meaning, for example (Quirk et al., 1972: 83):

> John could drive the car (ability or possibility).
> The car could be driven by John (possibility only).

However, the overriding factor seems to be that the initial rule is simplified primarily for the learner to get to grips with the concept of *possibility* in modal form and, in spite of its incompleteness it is difficult to see how those who study it can gain from it. Chalker (1994) makes a valid and noteworthy observation on the dynamics of rules:

> Much confusion is caused by a failure to distinguish between rules as a full and accurate description of how the system works, which all teachers should understand, and simplified rules intended as useful dos and don'ts for learners. (p. 32)

This perceptive comment illustrates the potential pedagogic rules possess as an aid for learners. The chief reason for the distinction between rules for teachers and simplified guidelines for learners is to enable students to improve their grammar, thereby increasing their confidence and, it is hoped, competence at communicating in the target language.

25.3.2 Modal Exercises Enhancing Swan's Pedagogical Stance

Here, specific exercises on modals are given to show how pedagogic rules can be helpful to learners, thus, supporting the position of basing a pedagogy on Swan's design criteria. Several types of modal tasks which maybe advantageous to learners exist: gap fills, word deduction, problem solving etc. Celce-Murcia and Hilles (1988) claim that activities and exercises "must be richly contextualised with a variety of examples" (p. 55) if the meaning and function of a modal or perfect modal is to be communicated. They recommend storytelling as an effective medium to teach modals. More recently, Ellis and Fotos (1991) have promoted consciousness-raising tasks whereby learners are required to solve structural problems in a communicative framework. Indeed, Fotos (1993) concludes that continual communicative exposure to "grammar structures presented through formal instruction tended to consolidate and increase the learners' accuracy" (p. 399). An attempt to assess the effectiveness of pedagogic rules which satisfy Swan's design criteria for learners when attempting such tasks will be made with reference to the following modal-focused gap-fill exercises (Ellis and Gaies 1999):

> **Complete the sentences. Use a modal verb or a simple present tense.**
>
> People with Alzheimer's disease *__forget__* things. They *__may prepare__* a meal
> (*forget*) (*prepare*)
> and then forget they cooked it. We all .... strange things sometimes,
> (*say*)
> but people with Alzheimer's disease .... things that do not make
> (*say*)
> any sense at all. Some people .... in strange ways but people
> (*dress*)
> suffering from Alzheimer's disease .... several shirts or dresses at
> (*put on*)
> the same time. They also .... some very odd things. For example,
> (*do*)
> someone with Alzheimer's .... an iron in a freezer. Everybody
> (*put*)
> .... sometimes, but people with Alzheimer's disease .... into
> (*cry*) (*burst*)
> tears for no reason at all. (p. 27)

Clearly, in order for learners to complete this task successfully, the reference rules as shown in the modals of possibility 3 (*ibid.*: 133) would be a vital accompaniment, which is equally true if the above exercise was set in the classroom or as homework. Furthermore, the proposal that such tasks increase proficiency is supported by numerous research projects (Ellis and Fotos 1991; Fotos 1993; Lightbown 1992); suggesting that there is a place for simplified guidelines in the EFL context. Whether such pedagogical rules are teacher-fronted or used as a reference, they complement pedagogical devices (as shown above) and, therefore, remain essential in a learners' development. Another example may confirm this assertion (Soars and Soars 1998):

> Which of the words in the right hand column can fit into the sentences on the left? Sometimes several will fit. Discuss the possibilities with a partner.
>
> (a) .... I ask you a question about this exercise? **must**
> (b) .... you help me with this exercise, please ? **can**
> (c) He'll .... hurry if he wants to get here in time. **may**

(d) I .... be able to come round and see you tonight.
(e) Sally .... read when she was only three.   **might**
(f) I .... be seeing Theo later this evening, but I'm not sure. **could**
(g) You .... be feeling very excited about your trip to Florida. **should**
(h) They .... have finished dinner by now.
(i) You .... pass the exam easily. You've worked really hard.   **will/'ll**
(j) She always .... leave work early on Fridays.
(k) That .... be the taxi.   **have/has to**

(p. 79)

Here, the task is pitched at a higher level, but the interesting point is that learners must discuss the different possibilities, which consolidates the notion that modal auxiliaries cover a semantically broad range. Moreover, the authors suggest that students consult the grammar reference while performing the task, demonstrating the tight relationship between pedagogical rules and some exercises. The former is essential if the rewards of the latter are to be realized, indicating that it would be extremely rash and impracticable to abandon pedagogical rules.

The above two example exercises infer a positive correlation between pedagogic rules and the successful performance of tasks, which, it is hoped, will, in turn, lead to a greater understanding and more confident use of the modal system. In light of this, it seems plausible to claim that the combination of tasks and simplified, but truthful, guidelines acts as a meaningful and useful tool towards acquisition.

25.4 CONCLUSION

This study has attempted to justify the argument for adopting Swan's design criteria for a pedagogic grammar in favour of Westney's perspective. With the use of various guidelines and exercises regarding modals, it has shown how pedagogic rules which largely conform to the six design criteria, can be helpful to rather than misleading learners, which leads to the assumption that to discard such rules would be unwise. Nevertheless, it is important to recognize the points raised by Westney, and acknowledge the problems his approach creates for the role of pedagogic rules; indeed, it remains difficult to refute the examples presented in his paper. Finally, however, it appears to be a question of human nature—optimism versus pessimism. Swan's view is of the former, making the most of a bad situation, whereas Westney asserts the uselessness of even attempting.

This chapter has shown that far from fruitless, certain modal pedagogic rules provide learners with a genuine chance to heighten their grammatical knowledge of the expansive and complex English modal system, and that it is difficult to fail to see how the study of such rules can be harmful to learners. It is also propitious to keep the role of guidelines for students in context and to remember that "there is no single pedagogical solution which is applicable in all classrooms" (Ellis 1990b: 67–68). The debate will no doubt continue, but there seems to be a scope for empirical research on the effects of learners studying pedagogic rules. In conclusion, this study holds that inadequacies are to be expected in generalisations, but the presentation of which is by no means futile as learners may well profit by them.

REFERENCES

Allen, J.P.B. (Ed.), *Pedagogic Grammar*, London: Oxford University Press, 1974. 59–92.

Bygate, M., Tonkyn, A., and Williams, E., *Grammar and the Language Teacher*, Hemel Hempstead: Prentice Hall, 1994.

Celce-Murcia, M., "Data-based language analysis and TESL," *Georgetown University Round Table on Language and Linguistics 1990*, J.A. Alatis (Ed.), Washington, D.C: Georgetown University Press, 1990, 245–259.

Celce-Murcia, M. and Hilles, S., *Techniques and Resources in Teaching Grammar*, Hong Kong: Oxford University Press, 1988.

Chalker, S., "Pedagogical Grammar: Principles and Problems," in Bygate, M.A. Tonkyn and E. Williams (Eds.), *Grammar and the Language Teacher*, London: Prentice Hall, 1994.

Corder, S.P. (Ed.) *Linguistics and the Language Teaching Syllabus*, London: Oxford University Press, 1973, 275–284.

Crystal, D., *A Dictionary of Linguistics and Phonetics*, Oxford: Blackwell, 1985.

Ellis, R., *Instructed Second Language Acquisition*, Oxford: Blackwell, 1990.

———, "Researching classroom language learning," *Research in the Language Classroom*, C. Brumfit and R. Mitchell (Eds.), London: Modern English Publications, 1990b.

Ellis, R. and Fotos, S., "Communicating about grammar: A task-based approach," *TESOL Quarterly* 25 (1991): 605–628.

Ellis, R. and Gaies, S., *Impact Grammar*, Hong Kong: Addison-Wesley Longman, 1999.

Fotos, S., "Consciousness raising and noticing through focus on form: Grammar task performance versus formal instruction," *Applied Linguistics* 14 (1993): 385–407.

Krashen, S.D., *Principles and Practice in Second Language Acquisition*, Oxford: Pergamon, 1982.

Lewis, M., *The English Verb—An Exploration of Structure and Meaning*, Hove, U.K: Language Teaching Publications, 1986.

Lightbown, P., "What have we here? Some observation of the influence of instruction on L2 learning," *Foreign Language Pedagogy Research: A Comemorative Volume for Claus Faerch*, R. Phillipson, E. Kellerman, L. Selinker, M. Sharwood-Smith, and M. Swain (Eds.), Clevedon: Multilingual Matters, 1992.

Odlin, T., *Perspectives on Pedagogical Grammar,* Cambridge: Cambridge University Press, 1994.

Palmer, F.R., *Modality and the English Modals,* London: Longman, 1990.

Powell, D. and McHugh, M., *Compact 2 Student's Book,* Great Britain: Nelson, 1992.

Quirk, R., Greenbaum, S., Leech, G., and Svartvik, J., *A Grammar of Contemporary English,* Great Britain: Longman, 1972.

Quirk, R., Greenbaum, S., and Svartvik, J., *A Comprehensive Grammar of the English Language,* Harlow: Longman, 1985.

Soars, J. and Soars, L., *New Headway Upper Intermediate Students Book,* Barcelona: Oxford University Press, 1998.

_____, *New Headway Upper Intermediate Teachers Book,* Barcelona: Oxford University Press, 1998.

Swan, M., "Design Criteria or Pedagogic Rules," in Bygate, M.A. Tonkyn and E. Williams (Eds.), pp. 45–55.

_____, *Practical English Usage,* Oxford: Oxford University Press, 1980.

Westney, P., "Rules and Pedagogical Grammar," in Odlin, T. (Ed.), pp. 72–96.

Part 8
DEVELOPING COMMUNICATION SKILLS

Chapter 26

DEVELOPING THE SPEAKING AND WRITING SKILLS AT TECHNICAL INSTITUTES
A Classroom Investigation with Suggestions

— S. Joseph Arul Jayraj

26.1 INTRODUCTION

This study has the following objectives:

1. Present an effective model of 'classroom research'/'action research'/'teacher-led research' for the teachers and the investigators to teach English effectively.
2. Give an idea of how a small scale investigation can be undertaken in activity-based English language teaching.
3. Present a model of a 'self-reflective inquiry' in a classroom in order to make the teachers of English and the investigators understand the usefulness of the language teaching practices with a view to improve the rationality of educational practices, and explain the situation in which these practices are carried out.
4. Persuade the teachers and the investigators to reflect over their language teaching practices and experiences and review their personal and professional development in a systematic way in order to lead them to potential change.
5. Empower the teachers and the investigators to release themselves from dependence on precepts handed down by trainers.
6. Encourage the teachers and the investigators to test for themselves the methods and materials they use in the classroom and see which are the most effective for them.
7. Enable the teachers and the investigators to indulge in the cyclic process of observing, diagnosing, planning, teaching, testing, reviewing, reflecting, re-teaching, and re-evaluating.

Language is a means of communication. If the user of a language has only knowledge of language rules and forms, he/she is said to have 'linguistic competence'. If he/she also has the knowledge to communicate functionally and interactively, then he/she is said to have 'communicative competence'. Communicative competence includes: (i) knowledge of the grammar and vocabulary of the language, (ii) knowledge of the rules of speaking, (iii) knowing how to use and respond to different types of speech acts such as requests, apologies, and thanks at different contexts, and (iv) knowing how to use the language appropriately.

In the L1 situation, one learns to speak at home. He/she is taught to read and write in the school. The teaching and learning practices prevalent in second language (L2) classroom consist of only writing tasks. The speaking skill is given scant attention. So, it becomes necessary to introduce the functional aspects of training the students to speak and write well in English in the syllabus and implement them in the classroom.

26.2 THE STRATEGY

In a language-learning situation, all language activities are language using because only in the process of using, a language can be learnt (Wilkins, 83). The whole point of language learning depends on how well the students are motivated towards attaining success in developing communicative skills (Wilkins, 85). The development of the English language skills in the students, therefore, involves remedial work on the deficiency of English language skills of the students. For example, "Students introduce themselves" was the language activity given to test the speaking skills of the students in the diagnostic test. Normally, a student writes as he/she speaks. So, a diagnostic test to test the writing skills of the students was not conducted. Their speaking test performance in the diagnostic test was not satisfactory. So, it was felt that there was a need to hone the competence of the students in speaking and writing in English. Therefore, suitable remedial language-learning activities were designed and taught. These remedial activities were carried out in the form of an intensive course for a stipulated period of 15 hours. They consisted of the Part-I of the Material Production which include:

- English sounds: Vowels and consonants,
- Use of 'a' and 'an',
- Naming words,
- One and many (singular and plural),
- Gender,
- One-word substitutes,
- Collective names,
- Doing words/action-words (verbs),
- Conjugation,

- Concord,
- Describing words (adjectives),
- Opposites,
- Joining words,
- Framing sentences, and
- Four type of sentences.

After doing the remedial language-learning activities, the students certainly gained confidence in doing the context-based language activities both in speaking and writing in English. The students were properly monitored and assisted in doing these activities.

If the teacher/investigator wants to give a functional thrust to develop the speaking and the writing skills in English as a second language, he/she should design need-based and activity-based language material. The package developed was used for teaching and testing. To be more comprehensive, to test appropriately and effectively, the following language activities were used under Part-II of the Material Production:

- Students greet each other,
- Students introduce themselves,
- Students introduce their friends,
- Describing animals/objects/places/persons,
- Picture description,
- Polite requests,
- Transforming assertions into negatives and questions,
- Add question tags,
- My family,
- My town,
- My school/college,
- My subject,
- My friend,
- The difference between life in a city and a village,
- Which mode of transport is comfortable? Why? and
- What are the advantages and disadvantages of sending goods by ship, train, lorry, airplane?

Part-III of the Material Production consisted of language activities such as: Describing the functions of:

- Water-tap,
- Air-pump,
- Refrigerator,
- Pressure cooker,
- Milk cooker,
- Stethoscope,
- Thermometer,

- Thermos flask,
- Geyser,
- Radio,
- Television,
- Cell phone/telephone,
- Wall-clock/wrist watch, and
- What are the uses of convex and concave lenses?

Part-IV of the Material Production consisted of the following language activities:

- How does a computer work?
- Name the different parts of a computer and explain their uses,
- What are the differences between electrical and electronic engineering?
- What are the differences between civil and mechanical engineering? and
- What are the differences between ordinary foundation and pile foundation?

The language activities that were designed and taught under Part-V of the Material Production were as follows:

- Delivering a welcome address,
- Introducing the chief guest,
- Proposing vote of thanks,
- Telling a story,
- Attending an interview,
- Participating in a group discussion (GD), and
- Delivering a talk on a given topic.

Mrs. Kamatchi and Mr. T. Selvakumar, Lecturers Selection Grade, Government Polytechnic, Thuvakkudy, Tiruchirappalli, were present in the classroom among the students throughout the experiment. The students were trained to speak and write in English on the topics presented in Parts II, III, IV, and V of the Materials produced in 45 hours in their presence. A series of Revision Tests both in the spoken and the written modes were conducted. After teaching the context-based language activities the students were tested periodically and evaluated. Based on their performance in each Revision Test, the activity-based language-teaching materials were re-taught effectively. On 24th September, 2004, a post-test was conducted for all students on various topics which were not taught in the class, in the presence of Mr. N. Rajendren, Head, Department of English, and Mrs. Kamatchi, Lecturer Selection Grade, Government Polytechnic, Thuvakkudy, Tiruchirappalli. The performance of the students in the post-test was noteworthy.

To accelerate the development of the speaking and the writing skills of the students in English, the context-based activities were taught with sufficient practice. The language environment encompassed everything the students heard, saw and did in English. Language could be best accomplished in contexts (Dalen 1973: 13). As the minds of the students were engaged predominantly in performing the language activities, the focal point was not on the language but on the tasks. In short, through this process, language habits were formed in the minds indirectly. Soon after the speaking activity was over, the students were asked to write it.

In this context, it is imperative for the teachers to try to use new aids of English language teaching in the classroom. Using expensive audio-visual aids may be suitable for use on a limited scale, and in selected classrooms. Instead, teachers can think of devising simple, capital-saving and more 'appropriate' technology by making use of indigenous materials to suit the needs of the students. 'Appropriate technology' does not mean an inferior technology, rather it is very useful in the prevailing local conditions (Alam 1983: 10–11); its application will not be easy, rather it will pose a clear challenge to the teachers. These techniques may be a bit taxing. Only a serious attempt of using such techniques extensively will improve the standard of language teaching (Alam 23).

Hazel Francis (1977) in his Preface to *Language in Teaching and Learning* alleges that many teachers are unable to see how problems of language use need to be related to actual classroom teaching-learning experiences. The problem can be sorted out either with the cooperation of the students themselves or with the experts because readymade solutions to the problems of the teachers/investigators and the students are not available. Therefore, textbooks that consist of context-based language activities can give confidence to the students in using English effectively, and such textbooks which suit the needs and standard of the students can be chosen. The textbooks have to be qualitative, need-based and indigenous.

Wilkins (1974) in his *Prologue* comments:

> What works is good; unfortunately, it is not at all easy to decide what works and what does not .... In some cases, the methods that are commonly discarded can be successful and the methods that are found useful can be a failure. The reason is that the principles that govern language learning are sufficiently general ..., which necessitate different approaches for different goals (p. 83).

Strictly speaking, while designing a language course or syllabus according to the availability of hours for teaching, the age, standard and the needs of the students—all are not taken into account. So, the course or syllabus fails to become need-based. According to Wilkins, the two important variables are the student and the teacher/investigator. The skill and the personality of the teacher are instrumental in creating conducive conditions for language learning. It depends on the teacher's proficiency of using the language and the pedagogical skills. The positive grooming in the personality of the teacher/investigator accelerates the pace of learning, which can result in formulating methodological principles in the teaching and learning processes (*ibid.*, 53–55).

While there are different methods, approaches, techniques and procedures already investigated, one should take stock of them. The proliferation of these shows the strength of English language teaching and reflects the teachers', investigators' and experts' commitment to find more efficient and effective ways of teaching English. As a result, the teachers of English have a variety of approaches and methodological options to choose, which may tend to baffle, confuse and bewilder them. Therefore, he/she faces conflicting opinions (Christophersen 1973: 11).

Though these methods, approaches, techniques and procedures are based on different views of what language is and how language is taught and learnt in the classroom and outside the classroom, these concepts and practices are described in such a way that they are difficult for the teacher to understand and implement. So, there is a need to make more concerted and concrete efforts to teach English. It is better to find out a much better workable method or approach than argue in support of or against one method or the other. So, the teacher/investigator has to employ all methods, approaches, techniques, procedures and classroom practices involving multiple approaches and methods. "In practice, most language teaching specialists are eclectic (holistic), as are the textbooks they write" (Paulston 1980: 30).

David Abercrombie insists on the necessity to

> ... Design a course for the beginner who knows exactly what he wants to do with the language and knows what is irrelevant to his purpose. It is a bigger problem to produce a satisfactory course for that great majority of beginners. (p. 16)

But the real problem is that the students are in such a position that they do not know what they want to do with the L2 learning and are unable to decide what is relevant or irrelevant to their purpose. This is the case with most of the teachers/investigators of English. It is not a mere exaggeration to state that the students who come to Polytechnics or Engineering Colleges from the vernacular medium are unable to read and understand sentences from their textbook. They are neither good in speaking nor writing in English. A teacher/investigator should not despair at this moment, for:

> ... a good teacher can get results whatever method he is using. It is best to have a method as sound as our present knowledge can make it. (*ibid.*)

Abercrombie suggests, the teacher should concentrate on making the students "... possess a relatively small active vocabulary ..." (*ibid.*, p. 18). So, it becomes necessary to design a beginners' course, which is well-graded and consists of a variety of context-based language activities for the students' active use. Thus, the language teaching processes can influence the selection of material to be taught and the method of teaching (*ibid.*, 23).

In this regard, the following suggestions, would be useful:

1. The objectives of the experiment can be stated clearly.
2. The activities in which the students' language competencies that have to be tested can be listed.

3. An educational plan with objectives can be laid out. It can be an outcome towards which an educational activity is directed.
4. Previously learnt structures can be reviewed and they can precede the introduction of new material (Wellman 1978: 53).
5. The performance of the students can be continuously tested and corrected.
6. Apart from being flexible, open-minded, friendly, inventive, enthusiastic and dedicated, the teachers/investigators need to design suitable remedial language-learning activities. The remedial work has to be carried out in the form of an intensive course in which the language components are integrated with methodology. The students will find it useful, while learning English.
7. The remedial materials prepared can consist of need-based, well-graded and skill-oriented language activities that are generally and fundamentally essential to equip the students with basic language skills for better understanding of the activities designed and will enable the students to "use the language in meaningful situations" (Corcoran 1970: 234).
8. The language units can be designed to impart certain basic knowledge and skills of English to the students. These language skills have to be taught only through activities, which when taught, will make the students learn with devout commitment, interest and enthusiasm. They are able to understand the concepts of these units and to put them to proper use. When they hear these exercises being described, they tend to forget; when they see these exercises being done by the teacher/investigator in the classroom and explained, they are likely to remember them well; and when they are given an opportunity to do these exercises themselves, they do understand. This fact is reminiscent of the concept of teaching and learning English as recommended by Bumpass (1963: 13).
9. The teacher/investigator can prepare supplementary materials which can assist the students a lot towards self-learning and provide them with a lot of opportunities to equip themselves with the competencies laid down in the syllabus. These competencies can serve as a model for teachers/investigators to imbibe these competencies first and ultimately enable the students to acquire them by involving them in the activity-based language learning process. These exercises can have

... a balanced compromise between structures and functions rather than grammatical structures; and allowing for plenty of practice and revision. (Holden 1980: 70)

It insists on the use of activity-based materials, wherein saying coincides with doing.

10. As Andrew Wright rightly points out, there is no "single ideal way" (p. 64), of teaching English. Bumpass (*op. cit.*) also shares the same point of view when he argues:

> There is no magic formula to help the teacher in accomplishing his task. But if he can learn to crystallize his thinking in the light of recent linguistic findings, he may be able to form a new 'attitude' towards what language learning and language teaching should comprise (p. 13).

Andrew Wright suggests that, according to linguists, if the teacher/investigator is interested, he/she can create a new and fruitful approach to English language learning by involving the students' observation and participation in the language-learning activities (*ibid.*: 64), it is desirable to follow the following checklist as proposed by him (*ibid.*: p. 66):

(a) The topic of interest chosen must be at the conceptual level of the students.
(b) The teacher/investigator must organize interesting types of participation for all students.
(c) The language the students have to produce must be known to them already or if new, they must be able to learn it easily.
(d) The language must be useable to the students.
(e) There must be plenty of opportunities to use the language at least in the classroom.

11. Drill, in army training, means planned and formal physical movements. In the field of education, it means the mode or method of teaching and learning with much practice through repetition. Guariento and Morley (2001) opine:

> Control over linguistic knowledge is achieved by means of performing under real operating conditions in meaning-focused language activities (p. 349).

12. A meaningful language activity is nothing but an attempt in making the activity-based language learning easy, participatory, useful and interesting. More than the infrastructure, it is the quality and committed teaching that certainly helps the students realize their language potentials and develop their language skills. A combination of spirit of research along with committed teaching introduces a breath of fresh air and enthusiasm. The learning activities must be presented in an interesting manner in which the students must have participatory learning experience. To make it happen, new organizing principles like creating a curiosity, an urge or a desire in the students to find out and learn have to emerge. These are certain essential steps to be taken to make teaching English effective and useful.

The students are like bulbs and the language activities are like a battery.

Without interplay of electricity between the bulbs and the battery, both will be inactive. The teacher/investigator is like an electrician. As soon as the teacher/investigator connects the students with the context-based language teaching and learning process, the bulbs are illuminated. As the driver ignites the engine by electrically firing the gases from the fuel, the students really have an urge to communicate. But they need the teacher/investigator to ignite it. Once their urge to communicate is ignited, the students do try to express themselves. To make it happen, Margy Whalley in her Foreword suggests that confident and competent practitioners are needed with a good understanding of the needs of the students who are able to promote the highest quality education and care for all students. The teachers/investigators need to be rigorous and reflective practitioners. She also advises them to pay close attention to students, offer appropriate help and create an encouraging and affectionate atmosphere (Lindon and Jennie 1977: 22).

13. The teachers/investigators of English should know how to appropriate the best pedagogical methods of the day and give the students an imprint of their own by 'adopting' and 'adapting' them to the needs of the students. They should be able to assimilate elements of their own pedagogy and mint it as their own coinage. To do so, they have to know how to inculturate English learning among the students. The task of teaching and learning English is confronted with a fundamental problem whether to pick up where it was left off and offer perhaps with a few modifications of the methods of a bygone era, or to inaugurate a new era with a new pedagogy. The problem remains with all its ambiguity. In such contexts, it is one's duty to pick up the thread again and to reweave the pedagogical fabric of English language teaching and learning according to the demands of the time and, if possible, with a more tough, battle-hardened spirit. The question that arises in this context is: Is this possible? To dream of a uniform pedagogy of teaching and learning English that would accelerate the students' speaking and writing skills and be accepted and equally practised in all technical institutions has turned out to be a true Utopia. Priority should be given to a more practice-oriented methodology of teaching and learning English.

It is not simply a matter of pedagogy. The underlying problem is the question of understanding the needs of the students and the new reality, the demands of the students and those of the society, which has surfaced in recent years. The teaching and learning of English today demands and urges one to prepare a new pedagogy that is suited to the needs of the teachers/ investigators and the students.

The idea of introducing a common pedagogy and a text to all technical institutions is in practice, but it is left to the choice of the teacher/investigator to determine how to implement it. In most technical institutions, the prescribed textbooks are not need-based. The educational programmes and methods of teaching and learning English are not suited to meet the demands of the students. Classes, daily schedule and language activities carried out can strictly be regulated.

It is time to embark upon a process of reflection and revision of all English teaching and learning practices in technical institutions. The teachers/investigators have to be subjected to serious questioning about their ability to teach English effectively. They have to accept the challenge and bravely start a process of evaluation of the existing practices and work for a transformation. Instructional design can be prepared based on definite objectives and as such framing objectives is the most important step for instructional design. If each objective gives its own general and specific characteristic behaviour, it will clearly communicate the behavioural outcome that will result in the students.

A teacher/investigator is supposed to know exactly what and how he/she is going to teach and what his/her students have to do, and should have a specific or particular objective for teaching each language activity. In this context, it will not be out of place to state that one should have knowledge of the aims and objectives of teaching English. It solves the problems such as what preparations he/she should make for his/her teaching and which method or approach he/she should adopt. This is possible only when the aims and objectives of teaching have been fixed in the beginning. The teacher/investigator has to be more clear and specific in his/her objectives of the teaching of English language because they give focus, concentration and progress to the work undertaken. They ensure the effectiveness of the English teaching experiment and help one know the levels of improvement of the knowledge and language skills of the students. They enable one to identify the areas where the students are slow and need help. They also help one evaluate the effectiveness of teaching at three levels, viz. knowledge, understanding and application.

The innumerable methods, materials and practices have been advocated in the field of English language teaching and learning "... at different times, and in terms of different problems and teaching objectives" (CIEFL 1995). These present before the teachers "a range of options" from which one can choose the suitable ones according to the need and practise them "in systematic and informed ways" (*ibid.*: 2–3). These methods are based on "rationales and theoretical explanations" (*ibid.*: 3). Moreover, they help in diagnosing the problems in teaching and learning English. They can empower the teachers/investigators and the students in developing skills and strategies to use them in different circumstances in order to solve the problems they face in the teaching and learning processes.

26.3 RECOMMENDATIONS—AVENUES OF CHANGES FOR IMPROVEMENT

1. It is a matter of rediscovering the direction of teaching and learning English in technical institutions in a new context of meeting the needs of the present day.
2. The teachers/investigators can better identify their talents, pool their resources of pedagogical formation and put them to proper use.
3. It can be done effectively only by the management and the teachers/investigators realizing their responsibilities and with the collaboration of their fellow workers in carrying out their duty diligently. To this end, the teachers/investigators should clearly establish their educational orientation and give their students enough opportunities and practice to learn and use English effectively.
4. The challenge for the teachers/investigators is to combine communicative skills in English with the students' knowledge in technical education and achieve effective access to teaching and learning of English.
5. One of the biggest challenges is the formation of teachers/investigators in the right pedagogical tradition. If success is obtained in getting cooperation from teachers/investigators in orienting them towards realizing their responsibilities to acquire language skills, their standard as well as that of the students will gradually improve.
6. The teachers/investigators need to develop a suitable pedagogical system of programmes and methodology, which are student-centred. The instruments with which the teachers/investigators can attain this goal are: the sense of unity, handwork, commitment and accountability. It is better to have a methodology of his/her own which is formulated from many novel approaches and methods suggested to be adopted in teaching rather than remain a willing slave to the formality of the predetermined pedagogical codes. The discovery and practice of these ideals will lead to the road of reaching one's goals successfully. It is a matter of not only teaching English but also applying the methods that are conducive to put English to use. It can flourish alongside the traditional, institutional as well as methodological forms.
7. To implement it successfully, a committed body of teachers/investigators who can work ceaselessly by realizing the need for their collective responsibility is necessary. They have to cooperate with one another wholeheartedly in fulfilling their duty.

To realize the above principles, the following suggestions can be implemented:

1. The average knowledge, the capacity, and the difficulties of the students in using English have to be assessed through the Diagnostic

Test. Poor performance can be remedied first by teaching them the required basic language operations. Experience shows that once the fundamentals are learnt, the learning process gets accelerated. If the students do not know the basics, it is futile to teach them activity-based language activities produced on various topics. Therefore, the learning experience can be planned to teach them the fundamentals of English.

2. Remedial teaching is not revising or re-teaching the topics that are already taught. It means to set the problem right by finding a solution to the problem of the students. In other words, it is diagnosing the areas of students' difficulties and gearing the language teaching tasks to tackle these difficulties.

3. Before designing the activity-based language teaching 'remedial and supplementary' material, the age, standard, and needs of the students have to be taken into consideration. Students can be incorporated as members of the Board of Studies and their suggestions can be taken into consideration. Only then, the language teaching material produced will be need-based and student-centred.

4. Teaching suitably designed and graded lessons, which are activity-based and properly monitored and assisted, definitely helps the students equip themselves with language skills within a short span of time.

5. Greater involvement, encouragement and ample chance for participative learning of language skills should be linked with real-life situation and with certain basic topics in major subjects of technical education can also be given for speaking practice followed by writing.

6. Specifically developed indigenous materials ought to be used to achieve the objectives of teaching English.

7. ELT experts in India can bring in a radical shift in material production and can also move away from Euro-American-centric texts to the texts more on native subjects, which are culturally familiar to the students. Textbook writers can be oriented in writing innovative and indigenous textbooks with a lot of context-based language activities in English, keeping in mind the classroom reality, the needs and culture of the students.

8. The teachers/investigators can be monitored and assisted ably by the managements and ELT experts for creating better English language teaching and learning atmosphere. Language experts can be hired and asked to observe the classroom reality and help the teachers and the textbook writers in designing suitable language teaching materials and in implementing curriculum and pedagogy.

9. Teachers of English, investigators, language experts, curriculum designers and the textbook writers of India can come together half-

yearly/annually and can focus their attention on the neglected area of English language teaching and learning. This problem can be easily tackled by their combined-efforts in designing appropriate materials and methods keeping in mind the classroom reality.

10. It can be made compulsory that the experts in the Regional Institutes of English (RIEs), Central Institute of English and Foreign Languages (CIEFL), National Council of Educational Research and Training (NCERT), and the State Institute of English Language Teaching (SIELT) can be asked to adopt educational institutions and thus monitor the English language teaching and learning processes.

11. Out of the methods suggested by the experts, the teachers/investigators can be required to choose and implement either method which suits their needs or design their own to overcome peculiar problems faced in their classrooms. Importance can be given to develop the speaking and the writing skills. The central and the state governments of India can take steps to introduce spoken English in the syllabus. The Teachers investigators, experts, curriculum designers and textbook writers in India must take necessary steps to redesign the English curricula and assign spoken English its due priority along with writing skills. Oral test can be included as an important component of evaluation in the continuous assessment of the English language skills.

12. Undergraduates or postgraduates in English Language and Literature with proper teacher training and pronounced fluency and accuracy in English can be appointed as teachers to teach English. Anglo-Indians with proper qualification can also be appointed as teachers in large numbers.

13. A basic intensive course in oral communication in English can be conducted for teachers. Orientation, refresher and In-service courses to the teachers of English in oral communication can be given every year. These training programmes can be revitalized with a lot of thrust to oral communication practice in English. The teacher-training syllabi can also be revised to include this component.

14. Research institutes such as RIEs, CIEFL and NCERT can be asked to undertake extensive classroom researches to develop the communicative language skills of the teachers and the students. The well-established research institutes and the State Governments can encourage such innovative and useful researches by giving support for infrastructure and finance.

15. If the students are assisted, facilitated and encouraged to communicate orally, first followed by writing in English in their classrooms, their communication skills can certainly be kept in operational efficiency.

REFERENCES

Abercrombie, David, *Problems and Principles: Studies in the Teaching of English as a Second Language*, London: Longman, 1956.

Alam, Qaiser Zoha, *Issues: Linguistic and Pedagogic Hints for the Teachers of English*, New Delhi: Sterling Publishers, 1983.

Andrew Wright quoted in Holden, Susan (Ed.), *Teaching Children*, London: Modern English Publications, 1980.

Bumpass, Faye L., *Teaching Young Students English as a Foreign Language*, New York: American Book Company, 1963.

Christophersen, Paul, *Second Language Learning: Myth and Reality*, London: Penguin, 1973.

CIEFL, *Methods of Teaching English: Block I and II*, Hyderabad: Latha, 1995.

Corcoran, Gertrude B., *Language Arts in the Elementary School: A Modern Linguistic Approach*, New York: Roland, 1970.

Dalen, Deobold Van, B., *Understanding Educational Research: An Introduction*, New York: McGraw-Hill, 1973.

Francis, Hazel, *Language in Teaching and Learning*, London: George Allen and Unwin, 1977.

Guariento, William and Morley, John, "Text and task authenticity in the EFL classroom," *The Journal of English Language Teaching* **55**.4 (October 2001), Oxford: OUP, 347–353.

Jayraj, Joseph Arul, S., *Teaching and Learning English as a Second Language at the Primary Level: A Study in Select Schools of Tiruchirappalli Town*, Ph.D. Thesis, Bharathidasan University, Tiruchirappalli, 2003.

Lindon, Lance and Lindon, Jennie, *Working Together for Young Children: A Guide for Managers and Staff*, London: Macmillan, 1977.

Paulston, Christina Bratt, *English as a Second Language*, Washington: A National Education Association Publication, 1980.

Wellman, Laurie, *Teacher of English As a Second Language*, Arco Teacher License Series, New York: Arco, 1978.

Wilkins, D.A., *Second-Language Learning and Teaching*, London: Edward Arnold, 1974.

Chapter 27

INTEGRATING SKILLS
Business Presentations for Business Students

— Vanessa Street

27.1 INTRODUCTION

It is well known that teaching English to business people is very different from teaching the language for the students at an educational institute. One of the skills that is usually required for the business professionals is the business presentation skill. Managers often have to present reports or projects where they are under time constraints to communicate their ideas clearly and succinctly. It is not just the language itself which is needed but also the presentation or communication skills. In fact, in many available resources for in-company language training, there is plethora of information, hints and practice tasks for teaching, how to present as well as the key language structures. This is a natural facet of teaching business English in the executive workplace and it forms part of the continuing trend for **content and language integrated learning** or **CLIL** as it is now known. Although it is rooted in the communication needs of the business world, there is a clear case for its application in the academic world.

This essay looks at the use of business presentations for a business English course at university level. It illustrates how the technique of presenting can be a catalyst for spoken communication and for integrating a variety of skills. For this particular university course, three kinds of skills were targeted.

1. Language skills — speaking in English
2. Communication skills — presenting ideas
3. Applied content knowledge — using business knowledge

This three-fold approach was intended to reflect the world into which business students hoped to participate after their studies. In effect, this essay, based on teaching experience at the Université du Littoral Côte d'Opale (ULCO)[1], aims to show that the CLIL techniques, which can be found so

---

1. ULCO is a regional university located in France. It is spread over three major sites: Boulogne-sur-Mer, Calais and Dunkerque. This course took place in the English Language Department at Boulogne-sur-Mer during the academic years 2006–2007 and 2007–2008.

easily in private business English language training, also have very tangible pedagogical benefits in public education.

27.2 CONTEXTS

Although using business presentations for language learning connects the academic world with the commercial world, there are nevertheless some very distinct differences between the two contexts that inevitably require an adjustment.

At the ULCO, the English element of the business course is split into written and spoken, as is usual with most academic establishments. Traditionally, the written part takes place in the first semester and the second semester focuses on 'oral' skills. The events this essay is based on took place during the second semester where the primary objective was to deliver a language course to business students at degree and master's levels which would focus on their spoken English.

Straightforward though this may seem, a significant difficulty arose with the extent of the class sizes. It is not unusual at the university to be faced with over 50 students and in this particular instance, one of the courses comprised in excess of 80 participants. This created a problem of engagement: how to ensure that the majority of students would be committed to the learning process and not just the nominated few who tend to be the strongest speakers anyway. In the business world, language classes tend to be much smaller and, in fact, mainly structured around individual courses or small group sessions. A smaller number of learners usually result in a more intensive but tailor-made teaching plan. Individuals can be supported according to their needs, even in small group sessions. This would not really be possible with such a large university class with heterogeneous ability levels.

It is not just class size that is very clearly different between the private and public sectors, important as it is. There are also other factors involved such as motivation, experience and objectives which require an adjustment on the part of the teacher.

Business people are generally very highly motivated because there is usually a practical reason for the language training. They need to communicate in English to perform certain functions of their job. Fulfilling work responsibilities is a strong motivational factor. We all wish to do well at our jobs for a number of reasons not least because of the monetary rewards it brings. On the other hand, motivation for the business student can be a more attenuated affair. English is often a compulsory element of a business degree course. However, it is normally ranked with respect to the other subjects of their degree such as marketing, company law, and economics. It may not even have the same importance, or be considered a core subject. It is usually a separate discipline, unrelated to their business subjects, that they need to pass in order to obtain the qualification or move up a year.

There is also a wealth of difference in the experience of a business professional compared to a university student. This touches upon the aspects of commercial knowledge, world experience, self-confidence or just simply being able to express language needs. Most business people unambiguously know what they want to do, for example, to participate in a meeting, and to socialize, negotiate, present findings, etc. whereas university students have been subjected to years of academic style teaching which has shaped their learning expectations. They are conditioned to expect certain activities, familiar practices and routines. Predictably within classes of this sort (and size), the lesson's activity might concentrate on reading a text and responding to spoken questions, maybe even group work on summaries with a spokesperson elected to read out the agreed text for discussion. There may be some role play or spoken games, etc. Thus, the business student may have unmistakable ideas about what they expect to experience in an English language course; and these expectations are not based on an assessment of their language needs but on what has previously been given to them by academic establishments.

Finally, there are the objectives. The business people come to the table with plainly defined communication goals. This is not just another aspect of communicative language teaching where communication is more important than language structure. Getting the message across is vitally important. But in business English teaching, there is a predominant communication skills element: how to present, how to participate in meetings, how to interface with the customer, etc. This is reminiscent of business management training and illustrates the integrated nature of content and language learning[2].

So, given how different the contexts are between private companies and public institutions, it may seem an improbable thing to do—to transfer the CLIL techniques used in business language training to business students. However, this rests upon the assumption that business students would not want to acquire the business communication skills which are so necessarily a part of the world of work—an assumption that appears illogical and which poses the question: Given the new technologies and the globalization of the world around us, are the goals between the private and public sectors very different after all?

27.3 RATIONALES

The relationship between the world of work and education was an important factor in determining the use of business presentations for this university course, but there were also pedagogical rationales for their usage. As mentioned above, the principal objective was to deliver a spoken English course to business students. Given the size of the classes, it appeared that group or team business presentations offered the best solution to the complex

---

2. In fact, the emerging integration between management training and teaching business English has now led to the development of cross-cultural or intercultural training. This is where language and culture are seen as interrelated when determining expectations in global business management.

problem of engagement. This would ensure that we would have a higher level of engagement in terms of quantity, i.e. all the students would have to get involved, to some degree, in the learning process and also, in terms of quality, through the integrated nature of the learning process. Consequently, to begin with, there was a combined practical and pedagogical rationale behind this decision.

More notably, the structure of presenting enforces a type of language discipline which is often associated with university education. Business presentations are an efficient means of communicating ideas within time limits. They force people into thinking about the content and structure of their message to present a unified and coherent argument. These are generic academic skills which all students need to acquire for both spoken and written documents. In addition, a business presentation was a good vehicle for this type of university class because it ensured that all students would participate in a spoken performance satisfying the 'oral' remit of the course and, at the same time, it would allow them to apply and demonstrate an application of their business knowledge. They would be able to use their content knowledge through the medium of English. So, in effect, they would not be performing for the sake of an oral English class but communicating their evaluation of a business idea or issue.

27.4 REDUCING PERFORMANCE STRESS

Finding a framework in which the majority of students would participate created the preliminary impetus for using business presentations. But this did not signify that there were not clearly identifiable language learning reasons, too.

The nature of a presentation provides the students with a certain amount of scaffolding. This means that the performance can be based, to a large extent, on preparation. The content of what they are communicating can be refined and prepared but, more critically, students can practise their performance beforehand. Speaking in front of peers in a second language is, of course, stressful. Stress as a factor in blocking performance has been well documented and researched by academics in the field[3]. However, being able to practise and focus on the presentation provided a secure platform for those most affected by psychological distress. In addition, it also formed a basis for other students to launch themselves into the more spontaneous aspects of language performance.

A group presentation also meant that the speaker had the support and help of his group mates; he was not out on a limb all alone. In fact, the use of groups provided for collaborative learning. Students could consult each other with regard to language structures like trying to get the best possible turn of phrase for the presentation or just with help in grammar and vocabulary. This

---

3. The most famous being Krashen's Affective Filter Hypothesis found in S.D. Krashen, *Principles and Practice in Second Language Acquisition*, Prentice Hall (1987).

would enhance peer teaching so that the weaker student would benefit from the language expertise of the stronger student. And on top of this, business ideas and analysis could be discussed so that a consensus of agreement would be reached. In fact, those who benefited from peer language advice tended to actively contribute to the presentation in terms of business knowledge and skills. This type of team work meant that everybody could play a part in the presentation and the learning outcome did not rest entirely upon the person who had the strongest grasp of English grammar or who had the highest levels of self-confidence.

Finally, as everybody could contribute something and no one student was individually responsible for the total outcome, a group business presentation has within it elements of security that, if managed carefully, can reduce language stress. These aspects of security were essential to move students out of their comfort zone into new learning practices.

27.5 APPLIED CONTENT KNOWLEDGE

Some of these new practices involved the application of students' business knowledge and their ability to manage information and knowledge. The ULCO presentations were a spoken performance lasting about 20–25 minutes (depending on group size) but this just represented the distilled result of the skilled work that was needed to produce it.

The students were given an open brief for the presentations. This meant that they had to find a way to satisfy the brief. It was not a closed question, but it allowed them to carry out research and make choices. At the outset, they would have to decide collectively how to respond to the subject and then select paths of investigation. It was also made very clear at the beginning of the course that it would not be sufficient just to obtain information. The students were encouraged to evaluate their research in the light of their business knowledge. This knowledge could be gleaned from other core subjects of their degree, their work experience or their own opinions on how to move a subject forward. Pulling reams of information from the Internet without interpreting or analyzing it was not an acceptable practice. Once the students had obtained the information they needed and decided upon their stance, they had to craft a presentation. The information had to be sorted and a selection made of which information they were going to use and how they were going to present it. The groups were also asked to put forward arguments or recommendations where possible.

These knowledge management skills, so evident in the business world, are not often made explicit in the English part of a business degree. But without them, the business presentation risked descending into a description of information or a manipulation of text (skills which students generally have in excess). So, it was very important to get the students use their content knowledge in an applied fashion by analyzing information and constructing arguments.

As the course continued, the students began to use their technology skills, which were taught in their information technology (IT) course for their performance. Using PowerPoint software, they started to put together written slides to support their presentation. This was done on their own initiative as presentations were accepted based on using the blackboard or handouts for visuals. Some presentations were even accompanied with video interviews as the students tried to make their presentations as professional as possible. Although technology skills were not part of the integrated skills originally conceived for this course, the students themselves unconsciously accepted its application as a natural dimension of their work. Technology as a language support is so readily a component of our world that it is easy to forget that it is, in some respects, a second-generation literacy skill.

27.6 THE STRATEGY

We have, thus, looked at the rationales for using business presentations for business students when trying to focus on oral competence in English. But how did this actually work in the classroom and what was the strategy employed? These we have to look into.

Essentially there were four facets to the classroom activity: (i) teamwork, (ii) teacher support, (iii) practice and (iv) evaluation.

27.6.1 Teamwork

Initially, the students worked in 'groups'—preferably there were four group members. There could be a maximum of 5 and in exceptional cases a group of 3 was accepted. The strategy was to form a gradual shift from the idea of 'group work' to the concept of 'teamwork', with all the connotations associated with team skills and management. The students were to remain in these teams for all work related to class presentations. As a result, this would not only satisfy the practical need to engage as many students as possible in the learning process, but it also had great value for life skills.

A key factor that really concentrated the students on teamwork was that their evaluations or grades would be based on the team and not the individual. This encouraged the teams to manage their strengths and weaknesses in all skill areas. It also contributed to the aspect of collaborative learning discussed above.

As a consequence of this strategy, the students were allowed to organise themselves, i.e. they would choose the members of their teams. The teacher would not decide who would be in which team. After the initial two weeks, the students were asked to provide written confirmation of the members of their team. Although such a strategy seemed to risk that students would wish to work only with the strongest speakers, in reality, this did not take place partly due to the mix of skills that were required to complete the tasks. In terms of purely language ability such as the understanding and use of language structures and vocabulary, the majority of the teams were of mixed ability.

27.6.2 Teacher Support

The teacher support was based around three main activities. The first one was fairly straightforward and familiar. It dealt with putting language structures into place, making sure that key vocabulary and technical terms were understood, verifying that students could express time sequencing, etc. Discussion of business topics for phrasal verbs, collocations and pronunciation were employed. In fact, this area of teacher support falls into the classic role of the language teacher.

The second activity dealt with the communication structure itself—the business presentation. Time was put aside to stress presentation skills, what was expected and what was not acceptable. Most students have an implicit appreciation already of what is needed because they are very media-savvy nowadays. The Internet and, to a lesser extent, television have created an international arena in which students have easy access to, and more importantly, easy participation. Thus, they already have clear ideas about what constitutes a business presentation. However, clear guidelines were still evidently needed as the variety of skills required did not fit into their years of training and expectation of language-learning activities. In short, it was not what they were used to doing in an English class and, as a result, explicit consolidation was required. For example the phrase 'everybody reads' was one of the defence mechanisms that had to be overcome in spite of the fact that they knew that 'reading' a script was more akin to giving a lecture than a presentation. Total memorization of the text also had to be discouraged as it led to some very slow and painful performances. Instead, consultation of notes rather than a four page hand-written script was recommended. Suggestions of how to use visual props was also given. This could be using a slide as a prompt or explaining a graph or table rather than reciting lists of statistics. Speaking and explaining were emphasised and encouraged by not having slides which were too busy or overloaded with text. To get the points across, examples of different types of presentations found on the Internet like 'YouTube' as well as using TV reality shows such as 'Dragon's Den' were recommended viewing in class.

The third aspect of teacher support was concerned with content-based tasks, activities which would naturally lead into the next presentation. For example, a market research presentation was first approached in class by looking at how market information is used and why it is necessary. This was then followed up with a task activity. A two-page report giving general market predictions for a variety of business sectors was read for comprehension, discussion and vocabulary. Then, working in their teams, the students were asked to plan how they would use this information if they were in a specific business, for example a potato farmer, a manufacturer of chilled products, and a health and beauty retailer. In essence, the idea was to come up with new product lines based on this information. Consequently, the students operating in English were asked to demonstrate how research information could be 'actioned'. This is just one of the many areas where language and content were integrated.

27.6.3 Practice

During the semester, the students carried out a series of presentations. The presentation practice was an essential element of classroom activity as it provided the 'training' by which the students would learn to implement their skills. During the course, there were three main presentations. The first one, a company presentation, was undoubtedly an easy task to do. The business students tend to do company presentations from their first year when they begin their university course. For the first class presentation, they could choose their own subject and this allowed them to use the work that they had previously carried out for another course.

Starting off with the familiar was a way on the one hand, to reassure the students; but on the other hand, for the teacher, the company presentation was primarily used as a vehicle to pick up on student misconceptions of what the course would entail. It provided a jumping off point for student preconceptions highlighting the new expectations and goals of the course.

The next presentation dealt with market research and class time was given over to exercises that would prepare the students for the various tasks required. This included the students deciding themselves which market they would like to investigate and which line of enquiry they would like to take up. They then had to conduct the research using skills which would have been dealt within their market research class. After that, they needed to sort the material, analyse it and select what they could use for their presentation. Students were also encouraged to put forward new trends for their particular business sector hence introducing the need for evaluation and not just description.

There were also smaller presentations that dealt with sales and new product development. Each class performance fed step-by-step into the final presentation. The latter required the teams to identify a niche gap in the student market and was particularly successful because it was a subject pertinent to their own lives. The teams had to come up with an idea based either around a new product or service or an existing product which needed improvement in some way. This activity required an identification of a demand in their market which was not satisfied and to which they could cater for. It gave the students a sense that they could solve a business problem by applying their content knowledge in a concrete and tangible fashion.

27.6.4 Evaluation Policy

Asking the students to put in so much work during the course was not easy. Although the benefits that would be accrued on a pedagogical level was clear, it was not necessarily given that all students would be motivated enough to spend a fair amount of time outside the classroom working on various English presentations. The way in which this difficulty was tackled was two-fold. Firstly, there was an explanation to the students about the learning outcome of this policy (a point I shall come to in more detail below) and secondly that the class presentations were evaluated and these evaluations would be used to back up their final grade if there was a problem during their exam. This meant that if one member of their team had flu or was feeling unwell, or their performance was impaired in some way for an unforeseeable event, the course assessments could be used to support their grades. This motivated the students to put in the necessary work as it gave them a utilitarian reason for engaging in the learning process. It also seemed a fairer system for an oral exam so that their result did not totally rest upon those thirty minutes of performance, important though they would be.

The final piece of the picture and for the students perhaps the most critical one was to know how they, as a team, would be evaluated; that is, how their grades would break down.

Key to encouraging the students to take on board the business presentation format was the emphasis put on communication and communication skills. For them, this really meant not being afraid of grammar, pronunciation mistakes or levels of accent. Of course if the clarity of the message was inefficient due to poor language structures than that would have to be taken into account. But they were not penalized for saying 'sit' instead of 'site' or forgetting a third person singular ending. However, at degree and masters level it is unusual not to have at least a lower intermediate level of grammar. But more importantly, it created a virtuous circle in that being free from the fear of mistakes led to an increase in self-confidence and the more self-confidence they had, the fewer mistakes they made. This meant better communication all round.

In technical terms, the evaluation policy could be broken down into three items: (i) the content of the presentation, (ii) how well the students communicated their argument and (iii) the language skills. These three elements reflect the integrated skills highlighted in the introduction of this essay. In real terms it implied that what the students said and how they said it was given almost equal value as their quality of English. This was fundamental to shifting the stress away from traditional deduction of points for grammar errors to promoting communication skills. And of course, the presentation skills they had practised would benefit them by structuring and focusing their spoken performance.

27.7 ISSUES

27.7.1 Resistance

At the beginning of this talk, we looked at the different contexts in the private and public sectors. A key difference centred on student expectations. Years of experience in national education tends to shape these expectations. For example, students would have been more familiar with a text for discussion and whole class work rather than teamwork for the majority of the course. Also, most business students would have had experience of presenting in front of a class and would have already set ideas on what they could or should do. However, these preconceptions had to be reset by asking them to accept new rules for business presentations such as:

- consulting notes,
- making eye contact,
- working in a team,
- focusing on communicating a message clearly, and
- providing analysis in the content

Ultimately students were asked to discard what they had done before and to move out of their comfort zone into an unfamiliar territory. At the same time, they were asked to make decisions and act upon them. They were not given individual subjects to present but guidelines or a brief, to which they had to respond. In fact, the students were asked to be very active in the decision-making process. This was not part of their natural expectations, or at least they were not used to participating in the management of their learning on a continuous basis. Therefore, given all this new activity and responsibility, there was a predictable initial resistance on the part of some students.

27.7.2 Reinforcement

This resistance was diminished by reinforcement both by tangible means and also by putting in place psychological structures to enhance motivation. As illustrated throughout this chapter, the students were supported by the teacher with gradual content-led, task-based activities as well as language support. A series of practice presentations in class were carried out with each performance requiring an application of content and language knowledge. As the semester progressed, the presentations became more and more business-like and professional in tandem with the recognised accumulation of skills.

Reinforcing students' belief in their ability and, therefore, overcoming resistance was an important part of the course. In a way, it not only required 'convincing' students that they 'could' carry out the tasks set but also explaining 'why' they should do it.

In business language training, the teacher is accountable to the client (the learner or his company). This normal but delicate aspect of private language training does not have a big place in national education as it hints at the students evaluating the teacher's teaching ability. But in this instance, pedagogical explanation and justification to the students was a key element in overcoming initial resistance to unfamiliar methodology. Although there are currently end of semester questionnaires for students to give their opinion of the teacher, here we are really talking about language learning and the whole aspect of learning how to learn. Once students grasped why they were doing business presentations in their English course and the language and communication skills they were enhancing, a psychological shift took place that helped to reinforce their motivation and overcome resistance to new practices and routines.

27.7.3 Reward

Once the students became comfortable operating under the above new expectations, the levels of confidence and motivation were increased. They began to perceive the rewards themselves of integrating their business knowledge and language skills to formally present an idea or a project.

At the end of the semester, the primary objective of delivering a spoken English course to a large class of business students was achieved through the format of business presentations as a vehicle for integrating skills. All the students were engaged in the learning process because all of them gave four or five presentations during the course. In addition, the levels of engagement rose to the extent that students began to take ownership of their ideas. For example, some of the teams wished to keep their presentation work as potential projects for their core business subjects. This really demonstrated that the students had bought into this type of content and language-integrated learning as they could themselves appreciate the learning benefits of it.

27.8 CONCLUSION

We have looked at the way business presentations have been used with business students to promote spoken English and also discussed how the content and language-integrated skills used in private business language training can be transferred to public university education in addition to many other issues in language teaching and learning.

Firstly, business communication skills, whose goal is often associated with the private sector, can work very well in the public sector and once the students see the value of what is being proposed, they take up the challenge. However, it requires transcending the mindset of the university student away from traditional academic teaching techniques to accepting new techniques as well as new responsibilities and expectations. This may bring resistance to change and resistance to the idea that most of the 'action' lies with the student and not with the teacher. The more active the student is required to be, the more autonomous he is. It is well known that fostering autonomy often provokes an initial resistance to change. The students or learners are comfortable with the idea that the teacher teaches and the learner learns through some act of giving and taking knowledge. However, language learning is not as easy or transparent as handing over an EFL reference book; it requires some form of 'process' knowledge. Integrating skills provides a framework in which this type of 'process' knowledge can be practised.

Secondly, important demands were made on the students to come up with ideas, make decisions and carry out research in fact to take on board the necessary workload that comes with giving a series of presentations. In order to justify this, some accountability had to be given. It was important for the students to know how they were learning and why they were doing a particular task. Business students are not usually uptodate with language learning theory being themselves specialists in other disciplines. However, by taking time to explain clearly and simply the pedagogical rationale behind the course as well as the practical communication skills, they are acquiring maintained motivation and engagement. With so many demands on the time of the student with regard to study, they have a 'utilitarian' perspective to their academic careers, mirroring perhaps the focused needs and objectives so often found in the business world.

Finally, the content and language-integrated teaching which is so natural a facet of in-company language training, worked here because it is specifically attuned to a particular course. The parallels between a business student and a company employee are obvious—the former is studying to end up working within a business environment. Throughout this chapter, the link between the business world and the academic world of the business student have been highlighted. Although they may seem to be two different learning contexts, I feel that integrated communication skills, so ubiquitous in our changing world, need to be part of the language programme we offer to our students.

On a final note, the way in which language is used in the real world should have an impact on our learning environments, too. This leads us back to the initial question posed at the beginning of this essay: Why assume that business students do not want the same business communication skills as their counterparts in the business world? This does not constitute a cry to discard what we have already achieved but an argument for adaptability. With the huge demands from India and China and other parts of the world shaping EFL, it is inevitable that new methods and strategies be developed. Language teaching needs to be part of the dynamics of a world changing through technology and globalisation or it risks being left on the academic shelf.

Part 9
MULTICULTURALISM IN ESL

Chapter 28

LINGUISTIC MIGRATIONS
Teaching English in Multicultural Contexts

— Esterino Adami

The impact of massive social phenomena like globalisation and migration plays a crucial role in the pedagogic context, which nowadays may also result in the variegated composition of learning environments, quite often represented by multiethnic classes. Since economies and societies need to build the capacity required to operate in a globalised world, education systems are in a state of rapid change and extensive curriculum reforms are taking place. In particular, the multiple role of English, considered not 'merely' as a foreign language, seems to emerge as a key notion, and this new scenario evokes the profound changes that concern the people who learn English, their motives for learning it and their communicative needs as learners. Along with the 'traditional' didactic concepts of approach, method, procedure and technique, the issue of teaching English in multicultural environments should also include a series of reflections and considerations about the nature and position of the language, the different typologies of students, as well as the political and social implications in the pedagogic activity. Therefore, emphasis ought to shift from 'what' to teach to 'how' to teach, on the basis of a holistic approach that considers the whole personality and idiosyncratic features of the learner. Here I deal with certain aspects of the global dimension of English language teaching against the backdrop of the migratory transformations that deeply affect societies and countries, focusing, in particular, on English in the contemporary mixed multiethnic class.

This chapter is concerned with a specific element embedded within the spread of English as a Global Language (EGL) and its didactic practices, namely, the implicit target of transnational or cosmopolitan citizenship, a significant element and the condition that currently surfaces the pedagogic implementation of linguistic teaching, especially in the multiethnic classroom where identities and histories are juxtaposed in an effort of formal mediation. Guilherme (2007) seems to extend the potentiality of the educational core of ELT and holds:

Considering that in most cases English is a foreign and dominant language, although still related to the power-negotiation process between languages, critical English teaching/learning nowadays cannot avoid reflecting on identity and citizenship discussions as related to regional, national and transnational spheres (p. 74).

In addition, the ideological implications of ELT as a hegemonic tool of power assertion on the world scale are today challenged and reshaped by efforts of interdisciplinary rethinking, in particular, via the promotion and realisation of projects concerning international partnership and cooperation, for which English is expected to function as a 'neutral' code. The spread of English as a Global Language EGL (or ELF) should allow, at least theoretically, more and more people to access education and resources. This vision may be too unrealistically positive, and teachers and language specialists have to extend the focus of their actions and research in order to implement the possible educational values of ELT.

Let us examine the scope of English language teaching, a kind of "world educational project" (to borrow Graddol's (2006) definition), whose contours still appear controversial. Traditionally, ELT refers to two prestigious varieties: (i) British English (Received Pronunciation) and (ii) General American (GA); but, for various reasons, trends show that these models, with their emphasis on the notion, or 'myth', of the native speaker, gradually seem no longer to provide the best goals for L2 learners. As Kramsch (1998) remarks: The 'native speaker' of linguists and language teachers is, in fact, an abstraction based on arbitrarily selected features of pronunciation, grammar and lexicon, as well as on stereotypical features of appearance and demeanor. As a matter of fact, the notion itself of the 'native speaker' nowadays seems to be more problematic than precise, given the emergence of different varieties of English (e.g. Australian English, Indian English, and South African English), and although the tests which are taken most seriously measure competence in relation to native speaker norms (let us think about the Cambridge Exams, for instance), learners may show different attitudes to the language. Perhaps they do not wish to sound like native speakers but prefer to consider—and acquire—English as an International Language (EIL) or English as a Lingua Franca (ELF). People who learn English could reject typical language courses drawing on a lot of UK/USA culture and with language samples mainly using one of the two varieties since they may be interested in mastering the language for international communication. It is a rather multifaceted arena in which people have to negotiate their different social positions and sociolinguistic attitudes, switching from their mother tongue to EIL. What emerges is a conflict between mutual intelligibility and identity markers: people aim to communicate with the world through English but at the same time, they may wish to maintain their cultural aspects, like accents, lexis and other peculiar traits.

Indeed, when we investigate the context of English language teaching/

learning, it is necessary to examine the ideological implications underlying its global dimensions since English still has connections with the postcolonial discourses that continue to reproduce colonial and exonormative perspectives. For example, the textbook *The Culture Puzzle*, which in the authors' (Deena et al. 1987) intention is "designed for use in English language classes both in the U.S. and abroad". In spite of the promising subtitle (which reads *Crosscultural Communication for English as a Second Language*), the writers specify in their Preface that "by the time students finish the text, they will have a basic understanding of commonly held American culture" and, therefore, explicitly show their orientation towards native models of language and culture. However, there are some attempts to expand the book's structures and materials so as to span over "differences in communication styles across cultures" (*ibid.*). To challenge the monolithic, and ethnocentric approaches with methodologies and materials promoted by the inner circle countries (i.e. territories with English as a First Language, the UK and the USA *in primis*), scholars like Braj Kachru and Peter Strevens suggest a paradigm shift in the teaching and testing of English, to reflect that the majority of people who learn and use English today are not native speakers and do not even use it to communicate between them. Moreover, especially in multiethnic classes, questions of cultural identity should be addressed properly in an effort to mediate between conflicting interpretations of human experience, or to avoid ethnocentric perspectives. The broad scope of the teaching practice, in this case, should enable learners not only to master communicative competences, but also allow them to acquire a critical vision, viz. a cosmopolitan or intercultural education and citizenship.

If the model of ELF or EGL is adopted, the intercultural competence, conceived as the apt combination of linguistic, sociolinguistic and discourse competences, must be a primary objective on the agenda. Therefore, some linguists and psychologists prefer the notion of "intercultural speaker" instead of "native speaker," which is based not on imitation but rather on comparison. In particular, Byram (1997) argues that in the foreign language classroom, due to the concomitance of many social and cultural aspects and characteristics, it would be appropriate to introduce the model of the intercultural speaker, namely, the subject able to employ at least "two broad and related categories—first, skills of interpretation and establishing relationships between aspects of the two cultures; and second, skills of discovery and interactions" (*ibid.*: 33). Another proposal, formulated by Patrick Boylan (in Bondi 2005), is centred on the model of the 'transcultured' speaker, according to a pedagogic vision that aptly matches together the values of both language and culture. In his opinion, special emphasis should be devoted to the student's personal sphere as well as the volitional, affective and cognitive components of knowledge:

> Language learners who undergo a 'transformation of the self' do not loose their identity: indeed, by being able to express themselves with

> feeling from within the new culture, they are able to make themselves understood far less ambiguously than if their knowledge of the target language/culture had been essentially cognitive. From this privileged vantage point, they are better able to appraise—critically—both their native and their acquired cultures. (*ibid.*: 65)

Thus, primary linguistic skills are not sufficient to interact successfully, but there is a need for integrative skills such as paraphrasing, summarising, and note-taking. In the area of interlinguistic skills in particular, translation operates as a paramount strategy, in both its written and impromptu forms, bearing in mind the relevant cultural component implied in the object of the translating process. Hence, according to Rizzo (2007):

> The new trends in translation theory and practice ultimately appear to be not only involved in an inter-exchange with issues of intercultural and cross-cultural communication, but are, in most cases, concerned with matters regarding the target readership, is culture and language at a synchronic level, i.e. according to the socio-cultural and political factors at a particular point in time. (p. 62).

In the multiethnic class, the activity of translation constitutes a vital resource of mediation, intermixing the different languages and fostering a climate of mutual identification and respect.

The language policies and educational practices of multilingual territories like Singapore can be observed as innovative experiments of English teaching in multicultural settings. This theme, thus, focuses on methods and cultures, and we ought to remember that our attitudes to the language and the way it is taught mirror the cultural biases and beliefs about how we should communicate and educate each other. Where there are differing beliefs or expectations, the teaching-learning experience can become problematic, and it is worth remembering that many approaches and teaching methods are based on a very "western" idea of what constitutes "good" learning and, consequently, in mixed classes and groups of learners, this attitude may generate tension and misunderstanding (Harmer 2001).

As a matter of fact, we cannot ignore the influence of multiculturalism on the teaching profession, and we should not consider it just in terms of encounter between different language and culture systems, but rather of encounter between individuals with their own meanings and cultural references. Within an intercultural approach, therefore prominence is laid upon the ability to gather knowledge about another culture as well as the skills of empathy, management of anxiety and adaptability (including the attitudes and skills of discovery, interpretation and relating). It is also important to distinguish this kind of engagement with otherness from the "tourist" approach of collecting experiences of the "exotic" (Byram 1997; Martin and Nakayama 2001). In fact, when Edelhoff (2006) affirms "Intercultural learning is understanding" (p. 117), she refers to a wide cognitive process of decoding signs and behaviours, combined with the capacity to interact. This becomes particularly salient in the circumstances of intercultural settings where the paradigms of closeness and distance between participants in communicative acts have to be interpreted not only as spatial (geographical) terms, but especially as cultural and social terms. We should bear in mind that reaching mutual understanding is a kind of "joint production" (Ponterotto in Bondi 2005).

In the outer circle countries, where English is taught as a foreign or international language, the case of multicultural classes, characterised by the presence of children from migrant families, is very common, and here teachers have to take into account not only elements like the personalities of the students, the issue of multiple intelligences (according to the model of Howard Gardner), their motivation factors (and implicitly all the affective filters slowing or preventing the learning process), learning styles and socio-cultural backgrounds, but also the distance between the mother tongue (L1) of the students, the English language used during the lesson activities as well as the official language of the host country (their 'new' L2). Equally significant and worth noticing are the resources available to students outside the classroom—which scholars tend to define either as "inter-subjective," for example, parents, friends or recreational contexts, or "subjective" like dictionaries, and libraries—the expectations deriving from the migratory process (social collocation, economic issues), or previous learning experiences in their homelands (type of schools in the migrants' native countries).

Moreover, teachers and pedagogues should also bear in mind the wide scope of the educational relationship as well as the psychological conflicts bound to the migrant's condition. Migrant subjects (children in particular) may have experienced different teaching/learning contexts and roles, and this type of situation can be further problematic owing to the identity negotiations that crucially characterise the burden of diaspora. As Martin and Nakayama (2001) argue:

> Identities do not develop as a smooth process and are created through communication with others. Also, they are multiple and develop in different ways in different cultures. They are dynamic and may be created for us by existing social contexts and structures and in relation to group membership. (p. 93).

Therefore, in the multiethnic class, a humanistic approach must take into account the wealth of personal, social and cultural elements that make up the uniqueness of every single learner/student, with the ultimate objective to enhance their developing interlanguage and promote effective communicative success.

A case study regarding a survey carried on in secondary schools in Milan, in northern Italy (Sekulić and Trovato 2006) is given now. This study focused on the perceptions of teachers with regard to the growing presence of migrant students (born within the migrant families living in Italy) and was mainly addressed to technical or vocational schools, where the pragmatic expectations of the parents are aimed at finding a job for their children, after completing the compulsory educational path. In such situations, English is seen as a third language since students have to employ and negotiate between both their original L1 (typically in the domain of family life) and their *acquired* L2 (Italian, in this case) for their practical (utilitarian) needs. In general, these students seem to find more difficulties with scientific subjects, but they often obtain better results with foreign languages. To a certain extent, their peculiar diasporic condition appears to bring them to reflect autonomously on some linguistic strategies—the ones they often use such as code-mixing, code-switching and lexical borrowing. To a certain degree, this act of language awareness affects positively their language learning/acquisition.

Given such intricate scenario, it is clear that teachers are not likely to find a univocal didactic solution to manage multicultural classes, but they should recognise a need for a personal methodology which, starting from precise methodological indications (for instance, a humanistic, affective and communicative approach), will have to be adopted and built bearing in mind the operational context. It is a creative effort of mediation between the set syllabus, the psychological dimension of the students and the environmental characteristics. Thus, the starting point should not be the theory, the method, the technique but rather the class perceived as a network of relations and individuals within an unthreatening environment (Caon 2005).

As a consequence, teachers ought to be oriented towards an active, experiential and experimental teaching activity in order to deal with the different affective, emotional, interpersonal, sensorial, cognitive characteristics of the students—pointing out the potentialities of both the individual and the group class in the phase of knowledge building and management, and coordinating the different types of savoir. Simultaneously, the teachers and educators should be aware of the social dimensions of the pedagogic context, and encourage pupils to develop their linguistic, cognitive, social, cultural and intercultural competences. This type of teaching, within an intercultural perspective, deems not only the 'products' (namely, the linguistic goals achieved by the students) but also the 'processes' through which students learn and approach the different topics. Consequently, the levels of motivation and self-reflection will increase and lead to student autonomy, emphasising the whole process of language acquisition. The methods and procedures can range from peer groups to self-learning (for instance, with materials like CD-ROMs) or the creation of interdisciplinary programmes. In so doing, the intercultural approach expresses, to a certain degree, its closeness to the methodology of Communicative Language Teaching (CLT) and its learner-centred focus, advocated by many scholars and linguists like Brumfit or Prabhu. Communicative and intercultural, activities are based on a desire to communicate, with special attention to the content and not the form, the varieties of the language and the communicative purpose. However, this kind of approach, with emphasis on the exposure to language in use and the importance given to linguistic functions, is sometimes criticised inasmuch as it highlights fluency excessively and does not concern proper formal accuracy.

Both productive and receptive skills (respectively, speaking/writing and reading/listening) have to be trained, but rather than drilling and repetition (i.e., the old-fashioned audio-lingual method; see Derrick 1966) that usually make the class a 'dull' place, for instance, the teachers could use task-based activities and then try to enhance attitudes like curiosity and openness in a measured and controlled way. We certainly should not condemn or abolish learning by rote *in toto* as it can be effective, but it is essential that it is included within a balanced methodological approach, benefiting from several didactic strategies. Teaching in a multicultural perspective may also draw from the Humanist Approach (let us think about Abraham Maslow) by considering the learner's feelings as important as their mental or cognitive abilities. Within such perspective (elaborated by Carl Rogers), the affective filters, that is the mental mechanisms that block that input from being absorbed and processed, students need to feel that what they learn is personally relevant to them. Thus, they have to be encouraged to speak about themselves in terms of personal identity, emotions and self-knowledge, although too personal or intimate questions have to be avoided while the teacher has to monitor the class constantly to mediate cultural, social, religious or personal conflicts. In multilingual contexts (India, for example), the teacher becomes the facilitator of the communicative processes as well as the needs analyst, the counsellor and the process manager. What emerges is a multiple role for the teacher, having to face radical transformations in the fast-changing global world/classroom.

Furthermore, it is significant to consider that the attention and time dedicated to migrant students is not of detriment to the rest of the class, but rather they can represent a fruitful chance to explore more complex themes with their cognitive, linguistic, social and cultural implications. In a multicultural approach, it is possible to promote the notion of difference considered not as a limiting threat, but as a source of new reciprocal learning. Let us briefly expand our issue: if we compare the dynamics of speakers' interactions in multiethnic settings with conversations held between the native and non-native speakers, interesting considerations arise. Research shows that typically native speakers tend to dominate conversations involving non-natives and natives, but recently scholars have noticed that this does not always occur, and that possibly non-native speakers can perform a central role in speech acts. Therefore, other variables affect communication when participants vie for the floor and the cultural weight in verbal interaction is prominent. As Ponterotto (in Bondi 2005) suggests,

> Negative stereotypes of cultural differences, including national, ethnic and gender-related attributions, will ghost, so-to-speak, interlocutors' cognitive representations and discourse strategies. (p. 262)

In pedagogic multiethnic and mixed contexts, the teachers cannot run the above risks and they have to elaborate methods for managing cultural conflicts and activate cooperation in the participant communication in order to negotiate a common breakdown. As teachers and language specialists, we also need to balance the interests of individuals against what is good for the group and to be aware of certain individual traits when putting students into pairs or groups. Teachers need to recognise those students who need more personal attention than others and those who need different kinds of explanations and practices of language. A personalised type of teaching, integrated within a wider didactic plan, can have a positive impact on the learning process and result.

Finally, it is important to underscore that teaching and learning constitute a contract between two parties for which both need to agree the terms. It is not a one-sided affair. Teachers need to understand the students' needs and expectations just as much as they are ready to adapt or change their own methodological beliefs. However, this does not necessarily mean that they just have to abandon their own theories because the students are not used to what their teachers want to do. Instead, some kind of accommodation has to be reached between what the two parties want and expect. It may mean, for example, starting gradually rather than with an instantaneous change. If the students are not used to giving instant opinions in class, for example, teachers can introduce the procedure gradually. Adopting accommodation between two cultures (which may involve moderating beliefs, and making comparisons) is part of what all teachers are required to do. In conclusion, we all should subscribe to Scrivener's (2005) remark:

> As language teachers, we are privileged to work with a vital and fascinating subject matter. Language is the way we express our very being. It is the way we come to terms with the world. It is the way we make our understanding of life concrete. It is the way we make contract with other human beings. (p. 380)

Within a multicultural perspective, the sociolinguistic and didactic context becomes even more challenging, but, at the same time, extremely rewarding if we project the value of education onto the future.

REFERENCES

Bondi, Marina, Maxwell, Nick (Eds.), *Cross-Cultural Encounters: Linguistic Perspective*, Rome: Officina Edizioni, 2005.

Byram, Michael, *Teaching and Assessing Intercultural Communicative Competence,* Clevedon: Multilingual Matters, 1997.

Caon, Fabio, "Didattica della lingua in classi multietniche e plurilivello: problemi e risorse," *LEND* **XLIII** (2005): 13–20.

Deena, R. Levine, Baxter, Jim, and McNulty, Piper, *The Cultural Puzzle, Cross-Cultural Communication for English as a Second Language*, Englewood Cliffs, New Jersey: Prentice Hall, 1987.

Derrick, June, *Teaching English to Immigrants*, London: Longman, 1966.

Edelhoff, Christoph, "Across borders—Understanding and communicating, Tasks for language teaching and learning in a wider and multicultural Europe", *LEND* **XXXV** 2006: 113–133.

Graddol, David, *English Next*, London: The British Council, 2006.

Guilherme, Manuela, "English as a global language and education for cosmopolitan citizenship," *Language and Intercultural Communication* **7**.1, 2007: 72–90.

Harmer, Jeremy, *The Practice of English Language Teaching*, Harlow, Essex: Pearson, 2001.

Kramsch, Claire, *Context and Culture in Language Teaching*, Oxford: Oxford University Press, 1996.

_____, *Language and Culture*, Oxford: Oxford University Press, 1998.

Martin, N. Judith and Nakayama, Thomas K., *Experiencing Intercultural Communication*, New York: McGraw-Hill Hinger Education, 2001.

Rizzo, Alessandra, *English across Disciplines*, Rome: Aracne, 2007.

Scrivener, Jim, *Learning Teaching*, Oxford: Macmillan, 2005.

Sekulić, Tatjana and Sara Trovato, "Studenti stranieri: una nuova sfida nella secondaria di secondo grado", *LEND* **XXXV**, 2006: 35–43.

Strevens, Peter, *Teaching English as an International Language*, Oxford: Pergamon, 1980.

Chapter 29

IDENTITY MAINTENANCE FOR NON NATIVE SPEAKERS OF ENGLISH

— Rebecca Belchamber

29.1 INTRODUCTION

Globalization affects a disparate yet interconnected range of elements in society; one of these is the English language. In the 21st century, English is evolving at an unprecedented rate. The native speakers must meet the challenge of keeping apace with these changes; for learners of English, there are added difficulties. This chapter considers the personal challenges of learning English as a Foreign Language (EFL). This issue is explored through an examination of the demands on the learner. To narrow the discussion, two aspects are examined: (i) the concept of identity and (ii) the ability to communicate effectively using English.

Identity, or a sense of self, is partly derived from group membership and often this arises from a sense of attachment to an ethnic or cultural group. The notion of culture and ethnicity will be examined with a view to how it relates to identity and the culture-language relationship. As one learns a foreign language, there can be a shift in this identity, either strengthening or weakening. When this language is English, the influence can be all the more widespread because of its popularity. However, identity need not be compromised with the learning of English. Finally, there is the aspect of communication; we consider the communication successful if the message, as intended by the sender, is understood by the recipient. What does it mean when the communication involves someone for whom English is not the L1 or when both/all those involved are not native speakers of English? This has implications for both the development of English and the practice of ELT.

Throughout the discussion, some alternative practices are reviewed, suggesting that learning EFL need not always cost the individual. The learner's readiness to compromise and the willingness of the dominant culture to accommodate can result in benefits and advantages to all concerned.

29.2 LANGUAGE, CULTURE AND IDENTITY

There are many ways of approaching the language-culture relationship. Does language construct culture or is it a means by which attitudes and practices are perpetuated? Alternatively, is language merely a reflection of culture? Miller (2004) deals with the broad perspective, noting that many language-related disciplines acknowledge that language is a means of self-representation which impacts on identity in a social setting.

Loveday (1982) defines culture as the subconscious knowledge of a society which enables its members to function according to the society's expectations. He argues strongly that language-culture interdependence does exist. Fishman (1999) claims language is a significant facet within the totality that contributes towards ethnicity. Wierzbicka (1985) investigates the speech acts and lexical choices of Polish and English speakers and illustrates how these reflect culturally-valued traits such as directness and intimacy. The issue of learning, or functioning in, a second language provides examples of the language-identity connection. Influences on identity are examined by Miller (2004) in a three-year study of 10 high school students from non-English speaking backgrounds. The challenges to identity involve changes in opportunity, and he explores this in relation to social contacts, chances to use the English language and the risk-taking behaviour with the L2:

> Being heard and acknowledged as a speaker of English, determines the extent to which a student may participate in social interactions, negotiation, and practices within the educational institution and in the wider society. (p. 294)

In another example, Bhatt (1990) describes how, after a visit to his birthplace Gujarat in Western India, he returned to England and found himself omitting to say please and being abrupt during service encounters. More tellingly, while in Gujarat, he hired a taxi and gave instructions in his native language. When the driver appeared to ignore the directions, Bhatt began to question his own competence in Gujarati. Then he realised that he had issued the instruction in Gujarati but overlaid it with an English communicative pattern—a command in the form of a request. The driver had expected him to be more direct.

Accepting that there is a strong language-culture connection, what happens as one begins to acquire a foreign or second language? Loveday (1982: 22) suggests that the process involves an intrusion on one's sense of ethnic identity. One response, according to Freeman (1998), is to redefine the negative characteristics. Where speech styles had been considered a mark of inferiority, the ingroup comes to take pride in its language variety. The reverse of this is to align with the outgroup, to assimilate, in an effort to gain a more positive social identity (that which is valued by the dominant society). These very different strategies strengthen or weaken the sense of ethnic identity and relate to the learner's orientation towards the L2.

The issue of integrative orientation is cited by Loveday (1982) as being relevant to L2 learning as linguistic aptitude. However, this is claimed to operate best when there is no threat to the status of the L1 community. In other circumstances, described by Loveday, the learner may deny knowledge of their L1 when in the wider community, associating it with a devalued culture; alternatively, the learner may deny knowledge of their L2 considering it a betrayal of community values. Both cases are an imbalanced reaction to the idea of integration, resulting in a loss of identity and opportunity, respectively. In some cases, there may also be an actual loss of the L1 due to a lack of institutional support for its maintenance. Muhlhausler (1994) argues that the spread of a minority of privileged languages occurs at the expense of a number of smaller, less powerful languages, resulting in the increased dependency of the learner. He asserts that bilingual education is merely transitional, leading to monolingualism in the dominant language by the final years of schooling though it could be argued that bilingual programmes prevent this. The loss of L1 would naturally have an impact on the sense of identity.

The above situations reflect a variety of cultural attitudes, both individual and community, which play a significant role in the sociolinguistics of learning. It is this area which both the target and learner's community needs to reappraise if the learner is to profit and not lose from the experience of acquiring an L2. These attitudes intertwine with our perceptions of what is acceptable English and appropriate ELT practice.

While not everyone learns English in the classroom, it is the place where many people are first exposed to a uniform or institutionally sanctioned, attitude to English teaching. Barrow (in Harrison 1990: 9) refers to teaching ELT as a service and a potential advantage. He claims that cultural imperialism is impossible (an exaggeration of our humble efforts), but nevertheless suggests it is inevitable and desirable. He sits at the functional end of the sociological continuum, ignoring the aspects of the power relations in society. If, for some groups, English is a key to new opportunities, a genuine "potential advantage," then it is to be welcomed. But if it is a means of maintaining the status quo (a workforce of menial labourers and a passive society), then the costs will be too great.

29.3 ATTITUDES TOWARDS STANDARD ENGLISH

In the next section I will look at some of the ways ELT is approached and the possible consequences are looked at. The spread of the English language, and ELT, originated in the colonial period as a means of facilitating centralized control, according to Phillipson (1988, in Pennycook 1989). The notion of a standard form of English developed as a model and a goal for learners. Over time, a normative philosophy towards the language emerged and any deviation was considered as an error or an aberration. Loveday (1982) argues that adherence to institutional norms conflicts with the need of the learner, which is to convey meaning immediately rather than to conform flawlessly.

This approach prevails in some classrooms where the lessons are more an exercise in problem-solving (grammar translation or manipulating structures) than communicating, and in some sections of the community where the non-standard forms are stigmatised. Both reactions hinder the learner's progress. In the classroom, this attitude can present as overcorrection instead of an informed teacher respecting the existence of interlanguage as essential to language development. In the community, a non-native speaker might be singled out (criticized or mocked) for their accent, turn of phrase or perceived lack of communicative competence.

However, citizens of some countries where English is an L2, and also is the lingua franca, have accepted that standard English is beyond realistic expectation and manage well with a local variety. Loveday (1982) cites the example of the broadcasting authorities and a school department head in Ghana who wanted their announcers and students, respectively, to sound like Ghanaians when speaking English. This is not always the case. How much better it would be for society to acknowledge that different varieties are acceptable so that all citizens have an opportunity to contribute rather than discriminating and marginalising sectors of the community.

The comments above relate to an overall approach to language; now I want to narrow the discussion to language features and aspects of ELT. We can find that, in both these realms, the learners may be disadvantaged by being outside the dominant sphere. Regarding language features, how standard should we expect students to be? Does it matter when students use the expression, for example, "Can I make a friend with you?" The meaning is clear and that is the ultimate goal after all.

There is so much a learner needs to master, so should we demand more than mutual intelligibility? This debate prompts Graddol (2006) to suggest that there may be a shift in the definition of what makes acceptable practitioners of ELT. Those who were once regarded as providing the authoritative standard and were seen as the best teachers now may be seen as a hindrance to the free development of global English. Graddol argues that native speaker teachers may not possess some of the skills required by learners, such as translation and interpreting. Also, he suggests that aspiring to the native speaker model makes it more costly and challenging to train teachers and as a result:

> In several Asian countries, the definition of 'native speaker teacher' has been relaxed to include teachers from India and Singapore. This ... represents a re-evaluation of the needs and aspirations of learners. (p. 115).

Ignoring this shift, or playing the part of a pedant, we are doing a disservice to learners and to ELT generally.

It is the non-native speaking (NNS) ELTs who should be accorded more recognition and be sought as a resource for the change in methodology that accompanies the reality of global English. Unfortunately, according to Seidlhofer (1999, cited in Ranta 2004), many non-native English teachers acknowledge the feelings of ineptitude or lack of self-confidence regarding their English language ability. Yet they are the very people who are best placed to empathise with, and be a model for, their students. Ranta (2004) discusses the positive attributes of NNS English teachers. Liu and Zhang (2007) list Medgyes's six positive characteristics of this group:

They (1) provide a good learner model to their students, (2) are able to teach language strategy very effectively, (3) are able to provide more information about the language to their students, (4) understand the difficulties and needs of the students, (5) are able to anticipate and predict language difficulties, and (6) can (in EFL settings) use the students' native language to their advantage.

Teaching approaches and the expectations on the learner are an area where demands are made based on valued behaviors. The communicative approach is currently promoted in many Western teaching situations. McKnight (1994) illustrates how this is disorientating for the Chinese learners, who are accustomed to the grammar translation approach. A further difference is the innovation, creativity and critical thinking encouraged by the Western educators compared with the rote learning and reproduction valued by the Chinese. Woodley (2007) argues that memorisation and chanting are legitimate methods of learning.

Without sensitive and accommodating teachers, it is often the L2 learner's ability to reconcile the conflicts they encounter which has a bearing on the success or failure of their goal, which is learning English. If unable to adjust, a personal cost will be their lack of linguistic competence and the social or economic disadvantages which follow. What is called for is a restructuring of a sense of self to deal with shifting realities. This should be a two-way process.

29.4 IMPLICATIONS FOR EDUCATORS

In this section, I briefly mention some of the solutions proposed by a selection of writers, many of whom adopt the critical perspective in which they suggest the empowerment of teachers and learners in the face of linguistic imperialism and its consequences. We have already seen in Section 29.3 that discrimination and criticism are the result of favouring the dominant patterns and cultural practices. How can we, as teachers, make learning EFL a positive, rewarding and enriching experience? Corson (1992) refers to the arguments of Pierre Bourdieu concerning the interdependence of language, power and education and suggests that discourses of resistance may be successful in counteracting the dominant ideologies. The aim is reciprocal power relations, or emancipation, which can only be achieved when the communication setting has validity for all participants. According to Corson (*ibid.*):

> Validity allows all participants to expect and receive truth, sincerity, appropriateness and comprehensibility in the exchange of all messages (p. 249).

This can operate at the level of school organisation, pedagogy or curriculum.

Corson offers a philosophical blueprint for change at the institutional level but I would question how realistic it is. Even Corson refers to it as an ideal setting. There are other smaller, albeit significant, changes which can be implemented at an individual level. The most obvious is the teacher's sensitisation to linguistic imperialism, and its implications. With this awareness, they can, as Loveday (1982) says:

> Be a skilled and sensitive cross-cultural interpreter capable of reducing the learners' ethnocentrism without damaging their self-image (p. 49).

Muhlhausler (1994) argues that the solution lies in adopting an ecological perspective, considering the effects of the introduction of English on both the other languages and their speakers. He states that the focus should be on the well being of the inhabitants and the maintenance of their language system; therefore, language teaching should empower the learners "by giving them knowledge and skills additional to rather than the replacement of what they already have" (p. 129).

In her account of L2 identity construction in Chicano literature, Solé (2004) comes to the conclusion that identities are dynamic, no longer constrained by geographical boundaries. They can be fluid and multiple; moreover, an L2 speaker has the potential to evolve a new identity using the foundations of their original one, but adding other dimensions. This is where the ELT teacher can be a positive support.

The goal here is cultural transformation. Auerbach and Burgess (1985) suggest that this can be achieved through a problem-posing approach where the learners are encouraged to examine issues in their lives, respond critically and act in a way to improve the situation, and so create a culture which is meaningful for them. Giroux (1983b, in Auerbach and Burgess 1985) states that the knowledge we give students has to be made problematic, and then discussed. This adds another dimension to the indoctrinating-informing continuum suggested earlier—not only should we inform students but we should develop critical thinking and promote debate.

Pennycook (1989) advocates Giroux and McLaren's (1989) concept of the teacher as a transformative intellectual, examining the power relationships that have a bearing on our practices and the social lives of our students, and acting as an agent to facilitate a more equitable society and a more significant culture (be it at the classroom level or in the wider community) for the students. To this end, culture teaching is promoted as an essential aspect of foreign language education. Thanasoulas (2001) reminds us that learning a language is more than acquiring knowledge of its linguistic forms, and that the goal of teaching culture involves more than conveying factual information about the target language group. He argues that the real communicative competence cannot be achieved without an insight into the speaker's culture. If our communicative aim understands, we need to be aware of those aspects which will either refine or hinder the interaction.

In our efforts to expose the English language students to other cultures and encourage their critical response, we must also remember that they need to explore their own culture *in English*. Lou and Chism (2005) make this point with respect to Taiwan, noting that most EFL teachers there rely on American textbooks. As a result, the Taiwanese students can discuss the world or specific American cultural features, but are less able to talk about their own culture because it has not been addressed in the classroom.

Graddol (2006) endorses a specific language-based approach to the necessity to interact in English, English as a Lingua Franca:

> Proponents of teaching English as a lingua franca (ELF) suggest that the way English is taught and assessed should reflect the needs and aspirations of the ever-growing number of non-native speakers who use English to communicate with other non-natives (p. 87).

A core principle is intelligibility, rather than native like accuracy. I recall a comment from a Korean student, who said that it was easier to understand other EFL students than a native speaker, because there was not so much linking of sounds! This observation is reinforced by van Essen (2004) who commented that NNSs may be encouraged as they are often better understood by one another than they understand NSs.

Once the notion of ELF has been accepted, it needs to be applied to curricula and classrooms alike. Two significant areas that have been researched are lexico-grammatical and phonological features by Seidlhofer and Jenkins (2005), respectively. Jenkins lists Seidlhofer's suggestions which are all based on the common errors that occupy much teaching time yet do not really impede communication, such as 'dropping' the third person present tense -s (as in 'She look very sad'). Jenkins proposes for example, the substitution of voiceless and voiced 'th' with /t/ or /s/ and /d/ or /z/ (so that 'think' becomes 'sink' or 'tink', and 'this' becomes 'dis' or 'zis'), for the same reason.

Another dimension to the focus on usage rather than perceived standards is reflected in the growing relevance of English corpora research. One example of practical use to the course book writers and teachers is the area of idioms. There seems to be an overwhelming number, yet reference to corpus studies can guide us as to the frequency of particular idioms and so inform our teaching choices.

Finally, Ranta (2004) refers to Seidlhofer's (2001) criticism that the actual practices in English language classrooms are lagging behind the changes that have occurred surrounding TEFL on a more theoretical level. Teachers acknowledge that English is an international language but have not built this notion into their lessons. There are many teachers still advocating native-speaker accuracy, and using texts where the content is predominately based on the native-speaker culture. Ranta discusses the situation in Finland and notes that despite the independence in producing English textbooks for Finnish students, there is still a long way to go. Yamaguchi (2002) outlines the issue of English in Japan and advocates that teachers should be preparing students across the range of varieties (e.g. International English, Standard English, Regional English, and Internet English) so they can make a choice depending on the situation.

To return to the notion of teaching culture, this is another area where the rhetoric is not in line with what actually happens. Sercu, Garcia and Prieto (2004) examined the Spanish EFL teachers and the degree to which they could be said to teach intercultural communicative competence. They concluded that although teachers were in favour of intercultural objectives, their teaching cannot yet claim to fully address that aim.

29.5 CONCLUSION

The above discussion reveals some potential costs related to learning EFL. Assuming a language-culture connection, learning a dominant language can often result in a loss of cultural identity or a struggle to maintain it. Other issues include discrimination, a loss of opportunity and self-esteem. Finally, there can be adverse effects on L2 development.

To counteract this, the students, educators and researchers need to be sensitized to alternative cultural values, to examine them critically and question whose interests are served. By examining the conventions of communication, sociolinguistics has come a long way in demystifying language, pointing out that there are many possibilities available to English speakers. Our particular conventions contribute to our identity, and sharing them within the group reinforces this. However, making them available to EFL speakers offers group membership to a wider community. Also, valuing the practices of other groups enlarges the community even further.

Began by inquiring into the challenges and conflicts surrounding learning EFL in this age of globalization, I would like to conclude the discussion with another question: What are the costs to us all, as global citizens, when the L2 speakers are marginalized and not given the opportunity to participate in, and contribute to, society?

REFERENCES

Auerbach, E.R. and Burgess, D., "The hidden curriculum of survival ESL," *TESOL Quarterly* **19**.3 (1985): 475–496.

Barrow, R., "Culture, values and the language classroom," *Culture and the Language Classroom: ELT Documents 132*, B. Harrison (Ed.), London: MEP and the British Council, 1990.

Bhatt, A., "A visit to Gujarat: A linguistic odyssey," *Culture and the Language Classroom*; *ELT Documents 132*, B. Harrison (Ed.), London: MEP and the British Council, 1990.

Corson, D., "Language, power and minority schooling," *Language and Education* 6. 2, 3 and 4 (1992): 231–253.

Essen, A., van, "The rise and role of English as an international language: Some educational consequences," *Humanising Language Teaching* **6**.4 (November 2004).

Fishman, J., *Handbook of Language and Ethnic Identity*, New York: Oxford University Press, 1999.

Freeman, R.D. *Bilingual Education and Social Change*, Multilingual Matters. Clevedon: United Kingdom, 1998.

Graddol, D., *English Next: Why Global English May Mean the End of 'English as a Foreign Language,'* 2006. Accessed December 24, 2007. http://www.britishcouncil.org/learning-research-english-next.pdf

Jenkins, J., "ELF at the gate: The position of english as a lingua franca," *Humanising Language Teaching* **7**.2 (2005). Retrieved June 7, 2008. http://www.hltmag.co.uk/mar05/idea.htm

Liu, M. and Zhang, L., "Student perceptions of native and non-native English teachers' attitudes, teaching skills assessment and performance," *Asian EFL Journal*, 2007. Accessed February 14, 2008. http://www.asian-efl-journal.com/Dec_2007_ml&lz.php

Lou, W. and Chism, R., "Integrating Chinese culture into the EFL classroom," *Academic Exchange Quarterly*, 2005. Accessed June 1, 2008. http://goliath.ecnext.com/coms2/gi_0199-5322541/Integrating-Chinese-culture-into-the.html

Loveday, L., *The Sociolinguistics of Learning and Using a Non-native Language*, New York: Pergamon Press, 1982.

McKnight, A., "Chinese learners of English: A different view of literacy," *Open Letter* **4**.2 (1994): 39–52.

Miller, J., "Identity and language use: The politics of speaking ESL in schools," *Negotiation of Identities in Multilingual Contexts*, A. Pavlenko and A. Blackledge (Eds.), Clevedon, UK: Multilingual Matters, 2004.

Muhlhausler, P., "Language teaching—Linguistic imperialism?," *ARAL* **17**.2 (1994): 121–130.

Pennycook, A., "The concept of method, interested knowledge, and the politics of language teaching," *TESOL Quarterly* **23**.4 (1989): 589–618.

Ranta, E., *International English—A Future Possibility in the Finnish EFL Classroom?*," 2004. Accessed February 14, 2008. http://www.uta.fi/laitokset/kielet/engf/research/elfa/research_er.pdf

Sercu, L., Méndez Garcia, M.C. and Castro Prieto, P., *Culture Teaching in Foreign Language Education, EFL Teachers in Spain as Cultural Mediators*, 2004. Accessed June 1, 2008 www.ugr.es/~portalin/articulos/PL_numero1/sercu.pdf

Solé, C., "Autobiographical accounts of L2 identity construction in Chicano literature," *Language and Intercultural Communication* **4**.4 (2004). Accessed June 1, 2008. http://www.multilingual-matters.net/laic/004/0229/laic0040229.pdf

Thanasoulas, D., "*The Importance of Teaching Culture in the Foreign Language Classroom*," 2001. Accessed June 1, 2008. http://radicalpedagogy.icaap.org/content/issue3_3/7-thanasoulas.html

Wierzbicka, A., "Different cultures, different languages, different speech acts," *Journal of Pragmatics* **9** (1985): 145–178.

Woodley, C., *Quality Matters Offshore: Issues in Vet and ELT in China*, 2007. Accessed January 6, 2008. http://www.idp.com/aiec/papers/Woodley%20Fri%201220%20B6.pdf.

Yamaguchi, C., "Towards international English in EFL classrooms in Japan," *The Internet TESL Journal* **8**.1 (2002). Accessed February 16, 2008. http://iteslj.org/Articles/Yamaguchi-Language.html

Chapter 30

PURSUING A POST-METHOD PEDAGOGY IN ENGLISH LANGUAGE INSTRUCTION IN INDIA

— MIGUEL MANTERO AND SIKARINI MAJUMDAR

30.1 INTRODUCTION

At the heart of every educational policy lie the questions: 'What is important to learn?' followed by 'How it would be best learned?' The same remains true while planning language policy in the field of education. Based on the state's approach to education, the curriculum is structured in order to build cohesion among philosophy, policy and pedagogy. This informs curriculum structuring and teaching methodology in the best possible ways to carry them out.

This research study examined the change in teaching methodology after a state in India reinstated English in the public schools in 2004, claiming globalization as the major reason. It offers a critique of the strategies employed by teachers which they identified as communicative methodology in teaching English as additional language, with the question: What and whose purpose is being served by the implementation of the present methodology?

The introduction of communicative methodology in teaching English as the compulsory, additional language, in the state of West Bengal in India made us examine 'how pedagogy helps in achieving the overall philosophical and policy goals of the Indian education as mentioned by the National Council of Education Research and Training (NCERT[1])' (NCERT 2005).

The results of this study will inform the Board of Secondary Education in West Bengal whether the methodology is consistent with the educational philosophy of the country as a whole and the language policy outlined in the Constitution of India. It will hopefully create a more informed approach to education under the current pressures of globalization and, perhaps, even offer

---
1. NCERT is an apex resource organization set up by the Government of India, with headquarters at New Delhi, to assist and advise the Ministry of Education and Social Welfare, the Central and State governments in the implementation of its policies and major programs in the field of education, particularly school education.

some insight to English as second language (ESL) policy and pedagogy in the U.S.

30.2 ENGLISH IN INDIA

India has a long history of teaching and learning English. The official introduction of English in India's education began during the British rule, with Macaulay's *Minute of 1835*. But even after the Independence, English remains to hold the position of associate official language of the country and serves the important role of the link language in this multilingual country. It is also an important language in the fields of education, business, commerce, law and finance. So, it is not surprising that "India has the third largest English-using population in the world, after the USA and the UK" (Hohenthal 2003). English has also been the language of the élite, of the administration, and of the pan-Indian press and, thus, a language associated with power.

The language policy in education (K-12) follows a 'Three-Language Formula' which includes:

1. Mother tongue or regional language—13 years
2. Official language—Hindi or English—8 years minimum
3. Other modern Indian or foreign language—3 years minimum (Khubchandani: 1981: 14). Khubchandani comments that the choice of second and third languages is very closely related to "the issues of languages privileges, cultural prestige, and socio-economic mobility".

As English serves a variety of purpose in the Indian context, most public schools have introduced English as an additional language to be learned from the first grade or Class I. In 1983, the ruling left-front government of West Bengal abolished the teaching of English in its primary/elementary schools citing reasons of educational equity and accessibility issues (Roy 2003). This gave rise to English-medium private schools and private coaching centres for teaching English (even in rural areas) and defeated the entire purpose of the Government's policy of establishing 'equal educational opportunity'. Increased loss of academically promising students from public schools and continued parental pressure forced the state government to establish a committee for solving the matter.

Based on the report of the first committee headed by Professor Pabitra Sarkar, the government announced that English was formally to be taught from Class III or the third grade from the scholastic year 2000–2001. The committee referred to economic liberalization and globalization as the two main reasons for bringing back English in the primary/elementary schools. (Sarkar Report 1998):

> ... the opening-up of the country's economy to foreign multi-national and trans-national corporations as a precondition for economic liberalization, has also contributed to the high profile of English which it enjoys (p. 35).

Later, under the recommendation of Prof. Ranjugopal Mukhopadhyay Committee on school education, English was decided to be reintroduced in Class I or the first grade. Anindita Chaudhuri on page one of *The Statesman* of 10 January 2004 reported:

> ... the state school education minister said today that English would be taught from Class I as the second compulsory language from the session beginning May 2004.

The report further added:

> When asked why the government felt it necessary to change its earlier decision of not teaching English at the primary level, Mr. Biswas, the State School Education Minister justified the reversal of policy, saying "the priorities have changed .... When we came to power, our priority was universal education .... He also felt that with the winds of change setting in with globalization and the advancement in IT, the need to communicate in English has acquired greater importance (Scrase, 2004: 10).

Hence, English was reinstated in public schools from Class I and communicative methodology was chosen for teaching English as an additional language.

30.3 PRIOR APPROACH TO TEACHING ENGLISH

The study of English literature became part of the Indian curriculum in the 1820s (Viswanathan 1990: 2) and served "the imperial mission of educating and civilising colonial subjects in the literature and thought of England"—in order to create a group of people who would be Indian in looks but British in thoughts and culture. She further insisted that the English literature was introduced to correct the negative view of the English colonial masters' behaviour (in Engler 2000). To establish the English as a cultured and superior race and continue having a mutually beneficial relationship[2] with the educated and influential Indian population it was necessary for them to do so. Even after Independence, the study of English literature continued along with the grammar and language. Authentic texts written mostly by the British writers were introduced to teach the cultural aspect of English and the use of grammar in writing. English continued to be studied as a compulsory second language that also met the requirement of foreign language education. Critically evaluated:

> English still commands authority *in absentia*, however lightly; it continues to be a powerful instrument of sociopolitical control ... in a country of 332 million illiterates (1991 Census of India) (Chandran 1996).

---

2. Personal trade relations were established between the English and the powerful Indians.

Educators kept the study of literature as:

> It can be especially valuable in generating intellectual growth, aesthetic appreciation, and an understanding of how experiences of people in the past and present can be represented (Cox 1991; West 1994 in Sivasubramaniam 2006).

Normally, in the English as an additional language classroom dialogic interaction remained missing and is still absent in the schools of Kolkata. Educators, thus, used literary texts as a source for developing students' imagination, and to have interactions and discussions based on them (Collie and Slater 1987; Duff and Maley 1990; McRae 1991). Since, text is considered both "a spoken and written language produced in discursive event" (Floriani 1994 in Mantero 2003), it opens up space for students to appropriate language leading to cognitive development.

The study of both language and literature in the additional language aided students to contextualize the form learnt in their grammar classes. Literature exposed the students to a linguistic culture foreign to them while providing them the opportunity to use the language contextually as experienced from reading the 'text'. It provided a chance to experience and see the world using a different pair of lenses, apart from their L1 culture that paved the way for understanding cultural differences without judging them.

30.4 COMMUNICATIVE APPROACH TO LANGUAGE TEACHING

The idea of communicative competence has been a foundational concept in the realm of L2 acquisition (Mantero 2006). Hymes' (1972) article titled "On Communicative Competence" that delivered the catch-phrase was written in order to reveal the limitation of the Chomskyan distinction between competence and performance. Hymes argued that communicative competence should be a crucial element in any linguistic theory. Since, the function of language is communication, "a pedagogically adequate grammar must at least take communication into account" (Thurgood 1981) in language teaching. Canale and Swain (1980) developed Hymes' concept that involved interaction among grammatical, psycholinguistics, socio-cultural and probabilistic sub-systems. Canale (1983) referred to communicative competence as "the underlying systems of knowledge and skill required for communication". Because communication takes place in a social setting and is a continuous process of meaning-making and negotiation, it becomes a part of sociolinguistics.

Different people have interpreted communicative language teaching differently (Savignon 1984; Harmer 1982). The meaning stretches from 'functional approach' and the use of 'notional-functional' materials to 'learner-centered' or increased learner participation in various activities (Savignon 1984). The diverse interpretation and opinion expressed on communicative language teaching are enough to create ample confusion for teachers to understand what it really means. But what is apparent from all the different interpretations is that the aim of communicative language teaching is to combine both the functional and structural aspects of language in a systematic way in order to fulfill the goal of foreign language teaching: communicative ability (Littlewood 1981). In addition, the very word 'communicative' indicates the presence of a speaker and a hearer processing language, negotiating and making meanings within a particular social context. So, it is evident that "language carries not only *functional* meaning, it also carries *social* meaning" (*ibid.*).

Berns (1984) identified the linguistic tradition of Sweet (1899), Jones (1917, 1918), and Firth (1957) as the functional approach to language teaching that observes language functioning in both linguistic and social or situational contexts and is based on an interest in performance or actual language use. With regard to the 'use' of language would mean interaction among persons, one person with him/herself and/or text and would follow Savignon's (1983) idea of communicative competence as "the expression, interpretation, and negotiation of meaning". This is a reflection of Hymes (1971) and Halliday's (1978) sociolinguistic approaches.

30.5 FORM IN COMMUNICATIVE LANGUAGE TEACHING

After examining the empirical studies conducted by Savignon (1972), Tucker (1974), and Upshur and Palmer (1974), Canale and Swain (1980) concluded that at the initial stage of L2 learning, neither meaning making nor grammatical accuracy should be given more importance than the other. Thus, some combination of emphasis on grammatical accuracy and emphasis of meaningful communication from the very beginning of language study is suggested. The focus on aspects of grammar should be based on the specific needs of learners at a given stage. Oller and Obrecht's (1968) stated, "... that from the very beginning of a second language program, aspects of grammatical competence should be taught in the context of meaningful communication". From a practical viewpoint, we could say that some learners would be unable to use the language without being comfortable in using the grammatical form. This would force us to consider the introduction of specific grammatical forms related to particular communicative functions and the learners' sociolinguistic needs in that particular context.

30.6 LITERACY IN ENGLISH AS SECOND LANGUAGE

An important issue that we need to take into account in the learning and teaching of an additional language is literacy. Since listening, speaking, reading, and writing are simultaneously introduced, it becomes necessary to teach "language-based strategies and skills that will later develop into literacy-based language proficiency" (Carrell 1992; Carrell et al. 1993; Mantero 2006). Arguably, the involvement of our psychological mechanism in determining how we communicate in different contexts and involve various strategies in producing both spoken and written languages requires more literacy-based instruction and less communicative approaches (Verhoeven 1994, Mantero 2006). Application of this methodology was made by Kern (2000) to ensure the expansion of the students' "available design". This means the learners are able to distinguish between the words such as 'see' and 'stare' and use them appropriately in their own sentences.

Flower (1990) distinguishes between two kinds of literacy—receptive and critical. Mantero (2006), Canale and Swain (1980) and Savignon (1972) have identified receptive literacy as the central component of communicative competency because of its importance in helping learners reproduce facts, patterns and information. Mantero (2006) refers to Flower's (1990) statement:

> Critical literacy is key to full membership in an academic discourse community because it provides access to the particular frames that individual typically use in interpreting and producing texts. (p. 5)

which Bachman (1990) addressed in his model. Gee (1994) opens up this line of thought by considering the instructor and students as members of a discourse community where the students are dynamic individuals able to process and transform the texts they read in class.

Language educators (Frawley and Lantolf 1985; Rogoff 1997) often mention the importance of ideas over language proficiency. In reality, we often find learners with limited L2 skills who are unable to express their ideas while interacting with texts in class. On this particular issue, we refer to Canagarajah's (2000) suggestion and study in making opportunities for learners of L2 to express their ideas and forming new knowledge by the use of L1 as and when required. He advises the instructors not to lower the learners' cognitive ability in the understanding of the text, which is too often observed in L2 classrooms.

30.7 APPLIED LITERACY IN L2 LEARNING

"Implicit within the concept of literacy in a second language is knowledge ... When knowledge is put to use, literacy begins to emerge" (Mantero 2006: 104). This very idea acknowledges the fact that the students are dynamic individuals and possess the ability to transform the texts while actively interacting with them. It also deconstructs the conventional L2 learning classroom based on communicative language teaching (CLT) where the teachers observe themselves as experts and "maximize their interpretations of the texts and lesson content" (Kumaravadivelu 2003, in Mantero 2006: 104). Scholars (Donato and Brooks 2004; Kramsch 1985; Mantero 2002; Mantero 2006) have recognized that discourse in a CLT environment reproduces the text and fails to produce dialogue in L2 involving learner-teacher negotiations of textual interpretations. The aim of applied literacy in L2 education is to enable the learners negotiate the meaning while interacting with texts and refining comprehension and production of the target language. This clearly establishes the difference in the aims of CLT and applied literacy in L2. The instructors of CLT pay more attention to their students' learning of vocabulary and acquiring lexical knowledge and later reading and comprehension involving linguistic issues than cognitive concerns (Kern 2000 in Mantero 2006). Freire (Freire and Macedo 1987) defined genuine literacy as "reading the word and the world," and helped open the door to a broader understanding of the term, from a simple decoding and reproducing of language into issues relating to the lived world. It refers to literacy as the ability to manipulate any set of codes and conventions—whether it is the words of a language, the symbols in a mathematical system, or images posted to the Internet in order to live a meaningful and productive life. According to Freire, "Reading the world always precedes reading the word, and reading the word implies continually reading the world" (*ibid.*: 35) and constructs literacy as an active phenomenon. But how a person reads or interprets the world through the words is deeply rooted to his/her cultural identity. The power of literacy enables a person to shape his/her life.

30.8 POLICY AND TEACHING METHODOLOGY

The language teaching methodology should be commensurate with the linguistic situation and language policy of the country and its education, so we need to examine the policy aspect to evaluate the instructional method. NCERT (2005) addresses the unique linguistic feature of India and the role it can serve in education in the following passage:

> Multilingualism, which is constitutive of the identity of a child and a typical feature of the Indian linguistic landscape, must be used as a resource, classroom strategy and a goal ... also a way of ensuring that every child feels secure and accepted, and that no one is left behind on account of his/her linguistic background. (p. 36)

The aim of teaching three languages in school is

> To promote multilingualism and national harmony ... and to develop language into an instrument for abstract thought and knowledge acquisition through literacy. (pp. 37–39)

stating clearly that the three-language policy does not exist for the sole purpose of learning three languages but to make students within the country's education system become literate in all of them. The goal is to enable the students use English, the compulsory additional language, in making meaning of the world.

In India, there are certain reasons to make students literate in the two additional languages and English in particular. One major reason is the history of the English language in the sub-continent. Till 1947, English had been the medium of instruction in education from K-12 and higher education. After Independence, implementing the language policy in this multilingual and multicultural country where the states are linguistically constructed turned out to be a complex endeavour and that left English to continue as the medium of higher education. The National Knowledge Commission (2007) has identified English language as an

> Important determinant of access to higher education, employment possibilities and social opportunities ... *and those who are*[3] not adequately trained in English as a language are always at a handicap in the world of higher education because almost always instruction is in English. (p. 48).

The commission has rightfully assessed the power of the English language educationally and socially both in India and abroad. However, being literate in an additional language which is also a foreign language would mean acquiring a medium of self-expression. A language becomes a part of the learner when he/she is able to use it to suit his/her culture—a language that "Can be profitably reconstructed into a vehicle for expressing socio-cultural norms and networks that are typically local" (Kumaravadivelu 2003: 539).

In the plurilingual country of India, English has been serving multiple functions since its inception: (i) it has, and continues, to provide the linguistic tool in maintaining the administrative cohesiveness of the country; (ii) it also serves as a language of wider communication (Kachru 1986a: 8). English functions in the Indian socio-cultural context to perform roles relevant and appropriate to the social, educational and administrative network of India (*ibid.*: 111). According to Kachru (1986c: 137), the power bases of English have to be seen in both material and psychological terms. English is supported in the Outer Circle particularly in India for cultural renaissance, spread of nationalism, pan-regional literary creativity and neutrality, and there is a strong emotional attachment to the language. The psychological factors are important also because they are vital for creating an identity and best reflected in its "nativization" (Kachru 1983: 182). Creative writers like Sulman Rushdie, Chinua Achebe, Bharati Mukherjee, Chitra Banerjee Dibakaruni, Arundhati Roy, Jhumpa Lahiri, Vikram Seth and others have proved that the English language can be successfully used to portray and communicate foreign socio-cultural nuances unknown to Western culture.

Communicative methodology fails to address the above issues relating to learning English as an additional language in the Indian context. The CLT in the US serves a particular purpose (Galloway 1993):

> They (learners) did not know how to communicate using appropriate social language, gestures, or expressions; in brief, they were at a loss to communicate in the culture of the language studied".

---

3. Emphasised by the Author.

The remark made with regard to the ESL learners in the U.S. helps understand the ESL speakers' requirement in an English speaking country. The learners need to acquire communicative competence in order to function in the society. Thus, it is the "basic interpersonal communicative skill" (Cummins 1979) along with the country's culture that L2 learners need to acquire for social survival. However, it does not ensure that all ESL students in the U.S. who have acquired social communicative skills in English have succeeded in school. In order to achieve school success, the students need to become functionally and critically literate in English.

It has been documented by researchers that the British colonizers used its colonies, especially India, to devise appropriate teaching methods (Pennycook 1998), testing techniques (Spolsky 1995), and literary canons (Viswanathan 1990) to fulfill their colonial agenda. The textbooks were specifically designed *to give* the Indians just enough English language skills "to produce clerks to run the colonial system" (Pennycook 1989: 593). We argue that by the indirect imposition of the 'communicative method' in teaching English, it pursues its neo-colonial agenda by ignoring local knowledge—particularly periphery communities in south Asia and southeast Asia where people have been teaching and learning foreign languages prior to the introduction of modern methods to the field.

30.9 CONCLUSION

We draw from Kumaravadivelu's (2003) post-method perspective and Canagarajah's (2002) post-colonial pedagogy to empower the practising teachers in developing appropriate pedagogy based on cultural knowledge and understanding of the learner community and its need. The communicative methodology with its target on 'native-like' speech accent marginalizes the non-native speakers and "seeks to preserve the dominance" of the centre over the periphery. Resisting the monolingual norms imposed by TESOL education such as:

1. Discouraging the use of learners' first language;
2. Introducing reading materials that portrays the superiority of Western knowledge by subjugating local knowledge; and
3. Superiority of native-speaking professionals over non-native ones;

can be possible by changing educational policies and the attitude of people. The nativization of English has helped in challenging the colonial construct of the language, but in order to resist the dominance in teaching the teachers need to develop macrostrategies as suggested by Kumaravadivelu (2003) by linking them to the sociolinguistic context and ways in which language is used in the culture.

Communicative language teaching focuses mainly on oral and aural development for social communication and language exchange which is required in English speaking countries or for people who require verbal communication with native English speakers. In India, English is still the requirement to access higher education. This has made certain marginalized and minorities perceive it as a goal to achieve "Equal Educational Opportunity" and also social opportunity. But it lacks an appropriate pedagogy of teaching and learning English as an additional language to realize these aims and goals. Tickoo (1994) has very aptly commented:

> English in India continues to be taught as though it were a language of social survival rather than a strong additional language whose unique contributions lie in relating scientific and technological developments to the country's socioeconomic needs, aspirations and challenges. (p. 332)

A well-balanced curriculum with English language and literature and the use of the spoken language in the additional language classrooms would provide the learners with the tools to develop linguistic, cognitive and literary goals of the additional language classrooms. The teachers of English need to develop appropriate methods and materials for the learners without accepting or importing them from the countries belonging to the Inner Circle because the aims and functions of the language totally differ within the countries in discussion.

Learning an additional language that has official status within the country and is also the language of globalization needs to engage specific social context and the ever changing nature of the components of the educational context. The educator, thus, needs to develop a pedagogy that would enable him/her to move beyond the politics of class, caste, gender and language in this plurilingual country, stressing the value of the country's goal to achieve "unity in diversity" by aiming to achieve 'equal educational opportunity' and empowering the learners through English education.

Since the publication of the first edition of this volume, English Language Policy and Instruction in India has continued to evolve to meet the needs of the community, the students, and the larger nation. We are pleased to note that the schools in India have started to address the 'periphery' much more than the 'center.' That is, as we noted in the first edition, English must be contextualized by the community in which is being taught rather than by societies which few students have or want access to in today's world.

Additionally, it is important to note that if we are to truly become a global society, then we as educators must understand how policy may be framed, and how it impacts instruction. Essentially, English language policy may influence instruction, addressing the construct of power in our communities. We then see how the process of democratization is influenced by education and learning English. This then may lead to increased number of individuals who willingly engage with the rest of the world.

At its core, language policy should serve to set the framework and foundation for teachers and institutions to develop the linguistic capacity of our students to the point where they become invested in cultivating patterns of linguistic interaction within schools in India which support broader, societal goals. As language policy comes alive in classrooms in India, we note that teachers and administrators have the responsibility to provide opportunities for curricular renewal and material development, based on their experiences in the community and not absent of meaning for the students. In other words, English language policy in India benefits from the potential of the live experiences of educators and students alike.

Needless to say, English is enjoying a special status across the globe and in India. And, arguably, this status is well-earned. However, it is the teachers who are responsible for initially portraying the purpose of English via their pedagogy. To this end, we still support the post method approach and perspective drawn from Kumaravadivelu (2003) and Canagarajah's (2002) work and insights where the learner and the local classroom serves as a foundation for language instruction via a locally-inspired pedagogy and not a text-bound approach to a language, which serves to further disembody the voices of our students. We invite the readers of this volume to reflect on the central elements in our proposition: Literacy, Knowledge, and Culture. Once we confirm that these exist together via our pedagogy, then we will remain on our path to a true post-method pedagogy.

REFERENCES

Bachman, L., *Fundamental Considerations in Language Testing,* Oxford: Oxford University Press, 1990.

Berns, M.S., "Functional approaches to language and language teaching: Another look," *Initiatives in Communicative Language Teaching: A Book of Readings,* S. Savignon and M.S. Berns (Eds.), Reading, PA: Addison-Wesley, 1984, 3–21.

Canagarajah, Suresh A., "Constructing hybrid postcolonial subjects: Code-switching in Jaffna classrooms," *Voices of Authority: Education and Linguistic Difference,* M. Heller and M. Martin-Jones (Eds.), London: Ablex, 2000.

Canale, M., "On some dimensions of language proficiency," *Issues in Language Testing Research,* J.W. Oller, Jr. (Ed.) Rowley, MA: Newbury House, 1983, 333–342.

Canale, M. and Swain, M., "Theoretical bases of communicative approaches to second-language teaching and testing," *Applied Linguistics,* **1**.1 (1980): 1–47.

Carrell, P.L., "Awareness of text structure: Effects on recall," *Language Learning,* **42** (1992): 1–20.

Carrell, P., Carson, J. and Zhe, D., "First and second language reading strategies: Evidence from Cloze," *Reading in a Foreign Language* **10**.1 (1993): 953–965.

Chandran, K.N., "English literature and India," *The Cambridge Quarterly* **25**.2 (1996): 197–200.

Collie, J. and Slater, S., *Literature in the Language Classroom*, Cambridge: Cambridge University Press, 1987.

Cox, B., *Cox on Cox: An English Curriculum for the 1990*, Seven Oaks, California: Hodder and Stoughton, 1991.

Cummins, J., "Cognitive/academic language proficiency, linguistic interdependence, the optimum age question and some other matters," *Working Papers on Bilingualism*, No. 19 (1979): 121–129.

Donato, R. and Brooks, F.B., "Literary discussions and advanced speaking functions: Researching the (dis)connection," *Foreign Language Annals* **37**.2 (2004): 183–199.

Duff, A. and Maley, A., *Literature*, Oxford: Oxford University Press, 1990.

Engler, Balz, "Englishness and English studies," *European English Studies: Contributions Towards the History of a Discipline*, Balz Engler and Renate Haas (Eds.), Leicester: The English Association for ESSE, 2000, 335–348.

Firth, J.R., *Papers in Linguistics 1934–1951*, London: Oxford University Press, 1957.

Floriani, A., "Negotiating what counts: Roles and relationships, texts and contexts, content and meaning," *Linguistics and Education* **5** (1994): 241–274.

Flower, L., "The role of task representation in reading-to-write," *Reading-to-Write: Exploring a Cognitive and Social Process*, V.S.L. Flower, J. Ackerman, M.J. Kantz, K. McCormick, and W.C. Peck (Eds.), New York: Oxford University Press, 1990.

Frawley, W. and Lantolf, J.P., "Second language discourse: A Vygotskyan perspective," in *Applied Linguistics* **6**.1 (1985): 19–44.

Freire, P. and Macedo, D., *Literacy: Reading the Word and the World*, South Hadley, MA: Bergin and Garvey, 1987.

Galloway, A., Communicative Language Teaching: An Introduction and Sample Activities. ERIC Clearinghouse on Languages and Linguistics, Washington DC: ED357642, 1993.

Gee, J.P., "First language acquisition as a guide for theories of learning and pedagogy," *Linguistics and Education* **6** (1994): 331–354.

Halliday, M.A.K., *Language as Social Semiotic*, London: Edward Arnold, 1978.

Harmer, J., "What is communicative?," *ELT Journal* **36** (1982): 164–168.

Hohenthal, A., "English in India: Loyalty and attitudes," *Language in India* **3**.5 (2003). Retrieved in 11/12/2007 from the website: http://www.languagein india.com/may2003/annika.html

Hymes, D.H. (1971), "On communicative competence," in J. Pride and J. Holmes (Eds.), *Sociolinguistics*, Harmondsworth: Penguin, 1972.

Jones, D., *An English Pronouncing Dictionary*, London: J.M. Dent and Sons, 1917.

———, *An Outline of English Phonetics*, Cambridge: Heffer, 1918.

Kachru, Braj B., *The Indianization of English: The English Language in India*, Oxford: Oxford University Press, 1983.

Kachru, Braj B., *The Alchemy of English: The Spread, Functions and Models of Non-Native Englishes,* Oxford: Pergamon Press, 1986a.

———, "The power and politics of English," in *World Englishes* **5**.2/3 (1986c): 121–140.

Kern, R., *Literacy and Language Teaching,* London: Oxford University Press, 2000.

Khubchandani, L.M., "Multilingual education in India, Pune: Center for Communication Studies," *Case Studies in Bilingual Education,* B. Spolsky, and R.L. Cooper (Eds.) Boston: Newbury House, 1981.

Kramsch, C., "Literary texts in the classroom: A discourse," *The Modern Language Journal* **69**.4 (1985): 356–366.

Kumaravadivelu, B., *Beyond Methods: Macrostrategies for Language Teaching,* London: Yale University Press, 2003.

Littlewood, W., *Communicative Language Teaching,* New York: Cambridge University Press, 1981.

Mantero, M., *Scaffolding Revisited: Sociocultural Pedagogy within the Foreign Language Classroom* (ERIC Document Reproduction Service No 459623), 2002.

———, "Appropriating literature in foreign language classrooms," *Academic Exchange Quarterly,* 2003.

———, "Applied literacy in second language education: (Re)-framing discourse in literature-based classrooms," *Foreign Language Annals* **3**.1 (Spring 2006): 99–114.

McRae, J., *Literature with a small 'l',* London: Macmillan, 1991.

National Knowledge Commission, *Recommendations on School Education,* 2007. Retrieved on 4/04/2008 from
http://knowledgecommission.gov.in/downloads/documents/nkc_se.pdf

NCERT 2005, "Curricular areas, school stages and assessment," *National Curriculum Framework* 2005. Retrieved on 2/14/2008 from the site:
http://ncert.nic.in/sites/publication/schoolcurriculum/NCFR%202005/contents2.htm

Oller, J.W., Jr. and Obrecht, Dean H., "Pattern drill and communicative activity: A psycholinguistic experiment," *International Review of Applied Linguistics* **6**.2 (1968): 165–174.

Pennycook, A., "The concept of method, interested knowledge, and the politics of language teaching," *TESOL Quarterly* **23**.4 (1989): 589–618.

———, *English and the Discourses of Colonialism,* London: Routledge, 1998.

Rogoff, B., "Evaluating development in the process of participation: Theory, methods, and practice building on each other," *Change and Development,* E. Amsel and A. Renninger (Eds.), Hillsdale, NJ: Erlbaum, 1997, 265–285.

Roy, J., "Abolition of teaching of English from primary schools in West Bengal, India: An evaluation," 2003. Retrieved on 04/12/2006 from the following website: http://www.arts.cornell.edu/econ/75devconf/papers/joydeeproy.pdf

Savignon, S.J., *Communicative Competence: An Experiment in Foreign Language Teaching,* Philadelphia: Center for Curriculum Development, 1972.

Savignon, S.J., *Communicative Competence: Theory and Classroom Practice; Texts and Contexts in Second Language Learning*, Reading, MA: Addison-Wesley, 1983.

―――, *Initiatives in Communicative Language Teaching: A Book of Readings*, Lebanon/Indiana: Prentice Hall, 1984.

Scrase, T., *The "New" Middle Class in India: A Re-assessment*, 2004. http://coombs.anu.edu.au/SpecialProj/ASAA/biennial-conference/2006/Scrase-Tim-ASAA2006.pdf

Sivasubramaniam, S., "Promoting the prevalence of literature in the practice of foreign and second language education: Issues and insights," *Asian EFL Journal* **8**.4 (2006).

Spolsky, B., *Measured Words: The Development of Objective Language Testing*, Oxford: Oxford University Press, 1995.

Sweet, H., *The Practical Study of Languages*, London: Oxford University Press, 1899.

Thurgood, G., "The communicative approach to language teaching," *TESOL Quarterly* **15**.3 (1981): 327–332.

Tickoo, M.L., "Kashmiri, a majority-minority language: An exploratory essay," *Linguistic Human Rights: Overcoming Linguistic Discrimination*, T. Skutnabb-Kangas and Robert Phillipson (Eds.), Berlin: Mouton de Gruyter, 1994, 317–334.

Tucker, R.D., "English Problems of Native Spanish Speaker," *Readings in Spanish/English Contrastive Linguistics*, R. Nash (Ed.), Puerto Rico: Inter-American University Press, 1974, 136–155.

Upshur, J.A. and Palmer, C.E., "Systematic Effects in the Rating of Second Language Speaking Ability: Test Method and Learner Discourse," *Language Testing*, **16** (1974): 82–111.

Verhoeven, L. (Ed.), *Functional Literacy: Theoretical Issues and Educational Implications*, Amsterdam/Philadelphia: John Benjamins, 1994.

Viswanathan, G., *Masks of Conquest: Literary Study and British Rule in India*, London: Faber and Faber, 1990.

West, A., "The centrality of literature," *Teaching English*, S. Brindley (Ed.), London: Routledge, 1994.

Chapter 31

UNDERSTANDING AND EXAMINING LINGUISTIC DIVERSITY IN AMERICAN CLASSROOM

— CHARLOTTE PASS AND MIGUEL MANTERO

31.1 INTRODUCTION

Through the years, multiple changes have influenced the culture of United States, including the influx of immigrant and refugee populations from around the globe, which has brought families of various ethnicities into American communities. Given the ever-changing landscape of the U.S. public school classroom, teachers must adapt or resign themselves to a lack of efficacy. In a curriculum that is already stretched to the seams, programs of teacher education must find ways to embed instruction about language development, the process of language learning, and the semiotic relationship between language and culture. Furthermore, to address the burgeoning English language learning (ELL) population, they must understand the language acquisition process to better assist ELLs in their classes (Van Patten 2003). Consequently, the necessary preparation and development must be provided to these classroom teachers to ensure their success, and the success of their students (Menken et al. 2001). To complement instruction about language acquisition, pre-service educators should receive instruction about multicultural pedagogy, particularly in view of the current statistics, which indicate that student diversity is increasing, while the teaching population becomes increasingly White (Hodgkinson 2000, 2002). Additionally, while the primary teachers (K-6) at least have the skills necessary to teach students the various components of reading, the secondary teachers, who have not been required to learn strategies to address emergent literacy, now must do that.

In addition, fundamental information about cultural differences and adapting the curriculum to address these essential topics must be offered. Additionally, with the federal mandates such as the *No Child Left Behind (NCLB) Act of 2001* (2002), many *teachers* are being left behind. Without appropriate training to meet the needs of this growing population of students who speak limited English and are learning English as an additional language, teachers are seeking the means by which they can successfully educate students from all cultural and linguistic backgrounds. Despite the pressing need to improve the education of ELLs, the mainstream classroom teachers may attend workshops or rely upon their personal efforts to learn about ESL instruction and become more effective (Fu 2004). To be effective instructors of ELLs, teachers must combine content area knowledge with knowledge of pedagogy as they attempt to meet the state-mandated, grade-level standards and to fulfill the intent of NCLB. Given this, we think it vital for classroom teacher to develop an approach and mindset that will assist them in understanding and investigating cultural differences in their classrooms.

31.2 INITIAL THEORETICAL UNDERPINNINGS

Given the current educational landscape, knowledge of second language acquisition is important for teachers (Van Patten 2003). Often, teachers represent for students the most important link between home and school. If a student believes that the school context, of which the teacher is an integral component, does not value his or her home language and culture, he or she may develop feelings of isolation (Brantley 2007). Consequently, every educator should consider the needs of English language learners (ELLs) (Williams 2001), a proposition endorsed by Handscombe (1989), who stated that all teachers should consider themselves ELL teachers. Unfortunately, as current literature indicates, too many teachers are not prepared adequately to teach culturally and linguistically diverse students (Gay 2002). One theory that frames this study is sociocultural theory and Vygotsky's (1978) characteristic zone of proximal development (ZPD) and zone of actual development (ZAD). This idea is foreshadowed by Wood et al. (1976), who endorsed the use of scaffolding—a modification of instruction that provides linguistically diverse students (in this case) with the assistance of a teacher or a more capable peer, and enables the student to expand as well as further develop and refine his or her ZAD and ZPD. The teacher also has ensured that the student will be able to internalize the ability to accomplish the task(s) independently (Dorn et al. 1998).

Krashen's (2003) ideas are important for establishing a fundamental knowledge of L2 learning in the instruction of mainstream content area teachers. These include (i) the acquisition-learning hypothesis, (ii) the input hypothesis, (iii) the affective filter hypothesis, and (iv) the interactionist hypothesis (*see* Peregoy and Boyle 2004).

The initial **acquisition-learning hypothesis** differentiates between the conscious and the subconscious learning. This precept suggests that language acquisition occurs subconsciously; one simply 'picks it up'. Language learning, on the other hand, implies a conscious, academic effort to learn a language. According to Krashen, the conscious learning is limited particularly when applying rules and grammar.

The second salient hypothesis, **the input hypothesis**, draws upon the efficacy of the classroom teacher. Based on this tenet, L2 learners learn most effectively when they are placed in natural communications situations and when the target language is comprehensible. For the content area teacher, this hypothesis suggests that the L2 learner can benefit from the use of any items that make content presentation more understandable, e.g., visual aids, graphic organizers, software such as Kidspiration and Inspiration, graphs, charts, photographs, and other instructional resources that reinforce verbal or print instruction.

An additional consideration for content area teachers working with ELLs is the assurance of a learning environment producing low anxiety, also known as Krashen's **affective filter hypothesis** (*see* Kottler and Kottler 2002; Peregoy and Boyle 2001; Richards and Rodgers 2001). If the learner is comfortable and experiences self-confidence, then he or she is more likely to listen to and understand the target language. Another important hypothesis, **the interactionist hypothesis** (Krashen 1981), posits that the purpose of teaching is to prepare ELLs for real-life communication. Therefore, the classroom should provide comprehensible language in an environment conducive to conversational competence that expands the student's knowledge through daily communicative situations and teacher scaffolding. The significant feature of this hypothesis is the natural interaction between native and non-native speakers as well as their "negotiation of meaning" (Peregoy and Boyle 2004).

31.3 TEACHING CULTURAL DIFFERENCES: REVIEWING CURRENT AND PAST PRACTICES

An English teacher's knowledge of the role of culture in language acquisition is significant but does not encapsulate all that should be relevant in the language classroom. Wexler and Cullicover (1980) stressed that all children learn the rules of language in the same sequence. McCune et al. (1999) provided teachers with guidelines for promoting diversity within the classroom. Their recommendations included the recognition by teachers that cultural diversity can be valued without requiring the criticism of Western values and traditions. Also, differences exist within groups, not only between groups of people. Teachers should remember that there exists a positive correlation between teacher expectations and the students' academic performance and that high standards of educational performance should be established for all students regardless of identity or background. Remembering that self-esteem and academic achievement are related is of paramount importance for teachers. Another salient point is that there is no single approach for meeting the educational needs of all the children in a multicultural classroom setting. The teacher and the student members of the majority culture must realize that multiculturalism is not exclusively a 'minority thing'; it encompasses everyone. And, finally, human understanding is a lifelong endeavor, thus, understanding culture transcends language learning.

Current educational research recommends that teachers expand their knowledge base of their ELLs' first languages and cultural backgrounds (Wong-Fillmore and Snow 2002; Zeichner 2003). When making initial inquiries of the case study teachers regarding the backgrounds of their ELLs, only one teacher could identify the countries of origin of her ELLs. The three remaining case study teachers stated that they believed that the responsibility for knowing and revealing that information lay with the ESL specialist. These teachers also could not reveal how long their ELLs had been in the country or if they had had any previous exposure to English in their home country. Garcia and Stritikus (2006) noted, "In order to educate them [ELLs], we must first educate ourselves about who they are and what they need to succeed" (p. 45).

To accomplish this task, the teachers must move beyond their own culture and belief systems:

> In contrast to racial, ethnic, and linguistic diversity among students, the vast majority of teachers and administrators are white and speak English as their native and only language (*ibid.*: p. 47).

This paradigm is aligned with Coulter and Smith's (2006) findings that schools expect ELLs to assimilate into the mainstream culture and to "act White".

Related to Coulter and Smith's (*ibid.*) study was the treatment provided by one teacher respondent to her two ELLs. One student had assimilated easily into the school culture, dressing like the other students in the school (with a predominantly white student enrollment), behaving like them, and being from a similar economic background (the students were mainly from middle- to upper-income homes). The other student's physical appearance, dress, language, and male-dominate social behaviors distinguished him from his peers. The teacher's reaction to these cultural differences was apparent. On the first day that the second ELL was in her class, he raised his hand to ask a question. When the teacher did not readily respond because she was on the other side of the classroom, he snapped his fingers and called her name. While she viewed his behavior as unacceptable and proceeded to tell him that he would *never* treat her in such a subordinate manner, he was simply confused by her response. What he deemed as an appropriate method of garnering her attention, she did not. His action elicited such a negative response that the teacher had a poor impression of him for the remainder of the school year. His behavior and her reaction contributed to his placement in the back of the classroom. Had the teacher made queries into the student's cultural background, she would have discovered that his response was a result of that and not intended as a gesture of disrespect. Because of his negative interactions with his teacher, this student completely disengaged academically in the class. The first student, however, was treated with great respect by the teacher and placed centrally in the front of the classroom. All his interactions with the teacher were positive, and he made great strides in language acquisition. In this case, by acting like the other white students in the class, the first student experienced greater success.

In Lee and Oxelson's (2006) study, the authors found that teachers with proficiency in an L2 were more sensitive to issues of diversity and language acquisition. Based on the aforementioned scenario, this may not be true. The teacher respondent involved in the cultural misunderstanding had learned a second language. Instead, the current study reveals that teachers who have traveled extensively beyond the United States demonstrate greater ethno-sensitivity and exercise greater effort to help ELLs learn English, and they enjoy doing so.

Harklau (1994) offered numerous strategies for effective verbal instruction for teachers of mainstream classes with ELLs. First, she described effective input as having an authentic communicative purpose; adjusting the speed and complexity of oral instruction; repeating the key points; pausing; providing comprehension checks; making abstract ideas concrete by using visual aids, including graphic organizers, photographs, and maps; avoiding puns and sarcastic or ironic comments; avoiding asides or distractions from the primary topic; providing ELLs with opportunities for authentic output and interaction with native speakers; and limiting use of the Initiation-Reply-Evaluation (IRE) format. Harklau also found that the teachers in her study lacked training in strategies for instructing ELLs. Consequently, their interaction with the students varied widely. Some learned strategies through trial-and-error, such as placing ELLs at desks near the front of the classroom and talking one-on-one with them. Others failed to speak to the ELLs for fear of embarrassing them.

Cartiera's (2006) guidelines recommended that teachers should be

1. aware of an ELL's L1 structure,
2. build fluency,
3. differentiate scaffolding,
4. read words,
5. build schema,
6. connect to students' background,
7. build vocabulary,
8. pre-teach vocabulary,
9. teach text structure,
10. teach phonics systematically,
11. embed phonemic awareness in writing activities,
12. provide a strong foundation in oral language before reading in English,
13. provide more time to complete activities and/or assignments,
14. offer students leveled books of high interest to read,
15. teach comprehension skills,

16. instruct in cooperative or small groups,
17. create a classroom environment that produces low anxiety,
18. teach inferencing,
19. explicitly teach pre-, during- and after-reading activities,
20. offer technology to support ELLs,
21. provide high quality instruction, and
22. use an ELL's native language as a foundation for L2 learning.

Many of the strategies identified as being exemplary practices for working with ELLs apply equally well to language learning. Trumbull and Farr (2005) contended:

> Language is a reflection of a culture's orientation to the world, of its needs and goals. There is no way to fully understand a language without also learning about the culture or the cultures in which it is spoken. (p. 7)

and that culture impacts one's approach to teaching and learning. As a result, it is not surprising that they fail to meet Cartiera's guidelines for exemplary teachers instructing language learners.

Of the list of 22 practices, the case study teachers demonstrated 10 at most. Those practices modeled to some degree by these teachers included: (i) differentiating scaffolding (minimally, at best); (ii) reading words; (iii) building schema (although only on a very limited scale, directed at native speakers rather than ELLs); (iv) building vocabulary; (v) pre-teaching vocabulary; (vi) providing more time to complete activities and/or assignments; (vii) teaching comprehension skills; (viii) instructing in cooperative/small groups (although the teachers did not provide instruction in small groups; instead, the students worked collaboratively in small groups); (ix) creating a classroom environment that produces low anxiety for the ELL (potentially treating them as though they were invisible members of the classroom); (x) explicitly teaching pre-, during-, and after-reading activities; and (xi) offering technology to support ELLs (a strength of one case study teachers). As Krashen (1981) advised, demonstrate input serving an authentic communicative purpose (since the greatest number of students in the classrooms were native speakers), but the majority of their strategies were used because they were good, general teaching strategies rather than strategies used specifically to benefit their ELL(s). In addition, because their instruction was directed toward the native speakers in the classroom, the teachers made few adjustments to their input (discourse) to make it more comprehensible to the ELLs. Cary (2000) posited that teachers can improve ELLs' comprehension of spoken discourse by using objects, videotapes, pictures, and movement; offering periodic summaries and paraphrases; developing key vocabulary and 'power' words; building and using student background knowledge; and including L1 support when possible. The teacher respondents included these strategies in their suggestions for working with ELLs, and in actual practice, the teachers did do a fair job of implementing these strategies.

Greater incorporation of the first language could have been accomplished by two of the teachers who offered students no L1 support.

Introducing the students to the hidden agendas of classroom culture also is significant. As with any student, the teachers should establish rapport and nurture an ELL's ability to learn at high levels. Making available a wide range of resources in the classroom that represents the heritage of all students serves to foster a positive learning community for everyone. Wheelock (1992) maintained that a need exists for combining language learning and content learning for ELLs using hands-on activities implemented by collaborative teacher teams. However, Cone (1992) argued that having ELLs as active participants in learning is not adequate. Instead, teachers must model content area knowledge and the target language. Harklau (1994) described similar concerns at her case study school:

> The content and course objectives of high school subject-area instruction presumed a relatively stable student population with a uniform knowledge base shaped by 8 or 9 years of previous instruction in U.S. elementary and middle schools. Thus, curriculum in subject areas depended on continuity, with content in any one course built upon a knowledge base that students were assumed to possess from previous courses in the sequence. (p. 257)

Kern's (2000) model of Available Designs illustrates the importance of the socio-cultural context in literacy and language teaching.

31.4 IMPLEMENTING A CLASSROOM-BASED RESEARCH STRATEGY: THE CASE STUDY APPROACH

Yin (2003) defined a case study as a research strategy comprising an "all-encompassing" (p. 14) method, including a particular design, specific data collection techniques, and certain approaches to data analysis. Researchers may elect to use the case study design to explore contextual conditions believing that they may be highly relevant to the focus of the study. Gerring (2007) declared the purpose of conducting case studies as gaining insight into the study participants. Hancock and Algozzine (2006) elaborated on this idea by maintaining that case studies differ from other forms of research because they provide intensive analyses and rich descriptions of a single unit or system as limited by space and time.

With the focus of this research upon teachers' perceptions of interactions with individuals from different ethnic and linguistic groups, the ELL and the native-speaking secondary teacher, the case study offered the most obvious method of choice since it provided "a detailed, in-depth examination of a person ... from a specific group" (Hubbard and Power 1999: 120).

Seliger and Shohamy (1989) suggested using the case study approach when the research interest is in some aspect of L2 performance or development of subjects as individuals. The premise is that observation of individual performance will be more revealing than studying large groups of people. Unlike observations performed in a qualitative design, those conducted for a descriptive research design begin with a deductive focus instead of the heuristic focus of qualitative observations. Seliger and Shohamy also suggested using various data collection methods for the validation and triangulation of the data. Consequently, the data collection from the four case studies (O'Malley and Chamot 1990, Oxford 1990, Chamot et al. 1990, Grenfell and Harris 1990) of exemplary mainstream secondary language arts teachers consisted of (i) observation, (ii) the transcription of videotaping and audiotaping, (iii) semi-structured interviews, (iv) questionnaires, and (v) field notes.

Controlling subjectivity also is a benefit of triangulation. To achieve triangulation, observations/comments of the researcher, teachers', and two nonparticipant external observers' were incorporated. The first external observer's specialty was ESL, and the second observer's expertise was secondary education language arts. These individuals were selected to review all data to ensure that the researcher did not draw erroneous conclusions.

Lincoln and Guba (1985) delineated the following items as requisite content for the case study:

1. an explanation of the problem or focus of the study,
2. the purpose of the study;
3. a "thick description" of the context; and
4. an explicit discussion of the activities or processes observed that are related to the problem.

Furthermore, they stressed the importance of including a discussion of the important factors identified at the study site and a discussion of the results of the study, i.e. the lessons to be learned. Also, the researcher may assume one of several roles from the nonparticipant observer to complete participant in the activities. MacMillan (2004) noted that as a complete observer, the researcher remains detached from the participants being observed. Subject effects, also known as reactivity, may occur due to the mere presence of the observer, impacting the behavior of the study participants (*ibid.*). To clarify what was seen and heard in observations, tape recording and videotaping techniques as recommended by Lincoln and Guba (1985) were employed.

Lincoln and Guba cautioned that interviews should be tape-recorded since all comments and observations cannot be hand-recorded. In this study, the researchers spoke informally to the teachers, eliciting additional information than what was provided during the formal interview process or during direct observations. The exchange of telephone calls and e-mails also served to provide the researcher with greater clarity. Also, according to Bogdan and Biklen (2003), field notes "[render] a description of people, objects, places, events, activities, and conversations" and "record ideas, strategies, reflections, and hunches, as well as [to] note patterns that emerges" (p. 110).

As noted, quality case studies result from careful, systematic work. According to Patton (2002), all raw data gathered for the case study must be organized into a case record for each teacher participant. This case record contains the data that have been condensed, organized, classified, and edited into a more manageable form. A draft case study narrative must be written from the case record that allows the researcher to understand the unique qualities of the case. Chronological or thematic organization may be used for presenting data in conjunction with essential background information that provides insights into the case. Each case study requires a final written narrative, which should offer a descriptive picture or story of the focus of the study that makes the unique qualities of each case understandable and accessible to the reader. Marshall and Rossman (2006) delineated the procedure for reducing the data collected into manageable pieces of information using seven steps:

1. Organize the data received from the various sources,
2. Plan for complete immersion in the data,
3. Create categories and themes,
4. Code the data and examine for patterns,
5. Generate potential interpretations,
6. Examine for alternate interpretations, and
7. Report the findings in a formal, written manner.

Zeichner (1996) advised that closing the achievement gap for diverse learners would require teachers to be of the opinion that all students had the ability to engage in in-depth learning and they are to communicate that notion to students. Proceeding as such would entail (i) offering students a curriculum teeming with equal opportunities to participate and to succeed, (ii) acknowledging students' background(s) when teaching content and (iii) cultural information sharing between cultural groups. In addition, teachers must create learning tasks and activities that are meaningful for all students. One technique for applying meaning to learning would be the scaffolding of students' learning to promote the understanding of complex material while encouraging them to be proud of their heritage.

31.5 CONCLUSION

For researchers and educators, culture is a domain of the mind (Lantolf 2000) that is accentuated and focused by the physical environment. This statement should never be reversed. Reversing it would mean that in order to be French all that a nation has to do is build an Eiffel Tower. Unfortunately, the contemporary classroom view of language and culture is truly one of product because understanding the process of culture formation may take more energy, effort, and time than standardized approaches to monolingual education. This approach, outside the United States, may not find serious support among other classroom teachers around the world.

Language learning and culture are intertwined. But the leap of faith comes when we use this concept in our content-based classrooms. Culture, in its true form, is a concept that cannot be defined within the realm of the classroom (Lakoff and Johnson 1980). And given the previous statement, many professionals believe that by presenting culture—either the dominant American culture or a minority culture—as purely product-based may assist language acquisition. While learning a first language, learning both culture and language is a process (Hanks 1996; Malinowski 1978). For the most part, American classrooms in the southeast view language learning as a process while culture is understood as a product. This is very different from L1 acquisition, and here is where we fall short in our leap of faith. There are certain humanistic goals that can be achieved if we present culture to our students as product—this is not in question. What is being challenged is the view of culture as a product when language learning is a process in content-based classrooms. Therefore, we call on the teacher to truly investigate his or her own lessons and surrounding using the aforementioned framework.

In this chapter, we attempted to provide a basic understanding and direction for classroom teachers to begin to investigate and further appreciate linguistic diversity in their own classrooms. Obviously, this is not a recipe which leads to one, single product. But it is an approach that if implemented, contextualized, and refined, will assist educators in appreciating and building on the strengths of their students who are learning to speak English as an additional language.

As American classrooms evolve, so must our approach to investigating linguistic diversity and important to underline several facts. First of all, teachers, for the most part, understand how to best approach content-area instruction for linguistically diverse learners. However, it could be argued that the reality of current educational settings prevent them from refining this understanding. And, since some teachers are already deemed to be good, effective teachers, there interaction with and instruction of linguistically diverse learners may not be further questioned by the administration, parents, or colleagues. And, this leads to teachers who may not want to explore their instruction even further.

It is vital that all teacher's reflect on and remember Coulter and Smith's (2006) findings when they examined eight English language learner's in an American high school to ascertain their experiences as immigrants attending a public school. Their study revealed the following:

1. ELLs were not provided the same access to mainstream school functions and/or extracurricular activities as were other students.
2. An inequity existed in the classroom resources, materials, field trips, and other learning requirements of the ELLs.
3. Opportunities for interaction with one another, with their native English-speaking peers, or with the content were not provided.

4. The school tracked ELLs into remedial classes where low expectations for academic achievement existed and where their academic success was undermined.
5. The school segregated ELLs from their native English-speaking peers.
6. The school community expected the ELLs to assimilate to the mainstream culture, foregoing their linguistic and cultural identity.
7. Neither the classroom instruction nor the school culture offered ELLs cultural relevance.

Current educational practice is producing predominantly monolingual teachers, who believe that they are overburdened, under supported by their schools, and are continually anxious about preserving their jobs and professional reputations. Add to that, the challenge of teaching multilingual students (with whom they are not even prepared to communicate) to speak, read, and write English, and to take federally mandated, standardized tests of in-depth knowledge in content area subjects during their second year of attendance in American public schools. This practice begs for reform that will create confident, efficacious teachers prepared to meet the ongoing challenges of diverse classroom contexts. Educational reform at the higher education level must supply future practitioners with the strategies, resources, and activities to become effective classroom researchers and instructors. As with all classrooms around the globe, American classrooms are in a constant state of change. Many of these changes come about by changes in our communities, schools, and the education policies which evolve every so many years.

Since the first, well-received, edition of this volume, schools in the United States have been coming to terms with a new framework for their classrooms: The Common Core Curricula. In the coming years, any investigating and understanding of linguistic diversity in American classrooms must include an in-depth understanding of these new policies, which are, at best, being heavily questioned by language educators and classroom teachers alike. Of importance is the proposal that our chapter still serves as a vital foundation and guide for investigating linguistic diversity in American Classrooms, but teachers and investigators are now faced with the challenge of understanding and examining linguistic diversity in these classrooms given the United States' shift in educational policy, which may impact how linguistic diversity is viewed in our schools.

REFERENCES

Bogdan, R.C. and Biklen, S.K., *Qualitative Research for Education: An Introduction to Theories and Methods*, 4th ed., Boston: Allyn and Bacon, 2003.

Brantley, D.K., *Instructional Assessment of ELLs in the K-8 Classroom*, Boston: Allyn and Bacon, 2007.

Cartiera, M.R., "Addressing the literacy underachievement of adolescent English language learners: A call for teacher preparation and proficiency reform," *The NERA Journal* **42**.1 (2006): 26–32.

Cary, S., *Working with Second Language Learners: Answers to Teachers' Top Ten Questions,* Portsmouth, NH: Heinemann, 2000.

Chamot, A.U., Barnhardt, S., El-Dinary, P.B. and Robbins, J., *The Learning Strategies Handbook,* New York: Longman, 1999.

Cone, J.K., "Untracking advanced placement English: Creating opportunity is not Enough," *Phi Delta Kappan* **73**.2 (1992): 712–717.

Coulter, C. and Smith, M.L., "English language learners in a comprehensive high school," *Bilingual Research Journal* **30**.2 (2006): 309–335.

Dorn, L.J., French, C., and Jones, T., *Apprenticeship in Literacy: Transitions Across Reading and Writing,* York, ME: Stenhouse, 1998.

Fu, D., "Teaching ELL students in regular classrooms at the secondary level," *Voices from the Middle* **11**.4 (2004): 8–15.

Garcia, E.E. and Stritikus, T., "Proposition 227 in California: Issues for the preparation of quality teachers for linguistically and culturally diverse students," *Preparing Quality Educators for English Language Learners: Research, Policies, and Practices,* K. Téllez and H.C. Waxman (Eds.), Mahwah, NJ: Lawrence Erlbaum, 2006, 45–69.

Gay, G., "Preparing for culturally responsive teaching," *Journal of Teacher Education* **53**.2 (2002): 106–116.

Gerring, J., *Case Study Research: Principles and Practices,* New York/ Cambridge: Cambridge University Press, 2007.

Grenfell, M. and Harris, V., *Modern Languages and Learning Strategies: In Theory and Practice,* London: Routledge, 1999.

Hancock, D.R. and Algozzine, B., *Doing Case Study Research: A Practical Guide for Beginning Researchers,* New York: Columbia University Press, 2006.

Handscombe, J., "A quality program for learners of English as a second language," *When They Don't All Speak English: Integrating the ESL Student into the Regular Classroom,* P. Riggs and V. Allen (Eds.), Urbana, IL: National Council of Teachers of English, 1989, 1–14.

Hanks, W., *Language and Communicative Practices,* Boulder, CO: Westview, 1996.

Harklau, L., "ESL versus mainstream classes: Contrasting L2 learning environments," *TESOL Quarterly* **28**.2 (1994): 241–272.

Hodgkinson, H.L., "High school demographics: Demand change," *The Education Digest* **66**.1 (September 2000): 10–14.

_____, "The demographics of diversity," *Principal* **82**.2 (2002): 15–18.

Hubbard, R. and Power, B.M., *Living the Questions: A Guide for Teacher-Researchers,* Portland, ME: Stenhouse, 1999.

Kern, R., *Literacy and Language Teaching,* Oxford: Oxford University Press, 2000.

Kottler, E. and Kottler, J.A., *Children with Limited English: Teaching Strategies for the Regular Classroom,* Thousand Oaks, CA: Corwin Press, 2002.

Krashen, S., *Second Language Acquisition and Second Language Learning,* Oxford,: Pergamon Press, 1981.

_____, *Explorations in Language Acquisition and Use,* Portsmouth, NH: Heinemann, 2003.

Lakoff, G. and Johnson, M., *Metaphors We Live By,* Chicago, IL: University of Chicago Press, 1980.

Lantolf, J., *Sociocultural Theory and Second Language Learning,* Oxford: Oxford University Press, 2000.

Lee, J.S. and Oxelson, E., "It's not my job: K-12 teacher attitudes toward students' heritage language maintenance," *Bilingual Research Journal* **30**.2 (2006): 453–476.

Lincoln, Y.S. and Guba, E.G., *Naturalistic Inquiry,* Beverly Hill, CA: Sage, 1985.

MacMillan, J.H., *Educational Research: Fundamentals for the Consumer*, 4th ed., Boston: Pearson Education, 2004.

Malinowski, B., *Coral Gardens and Their Magic,* New York: Dover Press, 1978.

Marshall, C. and Rossman, G.B., *Designing Qualitative Research,* 4th ed., Thousand Oaks, CA: Sage, 2006.

McCune, S.L., Stephens, D.E., and Lowe, M.E., *Barron's How to Prepare for the ExCET,* 2nd ed., Hauppage, NY: Barron's, 1999.

Menken, K., Antunez, B., Dilworth, M.E., and Yasin, S., *An Overview of the Preparation and Certification of Teachers Working with Limited English Proficient (LEP) Students,* Washington, DC: George Washington University, 2001.

National Clearinghouse of Bilingual Education. *No Child Left Behind Act of 2001,* Pub. L. no. 107–110, 115 Stat. 1425–2094, 2002.

O'Malley, J.M. and Chamot, A.U., *Learning Strategies in Second Language Acquisition*, Cambridge: Cambridge University Press, 1990.

Oxford, R.L., *Language Learning Strategies: What every teacher should know,* Boston: Heinle and Heinle, 1990.

Patton, M.Q., *Qualitative Research and Evaluation Records*, 3rd ed., Thousand Oaks, CA: Sage, 2002.

Peregoy, S.F. and Boyle, O.F., *Reading, Writing, and Learning in ESL: A Resource Book for K-12 Teachers,* 3rd ed., New York: Addison-Wesley Longman, 2001.

_____, *Reading, Writing, and Learning in ESL: A Resource Book for K-12 Teachers,* 4th ed., Boston: Allyn and Bacon, 2004.

Richards, J.C. and Rodgers, T.S., *Approaches and Methods in Language Teaching,* 2nd ed., Cambridge, MA: Cambridge University Press, 2001.

Seliger, H.W. and Shohamy, E., *Second Language Research Methods,* Oxford: Oxford University Press, 1989.

Trumbull, E. and Farr, B., *Language and Learning: What Teachers Need to Know,* Norwood, MA: Christopher-Gordon, 2005.

Van Patten, B., *From Output to Input: A Teacher's Guide to Second Language Acquisition,* Boston: McGraw-Hill, 2003.

Vygotsky, L.S., *Mind in Society: The Development of Higher Psychological Processes,* Cambridge, MA: Harvard University Press, 1978.

Wexler, K. and Cullicover, P.W., *Formal Principles of Language Acquisition,* Cambridge, MA: MIT Press, 1980.

Wheelock, A., *Crossing the Tracks: How "Untracking" Can Save America's Schools,* New York: New Press, 1992.

Williams, J., "Classroom conversations: Opportunities to learn for ESL students in mainstream classrooms," *Reading Teacher* **54**.8 (2001): 750–757.

Wong-Fillmore, L. and Snow, C., "What teachers need to know about language," *What Teachers Need to Know About Language,* C. Adger, C.E. Snow, and D. Christian (Eds.), McHenry, IL: Center for Applied Linguistics and Delta Systems, 2002, 7–54.

Wood, D., Bruner, J., and Ross, G., "The role of tutoring in problem solving," *Journal of Child Psychology and Psychiatry* **17** (1976): 89–100.

Yin, R.K., *Case Study Research: Design and Methods,* 3rd ed., Thousand Oaks, CA: Sage, 2003.

Zeichner, K.M., "Educating teachers to close the achievement gap: Issues of pedagogy, knowledge, and teacher preparation," *Closing the Achievement Gap,* B. Williams (Ed.), Alexandria, VA: Association for Supervision and Curriculum Development, 1996, 56–76.

_____, "Pedagogy, knowledge, and teacher preparation," *Closing the Achievement Gap: A Vision for Changing Beliefs and Practices,* 2nd ed., B. Williams (Ed.), Alexandria, VA: Association for Supervision and Curriculum Development, 2003, 99–101.

Chapter 32

CROSSTALK IN MULTILINGUAL INTERACTIONS AMONG NON-NATIVE SPEAKERS OF ENGLISH

— SVETLANA I. HARNISCH AND MAYA KHEMLANI DAVID

32.1 INTRODUCTION AND AIM

The non-native speakers of English use different variants of English partly due to first language (L1) influence. A number of varieties of English have, therefore, emerged and the differences can be at both the linguistic and pragmatic levels. Discourse among the non-native speakers of English can, therefore, lead to misunderstanding due to crosstalk arising from the use of regional Englishes. The standardization of international terminology and ways of enhancing mutual comprehension intelligibility between professionals, for whom English is not an L1, is essential for effective professional discourse to take place especially in the fields of technology and education. Implications of such informed knowledge for ESP courses are discussed in this chapter.

Since the end of the Second World War, English has become widely used all over the world. Today, it is the most functional working world language and is used in a wide number of professional sectors including international aviation and navigation. About 600,000 to one million people use English as a link language for communication in business and professional negotiations all over the world. This is due to its dominance in various fields such as politics, technology and science in English speaking countries like the USA. Globalization and technological advancements have also resulted in a higher demand for English. The expansion of English to various parts of the world has resulted in many varieties of English and this has resulted in crosstalk (misuse of English by non-native speakers).

Each variety creates its own standard. For example, American English has the General American (GE) as the standard while British English considers the Received Pronunciation (RP) as the standard. Other varieties also have developed their own standard English like standard Singapore English (SSE), and standard Philippine English (PE). These many standards of English have their own distinct linguistic and pragmatic features. Since every English variety is distinct in lexical, structural, prosodic and pragmatic features, problems in miscommunication and misunderstanding occur. The non-native speakers of English display L1 influence in the L2 English that they use. Besides, cultural norms also affect the forms for certain speech acts. Typologically different languages impose certain types of interference. In short, when people using different varieties of English communicate it can lead to misunderstanding and misinterpretation. LI interference influences the speaker's pronunciation, syntax, grammar and even pragmatics. Crosstalk may also arise due to variations in accent, intonation, pause, volume and timbre. Misunderstanding may also arise due to typologically grounded peculiarities of accent and influence of native languages as well as due to non-verbal codes in one culture being understood differently by another culture.

Both verbal and nonverbal codes in communication are influenced by the four K-components of any discourse, namely, (i) *content*, (ii) *context*, (iii) *communicants* and (iv) *comprehension*. Professional discourse emphasizes the first and the fourth K-components—-the content of talk and the mutual comprehension of interlocutors or speech partners in an interaction. Crosstalk or miscommunication occurs when one sign has various meanings (homonymy) or when a variety of signs has the same meaning (synonymy). The main task of this study is to compare crosstalk in two domains of communication, i.e. personal everyday talk (family and friends) and talk in professional spheres (colleagues and clients). Harnisch (2004) argues that crosstalk in professional discourse is hazardous, but it is also important to come across as polite in phatic communication.

To overcome the barriers in communication among professionals for whom English is not the first language, communicative strategies are used (*see* David 1993; David and Govindasamy 2002). One effective communicative strategy is the use of code-switching and code shifting. Jacobson (1990) discusses overt models of shifts with regard to their reasons, aims and effects on comprehension of a communicative act (David 2003 for existence and reasons for code switching in law courts in Malaysia).

Verbal discourse among professional links can display two models of code switching:

1. the *overt*—in the case of multilinguals as they shift from one language or dialect to another (*see* McLellan and David 2007) and
2. the *covert*—as a result of interference of a native language into a second language.

In this study, the covert model of code switching is analyzed based on several surveys conducted over different periods of time (Treskova 1989a, Harnisch 2004, 2006a). Harnisch's (2006b; 2006c) surveys on professional talk in multilingual environments have been used to specify the behavioral (social and psychological) and linguistic (choice and misuse of words) reasons for misunderstanding among the users of English as a non-native language.

Harnisch (2004) presents factual data of specific scientific terms used in professional discourse by non-native speakers of English in the work domain of foreign companies that have multiplied in new Russia. In addition, secondary data like that of Kirkpatrick (2008) is used to describe the miscommunication that takes place specifically among a range of ASEAN users of English, and for some of them English is a second language while for others it is a foreign language.

32.2 CROSSTALK: FOCUS ON ASIAN ENGLISHES

In some Asian countries where English is widely spoken and serves as an official language, the L1 interference is evident in the lexical, structural, and prosodic features of the new varieties of English. For instance, the variety of English used in Malaysia is known as Malaysian English (ME). This variety is widely used and has started to be codified and to be fully recognized as a distinct variety of English. ME has developed its own vocabulary, syntax and pronunciation which can be understood by Malaysians. Some words like 'cooling', 'auntie', 'uncle', 'borrow' are of English origin but have been given specific connotations in Malaysian English (Jamaliah 2000). Some examples of ME from Wikipedia (http://en.wikipedia.org/wiki/Malaysian_English) are given below:

bungalow — A villa or any semi-detached house regardless of the size or number of storeys.

chop — To stamp (with a rubber stamp), as well as the stamp itself.

condominium — A high-cost flat usually with common facilities.

la (h)! — The prominent trademark in Manglish, the colloquial Malaysian English, it is used for emphasis at the end of a sentence. E.g.: "Are you coming over to the party tonight?"—"Yes, of course lah".

pass up — To hand in.

send — To take somebody to somewhere. E.g. "I'll send you to the airport."

slippers — Japanese sandals; as in US and UK 'flip-flops,' and in Australia 'thongs'.

spoil — To be damaged. E.g. "This one, spoil, lah."

In the same way, the Philippine English (PE) too has developed its own distinct features. Bolton and Butler (2004) studied the dictionaries and the stratification of vocabulary towards a new lexicography for PE. The study revealed that the English in the Philippines is on its way towards legitimization of the PE. Moreover, the Webster unabridged dictionary has included some Anglicized Filipino lexis that are commonly used in education and the media. Anvil-Macquarie (2000) included some PE words like *academician, bed spacer, blowout, comfort room, and holdupper*. Some words taken from the PE dictionary for high school students (Anvil-Macquarie 2000) are the following:

Already — Filipinos like to insert this word to state that they have finished doing something, even though it was completed past the original deadline. In standard English, by contrast, 'already' is only used when something was completed ahead of schedule.

Bad trip — An unfortunate situation (E.g.: "Bad trip! I got into a car accident). In the U.S., a bad trip is usually reserved for drug addicts experiencing a bad experience on a drug high.

Bed spacer — A person, usually a college student, who pays rent for the use of a bed in a private home.

Blowout — Taking several people out to a restaurant and paying for everybody.

Boundary — An amount public transport drivers pay their operators daily; any excess that belongs to the driver as his daily wage.

Calling card — Refers to a 'business card', not a phone card.

It is clear that many of the PE lexical items can be understood only within the country but if they are used in other countries, problems in communication might occur.

Moving on from lexical variation to phonology it is clear that although the phonology of PE resembles that of the North American variant, there is a wide variation according to the speakers' location and their L1. Since many English phonemes are not found in most Philippine languages, pronunciation approximations are extremely common. Some examples of non-native pronunciations are:

Filipino — [pili'pino] or [pʰili'pʰino]

Vehicle — ['bɛhikel] or ['bɛhikol]

Find — ['pɐjnd] or ['pʰɐjnd]

Official — [o'pisʲɐl] or [o'pʰisʲɐl]

Very — ['bɛri] or ['bejri]

This list applies mainly to Tagalog speakers; a number of other indigenous languages in the Philippines employ phonemes such as [f], [v], and [z]. It should also be noted that this form of mispronunciation, caused by the limited sound inventories of most Philippine languages compared to English (which has more than 40 phonemes), is generally frowned upon by Anglophone Filipinos and businesses dealing with international clients.

These English varieties in southeast Asia are flourishing and have their own identity but do result in crosstalk even among the Asian users of English. Kirkpatrick (2008) discusses several examples of such crosstalk among the Asean speakers:

Examples of the **use of full vowels in unstressed syllables**:
　It is Officially launched.　(male Indonesian)
　When I first came TO Singapore.　(male Thai)

Examples of **stressing pronoun**:
　And HE has been in Singapore three times.　(female Burmese)
　I grew up with a lot of languages around ME.　(female Bruneian)

Examples of **heavy end stress**:
　We have the government schools and the private SCHOOLS.
　　　　　　　　　　　　　　　　　　　　　　(female Bruneian)
　And very few people speak ENGLISH.　(male Cambodian)

32.3　CULTURAL VARIATION IN PHATIC TALK

Phatic talk seems to be common among professionals particularly in acknowledging the presence of the other person. It may appear in a form of greetings and in the realization of words like 'Hello,' 'Hi,' and 'How are you?'. People from the same speech community will have no problem in understanding "Have you eaten?" as a greeting, but this question can be misunderstood as a greeting (David 2004). As phatic communication is culturally bound, there are possibilities of miscommunication and misunderstanding if both the speakers belong to different speech communities. The interlocutors' interpretation can be positive or negative depending on their communicative competence. Such competence is more complex to acquire as it goes beyond the lexical terms and includes pragmatic and cultural aspects. For example, Native speakers understand that a greeting like "How are you?" is but phatic talk, however, non-native speakers of English might interpret it as a form actually warranting detailed response and a sincere need to know one's condition.

32.3.1　Speech Acts

A speech act is the function performed by our utterances. For instance, greetings (*ibid.*), complimenting (David 2002), disagreement (*see* Jariah and David 1996); requests (David, et al. 2002; Kuang, et al. 2006), directives (David and Kuang 1999) are all examples of speech acts. The way a speech act is performed in any given language can be very culture specific. Culture-specific speech acts necessitate a familiarity with the value systems of the interlocutors in the interaction. In some cultures, an acceptance of the compliment is the norm, while in other cultures an acceptance would signify an infringement of the cultural norms. Such a breakdown in phatic talk results in misunderstandings across cultures.

32.3.2 Direct and Indirect Discourses

In some cultures, directness in discourse is deemed the polite norm. Time is not wasted and intentions are clearly stated. Yet, in other cultures, indirectness is deemed polite behavior and aids in conflict avoidance. "To be polite is saying the socially acceptable thing," says Lakoff (1975: 53). In some other cultures, it would not do to respond to a compliment with a mere "Thank you," for this would mean that one was openly acknowledging the fact; for example, 'that one was pretty,' and 'had a handsome husband' (*see* David 2002). It is important to note here that the language in which compliments are couched vary across cultures. In the Malaysian context, if a person says "You are like the moon," most young Malaysians will feel offended and may not perceive it as a compliment as they think that they are being told that they have gained weight.

In Malaysia, politeness is usually performed by an indirect form of discourse. This type of communication is perhaps rooted in the Malay culture. Jamaliah (1995, 1999, 2000) states that the Malays are overall an unassuming people whose most obvious trait is the need to be "subtle". She says:

> The use of indirectness in communication is an important aspect of Malay community life because one of its main intentions is conflict avoidance. (1995: 19)

Morais (1995: 103), while investigating how the employees of a business organisation communicate, states that the Malay workers "tend to be subtle and oblique in their approach and much of their true intention is left unstated and has to be inferred." Asmah (1995: 4) also maintains that Malays are more indirect (compared to the other ethnic groups in the country), are more subtle in putting their message forward (suggesting that they engage in euphemisms instead) and have a tendency to beat-around-the-bush (which she refers to as BAB) because they do not want to hurt the feelings of their interlocutors. On the other hand, the Malaysian Chinese are more open and direct in their ways although some may adjust and accommodate when in the company of Malay friends. David and Kuang (1999) found that the Chinese are more direct because of the commercial factor of "time being precious". Jamaliah mentions that the Chinese students in her study were "... more practical and objective" than their non-Chinese counterparts." It seems then that the Malaysian Chinese tend to be more direct in their discourse. Therefore, inevitably, crosstalk can occur even within a nation between those who favor direct talk as compared to those who deem it polite to be indirect.

Linguistic interference occurs due to typological difference between two language structures. It is usually one's native language that interferes with the non-native one at all levels of a language structure. An example of linguistic interference due to mispronunciation follows:

Occasional substitution [o:] with [ou] for o; [æ] with [ei]:

An Indian host to his guest: [*maj'dia frens sneik iz weitiŋ in houl*]. He wanted to say: ***My dear friends! Snack is waiting for you in hall.*** But what he said was: ***Me dear friends! Snake is waiting for you in hole.***

More often, **phonetic interference** occurs in a foreign language when substitution takes place, e.g. a Russian speaking in English tends to use [t] or [d] instead of the English thorns [ð] and [θ].

Semantic interference is the interference of notions and words when the same word can have different meanings in various languages. For example:

He has good command of English means He has good knowledge of English. This is wrongly translated into Russian *as **His command in English was good*** since Russian *команда* [komanda] means (i) *'a team'* and (ii) *order*.

Interference of cognition is the interference of concepts and terminology among either various kinds of professions or different methodology of approaches within the same domain of professional activity. Examples are:

1. Doublets
   (i) benzene // petroleum; Russian *нефть* [neft'] // English *oil*
   (ii) *English: **a car** //**automobile** // **machine**; Russian: **автомобиль**[*avtama'bil] // *машина* [ma'ʃina]
2. Triplet
   (i) In Azeri: ***tezlik** /chastota / frekvinsi* for 'frequencies' (**Tezlik** is Azeri. '**Chastota**' is borrowed from Russian and 'Frekvinsi' is borrowed from English).

32.4 METHODOLOGY

The survey was carried out in several stages. Firstly, factual data that led to crosstalk was obtained. One example is the doublets of a term, borrowed from different languages. The data was collected and examples highlighted. Secondly, a list of questions resulting from the analysis of the data was composed for the interviews with the L2 experts in technology and mass media. These experts had high English language proficiency and read professional literature in English. Finally, the data were verified by special dictionaries.

32.5 DATA ANALYSIS

The overview of collected and verified data has been conducted to classify the types of crosstalk that have been displayed by the respondents in the tests.

On the basis of our classification, the following two types of oppositions are specified:

1. **Factual (linguistic) opposition** when the same meaning of a term is presented by variables, e.g. the lexical, phonetical and morphological variables.
2. **Semantic opposition** is where when one and the same unit has several meanings.

32.6 ENGLISH FOR SPECIAL PURPOSES (ESP)

Let us start with scientific terminology—the origins of its formation. One way of coining a term is to **borrow** it from other languages. A number of terms in ESP come from Greek, e.g. *electricity,* and Latin, e.g. *calculation*. Most of the terms especially in electronics come from English. A scientific term can be calqued semantically. For instance, the Russian *zagruzhat* is a semantic calque from the English *to load.* A term can also be coined as semi-calques, for example, the Russian *televidenije* for television. Some lexical items in one language can, therefore, be scientific terms as a result of semantic calques. It should also be pointed out that some inventions have got the names of their inventors, e.g. Xerox, Roentgen, and Diesel. One of the writers when working in London was baffled by the term 'tipex' as it was referred to as blanco in Malaysia!

This study views the problem of origin and usage of scientific terms within the framework of two types of oppositions: (i) the factual opposition, where the same meaning of a term is presented by lexical, phonetic and morphological variables, and (ii) the semantic opposition.

32.6.1 Factual Opposition

Lexical duplets due to etymology of terms

It is argued that loans occur either with or without bilingualism and direct contact. The borrowed words usually go through some adaptation at different levels of a language due to internal or structural demands and this results in the same term sounding different in different Englishes. The English television [televizin] is loaned into Russian as a semi-calque телевидени [tele'videnije], in Japanese as [terebion] and in Malay as [talivesen]. Even those who have mastered English are non-native speakers of English, some interference or accent in their usage of English will emerge.

Phonetical duplets due to interference

English sounds are used in the speech of non-native speakers and hence undergo some phonetic adaptation due to a num-ber of causes, e.g.:

1. The similarities and differences between the two sound systems; and
2. The degree of assimilation of the loaned terminologies in one's native language.

Some English sounds have no analogy in other languages, e.g. English thorns [ð] and [θ]. The non-native speakers of English tend to substitute them with consonants such as [s], [z], [t], and [d] in their native language that may sound like English [ð] or [θ]. Thus, the Danish speakers of English would say *theory* as [siori] or [tiori] and *thriller* as [sriller] or [triller]; the Bulgarians would pronounce *theory* as [deori] and *thriller* as [driller]; the Japanese would say [seorii] to mean theory; and the Russians speaking English would prefer [t] instead of [θ]. They pronounce *theory* as [teori] and *thriller* as [triller].

Some languages, Turkish and Japanese, for instance, avoid sound junctions, so some vowels can be pronounced at the starting position of a word beginning with two consonants. If two consonants appear in the middle of a word, a vowel is used to divide the two consonants. Thus, English *screw* 'propeller' sounds like [uskur] in Turkish and *text* sounds like [tekisuto] in Japanese.

Since there is no phonological distinction between long and short vowels in Russian, the Russian speakers of English do not appear to worry about correct pronunciation of words like English *bit* and *beet*. Sometimes, they pronounce these words as if they were the same. In the same way, as the English speakers do not palatalize consonants, they hear no difference between the Russian быть [byt'] 'to be' and бить [bit'] 'to beat'. Also, since in Japanese the sounds [r] and [l] are not distinguished phonologically, consequently, it is possible to substitute them without any semantic effect. Thus, the English *right* and *light* may both sound as [rajto] in Japanese. The sound [v] is not phonologically significant for the Japanese and it can be substituted by the sound [b]. As a result, an English *volt* sounds as [boruto] in Japanese.

Morphological duplets due to different models of word formation

Some loans go through morphological adaptation. The English term *E-mail* (electronic post) is morphologically adapted in Russian and has its plural form [imejly] 'e-mails' and can be used as a verb, e.g. [imejlit'] 'to send e-mails'. The Russian verb копировать [kopirovat'] and the Japanese verb [kopii-suru] are used to mean the same English verb 'to copy'. Both words are coined by using the borrowed root [kopi] plus their own respective grammatical aids to arrive at a verb form. Such loans used in professional discourses (Treskova 1989) could cause crosstalk and communication breakdown.

Lexical oppositions: Compound terms versus abbreviations

A compound term made of two words can be of two types:

1. Noun + Noun, i.e. (N + N)
    e.g., *radio waves,* and *mass media*
2. Adjective + Noun (A + N)
    e.g., *high technologies,* and *direct impact*

Terms made of three or more words can be like (A1) + N1 + (A2) + N2 ... + A*n* + N*n* in which *n* means the number of words. Some nouns may not have adjectives. That is why (A) for an adjective is in parentheses. In order to avoid usage of compound terms, two types of abbreviation are used: (i) acronyms (made of letters) and (ii) morphemic. For example, English *laser* is an acronym for 'light amplification by stimulated emission of radiations'. Many languages have borrowed it as a term. The German [s] sounds as [z] in intervocalic positions are borrowed as *lazer* into Russian.

Professional colloquialisms versus standard terms

The principle of language economy works in verbal usage. Either a word or a word combination tends to be reduced if the frequency of use of a lexical item or unit increases (Martinet 1960: 178). This is also known as the language law of economy. For instance, the French *metro* is a shortened form for *chemin de fer metropolitain* (*ibid.*). Shortening the official term is one way to coin colloquial terms. The English *dynamo* is a shortened form of dynamo-electric machine. Similarly, the English *frig* refers to refrigerator, *tivi* to a TV-set and the Russian *auto* to automobile. The Japanese *terebi* is a shortened form for [terebion]—television.

The other way to invent colloquial terms is by the use of a metaphor. Metaphors are not alien in terminology for science. Thus, the English 'white noise' is a term to indicate distinctive limits of sensibility of technical devices towards noises in the channel. Professional colloquialisms are the result of the (i) conceptualization of new notions by experts and (ii) high frequency of usage of certain terms in a given domain. The use of metaphors is peculiar in various domains and in different tongues. That is why it is not always easy either to understand or translate professional colloquialisms from one tongue into another. In short, factual oppositions of verbal signs in professional thesauri are the result of three types of alternations:

1. An own term versus a loan;
2. A compound terms versus its abbreviations; and
3. An officially accepted term versus its colloquialisms.

Such oppositions can reduce comprehension especially if the speakers are non-native speakers of English and, moreover, their native tongues are typologically different.

32.6.2 Semantic Opposition

Semantic opposition occurs when one lexical item has several meanings. The semantic variables arise as a result of two tendencies. The first is the tendency of a language to adopt a foreign word according to its own phonetic and grammatical rules. The second is the tendency to conceptualize one and the same word differently. A word's semantic field can seldom be as narrow as to limit itself to only one meaning with the exception of functional words like yes, no, and, if, and when. Generally, however, a word has more than one meaning and/or connotation. In addition, one and the same word borrowed by several languages can sound differently or can go through morphological adaptation. The word can even have different meanings. For instance, the Russian words губернатор [gubernator], гувернант [guvernant] 'home teacher' and the term *cybernetics* as well as the English *Governor* have the same origin, i.e. the Greek κυβερνητης 'steersman'. This example shows how the same word can vary in its sound, grammar and even meaning when it is borrowed by different languages and used for various purposes.

32.6.3 Opposition between Verbal versus Nonverbal Signs

An opposition between verbal and nonverbal signs is usually seen as the opposition between linguistic and non-linguistic symbols, e.g. the English noun *water* and its chemical formula H_2O. A pictograph of running water from a tap can also be used to mean 'water'. Such opposition can be classified as factual opposition since different signs are used to refer to the same object. Nowadays, a number of nonverbal symbols are used internationally, for instance, the signs for traffic systems.

In the context of professional discourse, the main issue is an opposition between a term and its artificial symbol. One can use numbers, letters, symbols and pictures as signs of nonverbal code. Numbers are used in mathematics. Latin letters are used in Chemistry. Pictures and symbols are used by international aviation, traffic, tourism, etc. It is, therefore, important to have reliable and safe techniques for gauging the multilingual content of professional exchanges so as to prevent communication breakdown or misunderstanding.

32.7 DISCUSSION

Most interactions among non-native speakers of English may lead to miscommunication due to some differences in the lexical, phonological and structural features of the language and due to pragmatic breakdowns. Although one language (e.g. English) is used, the problem arises as the varieties of the target language are different and the influence of L1 on L2 also varies. This problem can become more complicated specifically in a context where both interlocutors are required to use their own professional registers.

Miscommunication and misunderstanding occur due to pragmatic factors and due to linguistic factors like lexical duplets due to etymology of terms, phonetical duplets due to interference, morphological duplets due to different models of word formation, compound terms, and different professional colloquialisms.

The aim of Harnisch's (2004) study was to determine how interference influences mutual comprehension in professional discourse. The results and data of the survey analysed focused on the factual and semantical oppositions. Factual and semantic verbal code switching was noted resulting in two models of code switching, viz. the overt and covert models being developed. The overt model is demonstrated by a switch from one language to another by a bilingual communicant and it occurs mainly due to communicative strategies. The covert types of code switching are mainly due to interference between two languages on contact. They are seen in the accent of a bilingual. In the English language performance of non-native speakers of English, they have both theoretical and applied importance. Theoretically, it is interesting to compare the cases of interference at different levels of language structure as displayed in the varieties of English used. Such informed knowledge can be used to teach English to L2 or foreign language users and textbooks, and bilingual dictionaries can be produced based on the results of such surveys.

In the case of English used in professional discourse by speakers of local languages, it is possible to distinguish between the elaborated and restricted versions of English. There are, therefore, educated experts in natural sciences who can speak good English as a foreign language. However, there are also a number of professionals who use English with incorrect pronunciation and with limited knowledge of grammar. As a result, code switching becomes common. The covert model is a peculiar type of language used in interactions amongst those for whom English is not an L1.

32.7.1 Pedagogical Implications: English for Specific Purpose

Since there is the need for verbal communication among professionals, a solid knowledge of some international language(s) is recommended especially for the technicians, operators and R&Ds. Hence, programmes of English for Special Purposes (ESP) must be introduced to students and adults as a part of their professional qualification.

English is adopted for special purposes as a link in international aviation and navigation. But its success depends not only on the pragmatic knowledge and communicative competence of non-native professionals who use English but also we have to bear in mind the influence of L1 on English at different linguistic levels—be it choice of words, accent, etc. Mutual understanding among communicators is essential in the case of professional discourse.

Since interference in English arises because of L1 influence, the following measures are recommended:

1. We should improve methods of English teaching to non-native speakers focusing on the needs of learners of ESP.
2. We need to introduce a course which discusses classified varieties of interference in English, especially in professional talk.
3. We should standardize special international terminologies and support the publishing of bilingual and multilingual dictionaries in professional fields.

32.8 CONCLUSION

Intercultural communication obviously occurs in intercultural contact settings. These settings, and the types of people who may be involved, can be variable. Naturally, intercultural communication occurs in a very wide range of domains, including education, international business, healthcare, the workplace, and the community.

This study aims to present the results of the survey of professional talk by R&Ds whose native languages differ from English and to specify two types of oppositions of a sign—factual and semantic—as the overt versus covert models of code switching and to demonstrate how interference of native tongues into a foreign language can cause misunderstanding in ESP.

Theories of code switching and methods of discourse analysis are noted in our survey of professional talk and validate the need for sociologists and linguists to work together in scientific research projects. Since innovations in technologies are constant and quick, some additional introduction of newly accepted terms and notions should be publicized in local, scientific and popular journals and manuals for students and experts. A database of professional and semiprofessional terms, idioms and colloquialisms should be developed. We also need to learn to analyze the factual and semantic types of oppositions displayed within professional spheres.

REFERENCES

Anvil-Macquarie, *Anvil-Macquarie Dictionary of Philippine English for High School*, Manila: Anvil Publishing, 2000.

Asmah, Haji Omar, "Indirectness as a rule of speaking among the Malays 47–60," *Rules of Speaking,* Zainab Abdul Majid and Loga Mahesan Baskaran (Eds.), Petaling Jaya: Pelanduk Publications, 1995.

Bolton, Kingsley and Butler, Susan, "Dictionaries and the stratification of vocabulary: Towards a new lexicography for Philippine English," *World Englishes* **23**.1 (2004): 91–112.

David, M.K., "'You look good': Responses of Malaysians to compliments," *Diverse voices 2: Selected Readings in English,* Rosli Talif et al. (Eds.) Serdang: Faculty of Modern Languages and Communication, Universiti Putra Malaysia, 2002, 111–119.

David, M.K., "Function and role of code switching in Malaysian courts," *Multilingua* **21** (2003): 1–20.

_____ (Ed.), "Greetings in multilingual Malaysia," *Language, Ethnicity and the Mind* 2, Adyghe State University, Maikop, Russian Federation: RIO AGU Publishers, 2004, 10–16.

_____, "Language and the law: Communicative strategies in a court of law—A Malaysian experience," *Legal Education in Malaysia—Quo Vadis?* Lake Tee Khaw (Ed.), 20th Anniversary Law Conference Proceedings, Kuala Lumpur: University of Malaya (1993), 109–116.

David M.K. and Govindasamy, S., "Communicative strategies and cross-cultural awareness: Core components for business English," *Teaching English for International Business*, 2002.

David, M.K. and Kuang, C.H., "Interethnic variations in the use of directives in Malaysia," *The Hong Kong Linguist* (1999): 19–20, 36–44.

David, M.K., Kuang, C.H. and Don Zuraidah Mohd., "Routines of request in an academic setting," in C. Lee and W. Littlewood (Eds.), *Culture, Communication and Language Pedagogy*, Language Centre: Hong Kong Baptist University, 2002, 11–24.

Harnisch, Svetlana, "Languages of technologies," *Yazyki i Transnational Problems (Languages and Transnational Problems)*, Moscow: Tambov, 2004, 100–112.

_____, "Education and language policy in a modern society," *Paper presented at the 16th World Congress of Sociology in Durban, SA*, 2006a. Details retrieved from website http://www./E:/rc25.htm/.

_____, "Language and education policy in a modern society," *The Quality of Social Existence in a Globalizing World*, Moscow Durban: Maska, 2006b, 155–162.

_____, "Technological networks in a multilingual environment," *Paper presented at the 16th World Congress of Sociology in Durban, SA*, 2006c. Details retrieved from website http://www./E:/rc25.htm/.

Jacobson, Rodolfo (Ed.), *Language Distribution Issues in Bilingual Schooling*, Clevedon, UK: Multilingual Matters, 1990.

Jamaliah, Mohd. Ali, *Verbal Communication: A Study of Malaysian Speakers*, Kuala Lumpur: Universiti Malaya Press, 2000.

_____, "The pragmatics of cross-cultural communication in a Malaysian context," *Rules of Speaking*, Zainab Abdul Majid and Loga Mahesan Baskaran (Eds.), Petaling Jaya: Pelanduk Publications, 1995, 112–124.

_____, "Indirectness in Malay Diplomacy with Particular Reference to Business Dealings and Labour Relations," *Jurnal Bahasa Moden* 9 (1999): 19–28.

Jariah, Mohd. Jan and David, M.K., "Oral skills: A need for acceptance of L1 cultural norms," *Pertanika Journal of Social Science and Humanities* **4** (1996): 11–19.

Kirkpatrick, Andy, "English as the official working language of the Association of Southeast Asian Nations (ASEAN): Features and strategies," *English Today* **94**.24 (2) (2008).

Kuang, C.H., David, M.K., and Don, Zuraidah Mohd, "Requests: Voices of Malaysian children," *Multilingua* **25** (2006): 27–42.

Lakoff, Robin, *Language and Women's Place*, New York: Harper and Row, 1975.

Martinet, Andr, *Elements of General Linguistics*, Trans. Elizabeth Palmer, London: Faber and Faber, 1960.

McLellan, J. and David, M.K., "A review of code-switching research in Malaysia and Brunei Darussalam," *Englishes in South East Asia*, A. Kirkpatrick, D. Prescott, I. Martin and A. Hashim (Eds.), Cambridge, UK: Cambridge Scholars Press, 2007.

Morais, Elaine, "Some preliminary observations of business communication in Malaysia: A cross-cultural perspective," *Rules of Speaking*, Zainab Abdul Majid and Loga Mahesan Baskaran (Eds.)," Petaling Jaya: Pelanduk Publications, 1995, 94–111.

Treskova, S.I., *Sots iolingvisticheskie problemy massovoi Kommunikats li*, Moskva: Nauka, 1989.

OTHER SOURCES

Mladenov, M., *Televizionnaja Zhurnalistika* (Journalism of Televroadcasting), Sofia, 1975.

Pokorny, Julius, *Indogermanisches Etymologisches Woerterbuch*, Bern, Munich: Francke Verlag, 1959.

Romaji-Dokuwa-jiten, *Deutsch-Japanisch Woerterbuch*, Verlag Euderle, 1984.

Technical Terms Dictionary, English-Russian, Moscow, 1962.

Technical Terms Dictionary, Russian-English, Moscow, 1951.

Turkic Terms of Automatic Control, Baku, 1971.

Wennreich, Robert, *International Dictionary of Abbreviations and Acronyms of Electronics, Electrical Engineering, Computer Technology, and Information Processing*, 1–2 vv, Munich, London, New York, Paris, 1992.

Part 10

CURRICULUM DEVELOPMENT

Chapter 33

UNIVERSALS IN THE PROCESS OF CURRICULUM DEVELOPMENT IN ELT

— E.A. Gamini Foneska

33.1 INTRODUCTION

This chapter addresses an awareness of some universals followed in the process of curriculum development that teachers and learners of ELT should have cultivated in the study of ELT methodology as well as in making decisions regarding educational management. Depending on the ethos of the institution, the aspirations of the clientele, the demands imposed by the social, cultural, academic and professional situations where the clients are supposed to move about in reality, the subject knowledge aimed at to be introduced in the course, the academic levels aimed at to be achieved in the course, the academic and professional background of the teachers, the facilities available within the institution, the methods of teaching aimed to be applied in classroom management, etc., the shape of one curriculum may differ from another though they both concentrate on a similar type of course in English. This implies that the rationale for a curriculum is circumstantial to these factors. Yet there are some universals which govern the process of curriculum development and the adherence to them is meant to preserve the systematicity of a course of study. This chapter introduces 'universals'—some principles and practices that are followed universally in curriculum development—and attempts to make a systematic presentation of these universals as it is realized that the knowledge of them will benefit the teachers, teacher educators, and teacher trainees.

33.2 DEFINITION OF CURRICULUM

In ELT literature, *curriculum* is defined by various authors in different ways. However, there is still room for improving the definitions already developed and used widely. An understanding of curriculum would be important for the decision makers as well as the teachers and the students who are concerned with the development and implementation of it. This is because the right conceptualization of the curriculum only guarantees a reasonable adherence to it by the teachers and students, and the success of a course lies in the successful implementation of the curriculum.

Richards et al. (1985: 70) define curriculum as (see also Brown 1992: 117)

> An educational programme which states: (a) the educational purpose of the programme (the ends); (b) the contents, teaching procedures and learning experiences which will be necessary to achieve this purpose (the means); (c) some means for assessing whether the educational goals have been achieved.

In this definition, the term "the educational purpose of the programme" focuses on a large number of processes and preliminary considerations involved in the actual development process of a curriculum, and it remains obscure because of its vast coverage. Yet the second part of the definition "the contents, teaching procedures and learning experiences which will be necessary to achieve this purpose" gathers prominence and saves the value of the definition because it addresses some actualities experienced and needed in the adherence to a curriculum. Again, the phrase that relates the third part of the definition "some means for assessing whether the educational goals have been achieved" implies that these 'means for assessing' the achievements are applied at a specific stage separate from the determination of 'the purpose' and 'the contents ... teaching procedures ... learning experiences' in the implementation of the curriculum. However, it is discernible that in this definition, the fundamentals of a curriculum are presented though in a vague manner.

In his definition of a curriculum, Christopher Candlin (1984; *see* Nunan 1998: 4) suggests:

> Curricula are concerned with making general statements about language learning, learning purpose and experience, evaluation, and the role of relationships of teachers and learners.

He makes a step further than Richards et al. (1985) by indicating the role of relationship of teachers and learners which is crucial in the successful completion of a course. This sheds light on the collaborative aspect of the curriculum. According to Candlin (*ibid.*), they will also contain banks of learning items and suggestions about how these might be used in class. Syllabi, on the other hand, are more localized and are based on the accounts and records of what actually happens at the classroom level as teachers and learners apply a given curriculum to their own situation.

The mention of "banks of items and suggestions" about the use of "learning purpose and experience, evaluation, and the role relationships of teachers and learners" (*ibid.*) as contents of a curriculum is of some importance as it implies that the curriculum is not just a policy document but a guide to a large process or a total mechanism.

Brown (1992: 117) has realized in his definition that curriculum and curriculum development cannot be separated. He has developed a model for curriculum emphasizing evaluation at the realization of every component of it: needs, objectives, materials, and methods of teaching and testing. In fact, the emphasis on evaluation at every stage of its evolution prevents it from being rigid, static, and arbitrary and allows it to be flexible, dynamic and participatory or collaborative. This is easily realized from the diagram (Figure 33.1) developed by Brown.

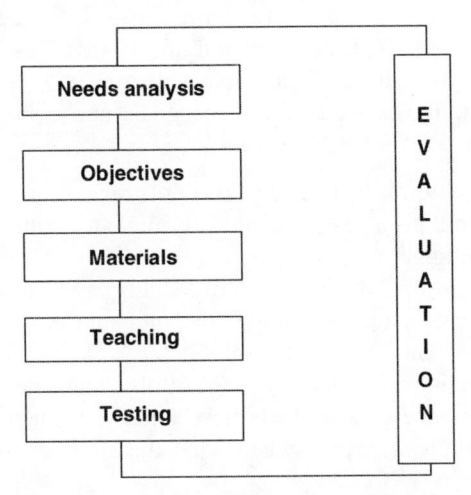

FIGURE 33.1 Curriculum development model.

A clearer view of the curriculum emerges from an excerpt from Richards (2001). According to him, the curriculum is a comprehensive, ongoing, cyclical process which determines:

> The needs of a group of learners; to develop aims or objectives for a program to address those needs; to determine an appropriate syllabus, course structure, teaching methods, and materials; and to carry out an evaluation of the language program that results from these processes. (p. 2)

The curriculum development process should reflect need analysis and ideologies about language, language teaching and learning.

33.3 DEVELOPMENT OF A CURRICULUM

In order to ensure that a suitable procedure is established for the development of a course of study, the following tasks are carried out (Snyder and Stoller 2003):

- Needs analysis
- Situation analysis
- Specification of goals, objectives and outcomes
- Syllabus design and course planning
- Materials selection and development

- Course "piloting"
- Course evaluation

These tasks are so interrelated with each other that none can be completed without carrying out the others in the order presented. They have been defined by Snyder and Stoller (*ibid.*) in the following way:

Needs analysis: It is a cyclical process—that takes place prior to, during, and after courses have been taught. It involves the collection of information that can be used to develop a profile of the needs of a group of learners for making decisions about the goals and contents of a language curriculum (and its courses).

- Determination of who the students are (e.g. their educational background, prior experiences with English, attitudes toward English and the English needs).
- Determination of the students' language abilities (e.g. their communicative abilities, pragmatic competence, strategic competence, and formal knowledge of English).
- Determination of which language skills, language strategies, content and experiences the students need and for what purposes.
- Identification of gap between what the students are able to do and what they need to do.
- Identification of perceived and present needs as well as potential and unrecognized needs.

Situation analysis: A continual/cyclical process that takes place prior to, during and after courses have been taught. It involves the collection of information about the broader context in which the instruction is given in order to be able to make decisions about the goals and contents of a language curriculum (and its courses).

- Identification of stakeholders (e.g. higher administration, program administrators, teachers, parents, educational and other government officials) and their attitudes toward English language instruction.
- Examination of societal factors in relation to language education.
- Examination of institutional factors that may facilitate or hinder change and innovation at the curricular level.
- Examination of teacher factors (e.g. language proficiency, teaching experience and skills, qualifications, morale, motivation, beliefs about language teaching, and language learning).

Specification of goals, objectives, and outcomes: Specification of goals (general purposes of a curriculum), objectives (more specific and concrete description of purposes/goals) and learning outcomes (what the students will have learned/ be able to do) based on the needs and situation analyses and ideologies about language learning and language teaching. The goals and objectives statements should provide guidelines for teachers, materials writers, test writers and learners, and focus for instruction and evaluation. They often focus on such learning areas as language, strategies, content and experiences.

Syllabus design and course planning: Translation of goals, objectives and targeted outcomes into a decision about the structure of courses within the curriculum, the distribution of course content, breadth and depth of content coverage at different levels, adaptation of different syllabus frameworks (e.g. grammatical, skills-based, task-based, content-based, and situational) to meet goals and objectives. The course syllabi will identify what, when and how it is to be taught (thereby providing additional guidance for teachers, materials writers, test writers, and learners).

Materials selection and development: The evaluation of commercial materials determines their appropriacy to previous steps in the curriculum-development process. Decisions about what commercial materials to adopt, what in-house materials should be created and how primary materials might be adapted and/or supplemented to accomplish goals, objectives, and targeted outcomes.

Course "piloting": Implementation of courses, with ongoing evaluation (thereby making almost all courses pilot courses) and fine-tuning in response to evolving student needs, teacher abilities, institutional goals and objectives, etc.

Curriculum evaluation: The ongoing cycle of (formative and summative) evaluation of all aspects of the curriculum in order to understand how successfully the program works and whether it, in all its complexity, is responding to students' needs, teachers' abilities, etc.

The procedure presented in the above order is considered to be effective in curriculum development. The definitions reveal the significance of each task carried out in this process in the light of successful classroom management aimed at providing an effective course of study. Yet it is important to examine the methodological principle behind each of them in order to realize the guarantee they can provide for the success of a course.

33.4 PEDAGOGICAL ANALYSIS OF CURRICULUM DEVELOPMENT PROCESS

It is realized that needs analysis takes place prior to, during and after a course has been taught. In a humanistic approach to teaching a language, while the learners are treated as humans, their learning needs have to be realized in all stages of a course. Therefore, needs analysis is vital at every stage of a course. It is of fundamental importance for a course to study the students' exposure to English, their present language abilities, their aspirations to learn specific language skills, the shift they aim at making in their progress in learning the language and the needs crucial for them, but unrecognized by the students, because the discoveries made in this sense support the maintenance of the relevance of a course. If the learner needs are ignored, the course has no bearing on their progress in life. Therefore, in order to make the other activities carried out in connection with a course, a careful needs analysis is always important.

Like needs analysis, situation analysis should take place before, during and after a course has been taught. The fund of intelligence gathered by the institution through situation analysis helps to be realistic in the decisions taken about the goals and contents of a language curriculum and about the instruction given in a broader context. Without realizing the attitudes of the stakeholders towards English language instruction, societal factors in relation to language education, institutional factors that may facilitate or hinder change and innovation at the curricular level, and teacher factors, an institution is unable to remain firm in its decisions about the conduction of a course. The stakeholders, the society, the institution, and the teachers, all have a significant share of responsibility towards the conduction of a course as its sustainability lies in their attitudes to it. The curriculum maintains its currency through the modifications it undergoes under the influence of these factors.

In formulating, marketing and managing a course, specification of goals, objectives, and outcomes is of great importance. A course is totally dependent on these as there is no syllabus without them. As clients can be attracted to a course only through a proper introduction to the goals, objectives and outcomes targeted at in it, there is no way of marketing a course without specifying them. Without any emphasis on these, there is no management of a course either. Therefore, if the course managers or leaders are not articulate about these, they will not be able to make any progress in the course's design, marketing and managing as they are meant to provide guidelines for teachers, materials writers, test writers and learners in determining inputs, strategies, contents and experiences which profess the goals, objectives and outcomes. On the other hand, the learners, too, can make their decisions based on their understanding of the programme by going through the goals, objectives and outcomes. Even in monitoring the conduction of a course, alertness to these is important. Therefore, their position next to situation analysis is very important.

Specialists in ELT interpret the act of syllabus design and course planning as the translation of goals, objectives and targeted outcomes into a decision about the structure of courses within the curriculum, the distribution of course content, breadth and depth of content coverage at different levels, adaptation of different syllabus frameworks leading to the achievements aimed at in the entire curriculum development endeavour (*ibid.*). The trend of the course to be grammatical, skills-based, task-based, content-based, or situational is determined in the event of designing the syllabus and planning the course.

> 'Curriculum' is concerned with the planning, implementation, evaluation, management, and administration of educational programmes. 'Syllabus,' on the other hand, focuses more narrowly on the selection and grading of content. (Nunan 1988: 8).

In fact, whatever transpires in class in terms of achieving knowledge, practice, experience, or expertise is realized through the contents of the syllabus.

The contents of the syllabus lead to two activities with regard to the learning materials used in a course: (i) selection and (ii) development. Materials are found in three different ways:

1. Recommending complete books produced by commercial publishers under the authorship of various experts,
2. Extracting materials from such sources and producing collections of materials to suit the syllabus or syllabuses and
3. Creating the institution's own materials based on their experience of the learner potentials.

This is a very crucial activity as it directly addresses the accomplishment of goals, objectives and targeted outcomes stipulated in the curriculum.

Armed with a thorough awareness of the learner needs, a clear perception of the situation, a logical syllabus design, and a portfolio complete with materials that match the syllabus contents, the teachers and educational managers carry out course piloting. By course piloting, Snyder and Stoller (*op. cit.*) mean the implementation of a course with on-going evaluation and fine-tuning it "in response to evolving student needs, teacher abilities, institutional goals and objectives, etc." Here, the implementation of a curriculum is endowed with an organic value as all aspects of it are recognized to be evolving, or growing, or changing in the course of time.

Like all other aspects of curriculum development, curriculum evaluation has a strong effect on the success of the curriculum implementation. As evaluation is carried out at all preliminary stages of curriculum development in a formative sense, and finally at the last stage in a summative sense, it guarantees the smooth conduction of a course. Evaluation helps understand how successfully a programme works and whether it, in all its complexity, is responding to the student needs, teacher abilities, etc. The evidence of success can be produced on the results earned at the evaluation and, therefore, evaluation requires to be considered indispensable in every stage of a course.

33.5 SUSTAINABILITY OF EFFECTIVE CURRICULUM DEVELOPMENT POLICY

In order to ensure the sustainability of a curriculum, an institution needs to develop an effective curriculum development policy that supports the efforts made for the development, change and innovation of curricula implemented. This cannot be done as a separate activity; rather it should embrace the entire management of the institution leading to the emergence of a powerful staff development mechanism in order to cultivate vital professional attributes and skills. The staff is not only a group of teachers, but it is also a group of individuals working as curriculum developers, syllabus designers, material developers, quality controllers and simply educational managers in a collaborative academic atmosphere. They should cultivate the professional attributes and skills in an interactive research-oriented staff development mechanism that make them:

- Evaluate alternative approaches and technologies in a range of learning contexts.
- Engage with relevant research, best practice and critical communities.
- Design, plan and take forward a curriculum development project.
- Work effectively with colleagues to identify and overcome difficulties.
- Motivate and support others in the development process.
- Evaluate progress against stated objectives.
- Critique organisational context and work appropriately to promote change.
- Communicate their findings and conclusions to relevant professional audiences.
- Assess and plan their own professional development needs.
- Reflect critically on their own practice, seek feedback and adapt appropriately.

(Adapted from Yorke 2004)

The institution should create an atmosphere where the staff cultivates the relevant professional attributes and skills which help all members operate in the above mode. They become reflective practitioners when they have a tendency to evaluate alternative approaches and technologies by engaging themselves with research and practice communities. Professionalism occurs only when the people are research-oriented and curious about new approaches, technologies and practices. Therefore, their constant interaction with similar interest groups instills in them the necessary confidence to design, plan and continue curriculum-development projects. This, enables them to work effectively with the others, engendering a high level of motivation and spirit of professionalism. Moreover, it helps them carry in a spontaneous way the institution into the future by evaluating the progress it achieves against the objectives stated in its curricula, analyse and critique the organizational context and help achieve the necessary innovations and changes and communicate their findings to the academic bodies. Once the academic body becomes articulate in their professional practices, they can assess and plan their own professional development needs and reflect critically on their own practices and, thus, improve further. In fact, the quality of the curriculum lies in the professional attributes and skills the members of the staff as curriculum implementation is a dynamic process which materializes through the operational behaviour of the staff.

33.6 STUDENT ENGAGEMENT IN THE IMPLEMENTATION OF CURRICULUM

The sustainability of quality in a curriculum, however, is not a responsibility unilaterally handled by the teachers or the members of the academic staff only. It is a responsibility of all persons who are engaged with it. That means, the students also have a role to play in the maintenance of quality in a curriculum. In order to attract student cooperation in the quality assurance, the institution should have a proper value system which recognizes the individuality of the students in a democratic academic atmosphere. After all, education is meant to create a decent society out of the individuals in a community and the ethos of an institution should focus on this function which it is avowed to carry out. Therefore, while focusing the needs of a democratic society, the institution should promote a system of values which enables it to attract the total cooperation of the student body in the successful implementation of the curriculum. Yorke (*ibid.*) has presented the following six values as crucial for an institution in the successful implementation of a curriculum:

Value 1: An understanding of how students learn

All teaching and academic administration should be informed by an understanding of how students learn and the conditions and processes that support student learning.

Value 2: A concern for students' development

Helping students learn must begin with recognition that all students have their own individual learning needs and bring their own knowledge and resources to the learning process. Work with students should empower them and enable them to develop greater capability and competence in their personal and professional lives.

Value 3: A commitment to scholarship

At the base of a teacher's competence is an awareness and acknowledgement of the ideas and theories of others. All teaching should be underpinned by a searching out of new knowledge—both about the subject/discipline and about good teaching and learning practices. All teaching should lead to students developing a questioning and analytical approach.

Value 4: A commitment to work with and learn from colleagues

Much of an academic's work is carried out as part of a team made up of teaching staff and academic support staff. The colleagueship and support of peers is as important as individual academic excellence.

Value 5: The practicing of equal opportunities

Teachers must see that students have equal opportunities irrespective of disabilities, religion, sexual orientation, race or gender. So, everything a teacher does should be informed by equal opportunities legislation, by institutional policy and by knowledge of best practice.

Value 6: Continued reflection on professional practice

Teachers should reflect on their intentions and actions. They should try to understand the reasons for what they see and for the effects of their actions. They, thus, continue to develop their understanding and practice and inform their own learning (*ibid.*).

Of the six values, the first helps all members of teaching and academic administration realize the conditions and processes that support student learning. Learner-centredness, which is in vogue in current methodologies, can be promoted only through an understanding of learner behaviour and the psychological, social, cultural and academic conditions intrinsic to learning. The second value in this structure is simply coincidental to the first. When an understanding of learner behaviour materializes, it leads to a concern for students' development. Without such a concern, the teachers are unable to exploit the learners' own individual learning needs in formulating learning strategies and to bring their own knowledge and resources to the learning process. Teachers also benefit from the possibilities for student empowerment and capacities building that accrue from close interaction with students. The third value gets established in the institutional atmosphere in terms of a commitment to scholarship only when student development becomes the teachers' main concern. Through commitment to scholarship they can achieve professionalism by updating their knowledge of the subject matter as well as by resorting to more sophisticated and effective practices in classroom management. This leads to a collective spirit among the academic staff which concerns the forth value—a commitment to work with and learn from colleagues. The exchange of new ideas and attitudes among the colleagues paves way for both institutional and individual academic excellence. The frustration, the monotony and the boredom that affect the professional zeal of the staff and that ruin institutions will disappear when team spirit is built up this way.

The development of the fifth value, the practicing of equal opportunities, allows the accommodation of students of all individual diversities—physical, social, cultural, gender, etc. All democratic policies in education which impose heavy demands on the academic staff for lofty spiritual values can become the hallmark of an institution only when there is no room for professional, academic, or social grievances and worries within the working milieu. The sixth value, continued reflection on professional practice, actualizes in the academic institution only if the other values have already got established. The self-realization the teachers achieve through the constant reflection on their intentions and actions, and on the effects of their actions transforms them into real reflective practitioners of teaching. All these values, as a whole, support in return the successful implementation of a curriculum. The awareness of learner behaviour, the concern for learner development, the commitment to scholarship and research, the engagement in collaborative academic ventures, the understanding of diversity within classroom dynamics, and the reflection on one's own professional practices for self-realisation professed in these values help create a suitable atmosphere for well-planned curricula.

33.7 CONCLUSION

The universals in curriculum development presented in this chapter do not concretise just because they are displayed in a document. The argument is that curriculum should exist beyond the document and be a part and parcel of the academic and administrative system of the institution as well as the clientele and the community concerned. While it lives on the energy of all the sectors involved in its implementation or the conduction of the course, it benefits them all in reciprocation of their commitment to it. When curriculum is realized this way the institution also has to have its resources—human, intellectual and infrastructural—fine-tuned to the demands it imposed on it. It is for this that the members of the institution need to cultivate the professional attributes, skills and the values enumerated under sustainability of a curriculum and student engagement in curriculum implementation. This chapter argues that the academic administration needs to adjust itself to the attitudinal and moral requirements imposed on it by the curriculum. Then only the entire exercise related to it implementation becomes a success.

REFERENCES

Brown, James Dean, "Social meaning in language curriculum, of language curriculum, and through language curriculum," *Georgetown University Round Table on Languages and Linguistics*, James T. Alatis (Ed.), Georgetown: Georgetown University School of Linguistics, 1992.

Candlin, C., "Design as a Critical Process," in C. Brumfit (Ed.), *General English Syllabus Design,* London: Pergamon Press and The British Council, 1984, pp. 29–46.

Nunan, David, *Syllabus Design*, Oxford: Oxford University Press, 1988.

Richards, Jack C., *Curriculum Development in Language Teaching,* Cambridge: Cambridge University Press, 2001.

Richards, Jack, John Platt and Weber, Heidi, *Longman Dictionary of Applied Linguistics,* Harlow, Essex, England: Longman, 1985.

Snyder, Bill and Stoller, Fredricka L., *Seminar on 'Curriculum Development,'* Ankara: Bilkent University, October 10, 2003.

    http://turkey.usembassy.gov/curriculum_development.html (Accessed on 12.06.2008)

Yorke, Jon, *ELT Professional Attributes, Skills and Values*', Integrated Masters Programme run by Educational Development at the University of Plymouth, Plymouth: University of Plymouth, 2004.

    http://www.educationaldevelopment.net/elt2/overview.htm (Accessed on 20-06-2007)

Chapter 34

COMMUNICATIVE LANGUAGE TEACHING: Problems of Designing Syllabuses and Producing Materials

— MADAN M. SARMA

34.1 INTRODUCTION

An approach to language teaching is shaped and influenced by a set of assumptions or beliefs about what language means, what learning is, how one usually learns a language, and what role the teacher/teaching plays in a formal language-learning situation. These assumptions are informed by the developments in the fields of linguistics, theories of language learning/acquisition and teaching methodology. The structural or grammatical approach, for example, viewed language as a structure, as a system of rules, and language learning as mastering the grammatical rules and a large part of the words and idiomatic expressions of the language. Communicative language teaching (CLT) is an approach to the teaching of second or foreign languages. It emphasizes that language is essentially a tool for communication and that it is learnt or acquired in the process of communication. The goal of second/foreign language learning is communicative ability.

34.2 EMERGENCE OF CLT

In the 1960s and 1970s, certain developments taking place in the ELT scenario in the U.K. and Europe eventually led to the emergence of CLT as an alternative approach to second/foreign language teaching. In the 1960s, a large number of students from the developing nations came to Britain for pursuing higher and specialized studies. Many of them needed competence in English to receive information and knowledge associated with their chosen specialized studies. In order to address specific needs of such groups of learners, need-based and function-based courses called English for Special Purposes (ESP) were introduced.

During the 1970s, the term 'communicative' was often used to describe the need-based ELT programmes that focused on language functions. This decade saw the emergence of CLT and a greater concern for communicative competence as the goal of L2 teaching. Communicative competence (Hymes 1972) or sociolinguistic competence implies the ability to use correct and acceptable utterances in different communicative, social contexts. In 1965, Noam Chomsky (1965) developed the concept of *competence* to refer to the abstract linguistic knowledge of a native speaker. He contrasted it with *performance*, the actual application of the rules of grammar while using language. Many linguists then pointed out that language occurs in social context and reflects social purposes. A child comes to acquire not only the grammatical knowledge of her language but also the knowledge required for using language appropriately in different social contexts. Hymes (*op. cit.*) coined the term *communicative competence* to emphasize that in social interaction, grammatical knowledge is not enough; one need to know what is appropriate and acceptable in a particular context. Communicative competence means the knowledge of "when and when not to speak, what to talk about with whom, when, where, and in what manner" (*ibid.*). One also needs to know when and how to take part in interaction and what linguistic repertoire is to be used in different contexts. One may have linguistic or grammatical competence in the L2, but he/she may not know how to use that competence in actual communicative situation—in social interaction. Experts have identified four components of communicative competence: (i) grammatical competence, (ii) sociolinguistic competence (ability to use appropriate language), (iii) discourse competence (ability to maintain cohesion and coherence), and (iv) strategic competence (the ability to use appropriate communication strategies) (Canale and Swain 1980).

A CLT programme aims at developing learners' communicative competence in the L2. It needs to be stressed that linguistic competence is a part of communicative competence. The assumptions underlying the communicative approach may be described as follows:

1. Language is communication.
2. Communication is learnt by making attempts to communicate, by taking part in verbal interaction in different communicative contexts.
3. For effective communication, mere linguistic or grammatical competence or knowledge is not enough; one has to develop sociolinguistic competence.
4. The learner's motivation, need for learning a language and efforts to learn are of crucial importance in learning and acquiring a language.
5. The teacher's role is that of a facilitator of learning; s/he creates conditions for learning to take place by involving learners in meaning-focussed activities. Students play the role of the manager of their own learning.

6. Authentic texts or learning materials that are *not* specifically meant to teach language should be used for developing learners' communicative competence.

34.3 SYLLABUS OPTIONS AND CLT

CLT brought about radical changes into language syllabus design and teaching methodology. The terms *curriculum* and *syllabus* are often used synonymously. In fact, the term curriculum has two interpretations. In its narrowest sense it is synonymous with the term syllabus. In this sense, curriculum is a specification of the learning content and the ordering of what is to be taught. In the widest sense, curriculum refers to planning, implementation and evaluation of the educational programme. It refers to the totality of educational experience. A curriculum contains the educational purposes, or objectives or outcomes of the programme, the content to be taught, the procedures to be followed in teaching and the learning experiences aimed at achieving the purpose or objectives. It also specifies the means of assessing and evaluating learner performance to ascertain whether the objectives have been achieved or not. A syllabus for a certain level is a specification of the content (what is to be taught/learnt). It first *selects* how much of something is to be taught and then it arranges what is to be taught in a *sequence*.

One can, perhaps, talk about broadly two types of language syllabuses: (i) form focused and (ii) function/meaning focused.

Form focused—Grammar-translation, audiolingual, structural, structural-situational.

Function/meaning-focused—Notional-functional, communicative.

Traditionally, units of learning a second or a foreign language like English have been defined in grammatical terms, assuming that language learning is learning grammatical rules. It has also been assumed that once a learner masters the linguistic forms s/he would automatically use the language for communication. So, whenever the questions of designing syllabuses and producing teaching-learning materials have arisen, there has been a tendency to assume that language items should be split up and taught as discrete items. Most conventional syllabuses like the grammar translation and the structural syllabuses, and most methods such as audio-lingual and structural methods have been based on this premise.

In a traditional grammar-based syllabus of English, the content is organized in terms of grammatical structures and vocabulary. Such a syllabus would list the structures (e.g. subject + be + present tense + main verb + ing—She is singing), and the words and phrases to be taught at different levels or classes/grades. Such a system of organizing or selecting and sequencing the content was discarded after the communicative approach to language learning/teaching became popular in the late 1960s and 1970s.

Grammatical syllabuses have certain obvious limitations. It may be useful to recall some of them:

1. Such a syllabus usually tends to take the learners through the grammatical system of the language, making them learn all parts of the grammatical systems, all types of constructions and rules. Many of these may not be required for immediate communicative purposes or may not be very useful to the L2 learner.
2. During the transaction of such a syllabus, one may tend to overemphasize grammatical forms than functions. As a result, learners may come to know the forms but may not be able to use them appropriately in communicative situations. The problem is how to make learners apply the grammatical rules in actual communication.
3. The presentation of sentences with similar structures, i.e. grammatically identical sentences in a lesson (say, sentences in the present progressive tense) prepared according to the specifications of a grammatical syllabus is too artificial.

As Wilkins (1979) rightly observes, "In real acts of communication, it is sentences that are alike in meaning and that occur together and not those that are alike in structure" are used more frequently (p. 83). So, a grammatical syllabus may not help learners to acquire communicative competence in the language.

The structural syllabus, introduced in a number of countries including India in the 1950s, is a grammatical syllabus. In this, the contents are arranged in terms of frequently occurring sentence structures of English and the selected vocabulary items used in the sentences. The principles followed in selecting and grading (that is, arranging systematically) sentence structures are frequency of use, level of complexity of the structure (simple sentence first, then sentences joined by coordinating conjunctions, then complex sentences containing main and subordinate clauses, etc.), creativity (a structure leading to/helping to learn another), teachability, etc. Similarly, in selecting the vocabulary items, the principles followed are frequency, usefulness, level of difficulty (words referring to concrete objects first, those referring to abstractions later), and creativity (the words that give more opportunity for teaching/learning many other words, e.g. a word 'bring'), etc.

A variation of the structural syllabus is the structural-situational syllabus. A situational syllabus emerged out of the realization that language occurs in social context or situation. The situational approach or method (as a component of structural-situational syllabus) is different; it is a method where teaching items are presented with *realia*, actions, etc. though the syllabus is essentially grammatical. A situational syllabus is based on the possible communicative situations in which the learner finds himself/herself (school, market, bank, post office, railway station, hotel, park, cinema, etc.). The linguistic contents may be arranged according to semantic demands of the learner as suggested by Wilkins (*ibid.*: 84).

A notional-functional syllabus is an attempt to address the deficiencies of a grammatical syllabus and the instructional mode associated with it. This is a meaning-based syllabus in which the language content is arranged according to the meanings a learner is required to express and the functions s/he will use the language for. It was developed by Wilkins (1976) and his colleagues. In this syllabus, 'notion' refers to "general concepts such as 'quantity', 'cause' and 'time'" (Littlewood 1981: 80), while 'function' indicates the use of language in performing interactional/communicative acts in a given context—greeting, requesting, describing, suggesting, etc. Notions (that is, concepts or meanings to be conveyed) and functions to be performed through the grammatical forms are selected in a notional syllabus. Wilkins grouped the categories of a notional syllabus into two sets. The first set is called *semantico-grammatical categories* which, according to him, interact with grammatical categories: time (point of time, duration, time relations, etc.), quality, space, matter, case, and deixis (person, time, place, and anaphora). The second set is described as *categories of communicative functions* (that is, the function of the utterances and the grammatical categories through which these functions are realized). They include modality (certainty, necessity, volition, etc.), moral and educative principles (judgement, approval, etc.), suasion, argument (agreement, assertion, disagreement, denial, and concession), rational enquiry and exposition (hypothesis, condition, conclusion, etc.), personal emotions (positive and negative), emotional relations (greeting, sympathy, gratitude, and hostility) and interpersonal relations (status and politeness). Widdowson (1990: 131) points out that the notional-functional syllabus was formulated on considerations not of language *learning* but of language *use*. The notional functional considerations were, however, expected to provide another dimension to the existing grammatical, and situational parameters.

CLT can be seen as an extension or development of the notional-functional syllabus. One must, however, note Widdowson's (*ibid.*) succinct observation: "There is no such thing as a communicative syllabus: there can only be a methodology that stimulates communicative learning" (p. 26).

In fact, CLT implies a set of principles about the goals of language teaching, about how learners learn a second/foreign language, and about the classroom activities that can facilitate language acquisition. Wilkins (1979), like many other experts, is against making too strong a claim for CLT:

> [W]e are quite simply woefully ignorant of the linguistic facts and will remain so for some time to come so that we would risk causing a reaction against the communicative movement in language teaching by making greater claims for it than we can justify. (p. 91)

He adds, "Greater concern should be given to seeing that what is learned has communicative value and that what has communicative value is learned ..." (p. 91)

CLT aims at developing the ability of the learners to manipulate the linguistic system to express message/meaning. It suggests procedures for helping learners develop strategies for relating linguistic structures to their communicative functions in real situations. Finally, it helps learners develop skills and strategies for using the linguistic repertoire at their command to communicate in different interpersonal situations and broader social contexts.

A traditional grammar-based syllabus can be called a 'content model' syllabus (Finney 2002) since the focus here is on organizing the content of language teaching/learning. The syllabus based on the objective model focuses primarily on objectives or purposes for which a language is learnt/taught, while the syllabus designed on the process model lays emphasis on enabling learners to progress towards self-fulfillment, taking into account learner needs, interest and development processes. The focus of CLT has all along been on learning processes, not on the content or end product of a language-teaching programme. A blending of content, objectives and process models is likely to be more useful and realistic (*ibid.*: 77). In fact, nowadays most language syllabuses seem to have incorporated elements/features from the three models. Because of the influence of CLT, the content of ESL/EFL curriculum has been expanded today to include "not only structures, situations, and themes or topics but also concepts (notions) and functions" (Dubin and Olshtain, 1986: 88). In recent times, tasks or activity-based language teaching has added new dimension to CLT.

3.4.4 Tasks and Activities

Any ESL programme designed today cannot ignore the insights gained from the principles and practices of CLT. Most syllabuses now incorporate elements of CLT methodology for devising meaningful classroom work. Tasks and/or activities have become an important part of an ESL classroom and many school textbooks suggest these for students throughout a particular lesson or text.

A task is an activity or action or work that involves students in processing or understanding language and then producing language. While performing a task, the students focus on meaning rather than form. Listening to an instruction and performing a command, looking at a picture and describing it, etc. are examples of tasks. Usually such tasks are called pedagogic tasks (Nunan 1989: 1-4). It is believed that successful language learning depends on engaging students in tasks or activities. In the process of performing a task, they negotiate meaning and take part in naturalistic communication.

Some of these activities are information gap and information transfer activities, role play, interview, language games, pair work, and various fluency-developing activities. Now we discuss some of these in brief as most textbooks tend to incorporate them.

Information gap

Information gap involves creating the need for exchanging information. If *A* possesses a piece of information which *B* does not, an information gap exists for *B*. In that case, an exchange between them can take place. In the classroom such an activity can be initiated by withholding some information from the students. The students are then forced to listen to something said by someone or read and understand something written, and make a verbal response.

    A: Do you know who won the football match last night?
    B: No. I didn't watch the match?
    A: Why? It was such an exciting match!
    B: I was so sleepy!

Information transfer

Information transfer is a communicative activity in which information is presented/available in one form or medium (say, in writing) and the students are required to present in another form or medium (say, by speaking).

    Teacher: Read these two advertisements of bicycles and explain which of these bicycles seems to be the better one. Give reason for your reply.

In this case, the students receive the information presented in written form and then interpret it and convey the interpretation by speaking.

Role play

Role play involves playing a part and using language to communicate as another person in a particular situation. A student may play the part of a seller, another of a buyer, and both can then try to simulate a transaction—selling and buying something. Both are forced to use appropriate language to play the roles.

    A (Salesperson): How can I help you?
    B (Customer): Do you have high-neck pullovers?
    A: Sure. Please come over here. I'll show the latest ones.
    ... ...

Such communicative activities that induce learners to use appropriate language in context can be made quite challenging.

It is obvious that in a language class, activity means *language-using activity*. It may mean saying something in response to someone (a teacher or a student), reading something alone or with others, writing something, and or performing some acts (standing up, walking up to the blackboard, and so on). Our beliefs about how a language is best learnt are behind what we do in the classroom. The purpose of some of the activities is to provide the students with language exercises. Some activities may be more or less communicative in nature.

It is believed that learners learn a language only when they use it in classroom activities. The teacher initiates or begins the activities and lets the learners get involved in such activities that demand some use of English. Some activities suggested in school textbooks may make them creative, too, because in performing an activity they use or try to use language in their own way. While taking part in an activity that can be regarded as *quasi-communicative,* they may consciously try to use linguistic forms they are learning or are familiar with. Truly, communicative or meaning-focused (or process-oriented) activity that demands unconscious application of linguistic knowledge may not be possible in all ESL classrooms. Many activities at the initial stage may be product-oriented. One has to remember that "wholesale denigration of product-oriented pedagogies has to be questioned" (Canagarajah 1999: 106).

34.5 DESIGNING AND IMPLEMENTING A CLT-ORIENTED SYLLABUS: PROBLEMS AND PROSPECTS

Classroom-oriented research in the 1980s helped syllabus designers and teachers to plan language-teaching programs in a more innovative manner. Problems of teaching English in bilingual and multilingual situations and teaching-learning traditions in different cultural settings came to attract greater attention from experts in the closing years of the 20th century. Consequently, CLT came to be reinterpreted and variously organized in different cultural contexts.

The influence of CLT can be distinctly noticed in the specification of objectives of teaching English, in the selection and organization of the learning content and also in the explicitly or implicitly suggested teaching strategies and classroom activities. A problem often encountered in the Indian CLT situation is how to find/produce suitable materials for communicative tasks or tasks that eventually lead to some kind of communication. The problem is compounded by the fact that in a large number of schools in the rural and semi-urban areas of India, most learners at the secondary level fail to acquire an understanding of how language operates in communication because they are hardly exposed to real-life communication in English. As Widdowson (1979) reminds us:

> Communication only takes place when we make use of sentences to perform a variety of different acts of essentially social nature. Thus, we do not communicate by composing sentences, but by using sentences to make statements of different kinds, to describe, to record, to clarify, and so on, or to ask questions, make requests, give orders (p. 118).

In most of our schools and colleges, most teachers of English still believe that once students have acquired the meaning which language items have *as elements in the language system*, they can use the meaning of these items *when they are used in actual commmunicative acts*. For example, most students know the meaning of words like *everything*, yet they would/could fail to make such a sentence as *how's everything with you?* in a communicative context. It is wrong to assume that students, at least in an acquisition-poor environment, would automatically make such a transfer. The solution lies in identifying and creating appropriate communicative acts which a student is required to perform inside and outside the class. However, the reality of the non-native, largely acquisition-poor, contexts (as in most parts of India) might necessitate certain changes within the CLT mode to be incorporated in syllabus design, materials production and classroom interactions. Some of the changes may take some or all the following forms:

1. One may be required to interpret communicative functions and acts with reference to the indigenous cultural contexts and think of including only those aspects of communicative protocols of English that are relevant to the learner needs. It will be wrong to accept a particular norm of communication as the ideal or the standard since different cultures may have different norms and strategies.
2. One needs to be aware of the fact that what may appear to be "authentic" materials/texts may, after all, be some form of simulated materials in situations where English is not the language naturally occurring in the learners' immediate environment.
3. The language-using activities that naturally go with CLT may, in a non-native, particularly Indian context, be *teacher-initiated and learning-centred* rather than learner-centred *at the initial stage*.
4. As most ESL learning in the Indian context takes place in an input-impoverished and acquisition-poor environment, some degree of emphasis on form, on conscious grammar learning seems to be essential. Otherwise, it might require a long time to induce learners to acquire a form or to arrive at the rules of grammar inductively through mere exposure and restricted interaction in such a context.

It needs to be remembered that a syllabus that lists notions and functions as well as grammatical structures may utilize principles and practices of CLT in presenting learning materials in a textbook and suggesting meaningful activities for the students because

> [I]t is also possible to find essentially grammar-based curricula that fit comfortably within the overarching philosophy of CLT (Nunan 1989: 10).

34.6 CLT: APPLICATION AND INNOVATION

It has been seen in practice that many learners achieve communicative fluency without gaining grammatical competence in the L2. Students may depend on familiar vocabulary items, memorized chunks of language and non-verbal strategies to communicate, apparently, with success. Some communicative activities may not result in the desired level of linguistic competence. That is why it is has been suggested that:

> ... there is a need to consider how a greater focus on grammatical form can be achieved during the process of designing and using tasks.
> (Richards 2002: 164)

It has, however, to be kept in mind that overemphasis on form-focused ESL instruction often results in a failure to ensure fluency, and most learners fail to advance from a stage of conscious learning to a certain stage in acquisition. Whether the learner will move towards fluency and stay where s/he depends to a great extent on the actual communicative-cognitive demand that English makes in a non-native/ESL context and also on the nature and degree of learner motivation. In a typical Indian context, such demands and motivations are virtually absent in a large number of learners at the early (school) stage during which most time and efforts at mastering English are expended. This implies that the teaching of English at upper primary and secondary levels needs to be reoriented. At these levels, the ability to manipulate the formal devices of the language is important. However, towards the end of the secondary stage, learners should be able to use the L2 as an instrument of thought. The National Curriculum Framework (NCF) adopted by the Government of India (NCERT 2005) reports:

> The goals for a second-language curriculum are twofold: attainment of a basic proficiency, such as is required in natural language learning, and the development of language into an instrument for abstract thought and knowledge acquisition through (for example) literacy .... The aim of English teaching is the creation of multilinguals who can enrich all our languages; this has been an abiding national vision. (p. 39)

In a multilingual, multi-cultural society, many ESL learners have the experience of learning and acquiring two, three or even four languages depending on the context of communicative and social needs. This experience of mastering languages other than the mother tongue should be utilized in learning English, too. In the process of acquiring languages other than their L1, young learners often master strategies that are likely to be used naturally in their ESL learning. Perhaps, there is some scope for inducing learners to bring some of the successful strategies from their unconscious to the conscious level. However, as Stern (1983: 405) observes, since our conventionally managed classrooms offer a very highly structured setting, allowing little flexibility to the teacher (at the school/college levels), students may not get the opportunity to make their learning strategies transparent. Even then, in the course of carrying out an activity, teachers may encourage learners to consciously use some of the strategies they find themselves using while acquiring another language spoken in their immediate environment.

The focus of English teaching at the tertiary level should be on functional-communicative competence and cognitive/academic language proficiency skills. The latter implies acquisition of adequate linguistic knowledge and literary skills usually required for academic work—work involving thought. The ability to use English as a cognitive tool, as a language of thought and reflection is as important as using it as a useful and important means/tool of communication. At this level, apart from the linguistic control, the students are required to acquire the basic ability to use language for receiving information, understanding concepts and for expressing their understanding of the special subjects and specialized skills. Keeping in mind the kind of skills and abilities required by the undergraduates in the Indian context, a number of universities have introduced courses in 'Communicative English,' which is obviously a CLT programme within the broad canvas. In India, students of science and technology at undergraduate and postgraduate levels need to use English as a tool in studying their subjects. Such students need a mastery of the language which is normally used to express scientific facts and concepts. They need to acquire such skills as reasoning, defining, classifying, generalizing, making hypotheses, drawing conclusions, and describing a process, a phenomenon, a mechanism, etc.

Many technical institutions have introduced a course designated as 'Functional/Communicative English,' focusing mostly on the development of communicative competence. In such a course the focus is more on 'functions' than on 'forms' of linguistic expressions and elements. The objective of such a course is to help learners develop their ability to use the linguistic resources of English available to them in carrying out communication effectively in a variety of real-life situations. It is assumed that the classroom activities that promote 'real' communication and lead learners to carry out meaningful tasks promote learning. For teaching communicative or functional use of English, then, the teacher needs to identify appropriate communicative acts which a student may be required to perform inside and outside the class.

Even a basically/essentially traditional humanistic course in English that requires students to study a sample of literary texts embodying humanistic values at the undergraduate level should have a functional/communicative component. Such a modification in syllabus design has been occasioned by the changing perception about the role of English in India. The role has two aspects: (i) cognitive which focuses on equipping students intellectually, and (ii) pragmatic which focuses on enabling students to use English effectively for some foreseen or unforeseen practical purposes. A course in Functional English, therefore, should ideally incorporate these two aspects.

In the classroom, the learners in ESL/EFL context may be involved in *simulated communicative activities.* The oral communicative activities may be of two types: (i) activities which promote listening and comprehension and (ii) activities which help the learner to carry out successful oral interaction.

The materials for the first type of activities have to be prepared by the teacher/instructor him/herself. They could be in the form of pre-recorded audio cassettes/compact disks containing popular lectures, conversations, group discussions and debates, recordings of TV and radio news, and films on both scientific and interesting non-scientific topics, etc.

For involving the learners in interactive activities that promote oral interaction, one could think of pair work and group work first using clue cards (or cards that contain very brief instructions and/or hints about what to say, how to respond to a speaker, etc., role plays) or samples provided in the textbook itself and, then, without giving any clues.

Sensitizing the teachers to CLT-oriented teaching practices should be one of the prime objectives of any ELT teacher-training programme in India. As in our context—non-natives teach English to non-natives—the teachers' actual proficiency in English rather than their ability to adopt some techniques (often done very mechanically) becomes very crucial. Further, when we suggest that in multilingual contexts a teacher utilizes the resources of the students' mother tongue, we assume that the teacher has the 'articulated' knowledge of L2 and also of a number of L1s. This rarely happens in reality, and it is not reasonable to expect an average teacher of English to possess such knowledge. A less ambitious approach towards utilizing multilingualism may, perhaps, involve such classroom activities as the following:

1. Engaging learners in group activities during which they perform some language-using tasks, and allowing them to use the languages known/familiar to them in the process of completing the task in English;
2. While discussing or clarifying a point of grammar, or illustrating the use of a vocabulary item, the teacher may refer to the L1 expressions containing the same/similar meanings and functions, and encourage the learners to come up with similar expressions from other languages spoken or known to them;
3. In teaching learners to communicate through English, the teacher may show how a particular communicative act or function (say, making a request) is usually performed in their languages.

Such activities may induce the learners, particularly at tertiary or advanced level, to utilize their L1 knowledge consciously and more effectively in learning an L2 whenever the occasion arises.

A large number of Indian students at various levels need communicative ability in English for different purposes. For designing effective courses and producing materials for them, the syllabus designers and teachers must be sensitive to the problems faced by most of them and be ready to innovate with a critical awareness of CLT and the ground realities of ELT in India.

REFERENCES

Canagarajah, Suresh A., *Resisting Linguistic Imperialism in English Teaching*, Oxford: Oxford University Press, 1999.

Canale, Michale and Swain, Merrill, "Theoretical bases of communicative approaches to second language teaching and testing," *Applied Linguistics* **1** (1980): 1–47.

Chomsky, Noam, *Aspects of the Theory of Syntax*, Mass.: MIT Press, 1965.

Dubin, F. and Olshtain, E., *Course Design: Developing Programmes and Materials for Language Learning,* Cambridge: Cambridge University Press, 1986.

Finney, Denise, "The ELT curriculum: A flexible model for a changing world," *Methodology in Language Teaching: An Anthology of Current Practice*, Jack C. Richards and Willy A. Renandya (Eds.), Cambridge: Cambridge University Press, 2002, 69–79.

Hymes, Dell, "On communicative competence," *Sociolinguistics*, J.B. Pride and J. Holmes (Eds.), Harmondsworth: Penguin Books, 1972.

Littlewood, William, *Communicative Language Teaching: An Introduction*, Cambridge: Cambridge University Press, 1981.

NCERT, *National Curriculum Framework 2005*, New Delhi, NCERT, Government of India, 2005.

Nunan, David, *Designing Tasks for the Communicative Classroom*, Cambridge: Cambridge University Press, 1989.

Richards, Jack C., "Addressing the Grammar gap in Task Work," Richards, Jack C. and Renandaya, Willy A. (Eds.), *Methodology in Language Teaching: An Anthology of Current Practice,* Cambridge: Cambridge University Press, 2002, 153–160.

Stern, H.H., *Fundamental Concepts of Language Teaching,* Oxford: Oxford University Press, 1983.

Wilkins, D.A., *Notional Syllabuses*, Oxford: Oxford University Press, 1976.

_____, "Grammatical, situational and notional syllabuses," *The Communicative Approach to Language Teaching*, C.J. Brumfit and K. Johnson (Eds.), Oxford: Oxford University Press, 1979, 82–90.

Widdowson, H.G., "The teaching of English as communication" in Brumfit and Johnson (Eds.), 1979, 117–121.

_____, *Aspects of Language Teaching*, Oxford: Oxford University Press, 1990.

Chapter 35

CONSTRUCTING CURRICULUM FOR AN INTENSIVE ENGLISH PROGRAM

— Natalie Hess and Elizabeth Templin

35.1 INTRODUCTION

As the ESL field grows and develops, teachers, researchers, materials writers, and administrators continue to aim toward greater professionalization. In the Intensive English Program (IEP), the issues of program change, evaluation, and structure are constantly being weighed, analyzed, and evaluated. Questions like those given below continually undergird our effort:

- How can we serve our students best?
- How can we work toward greater program vitality and relevance?
- How can we maximize our effectiveness and efficiency?

Thus, the building and restructuring of a viable IEP curriculum, as has been noted by various researchers in the field (Johnson 1982, 1994; Rogers 1994; Fitzpatrick 1995; Beane 1995; Berwick 1994; Elmore and Fuhrman 1994; Glatthorn 1994; Wiggins 1995), becomes the pivotal source from which both form and content of the IEP are evolved and nourished. In this study, we will describe and analyze one approach to curriculum as practiced by the Center for English as a Second Language (CESL) at the University of Arizona and consider how the model developed at this institute might be of use to the IEP structure.

At CESL, curriculum is perceived central to the IEP enterprise. Those of us most active in the shaping of the curriculum conceive it as a flexible backbone from which the program hangs and through which all its parts are joined and its boundaries determined. In the terms of Short and Burke (1991), the planners understand the curriculum to be a plan for putting ideas and beliefs into action. This chapter tells how such a curriculum emerged, how it developed, and how it continues to evolve and be redesigned.

35.2 BACKGROUND

CESL at the University of Arizona was established in 1968 with 55 students as a Center of English for Spanish Speaking People. Initially, the Center had only three proficiency levels: (i) beginning, (ii) intermediate, and (iii) advanced. In 1970, the institute was renamed The Center for English as a Second Language with students from many other countries. At this time, the institute introduced five proficiency levels.

During the following years, at various times, the student body consisted mainly of groups of students from Mexico, Brazil, Venezuela, Saudi Arabia, Iran, Lebanon, and Japan. Each group through its own needs and requests contributed to the development and evolution of the CESL curriculum. By 1978, the program had matured into seven levels of proficiency with a strong bent toward the audiolingual approach.

In the 1980s, the CESL curriculum moved away from audiolingualism to the communicative approach. As a result, names of courses were changed and the schedule of hours was rearranged to accommodate the demands of the new methodology. During this period of time, strategies and techniques changed as a result of diverse student needs. Many more students whose ultimate goal was acceptance at an American university were admitted to CESL and, at the same time, English requirements for university admission were being raised. Also, English instruction throughout the world became more emphasized and, as a result, students who enrolled at CESL came with a higher degree of proficiency. All these events and changes doubtlessly influenced the CESL curriculum.

35.3 THE PRESENT STRUCTURE

CESL is the self-supporting intensive English program at the University of Arizona. Students enrolled at CESL have, as a rule, not yet been admitted to the University. The program consists of seven levels of proficiency in which students study 22 hours a week in the classroom for two eight-week sessions each semester. In the three beginning levels, the four language skills are emphasized but not isolated. In other words, the approach is holistic, each skill playing its part in the totality of language development. Each skill supports and enhances all other skills. While a class may be called 'Writing,' it is clear that other skills, such as listening, reading, speaking, vocabulary development, and structure practice also play a part in classroom procedure, and within each of the skill specialties other skills remain integrated.

In the two intermediary levels, communication is stressed. We encourage students to express their ideas in the English they already know as they reach out for a more sophisticated language to express themselves. In the two advanced levels, academic skills gain prominence. Here students recycle old vocabulary, structure and expression and strive towards academic competence, using academic content.

Students are originally placed in their proficiency level according to their results on the Comprehensive English Language Test (CELT). At the end of each eight-week session, students move on to the next proficiency level, provided their grades meet the required grade point average (GPA)—for levels 10, 20, 30, and 40 this is 1.00; for levels 50 and 60, this is 2.00.

Chart 35.1 illustrates the process:

CHART 35.1 Levels and Procedures

Level of Proficiency	CESL Levels	Strategies and Procedures
Beginning	Levels 10, 20, 30	Emphasis is on skills—reading, writing, speaking, listening.
Intermediate	Levels 40, 50	Emphasis is on communication.
Advanced	Levels 60, 70	Emphasis is on academic skills.

35.4 HOW THE CURRICULUM COMES TOGETHER

At CESL, faculty and administration see curriculum as pivotal and fundamental to the mission of giving students the very best language instruction. Creating curriculum, as Taylor (1982) has noted, involves both form and content—the pedagogical, the philosophical and the procedural. Taylor's divisions have, to some degree, influenced our thinking at CESL. Under the rubric of procedural concerns, Taylor points to such issues as divisions of skill areas, size of enrollment, division of the instructional day, and access to resources and facilities. Under the classification of pedagogical and philosophical concerns, he places the setting of goals and objectives, and the choice of materials and the methodology. Chart 35.2 clarifies Taylor's categories.

CHART 35.2 Taylor's Categories

The Structural	The Philosophical	The Pedagogical
How should the skill areas be divided?	Should skill areas be divided or integrated?	How can the skill areas be taught best?
What size of class can we accommodate?	What is the optimal class size for good instruction?	How can we best adjust our methodologies to class size?
What resources are available to us?	From the resources available to us, which should we use and which should we reject and on what grounds?	What goals and objectives do we set for our pedagogy and our use of resources?

At CESL, we frequently find that Taylor's categories intersect and mesh. Recently, for example, the assistant director, in her attempt to construct a schedule, met with the Curriculum Committee to consult about the use of our new state-of-the-art multi-media laboratory. There were many curricular concerns to be considered:

- Should only certain teachers (those assigned to laboratory courses) use the new facility or should all teachers be involved?
- If all teachers were to use the lab, how often should they use the new facility?
- Should using the lab, and thus getting to know it, become a requirement for teachers, or should only those who were interested use the new laboratory?
- For which proficiency levels would the laboratory be of best use?
- Who should choose software, and how should such choices be made?

Many of these pedagogical and philosophical issues had to be ironed out and resolved before a seemingly procedural activity, like the construction of a schedule, could possibly be accomplished. One result of this particular meeting was that an ad hoc committee was set up to investigate software.

Ideas flourish at CESL. Teachers and students are involved in a constant stream of exchange and communication. Students may be bored with a certain textbook and express their dissatisfaction. A teacher has, perhaps, just seen a film that, he feels, would do wonders for the 50s curriculum. Another teacher has become enamored with wolves and shares her enthusiasm with her classes. Someone has attended a conference session on academic writing and is interested in revamping his/her course. How do all these ideas enter the classroom norm and become a curriculum? A central role obviously falls on the administration.

Pennington (1994) remind us that curriculum is of necessity a group process that requires careful facilitation and cooperation in order to ensure that not only needs of students are met but also the talents and abilities of faculty members are used to formulate the best possible curriculum design. The role of the administrator is to create and facilitate an atmosphere in which there is a great deal of faculty involvement and interest. Such administrative function is far from simple as it requires the kind of leadership that fosters creativity and cooperation. An administrator must have the willingness and ability to delegate authority, to gain trust, and foster a climate of cooperation. The administrator's role is to mediate between students and teachers as well as promote an atmosphere of cooperation. Brown (1995) offers the following advice to administrators:

- Involve as many teachers as possible in curriculum planning. Consult with teachers and actively seek their views.
- Do not assume the position of an all-knowing expert.
- Make sure that your demands on contributions of time are not unreasonable.
- Try not to make anyone feel on the defensive.
- Remember that discussion and mutual resolution usually work better than a dictated policy.

At CESL, Brown's advice is frequently followed in a social process of curriculum construction. Ideas emerge from many sources; they are talked about; they are proposed; they are tested; they are evaluated; they are worked on and improved; they are tested and re-evaluated; they enter the written curriculum and remain there until a more functional or more viable notion replaces them to restart the cycle.

Curriculum at CESL is a constantly growing and developing mechanism. It is the "shared vision" of achievement as recommended by Fitzpatrick (1995). We find it difficult to put it on paper as it must constantly meet new demands and bend to new directives. It is, however, that throughout this process of flux, one keeps the essential functions of a curriculum in mind. What then are the essential functions of a curriculum? At CESL, we perceive them to be to:

- Determine ultimate boundaries
- Set goals
- Prevent redundancies.

The curriculum, for one, is bounded by the mission CESL has been given by the university, which is to teach English at a high level and remain self-supporting. We are also restricted by our facilities, by the resources available to us, and by the training, skills, and personalities of our faculty. Within these restrictions, we seek ways to incorporate new and promising ideas. In order to be effective, a curriculum should draw substance from administration, faculty, and students. A top-down curriculum spurred mostly by administrative dictums, as noted by Fullan (1995), is overly concerned with structure and tends to ignore the process of education. A bottom-up curriculum, mostly generated by faculty concerns, on the other hand, tends to be too slow and might encounter resistance at the managerial level. Drawing of Pascale (1990), Fullan recommends a "sandwich Curriculum" (p. 192) in which there is managerial consensus as well as pressure and desire for change from the faculty. He envisions a dynamic, nonlinear continuous process of development, featuring high engagement and low bureaucracy.

The CESL structure is not just a series of courses, but rather an integrated program that includes many extracurricular components. In Pennington's (1991) terms, CESL has produced a "unified curriculum" that moves from needs analysis to the setting of goals, through testing to materials selection, to teaching and evaluation. We see our orientation process accompanied by such components as *The Student Handbook*, our international bazaars, school visits, wall newspaper, final luncheon ceremonies, and our outreach to both the University of Arizona and the Tucson community, such as our evening program and the summer teen program, as integral aspects of the unified curriculum. Since we assign significant value to such auxiliary concerns as those listed above, the members of the faculty, in addition to their class schedule, are at the beginning of each semester asked to sign up for participation on at least two of CESL's committees.

The core of CESL activity, of course, does take place in its classrooms, and it is the classroom curriculum that we shall next examine.

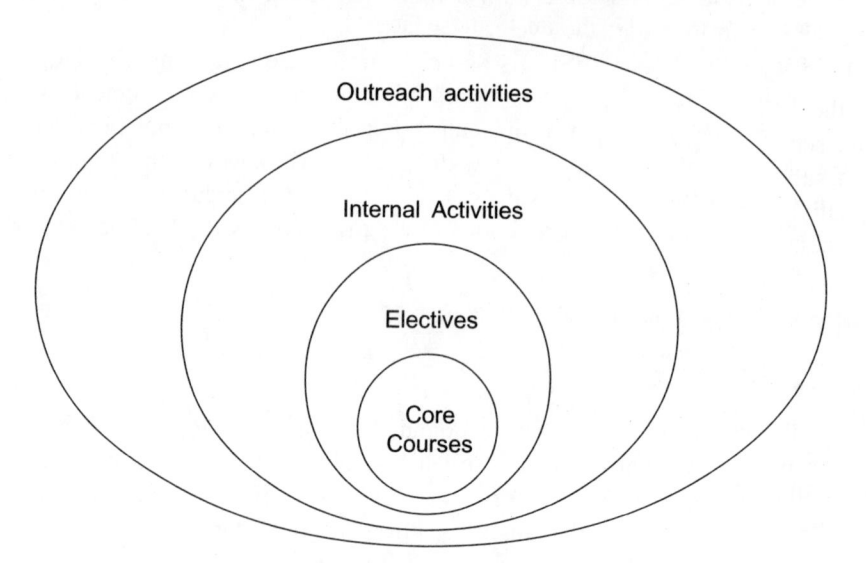

CHART 35.3   The Unified Curriculum

(Nested ovals from outermost to innermost: Outreach activities; Internal Activities; Electives; Core Courses)

35.5   HOW AN IDEA BECOMES A COURSE

As a rule, a group of teachers and administrators, perhaps in response to a student request, have discussed a new idea which may already have been tried out in the classroom as part of the existing curriculum. If there is sufficient interest, a faculty member will bring the suggestion to the Curriculum Committee. This committee, established on a yearly basis, consists of a group of teachers who have signed up to work on it together with the assistant director. Although the principal function of the Committee is to choose textbooks, it also oversees curricular issues and discusses curricular change.

If the Curriculum Committee is uncertain about the viability of the idea, they may assign an ad hoc committee to study it further. This committee will bring its report to the subsequent Curriculum Committee meeting where the issue will again be discussed and either accepted or rejected. If, after discussion and revision, the proposal is accepted by the Curriculum Committee, the faculty member or members who have suggested it refine it and write it up as a proposal. They submit their proposal to the CESL Council, an advisory group of appointed and elected faculty members that work with the director on pertinent issues. The Council discusses the proposal considering issues that pertain to scheduling and practical feasibility as well as usefulness and viability within the curricular boundaries. Below are some of the issues under consideration:

- How many faculty members will the proposal effect?
- Is the proposal financially viable?
- Has such an idea been tried at CESL before?
- Is it an idea that will prove beneficial to most students or only a few?
- Is the idea beneficial to most faculty members or only a few?
- Has the idea been tested out?

If the proposal is accepted by the CESL Council, the idea is incorporated into the schedule in the following session. If the proposal proves practical and workable, it remains within the program for a number of sessions and is finally placed in the written Curriculum Guide. Chart 35.4 illustrates the process.

35.6　HOW TEXTBOOKS ARE CHOSEN

As we have previously noted, choosing textbooks is one of the primary functions of the CESL Curriculum Committee. The textbook—a very essential tool in modern education—has been much maligned. Educators sometimes take the view that it is up to them to 'invent' their own course materials. It would certainly be very agreeable if IEPs could provide time and direction for all teachers to create and produce their own materials. But in real classroom life, this is of course an impossibility. If teachers are to teach, they cannot possibly also be materials writers. Textbook writers are, as a rule, serious professionals who have invested time and effort in compiling what they and their publishers envisioned as a suitable directive for the study of English. Textbooks, for better or worse, are definitely part of the IEP life, and it is the responsibility of the curriculum to be flexible enough to incorporate existing materials in an appropriate and useful manner. What we have said here, does not mean that teachers should be discouraged from developing interesting materials for their classes. But the choice of appropriate textbooks for each level lends continuity, stability, and integration of the program and is particularly useful for new teachers.

The faculty chooses textbooks at CESL. The assistant director looks through the many catalogues that arrive from publishers. Contacts with publishers have been made over the years at conferences or through personal communication. The assistant director then orders desk copies of books that seem appropriate or have been requested by teachers. These books are placed on a special shelf in the CESL faculty library or are circulated among teachers who have a particular interest in them. Teachers are encouraged to write comments regarding the appropriateness of books.

Textbooks have been chosen in two ways at CESL. One way has been to simply ask teachers to evaluate a textbook they have been using. They either recommend its use or suggest a replacement. Another way has been to have the Curriculum Committee host a book fair. At the time of such a book

CHART 35.4 How an Idea Becomes a Course

Steps of Entry into the CESL Curriculum	Example	Procedure
An idea emerges and is presented to the Curriculum Committee.	A faculty member suggests that a writing conference showcasing student writing be held every semester.	The Curriculum Committee discusses the idea and feels that it needs more information on how such a conference is to be organized. An ad hoc committee of three is appointed.
The ad hoc committee meets to plan out a procedure for the conference.	The conference will take place in the second session of each semester. The compositions used will be those that were submitted to an essay contest during the first session. Two faculty members will be in charge of the conference. Students in levels 60 and 70 will be the conference participants. All students from level 40 will be invited to the conference, which will deal with a theme of general interest and take place in four CESL classrooms.	The Curriculum Committee discusses the plans presented to it by the ad hoc committee. Two faculty members volunteer to take charge of the conference. The idea is approved and the faculty members in charge of the conference undertake to write a proposal.

Afternoon Session

The proposal is taken to the CESL Council.	The Council suggests that students use an overhead projector or a handout and talk through their papers rather than read them. A member of the Council suggests that refreshments be served.	The council discusses the proposal, makes suggestions, and accepts or rejects the proposal.
The proposal is tested.	A writing conference is held on the topic, 'Improving Our World'. Four speakers in each classroom talk about themes relating to the assigned topic. The subtopics are: The Situation of Women; Ecology; Education; and Health.	Faculty and students above level 40 have been encouraged to attend. Regular afternoon classes are canceled. Everyone chooses to attend the session that interests him/her most.
The proposal is evaluated.	In their writing classes, the day following the conference, students write evaluations on previously prepared evaluation forms. Members of the administration and of the faculty also give oral or written feedback.	The faculty members who planned the conference bring the evaluations to the Curriculum Committee and ask for suggestions.
The proposal is tested again (the following semester) incorporating the suggestions made by the students and the Curriculum Committee.	In order to allow more time for discussion and questions, there are only three presenters in each session, and there are three rather than four sessions.	The curriculum committee again discusses the proposal and suggests that it be incorporated into the written curriculum.

fair, all books that recently have arrived from publishers as well as books that teachers have found, used, and liked, or books that teachers wish to try out are displayed on tables. Teachers circulate, looking through books. They discuss the books with colleagues who teach the same level, and together choose an appropriate book for the next session. A member of the Curriculum Committee in charge of each level registers the titles, authors, publishers, and ISBN for each book chosen to be used in the following session. The Committee member checks to see that the books fit across the level—that is, that they match the requirements of the curriculum.

During the subsequent meeting of the Curriculum Committee, it is the responsibility of the group to see that the chosen books fit into the totality of curricular goals. The Committee needs to watch out for redundancies, for appropriate language level, for interest, and for pertinence.

It should be noted that what is valued is not merely the choice of book but also the professional interaction and discussion that naturally evolves as teachers study the materials that will become part of their teaching lives during the following session. It is important to note that all teachers are involved in choosing books and not just the teachers who happen to be using the particular text. This procedure is significant at CESL because all members of the faculty are expected to be able to teach all the CESL courses.

Although many books are used and reused at CESL, the constant search for more interesting and more relevant materials continually challenges us to stretch and develop our curriculum. Even when we use a different book for just one session and then decide that our previous choice really suited both of us and our class better, we have learned something new and valuable by working with a different text for a period of time.

35.7 HOW EVALUATION ENHANCES CURRICULUM

How well do we do our work? As professionals who strive for improvement, such knowledge is of vital interest to professionals at CESL. Pennington (1994) reminds us that faculty development is of utmost importance to both administrators and teachers. For administrators it means that the program is moving towards constant development and improvement, while for the individual faculty member it means an effort towards professional growth and advancement. Pennington recommends a strong "bottom-up impetus" (*ibid.*: 106) for faculty evaluation. The direct involvement of faculty in the evaluation process contributes greatly to faculty involvement and commitment to institutional growth. Short and Burke (*op. cit.*) tell us that the heart of the word 'evaluation' is 'value', and that in evaluating our work we consider giving value to our efforts.

At CESL, we follow a strong 'bottom up impetus' in our chain of evaluation procedures. There is no doubt that these procedures influence and propel the structure of our curriculum. The evaluation committee, one of the committees that teachers can choose to work on, with the help of a university evaluation professional, constructs a questionnaire, written in clear and simple English, for the students. At the end of each semester, students in each class fill out the questionnaire anonymously. The questionnaire is just one of our tools of evaluation. Others are:

- The self-summative review written by all faculty members at the conclusion of the academic year. The questionnaire for this review has been worked out by the evaluation committee and its appointed Peer Review Committee (PRC). The PRC is a group of three teachers who examine and evaluate the self-summative reports following an assigned point system. They tabulate the points earned by each faculty member and hand their computations, together with the summative essay written by each teacher, to the director.
- The director or assistant director also observes a lesson taught by each faculty member and the director writes each member of the faculty a yearly letter of evaluation. Needless to say, a good program depends on good teaching. In the words of Eskey (1982):

Despite the relatively low estate which teachers seem to have fallen into lately, teaching arguably remains the quintessential human activity. Since culture is learned, not inherited, every culture's first concern must be perpetuating itself. In this respect, teaching, the passing on of culture to each new generation of students, has a special importance and merits greater respect than most people now feel for a profession regarded as a home for 'those who can't' as opposed to 'those who can' and do. The trouble with the can/can't argument, however, is that those who can soon become those who could. George Bernard Shaw, who penned the original aphorism, has been dead for some time, and it is mainly thanks to teachers that a few cultured people still read his plays—and thanks to language teachers in particular that there are so many people in so many places who can understand the language that he wrote them. (p. 45)

The evaluation process, no doubt, contributes to teacher introspection and to the refinement of teaching skills as it enables faculty members to analyze their work, to plan ahead, and to set goals. Student evaluations are also helpful in determining the usefulness and interest of classes and materials. As a result, curricular goals change and curriculum develops.

Review of the administrators is done yearly by the faculty through a questionnaire prepared by the evaluation committee and the entire program is periodically evaluated by outside sources such as UCIEP (University Consortium of Intensive English Programs) and the University of Arizona.

The totality of evaluation procedures should help the director set goals for the future and upgrade such modules of the program that will benefit it most. Crucial to such upgrading is a continued teacher-development component. At CESL, this aspect is provided through faculty workshops, CESL Round Tables, faculty retreats, and through encouragement as well as financial support for faculty who are present at conferences.

35.8 THE WRITTEN CURRICULUM

In order to provide the guidance, stability, and sense of continuity for which it was intended, a curriculum must be written. However, as we previously stated, it is quite a perplexing exercise to pin down a text which persists in transfiguring itself and fluctuating. Perhaps, a loose-leaf curriculum might be a good idea.

Our written curriculum has in many respects followed the authoring cycle described by Short and Burke (*op. cit.*) who illustrate the growth of a curriculum from an envisioned curriculum to a paper curriculum, to an enacted curriculum, to a readjusted and evaluated curriculum, to a new paper curriculum, and to a constant repetition of this cycle. They see socialization as a central component of their curriculum planning and note that all human experience is rooted in exchange of ideas through communication.

Learning according to Short and Burke is based on curiosity, intentionality and sociability, and they recommend a curriculum that branches out in these three directions. Drawing on Vigotsky's notion of proximal development (1978), Short and Burke make the point that a curriculum needs to keep learners oriented in what they know and reaching out to what they don't know.

The written *CESL Curriculum Guide* is in a constant process of revision and provides a substantial guide to the policies and practices of CESL and is, no doubt, of great value to new faculty members. The introduction to the curriculum largely agrees with the recommendations of Short and Burke as it proposes its central design. The CESL curriculum follow the communicative approach primarily and is geared to the needs of students. CESL interprets learning as a social process in which students interact with one another, their material and, their facilitators. CESL encourages the implementation of activities that promote an enthusiasm for learning and the well being of the student. Learning is spiraled in that material is recycled and reformulated. The ever-changing needs of students help the faculty to find methodological perspectives encourage collaboration of teachers when they rethink these needs.

The curriculum then proceeds to outline each level by providing:

- A general overview
- A set of suggested activities
- A set of skills to be mastered
- A set of minimum requirements
- Suggested procedures for evaluation
- Suggested textbooks

Each CESL course is briefly described with suggestions on implementation. A CES Elective such as Current Events, for example, is open to 40 to 50 level students and offers videos and opportunities for the discussion of current events, readings from editorials, and field trips to local radio stations.

The written curriculum not only gives a sense of direction to new faculty members and a sense of equilibrium to continuing faculty members but it also, as Wiggins (*op. cit.*) demonstrates, prevents the kind of redundancy that often plagues school systems. Wiggins describes a case in a suburban school district where four teachers in four grade levels were teaching *Charlotte's Web* and were totally unaware of the fact that the book was in use elsewhere. He notes that a sense of seamlessness should pervade a curriculum both on the macro and on the micro levels. Primarily, he hopes that students feel the cohesive building plan of a curriculum and that they are well aware of why things are done.

At CESL, we provide a sense of seamlessness by looking at each course not only in its vertical position across the levels, but also its horizontal position within the level—that is, the courses in the scale of levels follow a progression while the courses in one level complement and supplement each other. We want to point out that the CESL *Curriculum Guide* is just that—a guide. It provides the goals and the boundaries expected, but does not proscribe specific activities. Within the guidelines, a professional teacher can best create a syllabus that fits his/her individual talents and the individual abilities and needs of the students in each class.

35.9 WHAT THE FUTURE HOLDS

CESL looks toward curricular changes. With the completion of our new multimedia interactive language laboratory, we are definitely moving in the direction of greater technological involvement. The institute has recently started a course in writing for graduate students and will perhaps become more active in the teaching of matriculated ESL students. A bridge course that incorporated college lectures in history was taught for two semesters and we are about to do such a course in astronomy. While CESL appears to be moving closer to the academic functions of the University of Arizona, we also host several short-term programs for both students and educators. Some of the most interesting of these groups are those from Japan, some of which come for a study period of 5–8 weeks for intensive English and American studies. Other groups come for an entire study-abroad year and receive credit at their home institutions. Recently, we have also hosted several groups of Latin American and European educators who came for periods of 3–7 weeks in order to hone and upgrade their teaching skills and to participate in the American education culture.

These programs have all brought us new challenges and opportunities, and we must continue to build a curriculum with sufficient firmness to uphold a set of principles and expectations and enough flexibility to bend with the winds of change.

REFERENCES

Beane, J.A., *Toward a Coherent Curriculum: 1995 Yearbook of the Association for Supervision and Curriculum Development*, Alexandria Virginia: Association for Supervision and Curriculum Development (ASCD), 1995.

Berwick, R., "Needs assessment in language programming: From theory to practice," in Johnson, R.K., *The Second Language Curriculum,* Cambridge: Cambridge University Press, 1994, 48–62.

Brown, J.D., *The Elements of Language Curriculum*, Boston: Heinle and Heinle, 1995.

Dewey, J., *Experience and Education*, New York: Collier Books, 1938.

Elmore, R.F. and Fuhrman, S.H., *The Governance of Curriculum*, Alexandria, Virginia: Association for Supervision and Curriculum Development (ASCD), 1994.

Eskey, D., "Faculty" in (Ed.) R.P. Barrett, *The Administration of Intensive English Programs*, National Association for Foreign Student Affairs, 1982, 39–45.

Fitzpatrick, K.A., "An outcome-based systems perspective on establishing curricular coherence" in J.A. Beane, 1995, 120–130.

Fullan, M.G., "Coordinating top-down and bottom-up strategies for educational reform," in R.F. Elmore and S.H. Fuhrman, 1995, 186–203.

Glatthorn, A.A., *Developing a Quality Curriculum*, Alexandria, Virginia: Association of International Educators (NAFSA), 1994.

Johnson, K., *Communicative Syllabus Design and Methodology*, Oxford: Pergamon Press, 1982.

Johnson, R.K., *The Second Language Curriculum*, Cambridge: Cambridge University Press, 1994.

Pascale, P., *Managing on the Edge*, New York: Touchstone, 1990.

Pennington, M.C., "Faculty development for language programs," in R.K. Johnson, 1994, 91–110.

Pennington, M., *Building Better English Language Programs*, Alexandria, Virginia: Association of International Educators (NAFSA), 1991.

_____, "Unifying curriculum process and curriculum outcomes: The key to excellence in language education," in M. Pennington, 1991, 57–74.

Rogers, T.S., "Syllabus design, curriculum development and polity determination," in Johnson, 1994, 24–34.

Short, K.G. and Burke, C., *Creating Curriculum*, Portsmouth, NH: Heineman Educational Books, 1991.

Taylor, B.P., "Curriculum design and the selection of teaching materials" in R.P. Barrett, 1982, 45–50.

Vygotsky L., *Mind in Society*, Cambridge, Mass.: Harvard University Press, 1978.

Wiggins, G., "Curricular coherence and assessment: Making sure that the effect matches the intent," in J.A. Beane, 1995, 101–119.

Part 11

LANGUAGE TESTING

Chapter 36

TESTING COMMUNICATIVE COMPETENCE

— Manish A. Vyas and Yogesh L. Patel

36.1 INTRODUCTION

Language learning/teaching is considered a continuous process. To maintain the continuity, a teacher needs to frequently assess learners' achievement and proficiency that he/she has attained during the 'learning process,' rather than after the lesson process is completed. Language teachers who consider language learning a continuous process stress that evaluation/testing is a continuous process, simultaneous with the lesson process.

However, it must be pointed out that language testing has not kept pace with the developments in the language teaching, and applied linguistics has done very little in this area. It is true that any language teaching techniques can be used for language testing. A traditional dictation task, translation work, reading assignment, any question-answer technique, an oral test and a close-test that uses the fill-in-the-gaps technique used for evaluation can become a language test. Davies (1968) once wrote, "a good test is an obedient servant since it follows and apes the teaching". Most of the language tests that are used are surface tests which test only surface problems in language. In such tests, the learners are asked to supply the correct forms as fill-in-the-blank types, spelling, etc. Often, even the surface tests are used only to supply what is given in the text. These text-based language tests evaluate only learner's ability to recall what they memorize; and hence, they are reproductive in nature.

Outside the text, people speak, listen, read, write, think, compose, describe, pray, promise and do meaning processing in order to achieve certain life-oriented goals and negotiate meaning as realized in pain and pleasure. Language testing in the communicative approach can open up a number of possibilities that are literally unlimited.

However, testing language has traditionally taken the form of testing knowledge about language—usually the testing of knowledge of vocabulary and grammar. Hymes (1971) proposes the concept of communicative competence, which refers to the ability to exchange information in a foreign language with native speakers of the language. He argued that a speaker can produce grammatical sentences that are completely inappropriate. In communicative competence, he included not only the ability to form correct sentences but also the ability to use them at appropriate times. Since Hymes proposed the idea in the early 70s, it has been expanded considerably and various types of competencies have been proposed. However, the basic idea underlying communicative competence is the ability to use the language appropriately, both receptively and productively, in real situation.

36.2 AN OVERVIEW OF A TEST

During the phase of structural linguistics, language was analyzed at several levels and into several components. Three levels of language analysis that were recognized are *Expression*, *Form* and *Content* of language. Based on this approach, the evaluation technique then recommended was the well known Discreet Point Evaluation technique. Carroll (1980) first named it Discreet Point as opposed to the tests of integrative skills. With the developments in the linguistics theories and approaches to language analysis, one finds that the structural grammar was replaced by Chomsky's (1966) Transformational Generative Grammar. And we are familiar with the reactions against his rather restricted views of 'competence'. Most of these reactions were primarily due to his argument to analyze language in isolation from its socio-cultural matrix. Objecting to Chomsky's notion of 'competence,' Halliday (1973) proposed a socio-semantic approach to language analysis, which includes the rules for use of language in appropriate context. With these developments in the field of linguistic theories and description, there are changes in approach to language teaching/learning process and testing theories.

36.2.1 Types of Test

Not all language tests are of the same kind. They differ with how they are designed, and what is the *method* and *purpose* of the test.

Discrete point tests

Early theories of test performance, influenced by structuralist linguistics, saw knowledge of language as consisting of mastery of the features of the language as a system. This position was clearly articulated by Robert Lado (1961). His testing theory focused on the learner's knowledge of the grammatical system, vocabulary and aspects of pronunciation. There was a tendency to atomize and decontextualize the knowledge to be tested and to test the aspects of knowledge in isolation. This practice of testing separate individual points of knowledge is known as **discrete testing**. The nature of discrete testing is objective.

Integrative test

After some decades, the necessity of evaluating the practical language skills of foreign students wishing to study in universities in abroad or to get employment in corporate sectors poised assessing the productive capacities of language. It focused on the integrated performance of the language user. The discrete point tradition of testing was seen as focusing too exclusively on the knowledge of the formal linguistic system for its own sake rather than on the way such knowledge is used to achieve communication. The new orientation resulted in the development of such tests that integrated knowledge of relevant systematic features of language with an understanding of context. This integrative test requires the candidate to combine many language elements in the completion of a task. This might involve writing a composition, making notes while listening to a lecture, taking a dictation, or completing close passage. But the problem with such integrative tests was that they tended to be expensive as they were time consuming and difficult to score (McNamara 2000). This also required trained raters and, sometimes, was potentially unreliable.

Pragmatic tests

Research carried out by John Oller (1971) in the 1970s seemed to offer a solution. The major traits of pragmatic tests are as follows:

- They require the learner to use language as in real-life context.
- The learner is required to process the meaning of discourse within a period of time which we would normally take in real life.
- They are integrative and adopt a holistic approach to language. However, it does not follow that all integrative tests are pragmatic.

Oller argued that certain kinds of more economical and efficient tests, particularly the close test (gap-filling reading tests), measured the same kind of skills as those tested in productive tests. Such tests were easy to construct, relatively easy to score, based on a compelling theory of language use, and expensive tests of the productive skills of speaking and writing. Thus, the cloze became very popular form of test in the 1970s and 1980s.

Unfortunately, further work soon showed that cloze tests on the whole seemed mostly to be measuring the same kind of things as discrete point tests of grammar and vocabulary. It seems that there are no short cuts in the testing of communicative skills.

36.3 COMPUTERS AND LANGUAGE TESTING

Rapid developments in computer technology have exerted a major impact on test delivery. Many important national and international language tests like NELTS, TOEFL and IELTS are moving to Computer Based Testing (CBT). Stimulus texts and prompts are presented not in examination booklets but on the screen, with candidates being required to key in their responses. The advent of CBT, however, has not necessarily involved any change in test content, remaining quite conservative in its assumptions, but often simply represents a change in the methods of testing. However, there are limitations and advantages of computer testing, especially productive skills which represent the social character of a language.

36.4 CHANGING PERSPECTIVES IN LANGUAGE TESTING

The communicative approach has ushered in radical changes in syllabus design, methodology and materials production. However, changes in testing have been rather slow. Hence we often find a mismatch between teaching and testing. The test model of the 60s and 70s adopted a linguistic approach to test construction. The skills were listening, speaking, reading and writing, with specific reference to phonology, structure and vocabulary.

36.5 COMMUNICATIVE LANGUAGE TESTS

From the early 1970s, a new theory of language and language use began to exert a significant influence on language teaching and, especially, on language testing. This was Hymes' (1971) theory of communicative competence, which greatly expanded the scope of what was covered by an understanding of language and the ability to use language in social context. Hymes saw that knowing a language was more than knowing its rules of grammar. There were culturally specific rules of use which related the language used to features of the communicative context. For example, the ways of speaking and writing appropriate to communication with close friends may not be the same as those used in communicating with strangers or in professional contexts. Communicative language tests had two features:

1. They were performance tests, which required assessment to be carried out when the learner or candidate was engaged in an extended act of communication, either receptive or productive, or both.
2. They paid attention to the social roles the candidates were likely to assume in real-world settings, and offered a means of specifying the demands of such roles in detail.

In this way, the communicative competence represented a profound shift from a psychological perspective on language, which views a language as an internal phenomenon, to a sociological one, focusing on its social functions.

The practical and imaginative response to the challenge of communicative language testing was matched by a continuing theoretical engagement with the idea of communicative competence and its implication for the performance requirement of communicative language testing. Various writers have tried to specify the communicative competence in L2s and their role in performance. Canale and Swain (1980) defined communicative competence in terms of four components:

1. **Grammatical competence:** words and rules.
2. **Sociolinguistic competence:** appropriateness.
3. **Discourse competence:** cohesion and coherence.
4. **Strategic competence:** appropriate use of communication strategies.

There has begun further specification of different components of knowledge that would appear to be included in communicative competence. Thus, Bachman (1990) has identified sub-categories of knowledge within the three broader categories of grammatical, discourse, and sociolinguistic competencies. Further, he divides it into the broad headings of (i) "organizational competence" which includes both grammatical and discourse (or textual) competence, and (ii) "pragmatic competence" which includes both sociolinguistic and *illocutionary* competencies.

36.5.1 What the Communicative Language Tests Measure

The communicative language tests are intended to measure how the testees are able to use language in real-life situations. In testing productive skill, emphasis is placed on appropriateness rather than on ability to form grammatically correct sentences, while in testing receptive skills, emphasis is placed on understanding the communicative intent of the speaker or writer rather than on picking out specific details. In fact, these two are often combined in communicative testing so that the testees must both comprehend and respond in real-time situations.

The tests are judged on the extent to which they stimulate real-life communicative situations rather than on how reliable the results are. In fact, there is an almost inevitable loss of reliability as a result of the loss of control. For example, if a test is intended to test the ability to participate in a group discussion for students who are going to a Cambridge University, it is impossible to control what the other participants in the discussion will say. Therefore, not every testee will be observed in the basic assumptions of communicative language testing. This is compensated for by the realism of the situation.

36.5.2 Designing a Communicative Test

Carroll's (1980) contribution to communicative language testing is of seminal importance. The ultimate criterion of language mastery is, therefore, the learner's effectiveness in communication for the settings he finds himself in.

Designing a communicative ability test is not like preparing a grammatical ability test. Rather, the design of such a test can be involving the answers to the following questions:

1. What are the performance operations we wish to test? (These are arrived at by considering what sort of things people actually use language for in the areas we are interested.)

2. At what level of proficiency will we expect the candidate to perform these operations?
3. What are the enabling skills involved in performing these operations? Do we wish to test control of these separately?
4. What sort of content areas are we going to specify? (This will affect both the types of operations and the types of 'text' which are inappropriate.)
5. What sort of format will we adopt for the questions we set? It must be one which allows for both reliability and face-validity as a test of language use.

36.5.3 Characteristics

According to Johnson and Morrow (1981), the following are expected to be the characteristics of a communicative test:

1. It will be criterion-referenced against the operational performance of a set of authentic language tasks. In other words, it will set out to show whether or not (or how well) the candidate can perform a set of specified activities.
2. It will be crucially concerned to establish its own validity as a measure of those operations to measure. Thus, content, construct and predictive validity will be important, but concurrent validity with existing texts will not be necessarily significant.
3. It will rely on the modes of assessment, which are not directly quantitative but qualitative. It may be possible or necessary to convert these into numerical scores, but the process is an indirect one and recognized as such.
4. Reliability which is clearly important will be subordinate to face-validity. Spurious objectivity will no longer be a prime consideration although it is recognized that in certain situations, test formats which can be assessed mechanically will be advantageous. However, the limitations of such formats will be clearly spelt out.

36.5.4 Examples of Communicative Test Tasks

There is necessarily a subjective element to the evaluation of communicative tests. The real-life situations do not always generate close-ended (true-false type) answers. So, there should be a description of the quality of the receptive or productive performances of the testee.

Testing listening

Task 1: Here are two sets of instructions. Listen carefully. Draw as you listen.

1. Draw a big square; put two small squares inside the vertical lines of the square; draw a rectangle on the base of the big square; draw a

triangle with the line of the big square as its base; put a circle beside the triangle; draw small lines around the circle.
2. Draw a small circle; draw another circle of the same size about half an inch away; draw an inverted triangle to the centre of the circles. Join the top corners of the triangle to the centre of each circle; draw a small line a cross the right corner of the triangle; draw a small circle on the left corner of the triangle.

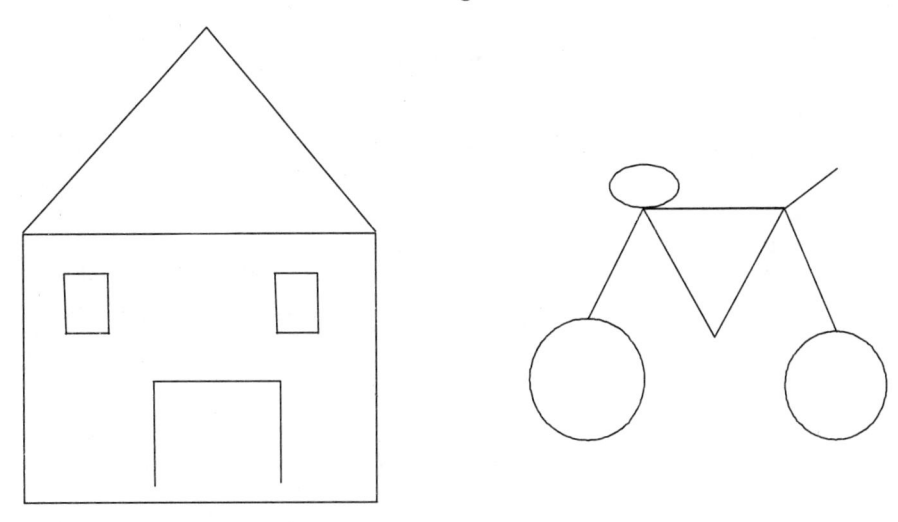

Task 2: The southwest monsoon has further withdrawn from east Rajasthan and the plains of west Uttar Pradesh. Today's INSAT picture shows a dense cloud mass over Andhra Pradesh, Tamil Nadu and Orissa.

Here is a warning. Heavy to very heavy rain is likely at one or two places in Andaman and Nicobar Islands.

Task sheet: Complete the grid by marking (√) in the relevant boxes:

	East Rajasthan	*Andhra Pradesh*	*Orissa*	*Tamil Nadu*	*Andaman and Nicobar*
S.W. Monsoon withdrawn					
Dense clouds					
Heavy rains					

Task 3: The temperatures recorded at the four major cities: Delhi had a maximum of 33.0°C and a minimum of 23.1°C; Kolkata 31.9°C and 26.2°C; Mumbai 30.6°C and 24.2°C; Chennai 30.1°C and 25.6°C.

Task sheet: Mark the temperatures recorded at the four major cities.

Delhi		Kolkata		Mumbai		Chennai	
Max.	*Min.*	*Max.*	*Min.*	*Max.*	*Min.*	*Max.*	*Min.*

Testing listening and writing/note taking

Listening and writing may also be tested in combination. In this case, the testees are given a listening text and are instructed to write down certain information from the text. Though it is not purely interactive, it should stimulate a situation where the information would be written down from a spoken text. An example of such a test is as follows.

Rahul and Bindu want to go to a movie. They call the local multiplex theater. Listen to their recording and fill in the missing information in the chart so that it can be discussed with other learners later.

Screen Number	*Movie*	*Show-time*
1	Singh is King	
2		
		11:45, 14:00, 18:00, 21:15
3		
		12:00, 14:45, 16:15, 19:30
4	Jhonny Gaddar	

Testing listening and speaking

Information gap: An information gap activity is one in which two or more testees work together. Each testee is given certain information, but lacks some necessary information. The task requires the testees to ask and give information. The task should provide a context wherein the testees can logically share information. The following is the example of information gap task.

A	*B*
A: Greet B.	A: ....
B:	B: Reciprocate A.
A: Ask what B is doing in the evening.	A: ....
B:	B: Give a suitable replay to A.
A: Invite B for a movie if B has nothing to do in the evening. If B is preoccupied, invite him for tomorrow.	A: ....
B:	B: Thank A.
A: Conclude the conservation.	

This kind of task would be evaluated using a system of band scales. The band scales would emphasize the testee's ability to give and receive information, express and elicit opinions, etc. It would not emphasize pronunciation, grammatical correctness, etc. The examiner should be an observer and would not take part in the activity. Also, the activity should be tape recorded so that it could be evaluated later.

Role play: In role play, the testee is given a situation to play out with another person. He/she is given information in advance about what his/her role is, what specific functions he/she needs to carry out, etc. A role play task would be similar to the above information gap activity except that it would not involve an information gap. Usually, the examiner or a confederate takes part in the role play.

Testing reading and writing

If we represent a set of tasks, we obtain the totality of sample of the candidate's ability and this way may have a beneficial backwash effect. Some tests combine reading and writing in communicative situations. The testees can be given a task in which they are represented with instructions to write a letter, memo, summary, etc.

Here is a test of writing about working in a summer camp for children in India. Look carefully at the information on this and follow the tasks given below.

YOUTH HOSTEL SUMMER CAMPS FOR CHILDREN
VOLUNTEERS WANTED FOR AUGUST 2009

We are looking for people to work as helpers in our Summer Camp in Mount Abu. You will be responsible for organizing games and activities for groups of children.

There is no salary, but travel and living expenses will be paid.

Write to us for more information and an application form.

Youth Hostel, Sector-15,
Gandhinagar-382015 Gujarat, India
Fax: 079-2434091

Task 1: You saw the advertisement for helpers. You write to Youth Hostel Summer Camp at the address in the advertisement.

In your letter, Find out about/ask:

- the start and finish dates
- the hours of work
- the type of accommodation
- for an application

Write your letter on the next page.

Task 2: You are now working in the Youth Hostel Summer Camp for Children in Mount Abu. You write in a postcard to your friend. On your postcard, tell your friend:

- Where you are
- Why you are there
- Two things you like about the Summer Camp.

Write on your postcard here.

POSTCARD

Communicative language tests test language in a way it is used in real communication. Though it is not always possible to make language tests communicative, it is possible to give them communicative elements. If students are encouraged to study for more communicative tasks, it will certainly have a positive effect on their language learning.

REFERENCES

Bachman, Lyle, *Fundamental Considerations in Language Testing*, Oxford: Oxford University Press, 1990.

Canale, Michale and Swain, Merrill, "The theoretical bases of communicative approaches to second language teaching and testing," *Applied Linguistics* **1** (1980): 1–47.

Carroll, B.J., *Testing Communicative Performance*, Oxford: Oxford University Press, 1980.

Chomsky, Noam, "Topics in the theory of generative grammar," in *Janua Linguarum*, The Hague: Mouton and Co., 1966.

Davies, A. (Ed.), *Language Testing Symposium: A Psycholinguistic Perspective*, Oxford: Oxford University Press, 1968, 5.

Halliday, M.A.K., *Explorations in the Functions of Language*, London: Edward Arnold, 1973.

Hymes, Dell, "On communicative competency," *Sociolingustics,* J.B. Pride and J. Holmes (Eds.), Penguin, 1971, 269–293.

Johnson, K. and Morrow, Keith, *Communication in the Classroom,* Harlow, Essex: Longman, 1981.

Lado, Robert, *Language Testing,* UK: Addison-Wesley Longman, 1961.

McNamara, Tim, *Language Testing,* Oxford: Oxford University Press, 2000, 15.

Oller, J.W., "Discreet point tests versus tests of integrative skills," *Focus on the Learner: Pragmatic Perspectives for the Language Teacher,* J.W. Oller and Richards, Jack C. (Eds.), Mass., Newbury House Publishers, 1971, 184–199.

AUTHOR INDEX

Abercrombie, David, 360
Allwirght, D., 194, 206

Bachman, Lyle, 491
Bailey, K.M., 197
Beale, J., 46
Belchamber, R., 54
Bhatt, A., 393
Bloomfield, L., 321
Brown, H.D., 262, 448
Brumfit, C.J., 37
Bygate M., 136

Canale, M., 402, 459, 490
Carrell, P.L., 407
Carroll, B.J., 488
Cartiera, M.R., 421
Carter, R., 292
Cary, S., 421
Chomsky, N., 46, 459, 488
Cook, V., 311, 312
Corria, I.L., 261
Corson, D., 297
Coulter, C., 419
Covey, S., 2
Crystal, D., 1, 113, 321, 345

Dalen, Deobold Van, B., 359
David, M.K., 221, 433
Davies, A., 487
Doughty, Catherine J., 219

Ellis, R., 137–140, 199, 220, 276, 340

Fishman, J., 393
Folse, K.S., 295
Foster, P., 136–139

Francis, Hazel, 359
Freeman, D., 207
Fu, D., 417

Gardner, H., 222
Gardner, R.C., 265
Gass, S., 138
Gay, G., 417
Gee, J.P., 239, 407
Godwin-Jones, 91, 92
Goodman, K., 229
Grieve, A. and Seebus, I., 166
Graddol, D., 395
Graustein, G., 172
Guerrero, R.G., 136
Guilherme, Manuela, 383
Gumperz, J., 311

Halliday, M.A.K., 406, 488
Harmer, Jeremy, 261–264, 386
Harsisch, Svetlana, 430, 440
Holmes, T.C., 223
Hussin, S., 183
Hymes, D., 46, 405, 487, 488, 490

Johnson, K., 492
Jung, J.U., 163

Kachru, B., 311, 409
Karshen, S.D., 341, 372, 417, 421
Kiefer, F., 167
Kramsch, Claire, 384

Labov, W., 310
Lambert, W.E., 265
Lewis, M., 200
Littlejohn, A., 262

Littlewood, W., 9, 37, 406, 462
Liu, M. and Zhang, L., 395
Long Michael, H., 219
Loveday, L., 393, 394
Lynch, T., 139

Maclean, J., 139
Martin, N.J., 386
Markham, Lois, 333
McDonald, K., 92
Menhert, U., 139
Miller, J., 393
Mohammed, M.F., 220
Morrow, Keith, 492
Muhlhausler, P., 397

Nakayama, T.K., 386
Nation, I.S.P., 280
Nattinger, J., 289
Nunan David, 37, 93, 463

Oller, J.W., 489
Omaggio Hadley, A., 164
O'Neill, R., 48

Palmer, F.R., 342
Pennycook, 215
Perkins, David, 249
Prabhu, N.S., 136
Prensky, M., 70, 106

Quirk, R., 49, 347

Richards, Jack C., 32, 194, 448
Rizzo, Alessandra, 386
Robert, Lado, 488
Rodgers, G., 32, 448

Roy, J., 403
Ruthorf, H., 222

Savignon, S.J., 406
Shannon, C.E., 221
Short, K.G. and Burke, C., 479
Sinclair, B., 289
Skehan, P., 136–139, 199
Smith, M.L., 419
Stern, H.H., 174, 467
Swan, M., 342
Swain, M., 136, 405, 459, 490

Tann, 194
Tarone, 194
Taylor, B.P., 473
Tickoo, M.L., 411

Ur, P., 261

Viswanathan, G., 404, 410
Vockell, E., 261
Vygotsky, L.S., 93, 310, 311, 481

Wang, Y.P., 35
Weaver, W., 221
Wendel, J.N., 154
Western, D., 222
Widdowson, H.G., 34, 40, 465
Willis, J., 39, 137
Wilkins, D.A., 356, 461
Woodley, C., 396

Yu, M., 163

Zhang, Z.Y., 26, 33

SUBJECT INDEX

Action research, 206
Audiolingual method, 45

Bilingualism, 218, 310
Blogs, 91
Bottom-up point of view, 221, 222
Bottom-up processing, 27, 222, 224, 231

Code mixing, 310–313, 315, 317–320
Code switching, 310–313, 315, 317–320
Cognitive processes, 221
Communicative Approach (CA), 57, 58
Communicative competence, 9, 21, 25, 27, 214
Communicative Language Teaching (CLT), 7–10, 22–24, 55, 57, 60, 62, 63, 458
Computer-assisted language instruction, 105
Computer-assisted Language Learning (CALL), 89, 90, 91, 93–95
Computer-based Testing (CBT), 489
Computer Meditated Communication (CMC), 93, 94
Communicative syllabus, 47
Context-based language activities, 359
Content and Language Integrated Learning (CLIL), 369, 371
Content-specific vocabulary, 297
Content-based Instruction (CBI), 129, 134
Cooperative environment, 26
Crosstalk, 430
Curriculum, 7, 447

Discourse competence, 45

Discourse Completion Task (DCT), 174
Digital Age Language Instruction (DALI), 105–123
Discrete point test, 488

English as a global language (EGL), 383
English as a link language, 429
English as a mother tongue, 49
English for special purpose, 50, 430
English as a Second Language (ESL), 9, 49, 63
English as a Foreign Language (EFL), 34, 35, 63
E-portfolio, 77
Exploratory practice, 206

Fluency development, 280
Foreign language learning, 260
Foreign Language Teaching (FLT), 9
Functional English, 468

Generative competence, 48
Grammar translation method, 26, 45
Grammatical competence, 45

Homophones, 291

Information and Communication Technologies (ICT), 69–71, 82, 84
Information gap, 464, 494
Input-hypothesis, 417
Inter-language, 218
Interference of cognition, 435

Knowledge transmission model, 194

Subject Index

Language acquisition, 218
L2 acquisition, 218
Learner centeredness, 212, 214
Learner-centred curriculum, 216
Learner autonomy, 212, 214
Language-focused learning, 280
Levelt's model of speech production, 137
Lexical competence, 285
Linguistics competence, 459
Linguistics interference, 434

Magnetic Response Imaging (MRI), 222
Meaning-focused input, 280
Meaning-focused output, 280
Mind mapping, 233
Motivation, 78
Mobile Phone Assisted Language Learning (MPALL), 95
Multi-modalities, 172
Multi-lingualism, 218

Narrative approach, 49
Native speaker, 395
Non-native Speaker (NNS), 395
Need analysis, 448
Notional-functional syllabus, 460

Personal learning environment, 74
Pokmon system, 239
Podcasting, 100, 101, 103, 104
Pragmatic competence, 491
Problem solving, 394

Realia, 461
Reflexive practice, 194
Reflexivity, 195
Retrieval, 232

Scanning, 38
Second Language Teaching (SLT), 9
Skimming, 38
Social environment, 169
Sociocultural competence, 45
Strategic competence, 45
Structural syllabus, 47
Student Centred Approach (SCA), 30
Sustain Silent Reading (SSR), 241

Task-based learning, 136
Task-based language Teaching (TBLT), 200, 201
Task-based learning and teaching, 34
Teaching of English to Speakers of Other Languages (TESOL), 55
Teacher centred approach, 36
Top-down point of view, 221–223
Top-down processing, 27, 222, 224, 228
Total Physical Response (TPR), 219

Universal grammar, 218

Vocabulary acquisition, 221
Vocabulary acquisition strategy, 295
Vodcasting, 102

Web 2.0 technologies, 69, 91–93, 96